The Future of World Evangelization

The Future of World Evangelization

Unreached Peoples '84

Edward R. Dayton
Samuel Wilson
Editors

ISBN: 0-912552-42-5
LC: 82-061991

Editors' Preface

Since the inauguration of the *Unreached Peoples* series in 1979, the concept of "people groups" and thinking about world evangelization in terms of such groups has now become popular. We are gratified by both the acceptance of the idea and the way in which numbers of churches and mission agencies around the world are utilizing it.

It has never been the purpose of this series to catalog *all* the unreached people groups of the world. Rather, it has been our desire to pass on that information which the Holy Spirit might use in motivating others. It is therefore appropriate that the 1984 volume should look back on the past ten years with gratitude and look forward to the next ten years with enthusiasm for the possibilities that lie ahead.

We wish to thank our many colleagues who have contributed to the preparation of this volume. In addition to the members of the Lausanne movement who have contributed articles, special recognition is due to Paul Hawley, who has been editorial manager of the volume, and to the many members of the MARC and World Vision staff who have contributed their time and their insight.

Edward R. Dayton
Samuel Wilson

Foreword

By the tenth and final day of the 1974 International Congress on World Evangelization at Lausanne, Switzerland, I was more convinced than ever that the world Church was stronger in more countries than perhaps at any time in the history of the Christian faith. I was also convinced that it was ready to accept the challenge of world evangelization.

Before Lausanne there had been the Berlin Congress of 1966 and, following Berlin, a number of regional conferences such as Singapore, Bogota and Amsterdam. My colleagues and I in the Billy Graham Evangelistic Association had the privilege of initiating, organizing and largely funding the Lausanne Congress, with the help of many friends and co-workers. Lausanne burst upon us like a bombshell. It became an awakening experience for those who attended and for the thousands in many countries who could only read about it. The Lausanne Covenant written and adopted there was almost a new charter for churches everywhere.

At Lausanne we saw the new possibilities of cooperation. We sensed that for perhaps the first time in history we had the tools at our disposal to evangelize the world in a relatively short time. We repented of our mistakes and failures and stood rebuked that nearly two billion people had never heard of Jesus Christ. We left Lausanne a more mature evangelical community with a renewed zeal and a new commitment to the cause of world evangelization. Since 1974 many events indicate that we may be on the verge of either a world holocaust or a worldwide spiritual awakening--perhaps both!

During my lifetime as an evangelist, I have seen many changes not only in the world and the Church, but also in the Church's special calling to evangelize. When I started proclaiming the gospel in the early '40s, the nerve of evangelism had been damaged from within and without. This often happens when Christians are conformed to the ease of this world, when materialism becomes too important. It happens when we lose sight of the urgency of the gospel message. It happens when we are diverted into secondary issues and so become preoccupied with things other than evangelism. However, it can also happen when we let the vastness of the task undermine the reality of the promises of God. When I started to evangelize, the Church found itself dead in some parts of the world, in turmoil and strife in other parts of the world, but more often impotent as far as evangelism was concerned.

World evangelization is now a possibility before the end of this century. The world in which we live, however, is totally different from the world at the beginning of this century. The twentieth century was called the "Christian Century," but the dreams of those well-meaning theologians were badly shaken by World War I and shattered by World War II. But there is no variableness or shadow of turning with God. The gospel has not changed. Christ never changes, the power of the Spirit to transform lives never changes, and man's desperate need for God has not changed. The Great Commission from our Lord to go and preach the gospel to every person is unchanged. Christ's promise that he is with us to the end of the age never changes.

Increasingly since the Lausanne Congress, evangelicals have been called upon to provide leadership in areas where they were either a small minority or almost did not exist before. Evangelism has taken on a new meaning. It is a time of great opportunity, but also a time of great responsibility. We are stewards of our evangelical heritage. We must evangelize at all costs while there is yet time. The night is coming when no one can work. We cannot look back. The world will not wait. World problems of poverty, overpopulation and the threat of nuclear war are mounting by the hour. As someone has said, the world is changing, it is restless, and it seems to be dying. Now is the time to establish thousands of new beachheads around the world for the gospel.

The Lausanne Committee for World Evangelization has already played and can continue to play a major part in helping to establish those beachheads by encouraging evangelism and social concern everywhere. Since 1974, the "spirit of Lausanne" has grown. It has moved leaders from many countries who are dedicated to working together. *The Future of World Evangelization: Unreached Peoples '84* helps us to see what God has done in the last decade and carries our vision forward to the future. My prayer is that this bold adventure we started on together a few years ago will continue to be used of God to fan the evangelistic fire of the Church until the day of our Lord's return.

Billy Graham

Contents

Editors' Preface   5

Foreword   7

Figures   15

Abbreviations   17

THE LAUSANNE MOVEMENT   19

The Lausanne Movement: What Is It?   31
by Bill Jefferson

Ten Historic Years   47
by Edward R. Dayton

Ten Years Later: The Lausanne Covenant   65
by John R. W. Stott

Evangelism and Social Responsibility   73
by John R. Reid

Theological Issues in World Evangelization   83
by Saphir P. Athyal

Theology and Strategy   91
by Peter Savage

THE IDEA SPREADS   97

The LCWE in Norway 105
by Kirsti Mosvold

The North American Lausanne Committee 109
by C. Peter Wagner

Lausanne and the Chinese Coordination Centre of 115
World Evangelism
by Thomas Wang

Ministry in Large Cities Since Pattaya '80 121
by Raymond J. Bakke

New Directions for Western Missions 131
by Warren W. Webster

COOPERATION IN WORLD EVANGELIZATION 139

Cooperation in Evangelism 143
by Gottfried Osei-Mensah

THE POWER OF PRAYER 157

A Foundation of Prayer 161
by Vonette Bright

PEOPLE GROUPS: A NEW NAME FOR AN OLD 167
IDEA

Lausanne and People Group Thinking 171
by Samuel Wilson

Seeing People Groups in Context 179
by Patrick J. Johnstone

The Communication Process of Evangelism   193
by Viggo Sogaard

RESOURCES   199

Resources for World Evangelization   203
by Edward R. Dayton

THE FUTURE OF WORLD EVANGELIZATION   217

The Ten Years Ahead   221
by Edward R. Dayton

The Future of the Lausanne Movement   263
by Leighton Ford

EXPANDED DESCRIPTIONS   281

Introduction to Expanded Descriptions   283

Expanded Descriptions   291

REGISTRY OF THE UNREACHED   347

Introduction to the Registry   349

Index by Group Name   351

Index by Receptivity   455

Index by Religion   485

Index by Language   517

Index by Country   577

APPENDICES   711

Appendix A Unreached Peoples Questionnaire   713

Appendix B Follow-Up Information   717

Figures

1. The Unfinished Task 25

2. Lausanne Committee for World Evangelization 40

3. Evangelism Conferences Since Lausanne '74 101

4. Urban Population and Growth 119

5. Definitions 129

6. Thailand Statement 148

7. Categories of People Groups 182

8. Peoples of Senegambia 183

9. Churches and Believers in Senegambia 184

10. Bible Translation in Senegambia 186

11. The Baluch 187

12. Peoples of Thailand 189

13. Church Planting Centers in Thailand 190

14. Cognitive Dimension of Evangelism 196

15.   Attitudinal Dimension of Evangelism   196

16.   A Journey Towards Christ   196

17.   Lausanne Publications   209

18.   Physical Quality of Life Index and Per Capita   229
      Gross National Product

19.   Evangelism Conferences Projected for the   249
      1980s

Abbreviations

ASEAN--Association of Southeast Asian Nations

CAG--Communications Advisory Group

CCCOWE--Chinese Coordination Centre of World Evangelism

CONELA--Confraternity of Latin American Evangelicals

COWE--Consultation on World Evangelization

EFMA--Evangelical Foreign Missions Association

GNP (Gross National Product)--Total domestic and foreign output. Includes Gross Domestic Product and factor incomes for residents from abroad, minus the income earned in the domestic economy accruing to persons abroad; no deductions are made for depreciation.

IAG--Intercession Advisory Group

ICOWE--International Congress on World Evangelization

IFMA--Interdenominational Foreign Mission Association

LCWE--Lausanne Committee for World Evangelization

LCWE/POF--Lausanne Committee for World Evangelization/Publication Order Form

LOP--Lausanne Occasional Paper

LTEG--Lausanne Theology and Education Group

MARC--Missions Advanced Research and Communication Center

PQLI (Physical Quality of Life Index)--Numeric value assigned to countries based upon an average life expectancy at age one, infant mortality and literacy rate for adults. One is a low rating and 100 is the highest.

SWG--Strategy Working Group

TWG--Theology Working Group (formerly LTEG)

WCE--World Christian Encyclopedia

WEC--Worldwide Evangelization Crusade

WEF--World Evangelical Fellowship

The Lausanne Movement

We, members of the Church of Jesus Christ, from more than 150 nations, participants in the International Congress on World Evangelization at Lausanne, praise God for his great salvation and rejoice in the fellowship he has given us with himself and with each other. We are deeply stirred by what God is doing in our day, moved to penitence by our failures and challenged by the unfinished task of evangelization. We believe the gospel is God's good news for the whole world, and we are determined by his grace to obey Christ's commission to proclaim it to all mankind and to make disciples of every nation. We desire, therefore, to affirm our faith and our resolve, and to make public our covenant.

Introduction
The Lausanne Covenant

With these words the 4000 participants at the International Congress on World Evangelization began what the next 10 years demonstrated was a historic document.

In the history of Christ's Church millions of events, both large and small, become part of the river of history that flows forth from the throne of God. At the time we had no way of assessing their importance in the future. Only as we recount the acts of God in history are we able to look back and see where his hand has been moving. And it is in the looking back that we are sometimes empowered by the Holy Spirit to be able to look forward.

Something happened at Lausanne, Switzerland, in the summer of 1974. It was as though a brightly burning fuse had suddenly reached a powder keg. What had seemed to be only a thinly burning flame of enthusiasm for world evangelization suddenly erupted in an explosion which triggered a chain reaction throughout the world. New forces and energies were released. Men and women in country after country saw the challenge of the unfinished task and believed God would give them the power to be part of his work of world evangelization.

This book looks back on what God has done and looks forward to the challenge that faces his Church. Its purpose is to open us up to what God is doing through one major instrument of his grace, which has become known as the "Lausanne movement."

THE AUTHORITY AND POWER OF THE BIBLE

We affirm the divine inspiration, truthfulness and authority of both Old and New Testament Scriptures in their entirety as the only written word of God, without error in all that it affirms, and the only infallible rule of faith and practice. We also affirm the power of God's word to accomplish his purpose of salvation. The message of the Bible is addressed to all mankind. For God's revelation in Christ and in Scripture is unchangeable. Through it the Holy Spirit still speaks today. He illumines the minds of God's people in every culture to perceive its truth freshly through their own eyes and thus discloses to the whole church ever more of the many-colored wisdom of God.

(II Tim. 3:16; II Pet. 1:21; John 10:35; Isa. 55:11; I Cor. 1:21; Rom. 1:16; Matt. 5:17,18; Jude 3; Eph. 1:17,18; 3:10,18)

Article 2
The Lausanne Covenant

THE URGENCY OF THE EVANGELISTIC TASK

More than 2700 million people, which is more than two-thirds of mankind, have yet to be evangelized. We are ashamed that so many have been neglected; it is a standing rebuke to us and to the whole church. There is now, however, in many parts of the world an unprecedented receptivity to the Lord Jesus Christ. We are convinced that this is the time for churches and para-church agencies to pray earnestly for the salvation of the unreached and to launch new efforts to achieve world evangelization. A reduction of foreign missionaries and money in an evangelized country may sometimes be necessary to facilitate the national church's growth in self-reliance and to release resources for unevangelized areas. Missionaries should flow ever more freely from and to all six continents in a spirit of humble service. The goal should be, by all available means and at the earliest possible time, that every person will have the opportunity to hear, understand, and receive the good news.

(John 9:4; Matt. 9:35-38; Rom. 9:1-3; I Cor. 9:19-23; Mark 16:15; Isa. 58:6,7; Jas. 1:27; 2:1-9; Matt. 25:31-46; Acts 2:44,45; 4:34,35)

Article 9a
The Lausanne Covenant

The Unfinished Task

CHRISTIANS

Presently, some 1.4 billion people consider themselves Christians and are associated with over 20,800 distinct denominations. However, the percentage of Christians to the world total population has been slowly declining from 34.4 percent of the world's population in 1900 to 32.8 percent in 1980.

Furthermore, it has been estimated that over half the 1.4 billion who consider themselves Christians are probably "nominal" or non-practicing Christians who still need to be evangelized. The churches of Europe and North America are losing 2,765,000 people per year (7,600 per day) to nominalism or unbelief.

NON-CHRISTIANS AMONG CHRISTIANS

There are roughly one billion non-Christians living among others who call themselves Christians. The majority of these are found within Western countries. Some theorists insist that these people are "evangelized" because they are surrounded by the marks of Christianity. Churches stand in their midst.

UNREACHED PEOPLES

There are over two billion people in the world who for a variety of reasons are separated from effective contact with the Church. No matter how the local church expands, these two billion will only be reached initially by some form of "cross-cultural" evangelism.

Presently there are not enough cross-cultural missionaries to reach the unreached people groups of the world. Most local churches and individual Christians do not recognize that the need for cross-cultural evangelists (missionaries) is greater than at any other time in history, and will continue to be so in the coming years.

Figure 1

Ten years later the 2700 million people now exceed 3000 million. And there must be over 1000 million people who call themselves Christians; there are millions whose Christianity is only nominal at best.

How do we respond to the urgency of the evangelistic task? There are at least six ways in which we attempt think God's thoughts after him and seek to do his will when faced with such a challenge:

We learn from history. In the same way Stephen recounted the acts of God to his listeners in chapter 7 of Acts, so we too must look back in history and try to see the foot-steps of God.

We learn from God's Word. We return again to the inex-haustable supply of Christian power. In the words of the Lausanne Covenant, "God's revelation in Christ and in Scripture is unchangeable. Through it the Holy Spirit still speaks today. He illumines the minds of God's people in every culture to perceive its truth freshly through their own eyes and thus discloses to the whole church ever more of the many-coloured wisdom of God" (Article 2).

We learn from each other. We come together to share our understanding of God's Word and the moving of his Spirit in our lives and to tell each other what we see God doing in our midst.

"We rejoice that a new missionary era has dawned. The dominant role of western missions is fast disappearing. God is raising up from the younger churches a great new

resource for world evangelization, and is thus demonstrating that the responsibility to evangelize belongs to
the whole body of Christ. All churches should therefore
be asking God and themselves what they should be doing
both to reach their own area and to send missionaries to
other parts of the world" (Lausanne Covenant, Article 8).

We learn from prayer. "We believe that we are engaged in
constant spiritual warfare with the principalities and
powers of evil, who are seeking to overthrow the church
and frustrate its task of world evangelization. We know
our need to equip ourselves with God's armour and to
fight this battle with the spiritual weapons of truth and
prayer" (Lausanne Covenant, Article, 12).

We learn from the Spirit. "We believe in the power of the
Holy Spirit. The Father sent his Spirit to bear witness to
his Son; without his witness ours is futile. Conviction of
sin, faith in Christ, new birth and Christian growth are all
his work. Further, the Holy Spirit is a missionary spirit;
thus evangelism should arise spontaneously from a
Spirit-filled church" (Lausanne Covenant, Article 14).

*We learn from understanding what God is doing in the world
both within and outside the Church.* We seek to learn what
tools are available for us to use, recognizing that it is not
the tools that are sinful but only people who use them for
wrong ends.

With this understanding we then turn to looking at that
part of history which has been the Lausanne movement,
to see how it has wrestled theologically to understand
the implications of God's Word for the day, to see how
the Church has been meeting to talk and discuss and

share and cooperate, to affirm again the power of prayer, to look at some of the new ideas that have been placed before us for our use in the task of world evangelization, and finally to look forward to the future.

THE UNIQUENESS AND UNIVERSALITY OF CHRIST

We affirm that there is only one Savior and only one gospel, although there is a wide diversity of evangelistic approaches. We recognize that all men have some knowledge of God through his general revelation in nature. But we deny that this can save, for men suppress the truth by their un-righteousness. We also reject as derogatory to Christ and the gospel every kind of syncretism and dialogue which implies that Christ speaks equally through all religions and ideolo-gies. Jesus Christ, being himself the only God-man, who gave himself as the only ransom for sinners, is the only mediator between God and man. There is no other name by which we must be saved. All men are perishing because of sin, but God loves all men, not wishing that any should perish but that all should repent. Yet those who reject Christ repudiate the joy of salvation and condemn themselves to eternal separation from God. To proclaim Jesus as "the Savior of the world" is not to affirm that all men are either automatically or ulti-mately saved, still less to affirm that all religions offer sal-vation in Christ. Rather it is to proclaim God's love for a world of sinners and to invite all men to respond to him as Savior and Lord in the wholehearted personal commitment of repentance and faith. Jesus Christ has been exalted above every other name; we long for the day when every knee shall bow to him and every tongue shall confess him Lord.

(Gal. 1:6-9; Rom. 1:18-32; I Tim. 2:5,6; Acts 4:12; John 3:16-19; II Pet. 3:9; II Thess. 1:7-9; John 4:42; Matt. 11:28; Eph. 1:20,21; Phil. 2:9-11)

Article 3
The Lausanne Covenant

The Lausanne Movement:
What Is It?

Bill Jefferson

In attempting to make sense out of the world in which we live, it is important to understand how the scene has changed for evangelical Christians in recent years. During the first half of the twentieth century, evangelicals often found themselves on the defensive against such ideas as universalism and unbiblical views of evangelism and the mission of the Church. Over the past few decades, however, a whole new era of cooperation for evangelicals has emerged. Today evangelicals around the world are called upon to provide leadership in many areas where they were either a small minority or almost did not exist before.

BERLIN 1966

Numerous factors have contributed to this changing scene, which began to emerge clearly in 1966. In the fall of that year some 1200 delegates from over 100 countries attended the World Congress on Evangelism held in Berlin. For some years, Dr. Billy Graham had carried the dream and vision of believers coming together from every corner of the earth for such a gathering. Initiated by the leadership of Dr. Graham and the support of the Billy Graham Evangelistic Association, the Congress was co-sponsored by the periodical *Christianity*

Today and its editor, Carl F. H. Henry. It gave evangelicals one of their first rallying events in decades. The theme, "One Race, One Gospel, One Task," provided clear direction for the Congress. It was time to unite for world evangelization.

Berlin was followed by national and regional evangelism conferences in Singapore, Minneapolis, Bogata, Ottawa and other places. These gatherings provided continuity between the Berlin Congress and the International Congress on World Evangelization (ICOWE) held in Lausanne, Switzerland, in 1974.

The nearly eight short years that separated Berlin and Lausanne, however, were anything but stable. The late '60s and '70s were a time of phenomenal world change-- economically, politically, socially and religiously. By the time of the 1974 Lausanne Congress, much of the Church world was looking for "new wine"; many of the old structures, the "old wineskins," were no longer relevant.

New forms of evangelism began to appear with a growing emphasis on the communication of life as well as the transmitting of content. Worldwide movements emphasizing the work of the Spirit were making a significant contribution to church renewal, while at the same time in the West the Jesus movement and other similar efforts brought literally tens of thousands of alienated young people into the Church. Numerous Bible translations were published, many with a goal of communicating to the grass roots. Likewise, specialized periodicals sprang up to meet the demand of readers in a growing Christian marketplace. By 1974, the tide was indeed turning for evangelism.

LAUSANNE 1974

It was in this climate that Dr. Billy Graham sensed that the time was coming for another even more representative gathering than the Berlin Congress. He personally wrote to 100 evangelical church leaders around the world and asked them: "Is there a need for another world congress on evangelization?" Nearly all responded affirmatively and enthusiastically. There was a feeling, however, that this congress should not be just a repeat of Berlin 1966. Rather, this should be a working congress dealing with practical issues and strategies, always spelling out the what, the why and the how of world evangelization.

The 2700 participants who accepted the invitation to come to Lausanne represented over 150 nations and came from a wide diversity of denominational backgrounds. Approximately 50 percent came from the Two-Thirds World. Counting observers, news media and guests, over 4000 Christians attended the Congress. *Time* magazine referred to the Congress as a "formidable forum, possibly the widest-ranging meeting of Christians ever held."

If there has ever been a moment in history when evangelicals were in tune with the times, it surely must have been in July of 1974. It became an awakening experience for those who attended and the thousands of Christians in numerous countries who read about it.

The participants left in a mood of expectation, determined under God that the vision of Lausanne should be fulfilled and the dream of world evangelization come true. The possibilities were so promising and numerous--the clear evidence of a new movement of the Holy Spirit in many areas together with modern technology, strategies for evangelizing specific people groups, international networks, regional congresses-- there appeared to be a renaissance of evangelistic thinking taking place. A new era of co-operation had emerged.

LAUSANNE COMMITTEE FOR WORLD EVANGELIZATION

The LCWE is the heart of an international movement--a global network of Christians who subscribe to the Lausanne Covenant and are committed to cooperation in world evangelization.

The Lausanne Committee does not take credit for evangelistic efforts taking place around the world. Rather, it seeks to discover those who are already at work on behalf of the kingdom and to stimulate and assist them through the resources of prayer, publications, information and resource personnel.

Lausanne Mandate

The mandate of the LCWE is to hasten the evangelization of all peoples of the world in obedience to the command of Jesus Christ and in anticipation of his return, by multiplying and strengthening the ways in which evangelical believers work together to accomplish this task through churches, missions and other Christian organizations.

Lausanne Objectives

1. To advance biblcal evangelization as reflected in the Lausanne Covenant among all the peoples, including those unreached people groups where the church has not yet taken root indigenously.

2. To promote spiritual renewal as foundation to world evangelization.

3. To be a motivator and facilitator for world evangelization through networks of relationship which encourage cooperation.

4. To measure progress in world evangelization so as to focus prayer and other resources in anticipation of further spiritual breakthroughs.

Lausanne Goals

The overriding goal of the Lausanne movement is to see men, women, children and communities come to know Jesus Christ as Savior and Lord. This desire translates into the following specific goals:

1. Promote cooperative evangelistic efforts based on the Lausanne Covenant which testifies to the biblical teachings for evangelization.

2. Promote and publish studies of biblical theology and strategies of evangelization, including methods the Holy Spirit is using.

3. Stimulate united and specific strategic praying for world evangelization.

4. Encourage stewardship of the Church's resources and stimulate sacrificial giving for world evangelization.

5. Share information, when appropriate, about the progress of evangelization in different parts of the world.

6. Sponsor or encourage meetings at all levels of Christian leaders to pray, plan and work together for world evangelization.

7. Commission those persons of vision and experience to share with an enlarged Christian community significant insights and useful models in evangelization.

8. Provide opportunities for Christians to engage in joint action and thus widen and enhance their common ministries for evangelization.

9. Encourage and support the research and development of the ministries of women and youth for world evangelization.

10. Intercede sympathetically for the liberty of some fellow believers who bear their evangelistic witness under conditions of oppression and persecution.

The LCWE sets policy, gives direction and overall guidance to the Lausanne movement. The committee consists of a chairman and 75 members who volunteer their time and are elected for three two-year terms ensuring the replacement of one-third of the members of each full meeting of the committee.

The Executive Committee

The 15-member Executive Committee of the LCWE gives oversight to the ongoing execution of LCWE policy, as well as initiating and overseeing long-range plans. It has representatives from all continents.

Membership as of 1983 subdivided by regions

Africa	8
Asia (East)	8
Asia (West and Mid-East)	6
Europe (West/UK/East)	13
Latin America and Caribbean	10
North America	14
Oceania	3
Youth Representation	4
Women Representation	5
Ex Officio	4

Offices: London, England--where a full-time executive secretary is based. Wheaton, Illinois--Communications Center responsible for all publications.

Theology Working Group

The Theology Working Group considers theological issues that are important to world evangelization and arranges for the future study of such issues as approved by the LCWE. This 10-member group uses consultations and gatherings to call together theologians, anthropologists, linguists, missionaries and others for study. This includes analyzing various contemporary movements and trends which are related to the mission of the Church.

The Consultation on Gospel and Culture in 1978 and the Consultation on the Relationship Between Evangelism and Social Responsibility in 1982 have made significant contributions to world evangelization, and the resulting reports have been widely read.

One of the most important functions of this group is to work closely with, and give theological input to, the Strategy Working Group. The Theology Working Group meets every one to two years.

Strategy Working Group

The purpose of the Strategy Working Group is to support the Lausanne Committee for World Evangelization by providing communication and motivational links between an international network of practicing missionaries, evangelists, churches and Christian organizations, and to help them develop strategies for evangelization which the LCWE may use to further the cause of world evangelization.

It gathers information about what these individuals and organizations are doing, the needs they have--along with their dreams and visions--and shares this information through the vehicle of a bimonthly *Lausanne Communique*. This information is stored in such a way that it can be made available to those who can be helped by it.

Like the Theology Working Group, the Strategy Working Group holds various consultations and gatherings to bring together individuals with expertise and experience in specific areas of missions and evangelism. The Strategy Working Group meets every one to two years and currently consists of ten members.

Intercession Advisory Group

Knowing the importance of prayer to world evangelization, the LCWE has established an Intercession Advisory Group which has the sole purpose of encouraging global prayer support. One of its main goals is to establish a worldwide network of individuals, churches and organizations that are committed to praying for world evangelization. This group promotes an annual World Day of Prayer (Pentecost Sunday), which is being increasingly observed around the world.

Communications Advisory Group

The Communications Advisory Group works in conjunction with the communications staff of the Lausanne movement to help develop strategies and plans for communicating to the various Lausanne constituencies. It provides valuable input toward the process of gathering and disseminating information pertaining to events, opportunities and needs related to world evangelization. The information provided by LCWE's monthly press service *World Evangelization Information Service* and the quarterly publication *World Evangelization* generates insight, vision and prayer around the world.

This group is also responsible for overseeing LCWE's publishing program. To date, some 24 Lausanne Occasional Papers (LOPs) have been published as a result of consultations sponsored by the Lausanne Committee.

Bill Jefferson is Special Assistant for Communications of the Lausanne Committee for World Evangelization.

Lausanne Committee for World Evangelization

(as of January 1984)

Chairman
Leighton Ford
2901 Coltsgate Road
Charlotte, NC 28211
U.S.A.

Honorary Chairman
Billy Graham
Box 937
Montreat, NC 28757
U.S.A.

Executive Secretary
Gottfried Osei-Mensah
Whitefield House
186 Kennington Park Road
London SE11 4BT, England

General Co-ordinator
A. Jack Dain
Box 4807 GPO
Sydney, 2001 Australia

MEMBERS (* Indicates Executive Committee Members)

Lucien Accad, Lebanon
Pierre Allard, Canada
Francisco Anabalon, Chile
Hakon Anderson, Norway
*Ramez Atallah, Egypt
*Saphir Athyal, India
Peter Beyerhaus, Federal Republic of Germany
Wim Bouw, Netherlands
Vonette Bright, U.S.A.
Clive Calver, England
David Chan, Republic of Singapore
*Chae Ok Chun, Korea
Wade T. Coggins, U.S.A.
Robert Coleman, U.S.A.
ma Djongwe Daidanso, Cameroon
A. Jack Dain, Australia
Nancy Leigh DeMoss, U.S.A.
Jonathan dos Santos, Brazil
Ajith Fernando, Sri Lanka
*Leighton Ford, U.S.A.
Juan Gili, Spain
David Gitari, Kenya
H. Richard Glaser, Brazil
Billy Graham, U.S.A.
Michael Griffiths, England
Fritz Hoffmann, Democratic Republic of Germany
*Bill Hogue, U.S.A.
*Donald E. Hoke, U.S.A.
George G. Hunter III, U.S.A.
Abd-el-Masih Istafanous, Egypt
Bashir Jiwan, Pakistan
James Katarikawe, Uganda
Victor A. T. Koh, U.S.A.

*Gordon Landreth, England
Ellie Lau, Hong Kong
Branko Lovrec, Yugoslavia
Costas Macris, Greece
Fred Magbanua, Philippines
D. Marini-Bodho, Zaire
*Horst Marquardt, Federal Republic of Germany
James Massey, U.S.A.
John J. Matulessy, Indonesia
Billy Melvin, U.S.A.
Kirsti Mosvold, Norway
Inoke Nabulivou, Fiji
Emilio Antonio Nunez, Guatemala
*Samuel Odunaike, Nigeria
Nathaniel Olutimayin, Nigeria
*Gottfried Osei-Mensah, England
Cho-Choon Park, Korea
Seikku Paunonen, Finland
Susan Perlman, U.S.A.
Michael P. Perrott, Northern Ireland
*John R. Reid, Australia
D. John Richard, India
Eduardo Ruan, Venezuela
Eliseu Simeao, Angola
Simon H. Sircar, Bangladesh
Alfredo Smith, Peru
Brian Stiller, Canada
Juliet Thomas, India
John Tooke, South Africa
C. Peter Wagner, U.S.A.
*Thomas Wang, Hong Kong
Esther Waruiru, Kenya
Warren Webster, U.S.A.
Ursula Wiesemann, Cameroon
Theodore Williams, India
*Thomas Zimmerman, U.S.A.

ALTERNATE MEMBERS

Tokunboh Adeyemo, Kenya
Paul Cedar, U.S.A.
Jonathan Chao, Hong Kong
Luke Chhoa, East Malaysia
David Cohen, Australia
Eric Gay, Switzerland
Michael Haynes, U.S.A.
Erwin Kolb, U.S.A.
Iqbal K. Massey, Cyprus
Caesar Molebatsi, Republic of South Africa
Mardoqueo Munoz, Guatemala
Victor Musa, Nigeria
Michael Nazir-Ali, Pakistan
John Olley, Australia
Samuel A. Olson, Venezuela
Marcelino Ortiz, Mexico
George Samuel, India
Rolf Scheffbuch, Federal Republic of Germany
Elon Svanell, Sweden
Carmelo Terranova, Argentina
Tite Tienou, Upper Volta
Agustin B. Vencer, Jr., Philippines

THEOLOGY WORKING GROUP

Chairman
John R. Reid
P.O. Box Q190
Queen Victoria Buildings
Sydney, NSW 2000
Australia

*Saphir Athyal, India
Wilson Chow, Hong Kong
Peter Kuzmic, Yugoslavia

43

Samuel H. Moffett, U.S.A.
Agne Nordlander, Sweden
*Emilio Antonio Nunez, Guatemala
Tite Tienou, Upper Volta
David F. Wells, U.S.A.

STRATEGY WORKING GROUP

Chairman
*Edward Dayton
World Vision International
919 W. Huntington Drive
Monrovia, CA 91016
U.S.A.

Patrick Johnstone, England
Victor A. T. Koh, U.S.A.
Gail Law, Hong Kong
Don M. McCurry, U.S.A.
Kirsti Mosvold, Norway
George Samuel, India
Peter Savage, Mexico
Viggo Sogaard, Denmark
Warren Webster, U.S.A.

INTERCESSION ADVISORY GROUP

Chairman
Vonette Bright
Arrowhead Springs
San Bernardino, CA 92414
U.S.A.

David Bryant, U.S.A.
Sun Ae Chou, Korea
Millie Dienert, U.S.A.
Fritz Hoffman, Democratic Republic of Germany

44

M. Mapalieij-Mantik SH, Indonesia
N. Lawrence Olson, Brazil
Jan-Aage Torp, Norway

COMMUNICATIONS ADVISORY GROUP

Chairman
*Horst Marquardt
Evangeliums-Rundfunk
Postfach 1444
D-6330 Wetzlar
Federal Republic of Germany

Sigurd Aske, Norway
Viggo Sogaard, Denmark

Ten Historic Years

Edward R. Dayton

1984 marks the tenth anniversary of the International Congress on World Evangelization (ICOWE)–held at Lausanne, Switzerland, in June 1974. In the same way it marks the tenth anniversary of what has now become known as the "Lausanne movement." To understand why Lausanne should be characterized as a movement rather than an organization, it is necessary to reexamine the mandate given to the Lausanne Committee for World Evangelization (LCWE) by the participants at Lausanne.

In the early months of 1974, Dr. Paul Little, the program director for the ICOWE, conducted an opinion survey of those already registered. This was an attempt to determine as early as possible whether those who would come felt there should be some kind of follow-up after the Congress. The survey produced a remarkable response. Replies came from every continent, over half coming from Asia, Africa and Latin America.

Bishop A. Jack Dain was the chairman of the Congress. In a report on the results of that survey, he writes, "Ninety-six percent of those replying requested short-term follow-up and eighty-four percent requested continuing follow-up after the forthcoming Congress. Eighty-nine percent of participants from Africa, Asia and Latin America requested continuing follow-up.

"During the hectic last days of the Congress itself a further questionnaire confirmed the earlier results. Eighty-eight percent of the 1600 replies affirmed the need for a post-Congress body. Eighty-four percent believed that such a continuing body should directly result from the Congress itself. In response to this clear, unequivocal mandate, regional groups were convened and received nominations for membership in a continuation committee. Nominations for the committee came from every major geographic and denominational interest."

But what kind of follow-on was desired? "The responses clearly showed a request not for an organizational structure, but for a committee that would act as a catalyst, enabling and not directing--providing a service to the cause of world evangelization and offering expertise in evangelism, missions, theology, mass communications, and planning of regional and functional congresses and conferences." The mandate given to what would become the Lausanne Committee for World Evangelization directed the Committee to focus its attention and efforts on the task of world evangelization and to do this without building a large organizational structure.

The Committee held its first meeting in Mexico City in January 1975. At this formative meeting the two major thrusts of the mandate given at Lausanne were reaffirmed. It was decided to maintain a very small permanent staff led by an executive secretary. The thought from the beginning was that this was to be a cooperative, volunteer organism based upon a web of relationships, rather than an organizational hierarchy.

At its first meeting the LCWE saw four major areas with which it should concern itself. These four concerns resulted in the appointment of four working groups: one for theology and education, a second for strategy, a third for communication within the body of Christ, and a fourth for prayer. Each of the original 48 members pledged himself or herself to become a catalyst within their local situation, within their country and within the geographic region of which they were a part.

It would be unfair to attribute to the LCWE members the amazing amount of activity that began immediately after the International Congress. However, the list of major congresses and consultations in Figure 3 amply demonstrates the results of the enthusiasm and spiritual motivation that both the members of the LCWE and the over 4000 participants observed from others who were at Lausanne.

The tasks assigned to the four working groups give us a way of considering all that has happened in these 10 years:

COMMUNICATION

Communication was the first thought of the day. Already there was a vast network of 4000 inspired men and women who had been given a new vision of the universality of the Church, who had a refilling of their spiritual energy and a new vision of what God might do through them in evangelizing their own countries. They returned to their churches, organizations and positions in society with hope and in many cases a determination to see the experience of Lausanne repeated in every region of the country. The appointment of Gottfried Osei-Mensah as the executive secretary provided the movement with an exceptionally gifted communicator and ambassador of goodwill. Gottfried Osei-Mensah's exposition of the Scriptures and irenic spirit became the key component of many of the follow-on congresses. At the same time a quarterly publication, *World Evangelization*, as well as a press service under the direction of Stan Izon were initiated. All over the world there were immediate efforts to translate the Lausanne Covenant into local languages. The Covenant became an umbrella under which men and women and churches and organizations could come together in the common cause of evangelization.

THEOLOGY

The Lausanne Covenant was the theological statement of the International Congress. In his chapter John Stott does an admirable job of describing the work of the Theology and Education Group (now known as the Theology Working Group) in bringing additional theological insights to bear on the Covenant. The continual "doing of theology" has been a major part of strengthening the Lausanne movement. Bishop John Reid, whose article on "Evangelism and Social Responsibility" appears elsewhere in this book, currently chairs the Theology Working Group.

In 1980 the LCWE convened a Consultation on World Evangelization (COWE) to assess the work of the LCWE to date. I will have more to say about that below. One recommendation of the COWE was that the Strategy Working Group and Theology Working Group should be brought more intimately together. In response to this, the next meetings of these two groups were held jointly, and the Theology Working Group set about the task of evaluating some of the strategy concepts of the SWG in greater depth. In his chapter "Theology and Strategy" Peter Savage deals with the relationship between strategy and theology. Saphir Athyal also utilizes the work of COWE as he discusses "Theological Issues in World Evangelization." Suffice it to say that a continual interaction is needed between theology and practice, and this is continuing at a good pace.

STRATEGY

Biblical theology can help us see *what* needs to be done. A second major task is deciding *how* to go about it. At the formation of the LCWE, C. Peter Wagner was asked to head up a Strategy Working Group. Dr. Wagner agreed, provided he could enlist the resources of the Missions Advanced Research and Communication Center (MARC) which had done the basic research on people groups and the Status of Christianity Country Profiles for the International Congress.

At Lausanne not only had we been challenged by the 2700 million people who had yet to be evangelized, but we had also recognized, perhaps for the first time, that there were as many as 2000 million people who were completely isolated from any effective Christian witness. There were millions of unevangelized people who could learn about Jesus from one of their neighbors. But these 2000 million would require specially called and equipped men and women to cross cultural and linguistic barriers to reach them.

The SWG set about the task of defining terminology that would help us communicate with others in order to focus a major portion of our evangelistic resources and personnel on these "unreached people groups." (See Figure 5 for definitions.) The usefulness of the people group concept is described by Samuel Wilson in the chapter entitled "Lausanne and

People Group Thinking." Along with the research and strategy staff of MARC the SWG began to publish in 1979 the *Unreached Peoples* series. Each volume featured a particular major emphasis (see Resources), with a cumulative Registry of the Unreached which attempted to challenge local Christians and churches everywhere with the task of reaching a specific unreached people group.

The SWG and MARC were not alone. Many others had been challenged at Lausanne to emphasize the same new approach to thinking about world evangelization. Ralph Winter, who had so challenged the participants at Lausanne with the unfinished task, founded the U.S. Center for World Mission, and that Center continued to popularize the unreached or "hidden" peoples and the need for "frontier mission" efforts to reach them. The results of these enterprises are well described in this volume by Warren Webster in his chapter entitled "New Directions for Western Missions."

As the LCWE looked forward to the future, the members felt it would be important to call a consultation to evaluate what had been done to date and the appropriateness of the plan and direction for the future, and to determine whether the LCWE should continue as an organized committee. Consequently, a Consultation on World Evangelization (COWE) was called to meet at Pattaya, Thailand, in June 1980. One thousand attended.

In effect the COWE was two consultations running in parallel. The one consultation was keyed to strategy. The second was keyed to an evaluation of progress to date. Of interest to us here is the appointment of 17 Coordinators who were asked to recruit Conveners on a particular focus of evangelistic need, such as Hindus, Muslims, large city dwellers, the poor, and nominal Christians. Hundreds of conveners met numbers of times to discuss strategies that would be effective in their areas of concern. At Pattaya, groups met both separately to discuss the results of their research and also in continental and regional groups to discuss how these particular strategies might fit together in context. In the coming months each of the Coordinators edited the Lausanne Occasional Paper on their findings (see Resources).

The research that was done varied greatly. In the providence of God the most interest was shown in urban evangelization. Over 5000 pages of research were brought together and presented by Raymond Bakke, the Coordinator for Large Cities. As Dr. Bakke indicates in his article entitled "Ministry in Large Cities Since Pattaya '80," the world is rapidly becoming urban, and we have often failed to realize that evangelism in the city requires some special insights and gifts.

But there were other major contributions by specific Coordinators and their Conveners. For example, the Chinese Coordination Centre of World Evangelism (CCCOWE) had already been established, and Thomas Wang, its executive director, utilized all the resources of that movement to share with others what was being done and what could be done among the Chinese of the diaspora.

The Consultation at Pattaya served to continue the momentum that had begun at Lausanne. But the LCWE was faced with a question of how to conserve that momentum. How could we utilize the vast number of men and women instrumental in the process that led up to Pattaya? The answer was the formation of a Lausanne Associates network which included the 17 Pattaya Coordinators and the working groups, plus a small but growing number of men and women who were already at the center of their own networks of relationships. Two "senior associates" were appointed, Raymond Bakke and Don McCurry, head of the Samuel Zwemer Institute. Don McCurry had been led of God to form a research and strategy organization to reach Muslims as a result of consultations sponsored by the North American Lausanne Committee at Glen Eyrie in 1978.

Ray Bakke's article tells the dramatic story of what happened as, under the sponsorship of LCWE, he visited 38 world-class cities in the three years following Pattaya. From all this one gets some impression of how Lausanne is attempting to build a strategy based upon cooperation, communication and relationships with others who are already at work in what God is doing.

To undergird the work of strategy, MARC produced a number of tools. The small book *That Everyone May Hear* by Edward R. Dayton was used as a study guide for Pattaya and has since been revised twice to reflect new insights that have been gained, both at Pattaya and by subsequent joint meetings of the Strategy Working Group and Theology Working Group. The initial audiovisual that accompanied the book has been modified four times not only to reflect a growing understanding of biblical strategy but also to adapt to different cultures. (For more information see Resources.)

In an effort to establish an ongoing "conversation" among those at Pattaya, the Strategy Working Group inaugurated the *Lausanne Communique*, an eight-page bimonthly newsletter which shares the work not only of those directly involved in the Lausanne movement but of others God is using in different places around the world. The *Lausanne Communique* is also used to share LCWE publications and other available tools.

In all this thinking about "strategy" there has been a continual attempt to recognize that means and methods are much less important than God's intentions. We need *biblical* strategies. We need strategies that have been passed through the fire of concerted prayer. We need strategies that are conceived and carried out by Spirit-filled men and women.

PRAYER

As Vonette Bright points out elsewhere in this volume in "A Foundation of Prayer," the Lausanne Covenant concludes with a commitment by the signers to "enter into a solemn covenant with God and with each other, to pray, to plan and to work together for the evangelization of the whole world." A portion of the statement that came out of the consultation at Pattaya reads, "We pledge ourselves to pray for the Church and for the world, that Christ will renew his Church in order to reach his world." God has gifted certain men and women with special abilities to pray. But too often evangelicals have been so concerned with "getting about God's business" that we have neglected to make prayer a basic part of our everyday living. The history of the Intercessory Advisory Group is the history of prayer as part of the Lausanne movement, and I commend Mrs. Bright's article to you for that history.

COOPERATION

As mentioned above, the Consultation on World Evangelization at Pattaya in 1980 was actually a two-track consultation. While one track focused on strategy, the second track dealt with an evaluation of the work of the LCWE to date and considered the value of continuing the work of the Committee. At the heart of this discussion was the relationship of LCWE to other Christian bodies. Accordingly a Commission on Cooperation had been formed to do the evaluation. This Commission presented to the plenary of the consultation a number of drafts of what eventually was affirmed as the Thailand Statement (see Figure 6). In his article on "Cooperation in Evangelism" Gottfried Osei-Mensah discusses how the Commission went on to study the entire area of church/parachurch relationships.

THE LAUSANNE COMMITTEE

Since the International Congress on World Evangelization in 1974 the Lausanne Committee has met biennially. During alternate years the Executive Committee has met to give direction to both the Working Groups and the Executive Secretary. At its January 1982 meeting the LCWE voted to expand its membership from 50 to 75 members. At that meeting it received a report from its Long-Range Planning Committee, headed by Tom Houston, which attempted to peer into the future to discern the potential usefulness of the Lausanne movement. Edward R. Dayton's article entitled "The Future of World Evangelization" shares with you some of the excitement the Committee felt. Leighton Ford's concluding article on "The Future of the Lausanne Movement" reflects hope that the Lausanne movement will continue to be a part of the "new thing" God is doing in proclaiming his kingdom throughout the world.

In the area of cooperation we are always faced with seeking a balance that serves the total Church in the task of world evangelization. We need to listen to all the voices. At the

International Congress itself there was a group that felt that the Lausanne Covenant did not go far enough. While rejoicing "in our membership by his Spirit in the body of Christ and in the joy and love he has given us in each other," they called us to recognize some of our shortcomings of the past and what at times is perceived to be our limited view of the future. The comprehensive reference volume *Let the Earth Hear His Voice*, that brings together all the papers and workshops of the ICOWE, includes a statement from one such group entitled "Theological Implications of Radical Discipleship."

At the COWE in Pattaya there were again those who felt we had not gone far enough in our statements. John Stott deals with a number of these issues in his article, "Ten Years Later: The Lausanne Covenant." Both the Working Groups and the Lausanne Committee will continue to listen with open hearts and minds to what the Spirit is saying to *all* the churches.

Edward R. Dayton is the founder of MARC and Vice President for Mission and Evangelism of World Vision International. He chairs the Strategy Working Group of the Lausanne Committee.

THE PURPOSE OF GOD

We affirm our belief in the one-eternal God, Creator and Lord of the world, Father, Son and Holy Spirit, who governs all things according to the purpose of his will. He has been calling out from the world a people for himself, and sending his people back into the world to be his servants and his witnesses, for the extension of his kingdom, the building up of Christ's body, and the glory of his name. We confess with shame that we have often denied our calling and failed in our mission, by becoming conformed to the world or by withdrawing from it. Yet we rejoice that even when borne by earthen vessels the gospel is still a precious treasure. To the task of making that treasure known in the power of the Holy Spirit we desire to dedicate ourselves anew.

(Isa. 40:28; Matt. 28:19; Eph. 1:11; Acts 15:14; John 17:6,18; Eph 4:12; I Cor. 5:10; Rom. 12:2; II Cor. 4:7)

Article 1
The Lausanne Covenant

One of the immediate responses of participants at the International Congress was to translate the Covenant into their own language. This process has moved so rapidly and so extensively that it has been impossible to keep track of all of the translations. However, one thing is certain: the Covenant has taken its place among the historic documents of the Church as an instrument that is widely used by Christians throughout the world as a statement of common purpose and intent. The vast number of congresses and consultations called together on the basis of the Covenant testify to this fact (see Figure 3).

One can go even further and say that the Lausanne Covenant was produced at a time in history uniquely suited to give it worldwide acceptance and utilization considerably beyond that of previous documents of the Church. This is not to prejudge the importance history will ascribe to the Covenant relative to other Church documents, but rather to say one must recognize that the Covenant was produced during a time when the rapid growth in communication technology made it possible, not only for over 4000 participants to come to Lausanne, but for those participants to rapidly disseminate the Covenant to their constituencies.

This same technology has permitted the Lausanne movement to operate much more as a web of relationships than as an organization. The unifying question of the Lausanne movement is not, "Do you belong to Lausanne?" but rather "Do you subscribe to the Covenant?"

Reverend John R. W. Stott has been greatly used by God in gathering and shaping the concepts that have flowed forth from both the International Congress and the subsequent consultations. In the preface to his *Exposition and Commentary* on the Lausanne Covenant (Lausanne Occasional Paper No. 3) he gives us a good overview of how the Covenant was produced and why it is called a "covenant" rather than a "declaration":

> A first and fairly short statement was produced two or three months before the Congress and submitted by mail to a number of advisers. Already this document may truly be said to have come out of the Congress (although the Congress had not yet assembled), because it reflected the contributions of the main speakers whose papers had been published in advance. The document was revised in the light of the advisers' comments, and this revision was further revised at Lausanne by the drafting committee. So what was submitted to all participants in the middle of the Congress was the third draft. They were invited to send in their contributions, either as individuals or as groups, and they responded with great diligence. Many hundreds of submissions were received (in the official languages), translated into English, sorted and studied. Some proposed amendments cancelled each other out, but the drafting committee incorporated all they could, while at the same time ensuring that the final document was a recognizable revision of the draft submitted to participants. It may truly be said, then, that the Lausanne Covenant expresses a consensus of the mind and mood of the Lausanne Congress. . . .

The word "covenant" is not used in its technical, biblical sense, but in the ordinary sense of a binding contract. For example, in seventeenth century Scotland there were the famous "Covenanters" who bound themselves by a "solemn league and covenant" to maintain the freedom of the church. The reason the expression "Lausanne Covenant" was chosen in preference to "Lausanne Declaration" is that we wanted to do more than find an agreed formula of words. We were determined not just to declare something, but to do something, namely to commit ourselves to the task of world evangelization . . . .

The same desire to let the Covenant speak for itself has led to the decision to omit a bibliography and references to other literature. The only quotations are from Congress papers and addresses (which are printed in full in the official Compendium, *Let the Earth Hear His Voice*) and from the Revised Standard Version of the Bible. Biblical references are numerous, for the Covenant will commend itself only in so far as it can show itself to be a true expression of biblical teaching and principles.

Bishop Jack Dain, Chairman of the Congress, has referred to Lausanne as "a process, not just an event." One important aspect of the continuing process will be the study of the Covenant both by individuals and by groups.

An audiovisual explaining the key points of the Covenant is now available (see Resources).

In the article that follows, John Stott gives us some insight into what has happened in the process of utilizing the Covenant.

Ten Years Later:
The Lausanne Covenant

John R. W. Stott

The Lausanne Covenant was an authentic utterance of the Lausanne Congress. Its early drafts reflected the contents of the Congress papers, and its final verson, as adopted by the Congress, incorporated hundreds of amendments proposed by participants. In the following months, as its text was translated into the world's major languages and studied, it received widespread acceptance, even acclaim. One theologian who teaches in Asia went so far as to say that the Covenant might prove to be "the most significant ecumenical confession on evangelism that the church has ever produced."

It did not escape criticism, however. Two examples may be given. Some evangelical leaders described the statement in paragraph 2 that Scripture is "without error in all that it affirms" as a subtle escape clause, designed to avoid a declaration of "inerrancy." The words were intended as a clarification, however, not an evasion. As I wrote in *The Lausanne Covenant--An Exposition and Commentary* (Lausanne Occasional Paper No. 3), "Not everything contained in Scripture is affirmed by Scripture. . . . It is important, therefore, in all our Bible study to consider the intention of the author, and what is being asserted. It is this, whatever the subject of the

assertion may be, which is true and inerrant." It was gratify-
ing, therefore, that--whether consciously or unconsciously--
the International Council on Biblical Inerrancy took up and
expanded the phrase in its first "Chicago Statement" as follows: "It is to be believed as God's instruction in all that it
affirms, obeyed as God's command in all that it requires, and
embraced as God's pledge in all that it promises." Thus biblical authority and biblical interpretation go together; we must
not evade the responsibility of seeking to determine what
Scripture is affirming, requiring and promising.

My second example concerns the statement of Dr. M. M.
Thomas at the fifth Assembly of the World Council of Churches (Nairobi 1975) that a "striking theological convergence"
in the understanding of evangelism was discernable in the
conferences held the previous year at Bangkok (Ecumenical),
Lausanne (Evangelical), Rome (Roman Catholic) and
Bucharest (Orthodox), though some "divergence" remained.
Genuine theological agreement, based on Scripture and
thoroughly tested, is exceedingly welcome. But some evangelicals were alarmed lest this talk of "convergence" concealed
our real (though regrettable) theological disagreement or
compromised our evangelical testimony. Was the Lausanne
Covenant clear and definite enough? I still think it was.
Although its thrust is positive and its tone irenic, it dissociates
itself from several viewpoints espoused in conciliar circles. It
outspokenly rejects "as derogatory to Christ and the gospel
every kind of syncretism and dialogue which implies that
Christ speaks equally through all religions and ideologies," and
instead makes an unequivocal affirmation of the uniqueness
and universality of Christ (para. 3). It also denies that social
action is "evangelism," and that political liberation is "salvation" (para. 5), while at the same time affirming that we
should be concerned for "the liberation of men from every

kind of oppression" and that "evangelism and socio-political involvement are both part of our Christian duty."

These two criticisms lack substance, therefore. The Lausanne Covenant was carefully framed. It has, in fact, been a unifying document among evangelicals. A number of groups have adopted it as their basis of faith.

At the same time, the Lausanne Committee has never claimed that the Covenant is a complete or definitive statement on Christian mission. On the contrary, the Lausanne Theology and Education Group (LTEG), now known as the Theology Working Group, was set up in 1976 "to promote theological reflection on issues related to world evangelization and, in particular, to explore the implications of the Lausanne Covenant." Between 1977 and 1983, therefore, it arranged four consultations.

The first topic chosen for discussion was the controversial "homogeneous unit principle." The colloquium brought five faculty members of Fuller Seminary's School of World Mission face to face, in the spirit of Christian brotherhood, with five discussants who wished to question certain aspects of their position. *The Pasadena Consultation--Homogeneous Unit Principle* was subsequently published as the first Lausanne Occasional Paper. It expresses the tension between theological principle (Christ's Church is a single, new, reconciled humanity) and evangelistic policy (in Donald McGavran's phrase, "people like to become Christians without crossing racial, linguistic or class barriers"). Concessions were made on both sides. It was agreed on the one hand that a homogeneous unit church "can be a legitimate and authentic church" and on the other that "it can never be complete in itself."

Just over six months later, in January 1978, a second consultation was held, this time at Willowbank in Bermuda, on gospel and culture. The topic of culture is mentioned in several paragraphs of the Lausanne Covenant, and these references brought it to the forefront of the evangelical agenda. So the Willowbank Consultation considered the place of culture in six spheres: in God's revelation, in our interpretation and communication of it, and in the response of the hearers as seen in their conversion, their churches and their ethical life-style. *The Willowbank Report--Gospel and Culture* is about 15,000 words in length and was published as Lausanne Occasional Paper No. 2.

The third consultation, which was jointly sponsored by LTEG and the World Evangelical Fellowship Theological Commission's Unit on Ethics and Society, took place in March 1980. It focused on the question of simple life-style, as expressed in the following sentences of the Lausanne Covenant which have occasioned much anxious concern and debate: "All of us are shocked by the poverty of millions and disturbed by the injustices which cause it. Those of us who live in affluent circumstances accept our duty to develop a simple life style in order to contribute more generously to both relief and evangelism" (para. 9). Here poverty and injustice, simplicity and generosity, relief and evangelism are brought together. Yet their mutual relations needed to be spelled out in greater detail. Hence the Consultation, which issued its statement under the title *An Evangelical Commitment to Simple Life-style*, on which Alan Nichols of Australia wrote an Exposition and Commentary, published as Lausanne Occasional Paper No. 20. Some have criticized the statement as unbalanced. But it is firmly grounded on the biblical doctrines of creation and stewardship, and on biblical attitudes to wealth and poverty.

It also contains an important paragraph on the relation between simple life-style and evangelism.

In June 1980 LCWE held at Pattaya its much larger Consultation on World Evangelization (COWE), at the conclusion of which the Thailand Statement was issued (see Figure 6). This alludes indirectly, at least in one paragraph, to an unofficial Statement of Concerns which had been circulated during the Consultation and expressed the view that the Lausanne Committee had been insufficiently concerned for social justice. The Thailand Statement included this paragraph: "Although evangelism and social action are not identical, we gladly reaffirm our commitment to both, and we endorse the Lausanne Covenant in its entirety. It remains the basis of our common activity, and nothing it contains is beyond our concern, so long as it is clearly related to world evangelization."

What most of the Pattaya participants did not know at the time was that LTEG's plans were already advanced for the Consultation on the Relationship between Evangelism and Social Responsibility (CRESR), to be jointly sponsored with the World Evangelical Fellowship. It took place in June 1982 and issued the Grand Rapids Report (Lausanne Occasional Paper No. 21) entitled *Evangelism and Social Responsibility: An Evangelical Commitment*. Nearly 20,000 words in length, it begins with a threefold call to worship and thanksgiving, to world evangelization and to social responsibility, and then goes on to affirm that social activity is a consequence of evangelism, a bridge to it and its partner. It sees the two related in an even more basic way by the gospel, and ends with some practical "Guidelines for Action."

This Consultation sought to complete some of the unfinished business of the Lausanne Congress. For the Lausanne Covenant had defined "The Nature of Evangelism" in paragraph 4 and "Christian Social Responsibility" in paragraph 5, without attempting to relate the two except by saying in paragraph 6 that "in the church's mission of sacrificial service evangelism is primary." The nature of this primacy was clarified at Grand Rapids.

That week convinced me yet again of the great value of representative international consultations, despite their cost in money, time and energy. It is only when we meet face to face, and struggle to hear and understand each other, that our typecast images of one another (developed in separation) are modified, and we grow in mutual respect and shared conviction. Nothing is more conducive to this health-giving process than what has been called "the Lausanne spirit," namely the spirit of openness, integrity and love.

John R. W. Stott is Rector Emeritus of All Souls Church, London, England. He served as chairman of the Drafting Committee of the Lausanne Covenant and has provided commentary on its significance. He chaired the Consultation on the Gospel and Culture and cochaired the Consultation on the Relationship Between Evangelism and Social Responsibility. He is a noted author, lecturer and Bible teacher.

CHRISTIAN SOCIAL RESPONSIBILITY

We affirm that God is both the Creator and the Judge of all men. We therefore should share his concern for justice and reconciliation throughout human society and for the liberation of men from every kind of oppression. Because mankind is made in the image of God, every person, regardless of race, religion, colour, culture, class, sex or age, has an intrinsic dignity because of which he should be respected and served, not exploited. Here too we express penitence both for our neglect and for having sometimes regarded evangelism and social concern as mutually exclusive. Although reconciliation with man is not reconciliation with God, nor is social action evangelism, nor is political liberation salvation, nevertheless we affirm that evangelism and socio-political involvement are both part of our Christian duty. For both are with man is necessary expressions of our doctines of God and man, our love for our neighbour and our obedience to Jesus Christ. The message of salvation implies also a message of judgment upon every form of alienation, oppression and discrimination, and we should not be afraid to denounce evil and injustice wherever they exist. When people receive Christ they are born again into his kingdom and must seek not only to exhibit but also to spread its righteousness in the midst of an unrighteous world. The salvation we claim should be transforming us in the totality of our personal and social responsibilities. Faith without works is dead.

(Acts 17:26,31; Gen. 18:25; Isa. 1:17; Psa. 45:7; Gen. 1:26,27; Jas. 3:9; Lev. 19:18; Luke 6:27,35; Jas. 2:14-26; John 3:3,5; Matt. 5:20; 6:33; II Cor. 3:18; Jas. 2:20)

THE CHURCH AND EVANGELISM

We affirm that Christ sends his redeemed people into the world as the Father sent him, and that this calls for a similar deep and costly penetration of the world. We need to break out of our ecclesiastical ghettos and permeate non-Christian society. In the church's mission of sacrificial service evangelism is primary. World evangelization requires the whole church to take the whole gospel to the whole world. The church is at the very centre of God's cosmic purpose and is his appointed means of spreading the Gospel. But a church which preaches the Cross must itself be marked by the Cross. It becomes a stumbling block to evangelism when it betrays the Gospel or lacks a living faith in God, a genuine love for people, or scrupulous honesty in all things including promotion and finance. The church is the community of God's people rather than an institution, and must not be identified with any particular culture, social or political system, or human ideology.

(John 17:18; 20:21; Matt. 28:19,20; Acts 1:8; 20:27; Eph. 1:9,10; 3:9-11; Gal. 6:14,17; II Cor. 6:3,4; II Tim. 2:19-21; Phil. 1:27)

We cannot hope to attain this goal without sacrifice. All of us are shocked by the poverty of millions and disturbed by the injustices which cause it. Those of us who live in affluent circumstances accept our duty to develop a simple life style in order to contribute more generously to both relief and evangelism.

Articles 5, 6 and 9b
The Lausanne Covenant

Evangelism and
Social Responsibility

John R. Reid

In response to the expressed need to look further at the relationship between evangelism and social responsibility, a consultation on this subject was held in Grand Rapids, Michigan, June 19-25, 1982. It was jointly sponsored by the Theological Working Group of the Lausanne Committee for World Evangelization and the Theological Commission of the World Evangelical Fellowship. Forty-seven persons were present as members of the Consultation, and in addition some representatives of the Church press.

The participants in the Consultation represented the major areas of the world and included leaders in evangelism and others noted for their leadership in social action as well as theologians. Among those present were people who had taken up declared and fixed positions on the topic. Their presence represented the widely varied views among evangelicals on the subject of evangelism and social responsibility. The positions evangelicals have taken on the subject had been expressed in various articles and books, and in one way or another all go back to the Lausanne Congress of 1974. In the Covenant both evangelism and social responsibility were affirmed as part of the Christian's duty and to be seen as expressions of our doctrine of God and man, of our love for our neighbor and our obedience to Christ. The Lausanne Covenant also affirmed that our responsibility in evangelism is primary. However, what it did not do was to explain the relationship between the two. The Consultation therefore was called to explore this unfinished agenda item from the Lausanne Congress.

The Consultation came at a time of considerable controversy and confusion among evangelicals. What was worse, it was being suggested that some who had a strong position on social responsibility had begun to desert the historic gospel of the grace of God. (It also became clear in the debate that a person's position is not only influenced by his or her doctrinal stance on the kingdom and eschatology but also by the social conditions which prevail in the country where he lives.) The Theology Working Group and the Theological Commission saw the importance of serious theological reflection on the topic which would be unhurried and would seek to face the different positions. To do this there was a blend of Bible study, prayer, and small group and plenary group discussions.

For four days of the Consultation, discussion was based on papers that had been previously circulated. These subjects took up major themes which bore upon the matter. Particular papers dealt with The Perspective of Church History; Perspectives of Evangelism and Social responsibility; Contemporary Theology; How Broad Is Salvation in Scripture; The Kingdom in Relation to the Church and the World; History and Eschatology, with a paper on evangelical views and a paper on non-evangelical views; and The Mission of the Church in relation to Evangelism and Social Responsibility.

A drafting Committee each day prepared a statement that reflected points of consensus as well as the divergences of opinion, and gradually this became the basis for a draft which was considered in plenary session by the whole Consultation for two days. Lausanne Occasional Paper No. 21, *Evangelism and Social Responsibility* is the result of that draft. In addition, the papers delivered at the Consultation are to be published as a book after suitable editorial work.

It was hard to see before the Consultation took place that it could produce positive achievements because the divergence and disagreements were so marked. To see the difficulties faced, we need to review the options which have been held on the relationship between evangelism and social responsibility. They range over these alternatives:

* Social responsibility is a distraction from or even a betrayal of evangelism. This view sees evangelism as the exclusive mission of the Church.

* Social responsibility is evangelism. It is argued that it is artificial even to distinguish them since they are so interrelated.

* Social responsibility is a manifestation of evangelism. In its most attractive form it makes the message significantly visible.

* Social responsibility is a consequence of evangelism, and it results from the teaching new converts receive.

* Social responsibility is a partner to evangelism, and both are expressions of love.

* Social responsibility and evangelism are two distinct components of the Church's ministry, and both are equal.

The Consultation had to pick its way through this jungle. It did so with patient listening to each other and by common study of the Scriptures. Differences of opinion remained to the end, but general good will was given to the report which reaffirmed the position of the Lausanne Covenant that evangelism has a priority over social responsibility. It is not necessarily a temporal priority but a logical one, since evangelism deals with a person's eternal destiny. The Consultation did not see a simple relationship between evangelism and social responsibility. It saw it as a set of relationships which could be expressed in these three ways:

1. Social responsibility is a *consequence* of evangelism. Evangelism should produce disciples who are zealous for good works.

2. Social responsibility is a *bridge* to evangelism. It is often possible to move from felt needs to the needs of the spirit.

3. Social responsibility is a *partner* to evangelism. Both stand as expressions for compassion for people's needs, and both can be seen in the ministry of Jesus where he preaches and feeds the hungry and heals the sick.

Reviews of the report are now appearing with both appreciation and criticism. Some are puzzled why so much attention was given to eschatology. Some regret has been stated about the section that deals with practical guidelines on how Christ's disciples can be effective agents for cultural, social and political change. One reviewer wrote, "There is strong encouragement in the document to engage in direct social and political action. It is very encouraging to see this from an 'official' evangelical source."

To my mind there is no doubt about the importance of face-to-face dialogue, as well as joint study of the Scriptures and prayer together as a means of elucidating difficult matters. So many of our attitudes are conditioned by our culture, traditions and social experiences, and it is therapeutic to be in the rough-and-tumble of a debate that forces us to bring all our convictions under the scrutiny of Scripture. This Consultation was not the last word in the debate, but it reduced for many the tensions which could have become hurtful in our fellowship together.

The Consultation ended with a service of the Lord's Supper. It was a fitting conclusion, for genuine love and respect for each other had united the members of the Consultation as they had sought to know the mind of the Lord.

John R. Reid is Bishop in the Diocese of Sydney, Australia. He is a member of LCWE and chairs the Theology Working Group.

The consultation Bishop Reid has described was fed by other streams. The same concerns that prompted some at the International Congress in 1974 to ask for a "more radical" statement of responsibility on the part of evangelicals eventually led to a conference called by the Unit of Ethics of the Theological Commission of the World Evangelical Fellowship directly before the jointly sponsored WEF/LCWE conference on simple life-style at Hoddesdon, England, in March 1980. This consultation on Theology of Development is described in the book *Evangelicals in Development: Toward a Theology of Social Change* edited by Ronald J. Sider (Westminster Press, Philadelphia, 1981). It in turn led to the formation of a steering committee to call a conference in June 1983 which would bring together practitioners and theoreticians under the theme "A Christian Response to Human Need." In its planning for the 1983 consultation the steering committee recognized the importance of the LCWE/WEF-planned consultation on the relationship. They wanted to make sure the streams of thinking that would converge at Grand Rapids would be foundational to future theory and practice. A number of those involved in A Christian Response to Human Need were also a part of the Grand Rapids discussions.

The steering committee later accepted the invitation of the World Evangelical Fellowship to be part of a larger three-track conference known as "I Will Build My Church--Wheaton '83." This gave an important interaction between those concerned with the practical and biblical outworkings of community development to evangelism.

The papers prepared for what now became known as the consultation on The Church in Response to Human Need are notable in their reflection of both Grand Rapids and the Lausanne Covenant. The statement issued by the consultation is worthy of quotation in part:

> We gladly reaffirm, therefore, our conviction that Jesus Christ alone is the world's peace, for he alone can reconcile people to God and bring all hostilities to an end (Eph. 2:14–17).

> We acknowledge, furthermore, that only by spreading the gospel can the most basic need of human beings be met: to have fellowship with God. In what follows we do not emphasize evangelism as a separate theme, because we see it as an integral part of our total Christian response to human need (Matt. 28:18–20). In addition, it is not necessary simply to repeat what the Lausanne Covenant and the report on the consultation on The Relationship Between Evangelism and Social Responsibility (CRESR, Grand Rapids, 1982) have all expressed . . . .

> Others in our Consultation, because of the difficulty in relating it to biblical categories of thought and its negative overtones, would like to replace "development" by another word. An alternative we suggest is "transformation," as it can be applied in different ways to every situation . . . .

We are concerned, however, that both the goals and the process of transformation should be seen in the light of the good news about Jesus, the Messiah . . . .

According to the biblical view of human life, then, transformation is a change from a condition of human existence contrary to God's purposes to one in which people are able to enjoy fulness of life and harmony with God (John 10:10; Col. 3:8-15; Eph. 4:13). This transformation can only take place with the obedience of individuals in communities to the gospel of Jesus Christ, whose power changes the lives of men and women by releasing them from the guilt, power and consequences of sin, enabling them to respond with love towards God and towards others (Rom. 5:5), and making them "new creatures in Christ" (II Cor. 5:17) (from *Social Transformation: The Church in Response to Human Need*, Summary Document of the Wheaton '83 Consultation "I Will Build My Church," August, 1983).

Thus we see the ongoing development of thought springing from many different movements of history, including Lausanne.

But what of the task of "transformation"? What is the relationship between discussing theology and philosophy and getting on with the work? In the following articles Saphir Athyal discusses the work that has been done and Peter Savage focuses in on "Theology and Strategy."

Theological Issues in World Evangelization

Saphir P. Athyal

Our commitment to world evangelization inevitably carries with it a twofold demand on us: first, to be faithful to the whole Bible, submitting to its authority; and second, to be faithful with a self-emptying love and sensitivity to the people to whom we witness. The Lausanne Committee for World Evangelization has earnestly attempted over the past decade to treat these two demands as interrelated and inherently belonging to each other. This is evidenced in the work of its two key committees, the Strategy Working Group and the Theology Working Group. The TWG clarifies the nature of our faithfulness to the Bible in our proclamation of the gospel and in the task of evangelism, while the SWG leads us to an increasingly practical understanding of the nature of our faithfulness to the people to whom we are sent. Evangelistic "strategy" is not some kind of tactics whereby people are lured into the Church, but rather practical ways of genuinely understanding the people to whom God sends us and of communicating the gospel in relevant terms so that it may be heard clearly enough for people to respond to it.

What has been the theological character of LCWE's evangelistic concerns and programs? World evangelism is unthinkable without the biblical theological basis. Except for the mandate given to us in the Bible, there is no evangelistic obligation placed upon us. Apart from the biblical message of salvation we have no evangelistic message or gospel to proclaim to the world. Except for what we know from the promises of God as to his final victory and establishment of his kingdom, the work of evangelism carries with it no sense of power and confidence.

The Work of the Theology Working Group

The general framework of LCWE's commitment to world evangelization is the Lausanne Covenant. Its 15 clauses are essentially our corporate confession of our deepest theological convictions as they relate to evangelization. When the Lausanne Theological and Educational Group (later named the Theology Working Group) was formed, the central mandate given to it was "to explore the implications of the Lausanne Covenant" and to promote the study of theological issues as "directly related to world evangelization."

This group sponsored a number of studies, several of them in cooperation with the Theological Commission of the World Evangelical Fellowship (WEF). (See also John Stott's article in this volume.) The first consultation was held in June 1977 in Pasadena on the homogeneous unit principle of the Church Growth philosophy. The important issue of the gospel and culture was effectively dealt with in an interdisciplinary consultation which brought together an equal number of theologians, missionaries and anthropologists of Willowbank in January 1978. A study was made on the place of culture in revelation, hermeneutics, evangelism, church planting and Christian life-style.

The place of world evangelization in theological education was explored on regional and national levels in order to promote the study of evangelism and mission in theological seminaries, Christian colleges and local churches. The WEF/LCWE-sponsored International Consultation on Simple Lifestyle held in Hoddesdon, England, in March 1980, discussed what should be the Christian attitude to possessions, and our responsibility to share with others more sacrificially what we have, in fuller obedience to the Lord.

Two studies of urgency and importance for the near future are "The Holy Spirit and Evangelization," to be held in Norway in June 1985, and "Conversion" in the following year.

The Consultation on World Evangelization

At the Consultation on World Evangelization (COWE) in Thailand in June 1980, seventeen mini-consultations met simultaneously, each of which studied the theological issues and strategies relating to reaching a major group of unreached people in the world. The following are some of the ways our theological concerns were expressed at COWE:

The people to be reached for Christ were seen in theological perspectives rather than purely in sociological terms. For example, from God's dealings with people in large cities as recorded in the Bible, we found principles upon which to draw for reaching our big cities today; we viewed nominal Christians in terms of biblical understanding of nominal Christianity; and we asked the question, "Why is it necessary to evangelize the Jews?"

COWE also attempted a biblical critique of our major strategies of evangelism today. Effective strategies are effective for theological and practical reasons; so also with strategies that fail. Most strategy questions are essentially theological issues, including our concept of an *effective* strategy. For example, should the focus of evangelism and conversion be always on individuals, or on groups, families, villages and tribes? Should conversion necessarily be followed by baptism in all cases? Is there a Christian way to practice ancestral respect without it becoming ancestral worship?

The gospel is given to us, and none can add to it or subtract from it; yet there are different ways of expressing it. To what extent can we use theological categories and patterns of thought commonly understood by our hearers but taken from non-Christian religions and ideologies, without making compromises? What teachings do we need to clarify and emphasize that might be sensitive and possibly even offensive to our hearers, such as the teaching on the Trinity in our witness to the Jews and the Muslims? Understanding the precise form of expression of the gospel of Jesus Christ in a given situation, and the practical implications of the gospel to a given people and culture, is a theological task. COWE also asked the basic theological question of what kind of people we should be in terms of our unity, if we would be effective witnesses of the gospel.

Our experience at COWE reiterated the importance we have given to having a controlling theology for all our strategies. As it met immediately after COWE, the Lausanne Committee decided that the TWG and the SWG should have closer working relationships and meet jointly for all major planning and decisions.

Theological Issues Today

It is difficult to say which are the key theological issues today in world evangelization. But we may list a few that continue to be in the forefront of contemporary debate.

One is *the meaning of salvation*. Among evangelicals themselves there always have been narrow and broad views of evangelism. A narrow view emphasizes the vicarious character of the atoning death of Christ appropriated by faith by each believer who is then regenerated. A broad view understands sin and salvation as having a corporate aspect as well and relating to social structures.

Related to this is the debate on *the nature of our mission*. The relationship between evangelism and social responsibility is still a crucial issue. The question of the nature of our mission to the people of other faiths is a lively issue in many African and Asian countries.

The relationship of *culture and evangelization* continues to be discussed. A great deal of study has already been done in this area. Because culture and religion are closely linked together, this raises several difficult problems. We need to delineate those elements in Christianity which are extra-biblical and derived from the western "Christian" culture. Also, we need to understand, respect and use the values in cultures of people who belong to other faiths.

While there is general agreement that *the people group concept* is an effective "tool" for evangelization, what bearing does this have on the planting and building of churches?

With the complexity of sociological and occupational group-ings and the intermixing of groups through rapid urbaniza-tion in the world, it is difficult to define the "people groups" and the "unreached." And who on earth are the "hidden peoples," let alone dealing with the gymnastics of arriving at their precise number? In the light of Christ's distinction between the people of Sodom and those of Capernaum on the judgment day, what is more tragic about "the hidden peoples" than, say, "the hardened peoples"? And what is their number? Such terminologies may be useful as practical communication tools, and probably that is all that has been intended; but then locally made tools in whatever part of the world may often be superior.

Evangelism is not simply a matter of "getting on with the job." Basic to what we do should be the continuing discipline of biblically understanding what indeed is our job, and making sure the way we carry it out is theologically sound.

Saphir Athyal is Principal of the Union Biblical Seminary in Maharashtra, India. He is Deputy Chairman of LCWE and a member of the LCWE Theology Working Group. He serves as General Coordinator of the Asia Theological Association.

THE POWER OF THE HOLY SPIRIT

We believe in the power of the Holy Spirit. The Father sent his Spirit to bear witness to his Son; without his witness ours is futile. Conviction of sin, faith in Christ, new birth and Christian growth are all his work. Further, the Holy Spirit is a missionary spirit; thus evangelism should arise spontaneously from a Spirit-filled church. A church that is not a missionary church is contradicting itself and quenching the Spirit. Worldwide evangelization will become a realistic possibility only when the Spirit renews the church in truth and wisdom, faith, holiness, love and power. We therefore call upon all Christians to pray for such a visitation of the sovereign Spirit of God that all his fruit may appear in all his people and that all his gifts may enrich the body of Christ. Only then will the whole church become a fit instrument in his hands, that the whole earth may hear his voice.

(I Cor. 2:4; John 15:26,27; 16:8-11; I Cor. 12:3; John 3:6-8; II Cor. 3:18; John 7:37-39; I Thess. 5:19; Acts 1:8; Psa. 85:4-7; 67:1-3; Gal. 5:22,23; I Cor. 12:4-31; Rom 12:3-8)

Article 14
The Lausanne Covenant

Theology and Strategy

Peter Savage

Theoreticians and practitioners have always struggled with each other; so also evangelists and theologians. In the Lausanne movement, there has been a real attempt to mesh the practice of the movement, through the development of strategies for evangelism, with its foundational base, biblical theology.

The Theology Working Group has wrestled with issues, seeking to establish what the mind of the Lord is on the matter. There has been a high view of Scripture and the Spirit, in the serious attempt to understand what the Word might say on each question, problem and issue. Scripture has been and is normative for the serious theological considerations that have been faced. Questions often arising from the "practice" of evangelism and mission, such as the cultural issues considered at Willowbank, the homogeneous unit questions discussed in Pasadena, or the social involvement addressed in Grand Rapids and Wheaton, have been faced biblically, theologically and missiologically.

As John Stott has discussed, the TWG consultations brought together key men and women within the Lausanne movement from all six continents that had specialized in the matters considered. Papers were presented and discussed, issues raised and faced, problems analyzed, and to some degree answers proposed. At times there were tensions, as differing groups emphasized opposite positions, but under the leadership of the Holy Spirit, and frequently under the able chairmanship of John Stott, the tide was turned, and together these formed part of a fast-moving current of one unbroken. stream of thought.

The Strategy Working Group (SWG) by contrast brought together those who had been involved in the practice and management of evangelism and mission. They were thirsty for action and results that would bring glory to God and extend his kingdom. Under the initial leadership of C. Peter Wagner and then Edward R. Dayton, the group focused first on the management question of "how to channel missionary endeavor into the front line of missionary action." Second, in light of increasingly complex as well as simple preindustrial societies, the question was raised: "What tools could be utilized to ensure a clear, communicable focus for the movement?" The notion of the people group was selected and refined in many a working gathering. Since then pastors, missionaries and students from all over the six continents have been locating, interviewing, and gathering and collating information on the many millions in "people groups" around the world.

Both the TWG and the SWG are aware that the great pressure in the Lausanne movement to see effective evangelization sometimes bypasses the careful and painstaking theological work such evangelization requires. In some contexts there is a pervasive rejection of the theological task. Some are not even aware that success in numbers of new decisions and increase in church members is not necessarily a sure proof of

God's will in evangelization. Oftentimes pragmatic under-
ones in evangelism betray a secular humanist attitude.

On the other hand, the sometimes painful theological task
cannot be a mere desk activity carried on by certain academic
experts. As the Church seeks to reach the whole world for
Christ through all expedient means it struggles with this
problem of contextualization and must not overlook faithful
theologizing in that process. At the Lord's ascension, he gave
gifts to his church; he gave teachers, whose responsibility is to
theologize in the context in which the church expresses itself
locally.

To theologize means to wrestle with the Word, under the
illumination of the Holy Spirit, to understand and perceive
the way forward in his missionary activity in a particular
context. Theology is a human activity that can never claim
an inspiration equal to that of the Scriptures. This requires
the Church in each generation to return to the Word and
allow it to dwell richly within, so the Church in its ministry
can discern the mind of the Lord.

Furthermore, the local church must also take account of the
Word, in each local context, so that God's mind on every
matter related to the church in that place, living in that
particular period of history, can be known. In this sense,
while there is only one Word, handed down in the Bible, many
churches around the world are reading, studying and finding
truths in it that meet each church in a given historical moment. This diversity in the work of the ministry and of
theology is rich, and like the colors of the rainbow, expresses
the common unity in the one light, but in multihued diversity
working out the fullness of the gospel.

Strategy is also a human activity, stimulated by the Holy Spirit, so that a church obedient to its Lord can follow through on a path of action. However, strategies speak of management, responsibility and accountability to the only manager of the Church, the Lord. The church in its local setting seeks to find ways into the surrounding social groups so that each may have the gospel. These strategies, or ways into a group of people who are distinct in identity, language, world view and social institutions, allow the church to open new doors for evangelization. For some, such laborious planning and research, even coupled with prayer, does not respond to the immediate and direct leadership of the Holy Spirit. They feel that innovation from the social sciences and business circles may drown out the creative whisper of the Holy Spirit. The SWG has been sensitive to these concerns and has attempted to grapple with both the direct and miraculous leadings of the Spirit, as well as the diligent search for those who have not yet been "reached" with the gospel.

Both theology and its practical management dimension, "strategy," respond to a historical perspective. The Lord's present reign is evident all over the world through those obedient communities where he is worshiped, obeyed and enjoyed. All these are working in mission with the joyous expectancy of the great consummation of his kingdom. This historical dimension is a helpful framework in which to do both theology and strategy. His coming in glory cannot be strategized, nor can its full dimensions be theologized. However, it is the central motivation for every Christian to see the world evangelized and every creature "reached" with the gospel before that great day of glory and triumph. This will be God's doing! "We shall see him."

Maranatha!

Peter Savage is the International Coordinator of the Latin American Theological Fraternity and serves as the Lausanne Coordinator for Reaching New Religious Movements. He is a member of the Strategy Working Group and also of the Executive Committee of the Theological Commission of the World Evangelical Fellowship.

The Idea Spreads

COOPERATION IN EVANGELISM

We affirm that the church's visible unity in truth is God's purpose. Evangelism also summons us to unity, because our oneness strengthens our witness, just as our disunity under-mines our gospel of reconciliation. We recognize, however, that organizational unity may take many forms and does not necessarily forward evangelism. Yet we who share the same biblical faith should be closely united in fellowship, work and witness. We confess that our testimony has sometimes been marred by sinful individualism and needless duplication. We pledge ourselves to seek a deeper unity in truth, worship, holiness and mission. We urge the development of regional and functional cooperation for the furtherance of the church's mission, for strategic planning, for mutual en-couragement, and for the sharing of resources and experience.

(John 17:21,23; Eph. 4:3,4; John 13:35; Phil. 1:27; John 17:11-23)

Article 7
The Lausanne Covenant

"We urge the development of regional and functional cooperation for the furtherance of the church's mission, for strategic planning, for mutual encouragement, and for the sharing of resources and experience." It is doubtful whether the framers of the Lausanne Covenant would have believed how rapidly their hopes for strategic planning, mutual encouragement and sharing of resources and experience would be realized. Kenya, Nigeria, Papua New Guinea, Hong Kong, Northern Europe, Guatemala, India, Ghana, Singapore, Norway--the list goes on in response to the moving of the Holy Spirit and the motivation of Lausanne. Congress after congress was called not only to reflect on the task of world evangelization but to get on with it. Figure 3 is a brief record of that spreading flame.

The spirit of Lausanne reached out across denominational distinctives and territorial prerogatives. Evangelization was the central theme: the task of the Church was to proclaim the good news of the kingdom. The Lausanne Covenant provided a way for Christians of different countries and diverse histories to affirm their common commitment to that proclamation. In the articles that follow, Kirsti Mosvold tells us what happened in Norway. Peter Wagner talks about the North American Lausanne Committee and its work. Thomas Wang shows how the Lausanne movement resulted in new cooperation to evangelize the Chinese of the diaspora. Raymond Bakke shares with us his report on visits to 38 cities and what he found God doing there. And finally, Warren Webster points us to the future with new directions for Western missions.

Evangelism Conferences Since Lausanne '74

1975 Nigerian Congress on World Evangelization

Formation meeting of the Lausanne Continuation Committee/Mexico City

Kenya Congress on Unreached Peoples/Lenana, Kenya

Executive Committee of the LCWE/London

1976 Seminar on Evangelism in Papua New Guinea and the Solomon Islands

Chinese Congress on World Evangelization (August)

Northern Europe Conference/Belgium (September)

PACLA/Nairobi (December)

LCWE meeting/Atlanta

Chinese Congress on World Evangelization/Hong Kong (August)

Executive Committee of the LCWE/Berlin

1977 Indian Congress of World Evangelization/Guatemala

All-India Congress on Mission and Evangelization/Devlali (January)

Pasadena Consultation on the Homogeneous Unit Principle/California (May)

Ghana Congress on Evangelization (July)

Chinese and Western Leadership Cooperation Seminar/Singapore (September)

Executive Committee of the LCWE/Montreal

1978 Nigerian Congress on World Evangelization/Nigeria

Norwegian Congress on Evangelization/Norway

Indian Congress of World Evangelization/Guatemala

101

1978   Consultation on Gospel and Culture/Willowbank, Bermuda (January)

Congress on Evangelism for Malaysia and Singapore (April)

Chinese World Missions Seminar/Philippines (May)

North American Conference on Muslim Evangelization/Glen Eyrie (October)

Executive Committee of the LCWE/Springfield, MO

ALCOE/Singapore (November)

1979   SACLA/Pretoria, South Africa (July)

Executive Committee of the LCWE/Ventnor, NJ

Venezuelan National Congress on Evangelization/Caracas (November)

1980   International Consultation on Simple Life-Style/London (March)

Stuttgart Congress on World Evangelization/West Germany (April)

Indian Congress of World Evangelization/Guatemala (April)

Consultation on World Evangelization (COWE)/Pattaya, Thailand (June)

COWE Follow-up Conference for Christian Leaders/Danvik, Norway (September)

Future Planning Consultation/Osaka, Japan (October)

Second Norwegian Congress on World Evangelization (November)

1981   Chinese Congress on World Evangelization (CCOWE)/Singapore (June)

Executive Committee of the LCWE/Old Jordan, UK

American Festival of Evangelism/Kansas City (July)

Third National Congress on Evangelism/Nigeria (August)

1981   Third Norwegian Congress on World Evangelization

1982   Consultation of Evangelicals in Latin America/Panama (April)

Executive Committee of the LCWE/Wheaton, Illinois (May)

Joint meeting of Theology Working Group and Strategy Working Group (May)

Lausanne Committee for World Evangelization/Wheaton, Illinois (May)

Consultation on the Relationship Between Evangelism and Social Responsibility/Grand Rapids, Michigan (June)

1983   Lausanne Committee for World Evangelization/San Bernardino (January)

Executive Committee of LCWE/San Bernardino, CA (January)

Canadian Consultation on Evangelism/Toronto (July)

Executive Committee of the LCWE/Amsterdam, Holland (July)

CONELA's Congress on Social Responsibility/Panama (July)

Brazil Congress on Evangelism/Belo Horizonte (October/November)

Chinese Mass Media Evangelization Seminar/Hong Kong (October)

The LCWE in Norway

Kirsti Mosvold

The thirty-five Norwegian church and mission leaders who attended the International Congress on World Evangelization in Lausanne back in 1974 returned home with a new burden for world evangelism in their hearts. How could this burden be shared with others who were not at Lausanne? How could Christians be mobilized to take a new share in the Great Commission and the task the Lord has set before us? There was a willingness and desire to pass on to others the vision that a few had experienced as a conference event.

The Norwegian Lausanne Congress attendees, led by bishop Erling Utnem, came together in May 1975, along with other key church and mission leaders, and formed the Norwegian Lausanne Committee (NLC). Today around thirty men and women serve on this committee. Each year five new members are appointed and five are "retired." This way we seek to secure both continuity and new input.

When the NLC was formed, there certainly was a felt need among church and mission leaders for a kind of fellowship that provided contact, information, inspiration and cooperation for the task of world evangelism, exactly as the young and fresh Lausanne movement had seemed to provide. Now the movement had come to Norway! Suddenly we had a fellowship with structures loose enough so that individuals and churches/parachurch organizations felt free to come together to share, listen, learn and inspire each other. A new resource for world evangelism was found--and founded.

The first point on the NLC agenda was to translate the Lausanne Covenant and have it distributed to the believers in our country for study and commitment. The Covenant was received with great appreciation by the church and mission leaders, as a significant missiological document of our time. The Covenant became the "starting point" as well as the guideline on what should be the concerns of the NLC. However, we have had to admit that the Covenant text is rather "heavy," so the response from the grass-roots level in the churches and parachurch agencies has been weaker than anticipated. This kind of document is just not what the ordinary church member tends to read. Therefore the NLC was born, and probably stayed, a movement primarily for leaders, and as such the Lord has blessed and used the Lausanne movement. Those leaders who are involved have gained a fresh outlook on the task of world evangelism, which is reflected in their teaching and preaching, and thus we believe that the grass-roots level has been touched as well.

In the '70s there was a debate in Norway as to whether the LCWE as an ecumenical movement ought to sharpen its critique of the World Council of Churches, or even become an alternative organization for those who are worried about the kind of ecumenism provided by the WCC. As these concerns were faced, there seemed to emerge a kind of consensus that neither of these are main purposes of LCWE, and we have grown to appreciate the special purpose and priorities of the LCWE, which in this context is to work in a constructive way for world evangelization, with a sharp focus on the main challenges in our time, e.g., the unreached peoples of the world, near and far.

So, the main purpose of the NLC has been to have a share in the LCWE, so that we can pass on the inspiration, challenges and information that flow towards us through the efforts and network of the LCWE. Our main tool to *pass on* and *reach out* is twofold. First, a national *Lausanne Newsletter* (in Norwegian) is printed four times a year and distributed to all members. A "member" is a person who has committed himself or herself to the Lausanne Covenant by signing the covenant and supporting the NLC with a small annual fee. Through this support we are able to pay the expenses for Norwegians who serve on the international committees and working groups, and also give a small support to the LCWE office in London.

Second, every other year since 1978, national conferences known as the Danvik Conferences have been sponsored, where 100 to 140 leaders have come together to study and share topics and concern that have been highlighted by the LCWE, such as focus on unreached peoples, church growth and church planting, and social responsibility. An important feature of these conferences has been the special contribution made by invited international speakers, such as Gottfried Osei-Mensah, John Stott and Chua Wee Hian. These servants of the Lord have provided us with a fresh understanding of what God is doing in the world today outside those contacts and networks that already are recognized between the churches/missions and their co-working partners overseas. In other words, we feel that the NLC has been a tool to broaden our scope, contacts, insight and share in world evangelism.

Along with the information and teaching that has been passed
on at Danvik, a primary outcome has been a deep sense of
fellowship in our Lord Jesus Christ among the attendees. The
sense of fellowship does not rule out our the different
denominational viewpoints. However, as an ecumenical
movement, our unity has been felt and perceived in the *goal*
we all share: the spreading of the Good News to all peoples in
the world, nearby and far away, and the coming of our Lord
Jesus.

Kirsti Mosvold is Executive Secretary of the Evangelical Lutheran Free Church in Norway, while studying theology in Oslo. She is a member of the Norwegian Missionary Council, a Lausanne Associate and a member of the Strategy Working Group.

The North American Lausanne Committee

C. Peter Wagner

The North American Lausanne Committee was formed short-ly after the International LCWE. One of the important fac-tors that has enabled the Committee to function was the decision made at the very beginning that the Committee would have no budget and no treasury. All participants have been required to raise their own expenses from their own sources. The result has been that many denominations and agencies have been drawn together through their financial contribution to individual members of the Committee. This same policy has applied to all the activities of the LCWE/NA, including events that it has sponsored.

Kenneth Chafin, pastor of the South Main Baptist Church of Houston, Texas, was the president for the first two years, 1974-1976. He was succeeded by Robert Coleman, now professor at Trinity Evangelical Divinity School, who served from 1976 to 1980. The current president is C. B. Hogue, pastor of Eastwood Baptist Church in Tulsa, Oklahoma.

The North American Lausanne Committee has sponsored two major events since the ICOWE and has a third one in the planning stage. In 1978 there was the North American Con-ference on Muslim Evangelization. In 1981 there was the

American Festival of Evangelism. The National Convocation on Evangelizing Ethnic America is scheduled for 1985.

The Gospel and Islam

The idea for this consultation originated in a paper written at the Fuller School of World Mission by Donald McCurry. McCurry had worked since the late 1950s as a missionary to Muslims in Pakistan. He came to study at the Fuller School of World Mission convinced that one of the greatest obstacles to Muslim evangelization was a lack of culturally congenial churches for Muslim converts. His broad experience and his personal warmth and sensitivity made him ideally suited to be director of this strategic conference. World Vision, through its MARC center, kindly provided office space, staff help and generous financial support to help make this project possible.

From the first, the organizers were committed to the concept of a "working" conference where participants would be carefully selected and thus highly motivated. Forty foundation papers were distributed to prospective participants in one-week intervals. The quality of the person's written response to these papers determined whether or not he or she would finally be chosen as one of the 150 participants at the conference itself!

A very special group of people, therefore, arrived at the Navigators Conference Center at Glen Eyrie, Colorado, on October 15, 1978. This was undoubtedly the first time so many people, representing so many different constituencies and types of ministries aimed at Muslims, had gathered together to pool their resources and learn from one another. The boldness and creativity of the foundation papers had already set the mood for a new freedom to grapple with the issues head-on to make honest evaluations of past and present efforts. The presence of various categories of people (missionaries, mission executives, anthropologists, Islamicists, communicators and Two-Thirds World consultants) allowed for a balanced and realistic discussion of new strategies and approaches.

One result of that significant conference has been published in *The Gospel and Islam: A 1978 Compendium* edited by Don M. McCurry and published by MARC. A second result was the organization of the Samuel Zwemer Institute for Muslim Studies located in Pasadena, California. McCurry is its founding president.

The American Festival of Evangelism

The idea for an American Festival of Evangelism began with a group of four or five Americans talking together on the banks of St. Lawrence River during a meeting of the LCWE in Montreal. Tom Zimmerman, General Superintendent of the U.S. Assemblies of God, was the person who directed the initial planning stages from his office in Springfield at the expense of the AOG. Subsequently, Paul Benjamin was appointed as executive coordinator with an office in Washington.

The Festival brought together over 14,500 participants. There were 200 specialists in evangelism conducting workshops and seminars on the themes of Evangelizing, Discipling and Equipping. Most of these presentations were subsequently put together in four reproducible notebooks and a host of cassette tapes. Special attention was given to evangelizing Native Americans, cults, refugees, the poor, political and community leaders, industrial workers, military personnel, professional athletes, businessmen, and alcoholics and drug addicts.

A wide range of seminars were given on discipling using a vast array of approaches and resources. For example, equipping dealt with how to prepare people to become evangelists, how to develop evangelistic strategies, how to prepare churches for evangelism outreach, how to teach the importance of evangelism in the church, how to use apologetics to evangelize, and the importance of intercessory prayer undergirding it all.

The National Convocation on Evangelizing Ethnic America-- Houston '85

The North American Lausanne Committee has now appointed a task force on reaching ethnic America which is in the process of doing research throughout the United States. The National Convocation on Evangelizing Ethnic America will be held in Houston, Texas, on April 15-18, 1985. The principal focus of Houston '85 will be the 18-20 different national families whose language and culture is other than English. It was during the planning for the 1981 American Festival of Evangelism that the North American Lausanne Committee became aware of the need for a similar effort among ethnic persons in the United States.

Oscar Romo, Director of the Language Mission Division of the Southern Baptist Home Mission Board, has been named chairman. C. Peter Wagner, a member of the LCWE and professor of church growth at Fuller Theological Seminary, is vice-chairman. Paul Landrey of the World Vision U.S. office is the coordinator. Under the general theme "Let Ethnic America Hear His Voice," Houston '85 will focus its efforts toward persons who have identified themselves with an ethnolinguistic group other than Anglo–American. It is understood that a similar event among American blacks is projected by the North American Lausanne Committee for the near future.

The basic objective for the convocation is to call key leadership of American churches and Christian organizations together for the specific purpose of uniting in prayer, research in the current ethnic realities in the United States, sharing lessons learned from successes and failures and mobilizing all U.S. churches in the exciting task of ethnic evangelization. The event will deal with Native Americans, Asians, Europeans, Hispanics, Middle Easterners, Caribbeans, and others.

C. Peter Wagner is Associate Professor of Church Growth at the School of World Mission, Fuller Theological Seminary. He is a founding member of LCWE and the first chairman of the Strategy Working Group. He served in Bolivia as a missionary and has written numerous books on missions and church growth.

Lausanne and the Chinese Coordination Centre of World Evangelism

Thomas Wang

The Lausanne movement, viewed from Asia, is one of the most significant spiritual movements God has raised up in the world in this century. It is a movement solely committed to the task of world evangelization. It is a spiritual movement, not structured as a rigid organization, but a joint endeavor among like-minded evangelicals to encourage and to motivate each other in the task of calling the world to repentance and acceptance of Christ as Savior.

The series of evangelism congresses in the past two decades (Berlin 1966, Singapore 1968, United States 1969, Lausanne 1974 and Thailand 1980) has significantly affected the evangelical world. Many of us still remember that until the middle part of this century, evangelical forces of the world were mainly on the defensive, if not in retreat. But by God's grace and through this series of congresses, the tide has turned: evangelicals are no longer retreating and have regained their confidence. The spiritual contribution of these congresses, with Lausanne as the apex, to the evangelical world as a whole is immeasurable.

Speaking of the Lausanne movement, I must, on behalf of the Chinese churches of the diaspora, express our words of affirmation. In 1974 over 70 Chinese church leaders attended the Lausanne Congress. We were overwhelmed by the spiritual impact of the occasion. The unity, the joy, the commitment to worldwide evangelism as well as the resounding declaration of the Lausanne Covenant by the 4000 evangelical leaders were things we had never witnessed before. We prayed together for one hour each morning for the Lord's mercy that something similar could also happen among the Chinese churches around the world. We confessed to God our sins of individualism, self-centeredness and self-righteousness. Before the Congress was over, we felt the Lord's leading that we should begin a movement of unity and evangelistic outreach among Chinese churches worldwide. And on the last day of the Lausanne Congress, we publicly declared that we would use the next two years to promote and to prepare for a Chinese Congress of World Evangelization (CCOWE) to be held in 1976 in Hong Kong.

The Hong Kong Congress was the first of its kind in Chinese church history. It was also a milestone in our commitment to world evangelization. Sixteen hundred Chinese evangelical leaders from over 20 countries participated in CCOWE '76. The blessings of God were so immense that the participants unanimously decided that the movement must go on and that a continuation office should be set up to further this unprecedented movement.

So in October 1976, the Chinese Coordination Centre of World Evangelism (CCCOWE) was formally established in Hong Kong. Since 1976 we have witnessed new and wonderful blessings of God among Chinese churches around the world.

The CCCOWE movement has brought to the Chinese churches a deeper sense of unity and greater commitment to world evangelization.

We have organized the 5000 Chinese churches in the diaspora into 39 geographic districts, each managed by a committee, which serve as an effective network and a cohesive force among Chinese churches worldwide. Through this network we are able to promote a 20-year ministry plan among the Chinese churches of the world. During the first 10 years (1981-1990) we envision a 300 percent growth of the Chinese churches in terms of converts, congregations and trained workers. During the second 10 years (1991-2000) we expect the Chinese churches to become responsible and substantial partners among the world force for evangelism and colaborers in evangelization to both the one billion people in China and other people groups requiring cross-cultural evangelism.

The Lausanne movement, in a short span of ten years, has been used by God to inspire and motivate numerous ethnic and national churches, denominations as well as parachurch groups, in a renewed vision, burden, confidence and determination to evangelize their own people and the peoples of the world. And the CCCOWE movement, one of the spiritual spin-offs of Lausanne, will serve as one of the supreme examples of what God has done through the Lausanne movement.

The Chinese church and its leaders cherish a deep appreciation of the Lausanne movement. Our prayer is that God will increasingly use this movement in a more profound yet practical way as an inspiration, motivation and rallying point among the world evangelical forces to fulfill together the Great Commission of our Lord Jesus Christ.

THE IDEA SPREADS

Thomas Wang is a member of the LCWE Executive Committee and is the General Secretary of the Chinese Coordination Centre of World Evangelism, Kowloon, Hong Kong.

Urban Population Relative to Population at Large
of Earth's Regions

| | 1975 | | 2000 | |
	Population (in millions) (1)	Urban Population (%) (2)	Population (in millions) (2)	Urban Population (%) (3)
Region				
World	3,967	39	6,130	51
Africa	401	27	851	42
Asia, East	1,006	29	1,488	45
Asia, South	1,250	25	2,077	37
North America	237	74	302	83
Latin America	324	65	564	76
Europe	473	69	511	78
USSR	255	62	309	74
Oceania	21	72	29	83

Sources:

(1) 1975 World Population Data Sheet of the Population Reference Bureau, Inc. – Population Estimate, mid-1975.

(2) 1983 World Population Data Sheet of the Population Reference Bureau, Inc. Estimates of % of urban population refer to some point in the '70s.

(3) Estimates supplied by the Population Reference Bureau, Inc. in telephone conversation on 11/3/83.

Figure 4a

Estimates of Growth in Selected Two-Thirds World Cities

	1960	1970	1975	2000
	millions of persons			
Calcutta	5.5	6.9	8.1	19.7
Mexico City	4.9	8.6	10.9	31.6
Greater Bombay	4.1	5.8	7.1	19.1
Greater Cairo	3.7	5.7	6.9	16.4
Jakarta	2.7	4.3	5.6	16.9
Seoul	2.4	5.4	7.3	18.7
Delhi	2.3	3.5	4.5	13.2
Manila	2.2	3.5	4.4	12.7
Tehran	1.9	3.4	4.4	13.8
Karachi	1.8	3.3	4.5	15.9
Bogota	1.7	2.6	3.4	9.5
Lagos	0.8	1.4	2.1	9.4

Source: <u>The Global 2000 Report to the President,</u> Vol. II, U.S. Government Printing Office, 1980, p. 242.

Figure 4b

Ministry in Large Cities Since Pattaya '80

Raymond J. Bakke

A Strategic Perspective of the City

For nearly two thousand years the Church has possessed the mandate to disciple all the peoples or nations of the world. Now, in this very generation, we are discovering where these peoples and nations are located: in the large cities of the world.

Urban pastors and missionaries need a global perspective to interpret the modern city. They need international skills to live and serve there. I believe this based on personal experience. Among the nearly 60,000 residents in my own inner-city Chicago neighborhood and nearby public high school, about 50 nations of the world are now represented (1980 Census) within an area of little more than one square mile.

Theologically, one might ask, "What is God trying to accomplish by the urbanization of his world and the internationalization of our cities?" The fact that he is doing it is undeniable. Could it be his way of showing us the priority now for urban evangelization?

"The Empire Strikes Back" is more than the title of a 1980 American movie. It is European urban reality. Without exception, capital cities of Europe which once served as administrative centers for empires in the colonial world abroad are now experiencing the usually painful role of caring for formerly colonialized peoples who have now come from the colonies to the new cheap labor markets. Although the dynamics in this process create enormous problems for old urban establishments in London, Paris, Amsterdam, Berlin and other cities, they also create exciting new potential for urban ministry and international evangelization. Every city now has links with populations "back home." To reach out to a person in the name of Jesus Christ in East London is simultaneously to reach out to the Punjab. In Paris it is to impact Algeria. Reaching out in Amsterdam affects Surinam, Goa or Indonesia. In Berlin, it affects Turkey and other places.

Strategies for Evangelism

Lamentably, we observe many single-strategy evangelization approaches to large cities. The evangelists, who represent a host of churches and agencies, do not recognize the need for multiple responses to the urbanization of the world. While Christian ministry strategies and responsibilities obviously begin with evangelism, they certainly do not stop there. God's people should seek to minister not only *in* the city, but *to* it as well.

Cities have inherited an unusual share of world problems and problem peoples who have dropped out of other places. As the old saying runs, "All roads lead to Rome . . . and all sewers also." Large numbers of urban individuals and institutions lie in ruin. Evangelism is most effective when the passion for evangelistic effectiveness is adorned with broad-ranging concerns and goals for the renewal of the whole of city life.

As in the days of old, urban evangelization is most effectively accomplished by those within the city itself. Jeremiah told the Babylonian exiles to "build houses and settle down and seek the prosperity of the city to which I have carried you into exile. Pray to the Lord for it, because if it prospers, you too will prosper" (Jer. 29:51). After the exile, Isaiah told the rebuilders of Jerusalem, "Your people will rebuild the ancient ruins and will raise up the age-old foundations; you will be called repairer of broken walls, restorer of streets with dwellings" (Isa. 58:12).

Is it not ironic that many contemporary Christians who claim a high view of Scripture continue to ignore the biblical truth stated plainly in hundreds of Old and New Testament texts dealing with urban mission? Surely "the blessed hope" is the Lord's intervention in the city, not the Church's continued flight from the presence and task of urban evangelization.

If our analysis is correct, evangelization of the cities today will impact the countryside tomorrow. Surely the cost accountants of mission budgets cannot fail to see the significance of urban mission as a high-growth investment, even though in the short run it often costs more than ministry in rural areas.

Ministry Since Thailand '80

Out of the mini-consultation on urban evangelization at Pattaya we conceived a three-year follow-on strategy. Since that time it has been my privilege to meet hundreds of the men and women who contributed to the process that led up to the Consultation on World Evangelization and reflect with them on how God might want to preach the Good News in the rapidly growing urban areas of the world.

It is appropriate to reflect on the total experience as background to planning any future multi-year strategies. What follows is a bare outline of reflections and recommendations.

Reflections

In my Associate role I have studied, corresponded, lectured, preached, consulted, strategized or directed consultations in 38 cities abroad and 18 large USA cities (plus a host of smaller ones). Since Pattaya the international list includes: Hong Kong, Tokyo, Caracas, Bogota, Lima, Quito, Santiago, Buenos Aires, Sao Paulo, Rio de Janeiro, San Jose, London, Amsterdam, Karachi, Calcutta, Bangkok, Seoul, Manila, Jakarta, Sydney, Melbourne, Medellin, Belo Horizonte, Mexico City, Toronto, Regina, Saint John, Wolfville, Halifax, Cairo, Nicosia, Singapore, Dacca, Bombay, Nairobi, Belgrade, Zagreb, Copenhagen and Oslo.

I am more convinced than ever of the validity of a Lausanne urban evangelization emphasis that focuses and empowers the Church in its mission to the "culturally distant unreached peoples" of large and rapidly growing cities. We need to understand that an unreached people group may live half a mile away from us, separated not only by towers of concrete and steel but by culture, class, thought form, and a variety of other attributes which enable us to discern a people group.

Urban anthropologists sometimes classify cities by roles: cultural, economic or administrative. These categories enable us to see obvious differences between most cities. For example,

Chicago, Sao Paulo and Bombay are clearly economic or industrial cities. Boston, Benares and Rio de Janeiro have primarily cultural roles in each of their countries. Washington, D.C., New Delhi, and Brasilia assume roles of governance.

No one can doubt that the structures of community life, histories, ethos, population profiles and expectations of these cities are broadly shaped or influenced by the roles they play in the larger society. On a smaller scale, numerous port cities, and market or county-seat towns, maintain similar roles with equal regional significance for those seeking to design ministry strategies within them. At a fundamental level, then, the differences between large cities and small cities or towns are differences in degree, not in kind. By comparison, the large city contains more human variety and functions at such speeds that its social life resembles the work of time-lapse photography.

Experience shows that six basic types of urban consultations have validity for future interaction in large cities. Each has its own unique size, venue, format, constituencies, planning and follow-up processes, costs and set of expected outcomes:

1. *The Urban Leaders Evangelization Consultation*, where four groups of key urban pastors, mission decision-makers, seminary professors or leadership developers, and lay professionals come together for two or three days of study, prayer, sharing and strategizing. This is appropriate for 20-50 persons generally.

2. *The Urban Evangelism Models and Strategies Conference*, where the varieties of urban ministry programs and resource persons are themselves the program and are presented in on-site visits or assessed in case study

workshops, so that these resources can be multiplied among other ministry designers who will be leaders also from groups chosen by invitation, up to perhaps 200 persons.

3. *The Urban Evangelism Conference*, an inspirational and informative lay event with plenary sessions and workshops on a range of personal evangelism issues and strategies by general invitation and with 500 to 1000 participants.

4. *The Regional Cities Leaders Evangelization Consultation*, where 20-50 denominationally diverse church and parachurch persons in teams of three or four per city come together in a process similar to 1.above but with a regional focus to the long-range strategy discussions.

5. *The Urban Ministry Congress*, where in a large national or regional format, model and strategy resources are brokered for the Church's total urban mission: worship, evangelism, discipleship, stewardship, fellowship and service.

6. *The Special Theme Urban Mission Conference*, where a single theme or a single constituency might be the fundamental organizing principle such as:

   a. The urban refugee.
   b. The elderly, youth, unemployed, etc.
   c. The chemically dependent unreached people.
   d. The lay professional in urban mission.
   e. The urban pastor.
   f. Media and communications.

g. Mission and institutions: hospitals, jails, schools, etc.
h. The gospel and the slum.
i. The urban family.

The emphasis is shifting away from data-filled, goal-directed, program-centered conferences, to process consultations that start where people say they are and focus on strengthening relationships, motivating for finding resources and strategizing to empower institutions.

One of the difficulties we face is that most urban Christian leaders plan for *events*, which become the end or goal, rather than a continuing *process*. We need to attract and support key local organizers who have a broad base of relationships and a kingdom perspective on urban mission.

Our major focus is Asia, Latin America, the Mediterranean and Africa where cities are huge and rapidly growing and the Church (if not evangelicals) are a clear minority. However, the new interest amid the re-paganizing cities of Europe and North America cannot be neglected for several reasons, not least because of the resources and influence of those cities.

For conceptualization and planning I am now thinking Lausanne's focus should be on the context of these urban regions:

1. North Asian Rim
2. Association of South-East Asian Nations (ASEAN)
3. India
4. Africa West
5. Africa South-Central

127

6. Mediterranean
7. East Bloc
8. Europe (West and North)
9. Hispanic (Miami and Mexico City to Lima)
10. Brazil
11. North America

We can inventory resources, do the urban demographics and plan our consultation strategies around each of these urban regions for 1984-1989. When I say "we," I obviously do not mean just the Lausanne movement. Joint-ventured sponsorships with joint funding will increase participation in the future consultations. Lausanne can promote them as a catalyst or resource. After all, that is what the Lausanne movement is all about!

Raymond J. Bakke serves on the faculty of Northern Baptist Theological Seminary, Lombard, Illinois. For the past three years he has traveled widely conducting urban ministry seminars in world-class cities. He serves as Lausanne Coordinator for Urban Ministry.

Definitions

People Group: a significantly large sociological grouping of individuals who perceive themselves to have a common affinity for one another. From the viewpoint of evangelization this is the largest possible group within which the gospel can spread without encountering barriers of understanding or acceptance.

Primary Group: the **ethnolinguistic** preference which defines a person's identity and indicates one's primary loyalty.

Secondary Group: a **sociological** grouping which is to some degree subject to personal choice and allows for considerable mobility. Regional and generational groups, caste and class divisions are representative.

Tertiary Group: casual associations of people which are usually temporary and the result of circumstances rather than personal choice such as high-rise dwellers, drug addicts, occupational groupings and professionals.

Unreached People Group: a people group among which there is no indigenous community of believing Christians with adequate numbers and resources to evangelize this people group without outside (cross-cultural) assistance. Also referred to as "hidden people group" or "frontier people group".

Reached People Group: a people group with adequate indigenous believers and resources to evangelize this group without outside (cross-cultural) assistance.

E-0 Evangelism: effort made to reach those already nominally part of the Christian movement.

E-1 Evangelism: ministry to those in the same culture but outside the Christian movement.

E-2 Evangelism: ministry outside the church's culture in an attempt to reach those of a similar culture. Requires the establishment of a new church to service the people of that culture and to reach the remainder of the culture.

E-3 Evangelism: effort to reach a culture that is distinct and remote from that within which the evangelizing church resides. The latter two types of evangelism call for cross-cultural skills in evangelism.

New Directions
for Western Missions

Warren W. Webster

Christian mission has been defined as the concern that where there are no Christians, there *should be* Christians. Where there are no living, growing churches, there should be reproducing communities of believers. This has been and always should be the concern of mission-minded followers of Christ.

Right from the beginning when our Lord gave the commission to "go and make disciples of all nations," some obeyed and went. Starting from Palestine, a tiny country that formed a land bridge between Africa, Asia and Europe, the gospel began to spread from people to people, country to country, continent to continent.

By the mid-twentieth century the Christian faith had achieved near-universal dimensions and was at least represented, if not deeply rooted, in nearly every country on the face of the earth. But that did not mean the task of world evangelization was complete. The International Missionary Council meeting at Whitby, Canada, in 1947 called for a partnership of younger and older churches to establish "pioneer work in all those parts of the world in which the gospel has not yet been preached and where the Church has not yet taken root."

Many established mission agencies had unconsciously become so absorbed in the "church development syndrome" with churches they had helped bring into being that they tended to minimize or neglect creative outreach to other as yet unreached and unevangelized peoples around them. On the other hand, there were voices calling Christians to recognize that one of the Church's top priorities must be getting the gospel to that one-third of the world's people who have not yet so much as heard the name of Christ. Wycliffe Bible Translators began in 1935 to focus on "Bibleless tribes," who had none of the Word of God in their language, as one category of unreached peoples. The very names of some other mission agencies founded during that era, such as Unevangelized Fields Mission (1931) and New Tribes Mission (1942), indicate their original commitment to plant the church where it could not already be found.

Both the World Congress on Evangelism in Berlin (1966) and the International Congress on World Evangelization in Lausanne (1974) added impetus to the evangelical commitment to biblical missions. Ralph Winter's paper at Lausanne on "The Highest Priority: Cross-Cultural Evangelism" was a landmark in mission strategy. It introduced the idea of separate "peoples" within a country, and popularized the concept of E-1, E-2, and E-3 evangelism measured in terms of *cultural* rather than *geographic* distance. (See Figure 5 for definitions). With the aid of the People Profiles prepared for the Congress by the Missions Advanced Research and Communication Center (MARC), Lausanne helped focus attention on the great task of world evangelization.

The major evangelical conferences that followed Lausanne (Figure 3) produced at least three major emphases or new directions that have influenced and characterized missions in the West over the past decade:

1. *A clearer understanding of biblical "nations" as "peoples."* The Hebrew and Greek words often translated as "nations" refer more to groupings of people (cultures) than to political territories. In biblical times, nation-states as political units with clearly defined geographic boundaries were not as common as they are today. When the Bible speaks of "nations," it is primarily referring to peoples--groups defined not so much by borders as by ethnic origin, language, group loyalty, custom and religion. Jesus' words in Matthew 28 can be translated (as in *Today's English Version*): "Go, then, to all peoples everywhere and make them my disciples." It is not enough to have a church in every country. We are also to endeavor to make disciples of the various ethnolinguistic "people groups" (*ta ethne*) which make up each country or nation-state. (See Definitions in Figure 5.)

This "people group" concept has proven to be a useful and powerful tool for churches and missions in conceptualizing the unfinished task and in planning workable strategies to fulfill our Lord's command.

2. *A renewed global thrust to evangelize "unreached peoples."* Lausanne brought to many for the first time a vivid awareness of the needs of the then "2.7 billion" people who did not call themselves Christians or profess the Christian faith in any form. Eighty percent of these non-Christians are allegedly reachable only through cross-cultural evangelism. Most of them can be found in five major blocs of humanity: Chinese, Muslim, Hindu, Buddhist and tribal (or animistic).

With reference to all unevangelized peoples everywhere Lausanne declared: "Let the Earth Hear His Voice."

Six years later a Consultation on World Evangelization was held in Pattaya, Thailand, a follow-up conference to Lausanne, met around the practical theme, "How Shall They Hear?" Pattaya '80 attempted to develop specific strategies for evangelizing major blocs of non-Christian peoples. Seventeen mini-consultations focused on communicating the gospel to various groups, such as nominal Christians among Protestants, Roman Catholics and Orthodox; members of cults and new religious movements; those of other faiths--Muslims, Hindus, Buddhists, Traditional Religionists; ethnic groups-- Jewish people, Chinese people; ideological groups--Marxists, secularists; and sociological groups--dwellers in large cities, urban poor, refugees. Some of the major groups for whom evangelistic strategies were designed at Pattaya are not, strictly speaking, "unreached peoples," because there is an active Christian presence in their midst. But they do represent significant segments of world society that remain relatively unevangelized and unincorporated into the Christian faith.

While Pattaya '80 took unreached peoples *seriously*, Edinburgh '80 was devoted to them *exclusively*. The World Consultation on Frontier Missions (conceived as agencies seeking to reach unreached people groups, which require missionaries to cross a linguistic or cultural "frontier"), held in October 1980 in Edinburgh, Scotland, focused on the frontier areas and peoples of the world which are currently beyond the reach of the gospel. By definition this includes "those cultural and linguistic subgroups, urban or rural, for whom there is as yet no indigenous community of believing Christians able to evangelize their own people." (Allan

Starling, editor, *Seeds of Promise*, Pasadena: William Carey Library, 1981, pp. 1-2). The slogan of Edinburgh '80 was "A Church for Every People by the Year 2000."

The thrust of these three major international conferences has had a significant effect on evangelical mission thinking and planning since 1974. The Strategy Working Group of the Lausanne Committee has prepared manuals, workbooks and audiovisuals for explaining and promoting these new insights and materials for "reaching the unreached." Scores of mission organizations are using the People Survey prepared by MARC to help in locating, describing and reaching neglected people groups. Several Christian organizations are cooperating in cataloging and computerizing the growing body of information about unreached peoples. Much of this data is made available through a series of *Unreached Peoples* directories published annually since 1979 by MARC and the Lausanne Committee's Strategy Working Group. The *Unreached Peoples* annuals incorporate and extend the directory materials first published for Lausanne 1974.

Responding to the challenge of unreached peoples, the North American Interdenominational Foreign Mission Association (IFMA) appointed a Frontier Peoples Committee, and the Evangelical Foreign Missions Association (EFMA) devoted two conferences to progress and problems in reaching the unreached. Between them these two associations represent some 20,000 North American evangelical missionaries. The U.S. Center for World Mission, established in 1976, has had commendable success in challenging and motivating students, clergy and lay persons to get behind frontier missions. An attractive new mission magazine entitled *World Christian* and the recently launched *International Journal of Frontier Missions* (see Resources) join in calling the Church to obedience in penetrating the last frontiers. Both are produced by youth and are evidence of new enthusiasm among potential candidates.

For hard data, however, on the "who" and "where" of people groups yet to be evangelized, we turn for help to the *Unreached Peoples* directories and to the research of David Barrett. In his monumental *World Christian Encyclopedia* (1982), using a "people group" structure based on an antropological and color differentiation, a different approach than that adopted by the SWG, Barrett reported identifying some 8990 basic people groups or cultures on earth, of which at least 8000 have to some degree been penetrated, if not permeated, by the Christian faith. The only peoples Barrett regards as clearly unreached are 636 groups (out of the 8990) which have from zero to less than .1% of their population as members of any church. Many of these are unreached peoples not because the Christian message has never reached them in any form but because they do not yet have a viable, indigenous, evangelizing community of believers. Dr. Barrett observes somewhat optimistically, "The dimensions of the unfinished task of world evangelization are in fact very much smaller than contemporary Protestant and Catholic missionary organizations realize." (It should be noted that Barrett's optimism is based on both his acceptance in the assessments of those who call themselves Christians according primarily to church affiliation and on his usage of the country unit to define the unfinished task.) He hopes to compile a *World Christian Atlas* covering 11,000 peoples and languages which promises to provide more information than we have ever had before concerning the spread of the gospel among the ethnic peoples of the world.

More and more mission agencies are conducting research, setting goals and committing resources to reach specific peoples than ever before. Overall, the ten years since Lausanne have seen significant progress in both understanding and beginning the next great thrust in world evangelization.

There is one further encouraging development of major significance for world evangelization.

3. *A growing partnership in completing the task.* The Lausanne Congress brought together 4000 participants from 150 countries. Nearly half of the official participants came from non-Western nations. The purpose of Lausanne included, among other things, a call "to share and strengthen our unity and love in Christ" and "to encourage cooperative strategies toward reaching all men for Christ." The Lausanne Covenant provides the basis for this cooperation without requiring formal organizational links; partially as a consequence, evangelical cooperation in world evangelization has been growing ever since!

One of the bright spots on the world scene is the work of the Holy Spirit in raising up a growing force of non-Western missionaries for new thrusts in cross-cultural evangelism within their own nations and beyond. In the last decade the number of missionaries rising out of the Two-Thirds World appears to have increased dramatically from 3000 to more than 15,000.

Whereas "Partnership in Mission" used to connote primarily Western mission/national church relationships, now we see many new patterns of partnership emerging as non-Western missions work with non-Western churches, with Western churches, with other non-Western missions, and with Western missions. Some of these partnerships develop along regional and geographic lines, others along denominational or special interest lines such as a common concern for Muslim evangelism. The various working arrangements all reflect something of the unity, the diversity and the vitality inherent in the body of Christ. Through partnership agreements they share ideas, personnel and finances as they send task forces, loan missionaries or assist in training disciples for cross-cultural ministries.

The mission of Christ worldwide will be immeasurably strengthened and extended into the future as leaders of both non-Western and Western mission agencies continue to help one another through fellowship in praying, thinking, planning, and sharing together in "reaching the unreached."

Warren W. Webster is General Director of the Conservative Baptist Foreign Mission Society and lives in Wheaton, Illinois. He serves on the Strategy Working Group of the Lausanne Committee.

Cooperation in
World Evangelization

CHURCHES IN EVANGELISTIC PARTNERSHIP

We rejoice that a new missionary era has dawned. The dominant role of western missions is fast disappearing. God is raising up from the younger churches a great new resource for world evangelization, and is thus demonstrating that the responsibility to evangelize belongs to the whole body of Christ. All churches should therefore be asking God and themselves what they should be doing both to reach their own area and to send missionaries to other parts of the world. A re-evaluation of our missionary responsibility and role should be continuous. Thus a growing partnership of churches will develop and the universal character of Christ's church will be more clearly exhibited. We also thank God for agencies which labor in Bible translation, theological education, the mass media, Christian literature, evangelism, missions, church renewal and other specialist fields. They too should engage in constant self-examination to evaluate their effectiveness as part of the Church's mission.

(Rom. 1:8; Phil. 1:5; 4:15; Acts 13:1-3; I Thess. 1:6-8)

Article 8
The Lausanne Covenant

Cooperation in Evangelism

Gottfried Osei-Mensah

The climax of Lausanne '74 came as over two thousand evangelical Christians from all over the world entered into a solemn covenant with God and with each other "to pray, to plan, and to work together for the evangelization of the whole world." Cooperation in evangelism is therefore the very essence of the "Lausanne spirit."

During the past ten years the Lausanne Committee for World Evangelization has sought to foster and spread this spirit of cooperation in evangelism among Christians worldwide. The Lausanne Covenant has been translated and distributed in scores of languages and has become widely accepted as a basis of cooperation in evangelism among evangelical Christians from diverse backgrounds. The existing forms of cooperation, inspired by the Lausanne movement, vary considerably. Some are regionally organized, such as the Confraternity of Latin American Evangelicals (CONELA) and the North American Lausanne Committee; others are nationally based--for example, Operation Good News in Nigeria, and similar evangelism committees in Norway, Sweden and Venezuela; still others are functional, linking groups concerned for the evangelization of specific peoples--the Chinese, Muslims, Jews, world-class city dwellers, etc. Where there are strong national evangelical fellowships with clear evangelistic concerns, they become the natural channels for cooperation in evangelism--as in India and Korea.

The Need for Cooperation

But the need for more cooperation in evangelism remains. In the prayer of our Lord Jesus Christ (John 17), he asked twice for the expressed unity of his people. First, he prayed the Father, "keep them in thy name . . . that they may be one, even as we are one" (v. 11). The Lord knows that in a hostile and unfriendly world, the joy and strength of his people lie in their covenant solidarity in him. Satan knows this too, and relentlessly seeks to weaken us by needless divisions. Hence the Lord's plea to the Father to keep us from the evil one (v. 15).

Christ's second petition for the expressed unity of his people had our evangelistic effectiveness in view, "so that the world may believe that thou hast sent me" (v. 21), "so that the world may know that thou hast sent me" (v. 23). The Good News unites both messengers and converts in the fellowship of Christ (v. 20, 21). When this oneness is expressed in common witness to the Savior, his unique reconciling power becomes unmistakably plain to those we seek to win for him.

One effective way to manifest authentic Christian unity is to work together toward specific objectives in world evangelization. The Lausanne Covenant provides the theological and biblical basis for our cooperation, as well as clarifying for us the nature of our common evangelistic responsibilities. God has used it mightily to build bridges between different expressions of the Church all over the world.

Commission on Cooperation

However, the obstacles in the way of cooperation in evangelism are not always theological or doctrinal. Stubborn attitudinal barriers to fellowship and cooperation must be faced and overcome in the interest of world evangelization. In order to deal with some of these barriers the LCWE appointed a Commission on Cooperation in World Evangelization, not only to discuss the essential problems internally but also to deal with them with others. A fine study by the Commission in the area of church/parachurch relationships has been edited and published as Lausanne Occasional Paper No. 24, *Cooperating in World Evangelization: A Handbook on Church/Para-church Relationships*. The Commission which sat during the Consultation on World Evangelization at Pattaya, Thailand, in 1980, examined the source and nature of difficulties in relationships between churches and Christian organizations, and recommended ways of dealing with them. The principles and guidelines drawn up also have a wider application to cooperation among individual Christians, organizations, churches and mission agencies. I commend this document to all who are concerned with cooperation in evangelism.

Ultimately people as well as organizations cooperate to the extent that they can trust each other. We build up trust by building up healthy personal relationships. In this respect the Lausanne Committee itself has become the model of cooperation in evangelism. Over the past ten years evangelical leaders from different denominations, nationalities and other backgrounds have come to know, love and appreciate one another on the Lausanne Committee and in the worldwide movement for evangelization as a whole. Because of the trust that has developed among them, members of the committee and its working groups are usually the strongest advocates for cooperation in evangelism in their own organizations and areas of influence. In country after country, the Lausanne movement provides the broadest platform for bringing together evangelical Christians from all backgrounds to cooperate in evangelism.

The Nature of Cooperation

LCWE has consistently attempted to work closely with the many expressions of the World Evangelical Fellowship (WEF). A number of consultations have been co-sponsored, including part of the Conference "I Will Build My Church." However, at the recommendation of the Commission on Cooperation, representatives of the executive committees of the LCWE and the WEF met together at Wheaton, Illinois, in June 1983. The group reviewed the relationship between the two bodies and agreed on recommendations affirming each other's distinctive ministry. Steps to increase cooperation between the commissions and working groups of the two bodies were also agreed upon. It is the intention of the Lausanne Committee to pursue the kind of active cooperation with the World Evangelical Fellowship and similar organizations that will further the cause of world evangelization.

The nature of the cooperation advocated by the Lausanne movement needs to be clearly understood. First of all, we believe in cooperation with a clear biblical basis. The Lausanne Covenant is the theological framework for the conferences and consultations sponsored by the Committee. Participants in Lausanne-sponsored activities are required to be in full agreement with the Lausanne Covenant, and other consultants and visitors are invited on the clear understanding that they recognize the framework of the Covenant.

In the second place, we recognize and respect the diversity of God-given ministries with their own distinctive contribution to world evangelism. The cooperation we promote carries no element of control by any central body. On the contrary, we are convinced that as evangelical Christians coordinate their efforts in evangelism--sharing their resources of ideas, skills and personnel--we can better achieve the goals of our own ministries working together than we can separately.

The Lausanne movement is only one of the many instruments God is using to declare his saving grace to the nations. It is our prayer that in all we do we will fit into the rest of the body of Christ in a way that builds and edifies that body and brings glory to its Head.

Gottfried Osei-Mensah serves as the Executive Secretary of the Lausanne Committee for World Evangelization while living in London. A citizen of Ghana, he is a respected pastor and Bible teacher.

Thailand Statement

We have gathered at Pattaya, Thailand, for the Consultation on World Evangelization, over 800 Christians from a wide diversity of backgrounds, nations and cultures.

We have spent 10 days together in a fellowship of study, praise and prayer. We have celebrated God's great love for us and for all humanity. We have considered before him and under his Word the command of our Lord Jesus Christ to proclaim the gospel to all people on earth. We have become freshly burdened by the vast numbers who have never heard the good news of Christ and are lost without him. We have been made ashamed of our lack of vision and zeal, and of our failure to live out the gospel in its fulness, for these things have lessened our obedience and compromised our witness. We have noted that there are hard places where opposition is strong and evangelism is difficult. At the same time, we have rejoiced to hear how God is at work in his world, and how he is making many peoples receptive to his Word.

Our consultation has been held in the ancient Kingdom of Thailand, and we are grateful for the welcome which we have received from the hospitable Thai people. In particular, we have enjoyed fellowship with Thai church leaders, and have sought to share the concern of their hearts that, after more than 150 years of Protestant missions, considerably less than 1% of their country's 46 million people confess Jesus Christ as Savior and Lord.

Close by, on the country's eastern border, are hundreds of thousands of refugees, from neighboring countries. They symbolize both the political ferment of the world and the tragic suffering of millions of human beings. We denounce the injustice of which they are victims, and have struggled to understand and feel their plight. We thank God for those Christians who have been among the first to go to their aid. We thank him also that growing numbers of them, uprooted from their ancestral homes and cultural inheritance, are finding in Jesus Christ a new security and a new life. We have made a solemn resolution to involve ourselves more actively in the relief and rehabilitation of refugees throughout the world.

THE MANDATE FOR WORLD EVANGELIZATION

We believe that there is only one living and true God, the Creator of the universe and the Father of our Lord Jesus Christ; that he has made all men, women and children in his own likeness; that he loves all those whom he has made, although they have rebelled against him and are under his judgment; and that he longs for their salvation. He sent his Son Jesus Christ to die for sinners and, having raised him from the dead, has given him universal authority, that every knee should bow to him and every tongue confess him Lord. This exalted Jesus now sends us, on whom he has had mercy, into the world as his witnesses and servants.

As his witnesses he has commanded us to proclaim his good news in the power of the Holy Spirit to every person of every culture and nation, and to summon them to repent, to believe and to follow him. This mandate is urgent, for there is no other Savior but Jesus Christ. It is also binding on all Christian people. As the Lausanne Covenant declares, the evangelistic task "requires the whole church to take the whole gospel to the whole world" (para. 6).

We are also the servants of Jesus Christ who is himself both "the servant" and "the Lord." He calls us, therefore, not only to obey him as Lord in every area of our lives, but also to serve as he served. We confess that we have not sufficiently followed his example of love in identifying with the poor and hungry, the deprived and the oppressed. Yet all God's people "should share his concern for justice and reconciliation throughout human society and for the liberation of men from every kind of oppression" (Lausanne Covenant, para. 5).

Although evangelism and social action are not identical, we gladly reaffirm our commitment to both, and we endorse the Lausanne Covenant in its entirety. It remains the basis of our common activity, and nothing it contains is beyond our concern, so long as it is clearly related to world evangelization.

THE PRIMACY OF EVANGELIZATION

The Lausanne Covenant declares that "in the church's mission of sacrificial service evangelism is primary" (para. 6). This is not to deny that evangelism and social action are integrally related, but rather to acknowledge that of all the tragic needs of human beings none is greater than their alienation from their Creator and the terrible reality of eternal death for those who refuse to repent and believe. If therefore we do not commit ourselves with urgency to the task of evangelization, we are guilty of an inexcusable lack of human compassion.

Some two-thirds of the world's four and a half billion people have had no proper opportunity to receive Christ. We have considered the value of thinking of them not only as individuals but also as "people groups" who perceive themselves as having an affinity with one another. Many are within easy reach of Christians. Large numbers of these are already Christian in name, yet still need to be evangelized because they have not understood the gospel or have not responded to it. The great majority of people in the world, however, have no Christian neighbors to share Christ with them. They can therefore be reached only by cross-cultural messengers of the gospel. We confidently expect that these will increasingly come from all countries, as the Christian mission becomes universalized, and we will work to keep this challenge before the churches.

SOME VITAL ASPECTS OF EVANGELIZATION

At Lausanne our theme was "Let the Earth hear his voice"; in Thailand it has been "How shall they hear?" So we have searched the Scriptures daily in order to learn more about the God who speaks, the message he has spoken, and the people to whom and through whom he speaks.

We have reaffirmed our confidence in the truth and power of God's Word, and our desire to let his voice penetrate our cultural defenses. We have recognized the local church as the principal agency for evangelism, whose total membership must therefore be mobilized and trained. We have heard the call to be sensitive to other people's cultural patterns and not to try to impose on them our own. We have also acknowledged the indispensable necessity of the work of the Holy Spirit, and of prayer to the sovereign Lord for boldness to speak for him.

For five of our ten days together we have divided into 17 mini-consultations, all of which have concentrated on how to reach particular peoples for Christ. These mini-consultations have built upon a lengthy study program in which hundreds of groups throughout the world have been involved. Our purpose has been to consider important issues of theology and methodology, in relation to our approach to different peoples, in order to develop realistic strategies for evangelism.

Many of the reports have called for a change in our personal attitudes. The following four have been particularly emphasized:

The first is *love*. Group after group has asserted that "we cannot evangelize if we do not love." We have had to repent of prejudice, disrespect and even hostility towards the very people we want to reach for Christ. We have also resolved to love others as God in Christ has loved us, and to identify with them in their situation as he identified himself with us in ours.

Secondly, *humility*. Our study has led us to confess that other people's resistance to the gospel has sometimes been our fault. Imperialism, slavery, religious persecution in the name of Christ, racial pride and prejudice (whether anti-black or anti-white, anti-Jewish or anti-Arab, or any other kind), sexual oppression, cultural insensitivity, and indifference to the plight of the needy and the powerless--these are some of the evils which have marred the church's testimony and put stumbling blocks in other people's road to faith. We resolve in future to spread the gospel with greater humility.

Thirdly, *integrity*. Several groups have written about the character and conduct of the message-bearer. Our witness loses credibility when we contradict it by our life or life-style. Our light will shine only when others can see our good works (Matt. 5:16). In a word, if we are to speak of Jesus with integrity, we have to resemble him.

The fourth emphasis has to do with *power*. We know that we are engaged in a spiritual battle with demonic forces. Evangelism often involves a power encounter, and in conversion Jesus Christ demonstrates that he is stronger than the strongest principalities and powers of evil by liberating their victims. Strategy and organization are not enough; we need to pray earnestly for the power of the Holy Spirit. God has not given us a spirit of fear, but of boldness.

COOPERATION IN WORLD EVANGELIZATION

We have been deeply concerned during our consultation to strengthen evangelical cooperation in global evangelization, for no single agency could accomplish this enormous task alone.

We joyfully affirm the unity of the Body of Christ and acknowledge that we are bound together with one another and with all true believers. While a true unity in Christ is not necessarily incompatible with organizational diversity, we must nevertheless strive for a visible expression of our one-ness. This witnesses to Christ's reconciling power and demon-strates our common commitment to serve him. In contrast, competitive programs and needless duplication of effort both waste resources and call into question our profession to be one in Christ. So we pledge ourselves again, in the words of the Lausanne Covenant, "to seek a deeper unity in truth, worship, holiness and mission" (para. 7).

It is imperative that we work together to fulfill the task of world evangelization. Cooperation must never be sought at the expense of basic biblical teaching, whether doctrinal or ethical. At the same time, disagreement on non-essentials among those equally concerned to submit to Scripture should not prevent cooperation in evangelism. Again, cooperation must never inhibit the exercise of the diverse gifts and ministries which the Holy Spirit gives to the people of God. Nor should the diversity of gifts and ministries be made an excuse for non-cooperation.

Yet obstacles to cooperation remain, which involve genuine problems and complex issues. Some of these reflect either the social, political, geographical and cultural circumstances or the ecclesiastical traditions from which we come. Others reflect tensions between different forms of ministry (e.g., between traditional church structures and those which are not directly accountable to churches) or between different evangelistic strategies and methodologies. These and other tensions are real and must be frankly faced. They do not release us, however, from our responsibility to explore with creativity different levels of cooperation in evangelism. We are determined to work more closely together. The Scripture urges us to "stand firm in one spirit, with one mind striving side by side for the faith of the gospel" (Phil. 1:27).

We believe that God has given a special role to the Lausanne Committee for World Evangelization to act as a catalyst for world evangelization. We desire therefore to give it a further mandate to stimulate evangelism throughout the world, on the basis of the Lausanne Covenant, and in growing cooperation with others of like mind.

OUR COMMITMENT TO CHRIST

In the light of his clear command to go and make disciples of all nations, his universal authority and his love for all humanity, we solemnly make the following commitment to Christ, which we shall seek his grace to fulfill:

1. We pledge ourselves to *live* under the lordship of Christ, and to be concerned for his will and his glory, not our own.

2. We pledge ourselves to *work* for the evangelization of the world, and to bear witness by word and deed to Christ and his salvation.

3. We pledge ourselves to *serve* the needy and the oppressed, and in the name of Christ to seek for them relief and justice.

4. We pledge ourselves to *love* all those we are called to serve, even as Christ loved us, and to identify with them in their needs.

5. We pledge ourselves to *pray* for the church and for the world, that Christ will renew his church in order to reach his world.

6. We pledge ourselves to *study* God's Word, to seek Christ in it, and to relate it to ourselves and our contemporaries.

7. We pledge ourselves to *give* with the generosity of Christ, that we may share with others what he has given to us.

8.   We pledge ourselves to *go* wherever Christ may send us, and never to settle down so comfortably that we cannot contemplate a move.

9.   We pledge ourselves to *labor* to mobilize Christ's people, so that the whole church may take the whole gospel to the whole world.

10. We pledge ourselves to *cooperate* with all who share with us the true Gospel of Christ, in order to reach the unreached peoples of the world.

11. We pledge ourselves to *seek* the power of the Spirit of Christ, that he may fill us and flow through us.

12. We pledge ourselves to *wait* with eagerness for Christ's return, and to be busy in his service until he comes.

We believe that God, who has uniquely exalted his Son Jesus Christ, has led us to make these pledges to him. With hope and prayer we invite all Christ's followers to join us in our commitment, so that we may work together for the evangelization of the world.

The Power of Prayer

Therefore, in the light of this our faith and our resolve, we enter into a solemn covenant with God and with each other, to pray, to plan and to work together for the evangelization of the whole world. We call upon others to join us. May God help us by his grace and for his glory to be faithful to this our covenant! Amen, Alleluia!

Conclusion
The Lausanne Covenant

A Foundation of Prayer

Vonette Bright

Prayer is the key to the greatest source of power known to humankind. Evangelism seldom produces revival, but revival always produces evangelism, and prayer produces revival. E. M. Bounds once said, "God shapes the world by prayer."

Strategies and plans are important, but prayer is foundational. John Wesley said, "God does nothing but in answer to prayer." We need to pray that, in spite of worldwide adversities, the work of evangelization will move forward everywhere. We need to pray for those involved in evangelization, both individual missionaries and mission organizations. We need to pray for the resources needed to accomplish the evangelization of the world.

Prayer has been woven into the events and meetings of the Lausanne Committee for World Evangelization during the past ten years. It began long before the first meetings in Lausanne in 1974, with Millie Dienert coordinating prayer efforts around the world, calling people to pray for that historic meeting.

The Lausanne Covenant concludes with a commitment by the signers to "enter into a solemn covenant with God and with each other, to pray, to plan and to work together for the evangelization of the whole world."

Each time the Lausanne Committee has met since 1974, the meetings have been surrounded by prayer, acknowledging that God is the giver of plans and strategies and asking for his guidance. As the Lausanne Continuation Committee met shortly after the Congress and defined its purpose, stimulating prayer for world evangelization was a constant consideration. After the January 1976 meeting of the Lausanne Committee, this function appeared in the minutes of the meetings:

A. Intercession

  1. To stimulate an increased concern among Christians worldwide for the fulfillment of the Great Commission to evangelize all lost peoples before Christ's Second Coming; through intercession, supplication and fasting with thanksgiving, asking him for his continuing help, particularly remembering those fellow Christians, who, on account of their evangelistic witness, or Christian identity, are now suffering persecution.

  2. To call upon Christians both to pray for the leaders of the nations, and to urge them to secure conditions of peace, justice, liberty, and racial equality, and to guarantee freedom of thought and conscience in which the Church may obey God's command to preach the gospel without interference.

This commitment was reaffirmed at the Consultation on World Evangelization in Pattaya, Thailand, in 1980. A portion of the Thailand Statement reads: "We pledge ourselves to pray for the Church and for the world, that Christ will renew his Church in order to reach his world."

The January 1976 meeting of the Lausanne Committee created a standing committee on prayer. What is now the Intercession Advisory Group evolved from that, with the late Armin Hoppler, then Bishop John Reid, and now Vonette Bright as successive chairpersons.

In 1977, under Armin Hoppler's leadership, the Intercession Advisory Group began to promote Pentecost Sunday as an annual Day of Prayer for World Evangelization. One of the primary functions of the Intercession Group is to distribute a packet of material which includes a brochure with suggestions for promoting the day. A possible sermon outline and photo-ready graphics for easy reproduction and translation in each country are also included.

In 1971 the Lord gave me a special burden for prayer. At that time, there seemed to be few people who regularly emphasized the need for united and specific prayer. Since the early '70s interest in prayer seems to have been increasing. Prayer ministries have been initiated all over the world, with a special and unique emphasis on uniting to pray for specific needs. International Intercessors, started by Frank Ineson of World Vision International, began to produce a monthly newsletter with daily prayer requests for physical and spiritual needs around the world. Evelyn Christenson began a ministry of uniting people through citywide prayer chains, to pray for church, family and community needs. Intercessors for America, under the leadership of John Beckett, has brought national concerns before believers for prayer.

Similar ministries exist in other countries. Women's prayer groups, such as Lydia Fellowship, under the leadership of Campbell and Shelagh McAlpine, have made profound impact in establishing neighborhood prayer groups. World Literature Crusade, under the leadership of Dick Eastman, established a Change the World School of Prayer, teaching prayer seminars in churches. Patrick Johnstone's book, *Operation World*, has done much to encourage prayer for the world. Frontier Fellowship, a prayer campaign aimed at people groups without a known Christian witness, seeks to involve a million Christians in a daily devotional discipline of prayer. The Great Commission Prayer Crusade, which I had the privilege of directing for over ten years, was founded with the encouragement of Mrs. Billy Graham, Mrs. Fred Dienert, Mrs. Harold Lindsell and Mrs. Howard Davison. It conducts prayer workshops to teach people how to pray unitedly, specifically and strategically, and encourages coordination of prayer in the church, city, province or state, and country. David Bryant of Inter-Varsity Missions is promoting "Concerts of Prayer" for revival and evangelization in strategic major cities. (See Part 6 – Resources for referrals to these and other prayer resources.)

These are only a few of the unique, dynamic emphases that God has brought into being since the early '70s. History records the impact of prayer upon the cause of Christ and the Church through the years. What we are experiencing in prayer today is simply building on the foundation laid by godly intercessors and great prayer movements of the past.

More people than ever before are talking about the need for prayer. The time seems ripe for an international conference devoted to prayer. For this reason, the Intercession Advisory Group is sponsoring an International Prayer Assembly for World Evangelization, to be held June 5-10, 1984, in Seoul, Korea. Korea was chosen, in part, because of the reports of revival taking place there, with all-night prayer meetings, prayer mountains, and regular early morning prayer meetings. The spiritual atmosphere of that nation is permeated with recognition that genuine spiritual advance is related to God. The purpose of this conference is to bring together and inspire movements of prayer in every continent, country, city and church of the world.

The Lausanne Committee for World Evangelization, during its ten years of existence, has endeavored to serve the Church by sharing evangelization strategies through congresses and publications. These are valuable tools in the hands of those who have a burden for the evangelization of the world in this generation. Basic to everything, however, is that directive from God which reminds us: "Not by might nor by power, but by my Spirit, says the Lord Almighty" (Zechariah 4:6 NIV).

Vonette Bright is the founder and director of the Great Commission Prayer Crusade and chairs the LCWE Intercession Advisory Group.

People Groups:
A New Name
for an Old Idea

THE NATURE OF EVANGELISM

To evangelize is to spread the good news that Jesus Christ died for our sins and was raised from the dead according to the Scriptures, and that as the reigning Lord he now offers the forgiveness of sins and the liberating gift of the Spirit to all who repent and believe. Our Christian presence in the world is indispensable to evangelism, and so is that kind of dialogue whose purpose is to listen sensitively in order to understand. But evangelism itself is the proclamation of the historical, biblical Christ as Savior and Lord, with a view to persuading people to come to him personally and so be reconciled to God. In issuing the gospel invitation we have no liberty to conceal the cost of discipleship. Jesus still calls all who would follow him to deny themselves, take up their cross, and identify themselves with his new community. The results of evangelism include obedience to Christ, incorporation into his church and responsible service in the world.

(I Cor. 15:3,4; Acts 2:32-39; John 20:21; I Cor. 1:23; II Cor. 4:5; 5:11,20; Luke 14:25-33; Mark 8:34; Acts 2:40,47; Mark 10:43-45)

Article 4
The Lausanne Covenant

EVANGELISM AND CULTURE

The development of strategies for world evangelization calls for imaginative pioneering methods. Under God, the result will be the rise of churches deeply rooted in Christ and closely related to their culture. Culture must always be tested and judged by Scripture. Because man is God's creature, some of his culture is rich in beauty and goodness. Because he is fallen, all of it is tainted with sin and some of it is demonic. The gospel does not presuppose the superiority of any culture to another, but evaluates all cultures according to its own criteria of truth and righteousness, and insists on moral absolutes in every culture. Missions have all too frequently exported with the gospel an alien culture, and churches have sometimes been in bondage to culture rather than to the Scripture. Christ's evangelists must humbly seek to empty themselves of all but their personal authenticity in order to become the servants of others, and churches must seek to transform and enrich culture, all for the glory of God.

(Mark 7:8,9,13; Gen. 4:21,22; I Cor. 9:19-23; Phil. 2:5-7; II Cor. 4:5)

Article 10
The Lausanne Covenant

Lausanne and People Group Thinking

Samuel Wilson

The Lausanne movement has made a strategic and powerful contribution to world evangelization by calling us to think in terms of people groups. By this I mean encouraging evangelizers to find a people group (see Figure 5 for a definition of "people group") and to define their approach by tailoring it to the needs and characteristics of the group. The idea of peoples has always been present in the intuition of evangelists who have operated cross-culturally; yet it has become powerful as it has become more deliberate and conscious, and as it is applied directly to evangelization.

The process related to Lausanne began with the twin stimuli of the MARC Status of Christianity Profiles and made available in a number of languages at the 1974 International Congress and the analysis of cross cultural commitment in Ralph Winter's paper "The Highest Priority: Cross-cultural Evangelism" with its subsequent discussion. C. Peter Wagner, as the first chairman of the Strategy Working Group, contributed greatly to making the concept an accepted way of developing strategy for evangelism through his early leadership, and MARC research and the *Unreached Peoples* series initially edited by Dayton and Wagner added fuel.

Why is "people group" a powerful concept? What is the source of the power?

The idea is inherently present in the way evangelism is done. The social structure which is part and parcel of life has a significant effect on the where and how of successful evangelism.

Most evangelists know this intuitively. I well remember the reaction of an outstanding architect in Peru whom I invited to take charge of home Bible study groups upon leaving for furlough. After joining an evening spent in the homes of a banker, a retired general and a wholesaler, the architect thought he could not take charge of work with "that class of people!" Though he was a recognized professional in his own right, he didn't think of those who were really his own peers as those among whom he could validly evangelize. At the time, he had become "comfortable" working among the marginated lower-class population in the sectors ringing the city.

But the point is, he had no trouble making the distinctions. His intuition and understanding were more or less automatic. The Lausanne process has shown a way to make these distinctions more visible and useful. The people group is the only currently recognized unit of social structure that is reasonably intelligible and provides the basis for a meaningful, prayerfully thought out plan of evangelism that can help us become "Greek to Greeks, and Roman to the Romans."

There are two major reasons seeing the world as people groups has been and is a powerful idea. A people group focus is important in the first instance for describing the job to be done, the business at hand. In the second place, the idea of people groups provides a workable basis for preparing and implementing plans for actual evangelism.

How Do We See the Task?

The heart that reflects the love of a redeeming Lord will respond deeply whenever it can identify the plight of groups of people who have no realistic possibility of seeing or experiencing Christ's love. When women and men are without Christ and without hope and promise, no further intellectual argument will be necessary. Their need, in and of itself, is a full stimulus to zeal. The description "unreached" has power to galvanize action. While we have been trapped by our mental categories at different times in history, and as church people have thus been unable to see, when the Church does see, it responds.

History is full of clear examples of how the significance of the social units in which people relate to one another has been met both by instinctive understanding and respect and by roughshod neglect on the part of would-be evangelists. Recognition of people groupings has always been a principal part of defining the missionary outreach of the Church of Jesus Christ. Paul undoubtedly recognized the Macedonian in his vision at Troas by his dress and perhaps the language used. I do not doubt that the man in the vision spoke the vernacular Greek of the empire with a Macedonian accent. Everything about him said, "I'm different." Paul recognized him and took ship to get to Macedonia. He did not go to look for this single convert. Luke tells us (Acts 16:10, NIV) "We got ready at once to leave for Macedonia, concluding that God had called us to preach the gospel to them."

PEOPLE GROUPS: A NEW NAME FOR AN OLD IDEA

Terms that accept people groups as right categories for ministry start right from Paul and run up to the present. Usage of such terms as "barbarian, Scythian" or "heathen, pagan," however derogatory they may be and whatever else they may communicate, also show ample and right awareness by the Church that the gospel requires disciplined proclamation and what we now call cross-cultural gifts to reach other peoples. These terms define where the gospel has not penetrated.

In the last century or so of mission contact with the peoples of the world, gospel missionaries have been acutely conscious of peoples and cultures. It is likely that the modern science of anthropology owes as much to the work of missionaries as it does to the fieldwork of scientists. Indeed, for the early period of the development of anthropology, European social scientists depended far more on facts and descriptions from missionaries than on any of their own fieldwork.

William Carey, with numerous dictionaries to his credit, hardly could be accused of a lack of people consciousness. The great wave of faith missions extending around the world to focus on ethnic groups and tribal language clusters for a while almost paralleled the selfishness inherent in the anthropologist's undue paternalistic pride in "my tribe." Colonialist errors aside, mission agencies instinctively selected peoples and planted churches among them. They discerned need and responded in terms of peoples. Two-Thirds World agencies today are notable for their ready recognition of peoples. In fact, many owe their existence and vision to the "discovery" of nearby, previously overlooked people groups. Peoples always have defined what we see as the mission task. They are the categories we use to determine what remains to be done.

At times the Church has taken other units as a focus for thought and action. A mistaken direction was followed when, for example, the modern nation-state was used in the 1950s and '60s as the basis of analysis. There was good reason for this. At the start of one decade, only two independent nations existed on the continent of Africa. By the end of the decade, there were nearly sixty newly independent nation states on this continent alone. Is it any wonder, then, that nations became the way to think about the task? Or that since churches existed within these artificial "national" boundaries, many wondered if the Western missions sending task was not over? As a consequence, through the late '60s and up until Lausanne, those who thought a major missions task remained were virtually defenseless before the argument that a church existed in practically every nation of the world, a moratorium was in order, and the missionary role as it existed in the romantic era of expansion was now passe.

After Lausanne examination of church presence and mission commitment among peoples, even in the restricted ethnolinguistic sense of peoples, clarified the situation and provided motivation for renewed sending. The artificiality of newly drawn borders came to light, and the need which had been obscured was again visible. The sending might occur from either the Two-thirds or One-Third Worlds, but again it was clear that there still were those for whom there was no possibility of seeing Jesus' life incarnated in visible behavior in human relations. Unfinished business was once more evident. Within modern nation-state boundaries whole people groups existed for whom there was no powerful witness of Christian love which transformed roles and values. Thinking in terms of people groups gave us back the power to see this task, a task that requires cross-cultural gifts in church planting.

But How Would They Hear?

The second way people group thinking is powerful is in giving focus to planning and action. There are few things as frustrating as trying to describe the total culture of a modern nation-state in terms that will prepare someone to do cross-cultural evangelism. But when someone describes the felt needs among members of a recognizable social group, approaches to evangelism seem to flow out almost naturally. The needs identified in a given group immediately begin to suggest possible kingdom ministries.

The ways people communicate with one another also suggest channels most natural for making the message known. This is true both of the means through which to communicate, and of the persons and circumstances for communication. The ways people associate with one another readily indicate ways for fellow members of the body of Christ to relate. The structure of the association networks allows us to visualize beforehand the organization of a local church expressed in appropriate social terms.

It is incontestable that the social divisions ordering people's lives serve either to favor or to hinder the development of the Church, and thus also to condition who can freely hear and respond to Christ's message given through a human church. The walls of entrapment in spiritual darkness are frequently social. They constitute the "establishment" behind individual reactions. The human shape of the church in any given local expression is also a utensil of clay dependent deeply on its social surroundings, whose members learn within a bounded social system. So from either the outside or the inside, the gates of the kingdom may also have social keys. Gang leaders, tribal chiefs or shamans may throw open or lock the doors of understanding and commitment to their followers. Attitudes and values of church members may either put off or draw in a lonely seeker.

The Strategy Working Group and the Lausanne movement have recognized the importance of praying plans into existence that build on an attempt to see the world in terms of the total life experience of the people group one is attempting to reach. The needs of the group are addressed as the principal focus. Many times evangelization has been guided by a "this has worked for me" mentality. Giving good news has at times been enslaved to method, whether this was a favorite method of proclamation or some agency-preferred method of entry or desired outcome. At other times, strategic decisions have depended on "where we are not" instead of where the *Church* is not. Instead we need to zero in on group need. This is the emphasis of Lausanne. We can minimize the compulsion to do evangelism in a certain standard way, or to reproduce a socially foreign structure, if we focus on meeting group needs and allow that to discipline our plans and action.

There is now general agreement on the need to contextualize the gospel in people group forms. When this is used to build on people group thinking, it can produce a vision of how best to establish a church that in turn can evangelize its local context. People group thinking thus makes strategy and planning meaningful under the guidance of the Holy Spirit, and in submission to the Lord of the Church who respects the integrity of the groups in which people learn who they are. The result is that in the human context others may also learn what Christians are like. This is and always has been the real goal of proclamation.

The Strategy Working Group and the MARC publications program have contributed to these processes and have provided us with a set of tools for prayerful planning with which to face the future, and the task that is newly before us (see Resources). In particular, people group thinking will enable us to see and define the unreached in the growing urban sectors of the world, and will continue to provide us with the means of bringing our limited resources to bear in kingdom ministry to extensive human need.

Lausanne has contributed to honing the vision of evangelistic need, to the development of strategic tools, and to the powerful concept of people group thinking which allows us, in dependence on the Holy Spirit, to see the task and to participate meaningfully in a more hopeful future which continues to efficiently utilize all the resources of the Church on all six continents.

Samuel Wilson is Director of MARC and a former missionary in Peru with the Christian and Missionary Alliance. He also served eight years as a professor at Nyack College and the Alliance School of Theology and Missions.

Seeing People Groups in Context

Patrick J. Johnstone

There has been such publicity concerning *people groups* that Christians all over the world are now realizing the significance of a "people group approach." Now many Christian leaders in missions and churches as well as concerned individuals are beginning to ask penetrating questions such as *"Where* are these people groups?" For such people a simple listing of people groups is insufficient. A list arouses Christians to their existence, but is inadequate for developing effective strategies for evangelizing and discipling them, and too abstruse and technical to stir potential evangelists to reach out to them with the gospel. What, then, is a possible next step?

THE VALUE OF MAPS AND DIAGRAMS

William Carey needed a map of the world to inspire his prayers and strategizing--even though it was crudely made out of leather. We, too, need to see as well as hear about the spiritual need of the peoples of the world. We now have amazing information at our disposal and the technology to put over the challenge in simple but effective terms that "he who runs may read."

PEOPLE GROUPS: A NEW NAME FOR AN OLD IDEA

Since I am an applied researcher, serving in the fellowship of a large mission committed to reaching out to unreached people groups, I have to keep my feet on the ground in developing strategies with my fellow workers and in communicating the vision to the Christian public. So over the last three years I have developed a wide range of maps and diagrams for use on overhead projectors and in slide form to depict the complex mosaic of differing needs of people groups in various parts of the world that enable people to see and hear.

Using maps and diagrams is a good discipline. I found it necessary to look at our definition of *people groups* more closely and make finer distinctions than those made previously. The following analysis and diagrams may prove illuminating.

CATEGORIZING PEOPLE GROUPS

It has helped me to classify people groups, as listed in the *Unreached Peoples* series, in three levels of identification; failure to distinguish between them has sometimes led to confusion and rejection of the valuable concept of people groups. Here are the three categories:

1. *Primary loyalty* - That which defines a person's identity, and what he himself claims to be, and what language he considers his mother/home tongue. This is the most basic category, and is primarily *ethnolinguistic*. Each person would have one primary loyalty that would rarely change throughout his life. Such a classification enables us to total the people of the world or a nation so that all are included once, and all the percentages total 100%. In such cases cross-cultural church planting, Bible translation, etc., in E-3 outreach is essential if no churches exist

within that group. (For an explanation of "E-3"and other terms in this chapter, see Figure 5.)

2. *Secondary loyalty* - Within a given ethnolinguistic people group, there are many horizontal divisions (age-groups, students, etc.) or vertical divisions (castes, classes, areas, provinces, etc.). In these there is considerable mobility and an element of choice. This is primarily a sociological category and, in complex societies, would probably embrace people in a *multiethnic* situation, but all sharing a common language of wider communication. The evangelization of such groups may be in need of either cross-cultural evangelism (E-2 or E-3) with the purpose of planting a specific type of culturally relevant church, or close-cultural evangelism by a local church to plant a variety of related churches, or else enlargement of a multisocial church.

3. *Tertiary loyalty* - Within both primary and secondary groups, there are often groups of people in casual associa-tion, brought together by circumstances rather than deliberate choice--e.g., occupations, professions, high-rise flat-dwellers, drug addicts, crowds in a Cairo traffic jam, etc. In most cases the idea of planting a specific church for them would be ridiculous. All these present superb E-1 evangelistic opportunities to local Christians, and help local churches develop specialized methods of outreach to draw them to the Savior, and ultimately into their own local churches.

Figure 7 may help to clarify these ideas.

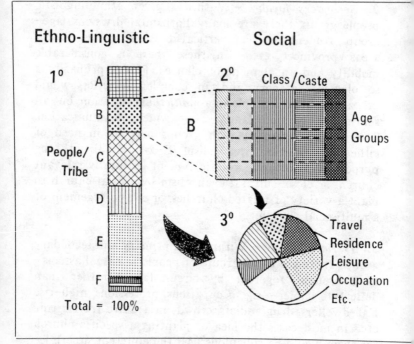

Categories of People Groups

Figure 7

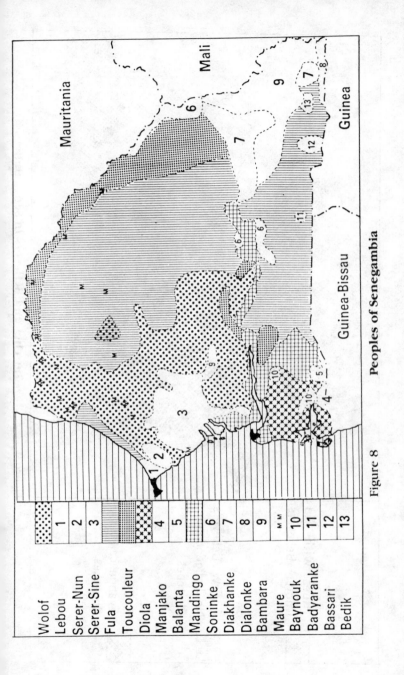

Figure 8   **Peoples of Senegambia**

Wolof	1
Lebou	2
Serer-Nun	3
Serer-Sine	
Fula	4
Toucouleur	5
Diola	
Manjako	6
Balanta	7
Mandingo	8
Soninke	9
Diakhanke	M M
Dialonke	10
Bambara	11
Maure	12
Baynouk	13
Badyaranke	
Bassari	
Bedik	

Mauritania

Mali

Guinea

Guinea-Bissau

183

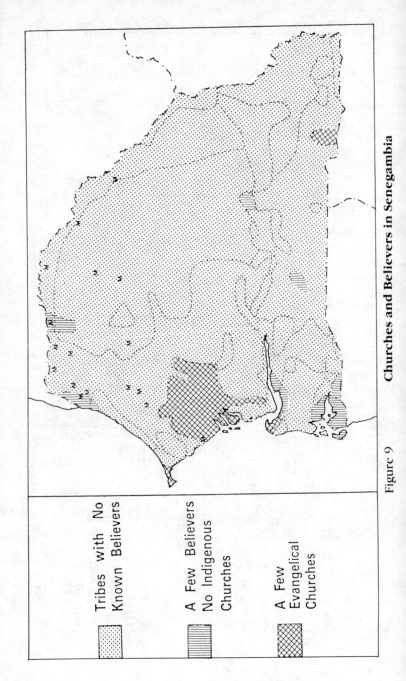

Churches and Believers in Senegambia

Figure 9

Tribes with No
Known Believers

A Few Believers
No Indigenous
Churches

A Few Evangelical
Churches

184

PRACTICAL APPLICATION IN USE OF MAPS.

1. *Ethnolinguistic Maps of Peoples Within a Nation.*

This is a straightforward case of a *primary people group*. This is very effective in illustrating the geographic concentrations, religions, spread of the gospel, amount of Bible translated, etc. Such an example is shown in Figure 8 and 9 Senegambia in West Africa.

These two maps indicate the approximate home areas of the 24 tribes or ethnolinguistic people groups in that country, and also the extent to which Protestant churches have been planted within each group. The need for Bible translation is underlined by the accompanying bar graph (Figure 10).

2. *Ethnolinguistic Maps of Transnational Peoples.*

We now move to a *primary loyalty people group but with sociopolitical implications of a secondary loyalty* (see Figure 11). Many of the world's peoples are not confined within the borders of a modern nation-state, and it is extremely important for us to know the areas in which a given people may best be reached so that a coherent strategy for evangelizing a whole people may be developed. The Baluch are such an example. Their territory spills over the borders of Iran, Pakistan and Afghanistan, but from Baluchistan many have emigrated to settle in surrounding territories such as Turkmenistan in the USSR, Oman, and other Persian Gulf states. There may be no more than two or three evangelical believers among these people, but Pakistan is the only country more or less open for their evangelization by conventional means.

People	Population in ,000 s	N.T.	O.T.
Wolof	2,000		
Lebou	70		
Serer-Nun Serer-Sine	950		
Fula	900		
Toucouleur	600		
Diola	320		
Manjako	50		
Balanta	40		
Mandingo	600		
Soninke	60		
Diakhanke	15		
Dialonke	14		
Bambara			
Maure	60		
Baynouk	4		
Badyaranke	1		
Bassari	12		
Bedik	1		

Translation Completed In Progress In Related Dialect

Bible Translation in Senegambia

Figure 10

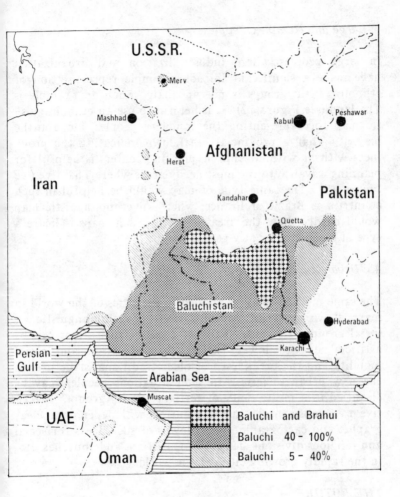

The Baluch

Figure 11

3. *Large and Complex Peoples.*

In large peoples where industrialization and urbanization have made a significant impact, a simple representation of ethnolinguistic groups is not adequate. Such an example is Thailand (see Figure 12). It is helpful to use an ethnolinguistic map for representing the minority peoples, but for the majority Thai, a provincial breakdown indicating the provinces with or without church-planting centers is helpful for planning advance to the most needy areas where Thai live (see Figure 13). The same type of map would be helpful in such countries as Brazil or France, where an ethnolinguistic map would hardly show the areas of need. Such maps indicate a type of secondary loyalty people group.

4. *Urban Agglomerations*

The same methods may be applied to the cities of the world in maps showing urban concentrations of ethnolinguistic or social groups. However, many of these classifications can be artificial due to lower barriers to association and social mobility and the breakdown of older traditional structures in the new urban societies. In such situations peoples may be classified in a multiplicity of tertiary loyalty groups. Effective evangelism and church planting will depend on clear graphic and cartographic breakdowns of such areas for social and religious divisions, density of Christians and churches, etc., in the rapidly growing cities of the world.

THE FUTURE

We are now at the point of being able to use computer graphics and plotters to produce maps and diagrams to clearly analyze the extent of the unfinished task. What an exciting

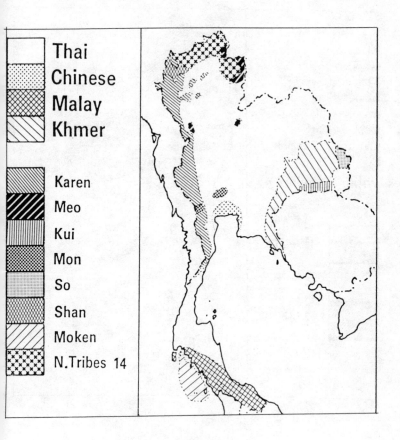

Peoples of Thailand

Figure 12

189

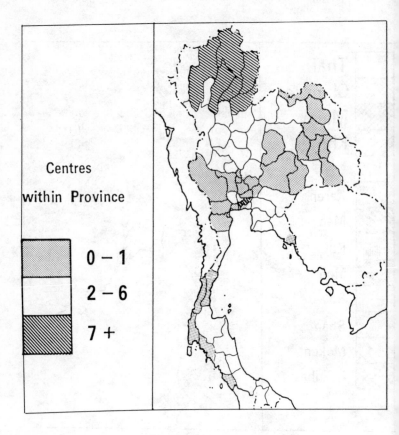

Church Planting Centers in Thailand

Figure 13

possibility! Let us use any means that help us to mobilize the Church worldwide to evangelize every people group.

Patrick J. Johnstone is International Research Secretary of the World Evangelization Crusade. He also serves as a member of the Strategy Working Group of the Lausanne Committee.

The Communication Process of Evangelism

Viggo Sogaard

Evangelization is a multidimensional process. The principal dimension, or we could say the foundation of evangelization, is the "hidden" work of the Holy Spirit. We cannot depict on graphs or scales the work of the Spirit--the wind blows where he wills--but we do know that all spiritual growth depends on it. On the other hand, there are dimensions of evangelization we can understand and illustrate as we try to conceptualize our task and plan new approaches. This helps us avoid the temptation of thinking of evangelism as an end in itself. The call of our Lord was to bear fruit, from all tongues, tribes and nations.

Evangelization is a process, not just an event. It is a communication process. As Christ came and communicated God to us, in all his fullness, so we are called to communicate Christ to others through life, words and deeds. The Lausanne movement has consistently recognized this. Experience makes quite obvious that we have not always been successful in making the gospel known and believed. Many people still seem to be without interest, if not directly opposed to the Christian message. Why is that?

We may often be tempted to look away from the hard and so-called unresponsive field and turn to the more obviously responsive areas. It is good, though, to remind ourselves that Christ asked us to go into all the world, and before turning away we should seek to discover the reasons for "unresponsiveness." What are the barriers and how did they get there? Have we really taken time to understand them? Do we communicate in a language, concepts and terms they do not understand? Have we failed to "incarnate" the message in life and blood? Have we actually constructed the barriers that turn people away from the church? Let us try to look beyond the barriers and try to build bridges across, reach out to where they are, rather than wait for them to come to us on our terms. A first prerequisite is for us to study the people God has called us to reach.

As Patrick Johnstone's article shows us, there is a vast mosaic of people groups around the world. Each requires a special strategy to reach them. (For further thinking on this, as well as further exposition on the diagrams used in this chapter, see *That Everyone May Hear* [third edition] by Edward R. Dayton, MARC, 1983. We need some ways to visualize the process of communication in the general way, an entry point for thinking about strategy.

The commission Christ gave us was to go out and make disciples. As stated above, disciple-making is a process. If we can somehow visualize that process, it will help us plan the evangelistic process accordingly. For this reason we use conceptual models. Models are not reality, but they help us understand reality. They are not finite or exclusive, but they serve as a frame of reference. Models never *do* the job for us, but experience shows it is easier to describe a situation by using a model. The model used here is an attempt to describe a possible situation, and then help us to develop integrated communication strategies for reaching a person, or a people group, and in so doing present the gospel to them. When a person accepts Christ as Lord and Savior, it is usually only one in a long series of steps. In that pilgrimage to Christ and his Church there have been steps of affective changes (attitude change) and steps of cognitive changes (new knowledge). It is a question of both knowing and feeling. The same is true of many people groups. They go through a *group* process which involves both attitude and knowledge.

Some people in our world will not even have an awareness of a living, personal God; others have some knowledge, and yet others have through school and church received ample knowledge about Christ. But they still do not know him. Others may be very negative, or directly hostile to the gospel; some are indifferent, and some may be actively seeking God. For the person with no awareness, our message must include plenty of cognitive content, and for those with a negative attitude, our message must seek a change of heart. Serious barriers of misunderstanding and prejudice may have to be bridged. It is important for us to understand where our listener is in relation to these dimensions.

Let us first try to illustrate the cognitive, or knowledge dimension of our model. Figure 14 illustrates a "scale" of steps that go from no awareness, through basic knowledge, more complete knowledge of the gospel, to a full understanding of the Word of God. This process should of course continue after a person has accepted Christ and become a member of a local church. We can never learn enough, or study the Word of God enough.

195

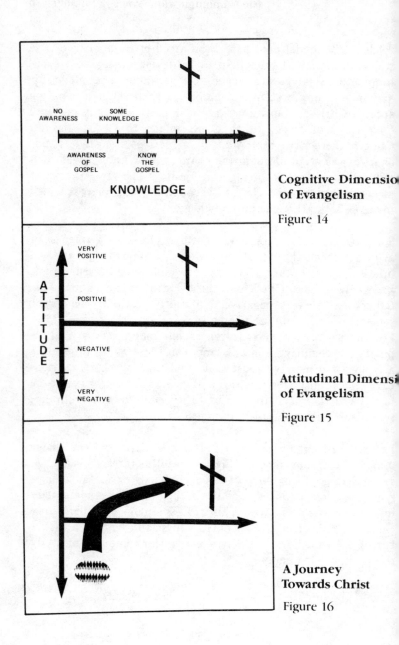

Cognitive Dimension of Evangelism

Figure 14

Attitudinal Dimension of Evangelism

Figure 15

A Journey Towards Christ

Figure 16

196

The second dimension of our model is the affective side, how one feels about the message presented (see Figure 15). We call this a person's attitudes towards Christ and his Church. If there are negative attitudes, there will most likely be negative decisions. Evangelization will often have to start here, changing attitudes that are based on misunderstandings, prejudices or negative experiences from the past. When we have a fairly good understanding of the position of a person or a people group in relation to Christ, we can begin to draw a "blueprint" for constructing a bridge on which one can travel to reach them and bring them to Christ (see Figure 16). We can also call this a strategy. It is a strategy of many steps, or an integrated process that may include several different ministries. For each step taken, the evangelization process has been effective if it has meant one step closer to Christ and his Church. As we minister, the Holy Spirit will work in hearts, bringing conviction and growth.

As we plan on reaching the unreached people groups for Christ, it will profit us to conceptualize their position in relation to Christ, and then visualize a possible journey they will have to take. This in turn will call us to make evangelistic approaches relevant to the situation.

Viggo Sogaard of the Strategy Working Group of the Lausanne Committee is a Danish specialist in communication theory and strategy, which he teaches as an adjunct faculty member at the School of World Mission, Fuller Theological Seminary. A former missionary in Thailand, he continues to minister in the Asian region through his participation in the Asian Institute of Christian Communication.

Resources for World Evangelization

EDUCATION AND LEADERSHIP

We confess that we have sometimes pursued church growth at the expense of church depth, and divorced evangelism from Christian nurture. We also acknowledge that some of our missions have been too slow to equip and encourage national leaders to assume their rightful responsibilities. Yet we are committed to indigenous principles, and long that every church will have national leaders who manifest a Christian style of leadership in terms not of domination but of service. We recognize that there is a great need to improve theological education, especially for church leaders. In every nation and culture there should be an effective training program for pastors and laymen in doctrine, discipleship, evangelism, nurture and service. Such training programs should not rely on any stereotyped methodology but should be developed by creative local initiatives according to biblical standards.

(Col. 1:27,28; Acts 14:23; Tit. 1:5,9; Mark 10:42-45; Eph. 4:11,12)

Article 11
The Lausanne Covenant

Resources for
World Evangelization

Barrett, David B., ed. *World Christian Encyclopedia*. Nairobi: Oxford University Press, 1982.

An exhaustive compendium of information about the spread of Christianity throughout the entire world with a country-by-country analysis of religion, including tables indicating change in the religious complexion of a country during the decade 1970-1980. Listing of Christian adherents and organizations and denominations accompany the analytical portions of the encyclopedia.

Beaver, R. Pierce, ed. *The Gospel and Frontier Peoples*. South Pasadena: William Carey Library, 1973.

Compendium of papers preceding and issuing from the Consultation on the Gospel and Frontier Peoples, December 1972.

Brierley, Peter, ed. *UK Christian Handbook* (1983 Edition). London: Evangelical Alliance, Bible Society and MARC Europe, 1982.

Four hundred thirty pages of data on Christian institutions in Great Britain including comprehensive statistics of churches, missionaries and agencies; articles evaluating the state of Christianity and the mission of the Church; and a directory of denominations and agencies throughout the British Isles.

Fraser, David A., ed. *The Church in New Frontiers for Missions.* Monrovia: Missions Advanced Research and Communication Center, 1983.

Prepared for the Wheaton '83 Conference, the volume brings together nineteen articles written since 1966, which deal with significant issues and methods in reaching unreached peoples.

Frontier Fellowship, *Daily Prayer Guide.* Pasadena: U.S. Center for World Mission; monthly subscription.

Issued monthly, these *Daily Prayer Guide* booklets are designed to be used by individuals to focus their devotional prayer life on a different unreached people group on each day of the month.

Grimes, Barbara, ed. *Ethnologue.* Huntington Beach: Wycliffe Bible Translators, 1978.

Lists over 5000 languages of the world by country. Includes the number of speakers of the language and status of Bible translation into the particular language described. Revision scheduled to be published in 1984.

International Journal of Frontier Missions. Pasadena: U.S. Center for World Mission; quarterly, $15.00/year.

This is a new publication which presents articles on mission theory, history and strategy with a view to promoting the concept of frontier mission among the unreached people of earth.

Johnstone, P.J. *Operation World.* Bromley, Kent: STL Publications, 1978.

A nation-by-nation practical prayer guide for world evangelization. National religious facts are presented along with several points for prayer for each nation.

Kane, J. Herbert. *Global View of Christian Mission.* Grand Rapids: Baker Book Co., 1971.

Comprehensive survey of the history of Christian missions and the status of churches and missions in each major country and area of the world.

Keyes, Lawrence E. *The New Age of Missions: A Study of Third World Missionary Societies.* Pasadena: William Carey Library, 1983.

An analysis of the emergence of hundreds of missionary sending societies in the non-Western world. The appendices to this published Ph.D. thesis contain the most updated listing of Third World mission agencies available.

Luzbetak, Louis J. *The Church and Culture.* South Pasadena: William Carey Library, 1970.

A collection of basic concepts and principles that hold for Christian interaction with all cultures.

Mission Handbook. Washington: United States Catholic Mission Association, Annual.

Inventory of U.S. Catholic personnel serving overseas during the year of publication. Catholic mission fields are then listed with distribution of personnel.

Missions Advanced Research and Communication Center (MARC). 919 W. Huntington Drive, Monrovia, CA 91016, U.S.A.

An international information center which conducts studies, consults with churches and agencies in the field and publishes materials on issues and strategies in world evangelization.

Pentecost, Edward C. *Reaching the Unreached.* South Pasadena: William Carey Library, 1974.

A brief, step-by-step strategy manual for evangelizing unreached people.

Read, William R., and Frank A. Ineson. *Brazil 1980: The Protestant Handbook.* Monrovia: Missions Advanced Research and Communication Center, 1973.

A clear-cut, definitive example of applied church growth thinking based on an accurate analysis of Protestant growth in one of the largest nations in the world.

To Every People.

This is a color film series produced for Inter-Varsity Christian Fellowship's Urbana '81. It features intoductions to four of earth's major groups of unreached peoples: tribal groups, Hindus, Muslims and Chinese. Write Twentyonehundred Productions, 233 Langdon, Madison, WI 53703 U.S.A.

Unreached Peoples Prayer Cards. Monrovia: Missions Advanced Research and Communication Center, 1983.

A set of sixty small cards each describing an unreached people group in various parts of the world.

U.S. Center for World Mission

The Center is devoted to the growth of a frontier missions movement through encouraging student awareness and involvement in frontier mission; marshalling the churches of North America to give, pray and strategize for the extension of the church where it does not presently exist; and creating new agencies for the express purpose of penetrating new frontiers for mission. Write 1605 E. Elizabeth St., Pasadena, CA 91104 U.S.A.

U.S. Frontier Mission Fellowship

This organization is designed to provide impetus for concerted prayer for the world's unreached peoples. Stimulation of unreached peoples programs among existing agencies is a further purpose of the fellowship. Located at the U.S. Center for World Mission.

Wagner, C. Peter. *Frontiers in Missionary Strategy.* Chicago: Moody Press, 1971.

Presents some guidelines for the development of a mission strategy that will be evangelical, biblically based, pragmatic and effective.

Wilson, Samuel, ed. *Mission Handbook: North American Protestant Ministries Overseas* (12th edition). Monrovia: Missions Advanced Research and Communication Center, 1980.

Contains results of a periodic survey of Protestant ministries accompanied by evaluative articles, analysis of the data collected, and a comprehensive directory of agencies engaged in overseas ministry.

World Christian. Pasadena: U.S. Center for World Mission; bimonthly subscription.

This is a popular bimonthly magazine devoted to promoting the concept of frontier missions among earth's unreached peoples.

You Can So Get There From Here. Monrovia: Missions Advanced Research and Communication Center, 1981.

A guide to those interested in pursuing a career in missions. Steps to take and issues to consider are presented sequentially with a series of resources for further information.

Dayton, Edward R. *That Everyone May Hear* (3rd Edition). Monrovia: Missions Advanced Research and Communication Center, 1983.

A revised and updated edition of a popular handbook designed in three parts to address the issues of people group evangelism, strategizing to reach them and planning for specific evangelism thrusts. Accompanying the text are two audiovisuals and a workbook.

_____, *That Everyone May Hear--A Workbook*. Monrovia: Missions Advanced Research and Communication Center and The Strategy Working Group 1983.

A companion to *That Everyone May Hear*, the workbook leads the user through a series of programmed steps in the planning process for evangelism.

Dayton, Edward R., and David A. Fraser. *Planning Strategies for World Evangelization*, Grand Rapids: William B. Eerdmans Publishing Co., 1980.

Social science data, management principles and missiological developments are brought together in this volume to point the way in both theory and practice to reaching the world's unreached peoples.

Douglas, J.D., ed. *Let the Earth Hear His Voice*. Minneapolis: World Wide Publications, 1975.

The proceedings of the historic Lausanne International Congress on World Evangelization held during 1974. Devotional messages, plenary papers and responses, and evangelistic strategy papers are included. Theological studies and national strategy reports round out the contents.

Fraser, David A., ed. *The Church in New Frontiers for Missions*. Monrovia: Missions Advanced Research and Communication Center, 1983.

Prepared for the Wheaton '83 Conference, the volume brings together sixteen articles written since 1966, which deal with significant issues and methods in reaching unreached peoples.

Hedlund, Roger E., ed. *World Christianity: South Asia*, Volume III. Monrovia: Missions Advanced Research and Communication Center, 1980.

Analyzes the status of Christianity in India, Sri Lanka, Pakistan, Nepal, Bhutan, Bangladesh and Afghanistan.

Holland, Clifton L., ed. *World Christianity: Central America and the Caribbean*, Volume IV. Monrovia: Missions Advanced Research and Communication Center, 1981.

Details of the Christian movement are presented for all the nations of Central America and the Caribbean.

Johnstone, P. J. *Operation World*. Bromley, Kent: STL Publications, 1978.

A nation-by-nation practical prayer guide for world evangelization. National religious facts are presented along with several points for prayer for each nation.

Keyes, Lawrence E. *The New Age of Missions: A Study of Third World Missionary Societies*. Pasadena: William Carey Library, 198 .

An analysis of the emergence of hundreds of missionary sending societies in the Two-Thirds World. The appendix gives a listing of these agencies.

Lausanne Communique. Strategy Working Group: bimonthly.

A newsletter containing valuable items on events, ideas and resources for world evangelization. Write Edward R. Dayton, chairman, Strategy Working Group, 919 W. Huntington Drive, Monrovia, CA 91016, U.S.A.

Lausanne Occasional Papers. Wheaton: Lausanne Committee for World Evangelization, 1975-.

A continuing series of booklets devoted to various topics and issues in world evangelization. The series now contains twenty-four volumes. Represents the theory and practice of the Lausanne movement since its inception.

1   The Pasadena Consultation--Homogeneous Unit Principle
2   The Willowbank Report--Consultation on Gospel & Culture
3   The Lausanne Covenant--An Exposition & Commentary
4   The Glen Eyrie Report--Muslim Evangelization

# 5	Thailand Report--Christian Witness to Refugees
# 6	Thailand Report--Christian Witness to the Chinese People
# 7	Thailand Report--Christian Witness to the Jewish People
# 8	Thailand Report--Christian Witness to Secularized People
# 9	Thailand Report--Christian Witness to Large Cities
#10	Thailand Report--Christian Witness to Nominal Christians Among Roman Catholics
#11	Thailand Report--Christian Witness to New Religious Movements
#12	Thailand Report--Christian Witness to Marxists
#13	Thailand Report--Christian Witness to Muslims
#14	Thailand Report--Christian Witness to Hindus
#15	Thailand Report--Christian Witness to Buddhists
#16	Thailand Report--Christian Witness to Traditional Religionists of Asia and Oceania
#17	Thailand Report--Christian Witness to Traditional Religionists of Latin America and Caribbean
#18	Thailand Report--Christian Witness to People of African Traditional Religions
#19	Thailand Report--Christian Witness to Nominal Christians Among the Orthodox
#20	An Evangelical Commitment to Simple Life-style-- Exposition and Commentary
#21	Grand Rapids Report--Evangelism and Social Responsibility An Evangelical Commitment
#22	Thailand Report--Christian Witness to the Urban Poor
#23	Thailand Report--Christian Witness to Nominal Christians Among Protestants
#24	Co-operating in World Evangelization: A Handbook on Church/Para-Church Relationships

Liao, David C.E., ed. *World Christianity: Eastern Asia*, Volume II. Monrovia: Missions Advanced Research and Communication Center, 1979.

Development of the Christian Church in East and Southeast Asia is evaluated and detailed in this volume.

McCurry, Don M., ed. *The Gospel and Islam: A 1978 Compendium*. Monrovia: Missions Advanced Research and Communication Center, 1979.

Contains papers prepared for the Glen Eyrie Conference dealing with the cultural and religious issues in reaching Muslims around the world. Christianity and Islam are treated in comparative analysis in a series of seminal essays.

_____, ed. *World Christianity: Middle East*, Volume I. Monrovia: Missions Advanced Research and Communication Center, 1979.

All the nations in the Middle East from Saudi Arabia to Iran are assessed with regard to the impact of Christianity on their peoples.

Sine, Tom, ed. *The Church In Response to Human Need*. Monrovia: Missions Advanced Research and Communication Center, 1983.

This collection of 14 papers moves the issue of evangelism and social responsibility along another step following the Consultation on the Relationship Between Evangelism and Social Responsibility held in Grand Rapids in June 1982.

Mission Handbook. Washington: United Stated Catholic Mission Association, 1982.

Inventory of U.S. Catholic personnel serving overseas during the year of publication. Catholic mission fields are then listed with field distribution of personnel indicated.

Unreached Peoples Prayer Cards. Monrovia: Missions Advanced Research and Communication Center, 1983.

A handy set of sixty small cards detailing unreached peoples in various parts of the world.

Wagner, C. Peter, and Edward R. Dayton, eds. *Unreached Peoples '79: The Challenge of the Church's Unfinished Business.* Elgin: David C. Cook Publishing Company, 1978.

The first volume of a yearly series devoted to identifying the world's unreached peoples. Explanation of the concept, five major case histories and detailed treatment of ninety unreached peoples are included along with a directory of those presently identified as unreached.

Wilson, Samuel, ed. *Mission Handbook: North American Protestant Ministries Overseas* (12th Edition). Monrovia: Missions Advanced Research and Communication Center, 1980.

Contains results of a periodic survey of Protestant ministries accompanied by evaluative articles, analysis of the data collected, and a comprehensive directory of agencies engaged in overseas ministry.

World Evangelization. Lausanne Committee for World Evangelization, quarterly news publication, P.O. Box 1100, Wheaton, IL 60187.

Details information on events and issues in world evangelization.

You Can So Get There From Here. Missions Advanced Research and Communication Center, 1981.

A guide to those interested in pursuing a career in missions. Steps to take and issues to consider are presented sequentially with a series of resources for further information.

The Future of
World Evangelization

SPIRITUAL CONFLICT

We believe that we are engaged in constant spiritual warfare with the principalities and powers of evil, who are seeking to overthrow the church and frustrate its task of world evangelization. We know our need to equip ourselves with God's armor and to fight this battle with the spiritual weapons of truth and prayer. For we detect the activity of our enemy, not only in false ideologies outside the church, but also inside it in false gospels which twist Scripture and put man in the place of God. We need both watchfulness and discernment to safeguard the biblical gospel. We acknowledge that we ourselves are not immune to worldliness of thought and action, that is, to a surrender to secularism. For example, although careful studies of church growth, both numerical and spiritual, are right and valuable, we have sometimes neglected them. At other times, desirous to ensure a response to the gospel, we have compromised our message, manipulated our hearers through pressure techniques, and become unduly preoccupied with statistics or even dishonest in our use of them. All this is worldly. The church must be in the world; the world must not be in the church.

(Eph. 6:12; II Cor. 4:3,4; Eph. 6:11,13-18; II Cor. 10:3-5; I John 2:18-26; 4:1-3; Gal. 1:6-9; II Cor. 2:17; 4:2; John 17:15)

Article 12
The Lausanne Covenant

The Ten Years Ahead

Edward R. Dayton

We have reviewed the ten exciting years that have just passed. We know where we have been, but where are we going? Any statement about the future is a statement of faith.

When Christians set goals, they are statements of faith. When we make plans, we do it in the full knowledge that "a man's mind plans his way, but the Lord directs his steps" (Prov. 16:9). But we have no choice but to think about the future, for the future is all that is left of life.

In an attempt to gain some understanding of the potential of the Lausanne movement for the future task of world evangelization and to suggest some steps that might be taken by the Lausanne Committee that would build up the body of Christ for this special task, the Long-Range Planning Committee of LCWE presented "A Long-Range Planning Context" to the full LCWE at its January 1983 meeting. What follows draws heavily upon that report.

In looking at the world, we first of all seek to see it in the light of God's revelation in the Bible. In the Bible there is unfolded God's action in "calling out from the world a people for himself and sending his people back into the world to be his servants and his witnesses for the extension of his kingdom, the building up of Christ's body and the glory of his name." In that action of God in his world, the Death, Resurrection and Ascension of the Lord Jesus Christ "declare with power" his deity and lordship and affirms his authority over his people for he commanded men to go into the whole world. Each generation of believers lives under that command.

The Death, Resurrection, Ascension of the Lord Jesus Christ reveal God's future purpose for the world. "This same Jesus who has been taken from you into heaven will come back." His second appearance will be the sign of God's great victory for his people when his kingdom will be fully established and his people will live in "a new heaven and a new earth, the home of righteousness." The second coming will also be the sign of God's judgment on all those whose names are not recorded in the book of life.

We seek to interpret our times as we live between the first and second coming of Christ. We look back to the first coming with gratitude for his redeeming love; we look forward to his second coming as our hope.

We seek to obey Christ's command in witness and sacrificial service with urgency and compassion as that day inevitably draws nearer. As we respond in faith to Christ's command, we are strengthened by the Holy Spirit who makes Christ's presence real to us and also equips us with gifts of grace which enable us to do his work of evangelization.

FUTURE TRENDS

What follows is an analysis of *possible* futures for the world in which we work and for the Church of which we are a part. It is divided into three major sections:

I.   THE WORLD IN WHICH WE LIVE AND WORK

   1. Religious Trends
   2. Economic and Social Conditions
   3. Population Trends

II.   WORLD EVANGELIZATION

   1. Status of Christianity
   2. Nominal Christians
   3. Non-Christians Among Christians
   4. Unreached Peoples
   5. The Force for Evangelism

III.   THE TASK OF WORLD EVANGELIZATION

   1. Approach to Evangelization
   2. Methods of Evangelism
   3. Cooperation in Evangelism

Throughout this analysis we have attempted to understand God's world in light of God's Word. For most of the trends and conditions that we note we have stated implications for the Church worldwide and for the Lausanne movement.

It must be remembered from the start that any statement about the future can only be an assumption. When we describe trends and future conditions, it is with the under-standing that the possible or probable futures described are the result of both outside research and consultation and the Spirit-led thinking of members of the LCWE.

I. *THE WORLD IN WHICH WE LIVE AND WORK*

1. *Religious Trends*

The spirit of militant Islam and militant Hinduism will seek to oppose Christian activity in countries which they dominate. They will be more aggressive in their focus on nominal Christian groups and individuals. Much of this aggressiveness will be reflected among the governments of the countries in which non-Christian religions predominate. The result will often be restrictions on the ability of the Church to preach the good news and to accept new members.

There is some indication that the strenuous at-tempts by some Islamic countries, such as Iran, to completely dominate the political and social struc-tures will have a backlash in other Islamic countries, perhaps leaving their people more open to change and thus to the gospel. The events of recent years have brought a new openness on the part of individuals who have been forced to doubt the ethical principles being demonstrated.

The oriental religions will continue to attract many from the West. However, a number of observers have noted that as Islam and Hinduism clarify their positions, their conclusions often seem bankrupt when placed alongside the claims of Christ.

The militancy of other religions may produce growing tension between the Church and these other religions.

Implications

What is needed is a deep understanding of the basic premises of these religions and a communication by the Church that it is our desire to understand them as people whom God loves, to confess our own failures to love in the past and to communicate not only by word but by a community life that the lord-ship of Jesus Christ is a powerful alternative.

At the same time the growing trend toward secularization of the Western countries will continue. This secularism will, on the one hand, produce more individualism and on the other hand a search for secular solutions, such as Marxism, to the dilemmas that the world faces. The commitment to Judeo-Christian ethics by most countries of the West will be negligible. An ever-increasing pluralism will make an appeal to "what is right" ever more difficult.

Implications

The implications for the Church are enormous. The worldwide spiritual unity that we claim for the body of Christ and the appeal of a community of people who support one another in love and have a compassionate concern for all in need can be extremely attractive to such a world.

2. *Economic and Social Conditions*

The spirit of nationalism will continue to grow in many countries and will hinder acceptance of programs originated or supported outside any given country. Patriotic Christians within these countries will often face the dilemma of allegiance to the Church Universal and to their own nationalistic instincts.

Economically, developing countries will continually be faced with the tension of wanting to become self-reliant and also to acquire the technical know-how of the economically developed countries. This tension will grow as communication between economically developing and developed countries rapidly improves. The majority of developing countries will be greatly attracted by technological modernization. The Western ideas of planning and controlling one's own future will continue to spread throughout the world as the only defense against rapid change brought about by modernization.

At the same time the number of multinational or transnational organizations that operate throughout the world, more or less independent from the control of any one government, will continue to increase. By moving their means of production from one country to another they effectively reduce the ability of any one government to control them through economic leverage. There are no international laws that govern such multinational and transnational organizations.

Implications

The implications for world evangelization are manifold. The ability of the gospel to permeate and transform cultures, while maintaining continuity with those aspects of the culture which are good and positive, should encourage us to seek unique programs of evangelization for each situation and to downplay "worldwide" or "standardized" approaches. At the same time there is a tremendous need for communication and understanding between churches.

The focus of encounters and meetings and conferences should be within countries and regional sections within countries.

Local churches should be viewed as the basic unit *of world evangelization. Non-parochial, "set-apart" organizations, such as mission agencies, should develop their strategies to work closely with existing local churches, not only to encourage local churches in the spontaneous expansion of the gospel but also to assist them in their own attempts to set apart people for non-parochial ministry to the over two billion people who have yet to receive a gospel witness.*

Economically and politically it is very difficult to peer into the future. One can forecast with some degree of assurance that the leadership of the U.S.

will decline and that economics will play a stronger role in international affairs than ideologies.

The "post-industrial era" will produce a United States whose primary product is information. Heavy industry and manufacture, such as steel and automobiles, will move to other countries.

At the moment there is little doubt that rich/poor polarities will increase both within nations and between nations. The number of hopelessly poor people in the world is increasing at a rate faster than the world population. The quality of life in many countries is deteriorating rapidly (see Figure 18).

There appear to be strong trends towards dictatorships of the left or the right. The pluralism which is the foundation of democratic societies appears to be less and less attractive to many of the world's peoples who are desperately seeking for some solution which will halt what appears to them to be a continuing slide towards chaos. Many peoples of the world appear ready to give up a great deal of their freedom in exchange for assurance of social and economic stability.

Implications

The Church and Lausanne must develop a presentation of the gospel which is faithful to its implications for the whole person.

Comparison of Physical Quality of Life Index (PQLI) and Per Capita Gross National Product (GNP) for Representative Two-Thirds World Countries

COUNTRY	PQLI	GNP
COSTA RICA	89	$1,476
TAIWAN	87	2,503
CYPRUS	86	3,759
SINGAPORE	86	5,220
SOUTH KOREA	85	1,720
CHILE	84	2,560
PANAMA	84	1,908
SRI LANKA	82	302
MEXICO	79	2,250
THAILAND	76	769
LEBANON	76	1,890
COLOMBIA	76	1,334
PHILIPPINES	73	789
BRAZIL	72	2,214
ECUADOR	72	1,171
EL SALVADOR	70	636
JORDAN	69	1,623
NICARAGUA	69	874
PERU	68	1,122
BELIZE	67	1,110
VIETNAM	65	190
SOUTH AFRICA	62	2,290
TURKEY	61	1,511
HONDURAS	61	591
SOLOMON ISLANDS	59	619
GUATEMALA	59	1,159
BURMA	59	183
DOMINICAN REPUBLIC	58	1,338
INDONESIA	55	519
KENYA	55	432

COUNTRY	PQLI	GNP
MOZAMBIQUE	38	$ 240
EQUATORIAL GUINEA	38	175
YEMEN, PEOPLE'S DEM. REP.	37	512
OMAN	35	5,924
BANGLADESH	35	144
TOGO	34	391
SUDAN	34	380
CENTRAL AFRICA REP.	34	328
BENIN	33	326
MALAWI	31	200
GABON	30	3,909
BURUNDI	30	235
GUINEA-BISSAU	29	185
NEPAL	28	156
GUINEA	28	298
MAURITANIA	27	484
SENEGAL	24	499
SIERRA LEONE	24	319
ETHIOPIA	24	142
CHAD	24	120
NIGER	23	336
BHUTAN	23	80
SOMALIA	23	282
MALI	23	185
ANGOLA	21	790
YEMEN, ARAB REP.	21	459
KAMPUCHEA	21	110
GAMBIA	20	348
UPPER VOLTA	18	237
AFGHANISTAN	17	170

Listed are representative countries having the highest and lowest physical quality of life indexes in the Two-Thirds World. Arranged in order of decreasing PQLI.

PQLI (Physical Quality of Life Index) refers to the numeric value assigned to countries based upon an average life expectancy at age one, infant mortality and literacy rates for adults. The range is from one (low) to 100 (high). GNP is per capita gross national product, 1981 (in US $).

Source – John P. Lewis and Valeriana Kallab, eds., *U.S. Foreign Policy and the Third World: Agenda 1983*, New York: Overseas Development Council, 1983, pp. 210-219.

*We must recapture a vision of the Church's respon-
sibility towards the poor. We must remember the
biblical admonition that God has a special concern
for the poor and demands justice for them.*

*As we continue to call individuals to accept a per-
sonal salvation, we must offer a vision of a new
community that comes forth as a result of lives
which are committed to Christ and his kingdom.*

Obviously if there is a nuclear holocaust or a total
collapse of the world economy, any speculation
about the role of the Church becomes somewhat
academic.

3. *Population Trends*

Demographic projections for world population show
radical shifts in the last two decades of the twentieth century. For example, although for the world
as a whole the percentage of those under 14 years
of age will decline, in Two-Thirds World countries
a 48 percent increase in school-age children is
predicted between 1975 and the year 2000.

A 36 percent increase is projected for the 15-64
age group in less industrialized countries by the
year 2000. This increase will mean a much larger
work force and will bring an increased demand for
employment and training.

Perhaps the most dramatic change within the world
population is the move towards urban centers.

Predictions indicate that by the year 2000 percentages of people living in cities will be: U.S., 94
percent; Europe, 82 percent; U.S.S.R. and Eastern
Europe, 80 percent; Latin America, 73 percent;
Australia, 85 percent; Asia, 60 percent; Africa, 45
percent. The examples of some cities are startling:
Mexico City is predicted to have a population of
31.6 million; Calcutta, 19.7 million; Greater Bombay, 19.1 million; Greater Cairo, 16.4 million;
Jakarta, 16.9 million; Seoul, 18.7 million; Manila,
12.7 million; Bogota, 9.5 million; and Lagos, 9.4
million. The results will be polyglot groupings of
people who will actually be members of many
diverse groups. (See Figure 4.)

Implications

*The Church's response to these population trends
must be to define the world in new terms. The type
of differentiation that was emphasized at Lausanne
needs to continue. The titles of some of the reports
given there indicate the trend. We heard reports on
evangelization among thinking people, secondary
school students, college and university students,
women, deaf, blind and handicapped, hippies and
other subcultures, urban poor, minority racial
groups, high-rise apartment dwellers, and so forth.
These are what Lausanne has termed "people
groups." The utilization of the people group as the
basic unit of evangelization has tremendous implications both for evangelization among communities where there are existing churches and for
cross-cultural mission efforts.*

A further implication for the Church and Lausanne is the urgent need to strengthen communication between existing Christian ministries in the world-class cities (those over one millon population). The very nature of the city tends to isolate local churches and Christian groups from one another. The Lausanne movement has already demonstrated that it can be an effective instrument in helping various expressions of the Church in large cities to know each other and appreciate each other's ministries better.

II. WORLD EVANGELIZATION

1. *Status of Christianity*

Presently, some 1433 million people consider themselves Christians and are affiliated among over 20,800 distinct denominations. The percentage of Christians to the world total population has been slowly declining from 34.4 percent of the world's population in 1900 to 32.8 percent in 1980. However, since the population of the world since 1900 has more than doubled, it is encouraging to know that there are twice as many Christians alive today as there were at the turn of the century.

Massive gains in the Two-Thirds World countries are being offset by growing apostasy in the One-Third World. For instance, there are six million new Christians in sub-Sahara Africa per year or about 16,400 per day. Churches in East Asia and South Asia are growing by 360,000 and 447,000 converts per year, respectively. Protestant Church membership is growing at an annual rate of ten percent in Central America. China may have between 25 and 50 million believers meeting in hundreds of thousands of house churches, compared to only hundreds of government-sanctioned churches in the entire country. (These recent estimates of the surprising growth of the church in China may offset the small statistical losses in total percentage mentioned above.)

However, the churches of Europe and North America are losing 2,765,000 people per year (7,600 per day) to nominalism or unbelief, which more than offsets the European and North American Evangelical Church growth.

Implications

We should rejoice over the demonstrated power of the Holy Spirit to bring new peoples to Christ.

Greater emphasis needs to be put on the reevangelization *of the Western world.*

2. *Nominal Christians*

Estimates as to the number of "nominal" or non-practicing Christians in the world are difficult to come by. But it is probably valid as a working assumption to assume that over one billion people who call themselves Christians need to be evangelized.

The evident strength of the Church in most places in the world also indicates that there are enough evangelical Christians to carry out the task of evangelization of this over one billion.

However, we can identify a number of hindrances to the task of evangelizing such nominal Christians. Some of these include the tendency on the part of many Western evangelicals to place an emphasis on preaching a gospel which calls people to salvation but does not place demands on them for a new life in Christ. The strong sense of individualism which tends to permeate Western society operates against local churches becoming effective *community* expressions of the love of Christ. There is doubt in the minds of many evangelicals as to whether they should attempt to evangelize those who already claim to be Christians. Many so-called "liberal" or "nominal" local Christian churches include in their membership those who are obviously born again and maturing Christians.

Other hindrances include the opinion of some that no one should have the privilege of "hearing twice" until everyone has had an opportunity to "hear once."

Finally, there is the generally observed natural tendency for every local congregation to become conformed to the world. Churches which do not multiply themselves evangelistically, either by growing in size of their own membership or establishing other churches easily turn from looking outward to looking inward.

Implications

Every church in every culture needs to continuously reexamine its response to that culture. The work that was done in studying the gospel and culture (LOP No. 4, The Willowbank Report) needs to be applied to our own cultures.

Local churches need to be challenged to the task of both spiritual and numerical growth.

3. *Non-Christians Among Christians*

There are roughly one-billion non-Christians living among others who call themselves Christians. The majority of these are found among Western countries. Some theorists insist that these people are "evangelized" because they are surrounded by the marks of Christianity. Churches stand in their midst. Christian radio broadcasts are present. Bibles are freely available. But no one can tell to what extent any individual has hardened his or her heart against the gospel to the point of having rejected Christ.

These non-Christians will be evangelized in one of two ways. First, there will be the spontaneous witness of local churches and Christians. Christians acting as Christians will spread the good news to those who are in the midst of their everyday lives.

Implications

If one asks what is the best way to multiply such evangelism, one can only reply, strengthen local churches and Christians in their daily walk. Let the church be the church.

Second, there is the *intentional* effort of evangelization carried out through local churches or evangelistic associations among the groups needing to be evangelized. Here we can talk about appropriate evangelistic methods and training those with the gift of evangelism to be good evangelists. It is important to understand that all the principles that apply to cross-cultural evangelism (missions) apply here. The best evangelistic methods are likely to be those which bear in mind a specific audience--a "people group," as defined by the Strategy Working Group. (See Samuel Wilson's "Lausanne and People Group Thinking.")

Such methods are tailored to the special needs of the group. This is not to change the content of the gospel. Christians have long since recognized such needs; they have formed evangelistic associations to reach businessmen, professionals, military personnel, particular occupations, as well as local neighborhoods. Most local churches recognize that if, for example, they are a middle-class church, and they want to evangelize a neighborhood of poor people, they are going to have to use different approaches than they would to evangelize people "just like them."

Implications

Lausanne materials and the Lausanne network can be just as effective in helping these local efforts as in stimulating attempts at reaching unreached people groups.

The basic strategy of attempting to see people as a people group and to attempt to discover God's unique plan for evangelizing this people group is equally applicable to local evangelization and cross-cultural evangelization.

4. *Unreached Peoples*

There are over two billion people in the world who for a variety of reasons are separated from effective contact with the Church. No matter how the local church expands, this over two billion will only be reached *initially* by some form of "cross-cultural" evangelism. These people exist in both ethnological and sociological groupings. Presently there are not enough cross-cultural missionaries to reach the unreached people groups of the world. Most local churches and individual Christians do not recognize that the need for cross-cultural evangelists (missionaries) is greater than at any other time in history, and will continue to be so in the coming years. The world situation needs to be clearly articulated in such a way that the Holy Spirit can motivate more Christians to this task of evangelizing those people who are separated from existing churches by marked social, cultural, linguistic and other barriers.

At the same time it needs to be well understood that although most of the unreached people groups in the world will be reached *initially* by cross-cultural evangelism, the greater part of world evangelization will depend upon the effectiveness of the local church which is planted in each group.

Implications

The thrust of world evangelization cannot stop at multiplying Christians. We must multiply propagators of the gospel. *All Christians are called to be involved in world evangelism, but not all are called to be evangelists. Consequently, we need to identify those who have specific calling and gifts.*

By and large the unreached peoples concept *has not been grasped* by the great majority of local churches and denominations. However, the growing number of missionaries from the Two-Thirds World, now estimated at over 15,000, as well as the broad acceptance by young college graduates in many Western countries of the people group concept, should be an encouragement to us. Many young people are committing their lives to specific unreached people groups and forming their own organizations to reach them.

In many places there is apathy about the unreached people of the world, which may increase because of the current world recession. On the other hand, oftentimes a financial stress tends to unite Christians to "give out of their poverty."

Implications

There is a need for increasing coordination and unity among evangelicals to make this situation in the world known and to motivate people toward it.

We should continue to challenge young people to be committed to the unreached of the world. We should encourage the emergence of mission agencies from among the younger churches. We should communicate what the Holy Spirit is already doing throughout the world.

5. *The Force for Evangelism*

One of the best measures of the health of the church is the number of those involved in actually building up the church and sharing the good news of the kingdom with others. During the last ten years we have seen a rapid growth in the number of cross-cultural missionaries. In North America in the four-year period between 1975 and 1979 the overseas mission force grew from 37,677 to 53,494 (*Mission Handbook: North American Protestant Ministries Overseas*, 12th Edition, 1980, pp. 24, 25). Most of these gains were the result of large growth in mission agencies catering to younger men and women and seeking new and innovative ways of cross-cultural ministry. The number of European young people attending the yearend biennial mission conference at Lausanne, Switzerland, sponsored by TEMA, continues to grow with over 7000 attending in December 1982. One finds new signs of revitalization in the United Kingdom with the latest edition of the *United Kingdom Christian Handbook* showing a turnaround in church attendance for the first time in a number of years (see Resources). One can sense a resurgence of interest in evangelism and mission that will continue in the immediate future. In the words of Vonette Bright, "Evangelism seldom produces revival, but revival always produces evangelism."

While growth in evangelism and mission continues in the West, an ever-increasing number of churches in the Two-Thirds World are producing their own cross-cultural mission agencies. Recent estimates indicate that there are at least 15,000 cross-cultural missionaries now working out of non-Western countries. There is every reason to believe this growth will continue.

The *World Christian Encyclopedia* (Oxford, 1982) identifies 247,763 full-time missionary personnel, 416 of whom are working in supposedly closed countries, 18,043 working in partially closed countries and 16,245 working in restricted situations. It also indicates that there are 2,680,349 men and women working in some form of full-time Christian service.

III. THE TASK OF WORLD EVANGELIZATION

1. Approach to Evangelization

The Lausanne Covenant becomes the firm basis on which we can consider the task of world evangelization. However, it is helpful to reemphasize some key concepts in our approach to world evangelization:

Jesus Christ is the model for evangelization as the evangelist *par excellence*. Ultimately the work of evangelization is the work of the Holy Spirit, but the Holy Spirit empowers the body of Christ, both individuals and groups of Christians, to carry out the task.

As was well described in *The Willowbank Report: Gospel and Culture*, in carrying out the task of evangelization the good news needs to be expressed in ways that make sense in each culture without sacrificing the essential content of the gospel as revealed in the Scripture.

Implications

This means that we must continually work to protect the purity of the message of the gospel even as we attempt to embody it in the indigenous terms that are available in the culture of the people that we are attempting to evangelize. This is just as true for those who are unreached people groups as it is for the 1000 million in people groups that now have churches in their midst.

Cultural adaptation implies that the way we render Christian service has to make sense to the particular people we are evangelizing. They have to see us as acting in a loving way.

Most individuals and groups normally go through a process which includes several changes of knowledge and attitude before they are ready to acknowledge Christ as Lord and Savior. Evangelization must begin and be related to that process, which will be quite different for different groups. The dimensions of this process are described in Viggo Sogaard's chapter "The Communication Process of Evangelism," as well as the Lausanne publication *That Everyone May Hear*.

Implications

Evangelization needs to be seen as a process in which we participate with the work of the Holy Spirit. The goal of this process should be the establishment of local churches which in turn are attempting to evangelize their own group, as well as send forth missionaries to reach other groups.

There is an intimate relationship between evangelism and social responsibility. It not only follows evangelism as a *consequence* and precedes it as a *bridge*, but also accompanies it as a *partner*. (See LOP No. 21, *Grand Rapids Report: Evangelism and Social Responsibility*.)

Implications

In our approach to evangelism we need to be aware that evangelization is always carried out within the context of a social situation. The two can never be divorced.

2. *Methods of Evangelism*

The key to effective evangelization is Spirit-filled people, not technology. At the same time we need to understand that technology at any point in history is God's gift to us and can be of great assistance to us. Evangelization must include modern means of communication such as TV, radios, cassettes and printed material. More importantly it needs trained and discipled men and women.

Implications

The continued development of the Lausanne Associates network should greatly enhance our awareness of the skills of others and new technical means of communicating the gospel.

Since evangelization involves the gifts of members of the whole body of Christ, using them depends on adequate communication about the evangelistic task. This may include the consolidation of existing training materials, the adaptation to local situations and the continual interplay and interaction between local and national churches throughout the world.

World trends indicate that in many areas of the world it will not be possible for people to go as specifically identified church planters.

Implications

The role of tentmaking ministries *in which committed Christians can move into such areas is
important.*

At the same time this should not deter us from
attempting to multiply the number of cross-
cultural missionaries.

Implications

*We need to develop cross-cultural missionaries both
within national boundaries and across national
boundaries. We need to use strategies which permit
us to build bridges between different national
groups.*

There is not only a need to identify non-Christians
in our midst and in distant places and to call people
to make a commitment to reach them. There is
also a need to do *the hard work of planning.*

In all of this *the role of prayer* cannot be overem-
phasized. The westernizing and modernizing trends
of the world are rapidly moving us away from
commitment to prayer and meditation upon the
Person of Christ. Tendencies towards action orientation work against community life.

Implications

*There must be a renewed emphasis on prayer and a
continuous calling of people to respond to God's*

command to pray. However, it is not enough to call people to prayer. We must also call them to a "community life in Christ" in which prayer and worship and listening to the Spirit are a natural part. Too often we have emphasized the commitment of the individual and failed to remember that individual gifts are given for the building up of the Church so that the Church can do the work of Christ. This needs to be explored more fully as to the implications for world evangelization and living out a life in community before unbelievers.

As has been noted earlier, we are living in a world which is rapidly changing. The "compression of history" has never been greater. It appears that the rate of change will increase.

Implications

A changing world means that we must keep on thinking of new ways of communicating the gospel *that will be meaningful to those we would win.*

For this reason it is important to keep asking questions *as well as applying answers. We can easily fall into standardized methods of evangelization which lose their effectiveness because of rapid social and communication changes in the world.*

Finally, as we think about the methods of world evangelization, we need to understand that God is at work in the minds and hearts of those who have yet to hear. Often the people we seek to evangelize may themselves be able to teach us the best methods *by which they can be most effectively evangelized. By this we do not mean that they can explain the gospel, but that they can teach us how the gospel can be best communicated to them in their context.*

3. *Cooperation in Evangelism*

The Lausanne movement is only one of many instruments that God is using to carry out the task of world evangelization. Figure 19 lists a large number of major conferences and consultations which have been identified, the majority of which are not at the moment directly related to the Lausanne movement. Each one of these is but the tip of an iceberg of tremendous activity going on among the churches and Christian agencies calling these conferences.

Implications

The idea of "Lausanne" as expressed in the Lausanne Covenant is an instrument to be used by the Holy Spirit as he will.

The Lausanne movement needs to be seen as a sharer of what has been learned by others in the task of world evangelization. It needs to bring light on what others are doing. It needs to remind itself and others that God is doing one thing, regardless of what we do. Yet at the same time there needs to be a mutual accountability to one another.

Lausanne needs to capitalize on its unique role in being able to attract committed evangelicals, both in the mainline and independent denominations whose loyalties to conciliar movements may differ.

It neither needs nor expects to take credit for the evangelistic efforts taking place around the world, but needs to be an encourager and a communicator of what God is doing through other groups.

It needs to establish a program that will contribute to coordination and reconciliation among the leaders of major Christian churches and organizations on a personal *and corporate basis.*

God has placed before us an open door. At no time in history has the Church had more resources to be about the task of world evangelization.

Let the Earth hear his voice!

Figure 19

Evangelism Conferences Projected for the 1980s

The following listing includes items not specifically initiated by the Lausanne movement. The roster of future conferences is provided as a service to those who may be interested in writing for details.

DATE	PLACE	EVENT	CONTACT
Jan. 5–8, 1984	Sydney, Australia	Planning Conf. for the Young Leaders 1986 Conference	B. Willersdorf 39A Excelsior Ave. Castle Hill 2154 Australia
Jan. 9–13, 1984	Bengal	Pastors' Conf.	Sam Kamaleson World Vision 919 W. Huntington Monrovia, CA 91016
Jan. 15–20, 1984	Stanwell Tops Sydney, Australia	LIFE Ministries Staff Conf.	Rev. G. Fletcher P.O. Box A399 Sydney S. 2000 Australia
Jan. 18–24, 1984	Harare, Zimbabwe	Int'l Association for Mission Studies	

Jan. 21–26, 1984	Stanwell Tops Sydney, Australia	National Student Conference	Student LIFE P.O. Box A399 Sydney S. 2000 Australia
Feb. 13–20, 1984	Tonga	Pastors' Conf.	Rev. G. Fletcher P.O. Box A399 Sydney S. 2000 Australia
March	Canberra	Explo	B. Willersdorf 39A Excelsior Ave. Castle Hill 2154 Australia
Mar. 5–9, 1984	Iloilo City, Philippines	Pastors' Conf.	Sam Kamaleson World Vision Int'l 919 W. Huntington Monrovia, CA 91016
Mar. 21–24, 1984	Berlin	Arbeitsgemein-schaft Miss. Dienste in der DDR	Dr. Paul Toaspern 1058 Berlin Schonhauser Allee 59

Mar. 26-29, 1984	Farmington, MI	Women in Mission Conference	Missionary Internship Box 457 Farmington, MI 48024
Apr. 2-6, 1984	Elbingerode/Harz	Annual Conf. of Evangelists in the GDR	Fritz Hoffman 3010 Magdeburg Karl-Marx-St 254
May 31-June 3, 1984	London, U.K.	Luis Palau Evangelistic Meeting	
June 4-10, 1984	Seoul, Korea	World Assembly of Prayer	IAG of LCWE Mrs. V. Bright Campus Crusade San Bernardino, CA 92414
June 10, 1984		Day of Prayer for World Evangelization	IAG of LCWE Mrs. V. Bright Campus Crusade San Bernardino, CA 92414

June 11–15, 1984	Manila, Philippines	Communicating Christ in Asia	Asia Christian Communications Fellowship Box 461 Serangooh Garden Postal Office Singapore 9155
June 19–23	Wellesley, MA	Evangelical Women's Caucus Meeting	
June 21, 1984	Essen, Germany	Evangelical Rallye Gemeindetag	Gen. Secr. Pastor Ulrich Parzany Hohenburgstr. 96 4300 Essen 1
June 24–29, 1984	Strassbourg, France	Mennonite World Conference	
July 4–12, 1984	Hawaii, USA	Ethnic Congress	CCCOWE P.O. Box 98435 Tsim Sha Tsui Kowloon, Hong Kong
July 10–15, 1984	Argentina	Youth Conference	Baptist Alliance 1628 16th St., N.W. Washington, DC 20009

July 15-18, 1984	San Diego, California (USA)	3rd World Anglican Chinese Clergy Fellowship Conf.	Rev. Luke Chhoa P.O. Box No. 811 Kota Kinabalu Sabah, E. Malaysia
July 23-27, 1984	Betel Camp	Pastors' Conf.	Orivaldo Lopes Visao Mundial Caixa Postal 848 30,000 Belo Horizonte, Brazil
Aug. 6-10, 1984	National Seminary Ampitiy, Kandy Sri Lanka	Pastors' Conf.	Sam Kamaleson World Vision 919 W. Huntington Monrovia, CA 91016
Aug. 6-10, 1984	Nairobi, Kenya	African Christian Communicators Conference	Richard Mukisa ACCC P.O. Box 20123 Nairobi, Kenya
Aug. 20-22, 1984	Hammons Center Springfield, Missouri (USA)	Conference on Holy Spirit	Tom Zimmerman Assemblies of God 1445 Boonville Ave. Springfield, MO 65802

253

Aug. 22–26, 1984	Bad Blankenburg GDR	Faith Conference of the Evangelical Alliance of the GDR	Manfred Kern 1156 Berlin Jacque–Duclosstr 10
September 1984	Cyprus	Middle East Christian Leadership Assembly	African Enterprise P.O. Box 988 Pasadena, CA 91102
Sep. 3–7, 1984	Bangladesh	Pastors' Conf.	Dr. Milton Coke World Vision P.O. Box 5024 Newmarket Dacca, Bangladesh
Sep. 9–14, 1984	Stuttgart Germany	LCWE Meeting	Mr. Bill Jefferson P.O. Box 1100 Wheaton, IL 60187
Sep. 10–14, 1984	Harare, Zimbabwe	Pastors' Conf.	Sam Kamaleson World Vision 919 W. Huntington Monrovia, CA 91016
Sep 10–15, 1984		EFMA/IFMA Conf.	Dr. Wade Coggins EFMA 1430 K St., NW Washington,DC 20005

Sep. 17–24, 1984	Congress on Evangelization of the Caribbean	University of West Indies Jamaica	
October 1984	International Theological Consultation on China		
Oct. 1–5, 1984	Pastors' Conf.	North India	Solomon Bodhan 209 M.G. Road Dilkusha Uttar Pradesh Lucknow, India
Oct. 25–28, 1984	Great Commission Convocation	St. Louis, Missouri (USA)	Erwin J. Kolb Lutheran Church Missouri Synod 1333 S. Kirkwood St. Louis, MO 63122
November	2nd National Congress of Evangelicals	Caracas, Venezuela	Fellowship of Evangel Ministers Apdo 80287 Prados del Este Caracas 1080 Venezuela

255

Date	Location	Event	Contact
Nov. 5-9, 1984	North Kerala, India	Pastors' Conf.	Sam Kamaleson World Vision 919 W. Huntington Monrovia, CA 91016
Nov. 12-16, 1984	South Kerala, India	Pastors' Conf.	Sam Kamaleson World Vision 919 W. Huntington Monrovia, CA 91016
Nov. 19-23, 1984	Hwa Nan Hotel Taipei, Taiwan	Pastors' Conf.	Rev. Jen-Li Tsai Bible Society 4E No.29 Jen-al Rd. Sect. 3 Taipei, Taiwan
Dec. 27-31, 1984	Urbana, IL	Urbana '84	Inter-Varsity 233 Langdon St. Madison, WI 53703
Jan. 7-11, 1985	St. Thomas School Kidderpore West Bengal	Pastors' Conf.	Dr. Sam Kamaleson World Vision 919 W. Huntington Monrovia, CA 91016
Jan. 7-11, 1985	Dallas, Texas	National Presbyterian Congress on Renewal	Dr. Ernest J. Lewis P.O. Box 202254 Dallas, TX 75220

Jan. 7–12, 1985	Stavanger, Norway	Finnish/Norwegian Lutheran Conf. on Mission Theology	Mission Theology School Stavanger, Norway
Feb. 10, 1985	Stuttgart, Germany	Youth Congress on World Evangelization	Winrich Scheffbuch Stitzenburgstr 13 7000 Stuttgart 1
Apr. 15–18, 1985	Houston, TX	Houston '85	Rev. Paul Landrey P.O. Box 3137 Arcadia, CA 91006
May 20–24, 1985	Norway	Holy Spirit Consultation	TWG of LCWE Rev. John Reid P.O. Box Q190 Queen Victoria Blvd NSW 2000
May 26, 1985		Day of Prayer for World Evangelization	
June 6, 1985	Stuttgart, Germany	Evangelical Congress	Dean R. Scheffbuch Burgstr. 42 7060 Schorndorf

Date	Location	Event	Contact
July 3–31, 1985	Manila, Philippines	Asian Institute of Christian Communication	ACCF Box 461 Serangoon Garden Post Office Singapore 9155
July 2–7, 1985	Switzerland	World Conference	Tom Zimmerman 1445 Boonville Ave. Springfield, MO 65802
October	Hong Kong	Chinese Culture and Evangelism	CCCOWE P.O. Box 98435 Tsim Sha Tsui Kowloon, Hong Kong
1985		Third Thailand Congress	
July 1986		Congress on Evangelism	CCCOWE P.O. Box 98435 Tsim Sha Tsui Kowloon, Hong Kong
Sept. 8–12, 1986		LCWE Meeting	Mr. Bill Jefferson P.O. Box 1100 Wheaton, IL 60187

Date	Location	Event	Organization
December 1987	Lausanne, Switzerland	Mission '87	European Missionary Association CH–1032 Romanel Switzerland
1987	Korea	Third Japanese Congress on Evangelism	
1989		ICOWE 1989 (proposed)	

FREEDOM AND PERSECUTION

It is the God-appointed duty of every government to secure conditions of peace, justice and liberty in which the church may obey God, serve the Lord Christ, and preach the gospel without interference. We therefore pray for the leaders of the nations and call upon them to guarantee freedom of thought and conscience, and freedom to practice and propagate religion in accordance with the will of God and as set forth in The Universal Declaration of Human Rights. We also express our deep concern for all who have been unjustly imprisoned, and especially for our brethren who are suffering for their testimony to the Lord Jesus. e promise to pray and work for their freedom. At the same time we refuse to be intimidated by their fate. God helping us, we too will seek to stand gainst injustice and to remain faithful to the gospel, whatever the cost. We do not forget the warnings of Jesus that persecution is inevitable.

(I Tim. 1:1-4; Acts 4:19; 5:29; Col 3:24; Heb. 13:1-3; Luke 4:18; Gal. 5:11; 6:12; Matt. 5:10-12; John 15:18-21)

Article 13
The Lausanne Covenant

The Future of the Lausanne Movement

Leighton Ford

"To prophesy is very dangerous--especially about the future."
So says a Chinese proverb. Yet to look to the future is one of
the distinctives the Creator has given us human beings. Man
is a creature who lives by foresight and planning and not just
by instinct and reaction.

As I sketch this possible future for the Lausanne movement, I
am aware of three basic attitudes we can take to the future.

We can treat the future with a kind of ignorance, agnosticism
or indifference. "Who knows? Who cares?" But *ignorance* is
not bliss; it is both dangerous and downright sinful. To remain ignorant is to descend to the animal level. The Lord
clearly tells us, "I will instruct you and teach you in the way
you should go; I will counsel you and watch over you. Do not
be like the horse or the mule which have no understanding"
(Ps. 32:8, 9).

Prudence is a second possible attitude. By prudence--a careful weighing of the alternatives--we rise from the animal
level to the human level. The writer of Proverbs often com-
mends prudence. "The plans of the diligent lead to profit as
surely as haste leads to poverty. The prudent man sees danger

and takes refuge, but the simple keep going and suffer for it" (Pro. 21:5; 22:3).

But as believers, we are called to a higher attitude, *obedience*. Obedience takes us from the human level of the weighing of alternatives to the spiritual level of discerning God's will. Proverbs qualifies prudence: "Many are the plans in a man's heart, but it is the Lord's purpose that prevails" (19:21). All our human foresight could not begin to understand "the mystery of his will" unless God had made known to us his purpose in Christ (Eph. 1:9). We are called to approach the future by seeking to know and obey God's will as he reveals it in Scripture, interprets it by his Spirit and works it out in his providence.

Prudence plus obedience makes a healthy combination, drawing together practical human sense with spiritual wisdom.

Jesus himself is the best example. He was quite clearly goal-oriented. When he was warned that Herod wanted to kill him, he sent word, "Go tell that fox, 'I will drive out demons and heal people today and tomorrow and on the third day I will reach my goal'" (Lk. 13:32). Yet Jesus' goal was very different from the success orientation that often dictates our future plans today. Jesus' goal in going to Jerusalem was to give up his life for our salvation and for the kingdom. "Surely no prophet can die outside Jerusalem!" (Lk. 13:33).

As we look to the future, the goal of the kingdom of God must always reign supreme. And the timing of the opportunities he opens to us is far more important than our schedules. *By no means* should we be ignorant; *by all means* we should be prudent; and *at any cost* we must be obedient.

A Focus for the Years Ahead

In the spirit of prudence and obedience, let me spell out some areas of evangelization which the Lausanne Committee has singled out for emphasis in the next few years. I have divided this tentative agenda into two parts—*the field of evangelization* and *the force for evangelization*.

The Field of Evangelization

At the 1974 Lausanne International Congress on World Evangelization, a focus on "unreached peoples" came to the forefront. The now well-known figure of 2.7 billion unreached people gained wide currency after Lausanne. The Lausanne Strategy Working Group suggested a strategy of reaching the world, not just a nation or a person at a time, but a people group at a time. *Time* magazine, in its December 1982 feature story on the new breed of missionary, reckoned that the people group strategy is the most significant development in missionary thinking in recent decades.

While the concept has been widely accepted by specialists, it is now beginning to filter down to the level of the local church. A program of education is a priority to help Christians at the grass-roots level direct their thinking, praying, planning and giving for a specific people group. The Lausanne Committee has prepared three audiovisual productions for this purpose. *That Everyone May Hear* explains in two parts how to think about people groups and how to develop a people group strategy. The third explains the basic concepts of the Lausanne Covenant and is available to local churches for study along with the Covenant itself. (See Part 6 Resources.)

Among the many "unreached peoples" let me select four major blocs as examples:

Cities. Those who think of biblical faith as a religion for green pastures need to remember that the Bible opens in a garden but closes in a city! The challenge of the cities through worldwide urbanization is undeniable. Predictions indicate that by the year 2000 percentages of people living in cities will be: U.S. 94%; Europe 82%; USSR and Eastern Europe 80%; Latin America 73%; Australia 85%; Asia 60%; Africa 45%. By the end of the century, Mexico City is predicted to have a population of 31.6 million.

As his chapter on "Evangelizing the Cities" adequately demonstrates, Raymond Bakke is diligently building a network of corresponding groups in some 150 world-class cities. Dr. Bakke is released for three months each year from teaching responsibilities at Northern Baptist Seminary to travel as a Senior Lausanne Associate. He brings together leaders in the great cities of the world to strategize with each other. His effective catalytic work in helping local Christians to "exegete" their own cities has set a pattern for the future and a model for similar networks. (See Lausanne Occasional Paper No. 9 *Christian Witness to Large Cities.*)

Islam. Isaiah's ancient prophecy of the day "when Israel will be the third along with Egypt and Assyria, a blessing on the earth" may startle many modern-day Christians. But God's future plan clearly embraces Arab as well as Jew (Isa. 19:24, 25).

It is surely more than a coincidence that the rise of the Middle Eastern powers to world economic might and the resurgence of fundamentalist Islam has made the secular news at the same time that a new Christian concern for Islam has been growing. Don McCurry, a veteran missionary to Pakistan and founder of the Samuel Zwemer Institute, has undertaken as a Senior Lausanne Associate an itinerant ministry aimed at those working with Muslims. This is similar to what Dr. Bakke is doing in the cities. It is a kind of apostolic ministry of carrying news from one area to another of what God is doing and how he is leading his people to witness among Muslims. Patrick Sookdheo is the Lausanne Associate for Coordinating Muslim Evangelization carrying out a similar task. (See L.O.P. No. 13, *Christian Witness to Muslims*; and *The Gospel and Islam* edited by Don M. McCurry, MARC 1979.)

The Secular West. High on the agenda for the future must be the reevangelization of the West. David Barrett's significant *World Christian Encyclopedia* points out that the burst of Christianity in the Two-Thirds World has been offset by defections due to Communism in the Eastern countries, secularism in Europe and materialism in America. A Church of England official briefing Billy Graham for "Mission England" told him he could expect more knowledge of the Bible in Nigeria than in England. An "Urgent Call to the Kirk" was circulated at the Church of Scotland's 1983 assembly, calling for the reevangelization of Scotland. In Canada, a study suggests the growth of evangelical churches may come less from the conversion of outsiders than by transfers from more liberal churches. Bishop Stephen Neill believes that evangelism in the West has largely meant starting at the center of a Christian ghetto and evangelizing to the fringes of that ghetto, without knowing how to move beyond to penetrate the truly secular world.

The West, too, is a mission field. To "go into all the world" means not only to go to nomadic tribes in Africa and cities in Asia, but to go into the world of business, university, industry and communications. Christians in the West must be taught not only to be faithful family and church members, but to think and live and speak as disciple makers in all the worlds in which they live.

There are welcome signs of renewal. "Mission England" is a three-year program of prayer, church growth, evangelism training and discipleship to prepare and follow up the 1984 Billy Graham crusades. Preliminary surveys indicate that a large proportion of the English population is interested in hearing his message. The spiritual renewal taking place in recent years in hundreds of U.K. churches may bear fruit in the current campaign. The North American Lausanne Committee is coordinating a special effort to reach the ethnic groups in North America. (See L.O.P.s No. 10 and 19, *Christian Witness to Nominal Christians Among Roman Catholics* and *Among the Orthodox.*)

The Poor. While the more affluent nations have gone through their own recession, the plight of the really poor has grown even more desperate. It is estimated that 10,000 people a day die of starvation.

In the Bible God makes plain his special concern for the poor. This does not mean that he does not equally desire the salvation of the rich. But when Jesus was asked by John the Baptist whether he was the Messiah, his response to John was, "The blind receive sight, the lame walk, those with leprosy are cured, the deaf hear, the dead are raised and *the good news is preached to the poor*" (Lk.7:22). The poor in the Bible are not only the economically poor who trust in God. The poor are

those helpless ones who have no hope except to cast themselves on the mercy and grace of God (see, for example, the
"poor" to whom Jesus brought good news in Luke 7: a Gentile
centurion, a bereaved widow, a sinful woman).

The Consultation on the Relationship Between Evangelism
and Social Responsibility, sponsored by LCWE and WEF in
1982, suggested three possible relationships between evangelism and social responsibility. (See L.O.P. No. 21, *Evangelism and Social Responsibility*.) First, evangelism is the seed
of which social responsibility is the fruit or consequence.
Second, Christian social action is a bridge of love across which
the gospel may move. Third, evangelism and social responsibility are partners, as the twin blades of a pair of scissors.

The report is sound, but will our deeds match our beliefs?
Will the followers of Marx show more concern for the poor
than the followers of Christ?

A close friend of mine has been an outstanding success in
business in the United States. An avid Bible reader, he told
me he had marked over 600 verses of Scripture which have to
do with our Christian responsibility to the weak and the poor.
He told me the moving story of a sort of vision which came to
him in the middle of the night in which God seemed to say to
him that he was giving the Church one last chance. The
churches in the U.S., he felt, have an opportunity to do what
governments could never do in terms of putting their resources to work. "God made it clear," he said, "that this would not
be for the sake of the poor, but for the sake of the Church."
Compelled by a heavenly vision, my friend has put his vision,
his energy and money into a program bringing together
church leaders in his city to provide job training and job
placement programs in the name of Jesus at a time of great

economic need. Such a concern is not a social gospel. It is biblical gospel, fully believed and obeyed.

The Force for World Evangelization

A second major concern is the renewal and equipping of the Church, for as the Lausanne Covenant says, "World evangelization requires the whole Church to take the whole gospel to the whole world. The Church is at the very center of God's cosmic purpose and is his appointed means of spreading the gospel" (para. 6).

Spirituality. Many years ago Archbishop William Temple laid down the principle that "the evangelization of those without cannot be separated from the rekindling of devotion of those within." Evangelical Christianity has gone through a widely publicized growth spurt in North America in recent years. But there is still a question whether this growing interest in personal salvation will be translated into a deep social and moral impact, and into a rising zeal for world evangelization. Those who try to raise money know it is fairly easy to raise funds for physical needs, but not nearly as easy to raise money for evangelism and missions. Could this be due in part to an absence of true spirituality?

Similarly, in some areas of the Two-Thirds World there has been remarkable statistical growth in the Church, but also a concern that this might result in nominal Christianity rather than in true discipleship. The best strategies for world evangelization will fail if we expect them to be implemented by carnal Christians.

This concern for a renewed spirituality lies behind some of the conferences to be sponsored by the Lausanne Committee.

In June 1984 the International Prayer Assembly for World Evangelization will be held in Seoul, Korea, sponsored by the Lausanne Intercession Advisory Group and hosted by the Korean Evangelical Fellowship. The year 1984 is a significant date for this assembly. It will be the centennial year of the Korean (Protestant) Church and will mark the tenth anniversary of the Lausanne Congress. Key people from various prayer ministries will seek to build a solid foundation of intercessory prayer for world evangelization in the years ahead.

Norway will be the site for a consultation on the Holy Spirit and World Evangelization in May 1985, while another consultation on Conversion and World Evangelization is scheduled for 1987. Both will be smaller, in-depth conferences with a theological emphasis.

The new emphasis does not imply a retreat from our Christian call to engage society and culture. Rather the forthcoming consultations complement the previous ones. It will take a renewed spirituality for a deep impact to be made upon our world whether in evangelism or social responsibility. As David Bryant has said, "Mission without renewal leads to burnout, while renewal without mission leads to copout."

Mobilization and recruitment. The rise of Two-Thirds World missions (so-called "emerging missions") has been an exciting development in the last two decades. The growing partnership between missionaries from all parts of the world must remain a top priority. Three other areas for the recruitment and mobilization of workers are bursting upon us.

Younger leaders. Historically, evangelism in missions has often been carried out through the visions of young men and women. This is also happening today. In Europe periodic missionary conferences have drawn increasing thousands of young people. Perhaps the largest evangelistic agency in the world is now Youth With A Mission (YWAM) which was founded in 1960. Today it has an estimated 14,000 young people involved in long or short-term outreach.

In many parts of the world we are in a period of transition. During the next few years a number of older leaders will move out of active service. At the same time we are seeing a number of creative young men and women beginning new and specific evangelistic thrusts. The 1990s will probably be a decade when the mantle of leadership is transferred in many groups. In anticipation, the Lausanne Committee is encouraging one or more conferences of younger leaders. We want the emerging young leaders to be exposed to the world scene, to know each other, to build friendships for future relationships, and to sharpen their skills in meeting one another.

Women. It is a fact of history that women have been widely used as missionaries but singularly ignored as leaders in the Church. The same women seem to be used again and again in regional or international conferences. This is not because capable women are not at work. Much of the finest evangelistic missionary work now as always is carried out by faithful and gifted women. When Bishop Festo Kivengere returned from exile to his native Uganda after Idi Amin was deposed, he found that the evangelistic work in his diocese had been carried on largely by women. In much of the world Christian women now find new opportunities for themselves in secular work and professions. The Church must increasingly enable these gifted women to be fellow laborers in the gospel. As Dorothy Sayers pointed out, women were the last at the cross and the first at the tomb, and therefore the first to proclaim the risen Christ in the gospel era.

Lay people. Similarly, world evangelization will be short-circuited without a far greater commitment to releasing the ministry of Christian lay people. J. Christy Wilson, professor of missions at Gordon-Conwell Seminary, recently wrote me to point out that Korean Christians working in the Middle East are the only available or effective missionaries in many of the Muslim countries! He urged special plans to equip and mobilize lay people.

Looking Forward--Cooperation and Unity

Biblical evangelism and biblical ecumenism have always belonged together. I use the work "ecumenism" in its biblical and classical sense of the worldwide church. The late John Mackay of Princeton pointed out that the modern ecumenical movement rose with the vision of the whole Church taking the whole gospel to the whole world. He then lamented that in later developments the ecumenical movement had become somehow detached from that evangelistic vision. We who call ourselves evangelicals should emulate the passion of Zinzendorf who once said he would travel anyplace in the world to further the spread of the gospel and the unity of believers. Even more important, we should seek to be part of the answer to our Lord's prayer, "that they may be one, that the world may believe" (John 17:21).

Billy Graham's evangelistic crusades have been used to bring tens of thousands into the kingdom of God. But future historians may see that his enormous influence has had as much an impact for evangelical unity as for evangelizing the unsaved. His crusades in many cities and countries have been a mobilizing factor that has brought evangelical Christians together. Many of the great international conferences: (Berlin 1966, Lausanne 1974, Amsterdam 1983) and scores of other national and regional conferences have grown from Dr. Graham's deep desire to see biblical evangelical Christians work, plan and pray together for world evangelization.

Since 1974 the central theme of the Lausanne continuing committee has been cooperation in world evangelization. The Lausanne Covenant has been an umbrella under which evangelical Christians have been able to meet together. "Lausanne" has become more than a place, an event, or a committee. It has become a symbol of a movement of like-minded believers who long to see the day when the gospel will be preached to the whole world and the Lord will return.

The Lausanne Committee recently adopted this purpose statement:

> "The mandate of the Lausanne Committee is to hasten the evangelization of all peoples of the world in obedience to the command of Jesus Christ and in anticipation of his return by multiplying and strengthening the ways in which evangelical believers work together to accomplish this task through churches, missions and other Christian organizations."

The Lausanne Committee has also expressed its belief that the time may be coming when there should be another international congress on world evangelization, a kind of "Lausanne II," perhaps before the end of this decade. Careful consultation will take place with a wide group of Christian leaders during 1983-84 before any concrete plans are made. If such a congress is held, we ought to pray that this might not just be a replay of 1974, a kind of spiritual "encore." Rather it should be a time to celebrate what God has done since 1974. It should be a meeting of the many streams of God's blessings which are pouring into the world. It should be an occasion to "pass the torch" to the leaders of the next generation of world evangelists.

Our Challenge

As Christians living near the end of the twentieth century, we have opportunities for world evangelization unique to our generation. It is up to us to make the most of these opportunities. No one knows what tomorrow may hold.

Over the past two decades we have seen the dawning of a whole new era of cooperation in world evangelization. On every continent, Christians are coming together, as never before, to pray, plan and work together. This spirit of cooperation, which has been so important in expanding the vision of Christians around the world, must continue, if we truly want to maximise our efforts in communicating the good news of Jesus Christ.

Today there are literally thousands of Christians throughout the world who receive Lausanne-related materials, who pray and work for world evangelization in their respective areas. They are linked not by membership, but rather by a covenant and commitment. And each person who holds high the vision of world evangelization, contributes a measure of hope both to the Church and this restless and dying world. Will you hold high the vision of world Evangelization?

The very nature of the task demands that the whole Church take the whole gospel to the whole world. True co-operation will not destroy individual initiative. On the contrary, those who recognize their place in the overall work of God are most likely to accomplish their goals and objectives.

In my firm belief that God has called us to this co-operative ministry, the Lausanne Committee is steadfast in its commitment to foster co-operation and hold high the vision of completing the task of world evangelization. We invite you, along with Christians everywhere, to participate in this ministry.

Let the earth hear His voice!

Leighton Ford is Vice President and Associate Evangelist of the Billy Graham Evangelistic Association. He serves as chairman of the Lausanne Committee for World Evangelization.

THE RETURN OF CHRIST

We believe that Jesus Christ will return personally and visibly, in power and glory, to consummate his salvation and his judgement. This promise of his coming is a further spur to our evangelism, for we remember his words that the gospel must first be preached to all nations. We believe that the interim period between Christ's ascension and return is to be filled with the mission of the people of God, who have no liberty to stop before the End. We also remember his warning that false Christs and false prophets will arise as precursors of the final Antichrist. We therefore reject as a proud, self-confident dream the notion that man can ever build a utopia on earth. Our Christian conscience is that God will perfect his kingdom, and we look forward with eager anticipation to that day, and to the new heaven and earth in which righteousness will dwell and God will reign for ever. Meanwhile, we rededicate ourselves to the service of Christ and of men in joyful submission to his authority over the whole of our lives.

(Mark 14:62; Heb. 9:28; Mark 13:10; Acts 1:8-11; Matt. 28:20; Mark 13:21-23; John 2:18; 4:1-3; Luke 12:32; Rev. 21:1-5; II Pet. 3:13; Matt. 28:18)

Article 15
The Lausanne Covenant

The
Unreached Peoples

Expanded Descriptions

Introduction to Expanded Descriptions

The following section contains descriptions of 27 people groups in alphabetical order. Each group has a data table printed above the written decription, containing information based on questionnaires completed by persons in the same country or otherwise knowledgeable about the people group. (Please see Appendix A for a sample of this questionnaire.)

In the data table, the most common name of the people group is given first, followed by the name of the country in which the group is located.

The following is a summary of the remaining data categories:

Alternate Names: Any alternate names or spellings for the people group.

Size of Group: Latest population estimate of the group.

MARC ID: An identification number by which information on the group is filed. Any correspondence sent to MARC dealing with a group, sending corrections, updates, additions or requests for further information, should refer to that number.

Distinctives: Distinctive features that unify this group. Many different things may make a group distinct or cause them to consider themselves a people. Often several factors give them some kind of affinity toward one another or make them different from other groups. Respondents to the unreached peoples questionnaire were asked to indicate the relative importance of various factors in making the group distinctive. Those factors were speaking the same language, common political loyalty, similar occupation, racial or ethnic similarity, shared religious customs, common kinship ties, strong sense of unity, similar education level, common residential area, similar social class or caste, similar economic status, shared hobby or special interest, discrimination from other groups, unique health situation, distinctive legal status, similar age, common significant problems, and "other(s)."

Social Change: This represents an estimate of the overall rate at which cultural and social change is taking place in the group--very rapid, rapid, moderate, slow or very slow.

Languages: Primary languages. Multilingual communities often use different languages in different situations. They may learn one language in school, another in the market, and yet another in religious ceremonies. Respondents were asked to indicate the major languages used by the group as well as the place or function of each language. These functions are indicated by the following codes:

V - vernacular or common language
T - trade language or lingua franca
S - language used for instruction in schools
W - language used for any current or past Christian witness
G - language most suitable for presentation of the gospel
P - language used in any non-Christian ceremonies

The percentages listed next to the headings *speak* and *read* indicate the percentage of the total group that speak and read the language listed.

Scripture: Indicates the availability of various forms of biblical literature in the main language of the group.

Recordings: Indicates the availability of recordings, records or cassettes in the main language of the group. Recordings can include Bible readings, Bible stories with gospel applications, culturally adapted gospel messages, or basic Christian teaching, as well as music. (Detailed information on recordings in specific languages can be obtained from Gospel Recordings U.S.A., 122 Glendale Boulevard, Los Angeles, California 90026, U.S.A.)

Christian Literacy:

This indicates the percentage of Christians among the people (if any) over 15 years of age who can and do read in any language.

Religion:

This indicates the primary religion(s) found among members of the group. The percentage shown next to *adherents* estimates the percentage of the group who would say that they follow the religion listed. The percentage next to *practicing* indicates the number who actively practice the religion listed (in the opinion of the researcher or reporter). Determining the percentage of those adhering to a certain religion versus the percentage of those practicing their faith is admittedly a subjective judgment. This figure is important, however, when considering Christian populations, because the definition of *unreached* used here depends on a measure of the church's strength, which must be drawn basically from its size and growth rate.

Churches and Missions:

This indicates the primary Christian churches or missions, national or foreign, that are active in the area where the people group is concentrated. The figure under *membership* is the approximate number of full members of this church or mission denomination from the people group. The figure under *community* is the approximate number of adherents (including children) to the denomination or mission from the people group. These are not *all* the churches and missions among this group, only the ones that have been reported.

Openness to Religious Change:

This is an estimate of how open the group is to religious change of any kind. Categories are very open, somewhat open, indifferent, somewhat closed and very closed.

Receptivity to Christianity:

This is an estimate of the openness of the group to Christianity in particular. Categories are very receptive, receptive, indifferent, reluctant and very reluctant.

Evangelism Profile: People tend to come to Christ in more or less well-defined steps. This scale (based on a scale developed by Dr. James Engel of the Wheaton Graduate School) indicates the approximate percentage of the group at various levels of awareness of the gospel. The scale ranges from people with no awareness of Christianity to those who are active propagators of the gospel. A further explanation of this useful tool may be found in Edward Dayton's article "To Reach the Unreached" in *Unreached Peoples '79.*

Not Reported (nr): Whenever this appears in any category, it indicates that the information has not yet been received by the MARC computers. In future volumes of this series, information will be added as it becomes available.

Validity Code: An estimate of the accuracy and completeness of the data on a scale from one to nine. The code is:

1. The only information available at this point is the group name, country, language, population and primary religion. The percentage listed under practicing Christians is at best a rough estimate.

2. There has been more data collected than the "baseline" information in 1, but it is scanty or of poor quality.

3. About half of the information on the unreached peoples questionnaire (Appendix A) has been collected, and information on the Christian community, if any, is missing or probably inaccurate.

4. Almost all the data on the unreached peoples questionnaire has been collected, *or* the source document has supplied most of the necessary information.

5. Information has been supplied by a completed unreached peoples questionnaire *and* at least one other document.

6. In addition to 5, there is enough detailed information about the people group to write an accurate, up-to-date description.

7. There exists an extensive description of the people group in secular or Christian literature.

8. There has been a major research study (thesis or dissertation quality) done on the group which includes detailed information on the Christian community.

9. In addition to 8, the study includes a thorough exploration of evangelism strategy for the particular group, based on first-hand experience.

Following the data table with the basic information about the people group are several paragraphs further detailing characteristics of the group.

A complete listing of all unreached people groups currently identified in the MARC files can be found in the Registry of the Unreached following these descriptions. For many of these groups more information is available. To obtain the data on a particular group, just send in the reply page located in the back of this book.

Index of People Groups
With Expanded Descriptions

Badui (Indonesia) 293

Bengali, Los Angeles area (United States of America) 295

Bengali Sufis (Bangladesh) 297

Black Caribs (Honduras) 299

Blind, N.E. Thailand (Thailand) 301

Boni of Lamu (Kenya) 303

Caribs (Dominica) 305

Cherkess (Jordan) 307

Chinese (Mauritius) 308

Digo (Kenya) 310

English speakers, Guadalajara (Mexico) 312

Filipino Migrant Workers (Saudi Arabia) 314

Indo-Canadians, Vancouver (Canada: British Columbia) 316

291

EXPANDED DESCRIPTIONS

Llaneros (Colombia) 318

Military Officers (Ecuador) 320

Phu Thai (Thailand) 322

Rural Vodun Believers (Haiti) 324

Samburu (Kenya) 326

Sanga (Zaire) 328

Sundanese (Indonesia) 330

Thai Immigrants, Los Angeles (United States of America) 332

Urban Street Women/Los Angeles (United States of America) 334

Wandering Homeless (United States of America) 336

Water Surface People (Hong Kong) 338

Yami of Orchid Island (Indonesia) 340

Yao (Malawi) 343

Zanskari (India) 345

Badui (Indonesia)

ALTERNATE NAMES: Baduj; Kanekes

SIZE OF GROUP: 5,000   **MARC ID:** 4812

DISTINCTIVES: language; ethnicity; kinship; religion; education; discrimination; residence; sense of unity

SOCIAL CHANGE: very slow

LANGUAGES: Badui (100% speak; V,G); Indonesian (60% speak/ 5% read; T)

SCRIPTURE: none   **RECORDINGS:** not reported

CHRISTIAN LITERACY: not reported

RELIGION: Animism (100% adherents/100% practicing); Christianity (<1% practicing)

CHURCHES AND MISSIONS: not reported

OPENNESS TO RELIGIOUS CHANGE: very closed

RECEPTIVITY TO CHRISTIANITY: very reluctant

GROWTH OF CHRISTIAN COMMUNITY:: not reported

EVANGELISM PROFILE: not reported   **VALIDITY:** 4

Western Java is populated primarily by Sundanese Muslims, but located in the western sector are the Badui people, a remnant of archaic Sundanese society, speaking an old dialect of Sundanese. The Badui purposely isolated themselves in this mountainous region when Java became predominantly Muslim in religion. They have maintained a rigid, caste-like system of social stratification. Descent is traced through both parents, but the nuclear family is not as strong as among the major ethnic group of Java. Village patterns consist of approximately 35 small clusters of houses interspersed among fields of swidden-rice cultivation. Three villages have remained completely isolated from non-Badui contacts.

Due to this withdrawal, they have refused to educate their offspring in the Indonesian public schools. The government has not enforced education, and consequently they remain illiterate and primitive. Badui men are reportedly allowed to ride the trains free of charge. The men wear dark blue or black shirts and sarongs and wrap their waist-length hair up under black cloth on their heads. Picture-taking is taboo.

Folk religion is the dominant spiritual force in their daily lives. Exposure to Christianity has been minimal within Baduiland because it is so isolated. During the

293

EXPANDED DESCRIPTIONS

1970s a zealous Sundanese Christian made several trips to Badui and many converts were reported. His life was in jeopardy at times and he had to flee the area. That contact has not persisted, and there remains no Christian witness. Even when the gospel contact was made, the people were strongly opposed. The only outside contact with these people now is a nearby entrepreneur who employs some Badui to demonstrate cultural artifacts and customs.

A major difficulty is to penetrate Badui territory. Perhaps the first step would be to establish a contact point on the fringe and begin to befriend some Badui. The most natural contact would be the Sundanese rather than foreigners. Workers should be prepared with some good culturally-oriented gospel visuals since the people cannot read. The people's black magic and fetishes mean one should be prepared for power-encounter situations. Healing and exorcism ministry would be appropriate to accompany preaching of the gospel. A foreign Christian linguist/translator could be placed in the area to work on the language with low-key gospel input initially.

Ways should be sought to reach a mobile Badui who has natural relationships on the inside. Other ethnic Christians could then be introduced. The few Badui associated with the entrepreneur are an example of those with outside contacts. A risk would be the alienation of those contacts. The youth would be a receptive target audience. Those who have traveled outside and been exposed to non-Badui life are candidates for change. However, the culture could easily face disequilibrium if the older people are bypassed. Workers must befriend them and discover felt needs unique to their isolated life-style. Later a more complete strategy can be formed to reach the whole tribe.

Bengali, Los Angeles area (United States of America)

ALTERNATE NAMES: not reported

SIZE OF GROUP: 4,000　　　　　　　　　　**MARC ID:** 4818

DISTINCTIVES: language; occupation; education; economic status; age; residence

SOCIAL CHANGE: very rapid

LANGUAGES: Bengali (98% speak/ 98% read; V,W,T,G); English (98% speak/ 98% read; V,T,S,W)

SCRIPTURE: Bible　　　　　　**RECORDINGS:** not reported

CHRISTIAN LITERACY: 99%

RELIGION: Islam (93% adherents); Hinduism (6% adherents); Protestant (1% adherants/ <1% practicing)

CHURCHES AND MISSIONS	BEGAN	MEMBERSHIP	CMTY
Pasadena First Baptist	1982	20	nr

OPENNESS TO RELIGIOUS CHANGE: somewhat open

RECEPTIVITY TO CHRISTIANITY: receptive

GROWTH OF CHRISTIAN COMMUNITY: stable

EVANGELISM PROFILE: not reported　　　　**VALIDITY:** 4

Bangladesh, a country about the size of Illinois, is the world's eighth most populous nation, with a population density 26 times that of the United States. Its total output in 1980 was about $130 per person. Roughly one-fourth of the population is literate, and the life expectancy at birth is 46 years. One in seven children never reaches a first birthday. Due to recent price declines, Bangladesh is on the verge of bankruptcy.

In contrast to the country of origin, nearly 4000 persons of Bengali descent now live in Pasadena, South Pasadena, Covina, West Covina, San Gabriel, Los Angeles, Monterey Park, Glendale and San Marino, all of which are a part of Los Angeles county in California. In general, this group of primarily middle-aged people (30-45 years) are bilingual, well educated and entering professional careers such as engineering. They are thankful to live in America, but still cling to many customs and mores of Bangladesh. Nearly all these immigrants can read English, and the Bible is available to them in print in Bengali. They are somewhat open to the claims of Jesus Christ, but very few Christian workers are attempting to reach them. Of these 4000 people, only 25 families are Christians. In other words, less than one percent of them have accepted Jesus Christ as Lord and have become responsible church members.

One believer, however, is trying to change this situation. His name is John Biswas. John, in conjunction with the First Baptist Church in Pasadena, has dedicated count-less hours toward spreading the love of Christ with his fellow people. His activities include: personal visitation, providing transportation to church, and programs which include swimming lessons, picnics, trips to the zoo and Disneyland. He leads a lan-guage correspondence school program in Bengali. In addition, John dreams of start-ing a nursery school and day-care center to aid the many working Bengali parents. He also hopes to work in drug rehabilitation, medical care and stop-smoking pro-grams. His motto is, "In service with love, affection and responsibility." John desper-ately needs assistance both in personnel and finances. The only effective way to reach these southern California Bengali people is first through prayer, and second through an outpouring of the Holy Spirit. They tenaciously cling to their Hindu or Islamic roots. Workers are needed to join John Biswas in tangible demonstration of the abundant, forgiving love of Jesus Christ which is able to penetrate the barriers that now separate them.

Bengali Sufis (Bangladesh)

ALTERNATE NAMES: not reported

SIZE OF GROUP: 70,000   **MARC ID:** 4820

DISTINCTIVES:

SOCIAL CHANGE: moderate

LANGUAGES: Bengali (100% speak; V,G,S); English (T,S)

SCRIPTURE: Bible   **RECORDINGS:** not reported

CHRISTIAN LITERACY: not reported

RELIGION: Islam (100% adherents/100% practicing)

CHURCHES AND MISSIONS: not reported

OPENNESS TO RELIGIOUS CHANGE: somewhat open

RECEPTIVITY TO CHRISTIANITY: receptive

GROWTH OF CHRISTIAN COMMUNITY: not reported

EVANGELISM PROFILE: not reported   **VALIDITY:** 4

Sufis are religious leaders who believe it is essential to draw close to Allah in a personal and often mystical way. When they are successful in attaining union with Allah, they have power to heal, give sound advice, and intercede for devout Muslims. Sufis have often been the most fervent missionaries and have been primarily responsible for the conversion of Bengalis to Islam. The Sufi movement prevails in Bangladesh to a greater degree than in most other Muslim countries.

Sufis seek truth through an active and growing relationship with Allah rather than through strict adherence to Islamic law. Bengali Muslims tired of lifeless traditions turn to Sufi leaders as mentors in developing a more personal religious life. Many of the mystical practices are learned from individual Sufis, which leads to a great deal of diversity. Some have studied the Quran extensively and are well educated; others are quite uneducated and rely heavily on the experiential.

Sufis rely on supernatural events to prove their "barakat" or personal holiness, which is accompanied by obvious spiritual powers. Some have assimilated Hindu traditions, Buddhist practices, and occult activities in their teachings. Others have separated themselves from Islam and lead new cults. Most are fervent in their devotion to Allah and their careful study of the Quran. They usually belong to one of the four orders which give structure to the movement.

EXPANDED DESCRIPTIONS

The status of Sufi leaders rises as their supernatural powers become more pronounced. Disciples are taught the disciplines of a holy life. When a Sufi leader dies, his tomb often becomes a shrine, and disciples who have attained personal "barakat" carry on the ministries of intercession and healing in the vicinity. Followers of Sufism in turn tend to frequent shrines when they need a miracle.

Many Bengali Muslims feel that traditional teachers instruct them to fear Allah while Sufi teachers encourage them to love Allah. More traditional Islam which prescribes strict obedience to the law is balanced by Sufi tradition which demonstrates the power of a loving God who wants to act for believers. Christians who recognize the principles and practices of Sufism will be able to speak persuasively for the gospel.

Black Caribs (Honduras)

ALTERNATE NAMES: Garifuna; Morenos

SIZE OF GROUP: 80,000   **MARC ID:** 245

DISTINCTIVES: language; ethnicity; religion; kinship; sense of unity; residence; social class; discrimination

SOCIAL CHANGE: moderate

LANGUAGES: Garifuna (100% speak/ 20% read; V,G); Spanish (85% speak/ 40% read; T,S); English (2% speak; T)

SCRIPTURE: New Testament   **RECORDINGS:** not reported

CHRISTIAN LITERACY: 75%

RELIGION: Christo-Paganism (90% adherents/ 90% practicing); Protestant (1% adherents/ <1% practicing); Secularism (9% adherents/ 9% practicing)

CHURCHES AND MISSIONS	BEGAN	MEMBERSHIP	CMTY
Plymouth Brethren Church	nr	nr	nr
United Brethren in Christ	nr	nr	nr
Mennonite Church	1960	50	150
Conservative Baptists	1950	15	25
Seventh-Day Adventist	nr	50	150

OPENNESS TO RELIGIOUS CHANGE: somewhat closed

RECEPTIVITY TO CHRISTIANITY: indifferent

GROWTH OF CHRISTIAN COMMUNITY: slow growth

EVANGELISM PROFILE: not reported   **VALIDITY:** 5

The Black Caribs of Honduras live in some 42 villages along the beaches of the north coast. These villages extend from near the Guatemalan border on the west to the Miskito Coast on the east. In addition there is one village on the northeast end of Roatan Island. The Black Caribs call themselves and their language Garifuna. They are known among the Spanish-speaking population as Morenos and their language is called Moreno. Most anthopologists prefer to call them Garifuna. It is estimated that about 80,000 of them live in Honduras.

The settlement on Roatan known as Punta Gorda is the site of the first settlement of Black Caribs in Central America. From there they spread to Belice, Guatemala, and Nicaragua as well as to the Honduran coast.

EXPANDED DESCRIPTIONS

In 1797 the British government forcibly moved 5000 of them to Roatan from St. Vincent Island in the Lesser Antilles. They had come to St. Vincent as escaped or shipwrecked slaves. There they came in contact with the Carib Indians. Apparently they did not intermarry with the Caribs, but they adopted their language and culture. However, they have maintained some aspects of African culture.

The Black Caribs of Honduras converted to Catholicism during the second half of the nineteenth century, but they have combined it with their former religion. They believe in a hierarchy of spiritual beings which must be appeased. The spirits of the dead are identified with angels. Other spirits live in the ocean and in various other aspects of nature, and they may live in people as well. Some people are said to sign contracts with the devil. The Black Caribs are well known for their elaborate religious ceremonies carried on by diviners, curanderos and practitioners of magic.

There are a few small evangelical congregations among the Black Caribs. For years an independent American missionary family lived in Limon, east of Trujillo. They retired about six years ago and no replacement has been found. About all that remains of this work are decaying buildings and a few Spanish-speaking Ladino believers. There is a small Mennonite congregation in Santa Fe to the west of Trujillo. An independent Baptist missionary is working in San Juan near Tela. The Adventists have an active congregation in Punta Gorda on Roatan and there is also a small Conservative Baptist church there. There are a few Black Caribs in some of the Spanish-speaking congregations along the coast. The Church of God (Cleveland) is attempting to begin churches in some places. There may be additional churches in other villages as well.

There is a rather high level of prejudice between the Black Caribs and the dominant Honduran culture. For this reason it may be difficult to count on the Spanish-speaking churches to evangelize them. Most Hondurans say that the Caribs are hard to reach with the gospel. Missionaries from the U.S. with experience with American Indians or missionaries who have had experience in Africa among animistic peoples may well be a suitable force for evangelism. Even better would be African missionaries. It could be that a culturally sensitive Honduran could have an effective ministry among them.

Whoever works among them should take the time to learn their culture and the Garifuna language. Although many of them speak Spanish, the heart language is Garifuna. Since the culture seems to be a well integrated culture, it will be essential to have a good understanding of the felt needs of the Caribs in order to see a growing church among them.

Blind, N.E. Thailand (Thailand)

ALTERNATE NAMES: not reported

SIZE OF GROUP: 100,000   **MARC ID:** 4810

DISTINCTIVES: significant problems; health situation; discrimination; ethnicity; language; social class; religion; kinship

SOCIAL CHANGE: rapid

LANGUAGES: Northeast Thai (98% speak/ 2% read; V,G); Thai (20% speak/ 2% read; T,S)

SCRIPTURE: portions   **RECORDINGS:** not reported

CHRISTIAN LITERACY: 100%

RELIGION: Buddhist-Animist (95% adherents); Secularism (4% adherents); Protestant (<1% adherents/ <1% practicing)

CHURCHES AND MISSIONS	BEGAN	MEMBERSHIP	CMTY
Chr. Home of Educ./Blind Indep	1978	100	200

OPENNESS TO RELIGIOUS CHANGE: somewhat closed

RECEPTIVITY TO CHRISTIANITY: reluctant

GROWTH OF CHRISTIAN COMMUNITY: slow growth

EVANGELISM PROFILE: not reported   **VALIDITY: 4**

A crowd of curious people mill around a group of young men and boys. They are attracted by the familiar sound of indigenous Thai musical instruments accompanying a chantstyle singing. It is evident to them that each of these performers is blind! These musicians are among the favored few of the blind of Thailand who have found fulfillment in life.

An estimated 100,000 people are afflicted with blindness in Northeast Thailand. This is based on a random sampling survey conducted by two Thai University students.

The Northeast contains approximately one-third of the land area of Thailand (66,000 square miles), with a population of 17 million. One out of every 173 persons is blind. Medical authorities feel that the blindness is due to vitamin deficiency, venereal disease, accidents and indiscriminate use of medicine, in that order of prevalance. There is a widespread lack of basic medical knowledge.

EXPANDED DESCRIPTIONS

The highest incidence of blindness occurs among the peasant farmers. However, it is found in every stratum of Thai society. Some are born blind; many lose their sight in infancy or early childhood, a few as adults.

These sufferers are isolated and neglected. This is due in part to a Buddhist religious bias. The average parent holds the religious concept that the child's blindness is a result of sins committed in a previous incarnation. Many of the blind remain hidden in their homes, unable to care even for their own bodily needs.

These blind people live in the same geographic area. They speak the Northeastern Thai dialect. Due to their common affliction they have experienced almost complete social ostracism. The prevailing religious attitude produces a mutual reaction of shame and inferiority. Consistently, for generations, they have been denied the most basic opportunities of life, such as social interaction, education and job opportunities. The blind share a common felt need for self-worth, educational advantages, acceptance into Thai society and a purpose in life.

These young musicians were trained and sent out as a gospel team by the Christian Home of Education for the Blind, begun in Northeast Thailand. The director himself is blind. The training program provides the blind with mobility, the ability to read and write braille, and vocational skills. As soon as possible each student is integrated into regular Thai government schools. All their textbooks are transcribed into braille by trained secretaries. Currently 33 students of both sexes are enrolled in elementary to university levels. Graduates of the Home are self-supporting and are productive members of society.

A Christian Foundation for the Blind has been registered with the Thai government. Five acres of land are being developed. It will soon be possible to house up to 200 coeducational students at the home. The financial and material support of the local townspeople has been unprecedented. The King of Thailand has recognized and commended this revolutionary new approach to develop blind people into self-supporting members of Thai society. The Home is being supported by people in West Germany, the Netherlands, Canada and Australia. The program has attracted favorable attention from the governor and educational officials of Khon Kaen province.

As a result of exposure to the message of salvation in Christ Jesus through this training program, many blind students have been very responsive to the gospel. There is every reason to expect that as others are similarly exposed and hear the redemption message articulated by their fellows, this climate of general approval will continue and receptivity increase.

Boni of Lamu (Kenya)

ALTERNATE NAMES: not reported

SIZE OF GROUP: 2,500   **MARC ID:** 4803

DISTINCTIVES:

SOCIAL CHANGE: not reported

LANGUAGES: Boni (100% speak; V)

SCRIPTURE: not reported   **RECORDINGS:** not reported

CHRISTIAN LITERACY: not reported

RELIGION: Islam-Animist ; Christianity

CHURCHES AND MISSIONS: not reported

OPENNESS TO RELIGIOUS CHANGE: not reported

RECEPTIVITY TO CHRISTIANITY: not reported

GROWTH OF CHRISTIAN COMMUNITY: not reported

EVANGELISM PROFILE: not reported   **VALIDITY:** 4

Hunting and gathering are the primary sources of recreation and sustenance for these people. If government regulations did not prohibit hunting, they would probably be full-time hunters. As it is, they remain aloof, live as they like, and watch out for government officials. Status and recognition in the Boni culture are based on performance in hunting. Boys are accepted as men when they kill an elephant, lion, buffalo, rhino or hippopotamus. The Boni are nostalgic and do what they can to preserve their carefree way of life.

Recent observations by researchers indicate that the Boni are inclined to pick up and move for little apparent reason. They maintain permanent villages to grow maize, but they set up temporary camps in areas where wild fruits are available. They enjoy harvesting *mkamwa*, a red fruit which is dried and pounded into flour. During excursions into the bush they gather wild honey, hunt small game and brew homemade beer. When their two-to-three-month vacation is over, they return to their villages and plant crops of beans and maize. The men clear the land, and the women sow and weed.

The Boni learned to farm by working on Arab farms. They imitated their wealthy landlords by adopting Islam. As they settled in permanent villages, they built mosques and schools where itinerant Muslim teachers and leaders explain the Koran. Few Boni have a keen interest in Muslim doctrine despite their acceptance of Islamic customs and names. They have reduced their consumption of alcohol and sought to perform appropriate rituals, but Islam has affected little beyond their external behavior. Most Boni also learn and observe their traditional tribal customs and values, particularly when they are out in the bush.

As government regulations become more strict, and as the 21st century catches up with the Boni, they will undoubtedly settle and modify their life-style. For the present, though, they are not being reached by Christians who are presenting a culturally appropriate explanation of Christianity. They have had contact with Christian game wardens, for example, but such contacts are mutually avoided. A Christian team needs to commit itself to praying, planning and developing strategy to reach the Boni.

Caribs (Dominica)

ALTERNATE NAMES: not reported

SIZE OF GROUP: 2,500   **MARC ID:** 4825

DISTINCTIVES: language; ethnicity; religion; residence; legal status

SOCIAL CHANGE: slow

LANGUAGES: English (V); Patois (T)

SCRIPTURE: Bible   **RECORDINGS:** yes

CHRISTIAN LITERACY: not reported

RELIGION: Animism; Roman Catholic

CHURCHES AND MISSIONS: not reported

OPENNESS TO RELIGIOUS CHANGE: indifferent

RECEPTIVITY TO CHRISTIANITY: indifferent

GROWTH OF CHRISTIAN COMMUNITY: stable

EVANGELISM PROFILE: not reported   **VALIDITY:** 4

The Caribs are the last indigenous race of the West Indies. They will probably vanish within this century, primarily because of intermarriage with other groups. They live in a continuous belt of six villages along the eastern coast of Dominica in the Caribbean. The "pure" Caribs are concentrated in two of the older villages: Bataka and Sineku.

There is no private property among the Caribs and people live on any land that they work. Like most Dominicans, the Caribs are mainly farmers, with bananas and coconuts as their major crops. Their origins are unclear, but they are thought to have come from the Orinoco River area in South America. They conquered the Arawak peoples who populated the West Indies at that time. Much intermarriage has occurred since then and this has resulted in two languages: one spoken by the women (Arawak) and one by the men (Carib). These two languages have merged as the groups dwindled. By the time the common language was abandoned around the turn of the century, it was more Arawak than Carib. This is due primarily to the influence that the dominant Arawak culture had over the Caribs.

In the 1700s, the Caribs resisted European attempts to enslave them. It is said that captured Caribs simply ate dirt until they died. The Caribs were poor subjects for conversion, although some are nominal Roman Catholics. There is a belief in witchcraft among the Caribs, and also a widely believed legend of the Great Snake "Tete-

EXPANDED DESCRIPTIONS

Chienn," whose passage caused a long staircase of rock to the sea. Thus, most Caribs can be considered animists, focusing their religious attention on natural objects in the environment. There is a great need for a Christian witness among this group that will help them to overcome their superstitions and believe in the truth of the gospel.

Cherkess (Jordan)

ALTERNATE NAMES: Sharkas

SIZE OF GROUP: 60,000   **MARC ID:** 4814

DISTINCTIVES: language; political loyalty; ethnicity; sense of unity

SOCIAL CHANGE: moderate

LANGUAGES: Sharkas (100% speak; V); Arabic (98% speak/ 50% read; T,S,G,W)

SCRIPTURE: Bible   **RECORDINGS:** not reported

CHRISTIAN LITERACY: 75%

RELIGION: Orthodox

CHURCHES AND MISSIONS	BEGAN	MEMBERSHIP	CMTY
Christian Missionary Alliance	1923	nr	nr
Free Evangelical	1940	nr	nr
Baptist Church	1950	nr	nr

OPENNESS TO RELIGIOUS CHANGE: indifferent

RECEPTIVITY TO CHRISTIANITY: indifferent

GROWTH OF CHRISTIAN COMMUNITY: stable

EVANGELISM PROFILE: not reported   **VALIDITY:** 4

This people group is a minority and composes only about 2 percent of the population of Jordan (3,000,000). They came into Amman in 1905. They own large areas of the city and are, in general, well-to-do people. They have very good relations with the royal family, and the Royal Guards are all from this people group.

They see themselves only as part of the Jordanian people, unlike the majority of the Jordanians who see themselves as part of the greater Arabic nation. And because they admit that their original religion is Christianity and because there are cultural barriers between them and the Arab Muslim majority, bridges could perhaps be easily built between them and the other evangelical minorities. Christian believers whose background is Greek Orthodox (like the Cherkess people) are the best ones to reach them for Christ.

Chinese (Mauritius)

ALTERNATE NAMES: not reported

SIZE OF GROUP: 30,000   **MARC ID:** 4811

DISTINCTIVES: language; occupation; ethnicity; religion; kinship

SOCIAL CHANGE: slow

LANGUAGES: Creole (70% speak; V,G); Hakka (30% speak; V,G,W); English/French (70% speak/ 50% read; T,S); Cantonese (30% speak; V)

SCRIPTURE: Bible   **RECORDINGS:** not reported

CHRISTIAN LITERACY: 60%

RELIGION: Buddhist-Animist (64% adherents); Roman Catholic (30% adherents/ <1% practicing); Protestant (5% adherents/ 1% practicing); Secularism (1% adherents/ 1% practicing)

CHURCHES AND MISSIONS	BEGAN	MEMBERSHIP	CMTY
Chinese Chr. Fell. of Maurit	1955	100	130
Youth Fellowship	1977	60	60

OPENNESS TO RELIGIOUS CHANGE: somewhat open

RECEPTIVITY TO CHRISTIANITY: receptive

GROWTH OF CHRISTIAN COMMUNITY:: slow growth

EVANGELISM PROFILE: not reported   **VALIDITY:** 4

Some 80 percent of the Chinese in Mauritius are descended from Chinese immigrants of the 19th and 20th centuries. The rest are recent immigrants from Mainland China, Hong Kong and Taiwan. English, French and a local dialect (Creole) are commonly spoken by the younger generation. The immigrants and older generation speak Hakka (70%) and Cantonese (30%). A typical young man may learn French at school, speak English in the market, hear his parents speak Hakka to him at home and reply to them in Creole.

About 70 percent of the Chinese are engaged in commerce and local retail stores. Recently, about 300 people arrived from Hong Kong to start small factories. More than 60 percent of the people believe in a mixture of Confucian, Buddhist and Taoist religion with animistic religious practices. Since the local government subsidizes individual Catholics and the Catholic church permits ancestor veneration, about 30 percent of the Chinese people are at least nominally Catholic.

The Protestant population is very small. The Chinese Anglican church had 1800 adherents at one time, but only 10 people attended Sunday worship service. Thus, most of the congregation have departed and some joined the local Anglican churches. A Chinese Christian Assembly was established in 1955 by two medical doctors from Hong Kong. It grew slowly after they departed, only recently revived by a short-term missionary group headed by Rev. and Mrs. Cyrus Lam (both students at Fuller School of World Mission). One member of the group, Mr. Sing-fung Wong, decided to stay behind after the tour to pastor this church. In 1982, more than 100 attenders built a church building. The third Protestant group is a youth fellowship of 50 to 60 members which meets weekly since 1977 at the home of a retired OMF missionary, pastor Percy King. With a total of about 230 committed Christians, the Chinese in Mauritius are only initially reached.

The first step to plan an effective evangelistic strategy for reaching this people is to identify their needs. Obviously, a minority in a predominantly Indian and European society needs to find and maintain identity and cohesion. With the increasing trend toward Westernization, the gap between the young and the old grows even wider. The high competitiveness in the business community also brings stress, anxiety, loneliness and secular and materialistic life-styles. All these can point to avenues for the message of the gospel to reach their hearts.

In order to disciple these 30,000 persons, the following methods of evangelism might be employed:

1. The small group of committed Christians should be trained in personal evangelism techniques so they can reach their family members, fellow workers and near neighbors.

2. Chinese churches in South Africa, Hong Kong, Taiwan, Singapore and North America should organize more short-term missionary tours of professionals to seek identification with the local residents.

3. Two to four missionary couples fluent in Hakka and English with basic cross-cultural missionary training should be sent to this fertile soil. By planting new churches in various cities, the Chinese churches can serve as bridges to reach the rest of the population as well as the 15,000 Chinese in nearby Reunion Island.

4. Since the traditional Chinese family system is weakened considerably, with the language gap between the younger and older generation ever widening, different types of churches should be planted for them. But in order to maintain the cultural identity, the better way is the establishment of multi-congregations under one roof.

5. The large student body (up to 50%) is the most receptive bracket among this people group. This group can be reached by Western missionary teachers who are willing to do cross-cultural missions among this strategic people who are waiting to be reached by the gospel of our Lord.

Digo (Kenya)

ALTERNATE NAMES: not reported

SIZE OF GROUP: 168,000   **MARC ID:** 4050

DISTINCTIVES: occupation; ethnicity; religion; social class

SOCIAL CHANGE: moderate

LANGUAGES: Digo (90% speak/ 5% read; V,G); Kiswahili (T,G); English (S)

SCRIPTURE: not reported   **RECORDINGS:** not reported

CHRISTIAN LITERACY: not reported

RELIGION: Islam (95% adherents); Christianity (<1% practicing); Animism (4% adherents)

CHURCHES AND MISSIONS	BEGAN	MEMBERSHIP	CMTY
Norwegian Lutherans	1978	nr	nr
Grace Brethren	1978	nr	nr
Anglican Church	1844	nr	nr
Methodist Church	nr	nr	nr

OPENNESS TO RELIGIOUS CHANGE: indifferent

RECEPTIVITY TO CHRISTIANITY: reluctant

GROWTH OF CHRISTIAN COMMUNITY: not reported

EVANGELISM PROFILE: not reported   **VALIDITY:** 4

Islam has become more widely accepted among the Digo than among any other of the Mijikenda tribes of Kenya. Whereas many of the Duruma, Kamba, Kikuyu and Luo and Luhya have become Christians, most Digo have become Muslims.

Many of their traditional animistic beliefs have been preserved through traditional cultural practices. Islamic influence during the past 80 years has altered their religious and political structure. The people have adopted new attire and diets from Muslim Arab neighbors. Few Digo have studied Islam in any depth, however, and most only have a superficial knowledge of the principles and doctrines of Islam. A folk Islam has resulted. Dead ancestors are still venerated and spiritism is practiced. Witchdoctors are consulted regularly and play an important role in Digo society.

Agriculture, fishing and trade have all been sources of livelihood. Heads of homesteads now have official title to lands they occupy, and the sale of land is gaining importance. The Digo have long been involved in trade with Muslim Arabs and enjoy a higher standard of living than many other neighboring tribal peoples.

The Digo are concentrated on the Southern coastal strip of Kenya. They have established numerous villages along the Mambasa-Lunga road and in the coastal plain
between the road and the ocean.

Rice, maize and cassava are important cash crops. Palm trees provide the source for
palm wine, a lucrative and controversial business. Since the Digo have been
economically self-sufficient they have not been reached through traditional social
programs sponsored by Christian agencies and churches. There are many Christian
churches in areas close to Digo settlements but effective outreach to the Digo has not
been effective. Materialism and secularism are becoming increasingly widespread
and in the absence of a Christian alternative the Digo are influenced in these ways.
Few have shown interest in Christianity. This group will require considerable study,
planning and strategizing to relate the gospel to them in a contextualized manner.

English speakers, Guadalajara (Mexico)

ALTERNATE NAMES: not reported

SIZE OF GROUP: 25,000   **MARC ID:** 4816

DISTINCTIVES: language; ethnicity; residence; economic status

SOCIAL CHANGE: slow

LANGUAGES: English (100% speak/100% read; V,S,G); Spanish (10% speak/ 10% read; T,S)

SCRIPTURE: Bible   **RECORDINGS:** yes

CHRISTIAN LITERACY: 100%

RELIGION: Secularism (85% adherents); Protestant (10% adherents/ 10% practicing); Roman Catholic (5% adherents/ 5% practicing)

CHURCHES AND MISSIONS	BEGAN	MEMBERSHIP	CMTY
Gethsemane Baptist Church	nr	nr	150
United Methodist Church	nr	nr	100
Lutheran Church	nr	nr	100

OPENNESS TO RELIGIOUS CHANGE: indifferent

RECEPTIVITY TO CHRISTIANITY: indifferent

GROWTH OF CHRISTIAN COMMUNITY: slow growth

EVANGELISM PROFILE: not reported   **VALIDITY:** 3

A large community of North Americans live in Guadalajara, Mexico. The largest number are retired U.S. and Canadian citizens; most of the others are medical school students, and the remaining few are businessmen whose work requires that they live in Mexico. They have several things in common: they speak English, they live in a few well-defined areas of the city, and they are largely unchurched.

The great majority of these people have some basic knowledge of the gospel, since almost all of them grew up in churched areas. However, three English-speaking Protestant churches and an English-language Roman Catholic chapel have a combined attendance that barely exceeds 1 percent of this population. Two of the three churches do not have a theology of ministry that encourages evangelistic outreach; the other is part of an evangelistic denomination, but the pastor is a busy man and cannot give first priority to evangelism concerns among English-speaking North Americans.

A strategy to reach them should consider the following facts:

1. There are basically two homogeneous units: retired persons (living primarily in Chapalita, La Cama and Las Fuentes areas) and medical students (living usually near the school). All three churches are situated in other parts of town, where Americans may have lived years ago.

2. The only viable growth-oriented church is Gethsemane Baptist, a congregation pastored by a man appointed by the Southern Baptist Foreign Mission Board. Since it is probably the only church (barring revolutionary renewal in the others) which would welcome and sustain an evangelistic outreach, whatever effort is put forth should probably be related to it.

3. Because the retired community is somewhat gregarious--and because they are somewhat distant from the church building--it may be practical to initiate Bible study groups in homes in an attempt to reach them. A social event-based approach would have a good chance of success.

4. A Campus Crusade/Inter-Varsity type outreach might be effective with the medical school students, particularly since they are similar to other groups already targeted by these organizations and because they generally lack the social activities characteristic of an American university setting.

Filipino Migrant Workers (Saudi Arabia)

ALTERNATE NAMES: not reported

SIZE OF GROUP: 132,000   **MARC ID:** 4815

DISTINCTIVES: language; occupation; ethnicity; religion; economic status; health situation; significant problems

SOCIAL CHANGE: rapid

LANGUAGES: Tagalog (99% speak; V,G); English (75% speak; T,G)

SCRIPTURE: Bible   **RECORDINGS:** yes

CHRISTIAN LITERACY: not reported

RELIGION: Roman Catholic (99% adherents/ 50% practicing)

CHURCHES AND MISSIONS: not reported

OPENNESS TO RELIGIOUS CHANGE: somewhat open

RECEPTIVITY TO CHRISTIANITY: receptive

GROWTH OF CHRISTIAN COMMUNITY: not reported

EVANGELISM PROFILE: not reported   **VALIDITY:** 4

There are an estimated 132,000 Filipinos in Saudi Arabia, most of them heavy construction workers. Others work as service workers in hotels, as domestics and at other jobs related to production processes.

An estimated 16,000 Filipinos leave the Republic of the Philippines annually in search of overseas employment. Of the others in various countries:

"Those who go to Europe are often employed as domestic helpers, as are those in Hong Kong and Singapore. The United States and Canada are of course the traditional havens of Filipino nurses, doctors and other medical workers. Those with musical talent can be found in the honky tonk districts of Tokyo, Osaka and other cities of Japan. Then there are some 60,000 Filipino sailors who sail the seven seas under the flags of some 110 countries" (*Philippine Panorama*, September 26, 1982, p.10).

The move to the Middle East (mainly Saudi Arabia) began as a trickle in 1977 but presently the wave of migrant departures has left entire segments of squatter communities deprived of their male population. Although not the subject of this report, an entire group of unreached people is left behind in the persons of the husbandless wives and fatherless children. Catholic social agencies are already taking steps to aid those left behind.

For those men who must go abroad, however, there are unique sets of problems. Like their families at home, the principal problem is loneliness. Many workers, unprepared for the cultural and psychological shock, have been driven by their homesickness to deliberately break laws or cause trouble for their employers just to be sent back home. For those who remain, sometimes up to two or three years at a time, there are further problems: a very harsh climate; difficult working conditions; conflicts arising from employers' non-compliance with contract agreements; boredom; and the insecurity of not hearing often enough from their spouses (mail sometimes takes a month from Manila).

It must still be determined to what degree these men are literate and what dialects are represented among them. Most likely, in order to work these jobs, they speak and understand English. All of them would communicate in Pilipino, the national language of their home country. Most of them are from traditional Roman Catholic backgrounds though many may be turning to secularism since they are outside of the Philippines in a non-Roman Catholic environment. Since they are not in an "open" country, evangelistic efforts must be creative. A force for evangelism can be mobilized both within and outside Saudi Arabia. There are some believers from North America and Europe working as professionals, and laborers, in Saudi Arabia. In addition, there is a sizable number of Koreans among whom there are also a good percentage of practicing Christians. From the outside, evangelical churches and agencies in the Philippines should encourage Filipino believers to consider going to Saudi Arabia as "tentmakers." These could be recruited from among the committed young people in seminaries, Bible schools and churches.

Evangelistic strategies could involve such things as establishing friendships, helping provide legal counsel, sharing reading material or cassettes with gospel messages, and finding Christian "pen-pals" in the Philippines and other English-speaking countries, who would write these lonely people. A social center could be established (like a USO) with activities, recreational programs, dinners and other fellowship which would provide an impetus for evangelism among web relationships.

Indo-Canadians, Vancouver (Canada: British Columbia

ALTERNATE NAMES: not reported

SIZE OF GROUP: 70,000   **MARC ID:** 9127

DISTINCTIVES: language; ethnicity; occupation; sense of unity

SOCIAL CHANGE: not reported

LANGUAGES: English (V,T,S); Punjabi (V); Urdu (V); Hindi (S)

SCRIPTURE: Bible   **RECORDINGS:** yes

CHRISTIAN LITERACY: not reported

RELIGION: Sikhism (60% adherents); Hinduism; Islam; Buddhism; Jain

CHURCHES AND MISSIONS	BEGAN	MEMBERSHIP	CMTY
Indo-Canadian Chr. (Bapt. Gen)	nr	nr	nr
Hindu-Punjabi Gospel Chapel	nr	nr	nr
South Abbotsford Mennonite Br.	nr	nr	nr
Gen. Conf. Mennonite Mission	nr	nr	nr
Council Indo-Canadian Chr. Mis.	nr	nr	nr

OPENNESS TO RELIGIOUS CHANGE: not reported

RECEPTIVITY TO CHRISTIANITY: not reported

GROWTH OF CHRISTIAN COMMUNITY: not reported

EVANGELISM PROFILE: not reported   **VALIDITY:** 3

The National Association of Canadians of Origin in India estimates there are 300,000 Canadians of East Indian extraction living in the country. Eighty representatives from India, Pakistan, Sri Lanka, Fiji, Uganda and the Carribbean met recently in Winnipeg to discuss race relations, labor issues, and the changing values in child-rearing.

In the Vancouver area there are approximately 70,000 of East Indian extraction. They prefer to be called Indo-Canadians. Forty thousand of these are from Fiji; their major language is English, though some have studied Hindi at university as a foreign language. There are more than 12,000 Sikhs (some say as many as 75 percent of the 70,000 are Sikhs), and they are highly visible because of the turbans the men wear. They have become the target for a new wave of racism with beatings and gasoline bomb attacks, particularly in East Vancouver and Surrey. "The current 'niggers' of British Columbia are East Indians," comments lawyer Calvin Sandborn of the Fraser Valley Legal Service Project.

Approximately 90 percent of 12,000 farm laborers are East Indian, many of them Sikhs (whose language is Punjabi, Hindi or English), and locals consider it quaint to see the hundreds of workers wearing turbans, saris or coolie hats stooped in the fields alongside BC highways. Living conditions are scarcely minimal: in the best times they earn $1.30 to $2.50 per hour, and when the picking gets leaner, an hour's hard work might yield 50 cents. While some farmers have erected motel-like accommodation for their workers, at least one-third are housed in converted barnstalls and dilapidated outbuildings. Farm machinery generally needs repair, and workers are not adequately trained in its use, resulting in a high number of preventable accidents: 64 people have died in BC in work-related accidents during the last five years.

The Sikhs have also established themselves in the BC forest industry; for centuries their people have been expert loggers on the upper reaches of the five rivers of the Punjab where Himalayan evergreens thrive. Canada's richest Sikh is the multimillionare head of a logging empire with headquarters in Duncan. In Lake Cowichan, almost one-third of the 2400 residents are Punjabi. The first Sikh forest workers arrived in the early 1900s; then in 1907 the Natal Act classified "Hindus" with Japanese and Chinese as "undesirables" and their ships were turned back to India. Through various loopholes the East Indians continued to trickle into BC, but not until 1967 were they allowed into Canada under the point system and the East Indian population in the Vancouver area boomed.

The Sikhs worship in Sikh Temples. Their religion is based on the Punjab writings of Guru Nanak, a contemporary of Martin Luther who insisted on the equality of the sexes, the oneness of God and the free access of the soul to God without intermediaries. It was a compromise gospel intended to sweep away both the ritual and taboos of the Hindu cults and the strict regulations of the Muslims. Later the five "Ks" were introduced which orthodox Sikhs cling to: Kes, the uncut hair; Kanga, the comb; Kach, the short trousers that are never completely removed; Kara, the iron bangle; and Kirpan, the sword or knife that is worn as a symbol of readiness to fight "for the pure way." The name most Sikhs bear, Singh, means "lion" and stems from the transformation of a Punjabi pacifist sect into a warrior people.

This warrior element has drawn additional antagonism when political factions from India get embroiled in bloody outbreaks of violence in Canada. An international Sikh secessionist movement aimed at taking control of the state of Punjab and the establishment of an independent Sikh nation of "Khalistan" has opened a consulate in Vancouver and is issuing passports. They are also giving military training in BC to young Sikhs. Yet the majority of Sikhs in Canada reportedly want to lead normal lives and feel that if these people want to fight for Khalistan, they should return to India to do it.

--from *Reaching Canada's Unreached*,
World Vision Canada, 1983

Llaneros (Colombia)

ALTERNATE NAMES: Cattle Ranchers

SIZE OF GROUP: 25,000   **MARC ID:** 4807

DISTINCTIVES: political loyalty; occupation; social class; economic status

SOCIAL CHANGE: rapid

LANGUAGES: Spanish (100% speak/ 60% read; V,S,T,G)

SCRIPTURE: Bible   **RECORDINGS:** yes

CHRISTIAN LITERACY: 80%

RELIGION: Christo-Paganism (95% practicing); Secularism (5% adherents); Protestant (<1% adherents/ <1% practicing); Roman Catholic (95% adherents/ 5% practicing)

CHURCHES AND MISSIONS	BEGAN	MEMBERSHIP	CMTY
Asociacion Col. de Igl. Crist.	1967	400	800
Mision Panamericana	nr	nr	nr
Roman Catholic Church	nr	nr	nr

OPENNESS TO RELIGIOUS CHANGE: somewhat closed

RECEPTIVITY TO CHRISTIANITY: indifferent

GROWTH OF CHRISTIAN COMMUNITY: slow decline

EVANGELISM PROFILE: not reported   **VALIDITY:** 4

Scattered throughout the Colombian Llanos with its great savannas are numerous cattle ranches. Here the life of cattle ranchers or llaneros remains reminiscent of that popularized by the novel *Dona Barbara* years ago. It is a sparsely populated region. One obvious reason is the harshness of the tropical climate with seasonal dry heat and heavy rains. Little grows in the poor soil except some types of grass, and even that provides only sparse food for the herds of cattle which must graze over vast areas. Both a cause and a result of the sparse population is the great lack of roads (especially a problem in the rainy season due to flooding of streams).

This sparse population has resulted in distinct social structures. The people, for the most part, live on the large ranches called "hatos." At the ranch there lives the rancher and his family, which may often include older married sons, and also the permanent and temporary ranchhands. Those living at a large ranch may number fifty or more. Also there are some very small towns with populations under one thousand. Where these exist they also form the only real connection to Christianity through the small Catholic chapels where a priest may visit once or twice a year.

Because of the harsh conditions the llaneros have also developed a life-style distinct from the rest of Colombia. They possess a pioneer spirit and a rough and tough character. To live on the Llanos they must be hardy people just as they must have hardy cattle. For many the greatest ideal is a life riding a favorite horse under a beautiful blue sky amid miles of savanna dotted by cattle and infrequent people. The llanero is the Colombian version of the cowboy. When he comes together with friends it is to have a good time and frequently to sing the "joropos" (indigenous singing chant) accompanied by harp, guitar, and "cuatro" (a fourstringed instrument similar to a ukulele).

For years the llaneros lived unaffected by the happenings in the rest of the country. Within the last twenty years they have become increasingly affluent. Though they could be considered a part of the middle class, their life-style would not put them naturally on a par with Colombians of similar financial status living in the city. Small aircraft can overcome many transportation problems and incorporate them better in the broader life of the country. Villavicencio (a town of 150,000 on the northeastern corner of the Llanos) is becoming more and more the social center. It is said that in a one-block plaza of outdoor taverns one can find any friend from the Llanos (an area half the size of the state of Texas).

The force for evangelization presents a great challenge. Because the ranchers' life-style and occupation are much of what makes them a people group, they would be best reached by those who can identify with this type of person and their needs. The gospel needs to be communicated to appeal to the heads of the families and must be understood to be worthy of a "man's" involvement. Other groups with a similar background would be the llaneros of Venezuela; the gauchos of Argentina, Uruguay or Brazil; and possibly North American missionaries with this type of background.

Military Officers (Ecuador)

ALTERNATE NAMES: not reported

SIZE OF GROUP: 1,000   **MARC ID:** 4817

DISTINCTIVES: education; sense of unity; legal status; political loyalty; occupation; significant problems

SOCIAL CHANGE: moderate

LANGUAGES: Spanish (100% speak/100% read; V,T,G,W)

SCRIPTURE: Bible   **RECORDINGS:** yes

CHRISTIAN LITERACY: 100%

RELIGION: Roman Catholic (95% adherents/ 5% practicing); Protestant (<1% adherents/ <1% practicing)

CHURCHES AND MISSIONS: not reported

OPENNESS TO RELIGIOUS CHANGE: indifferent

RECEPTIVITY TO CHRISTIANITY: indifferent

GROWTH OF CHRISTIAN COMMUNITY: stable

EVANGELISM PROFILE: not reported   **VALIDITY:** 3

For years a military dictatorship ruled Ecuador. The three heads of the Army, Navy, and Air Force held the reins of power choosing one of themselves to be the titular president. Although the country now has a civilian president, elected democratically by the people, the military is still part of the power structure.

Members of the military serve in the cabinet, and presidential aides in military uniform are highly visible at public functions. A major share of the national budget goes to the armed forces, and public parades feature them. The upper echelon of the officers would rank in the upper middle class economically, but few of them fit easily into this social bracket. Military policy dictates that changes of assignment be frequent resulting in relocation in different parts of the country. To provide continuity the family often lives in urban centers while the officers serve in faraway camps. Enforced isolation from the family creates tensions which often lead to severe marital conflicts. Infidelity and alcoholism are two major problems of military personnel.

Highly literate, these educated officers return to the urban centers for additional training. Because of their rank they are highly influential in government and industry, but fear and suspicion of their power isolates them from society. Casual social contacts are infrequent since officers fear being used for personal advantage. Within one's rank there develops an *esprit de corps*, but across rank boundaries the officer class system isolates men from each other. "Getting ahead" means a promotion to a higher rank with resulting prestige, power and economic rewards, but the survivors of this competition pay a high price personally and emotionally. The tragic toll of broken homes is mute evidence of the greater emotional and psychological toll which often results in tragic escape into alcoholism.

Some might consider military officers as a resistant group. For this reason little effort has been made to reach them with the gospel. Counseling centers could minister to them on the basis of their felt needs. Seminars on the home and family relationships might open many new doors which previously were thought to be closed. Home Bible studies, breakfast fellowships, and various activities that would reach men would be productive. Middle and upper-class civilians must reach out to these people in friendship and demonstrate love. A bridge might be made through their own families and circle of civilian friends. Literature and radio could have a softening effect and create an openness to the gospel.

Phu Thai (Thailand)

ALTERNATE NAMES: Pu Tai

SIZE OF GROUP: 80,000   **MARC ID:** 4809

DISTINCTIVES: language; discrimination; ethnicity; religion; kinship; sense of unity

SOCIAL CHANGE: rapid

LANGUAGES: Phu Thai (100% speak/ 50% read; V,G); Thai (50% speak/ 25% read; T,S)

SCRIPTURE: none   **RECORDINGS:** not reported

CHRISTIAN LITERACY: 100%

RELIGION: Buddhist–Animist (99% adherents/ 99% practicing); Christianity (1% adherents/ <1% practicing)

CHURCHES AND MISSIONS	BEGAN	MEMBERSHIP	CMTY
Gospel Church of Thailand	1953	75	225

OPENNESS TO RELIGIOUS CHANGE: somewhat closed

RECEPTIVITY TO CHRISTIANITY: reluctant

GROWTH OF CHRISTIAN COMMUNITY: slow decline

EVANGELISM PROFILE: not reported   **VALIDITY:** 4

Paw Huck was excited! At last someone was explaining what the word baptism meant. Seventeen years had passed since "Yasu" had become his God. In his capacity as area policeman he had contact with those outside Phu Thai land. A book of God, Luke by name, had been purchased by a friend who knew of Paw Huck's desire for moral teaching and had given it to him.

The gospel portion induced Paw Huck to call his children and relatives together and teach them from the book how to follow "Yasu" and his teachings. Now they all had "Yasu" as their God. But no one had ever been able to discipher what baptism meant. Now his heart was full. He would be baptized and then baptize his extended family.

The Phu Thai are located in the rolling hills of three northeastern Thai provinces with common borders. Some Thai historians maintain that they preceded the Thai people in their migration southward out of Yunan province in Southern China. They retreated from the cultivated rice fields of the lowlands to the surrounding hills as the Thai advanced. Their language has a distinctive lilting sound, different from Thai or Lao. Some words they have in common are pronounced differently utilizing an entirely dissimilar tonal pattern. The distinctive dress of the Phu Thai women easily identifies them at a distance. A black blouse and skirt trimmed with red is the main feature. Their heavy silver necklaces and wrist bracelets are very similar to those found among the Hmong tribeswomen of Southeast Asia.

Phu Thai marriage customs differ from those of their Thai cousins. Moral ethics and standards are also much stricter. Court cases and divorce are rare. Intermarriage with the Thai is not common. If, however, it occurs, the wife will remain with her Northeastern Thai husband and not move with her people to the new site.

In a sense the Phu Thai are still retreating from the Thai. They are continually withdrawing into the hinterland to escape contact with non-Phu Thai. A village will move to a new location if a new road makes the present site easily accessible. Phu Thai villages are usually small (20-30 houses) and located within walking distance of related kin groups. The Thai central government regulations enforce the use of the Thai language in the education system so the younger generation is bilingual. The people are very industrious. They produce intricate needlework in blankets, shawls and pillows. Black, red and white are the predominant colors. These Phu Thai people share the same heart language, live within the same geographic area and share a high moral sense. Distinctive customs and dress characterize their people. The outside world of change continues to press in upon them. Their integrity as a people is being threatened. And more receptive people like Paw Huck can be found among them. The tragedy is that the scene described above transpired 34 years ago. Today (1983) a few of Paw Huck's relatives remain Christian. They can and must be nurtured and trained to evangelize their own Phu Thai people. The harvest is ripe.

Rural Vodun Believers (Haiti)

ALTERNATE NAMES: not reported

SIZE OF GROUP: 5,400,000   **MARC ID:** 4819

DISTINCTIVES: significant problems; ethnicity; language; religion

SOCIAL CHANGE: rapid

LANGUAGES: Creole (100% speak/ 15% read; V,S,G); French (15% read; T,S,W)

SCRIPTURE: Bible   **RECORDINGS:** not reported

CHRISTIAN LITERACY: not reported

RELIGION: Animism (100% adherents); Roman Catholic

CHURCHES AND MISSIONS: not reported

OPENNESS TO RELIGIOUS CHANGE: indifferent

RECEPTIVITY TO CHRISTIANITY: receptive

GROWTH OF CHRISTIAN COMMUNITY: not reported

EVANGELISM PROFILE: not reported   **VALIDITY:** 4

Poverty is a powerful force in the lives of thousands of rural Haitians. They have never known anything else and have virtually no hope for a better future. They live under the suppressive control of a self-appointed dictator who has little or no interest in meeting their needs. Poverty leaves 88 percent of the population vulnerable to natural and human-caused calamities. Shelter is tenuous at best and quite insecure during hurricanes and storms. Such natural disasters strike rural Haiti with relentless frequency.

The government has prohibited freedom of speech and democracy for so long that the people have lost dignity and individuality. They have no recourse in dealing with social injustice, but rather fear the reprisals of policy enforcement officers--with good reason: they have seen fellow workers battered and eliminated.

Fear keeps these rural Haitians bound to archaic traditions. Vodun has arisen as a popular movement among them. They deal with their fears by calling upon the presence of evil spirits and by seeking to maintain a peaceful relationship with forces of the supernatural world. Vodun provides an outlet for the people, but also traps them in the crossfire of spiritual warfare. Rural Haitians are well aware of the power of Satan and seek to protect themselves by venerating and appeasing the spirits.

Literacy training would enable many more of these people to become aware of the power available through Christ to deal with their adverse circumstances. Power encounter will doubtless be an aspect of successful church planting efforts among these needy people. Leadership training will offer the possibility of dynamic nationals witnessing to Christ's Lordship and able to evangelize powerfully among their own people.

Samburu (Kenya)

ALTERNATE NAMES: not reported

SIZE OF GROUP: 74,000   **MARC ID:** 535

DISTINCTIVES: language; ethnicity

SOCIAL CHANGE: not reported

LANGUAGES: Maasai, Samburu (100% speak; V)

SCRIPTURE: portions   **RECORDINGS:** not reported

CHRISTIAN LITERACY: not reported

RELIGION: Animism (97% adherents); Christianity (3% adherents/ 3% practicing)

CHURCHES AND MISSIONS	BEGAN	MEMBERSHIP	CMTY
Bible Churchmen's Msy. Society	nr	nr	nr
Anglican Church	nr	nr	nr
Consolata Catholic Mission	nr	nr	nr
Church Army in Kenya	nr	nr	nr

OPENNESS TO RELIGIOUS CHANGE: not reported

RECEPTIVITY TO CHRISTIANITY: receptive

GROWTH OF CHRISTIAN COMMUNITY: not reported

EVANGELISM PROFILE: not reported   **VALIDITY:** 4

Attempts to reach the Samburu are well under way. Individuals ministering among them are beginning to see rewards for their sacrificial efforts and signposts directing them toward new avenues of effective outreach. The thorough research by Daystar Communications allows us to observe new strategies as they are developed. Here we will highlight some of the social and cultural factors which have direct implications for any strategy.

Approximately 74,000 Samburu live slightly south of Lake Turkana in the Rift Valley Province of Kenya. They have traditionally herded cattle, goats and sheep in an arid region with sparse vegetation. A nomadic life-style is essential for their survival since attempts to settle down in permanent locations have reduced their self-sufficiency and ability to maintain their traditional values and practices.

Generally between five and ten families set up encampments for five weeks and then move on to new pastures. Adult men care for the grazing cattle which are the major source of livelihood. Women are in charge of maintaining the portable huts, milking cows, obtaining water and gathering firewood.

Natural disasters and insensitive government mandates have plagued the Samburu. Droughts reduce the amount of available pasture and the number of cattle is reduced through natural, though at times abnormal, selection with resulting reduction of the wealth, status and stature of family groups. If individuals are forced to sell their cattle or lose them through natural cause, they lose their means of self-sufficiency. They are then reduced to welfare help provided by national and religious organizations. A few development projects have provided new means of establishing settlements based on agriculture as well as hunting and gathering; this implies a sedentary agricultural life-style as well as a loss of status among the Samburu, who have traditionally held their nomadic life-style to be superior. Thus economics and survival are directly affecting the Samburu. Linguists have debated the distinction between the Samburu and Maasai languages for decades. In normal conversation one who speaks one of these languages can understand the other language 95 percent of the time. The Samburu tongue is also related to Turkana, Suk and Rendille.

The Boni recognize Islam as the religion of the enemy Boran and Somali. Thus virtually no Samburu have become Muslims. Their own tribal religion is based on animism with many spirits performing different tasks.

Increasing numbers have become Christians. New missionary teams sent out as itinerant evangelists have been effective in reaching nomadic groups by becoming nomadic themselves. Other Samburu become Christians as a result of relief efforts provided by Christian groups who meet the needs of those who have become sedentary. Significant changes in social, cultural and economic traditions have created many opportunities for Christians to explain the gospel.

Thirteen denominations are ministering to Samburu in 130 distinct "congregations." The elders and leaders have been resistant to change, so most Christians are women or young men and boys. Strategies are needed to reach the men, who spend their time with cattle and do not meet with women and children. Many medical facilities, development projects and educational institutions are operated by Christians, so Christians have regular contact with Samburu persons.

Sanga (Zaire)

ALTERNATE NAMES: not reported

SIZE OF GROUP: 35,000   **MARC ID:** 5765

DISTINCTIVES: language; occupation; ethnicity; kinship; education; residence; social class; economic status

SOCIAL CHANGE: slow

LANGUAGES: Sanga (100% speak/ 65% read; V,S,G,W); Swahili (85% speak/ 65% read; T,S,G,W); French (20% speak/ 15% read; S)

SCRIPTURE: Bible   **RECORDINGS:** yes

CHRISTIAN LITERACY: 70%

RELIGION: Roman Catholic (55% adherents); Protestant (25% adherents); Animism (10% adherents); Other Christian (5% adherents)

CHURCHES AND MISSIONS	BEGAN	MEMBERSHIP	CMTY
Roman Catholic Church	1890	nr	nr
Geranganzi (Brethren)	1900	nr	nr
Methodist Church	1910	nr	nr

OPENNESS TO RELIGIOUS CHANGE: very open

RECEPTIVITY TO CHRISTIANITY: very receptive

GROWTH OF CHRISTIAN COMMUNITY: slow growth

EVANGELISM PROFILE: not reported   **VALIDITY:** 4

The Sangas live in the southernmost Shaba Province of Zaire. Their language seems to be a cousin to the Luba language. Swahili has become the lingua france between tribes. The many tribes in this area are coming together because of the mines. Most of the people are small subsistence farmers who also sell produce in the nearby mining towns.

There are strong kinship ties within clans but very little unity on the tribal level. Under the tribal chief, smaller village chiefs are always at odds with one another. It is a matriarchal society with the husband coming to live in the wife's village. There is therefore not much migration and the people stay in the same area as farmers; the economic system makes for fairly even distribution of wealth. The Sangas have been subjugated by many tribes so they don't have any strong political loyalties. They are not an aggressive people and take changes in stride.

Originally the Sangas were animists and practiced their own folk religion. With the Belgians came a very strong Roman Catholic presence. Today about 55 percent of the tribe belongs to this church. Presently there is one bishop from this tribe. Not many have become priests because of the celibacy issue. Most of the training has therefore been on the lay level. Priests serving in the villages are usually from Belgium or Spain.

There have been two Protestant works. Around the turn of the century the Geranganzi Mission (Brethren) composed of mostly English and Australians started their work. They have worked to train African pastors to their people. They have translated the Bible into the Sanga language and produced a Sanga hymnbook. The Methodists came in around 1910 and likewise have raised up many Sanga pastors. The director of the Methodist Seminary at Mulungwishi is from this tribe. There are also some outstanding pastors and evangelists. About 25 percent of the tribe are members of one of these two groups. There are also small numbers of Orthodox in the cities, Kimbanguists, and recently Jehovah's Witnesses. All of this shows that the Sanga are open to religious change and are favorable towards Christianity. Since most of the tribe is incorporated into the Church, the evangelistic thrust should be in terms of renewal from nominalism. It should also take account of the desire to use folk religions for everyday decisions. Christianity needs to be presented in terms of power to meet the spiritual powers the people are dealing with.

When the church came in, especially the Roman Catholic and Methodists, schools were established as part of the church program. Consequently, there is a high literacy rate among the people in Sanga and Swahili. In addition, mainly the youth who have gone to high school can use French. A revision of the Sanga Bible is being done by the Roman Catholics, the Garanganzi and the Methodists in conjunction with the Bible Society. The Scriptures are also available in Swahili but it is a refined Swahili of East Africa and Eastern Zaire. The Shaba Swahili is not as polished.

The Catholics, Garanganzi and Methodists can all use Sanga. The most effective work can be done with this tribe amongst the Protestants by Sanga pastors. These pastors operating in the power of the Holy Spirit can best reach those in the Church who live in both worlds.

Sundanese (Indonesia)

ALTERNATE NAMES: Orang Sunda

SIZE OF GROUP: 20,000,000   **MARC ID:** 273

DISTINCTIVES: language; ethnicity; religion; residence

SOCIAL CHANGE: not reported

LANGUAGES: Sundanese (100% speak/ 30% read; V); Indonesian (60% speak; T); Dutch (5% speak; T)

SCRIPTURE: Bible   **RECORDINGS:** not reported

CHRISTIAN LITERACY: 50%

RELIGION: Islam-Animist (99% adherents); Christianity (1% adherents/ <1% practicing)

CHURCHES AND MISSIONS	BEGAN	MEMBERSHIP	CMTY
Christian & Msny. Alliance	1970	nr	100
Indigenous Churches	nr	nr	300
Methodist Church	1971	nr	100
Pentecostal Churches	1910	nr	nr
Sundanese Reformed Church	1940	nr	nr

OPENNESS TO RELIGIOUS CHANGE: somewhat open

RECEPTIVITY TO CHRISTIANITY: receptive

GROWTH OF CHRISTIAN COMMUNITY: not reported

EVANGELISM PROFILE: not reported   **VALIDITY:** 6

A significant movement which seeks to mobilize Christians to pray and fast one day each month for a year is in effect four years after the initial expanded description of the Sundanese people appeared in this series. So far little progress is evident in this overwhelming task. Miraculous results are expected, however, because the power of the Holy Spirit is being sought on behalf of Sundanese Muslims.

A new missionary force is also being motivated, mobilized and trained. According to Islamic leaders, up to 40 percent of the Sundanese are merely nominal Muslims, and it is likely that 60 percent do not regularly practice any Muslim rituals other than those incorporated in their cultural traditions. Thus Islam has little bearing on what the people believe; it merely dictates how they act. Within the scenario there will be ample opportunity for thousands or even millions of Sundanese to become Christians.

The forces of modernization are moving at full speed in Indonesia, and the people are being exposed to contemporary material goods and systems of thought. Many are ready to commit themselves to a life of materialism and secularism; perhaps they can be given an alternative. The gospel is being transmitted in a variety of ways through radio programs. Literature distribution is increasing rapidly as materials become available. The major hindrance is the lack of capable persons. It is evident that the people are about to be reached. They need personal encounter with committed Christians.

The forces and followers of Satan are rumbling also. Many feel that open spiritual warfare will take place over the Sundanese. There is every reason to expect a decade of revolutionary conversion and growth within the church among the Sundanese.

Many of the theories and dreams of contemporary missiology will be field-tested, fine-tuned and refined as new workers are mobilized and actually get involved in ministries. Muslim leaders in Indonesia are seeking to prevent evangelism, so the task will not be easy.

Most adult Sundanese do not read or write any language, so new forms of adult education are essential to effectively evangelize them. Discipleship will no doubt be a prerequisite to developing capable Christian leaders and widespread church growth. Responsive persons are eagerly awaiting the arrival of trained Christian laborers who will learn their language, spend time with them and explain the whole gospel message. It is not a time for shoddy preparation or hit-and-run evangelism. Well-trained, committed Christians actively supported by experienced prayer warriors are now needed in this new people movement. Many are excited by the prospect of a vital church ten years in the future; the time is right for others excited about the opportunity to get involved personally now in this movement. For further information write to the Sundanese Connection, 141 East Duarte Road, Arcadia, CA 91006.

Thai Immigrants, Los Angeles (United States of America)

ALTERNATE NAMES: not reported

SIZE OF GROUP: 60,000   **MARC ID:** 4813

DISTINCTIVES: language; religion; sense of unity; ethnicity

SOCIAL CHANGE: slow

LANGUAGES: Central Thai (100% speak/ 98% read; V,T,S,G)

SCRIPTURE: Bible   **RECORDINGS:** yes

CHRISTIAN LITERACY: 100%

RELIGION: Buddhism (96% adherents/ 25% practicing); Protestant (1% adherents/ <1% practicing); Roman Catholic (<1% adherents/ <1% practicing); Islam (<1% adherents/ <1% practicing); Other (3% adherents)

CHURCHES AND MISSIONS	BEGAN	MEMBERSHIP	CMTY
Thai Outreach Church, Pasadena	1979	30	80
North Hollywood Thai Church	1973	30	100
Duarte Thai Church	1982	20	30

OPENNESS TO RELIGIOUS CHANGE: somewhat open

RECEPTIVITY TO CHRISTIANITY: indifferent

GROWTH OF CHRISTIAN COMMUNITY: slow growth

EVANGELISM PROFILE: not reported   **VALIDITY:** 4

The Thai are an unreached people in America. The majority of them came to America during the '70s after the fall of Vietnam, Cambodia and Laos. Prior to this period, the Thai in the U.S. were mainly students seeking higher education.

There are around 120,000 Thai today in America. All of them can speak central Thai. And probably 98% of them can read Thai. At least 60% of them live in California--due to attractive climate and opportunity for employment and education. Around 60,000 of them live in Los Angeles and Orange County alone. The areas of their concentration are downtown Los Angeles and North Hollywood. In Los Angeles there are around 50 Thai restaurants, two Thai newspapers, one Thai radio program, at least one Thai bookstore, a movie theater that shows Thai movies and a Buddhist temple. Several supermarkets sell Thai food and groceries. The Thai can find almost every kind of Thai food here.

Other cities that have significant numbers of Thai are New York, Chicago, Baltimore and San Francisco. Some are beginning to settle in Seattle, Washington and Michigan.

Approximately 70% of the Thai in America are Chinese born in Thailand and consider themselves Thai citizens. Most of this group speak and read Thai fluently. This group of Thai is more open to change.

Around 60% of all the Thai here are students. Most of them are doing their graduate study; a few are in high school. The majority are from the middle class. Many of them are children of well-to-do and prominent families. Some are government officials and scholars. They are proud of their country and nationality and must never be mistaken as refugees. Around 35 percent of the Thai are seeking employment here. Another 5 percent are temporary visitors.

Among the Thai, students are most receptive to the gospel and many have become Christians. Around 40% of the students will eventually go back to Thailand. Thai students in America are therefore a strategic group to be reached.

Of all the Thai in America, around 96% are adherents to Buddhism. But probably only 25% are committed or practicing Buddhists. Around 1% are Protestant Christian, 0.5% Roman Catholic, 0.2% Islamic and 2.5% other. Compared to the Thai in Thailand, the Thai here are more open to the gospel, but they are not necessarily responsive. Their attitude is still mainly indifferent to Christianity due to their strong identification with Buddhism. To them it is part of Thai culture.

The Thai are in the process of settling down in America. Most of them have social and emotional needs as a result of required adjustments. Many of them are looking for employment. A lot of families have a problem adjusting relations internally. They feel insecure and lonely. Many become Christians because of the genuine love found among believers. The message of peace, hope, security, love and the divine providence usually attracts the Thai.

For initial steps in evangelism, the American church can be a strong force by showing personal interest, love and concern for their welfare. American Christian home contact can be effective in outreach. Friendship evangelism is probably the most effective for cross-cultural situations, though the Thai church in America would probably have an even stronger evangelistic influence.

There are at least three organized Thai churches in Los Angeles--in North Hollywood, Pasadena, and Duarte. Thai Christians need to be encouraged and trained to evangelize the other 98% of Thai citizens in America. Other non-Thai can help support the work financially, through prayer, training materials, and instruction.

Urban Street Women/Los Angeles (United States of America)

ALTERNATE NAMES: not reported

SIZE OF GROUP: 100   **MARC ID:** 4826

DISTINCTIVES: economic status; health situation

SOCIAL CHANGE: very rapid

LANGUAGES: English (V); Spanish (V)

SCRIPTURE: Bible   **RECORDINGS:** yes

CHRISTIAN LITERACY: not reported

RELIGION: Secularism; Christianity

CHURCHES AND MISSIONS: not reported

OPENNESS TO RELIGIOUS CHANGE: somewhat closed

RECEPTIVITY TO CHRISTIANITY: reluctant

GROWTH OF CHRISTIAN COMMUNITY: slow decline

EVANGELISM PROFILE: not reported   **VALIDITY:** 4

Today there are homeless women in virtually every major American city. Often called "bag ladies," they are conspicuous with their shopping bags or grocery carts, which contain all their worldly possessions. They live on the streets of the cities, and find shelter wherever they can, often mingling with other travelers in bus depots and train stations, and spending the night in public lavoratories when the weather is cold. Their clothing is usually torn and dirty and their hair is matted. Though the number of homeless women in America is impossible to estimate, it seems that their numbers are rising.

A recent survey indicated that 30 percent of these homeless women have mental problems. Their poor existence aggravates this condition, and many are refused hospitalization because of the rigid admission requirements. With no one to care for them, they usually wander the streets talking only to themselves. Their needs are many. In addition to the psychological and emotional support that every human requires, they are deprived of the basic comforts that the average American takes for granted.

Their health is a major problem. Many have lice and swollen legs. Circulation in their legs decreases causing fluid retention and eventual tissue damage from trying to stand up while sleeping. There are soup kitchens and mission homes, but most of these are for men. The few jobs that are available for people like this are usually reserved for men too, such as washing cars or dishes, delivering lunches, or passing out handbills. Many of the "bag ladies" actually seem to prefer their poor life-style, and refuse all efforts by others to help them. They tend to be isolated, even from other women like themselves. They rarely will ask for handouts, but prefer to wait around fast-food restaurants to clean out their garbage cans.

Some of these homeless women are actually frightened of living in buildings. By staying out on the streets they can avoid the responsibility of paying rent and interacting with others. Thus, their isolation is heightened and the chances for improving their situation decrease even further. Working with homeless women is very difficult, and yet many volunteers are happy to help at the centers where the women can get off the streets. Locations like the Downtown Women's Center in Los Angeles, and the Antonio G. Olivieri Center for Homeless Women in New York, are doing good work with this group. They hope to provide an alternate life-style for these women, and eventually reintegrate them into society.

The spiritual needs of this people group are obviously very great. There is a need for the development of unique ministries, preferably by other women. This ministry would have to address the physical as well as the spiritual needs of the homeless women in America, since many have had bad experiences with "formal religion." The opportunities and potential for evangelization among this unreached people appear to be very great.

Wandering Homeless (United States of America)

ALTERNATE NAMES: Freeway Trolls; Street People; Modern Nomads

SIZE OF GROUP: 15,000   **MARC ID:** 4804

DISTINCTIVES: occupation; residence; economic status; discrimination

SOCIAL CHANGE: not reported

LANGUAGES: English (V,T,S)

SCRIPTURE: Bible   **RECORDINGS:** yes

CHRISTIAN LITERACY: not reported

RELIGION: Secularism; Protestant; Roman Catholic; Judaism

CHURCHES AND MISSIONS	BEGAN CMTY	MEMBERSHIP	
Christian Temp. Housing Facil.	nr	nr	nr
Travelers Aid	nr	nr	nr
Salvation Army	nr	nr	nr

OPENNESS TO RELIGIOUS CHANGE: not reported

RECEPTIVITY TO CHRISTIANITY: not reported

GROWTH OF CHRISTIAN COMMUNITY: not reported

EVANGELISM PROFILE: not reported   **VALIDITY:** 4

An estimated 200,000 adults are roaming the streets throughout the United States without homes and without jobs, and the problem is mounting. This scene resembles the Great Depression of the 1930s when many lost their jobs because of a failing economy.

Experts say most of America's hobos today are mentally ill persons or hopeless alcholics who cannot cope with society. Scores die each year due to exposure, starvation, disease or thieves.

Without proper identification, a fixed address or a job history these people cannot qualify for government relief. Efforts to provide food and shelter cost millions of dollars, which come from charities and taxpayers. Many who do qualify for welfare benefits are too socially alienated to stand in line to fill out a form or cash a check.

The numbers of vagrant Americans began to climb in the 1960s when government agencies started releasing mental patients who, they felt, posed no threat to society or to themselves. Down from nearly 560,000 in the mid-1950s, only about 138,000 are confined today. It was planned that most could be treated as outpatients but many former patients, because of their condition, could not find their way to the centers for help. San Francisco, California, reports 4000 of these street wanderers. When interviewed, they say they have no interest in returning to a normal place in society. They believe it would be too hard and not worth the trouble.

Street life is marked by not only deprivation but also by violence. The weak are robbed and assaulted by the strong. Women are easy prey for rapists. The young and aggressive take areas of warmth and shelter from the old and weak.

In early 1983 the U.S. Labor Department reported that 12 million Americans were out of work in December 1982. Many once solid middle-class families have had to gather their belongings and set out on the road in search of jobs. Some families are forced to sleep in their cars, at campgrounds or in makeshift tents pitched along the roadside. Finding shelter under freeway overpasses is a growing practice.

Ohio reports the largest number of displaced Americans. However, informal surveys reveal that Michigan, New York, and Indiana are heavily represented as well. Tent City, some 30 miles south of Houston, Texas, is a recently redeveloped makeshift community of local drifters and job seekers from throughout Texas and elsewhere. They burn wood scraps in 55-gallon drums to keep warm, use highway department grills for cooking, and drink water from donated barrels. These people are on the road not by choice but out of desperation.

Water Surface People (Hong Kong)

ALTERNATE NAMES: Shiu Min Yan; Tanka (derog)

SIZE OF GROUP: 11,000   **MARC ID:** 4822

DISTINCTIVES:

SOCIAL CHANGE: not reported

LANGUAGES: Cantonese dialects (V)

SCRIPTURE: not reported   **RECORDINGS:** not reported

CHRISTIAN LITERACY: not reported

RELIGION: Islam-Animist

CHURCHES AND MISSIONS: not reported

OPENNESS TO RELIGIOUS CHANGE: not reported

RECEPTIVITY TO CHRISTIANITY: not reported

GROWTH OF CHRISTIAN COMMUNITY: not reported

EVANGELISM PROFILE: not reported   **VALIDITY:** 3

Small watercraft offer both a means of livelihood and place of residence to thousands of people in Hong Kong's busy harbor. About half of these people are fisherfolk; the rest serve as cargo carriers or pilots, or wander aboard sampans.

One significant feature of this group is their vocabulary. Since they live and work aboard boats, they use many technical terms for articles and actions related to life at sea. Although their spoken language (Cantonese) is the same used by Hong Kong residents on land, there is often difficulty in communicating because of the differences in interests and occupations.

Water surface people have historically been regarded as a lower-class group. They have few belongings, and few adults ever attended schools. The availability of efficient diesel engines has increased the productivity of many small craft; income has risen and children can now attend schools.

The hardest-working individuals and those able to earn large amounts of money are buying or renting flats on land where their families and elderly relatives can reside. This provides opportunity for improved health care and education. Once they settle in flats, their lives are significantly changed. No longer are the women subjected to dismal conditions like unsafe kitchens, cramped quarters, rickety decks, and bouts with seasickness, nor must they contend with the absence of amenities such as running fresh water. Better food is available on land, and school uniforms with shoes become status symbols.

For families who remain at sea, life remains as before. Mothers anxiously watch toddlers lest they fall overboard; children go off to work with their fathers where they learn the jargon and skills of sea life. The Hong Kong Government now requires the licensing of pilots, so many more adults are receiving some schooling and upgrading their businesses. Educated children are developing new ways to offer products and services related to harbor life.

A "church afloat" is needed for these people, who have very limited contacts with Christians. Itinerant workers who understand their problems and lifestyle can reach them. Education may be the means to both help these people integrate with the land-based population and also reach them with the gospel.

Yami of Orchid Island (Indonesia)

ALTERNATE NAMES: not reported

SIZE OF GROUP: 2,200   **MARC ID**: 4805

DISTINCTIVES: ethnicity; language; religion; residence

SOCIAL CHANGE: slow

LANGUAGES: Yami (V); Mandarin (S)

SCRIPTURE: portions   **RECORDINGS**: not reported

CHRISTIAN LITERACY: not reported

RELIGION: Christianity

CHURCHES AND MISSIONS	BEGAN	MEMBERSHIP	CMTY
Baptist Bible Fellowship	nr	700	nr
Presbyterian Ch. of America	nr	nr	nr

OPENNESS TO RELIGIOUS CHANGE: not reported

RECEPTIVITY TO CHRISTIANITY: not reported

GROWTH OF CHRISTIAN COMMUNITY: not reported

EVANGELISM PROFILE: not reported   **VALIDITY**: 4

The Yami are a sedentary group of Indonesian farmers, fishers and boat builders who inhabit the small island of Lanyu (also known as Orchid Island). They have been among the most geographically isolated of all Indonesia's aboriginal groups. Their island is located some 40 miles off the southern tip of Formosa. Their name, "Yami," was probably derived from the Batanese word "i-ami" meaning "people from the North." Although today's Yami have little knowledge of or interest in the island of Formosa, it is likely that their history is closely linked to the people of its eastern coast.

Japanese colonial rule protected and secluded the Yami from outside contact, although the post-World War II period has introduced Taiwanese immigration, schools and missions. They have proven resistant to social change. Their life-style varies little from that of their ancestors. The digging stick is still the primary agricultural tool. Few animals are used for labor; nor do they fertilize their fields. Fishing and shellfish provide an important segment of their diet.

The Yami believe they originated from the sea. They participate in a semiannual religious festival revolving around "the god of the sea." They believe the soul is good by nature as long as it resides within the body, but at death, when it is released, it becomes evil. To protect themselves from the evil souls of the dead, they observe various taboos and use charms. Their swords and spears are used more as talismans against bad fortune than for fighting.

The Yami recognize property rights over fishing grounds, pasture lands, house lots and fields. Each is named individually and boundaries are made well-known. Certain natural resource areas are often owned by a village or a family rather than an individual. Anything movable, however, always belongs to one person.

A newly married couple may share the home plot of the groom's father, but the birth of the first child marks complete independence from both sets of parents. A change of name, house and status mark the event. A new home is built accompanied by serious ceremonial consecration. The feast that accompanies this ceremony requires several years of planning and accumulation of food. The Yami do not practice adoption when a couple cannot have children. Very little importance is placed on continuing a family line. Most households consist only of nuclear family members; there are no clans.

Divorce initiated by either spouse has become relatively common within their culture; marriages are not stable until the birth of the first child. Divorces are caused by conflict between the bride and her new mother-in-law, or adultery on either side. Second marriages are permissible. The practice of brothers marrying a dead brother's wife, or a widowed sister marrying her brother-in-law, is discouraged, but it does occur occasionally, after the payment of a ritual fine.

Wealth is a major factor in individual and family prestige and status; wealthy men have considerable influence in village affairs. In fact, the dynamics of Yami culture are largely associated with the accumulation, display and distribution of wealth, particularly in the form of foodstuffs. There are periodic feasts of merit at which family members wear elaborate silver and wood ritual helmets, gold and silver breast ornaments and strings of beads, holding ritual staffs and ancient jars. Some believe there are spiritual advantages to having a lot of social prestige, therefore reinforcing the community's felt need for these occasional merit ceremonies for recognition.

Most forms of injustice in the Yami culture are dealt with through community elders and chieftains who mediate in negotiations and payment of compensation. If negotiations fail, then physical conflict may ensue which consists more of noise and bravado than bloodshed. In the case of accidental death, however, formal blood vengeance is expected from the group of the fallen person. Unlike the majority of the tribes on the Formosa mainland, the Yami have never been known to practice headhunting.

The traditional Yami religion conceives of a layered upper world ruled by deities known as the "people above." These deities are believed to rule the earth via natural elements like fires, rain and thunderstorms. They are honored annually in ceremonies and food offerings. The Yami also apparently acknowledge an underworld inhabited by evil spirits other than those of the dead. These spirits and ghosts are greatly feared and are therefore given innumerable offerings; exorcism rites are spectacular attempts to control their malevolent influence.

EXPANDED DESCRIPTIONS

Certain individuals are respected as having supernatural powers and abilities to enter the spiritual worlds, foretell the future and heal the sick. Most of these ceremonies are conducted by heads of households: the role of priests has never developed significantly among the Yami.

A person's soul is believed to dwell in the head, leave the body at death and travel to a land said to be on two small islands within the Bataan Archipelago. At death, the burial party is kept small (usually only the close male relatives) because of their overwhelming fear of cemeteries and contact with the dead. Members of the burial party wear full armor and brandish spears. The family mourns for three days, participating in stringent taboos, and culminating the activities with a farewell feast, which also serves to resolidify surviving family members. A man or woman who has lived a decent life will usually be kept at home to die and be buried in the village cemetery. Those who die "bad" deaths are kept away from other family members and their bodies exposed on ledges near the sea. They no longer practice the Chinese tradition of being buried in jars.

In February of 1983 MARC received exciting news concerning Orchid Island. A church has been planted and now reports a thriving membership of 700 (a third of the population). The New Testament books of Mark and James and sections of Acts have been translated into the Yami language. However, translation ceased in 1981 pending the arrival of another translator to continue the work. Chinese is currently the language in which Scripture is being distributed.

Yao (Malawi)

ALTERNATE NAMES: Ayao

SIZE OF GROUP: 600,000   **MARC ID:** 1006

DISTINCTIVES: language; ethnicity; religion; social class

SOCIAL CHANGE: rapid

LANGUAGES: Chiyao (95% speak/ 5% read; V,G,W); Chichewa (80% speak/ 60% read; T,W); English (40% speak/ 30% read; W); Arabic (P)

SCRIPTURE: Bible   **RECORDINGS:** not reported

CHRISTIAN LITERACY: 10%

RELIGION: Islam-Animist (96% adherents); Roman Catholic (2% adherents/ 1% practicing); Protestant (2% adherents/ 1% practicing)

CHURCHES AND MISSIONS	BEGAN	MEMBERSHIP	CMTY
Anglican Church	1900	500	nr
Presbyterian Church	1920	500	nr
Roman Catholic Church	1920	500	nr
Baptist Church	1950	100	nr
Lutheran Church	1960	50	nr

OPENNESS TO RELIGIOUS CHANGE: somewhat open

RECEPTIVITY TO CHRISTIANITY: receptive

GROWTH OF CHRISTIAN COMMUNITY: not reported

EVANGELISM PROFILE: not reported   **VALIDITY:** 4

The Yao of Malawi, Southeast Africa, are a Central Bantu people. Their traditional homeland is between the Lujendu and Rovuma rivers east of Lake Malawi.

Rapid spread of Islam among the Yao seems to have been due chiefly to their long association with Arabs. The Yao were active as traders and handled the wares of Arabs including ivory, slaves, beeswax, tobacco, gunpowder and cloth. They were traditionally suspicious of Europeans, particularly Christian missionaries who spoke out against their involvement in the slave trade. Negative sentiment has been passed from generation to generation and the Yao remain resistant to Christianity.

Traditional Yao villages are small and each has a strong, dominant headman. Yao are predominantly Sunni Muslims of the Shafi school. Elements of animism are syncretized with Islam. Ancient beliefs relating to ancestral spirits are preserved.

In Islam, patrilineal descent is stressed, but many Yao remain committed to matrilineal descent patterns. Few Yao of Malawi have made the pilgrimage to Mecca and few are militant, deeply committed orthodox Muslims.

As the Yao rub shoulders with Christians in the cities and towns, they have opportunity to receive a personal word of testimony from fellow countrymen. There is no concerted effort to reach Muslims who live in the remote villages of Malawi. Those who live in cities have the opportunity to hear of Christ's love but they rarely receive a personal invitation to meet Christ.

Malawi is one nation where Christians could develop a unique and effective strategy to reach Muslim neighbors such as the Yao who live among them.

Zanskari (India)

ALTERNATE NAMES: not reported

SIZE OF GROUP: 8,000   **MARC ID:** 4834

DISTINCTIVES: language; ethnicity; religion; residence

SOCIAL CHANGE: not reported

LANGUAGES: Zanskari (100% speak; V) Tibetan (T)

SCRIPTURE: none   **RECORDINGS:** not reported

CHRISTIAN LITERACY: not reported

RELIGION: Buddhism (100% adherents/100% practicing)

CHURCHES AND MISSIONS:	BEGAN	MEMBERSHIP	CMTY
Youth With A Mission	nr	nr	nr

OPENNESS TO RELIGIOUS CHANGE: not reported

RECEPTIVITY TO CHRISTIANITY: not reported

GROWTH OF CHRISTIAN COMMUNITY: not reported

EVANGELISM PROFILE: not reported   **VALIDITY:** 3

The Zanskari are isolated from any major population center 6-8 months of every year. The 8000 men, women and children who live in the rugged Himalaya mountains along the boundary of Tibet and northern India have learned to adapt to the extreme temperatures and hostile environment. They are able to grow barley and peas during the brief summer growing season. They rely on yak livestock for milk, manure and clothing. The milk is given to the children or mixed with barley flour for staple meals. The manure is used for cooking and heating. A slightly fermented barley broth is the only beverage other than salted Tibetan tea with yak butter.

Life is not easy for the Zanskari. The men travel long frozen rivers to reach other villages in winter. Otherwise families stay in the lower levels of two-story buildings where yak reside and radiate warmth to keep the rooms livable. In summer the families move to the second story.

Sixty Buddhist monks have settled in a high rock outcropping called the Eagle's Nest. They have many health problems due to lack of trained medical personnel and the scarcity of food and supplies. These individuals are responsible for all spiritual needs of the people and appear to be the only educated few in the Zanskar region. A few of the monks came from other parts of the Buddhist world and have learned English. Otherwise everyone speaks Zanskari, a language related to Tibetan.

Reports from Christians who have contacted the Zanskari monks reveal a small percentage yet high receptivity to the gospel, especially when presented in written form. It appears easy to share the gospel after confidence is established by providing medical attention and food. Because of their position as respected religious leaders among the villagers, monks who become Christians should then be trained to introduce the gospel to the other Zanskari.

Registry
of the Unreached

Introduction
to the Registry

The information on the 3815 unreached peoples in the registry is presented in five different lists. Each list organizes the information differently. The first list, which indexes the peoples alphabetically by group name, and the last one, arranged by country, include the estimated percentage of those that practice Christianity and a code that indicates the overall accuracy of the data. A more detailed explanation of the information contained in the following lists may be found at the beginning of each section.

Groups are also listed by receptivity to the gospel, principal professed religion, and language. All five lists indicate those groups that are reported to be very receptive (***), receptive (**) or indifferent (*) to Christianity. There is also another code (79, 80, 81, 82, 83 or 84) attached to the group name to indicate that a description has been written about this people group in the *Unreached Peoples* volume of that year.

A comparison with the indexes in previous volumes in this series will show that some early data has been changed. In a few cases, the group has been removed because of more accurate information. This reflects the ongoing nature of this data collection and research.

Index by Group Name

This is a basic listing of people groups in this registry. Peoples are listed by their primary *name*, and effort has been made to standardize names and use the most commonly accepted English spelling. This listing includes the *country* for which the information was provided, principal vernacular *language* used by the group, population estimate of the *group size* in the country listed and principal professed religion (*primary religion*), which in some cases is less than 40 percent of the total group membership.

In addition, this index includes the estimated percentage of the group that practices Christianity in any recognized tradition (*% Chr*). Included in this percentage are Protestant, Roman Catholic, Orthodox, African Independent and other Christian groups. Excluded from this percentage are Christopagans and Christian cultic groups. It is important to note that this figure is the estimated percentage of *practicing* Christians within the group. If the group was listed in *Unreached Peoples '80* or earlier, the figure recorded here will most likely be different, because those volumes recorded the percentage of *professing* Christians (or adherents), which most often will be a higher number. Thus, these figures should not be compared or used as a time series, since the changes indicate a different kind of data. Differences might also be due to a new and better data source or revised data, since we are continually updating our files.

This index also lists a validity code (*V*) which estimates the accuracy and completeness of the data on a scale from 1 to 9. See the introduction to the expanded descriptions for an explanation of this code.

The column labeled *Vol U.P.* indicates the year of the volume of *Unreached Peoples* in which a description of the group appears. The final column (*ID*) shows the identification number by which information on the group is filed in the unreached peoples database. Any correspondence sent to MARC dealing with the group should refer to that number.

NAME	COUNTRY	LANGUAGE	GROUP SIZE	PRIMARY RELIGION	% CHR	V	VOL UP ID
Abaknon	Philippines	Abaknon	10,000	Christo-Paganism	<1%	1	3239
Abanyom	Nigeria	Abanyom	4,000	Aninism	<1%	1	2311
Abau	Indonesia	Abau	3,000	Aninism	<1%	1	2852
Abau	Papua New Guinea	Abau	3,000	Aninism	<1%	1	5900
Abazin	USSR	Abazin	25,000	Islam	0%	1	5821
Abe	Ivory Coast	Abe	30,000	Islam-Aninist	<1%	1	2273
Abialang	Sudan	Abialang	7,000	Islam	0%	1	5464
Abidji	Ivory Coast	Adidji	23,000	Islam-Aninist	<1%	1	2274
Abie	Papua New Guinea	Abie	600	Aninism	<1%	1	5901
Abkhaz	Turkey	Abkhaz	12,000	Islam	<1%	1	2540
Abkhaz	USSR	Abkhaz	83,000	Unknown	0%	1	5822
Abong	Nigeria	Abong	1,000	Islam	<1%	1	2312
Aborigines in Brisbane	Australia	English	8,000	Secularism	6%	6 82	5000
Abou Charib	Chad	Abou Charib	25,000	Islam-Aninist	<1%	1	2208
Abu Leila	Sudan	Abu Leila	4,000	Islam	0%	1	5505
Abua	Nigeria	Abua	24,000	Aninism	<1%	1	2313
Abujmaria (Madhya Pradesh)	India	Abujmaria	11,000	Hindu-Aninist	<1%	1	2600
Abulas	Papua New Guinea	Abulas	33,000	Aninism	<1%	1	5902
Abure	Ivory Coast	Abure	25,000	Islam-Aninist	<1%	1	2275
Ach'ang	China	Ach'ang	10,000	Traditional Chinese	<1%	1	2807
Achagua	Colombia	Achagua	100	Aninism	<1%	1	2178
Achehnese	Indonesia	Achehnese	2,200,000	Islam	<1%	6 80	97
Acheron	Sudan	Acheron	1,000	Islam	0%	1	5506
Achi, Cubulco	Guatemala	Achi, Cubulco	15,000	Aninism	<1%	1	8000
Achi, Rabinal	Guatemala	Achi, Rabinal	21,000	Aninism	<1%	1	8001
Achipa	Nigeria	Achipa	4,000	Islam	<1%	1	2314
Achode	Ghana	Achode	5,000	Islam-Aninist	<1%	1	5319
Acholi	Uganda	Acholi	nr	Aninism	<1%	1	5638
Achual	Peru	Achual	5,000	Aninism	<1%	5	3162
Adamawa	Cameroon	Fulani	380,000	Aninism	<1%	1	507
Adele	Togo	Adele	3,000	Islam-Aninist	0%	1	5620
Adhola	Uganda	Adhola	200,000	Aninism	0%	1	5639
***Adi	India	Adi	80,000	Aninism	2%	4	1027
Adiyan in Kerala	India	Adiyan	3,000	Hinduism	<1%	1	2601
**Adja	Benin	Ge	250,000	Aninism	5%	4	423
Adjora	Papua New Guinea	Adjora	2,000	Aninism	<1%	1	5903

NAME	COUNTRY	LANGUAGE	GROUP SIZE	PRIMARY RELIGION	% CHR	V	VOL	UP ID
Adygei	USSR	Adygei	100,000	Islam	0%	1		5811
Adyukru	Ivory Coast	Adyukru	51,000	Islam-Animist	<1%	1		2276
Aeka	Papua New Guinea	Aeka	3,000	Animism	<1%	1		5904
Aeta	Philippines	Aeta	500	Christo-Paganism	<1%	1		3240
Afar	Ethiopia	Afar	300,000	Islam-Animist	1%	6	79	21
*Afawa	Nigeria	Afanci	10,000	Animism	1%	6	80	559
**Afghan Refugees (NUFP)	Pakistan	Dari	1,835,000	Islam	<1%	4		9004
Afitti	Sudan	Afitti	3,000	Islam	0%	1		5439
**Afo	Nigeria	Eloyi	25,000	Animism	1%	6	80	558
***African Students in Cairo	Egypt	Various dialects	700	Islam	9%	4		2100
Afshars	Iran	Afshari	290,000	Islam	0%	4		2035
Agajanis	Iran	Agajanis	1,000	Islam	0%	3		2065
Agarabi	Papua New Guinea	Agarabi	12,000	Animism	<1%	1		5905
Agariya in Bihar	India	Agariya	12,000	Hinduism	<1%	1		2602
Age	Cameroon	Age	5,000	Animism	0%	1		5206
Aghem	Cameroon	Aghem	5,000	Animism	0%	1		5207
Aghu	Indonesia	Aghu	3,000	Animism	<1%	1		2853
Agob	Papua New Guinea	Agob	1,000	Animism	0%	1		5906
Agoi	Nigeria	Agoi	4,000	Animism	<1%	1		2315
Aguacateco	Guatemala	Aguacateco	16,000	Animism	25%	2		8002
Aguaruna	Peru	Aguaruna	22,000	Animism	<1%	1		3163
Agul	USSR	Agul	9,000	Islam	0%	1		5823
Agutaynon	Philippines	Agutaynon	7,000	Islam-Animist	<1%	1		3241
Aguagwune	Nigeria	Aguagwune	20,000	Animism	<1%	1		2316
Ahir in Maharashtra	India	Ahir	133,000	Islam	<1%	1		2603
**Ahl-i-Haqq in Iran	Iran	Kurdish dialects	500,000	Islam	0%	6	79	1237
Ahlo	Togo	Ahlo	3,000	Islam-Animist	0%	1		5621
Ahmadis in Lahore	Pakistan	Panjabi	60,000	Islam	0%	6	82	5016
Aibondeni	Indonesia	Aibondeni	200	Animism	<1%	1		2854
Aiku	Papua New Guinea	Aiku	800	Animism	0%	1		5907
Aikwakai	Indonesia	Aikwakai	400	Animism	0%	1		2855
Ainol in Assam	India	Ainol	100	Hindu-Animist	<1%	1		2604
Aiome	Papua New Guinea	Aiome	900	Animism	<1%	1		5908
Aion	Papua New Guinea	Aion	800	Animism	<1%	1		5909
Airo-Sumaghaghe	Indonesia	Airo-Sumaghaghe	2,000	Animism	<1%	1		2856
Airoran	Indonesia	Airoran	400	Animism	<1%	1		2857

REGISTRY OF THE UNREACHED

NAME	COUNTRY	LANGUAGE	GROUP SIZE	PRIMARY RELIGION	% CHR	VOL V	UP ID
Aja	Sudan	Aja	1,000	Islam	0%	1	5440
Ajmeri in Rajasthan	India	Ajmeri	600	Hindu-Animist	<1%	1	2605
Aka	India	Aka	2,000	Animism	0%	3	1036
Akan, Brong	Ivory Coast	Akan, Brong	50,000	Islam-Animist	<1%	1	2277
Akauaio	Guyana	Akauaio	3,000	Christo-Paganism	<1%	1	5115
Ake	Nigeria	Ake	300	Animism	<1%	1	2317
**Akha	Thailand	Akha	10,000	Ancestor Worship	1%	6	79 609
Akhavakh	USSR	Akhavakh	5,000	Unknown	0%	4	5824
***Akhdan	Yemen, Arab Republic	Arabic	nr	Islam-Animist	0%	4	4064
Akpa-Yache	Nigeria	Akpa-Yache	15,000	Animism	<1%	1	2318
Akpafu	Ghana	Akpafu	8,000	Islam-Animist	0%	1	5320
Akrukay	Papua New Guinea	Akrukay	200	Animism	<1%	1	5910
Alaba	Ethiopia	Alaban	50,000	Islam	3%	4	358
Aladian	Ivory Coast	Aladian	15,000	Islam-Animist	<1%	1	2278
Alago	Nigeria	Alago	35,000	Animism	2%	5	1058
Alak	Laos	Alak	8,000	Animism	<1%	1	112
Alamblak	Papua New Guinea	Alamblak	2,000	Animism	<1%	1	5911
Alangan	Philippines	Alangan	6,000	Christo-Paganism	<1%	1	3242
*Alars	India	Allar	400	Folk Religion	0%	4	2017
Alas	Indonesia	Gayo	30,000	Islam-Animist	0%	4	1133
Alatil	Papua New Guinea	Alatil	400	Animism	0%	1	5912
Alauagat	Papua New Guinea	Alauagat	300	Animism	0%	1	5913
*Alauites	Syria	Arabic	600,000	Islam	0%	6	79 1104
*Albanian Muslims	Albania	Albanian Tosk	1,700,000	Islam	0%	6	80 4000
*Albanians in Yugoslavia	Yugoslavia	Albanian (Gheg)	1,500,000	Islam	<1%	5	4036
Alege	Nigeria	Alege	1,000	Animism	<1%	1	2319
Algerian Arabs in France	France	Arabic	800,000	Islam	0%	3	1086
Alor, Kolana	Indonesia	Alor, Kolana	90,000	Animism	<1%	5	81 2858
Alutor	USSR	Alutor	2,000	Unknown	0%	1	5825
Ama	Papua New Guinea	Ama	400	Animism	<1%	1	5914
Amahuaca	Peru	Amahuaca	2,000	Animism	<1%	1	2203
Amaimon	Papua New Guinea	Amaimon	400	Animism	<1%	1	5915
Amanab	Indonesia	Amanab	3,000	Animism	<1%	1	2859
Amanab	Papua New Guinea	Amanab	3,000	Animism	<1%	1	5916
Amar	Ethiopia	Amar	23,000	Animism	<1%	1	3190
Amarakaeri	Peru	Amarakaeri	500	Animism	<1%	1	3164

NAME	COUNTRY	LANGUAGE	GROUP SIZE	PRIMARY RELIGION	% CHR	V	VOL UP	ID
Anasi	Cameroon	Anasi	10,000	Animism	0%	1		5208
Anbai	Indonesia	Anbai	6,000	Animism	<1%	1		2860
Anbasi	Papua New Guinea	Anbasi	500	Animism	<1%	1		5917
Anber	Indonesia	Anber	300	Animism	<1%	1		2861
Anberbaken	Indonesia	Anberbaken	5,000	Animism	<1%	1		2862
Anbo	Zambia	Anbo	1,000	Animism	0%	1		5786
Anbonese	Indonesia	Anbonese	80,000	Animism	<1%	1		2863
	Netherlands	Anbonese	30,000	Animism	2%	4		67
*Americans in Geneva	Switzerland	English	45,000	Secularism	<1%	1		4118
*Ani	Taiwan	Ani	99,000	Buddhist-Aninist	2%	5	81	7032
Ano	Nigeria	Ano	4,000	Animism	<1%	1		2320
**Anpeeli	Papua New Guinea	Ampale	1,000	Christo-Paganism	1%	4		411
Amsterdam Boat Dwellers	Netherlands	Dutch	8,000	Secularism	0%	3		4159
Anto	Papua New Guinea	Anto	200	Animism	<1%	1		5918
Anuesha	Peru	Anuesha	5,000	Animism	<1%	1		3165
Anuzgo, Guerrero	Mexico	Anuzgo, Guerrero	20,000	Christo-Paganism	<1%	1		8015
Anuzgo, Oaxaca	Mexico	Anuzgo, Oaxaca	5,000	Christo-Paganism	<1%	1		8016
Ana	Togo	Ana	36,000	Islam-Aninist	0%	1		5622
Anaang	Nigeria	Anaang	246,000	Animism	<1%	1		2321
Anal in Manipur	India	Anal	7,000	Animism	<1%	1		2607
*Anatolian Turks-Istanbul	Turkey	Turkish	2,000,000	Islam	0%	5	82	5041
Andarum	Papua New Guinea	Andarum	700	Animism	<1%	1		5919
Andha in Andhra Pradesh	India	Andha	65,000	Animism	<1%	1		2608
Andi	USSR	Andi	9,000	Unknown	0%	1		5826
Andoque	Colombia	Andoque	100	Animism	<1%	1		2179
Anem	Papua New Guinea	Anem	1,000	Animism	<1%	1		5920
Anga in Bihar	India	Anga	424,000	Hinduism	<1%	1		2609
Angaataha	Papua New Guinea	Angaataha	800	Animism	<1%	1		5921
Angal Heneng, South	Papua New Guinea	Angal Heneng, South	15,000	Animism	<1%	1		5922
Angal Heneng, West	Papua New Guinea	Angal Heneng, West	25,000	Animism	<1%	1		5923
Angal, East	Papua New Guinea	Angal, East	10,000	Animism	<1%	1		5924
Angas	Nigeria	Angas	100,000	Animism	<1%	1		2322
Angaua	Papua New Guinea	Angaua	2,000	Animism	<1%	1		5925
Anggor	Papua New Guinea	Anggor	1,000	Animism	<1%	1		5926
Angoran	Papua New Guinea	Angoran	4,000	Animism	<1%	1		5927
Animere	Togo	Animere	300	Islam-Aninist	0%	1		5623

NAME	COUNTRY	LANGUAGE	GROUP SIZE	PRIMARY RELIGION	% CHR V	VOL UP ID
Ankave	Papua New Guinea	Ankave	2,000	Animism	0% 1	5928
Ankwe	Nigeria	Ankwai	10,000	Animism	1% 4	557
Anor	Papua New Guinea	Anor	600	Animism	1% 4	5929
Ansar Sudanese Refugees	Ethiopia	Arabic	11,000	Islam	1% 4 83	9010
Ansus	Indonesia	Ansus	3,000	Animism	1% 1	2864
Anuak	Ethiopia	Anuak	52,000	Animism	1% 5	516
Anuak	Sudan	Anuak	30,000	Animism	4% 5	584
Anuki	Papua New Guinea	Anuki	500	Animism	1% 1	5930
Anyanga	Togo	Anyanga	3,000	Islam-Animist	0% 1	5624
Apalai	Brazil	Apalai	100	Animism	1% 1	2145
**Apartment Residents-Seoul	Korea, Republic of	Korean	87,000	Folk Religion	11% 4	301
**Apatani in Assam	India	Apartani	11,000	Animism	1% 4	1026
**Apayao	Philippines	Ismeg	12,000	Christo-Paganism	9% 6	1201
Apinaye	Brazil	Apinaye	1,000	Animism	1% 1	2146
Apurina	Brazil	Apurina	1,200	Animism	1% 1	2147
Ara	Indonesia	Ara	75,000	Islam	1% 1	2865
Arab Immigrants in Bangui	Central African Republic	Arabic	5,000	Islam	0% 5 82	5045
Arab-Jabbari (Kamesh)	Iran	Arabic	13,000	Islam	0% 3	2044
Arab-Shaibani (Kamesh)	Iran	Arabic	16,000	Islam	0% 3	2045
Arabela	Peru	Arabela	200	Animism	1% 1	3166
**Arabs in New Orleans	United States of America	Arabic	1,000	Islam	nr% 5 82	5008
Arabs of Khuzestan	Iran	Arafundi	520,000	Islam	1% 4	2034
Arafundi	Papua New Guinea	Arafundi	1,000	Animism	0% 1	5931
Aranadan in Tamil Nadu	India	Aranadan	600	Hindu-Animist	1% 1	2610
Arandai	Indonesia	Arandai	2,000	Animism	1% 1	2866
Arapaco	Brazil	Tucanoan	300	Animism	1% 1	2148
Arapesh, Bumbita	Papua New Guinea	Arapesh, Bumbita	2,000	Animism	1% 1	5932
Arapesh, Mountain	Papua New Guinea	Arapesh, Mountain	5,000	Animism	1% 1	5933
Arapesh, Muhiang	Papua New Guinea	Arapesh, Muhiang	8,000	Animism	1% 1	5934
Arawa	Nigeria	Hausa	200,000	Islam	1% 4	644
Arawak	Guyana	Arawak	5,000	Christo-Paganism	1% 1	5116
Arawe	Papua New Guinea	Arawe	2,000	Animism	1% 1	5935
Arbore	Ethiopia	Arbore	2,00	Animism	1% 1	3191
Archin	USSR	Archin	900	Unknown	0% 1	5827
Arecuna	Venezuela	Arecuna	14,000	Animism	1% 1	5134
Argobba	Ethiopia	Argobba	3,000	Animism	1% 1	3192

NAME	COUNTRY	LANGUAGE	GROUP SIZE	PRIMARY RELIGION	% CHR	V	VOL UP ID
Arguni	Indonesia	Arguni	200	Animism	<1%	1	2867
Arifama-Miniafia	Papua New Guinea	Arifama-Miniafia	2,000	Animism	1%	1	5936
Arigibi	Papua New Guinea	Arigibi	300	Animism	0%	1	5937
Arinua	Papua New Guinea	Arinua	2,000	Animism	0%	1	5938
*Arnatas	India	Aranatan	700	Animism	<1%	4	2014
Arop	Papua New Guinea	Arop	2,000	Animism	<1%	1	5939
Aruop	Papua New Guinea	Aruop	500	Animism	0%	1	5940
Arusha	Tanzania	Arusha	110,000	Animism	8%	5	142
Arutani	Venezuela	Spanish	100	Animism	0%	1	5135
Arya in Andhra Pradesh	India	Arya	3,000	Hinduism	<1%	1	2611
Asaro	Papua New Guinea	Asaro	12,000	Animism	<1%	1	5941
Asat	Papua New Guinea	Asat	2,000	Animism	<1%	1	5942
*Asian Students	Philippines	English	2,000	Islam	2%	4	2101
Asienara	Indonesia	Asienara	700	Animism	<1%	1	2868
*Asmat	Indonesia	Asmat	30,000	Animism	7%	6 79	205
Assumbo	Cameroon	Assumbo	10,000	Animism	<1%	1	5209
Asu	Tanzania	Asu	110,000	Animism	0%	1	5533
Asuri in Bihar	India	Asuri	5,000	Animism	<1%	1	2613
Ata	Papua New Guinea	Ata	1,000	Animism	4%	4	5943
*Ata of Davao	Philippines	Manobo	10,000	Animism	<1%	1	627
Aten	Nigeria	Aten	4,000	Islam	<1%	1	2323
Ati	Philippines	Ati	2,000	Christo-Paganism	<1%	1	3243
Atoc	Sudan	Atoc	5,000	Islam	0%	1	5459
Atruahi	Brazil	Atruahi	500	Animism	<1%	1	2149
Atsi	China	Atsi	50,000	Traditional Chinese	<1%	1	2808
*Atta	Philippines	Atta	2,000	Animism	1%	5	634
Attie	Ivory Coast	Attie	160,000	Islam-Animist	<1%	1	2279
Atuot	Sudan	Atuot	8,000	Islam	0%	1	5441
*Atye	Ivory Coast	Atye	210,000	Animism	9%	4	4127
Au	Papua New Guinea	Au	4,000	Animism	<1%	1	5944
Au ei	Botswana	Au ei	5,000	Animism	0%	1	5173
Aunalei	Papua New Guinea	Aunalei	2,000	Animism	0%	1	5945
Auyana	Papua New Guinea	Auyana	7,000	Animism	0%	1	5946
Avatine	Ghana	Avatine	10,000	Islam-Animist	<1%	1	5321
Avikan	Ivory Coast	Avikan	8,000	Islam-Animist	<1%	1	2280
Avukaya	Sudan	Avukaya	5,000	Islam	0%	1	5442

NAME	COUNTRY	LANGUAGE	GROUP SIZE	PRIMARY RELIGION	% CHR	VOL V	UP ID
Awa	Papua New Guinea	Awa	2,000	Animism	<1%	1	5947
Awadhi	Nepal	Awadhi	317,000	Hindu-Buddhist	0%	1	6501
Awar	Papua New Guinea	Awar	600	Animism	<1%	1	5948
Awara	Papua New Guinea	Awara	900	Animism	<1%	1	5949
Awin	Papua New Guinea	Awin	7,000	Animism	<1%	1	5950
Aungi	Ethiopia	Aungi	50,000	Islam	<1%	1	3193
Awutu	Ghana	Awutu	85,000	Islam-Animist	0%	1	5322
Auyi	Indonesia	Auyi	400	Animism	<1%	1	2870
Auyu	Indonesia	Auyu	18,000	Animism	<1%	1	2871
Ayana	Kenya	Ayana	5,000	Islam-Animist	0%	3	4133
**Aymara	Bolivia	Aymara	850,000	Animism	7%	5	8
Aymara, Carangas	Chile	Aymara, Carangas	20,000	Christo-Paganism	0%	1	5113
Ayoreo	Paraguay	Ayoreo	700	Animism	<1%	1	5120
Ayu	Nigeria	Ayu	4,000	Islam	<1%	1	2324
Azera	Papua New Guinea	Azera	400	Animism	<1%	1	5951
**Azerbaijani	Afghanistan	Azerbaijani	5,000	Islam	<1%	1	2545
Azerbaijani Turks	Iran	Azerbaijani Turkish	6,000,000	Islam	0%	5 80	2026
***Azteca	Mexico	Nahuatl, Hidalgo	250,000	Christo-Paganism	2%	6 79	284
Baali	Zaire	Baali	38,000	Animism	0%	1	5688
Babajou	Cameroon	Babajou	500	Animism	0%	1	5210
Babri	India	Babri	10,000	Hinduism	0%	1	2624
**Babur Thali	Nigeria	Bura (Babur)	75,000	Animism	3%	6 80	1057
Baburiwa	Indonesia	Baburiwa	200	Animism	<1%	1	2872
Bachama	Nigeria	Bachama	20,000	Islam	<1%	1	2325
**Bachelors in Lagos	Nigeria	Tribal Languages	25,000	Secularism	nr%	6 82	5013
Bada	India	Bada	10,000	Animism	<1%	1	2326
Badagu in Nilgiri	India	Badagu	110,000	Animism	<1%	1	2614
Bade	Nigeria	Bade	100,000	Islam	<1%	1	2327
Badjao	Philippines	Badjao	4,900	Islam	0%	3	4832
Badui	Indonesia	Badui	5,000	Animism	%	4 84	4812
Badyara	Guinea-Bissau	Badyara	10,000	Islam	0%	1	5347
Bafut	Cameroon	Bafut	25,000	Animism	<1%	1	5211
Bagelkhandi in M.P.	India	Bagelkhandi	230,000	Hindu-Animist	<1%	1	2616
Baghati in H.P.	India	Baghati	4,000	Animism	<1%	1	2617
Bagirmi	Chad	Bagirmi	40,000	Islam-Animist	<1%	1	2209
***Bagobo	Philippines	Bagobo	35,000	Christo-Paganism	14%	5	4072

NAME	COUNTRY	LANGUAGE	GROUP SIZE	PRIMARY RELIGION	% CHR	V	VOL UP	ID
Bagri	Pakistan	Bagri	20,000	Hinduism	1%	4		268
Baguio Area Miners	Philippines	Ilocano	40,000	Nominal Christian	15%	5	81	7004
Bahais in Teheran	Iran	Farsi	45,000	Bahaism	0%	6	82	5037
Bahan	Indonesia	Bahan	500	Animism	<1%	1		2873
Baharlu (Kanesh)	Iran	Turkish	8,000	Islam	0%	3		2046
Bahawalpuri in M.P.	India	Bahawalpuri	600	Animism	<1%	1		2618
Bahinemo	Papua New Guinea	Bahinemo	300	Animism	<1%	1		5952
Bai	Sudan	Bai	3,000	Islam	0%	1		5443
Baibai	Papua New Guinea	Baibai	300	Animism	0%	1		5953
Baiga in Bihar	India	Baiga	11,000	Animism	<1%	1		2619
Baining	Papua New Guinea	Baining	5,000	Animism	<1%	1		5954
Bajania	Pakistan	Gujarati Dialect	20,000	Hinduism	1%	6	79	263
Baju, Indonesian	Indonesia	Bajau, Indonesian	50,000	Islam	1%	1		2874
Bajau, Land	Malaysia	Bajaus	90,000	Islam-Aninist	0%	2		4091
Baka	Cameroon	Baka	15,000	Animism	<1%	1		5212
Baka	Zaire	Baka	3,000	Animism	0%	1		5689
Bakairi	Brazil	Bakairi	300	Animism	<1%	1		2150
Bakhtiaris	Iran	Bakhtiaris	590,000	Islam	0%	5	80	2031
Bakongo Angolan Refugees	Zaire	Kikongo	600,000	Animism	n/r%	4	83	9026
**Bakuba	Zaire	Tshiluba	75,000	Animism	14%	5		1188
Bakwe	Ivory Coast	Bakwe	5,000	Islam-Aninist	<1%	1		2281
**Bakwele	Congo	Bakwele	8,000	Animism	0%	1		5291
Balangao	Philippines	Balangao	5,000	Christo-Paganism	3%	4		633
Balangaw	Philippines	Balangaw	5,000	Animism	<1%	3		3246
Balanta	Senegal	Balanta	50,000	Animism	0%	3		1142
Balanta Refugees	Senegal	Balanta	60,000	Animism	<1%	4		9030
Balantak	Indonesia	Balantak	125,000	Islam-Aninist	<1%	1		2875
Balante	Guinea-Bissau	Balanta	100,000	Islam-Aninist	7%	4		594
Bali	Nigeria	Bali	7,000	Islam-Aninist	<1%	1		2328
Bali-Vitu	Papua New Guinea	Bali-Vitu	7,000	Animism	<1%	1		5955
Balinese	Indonesia	Balinese	2,000,000	Hindu-Animism	1%	5		1094
Balkars	USSR	Balkar	60,000	Islam	0%	1		5813
Balmiki	Pakistan	Hindustani	20,000	Hinduism	1%	5		254
Balong	Cameroon	Duala	5,000	Animism	<1%	1		5213
**Balti	Pakistan	Balti	80,000	Islam	<1%	4		4802
Balti in Jammu	India	Balti	40,000	Animism	<1%	1		2620

NAME	COUNTRY	LANGUAGE	GROUP SIZE	PRIMARY RELIGION	% CHR	V	VOL UP	ID
Baluchi	Iran	Baluchi	1,100,000	Islam	0%	6	80	2030
Ban	Papua New Guinea	Ban	600	Animism	0%	1		5956
Bambara	Ivory Coast	Banbara	1,000,000	Islam-Animist	<1%	1		2282
	Mali	Banbara	1,000,000	Islam	<1%	5		604
Banbuka	Nigeria	Banbuka	10,000	Islam	<1%	1		2329
Banougoun-Bamenjou	Cameroon	Banougoun-Bamenjou	31,000	Animism	0%	1		5214
Banum	Cameroon	Banum	75,000	not reported	nr%	1		5215
**Banai	Bangladesh	Bengali	2,000	Buddhist-Animist	1%	4		63
***Banaro	Papua New Guinea	Banaro	3,000	Animism	5%	4		195
Bandawa-Minda	Nigeria	Bandawa-Minda	10,000	Islam	<1%	1		2330
Bandi	Liberia	Bandi	32,000	Animism	6%	4		555
Bandjoun	Cameroon	Bandjoun	60,000	Animism	0%	1		5216
Banen	Cameroon	Banen	28,000	Animism	0%	1		5217
Banga	Nigeria	Banga	8,000	Islam	<1%	1		2331
Bangangte	Cameroon	Local Dialects	475,000	Unknown	<1%	1		5218
Bangaru in Punjab	India	Bangri	4,000,000	Hindu-Animist	<1%	1		2621
Bangba	Zaire	Bangba	29,000	Animism	0%	1		5692
Banggai	Indonesia	Banggai	200,000	Islam	<1%	1		2876
Baniwa	Brazil	Baniwa	3,000	Animism	<1%	1		2151
Banoni	Papua New Guinea	Banoni	1,000	Animism	<1%	1		5957
Bantuanon	Philippines	Bantuanon	50,000	Christo-Paganism	<1%	1		3244
***Banyarwanda	Rwanda	Kinyarwanda	4,000,000	Animism	6%	5		4027
Banyun	Senegal	Banyun	9,000	Islam-Animist	0%	1		5421
Baule	Guinea-Bissau	Baule	15,000	Animism	6%	4		593
***Banyun	Ivory Coast	Banyun	1,200,000	Animism	9%	4		407
Barabaig	Tanzania	Tatoga	49,000	Animism	2%	5	79	573
Baral	Papua New Guinea	Baral	2,000	Animism	<1%	1		5958
Barambu	Sudan	Barambu	46,000	Islam	0%	1		5444
Barasano, Northern	Colombia	Barasano	400	Animism	<1%	1		2180
Barasano, Northern	Colombia	Barasano, Northern	450	Animism	3%	5		474
Barasano, Southern	Colombia	Janena	400	Animism	2%	4		289
Barau	Indonesia	Barau	300	Animism	<1%	1		2877
*Barbers in Tokyo	Japan	Japanese	220,000	Buddhism	1%	6	82	5009
Bare'e	Indonesia	Bare'e	325,000	Animism	<1%	1		2878
Bareli in Madhya Pradesh	India	Bareli	230,000	Hinduism	<1%	1		2622
Bari	Sudan	Bari	340,000	Islam	0%	1		5445

Index by Group Name

NAME	COUNTRY	LANGUAGE	GROUP SIZE	PRIMARY RELIGION	% CHR	V	VOL UP	ID
Bariai	Papua New Guinea	Bariai	3,000	Animism	<1%	1		5959
*Bariba	Benin	Bariba	400,000	Animism	4%	6	80	246
Bariba	Nigeria	Bariba	55,000	Islam-Animist	<1%	1		7041
Bariji	Papua New Guinea	Bariji	300	Animism	<1%	1		5960
Barin	Papua New Guinea	Barin	600	Animism	<1%	1		5961
Barok	Papua New Guinea	Barok	1,000	Animism	<1%	1		5962
Baruga	Papua New Guinea	Baruga	1,000	Animism	<1%	1		5963
Baruya	Papua New Guinea	Baruya	4,000	Animism	<1%	1		7063
Basaa	Cameroon	Basaa	170,000	Unknown	0%	1		5219
Basakomo	Nigeria	not reported	60,000	Animism	12%	4		550
Basari	Guinea	Basari	4,000	Animism	0%	1		5341
Basari	Senegal	Basari	8,000	Animism	0%	1		5422
	Togo	Basari	100,000	Animism	10%	5		599
Bashar	Nigeria	Bashar	20,000	Animism	<1%	1		2333
Bashgali	Afghanistan	Bashgali	10,000	Islam	<1%	1		2546
Bashkir	USSR	Tatar	1,200,000	Islam	0%	5	80	5625
Basila	Togo	Basila	5,000	Islam-Animist	0%	1		4001
Basketo	Ethiopia	Basketo	9,000	Animism	<1%	1		3194
***Basotho, Mountain	Lesotho	Southern Sesotho	70,000	Animism	8%	6	79	232
*Bassa	Liberia	Bassa	200,000	Animism	11%	5		366
**Bassa	Nigeria	Bassa	100,000	Animism	8%	5		1056
Bata	Indonesia	Bata	30,000	Islam-Animist	<1%	1		2334
*Batak, Angkola	Indonesia	Batak, Angkola	nr	Islam	6%	6	80	4002
Batak, Karo	Philippines	Batak, Karo	400,000	Animism	<1%	1		2879
Batak, Palawan	Philippines	Batak, Palawan	400	Christo-Paganism	<1%	1		3245
Batak, Simalungun	Indonesia	Batak, Simalungun	800,000	Animism	<1%	1		2880
Batak, Toba	Indonesia	Batak, Toba	1,600,000	Animism	<1%	1		2881
Batanga-Ngolo	Cameroon	Batanga-Ngolo	9,000	Animism	<1%	1		5220
**Batangeno	Philippines	Tagalog	nr	Nominal Christian	16%	4		4073
Bateg	Malaysia	Bateg	400	Animism	0%	2		4114
Bathudi in Bihar	India	Bathudi	74,000	Hinduism	<1%	1		2623
Batsi	USSR	Batsi	3,000	Unknown	0%	1		5828
Batu	Nigeria	Batu	25,000	Islam	<1%	1		2335
Bau	Papua New Guinea	Bau	3,000	Animism	<1%	1		5965
Baushi	Nigeria	Baushi	3,000	Islam	<1%	1		2336
Bauwaki	Papua New Guinea	Bauwaki	400	Animism	<1%	1		5966

NAME	COUNTRY	LANGUAGE	GROUP SIZE	PRIMARY RELIGION	% CHR	VOL V UP	ID
Bavenda	South Africa	Tschievenda	360,000	Animism	nr%	4	6564
Baum	Bangladesh	Baum	7,000	Islam	<1%	1	2561
Bauoyo	Zaire	Kiwoyo	10,000	Nominal Christian	20%	4	6571
Bayats	Iran		nr	Islam	<1%	3	2067
Bayot	Gambia	Bayot	4,000	Islam-Animist	<1%	1	2266
	Guinea-Bissau	Bayot	3,000	Islam-Animist	0%	1	5348
	Senegal	Bayot	4,000	Islam-Animist	0%	1	5423
Bazigar in Gujarat	India	Bazigar	100	Animism	<1%	1	2626
Bebeli	Papua New Guinea	Bebeli	600	Animism	<1%	1	5967
Bediya in Bihar	India	Bediya	32,000	Animism	<1%	1	2627
Bedoanas	Indonesia	Bedoanas	300	Animism	<1%	1	2882
Beja	Ethiopia	Beja	39,000	Islam	<1%	1	3195
	Sudan	Beja	91,000	Islam	0%	1	5446
Bekwarra	Nigeria	Bekwarra	34,000	Animism	<1%	1	2337
Bembe	Zaire	Bembe	50,000	Animism	0%	1	5693
Bembi	Papua New Guinea	Bembi	400	Animism	0%	1	5968
Bena	Tanzania	Bena	150,000	Animism	0%	1	5534
Benabena	Papua New Guinea	Benabena	14,000	Animism	<1%	1	5969
Bencho	Ethiopia	Bencho	5,000	Animism	<1%	1	3196
Bende	Tanzania	Bende	9,000	Animism	0%	1	5535
Bene	Cameroon	Bene	60,000	Animism	0%	1	5221
Benga	Gabon	Benga	nr	Animism	0%	1	5306
Bengali Refugees, Assam	India	Bengali	4,000,000	Islam	<1%	3	9054
**Bengali Sufis	Bangladesh	Bengali	70,000	Islam	0%	4 84	4820
**Bengali, Los Angeles area	United States of America	English	4,000	Islam	<1%	4 84	4818
Bengalis in London	United Kingdom	Bengali	15,000	Islam	0%	5 82	5038
Bengkulu	Indonesia	Bengkulu	25,000	Islam	0%	1	6563
Berba	Benin	Berba	44,000	Animism	0%	1	5165
Berik	Indonesia	Berik	800	Animism	<1%	1	2883
Berom	Nigeria	Berom	116,000	Animism	<1%	1	2338
Besisi	Malaysia	Besisi	7,000	Animism	0%	2	4109
Bete	India	Bete	3,000	Animism	<1%	1	7049
*Bete	Ivory Coast	Bete	300,000	Animism	<1%	5	4128
Bethen	Cameroon	Bethen	10,000	Animism	0%	1	5222
Betsinga	Cameroon	Betsinga	10,000	Animism	0%	1	5223
Bette-Bende	Nigeria	Bette-Bende	40,000	Animism	<1%	1	2339

NAME	COUNTRY	LANGUAGE	GROUP SIZE	PRIMARY RELIGION	% CHR	V	UP	VOL ID
Bhakta	India	Bhakta	55,000	Hindu-Animist	<1%	1		2615
Bharia in Madhya Pradesh	India	Bharia	5,000	Animism	<1%	1		2628
Bhatneri	India	Bhatneri	200	Islam	<1%	1		2629
Bhattri	India	Bhattri	100,000	Hindu-Animist	<1%	1		7047
**Bhil	Pakistan	Marwari	800,000	Hinduism	1%	6		35
**Bhilala	India	Bhilala	247,000	Hindu-Animist	<1%	1		7048
**Bhils	India	Dangi	800,000	Animism	1%	6	79	291
*Bhojpuri	Nepal	Bhojpuri	810,000	Hinduism	1%	4		670
Bhoyari in Maharashtra	India	Bhoyari	5,000	Hindu-Animist	<1%	1		2632
Bhuiya in Bihar	India	Bhuiya	5,000	Animism	<1%	1		2633
Bhumij in Assam	India	Bhumij	50,000	Hindu-Animist	<1%	1		2634
Bhunjia in Madhya Pradesh	India	Bhunjia	5,000	Hindu-Animist	<1%	1		2635
Bhutias	Bhutan	Sharchagpakha	780,000	Buddhism	1%	6		2022
Biafada	Guinea-Bissau	Biafada	15,000	Animism	6%	4		592
Biak	Indonesia	Biak	40,000	Animism	<1%	1		2884
Biaka	Papua New Guinea	Biaka	400	Animism	<1%	1		5970
Biangai	Papua New Guinea	Biangai	1,000	Animism	<1%	1		5971
Bibling	Papua New Guinea	Bibling	1,000	Animism	<1%	1		5972
**Bidayuh of Sarawak	Malaysia	Biatah	110,000	Christo-Paganism	<1%	5	81	2123
**Biduanda	Malaysia	Biduanda	4,000	Animism	0%	2		4098
**Bijogo	Guinea-Bissau	Bidyogo	25,000	Islam	8%	4		591
Bijori in Bihar	India	Bijori	2,000	Hindu-Animist	<1%	1		2638
Biksi	Indonesia	Biksi	200	Animism	<1%	1		2885
Bilala	Chad	Bilala	42,000	Islam-Animist	<1%	1		2210
**Bilan	Philippines	Bilaan	75,000	Animism	<1%	5		1025
Bile	Nigeria	Bile	1,000	Islam-Animist	<1%	1		2340
Bilen	Ethiopia	Bilen	32,600	Islam	<1%	1		3197
Biliau	Papua New Guinea	Biliau	600	Animism	<1%	1		5973
Bimanese	Indonesia	Bima	300,000	Islam	1%	5		1096
Binin	Papua New Guinea	Binin	400	Animism	<1%	1		5974
Bimoba	Ghana	Bimoba	50,000	Islam-Animist	<1%	1		5323
	Togo	Bimoba	70,000	Islam-Animist	<1%	1		5626
Binahari	Papua New Guinea	Binahari	800	Animism	<1%	1		5975
Binandere	Papua New Guinea	Binandere	3,000	Animism	<1%	1		5976
Binawa	Nigeria	Binawa	2,000	Islam	<1%	1		2341
Bine	Papua New Guinea	Bine	2,000	Animism	<1%	1		5977

NAME	COUNTRY	LANGUAGE	GROUP SIZE	PRIMARY RELIGION	% CHR	V	VOL	UP ID
Binga	Sudan	Binga	1,000	Islam	0%	1		5450
Bingkokak	Indonesia	Bingkokak	150,000	Islam	<1%	1		2886
Binjhwari in Bihar	India	Binjhwari	49,000	Hindu-Animist	<1%	1		2639
Binji	Zaire	Binji	64,000	Animism	0%	1		5694
Binumarien	Papua New Guinea	Binumarien	200	Animism	<1%	1		5978
****Bipim	Indonesia	Bipim	500	Christo-Paganism	5%	4		1119
Bira	Indonesia	Bira	75,000	Islam-Animist	<1%	1		2887
Birhor	India	Birhor	600	Hindu-Animist	<1%	1		2640
Birhor in Bihar	Ghana	Birifor	40,000	Animism	3%	5		1075
Birifor	Upper Volta	Birifor	50,000	Islam-Animist	<1%	3		5664
Bisa	Zambia	Bisa	83,000	Animism	0%	1		5789
Bisaya	Malaysia	Bisaya	3,000	Animism	nr%	6	81	7022
Bisis	Papua New Guinea	Bisis	400	Animism	0%	1		5979
Bitara	Papua New Guinea	Bitara	100	Animism	0%	1		5980
Bitare	Cameroon	Bitare	50,000	Animism	0%	1		5224
Bitare	Nigeria	Bitare	3,000	Islam-Animist	<1%	1		2342
Biti	Sudan	Biti	300	Islam	0%	1		5509
Biyom	Papua New Guinea	Biyom	400	Animism	0%	1		5981
**Black Caribs, Belize	Belize	Garifuna	10,000	Christo-Paganism	1%	6	79	252
**Black Caribs, Guatemala	Guatemala	Garifuna	2,000	Christo-Paganism	1%	5	84	251
*Black Caribs, Honduras	Honduras	Garifuna	80,000	Christo-Paganism	<1%	5	84	245
Blind, N.E. Thailand	Thailand	Northeast Thai	100,000	Buddhist-Animist	<1%	4	84	4810
Boanaki	Papua New Guinea	Boanaki	2,000	Animism	<1%	1		5982
Boat People	Japan	Vietnamese	1,800	Ancestor Worship	nr%	4		9036
Bobe	Cameroon	Bobe	600	Animism	0%	1		5225
Bobo Fing	Mali	Bobo Fing	3,000	Animism	<1%	1		5373
Bobo Wule	Mali	Bobo Wule	366,000	Animism	<1%	1		5374
**Bodo Kachari	India	Bodo	610,000	Hindu-Animist	2%	4		2007
Bodo in Assam	India	Bodo	510,000	Animism	2%	4		2641
Boghom	Nigeria	Boghom	1,000	Animism	<1%	1		2343
Bohutu	Papua New Guinea	Bohutu	1,000	Animism	<1%	1		5983
Boikin	Papua New Guinea	Boikin	31,000	Animism	<1%	1		5984
**Boko	Benin	Boko (Busa)	40,000	Animism	2%	4		444
Bokyi	Cameroon	Bokyi	43,000	Animism	<1%	1		5226
Bokyi	Nigeria	Bokyi	44,000	Animism	<1%	1		2344
Bola	Papua New Guinea	Bola	5,000	Animism	<1%	1		5985

Index by Group Name

NAME	COUNTRY	LANGUAGE	GROUP SIZE	PRIMARY RELIGION	% CHR	V	UP	VOL ID
Bole	Nigeria	Bole	32,000	Islam	<1%	1		2345
***Bolinao	Philippines	Bolinao	26,000	Nominal Christian	19%	4		4058
Bolon	Upper Volta	Bolon	4,000	Islam-Animist	<1%	1		5661
Bolondo	Zaire	Bolondo	1,000	Animism	0%	1		5696
Bom	Papua New Guinea	Bom	1,000	Animism	<1%	1		5986
Boma	Zaire	Boma	15,000	Animism	<1%	1		5697
Bomboko	Cameroon	Bomboko	3,000	Animism	<1%	1		5227
Bomou	Cameroon	Bomou	15,000	Islam-Animist	<1%	1		2211
Bondei	Tanzania	Bondei	30,000	Islam	0%	1		5536
Bondo in Orissa	India	Bondo	2,000	Hinduism	<1%	1		2642
Bonerif	Indonesia	Bonerif	100	Animism	<1%	1		2888
Bonggo	Indonesia	Bonggo	400	Animism	<1%	1		2889
Bongili	Congo	Bongili	4,000	Animism	<1%	1		5292
Bongo	Sudan	Bongo	2,000	Islam	0%	1		5451
Bongu	Papua New Guinea	Bongu	400	Animism	<1%	1		5987
Boni of Lamu	Kenya	Boni	2,500	Islam-Animist	nr%	4	84	4803
Bonkeng-Pendia	Cameroon	Bonkeng-Pendia	2,000	Animism	0%	1		5228
Bonkinan	Papua New Guinea	Bonkinan	2,300	Animism	<1%	1		5988
**Bontoc, Central	Philippines	Bontoc, Central	20,000	Islam	1%	5	81	632
**Bontoc, Southern	Philippines	Southern Bontoc	12,000	Christo-Paganism	4%	5		1060
Bor Gok	Sudan	Bor Gok	6,000	Islam	0%	1		5463
Bora	Colombia	Bora	400	Animism	<1%	1		2181
Borai	Indonesia	Borai	1,000	Animism	<1%	1		2890
Boran	Ethiopia	Boran	95,000	Islam-Animist	<1%	1		3198
**Boran	Kenya	Boran	37,000	Islam-Animist	3%	5		4077
Bororo	Brazil	Bororo	500	Animism	1%	1		441
Bosavi	Papua New Guinea	Bosavi	400	Animism	0%	1		5989
Bosilewa	Papua New Guinea	Bosilewa	400	Animism	<1%	1		5990
Bosngun	Papua New Guinea	Bosngun	700	Animism	<1%	1		5991
*Bosnian	Yugoslavia	Serbo-Croation	1,740,000	Islam	1%	6	80	4004
Bote-Majhi	Nepal	Bote-Majhi	6,000	Buddhist-Animist	0%	1		6502
Botlikh	USSR	Botlikh	4,000	Unknown	4%	1		5829
Bousansi	Upper Volta	Bisa	140,000	Islam-Animist	<1%	1		5660
Bovir-Ahmadi	Iran	Lori	110,000	Islam	0%	1		2040
Bouili	Togo	Bowili	3,000	Islam-Animist	0%	1		5627
Boya	Sudan	Boya	15,000	Animism	<1%	4		703

NAME	COUNTRY	LANGUAGE	GROUP SIZE	PRIMARY RELIGION	% CHR	V	UP	VOL ID
Bozo	Mali	Bozo	nr	Animism	0%	1		5375
Brahui	Pakistan	Brahui	745,000	Islam	<1%	5		4049
Braj in Uttar Pradesh	India	Braj	6,000,000	Animism	<1%	6		2643
Brao	Laos	Brao	18,000	Animism	<1%	6	79	108
Brat	Indonesia	Brat	20,000	Animism	<1%	1		2891
Breri	Papua New Guinea	Breri		Animism	0%	1		5992
Bruneis	Malaysia	Bruneis	25,000	Animism	0%	2		4092
Bua	Chad	Bua	20,000	Animism	0%	3		513
Bual	Indonesia	Bual	150,000	Islam	<1%	1		2892
Buang, Central	Papua New Guinea	Buang, Central	6,000	Animism	<1%	1		5993
Buang, Mangga	Papua New Guinea	Buang, Mangga	3,000	Animism	<1%	1		5994
Bube	Equatorial Guinea	Bube	20,000	Animism	0%	1		5303
Budibud	Papua New Guinea	Budibud		Animism	<1%	1		5995
Budug	USSR	Budug	2,000	Unknown	0%	1		5830
Budugum	Cameroon	Masa	10,000	Animism	<1%	4		506
Buduna	Nigeria	Buduna	80,000	Islam	<1%	1		2346
Bugis	Indonesia	Bugis	3,500,000	Islam-Animist	<1%	6	80	7
Buglere	Panama	Buglere	2,000	Christo-Paganism	<1%	1		5112
Bugombe	Zaire	Bugombe	12,000	Animism	0%	1		5699
Buhid	Philippines	Buhid	6,000	Christo-Paganism	<1%	1		3249
Builsa	Ghana	Buli	97,000	Animism	<1%	1		522
Buin	Papua New Guinea	Buin	9,000	Animism	<1%	4		5996
Buja	Zaire	Buja	200,000	Animism	0%	1		5700
Buka-khwe	Botswana	Bukaua	9,000	Animism	0%	1		5174
Bukaua	Papua New Guinea	Bukaua	5,000	Animism	0%	1		5997
**Bukidnon	Philippines	Manobo, Binukid	100,000	Animism	15%	5		1063
Buli	Indonesia	Buli	1	Islam-Animist	<1%	1		2893
Buli	Upper Volta	Buli	60,000	Islam-Animist	0%	1		5662
Bulia	Zaire	Bulia	45,000	Animism	0%	1		5701
Bullom, Northern	Sierra Leone	Bullom, Northern	167,000	Islam-Aninist	<1%	1		5428
Bullom, Southern	Sierra Leone	Bullom, Southern	40,000	Islam-Animist	<1%	1		5429
Bulu	Papua New Guinea	Bulu	200	Animism	0%	1		5998
Buna	Papua New Guinea	Buna	900	Animism	0%	1		5999
Bunabun	Papua New Guinea	Bunabun	500	Animism	0%	1		6000
Bunak	Indonesia	Bunak	50,000	Animism	<1%	1		2894
Bunana	Papua New Guinea	Bunana	5,000	Animism	<1%	1		6001

Index by Group Name

NAME	COUNTRY	LANGUAGE	GROUP SIZE	PRIMARY RELIGION	% CHR	V	VOL	UP ID
Bunann in Kashmir	India	Bunan	2,000	Animism	<1%	1		2644
Bungku	Indonesia	Bungku	180,000	Animism	<1%	1		2895
Bunu	Nigeria	Bunu	150,000	Animism	<1%	4		549
Bura	Cameroon	Bura	100,000	Animism	<1%	1		5229
Burak	Nigeria	Burak	2,000	Islam	<1%	1		2347
Buraka-Gbanziri	Congo	Buraka-Gbanziri	1,000	Animism	0%	1		5293
Buriat	China	Buriat	30,000	Traditional Chinese	<1%	1		2809
Buriat	USSR	Buriat	315,000	Buddhist-Animist	<1%	1		5831
Burig in Kashmir	China	Burig	148,000	Traditional Chinese	<1%	1		2810
Burig in Kashmir	India	Burig	132,000	Animism	<1%	1		2645
Burji	Ethiopia	Burji	20,000	Animism	<1%	1		3199
Burmese Muslin Refugees	Bangladesh	Bengali	200,000	Islam	0%	3	83	9001
Burum	Indonesia	Buru	6,000	Animism	<1%	1		2896
Burum	Papua New Guinea	Burum	3,000	Animism	<1%	1		6002
Burun	Sudan	Burun	5,000	Islam	0%	1		5452
Burundian Hutu Refugees	Tanzania	Kirundi	120,000	Animism	0%	4	83	9006
Burungi	Tanzania	Burungi	20,000	Animism	7%	4		493
**Bus Drivers, South Korea	Korea, Republic of	Korean	26,000	Unknown	8%	4		1195
**Bus Girls in Seoul	Korea, Republic of	Korean	50,000	Secularism	8%	6	82	5023
Busa	Nigeria	Busa (Bokobarn Akiba)	50,000	Islam	1%	6	80	1055
Busah	Papua New Guinea	Busah	200	Animism	1%	6		6003
Busani	Indonesia	Busani	400	Animism	<1%	1		2897
**Busanse	Ghana	Bisa (Busanga)	50,000	Animism	2%	5		1082
Bushmen (Heikum)	Namibia	Heikum	16,000	Animism	6%	4		563
*Bushmen (Hiechware)	Zimbabwe	Kwe-Etshari	2,000	Animism	6%	5		588
*Bushmen (Kung)	Namibia	Xu	10,000	Animism	6%	6	79	562
Bushmen in Botswana	Botswana	Buka-khwe	30,000	Animism	7%	4		509
Bushoong	Zaire	Bushoong	1	Animism	<1%	1		5702
Bussa	Ethiopia	Bussa	200,000	Animism	<1%	1		3200
Butawa	Nigeria	Buta	16,000	Islam-Animist	<1%	5		548
Butung	Indonesia	Butung	6,000	Animism	<1%	1		2898
**Bwid	Philippines	Buwid	200,000	Animism	8%	5	81	4161
Bviri	Sudan	Bviri	16,000	Islam	0%	1		5453
Bua	Upper Volta	Buamu (Bobo Wule)	140,000	Animism	9%	6	80	468
Bua	Zaire	Bua	35,000	Animism	<1%	6		5703
Buaidoga	Papua New Guinea	Buaidoga	5,000	Animism	<1%	1		6004

REGISTRY OF THE UNREACHED

NAME	COUNTRY	LANGUAGE	GROUP SIZE	PRIMARY RELIGION	% CHR	VOL V	UP ID
Buisi	Zaire	Buisi	6,000	Animism	0%	1	5704
Byangsi	Nepal	Byangsi	2,000	Buddhist-Animist	0%	1	6503
Cacua	Colombia	Cacua	200	Animism	<1%	1	2182
Caiwa	Brazil	Caiwa	7,000	Animism	<1%	1	2152
Cakchiquel, Central	Guatemala	Cakchiquel, Central	300,000	Animism	<1%	1	8003
Caluyanhon	Philippines	Caluyanhon	30,000	Christo-Paganism	<1%	1	3250
*Cambodians	Thailand	Northern Kaner	1,000,000	Buddhist-Animist	1%	5	606
Canpa	Peru	Canpa	5,000	Animism	<1%	1	2204
Cansa	Colombia	Cansa	2,000	Animism	<1%	1	2183
Candoshi	Peru	Candoshi	3,000	Animism	<1%	1	3167
Canela	Brazil	Canela	1,500	Animism	<1%	1	2153
Capanahua	Peru	Capanahua		Animism	<1%	1	2205
Cape Malays in Cape Town	South Africa	Afrikaans	150,000	Islam	7%	6	82	5006
Carapana	Colombia	Carapana	200	Animism	<1%	1	2184
*Caribs	Dominican Republic	English	2,500	Animism	nr%	4	84	4825
Cashibo	Peru	Cashibo	2,000	Animism	<1%	1	3168
*Casiguranin	Philippines	Casiguranin	10,000	Nominal Christian	17%	4	4055
*Casual Laborers-Atlanta	United States of America	English	3,000	Secularism	nr%	5	82	5048
Cayapa	Ecuador	Cayapa	3,000	Animism	<1%	1	3158
***Cebu, Middle-Class	Philippines	Cebuano	500,000	Christo-Paganism	12%	5	1079
*Central Thailand Farmers	Thailand	Thai	5,000,000	Buddhist-Animist	1%	5	81	645
Cewa	Zambia	Cewa	200,000	Animism	0%	1	5803
Ch'iang	China	Ch'iang	77,000	Traditional Chinese	<1%	1	2811
***Ch'ol Sabanilla	Mexico	Ch'ol	20,000	Christo-Paganism	5%	4	114
Ch'ol Tila	Mexico	Tila Chol	38,000	Animism	<1%	5	1216
Chacobo	Bolivia	Chacobo	300	Animism	<1%	1	2132
Chad's Refugees from N'Djanena	Cameroon	Tribal Languages	100,000	Islam	<1%	4	83	9005
Chadian Refugees	Nigeria	Arabic	3,000	Islam	<1%	4	83	9043
Chagga	Tanzania	Chagga	800,000	Animism	0%	4	5537
Chaghatai	Afghanistan	Chaghatai	300,000	Islam	<1%	1	2547
Chakfem-Mushere	Nigeria	Chakfem-Mushere	5,000	Animism	<1%	1	2348
*Chakmas of Mizoram	India	Chakma	20,000	Buddhist-Animist	<1%	5	81	2011
Chakossi in Ghana	Ghana	Chakossi	31,000	Animism	1%	5	524
Chakossi in Togo	Togo	Chakossi	20,000	Animism	3%	4	598
Chala	Ghana	Chala	1,000	Islam-Animist	0%	1	5324
Chan	Viet Nam	Chan	45,000	Hindu-Animist	1%	5	272

NAME	COUNTRY	LANGUAGE	GROUP SIZE	PRIMARY RELIGION	% CHR	VOL V UP	ID
					0% 6 83		91
*Chan Refugees from Kampuchea	Kampuchea, Democratic	Cham	20,000	Islam	0%	1	5121
Chanacoco, Bahia Negra	Paraguay	Chanacoco, Bahia Negra	1,000	Animism	<1%	1	5832
Chanalin	USSR	Chanalin	6,000	Unknown	0%	1	2647
Chanari in Madhya Pradesh	India	Chanari	5,000	Hindu-Animist	<1%	1	2349
Chamba Daka	Nigeria	Chamba Daka	66,000	Islam-Animist	<1%	1	2350
Chamba Leko	Nigeria	Chamba Leko	30,000	Islam-Animist	<1%	1	6005
Chambri	Papua New Guinea	Chambri	900	Animism	0%	1	2648
Chameali in H.P.	India	Chameali	53,000	Hindu-Animist	<1%	1	2186
Chani	Colombia	Chani	3,000	Animism	<1%	1	3169
Chanicuro	Peru	Chanicuro	200	Animism	<1%	1	1001
Chanorro	Pacific Trust Islands	Chamorro	15,000	Christo-Paganism	10%	4	162
Chanula	Mexico	Tzotzil (Chamula)	50,000	Christo-Paganism	10%	6 79	7011
*Chang-Pa of Kashmir	India	Tibetan Dialect	7,000	Buddhist-Animist	0%	5 81	3201
Chara	Ethiopia	Chara	6,000	Animism	<1%	1	8017
Chatino, Nopala	Mexico	Chatino, Nopala	8,000	Christo-Paganism	<1%	1	8018
Chatino, Panixtlahuaca	Mexico	Chatino, Panixtlahuaca	5,000	Christo-Paganism	0%	1	8019
Chatino, Tataltepec	Mexico	Chatino, Tataltepec	2,000	Christo-Paganism	<1%	1	8020
Chatino, Yaitepec	Mexico	Spanish	2,000	Christo-Paganism	<1%	1	8021
Chatino, Zacatepec	Mexico	Chatino, Zacatepec	500	Christo-Paganism	0%	1	8022
Chatino, Zenzontepec	Mexico	Chatino, Zenzontepec	4,000	Christo-Paganism	0%	1	6504
Chaudangsi	Nepal	Chaudangsi	2,000	Buddhist-Animist	<1%	1	2568
Chaungtha	Burma	Chaungtha	40,000	Buddhist-Animist	<1%	4	547
Chawai	Nigeria	Chawai	30,000	Animism	11%	4	84
**Chayahuita	Peru	Chayauita	6,000	Christo-Paganism	0%	1	6006
Chenapian	Papua New Guinea	Chenapian	200	Animism	<1%	1	2649
Chenchu in Andhra Pradesh	India	Chenchu	18,000	Hindu-Animist	<1%	1	6505
Chepang	Nepal	Chepang	10,000	Buddhist-Animist	0%	1	4814
*Cherkess	Jordan	Sharkas	60,000	Nominal Christian	nr%	4 84	5814
Cherkess	USSR	Cherkess	40,000	Islam	0%	1	2650
Chero in Bihar	India	Chero	28,000	Animism	<1%	1	5029
**Chicanos in Denver	United States of America	Spanish	121,000	Nominal Christian	nr%	5 82	5641
Chiga	Uganda	Chiga	272,000	Animism	0%	1	2651
Chik-Barik in Bihar	India	Chik-Barik	30,000	Animism	<1%	1	9031
*Chilean Refugees	Argentina	Spanish	1,850	Nominal Christian	nr%	4 83	9023
*Chilean Refugees, Toronto	Canada:Ontario	Spanish	10,000	Nominal Christian	nr%	4 83	2812
Chin	China	Chin	100,000	Traditional Chinese	<1%	1	

REGISTRY OF THE UNREACHED

NAME	COUNTRY	LANGUAGE	GROUP SIZE	PRIMARY RELIGION	% CHR	V	VOL	UP ID
Chin, Falam	Burma	Chin, Falam	92,000	Buddhist-Animist	<1%	2		2570
Chin, Haka	Burma	Chin, Haka	85,000	Buddhist-Animist	<1%	2		2571
Chin, Khumi	Burma	Chin, Khumi	30,000	Buddhist-Animist	nr%	2		2572
Chin, Ngawn	Burma	Chin, Ngawn	5,000	Buddhist-Animist	<1%	1		2573
Chin, Tiddin	Burma	Chin, Tiddin	38,000	Buddhist-Animist	<1%	1		2574
Chinanteco, Tepinapa	Mexico	Chinanteco, Tepinapa	3,000	Christo-Paganism	0%	1		8033
Chinanteco, Ayotzintepec	Mexico	Chinanteco, Ayotzintepec	2,000	Christo-Paganism	0%	1		8023
Chinanteco, Chiltepec	Mexico	Chinanteco, Chiltepec	3,000	Christo-Paganism	0%	1		8024
Chinanteco, Comaltepec	Mexico	Chinanteco, Comaltepec	2,000	Christo-Paganism	<1%	1		8025
Chinanteco, Lalana	Mexico	Chinanteco, Lalana	10,000	Christo-Paganism	<1%	1		8026
Chinanteco, Lealao	Mexico	Chinanteco, Lealao	5,000	Christo-Paganism	<1%	1		8027
Chinanteco, Ojitlan	Mexico	Chinanteco, Ojitlan	10,000	Christo-Paganism	<1%	1		8028
Chinanteco, Palantla	Mexico	Chinanteco, Palantla	11,000	Christo-Paganism	<1%	1		8029
Chinanteco, Quiotepec	Mexico	Chinanteco, Quiotepec	7,000	Christo-Paganism	<1%	1		8030
Chinanteco, Sochiapan	Mexico	Chinanteco, Sochiapan	2,000	Christo-Paganism	<1%	1		8031
Chinanteco, Tepetotutla	Mexico	Chinanteco, Tepetotutla	1,000	Christo-Paganism	<1%	1		8032
Chinanteco, Usila	Mexico	Chinanteco, Usila	21,000	Christo-Paganism	<1%	1		8034
**Chinbok	Burma	Chinbok	30,000	Buddhist-Animist	2%	1		2575
**Chinese	Mauritius	Hakka	10,000	Traditional Chinese	2%	2	84	4811
Chinese Businessmen	Hong Kong	Cantonese	500,000	Traditional Chinese	8%	5	81	2111
Chinese Factory Workers	Hong Kong	Cantonese	4,000	Traditional Chinese	2%	3		744
Chinese Fishermen	Malaysia	Hokkien	1,750,000	Traditional Chinese	0%	3		4142
**Chinese Hakka of Taiwan	Taiwan	Hakka	2,000,000	Traditional Chinese	1%	6	79	746
*Chinese Mainlanders	Taiwan	Mandarin	45,000	Traditional Chinese	8%	4		85
Chinese Muslims	Taiwan	Mandarin	100,000	Islam	<1%	5	81	7019
**Chinese Refugees in Macau	Macau	Cantonese	100,000	Traditional Chinese	1%	5	81	129
*Chinese Refugees, France	France	Mandarin	50,000	Traditional Chinese	1%	4	79	1226
*Chinese Restaurant Wrkrs.	France	Won Chow		Traditional Chinese	2%	4		1227
**Chinese Stud., Australia	Australia	Chinese Dialects	6,000	Secularism	2%	4		2119
**Chinese Students Glasgow	United Kingdom	Mandarin	1,000	Traditional Chinese	5%	4		2078
Chinese Students, Thunder Bay	Canada:Ontario	Mandarin	500	Secularism	15%	2		9113
Chinese Villagers	Hong Kong	Cantonese	500,000	Traditional Chinese	1%	3		742
*Chinese in Amsterdam	Netherlands	Cantonese	15,000	Unknown	1%	3		735
**Chinese in Australia	Australia	Cantonese	30,000	Traditional Chinese	8%	4		747
*Chinese in Austria	Austria	Mandarin	1,000	Traditional Chinese	5%	4		753
**Chinese in Boston	United States of America	Mandarin	20,000	Secularism	4%	6	82	5019

NAME	COUNTRY	LANGUAGE	GROUP SIZE	PRIMARY RELIGION	% CHR	VOL V	UP ID
**Chinese in Brazil	Brazil	Hakka	45,000	Traditional Chinese	8%	4	755
*Chinese in Burma	Burma	Mandarin and dialects	600,000	Traditional Chinese	2%	4	751
*Chinese in Costa Rica	Costa Rica	Cantonese	5,000	Unknown	1%	3	736
	Costa Rica	Mandarin	4,000	Unknown	1%	3	4141
*Chinese in Holland	Netherlands	Mandarin	35,000	Secularism	1%	3	734
*Chinese in Indonesia	Indonesia	Indonesian	3,600,000	Traditional Chinese	6%	4	733
*Chinese in Japan	Japan	Mandarin	50,000	Traditional Chinese	1%	4	738
*Chinese in Korea	Korea, Republic of	Mandarin	20,000	Secularism	5%	4	298
*Chinese in Laos	Laos	Mandarin	25,000	Secularism	1%	4	101
*Chinese in Malaysia	Malaysia	Chinese dialects	4,000,000	Traditional Chinese	8%	5	408
**Chinese in New Zealand	New Zealand	Cantonese	13,000	Traditional Chinese	4%	4	752
*Chinese in Panama	Panama	Spanish	25,000	Traditional Chinese	1%	3	4140
Chinese in Puerto Rico	Puerto Rico	Hakka	200	Traditional Chinese	0%	2	748
**Chinese in Sabah	Malaysia	Hakka	180,000	Traditional Chinese	10%	4	740
**Chinese in Sarawak	Malaysia	Mandarin and dialects	330,000	Traditional Chinese	7%	4	737
*Chinese in Saudi Arabia	Saudi Arabia	Arabic	20,000	Islam	0%	3	4135
*Chinese in South Africa	South Africa	Cantonese	9	Traditional Chinese	9%	4	756
*Chinese in Thailand	Thailand	Hakka	3,600,000	Traditional Chinese	2%	4	749
**Chinese in United Kingdom	United Kingdom	Mandarin	110,000	Traditional Chinese	3%	4	1225
*Chinese in United States	United States of America	Mandarin	550,000	Traditional Chinese	9%	4	750
*Chinese in West Germany	German Federal Rep.	Mandarin	5,000	Secularism	2%	4	1228
*Chinese of W. Malaysia	Malaysia	Cantonese	3,500,000	Traditional Chinese	4%	4	757
Chinese, Calgary	Canada:Alberta	English	30,000	Traditional Chinese	nr%	2	9171
Chinese, Halifax	Canada:Nova Scotia	Mandarin	3,000	Buddhism	0%	2	9120
Chinese, Metro Toronto	Canada:Ontario	English	40,000	Buddhism	nr%	2	9100
Chinese, Thunder Bay	Canada:Ontario	Various dialects	1,000	Buddhism	nr%	2	9109
**Chinese, Vancouver	Canada:British Columbia	Cantonese	80,000	Traditional Chinese	6%	4	758
Chinga	Cameroon	Chinga	13,000	Animism	0%	1	7050
Chingp'o	China	Chingp'o	100,000	Traditional Chinese	<1%	1	2813
Chip	Nigeria	Chip	6,000	Animism	<1%	1	2351
Chipaya	Bolivia	Chipaya	100	Animism	<1%	1	2133
Chiquitano	Bolivia	Chiquitano	20,000	Animism	<1%	1	2134
**Chiriguano	Argentina	Guarani (Bolivian)	23,000	Animism	8%	5	14
Chitralis	Pakistan	Khuwar	120,000	Islam	0%	6 79	1234
Chocho	Mexico	Spanish	3,000	Christo-Paganism	0%	1	8035
Chodhari in Gujarat	India	Chodhari	139,000	Hindu-Animist	<1%	1	2654

NAME	COUNTRY	LANGUAGE	GROUP SIZE	PRIMARY RELIGION	% CHR	V	VOL UP ID
Chokobo	Nigeria	Chokobo	400	Animism	<1%	1	2352
Chokue	Zambia	Chokwe	25,000	Animism	0%	2	5782
Chokwe (Lunda)	Angola	Chokwe	400,000	Animism	9%	5	149
Chola Naickans	India	Canarese	100	Animism	0%	3	124
Chopi	Mozambique	Chopi	400,000	Animism	<1%	1	5390
Chorote	Paraguay	Chorote	nr	Animism	<1%	1	5122
Chorti	Guatemala	Chorti	25,000	Animism	<1%	1	8004
**Chrau	Viet Nam	Jro	15,000	Animism	14%	4	394
Chuabo	Mozambique	Chuabo	259,000	Animism	9%	4	566
Chuang	China	Chuang	12,000,000	Animism	0%	5	7014
Chuave	Papua New Guinea	Chuave	20,000	Animism	<1%	2	6007
Chuj	Guatemala	Chuj	30,000	Animism	17%	2	8005
Chuj, San Mateo Ixtatan	Mexico	Chuj, San Mateo Ixtatan	3,000	Christo-Paganism	<1%	1	8036
Chukot	USSR	Chukot	14,000	Unknown	0%	1	5833
Chulupe	Paraguay	Chulupe	8,000	Christo-Paganism	<1%	1	5123
Chungchia	China	Chungchia	1,500,000	Traditional Chinese	<1%	1	2814
Churahi H.P.	India	Churahi	35,000	Hindu-Animist	<1%	1	2655
Chwang	China	Chwang	7,800,000	Traditional Chinese	<1%	1	2815
Cinta Larga	Brazil	Cinta Larga	500	Animism	<1%	1	2154
Circassian	Turkey	Circassian		Islam	<1%	1	2541
Circassians in Amman	Jordan	Arabic	17,000	Islam	0%	5	5018
Cirebon	Indonesia	Javanese, Tjirebon	2,500,000	Islam-Animist	<1%	5	1135
***Citak	Indonesia	Citak (Asmat)	18,000	Animism	<1%	5	1166
Cocama	Peru	Cocama		Animism	<1%	1	3170
Cocopa	Mexico	Cocopa	900	Christo-Paganism	0%	1	8037
Cofan	Colombia	Cofan	300	Animism	<1%	1	2188
Cogui	Colombia	Cogui	4,000	Animism	<1%	1	2189
*Coloureds in Eersterust	South Africa	Affikaans	20,000	Secularism	15%	6	5040
***Copacabana Apt. Dwellers	Brazil	Portuguese	400,000	Nominal Christian	11%	4	4116
Cora	Mexico	Cora	8,000	Christo-Paganism	<1%	1	8038
**Coreguaje	Colombia	Coreguaje	500	Animism	<1%	4	397
Cubeo	Colombia	Cubeo	2,000	Animism	<1%	1	2191
Cuiba	Colombia	Cuiba	2,000	Animism	<1%	1	2192
Cuicateco, Tepeuxila	Mexico	Cuicateco, Tepeuxila	10,000	Christo-Paganism	<1%	1	8039
Cuicateco, Teutila	Mexico	Cuicateco, Teutila	6,000	Christo-Paganism	<1%	1	8040
Cujareno	Peru	Cujareno	100	Animism	<1%	1	3171

374

Index by Group Name

NAME	COUNTRY	LANGUAGE	GROUP SIZE	PRIMARY RELIGION	% CHR	V	VOL UP	ID
Culina	Brazil	Culina	800	Animism	<1%			2155
*Cuna	Colombia	Cuna	600	Animism	7%	5	79	9
Curipaco	Colombia	Curipaco	3,000	Animism	<1%	1		2194
Cuyonon	Philippines	Cuyonon	49,000	Christo-Paganism	<1%	1		3251
Daba	Cameroon	Daba	31,000	Animism	<1%	1		7051
Dabra	Indonesia	Dabra	100	Animism	<1%	1		2900
Dadibi	Papua New Guinea	Dadibi	6,000	Animism	<1%	1		6008
Dadiya	Nigeria	Dadiya	2,000	Islam	<1%	1		2353
Daga	Papua New Guinea	Daga	6,000	Animism	<1%	1		6009
Dagada	Indonesia	Dagada	30,000	Animism	<1%	1		2901
Dagari	Ghana	Dagari	200,000	Animism	<1%	4		523
**Dagomba	Upper Volta	Dagbanli	150,000	Islam-Animist	<1%	4		5563
**Dagomba	Ghana	Dagbanli	350,000	Islam-Animist	1%	4		525
Dagur	China	Dagur	23,000	Traditional Chinese	<1%	1		2816
Dahating	Papua New Guinea	Dahating	900	Animism	<1%	1		6010
Dai	Burma	Dai	20,000	Buddhist-Animist	<1%	3		2576
Dair	Sudan	Dair	200	Islam	0%	1		5454
Daju of Dar Dadju	Chad	Daju of Dar Dadju	27,000	Islam-Animist	<1%	1		2213
Daju of Dar Fur	Sudan	Daju of Dar Fur	12,000	Animism	0%	1		5455
Daju of Dar Sila	Chad	Daju of Dar Sila	33,000	Islam-Animist	<1%	1		2214
Daju of West Kordofan	Sudan	Daju	6,000	Islam	0%	1		5456
*Daka	Nigeria	Dakanci	10,000	Animism	3%	4		546
Dani	Papua New Guinea	Dani	1,000	Animism	<1%	1		6011
***Dan	Ivory Coast	Dan	270,000	Animism	2%	5		4126
Dan	Liberia	Dan	94,000	Islam-Animist	<1%	1		5359
*Danchi Dwellers in Tokyo	Japan	Japanese	2,500,000	Secularism	2%	5	82	5005
Dangaleat	Chad	Dangaleat	20,000	Islam-Animist	<1%	1		2215
*Dani, Baliem	Indonesia	Dani, Grand Valley	50,000	Animism	3%	6	79	1219
Danu	Burma	Burmese	70,000	Buddhism	0%	2		4148
Daonda	Papua New Guinea	Daonda	100	Animism	0%	1		6012
Darai	Nepal	Darai	3,000	Buddhist-Animist	0%	1		6506
Dargin	USSR	Dargin	231,000	Islam	0%	1		5834
Darmiya	Nepal	Darmiya	2,000	Buddhist-Animist	0%	1		6507
Dass	Nigeria	Dass	9,000	Islam-Animist	<1%	1		2354
Dathanik	Ethiopia	Dathanik	18,000	Animism	<1%	1		3202
Davaweno	Philippines	Davaweno	13,000	Christo-Paganism	<1%	1		3252

NAME	COUNTRY	LANGUAGE	GROUP SIZE	PRIMARY RELIGION	% CHR	V	UP	ID
Dawawa	Papua New Guinea	Dawawa	2,000	Animism	<1%	1		6013
Dawoodi Muslims	India	Gujarati	225,000	Islam	0%	4		2004
Day	Central African Republic	Day	2,000	Animism	<1%	1		5180
Daza	Chad	Dazaga	159,000	Islam	0%	5		4044
Dead-End Kids - Amsterdam	Netherlands	Dutch	30,000	Secularism	0%	6	82	5034
Deccani Muslims	India	Dakhni (Urdu)	nr	Islam	<1%	6	82	4047
Deccani Muslims-Hyderabad	India	Dakhni	500,000	Islam	0%	1		5027
Dedua	Papua New Guinea	Dedua	4,000	Animism	0%	1		6014
Degema	Nigeria	Degene	10,000	Animism	<1%	1		2355
Degenan	Papua New Guinea	Degenan	500	Animism	<1%	1		6015
Dem	Indonesia	Den	2,000	Animism	<1%	1		2902
Denta	Indonesia	Denta	800	Animism	<1%	1		2903
Dendi	Benin	Dendi	40,000	Islam	0%	3		445
Dengese	Zaire	Dengese	4,000	Animism	0%	1		5705
Deno	Nigeria	Deno	10,000	Islam	<1%	1		2356
*Dentists, Fukuoka	Japan	Japanese	4,500	Secularism	nr%	4		4808
Deori in Assam	India	Deori	15,000	Animism	<1%	1		2656
Dera	Nigeria	Dera	20,000	Islam	<1%	1		2357
*Desano	Brazil	Desano	1,000	Animism	<1%	1		2156
*Deviant Youth in Taipei	Taiwan	Chinese, Min-Nan	80,000	Folk Religion	nr%	5	82	5044
*Dewein	Liberia	De	5,000	Islam	1%	4		690
*Dghwede	Cameroon	Dghwede	13,000	Animism	<1%	5		7052
*Dghwede	Nigeria	Zighvana (Dghwede)	13,000	Animism	1%	5		1179
Dhaiso	Tanzania	Dhaiso	12,000	Animism	<1%	1		5538
Dhanka in Gujarat	India	Dhanka	10,000	Animism	<1%	1		2657
Dharwar in Madhya Pradesh	India	Dharwar	21,000	Animism	<1%	1		2658
Dhimal	Nepal	Dhimal	8,000	Buddhist-Animist	0%	1		6508
**Dhodias	India	Dhodia Dialects	300,000	Hindu-Animist	1%	4		700
Dhurwa	India	Parji	20,000	Hindu-Animist	0%	4		4059
Dia	Papua New Guinea	Dia	2,000	Animism	<1%	1		6016
**Dida	Ivory Coast	Dida	120,000	African Independent	7%	4		4138
Didinga	Sudan	Didinga	30,000	Animism	<1%	4		583
Didoi	USSR	Didoi	7,000	Unknown	0%	1		5835
Digo	Kenya	Digo	168,000	Islam	<1%	4	84	4050
Digo	Tanzania	Digo	30,000	Animism	0%	1		5539
Dimasa in Cachar	India	Dimasa	38,000	Animism	<1%	1		2659

NAME	COUNTRY	LANGUAGE	GROUP SIZE	PRIMARY RELIGION	% CHR	V	UP ID	VOL
Dine	Ethiopia	Dine	2,000	Animism	<1%	1		3203
Dimir	Papua New Guinea	Dimir	1,000	Animism	<1%	1		6017
Dinka	Sudan	Dinka	1,940,000	Animism	4%	5		582
Dinka, Agar	Sudan	Dinka, Agar	16,000	Islam	0%	1		5458
Diodio	Papua New Guinea	Diodio	1,000	Animism	<1%	1		6018
Diola	Guinea-Bissau	Diola	15,000	Islam	3%	5	80	590
	Senegal	Diola	266,000	Islam-Animist	1%	5		434
Dirin	Nigeria	Dirin	11,000	Islam-Animist	<1%	1		2358
Dirya	Nigeria	Dirya	4,000	Islam	<1%	1		2359
Divehi	Maldives	Divehi	120,000	Islam	0%	6	80	4005
**Djandeau	Zaire	Tribal dialects	26,000	Animism	3%	4		6559
Djuka	Surinam	Djuka	20,000	Christo-Paganism	<1%	1		5129
Dobu	Papua New Guinea	Dobu	8,000	Animism	0%	1		6019
Doe	Tanzania	Doe	8,000	Animism	0%	6	81	5540
*Dog-Pa of Ladakh	India	Shrina	2,000	Animism	0%	1		7005
Doga	Papua New Guinea	Doga	200	Animism	<1%	1		6020
Doghosie	Upper Volta	Doghosie	8,000	Islam-Animist	0%	1		5665
*Dogon	Mali	Dogon	312,000	Animism	10%	6	79	150
Dogoro	Papua New Guinea	Dogoro	100	Animism	0%	1		6021
Dolgans	USSR	Dolgan	5,000	Unknown	0%	1		5816
Dom	Papua New Guinea	Dom	9,000	Animism	<1%	1		6022
Dompago	Benin	Dompago	19,500	Animism	7%	4		515
Donu	Papua New Guinea	Donu	500	Animism	<1%	1		6023
Donung	Papua New Guinea	Donung	900	Animism	<1%	1		6024
Dongjoi	Sudan	Dongjoi	9,000	Islam	0%	1		5465
Dongo	Zaire	Dongo	100	Islam	0%	1		5490
**Doohwaayo	Cameroon	Doohyaayo	5,000	Animism	0%	1		5706
Dorlin in Andhra Pradesh	India	Dorli	15,000	Animism	12%	5		5
Dorobo	Kenya	Nandi	24,000	Hindu-Animist	1%	5		2661
	Tanzania	Hadza	22,000	Animism	1%	5		151
Doromu	Papua New Guinea	Doromu	3,000	Animism	<1%	1		6025
Dorze	Ethiopia	Dorze	800	Animism	<1%	1		3204
Doura	Papua New Guinea	Doura	3,000	Animism	<1%	1		6026
*Drug Addicts in Sao Paulo	Brazil	Portuguese	200,000	Nominal Christian	nr%	5	82	5022
Druzes	Israel	Arabic	33,000	Folk Religion	0%	6	79	1230

REGISTRY OF THE UNREACHED

NAME	COUNTRY	LANGUAGE	GROUP SIZE	PRIMARY RELIGION	% CHR	V	VOL	UP ID
Duau	Papua New Guinea	Duau	7,000	Animism	<1%	1		6027
**Dubla	India	Gujarati	200,000	Hindu-Animist	4%	4		122
Dubu	Indonesia	Dubu	100	Animism	<1%	1		2904
Duguir	Nigeria	Duguri	12,000	Islam	<1%	1		2360
Duguza	Nigeria	Duguza	2,000	Islam	<1%	1		2361
**Duka	Nigeria	Dukanci	10,000	Animism	1%	5		1054
Dukue Refugee Camp Residents	Botswana	Tribal Languages	800	Animism	nr%	4	83	9022
Duna	Gabon	Duna	10,000	Animism	0%	1		5307
*Dumagat, Casiguran	Philippines	Dumagat	1,000	Animism	3%	6	81	2
Duna	Papua New Guinea	Duan	11,000	Animism	<1%	1		6028
Dungan	USSR	Dungan	39,000	Islam	0%	1		5836
Duru	Cameroon	Duru	20,000	Animism	6%	4		7040
Dusun	Malaysia	Kadazan	160,000	Animism	nr%	6	81	7023
Duvele	Indonesia	Duvele	500	Animism	<1%	1		2905
Dyan	Upper Volta	Dyan	8,000	Islam-Animist	<1%	1		5666
Dyerma	Niger	Dyerma	1,000,000	Islam-Animist	1%	6	80	4014
Dyola	Nigeria	Dyola	50,000	Islam	0%	1		2362
Dyola	Gambia	Dyola	216,000	Islam-Animist	<1%	1		2267
Ebira	Nigeria	Ebira	325,000	Islam-Animist	<1%	1		2363
Ebrie	Ivory Coast	Ebrie	50,000	Islam-Animist	<1%	1		2287
Edawapi	Papua New Guinea	Edawapi	4,000	Animism	0%	1		6029
Edo	Nigeria	Edo	430,000	Animism	<1%	1		2364
Efik	Nigeria	Efik	30,000	Animism	<1%	1		2365
Efutop	Nigeria	Efutop	10,000	Animism	<1%	1		2366
Eggon	Nigeria	Eggon	80,000	Animism	12%	5		146
Eivo	Papua New Guinea	Eivo	1,000	Animism	<1%	1		6030
Ejaghan	Nigeria	Ejaghan	100,000	Animism	<1%	1		2368
Ekagi	Indonesia	Ekagi	100,000	Animism	<1%	1		2906
Ekajuk	Nigeria	Ekajuk	15,000	Animism	<1%	1		2369
Eket	Nigeria	Eket	22,000	Animism	<1%	1		2370
Ekpeye	Nigeria	Ekpeye	30,000	Animism	<1%	1		2371
El Molo	Kenya	Samburu	1,000	Animism	3%	4		533
Eleme	Nigeria	Eleme	16,000	Animism	<1%	1		2372
Elkei	Papua New Guinea	Elkei	1,000	Animism	<1%	1		6031
Enai-Iuleha-Ora	Nigeria	Enai-Iuleha-Ora	48,000	Animism	<1%	1		2373
Embera, Northern	Colombia	Embera	2,000	Animism	<1%	1		2196

NAME	COUNTRY	LANGUAGE	GROUP SIZE	PRIMARY RELIGION	% CHR	V	VOL UP ID
Enerum	Papua New Guinea	Enerum	500	Animism	0%	1	6032
Emira	Papua New Guinea	Emira	4,000	Animism	<1%	1	6033
Emumu	Indonesia	Emumu	1,000	Animism	<1%	1	2907
Endangen	Papua New Guinea	Endangen	500	Animism	0%	1	6034
Enga	Papua New Guinea	Enga	110,000	Animism	<1%	1	6035
Engenni	Nigeria	Engenni	10,000	Animism	<1%	1	2374
*English speakers, Guadalajara	Mexico	English	25,000	Secularism	15%	3 84	4816
Enya	Zaire	Enya	7,000	Animism	0%	1	5707
Eotile	Ivory Coast	Eotile	4,000	Islam-Animist	<1%	1	2288
Epie	Nigeria	Epie	12,000	Islam-Animist	<1%	1	2375
**Equatorial Guin. Refugees	Gabon	Tribal Languages	60,000	Nominal Christian	nr%	4 83	9033
**Eritrean Refugees	Djibouti	Somali	25,000	Islam	<1%	4 83	9018
**Eritrean Refugees	Sudan	Galla	150,000	Islam	nr%	4 83	9007
Erokwanas	Indonesia	Erokwanas	300	Animism	<1%	1	2910
Esan	Nigeria	Esan	200,000	Animism	<1%	1	2376
**Ethiopian Refugees	Somalia	Oromo	700,000	Islam	<1%	4 83	9027
**Ethiopian Refugees, Yemen	Yemen, Arab Republic	Tigre	480	not reported	nr%	3	9040
Eton	Cameroon	Eton	112,000	Animism	0%	1	7053
Etulo	Nigeria	Etulo	3,000	Animism	<1%	1	2377
Evant	Nigeria	Evant	5,000	Animism	<1%	1	2378
Evenki	China	Evenki	7,000	Traditional Chinese	<1%	1	2817
Evenks	USSR	Evenk	25,000	Buddhist-Animist	0%	1	5837
Ewage-Notu	Papua New Guinea	Ewage-Notu	10,000	Animism	<1%	1	6036
Ewenkis	China	Altaic	10,000	Animism	0%	5 81	7020
**Ex-Mental Patients in NYC	United States of America	Spanish	20,000	Secularism	nr%	5 82	5007
Ex-Mental Patients, Hamilton	Canada:Ontario	English	800	Secularism	0%	2	9116
*Expatriates in Riyadh	Saudi Arabia	English	nr	Secularism	<1%	5 82	5024
Fa D'Ambu	Equatorial Guinea	Fa D'Ambu	2,000	Animism	0%	1	5304
*Factory Workers	Hong Kong	Cantonese	40,000	Unknown	5%	6	1010
Fagululu	Papua New Guinea	Fagululu	400	Animism	<1%	1	6037
Faiwol	Papua New Guinea	Faiwol	3,000	Animism	<1%	1	6038
**Fakai	Nigeria	Faka	15,000	Animism	1%	5	1053
**Falasha	Ethiopia	Agau	30,000	Judaism	7%	7 79	159
*Fali	Cameroon	Fali	50,000	Islam	<1%	1	7054
**Fali	Nigeria	Fali	25,000	Animism	2%	5	1052
Fas	Papua New Guinea	Fas	2,000	Animism	<1%	1	6039

REGISTRY OF THE UNREACHED

NAME	COUNTRY	LANGUAGE	GROUP SIZE	PRIMARY RELIGION	% CHR	V	VOL	UP ID
Fasu	Papua New Guinea	Fasu	900	Animism	<1%	1		6040
*Favelados-Rio de Janeiro	Brazil	Portuguese	600,000	Christo-Paganism	<1%	5	82	5043
Feroge	Sudan	Feroge	3,000	Islam	0%	1		5471
**Filipino Migrant Workers	Saudi Arabia	Tagalog	132,000	Nominal Christian	50%	4	84	4815
Finungwan	Papua New Guinea	Finungwan	400	Animism	0%	1		6041
Fipa	Tanzania	Fipa	78,000	Animism	0%	1		5541
Fishing Village People	Taiwan	Amoy	150,000	Traditional Chinese	2%	4		2107
Foau	Indonesia	Foau	200	Animism	<1%	1		2911
Foi	Papua New Guinea	Foi	3,000	Animism	<1%	1		6042
Foran	Papua New Guinea	Foran	800	Animism	<1%	1		6043
Fordat	Indonesia	Fordat	10,000	Animism	<1%	1		2912
Fore	Papua New Guinea	Fore	16,000	Animism	<1%	1		6044
Fra-Fra	Ghana	Fra-Fra	230,000	Animism	<1%	4		656
French, St. Pierre & Miquelon	Canada:Newfoundland	French	6,000	Nominal Christian	nr%	1		9159
Fula	Guinea	Fula	1,500,000	Islam	1%	5		406
	Sierra Leone	Fula	250,000	Islam	0%	5		4035
	Upper Volta	Fula	250,000	Islam-Animist	<1%	1		5667
Fula, Cunda	Gambia	Fula	70,000	Islam-Animist	<1%	1		2268
Fula, Macina	Mali	Fula, Macina	50,000	Animism	<1%	1		5376
Fula, Peuhala	Mali	Fula, Peuhala	450,000	Animism	0%	1		5377
Fulani	Upper Volta	Fulani	300,000	Islam	1%	4		140
*Fulani	Benin	Fulani	70,000	Islam-Animist	1%	4		446
*Fulbe	Cameroon	Fulani	250,000	Islam-Animist	1%	5	79	37
Fuliro	Zaire	Fuliro	6,000	Islam-Animist	0%	5		1081
Fulnio	Brazil	Fulnio	56,000	Animism	0%	1		5708
Fungom, Northern	Cameroon	Fungom, Northern	2,000	Animism	<1%	1		2157
Fungor	Sudan	Fungor	15,000	Animism	0%	1		7055
Fur Trappers	Canada:Ontario	French	5,000	Islam	0%	1		5472
Furu	Zaire	Furu	8,000	Secularism	0%	2		9115
Fuyuge	Papua New Guinea	Fuyuge	5,000	Animism	0%	1		5709
Fyan	Nigeria	Fyan	13,000	Animism	<1%	1		6045
Fyer	Nigeria	Fyer	14,000	Animism	<1%	1		2379
Ga-Dang	Philippines	Ga-Dang	3,000	Animism	<1%	1		2380
Gaanda	Nigeria	not reported	6,000	Animism	1%	5		631
	Nigeria		10,000	Nominal Christian	<1%	1		2381
*Gabbra	Ethiopia	Gabrinja	nr	Folk Religion	<1%	4		234

NAME	COUNTRY	LANGUAGE	GROUP SIZE	PRIMARY RELIGION	% CHR v	VOL UP ID
Gabbra	Kenya	Galla	12,000	Folk Religion	1% 4	715
Gabri	Chad	Gabri	20,000	Islam-Animist	<1% 1	2216
Gadaban in Andhra Pradesh	India	Gadaba	20,000	Hindu-Animist	<1% 1	2662
Gaddi in Hinachal Pradesh	India	Gaddi	70,000	Hindu-Animist	<1% 1	2663
Gade	Nigeria	Gade	25,000	Animism	1% 4	545
Gadsup	Papua New Guinea	Gadsup	7,000	Animism	<1% 1	6046
Gagauzes	USSR	Gagauz	157,000	Christo-Paganism	<1% 1	5838
**Gagre	Pakistan	Punjabi	40,000	Animism	1% 4	264
Gagu	Ivory Coast	Gagou	25,000	Animism	1% 4	480
Gahuku	Papua New Guinea	Gahuku	8,000	Animism	<1% 1	6047
Gaikundi	Papua New Guinea	Gaikundi	700	Animism	<1% 1	6048
Gaina	Papua New Guinea	Gaina	1,000	Animism	<1% 1	6049
Gal	Papua New Guinea	Gal	1,200	Animism	<1% 1	6050
Galambi	Nigeria	Galambi	1,000	Islam	<1% 1	2382
Galeshis	Iran	Galeshi	2,000	Islam	0% 3	2057
*Galla (Bale)	Ethiopia	Galla	750,000	Islam-Animist	7% 5	277
Galla of Bucho	Ethiopia	Gallinya (Oromo)	2,000	Christo-Paganism	<1% 3	404
Galla, Harar	Ethiopia	Gallinya	1,310,000	Islam	1% 5	367
Galler	Laos	Galler	50,000	Animism	1% 4	111
Galong in Assam	India	Galong	37,000	Hindu-Animist	<1% 1	2664
Ganbal	Chad	Ganbal	200,000	Islam-Animist	<1% 1	2217
Ganei	Papua New Guinea	Ganei	900	Animism	<1% 1	6051
Ganti in Gujarat	India	Ganti	140,000	Hindu-Animist	<1% 1	2665
Gane	Indonesia	Gane	4,000	Islam-Animist	<1% 1	5668
Gan	Upper Volta	Gan	2,000	Animism	<1% 1	2913
Gangam	Togo	Gangam	16,000	Islam-Animist	0% 1	5628
Ganglau	Papua New Guinea	Ganglau	200	Animism	<1% 1	6052
Gangte in Assam	India	Gangte	6,000	Hindu-Animist	<1% 1	2666
Garuh	Papua New Guinea	Garuh	2,000	Animism	<1% 1	6053
Garus	Papua New Guinea	Garus	2,000	Animism	<1% 1	6054
Garuwahi	Papua New Guinea	Garuwahi	200	Animism	<1% 1	6055
Gawar-Bati	Afghanistan	Gawar-Bati	8,000	Islam	<1% 1	2548
Gawari in Andhra Pradesh	India	Gawari	21,000	Hindu-Animist	<1% 1	2668
Gawuada	Ethiopia	Gawuada	4,000	Animism	<1% 1	3205
Gayo	Indonesia	Gayo	200,000	Islam-Animist	0% 4 80	1132
Gays in San Francisco	United States of America	English	150,000	Secularism	0% 6 82	5010

REGISTRY OF THE UNREACHED

NAME	COUNTRY	LANGUAGE	GROUP SIZE	PRIMARY RELIGION	% CHR	V	VOL UP ID
Gbande	Guinea	Bandi	66,000	Animism	3%	4	477
Gbari	Nigeria	Gbari	500,000	Animism	2%	6 80	158
Gbaya	Nigeria	Gbaya	350,000	Islam	<1%	1	2384
Gbaya-Ndogo	Sudan	Gbaya-Ndogo	2,000	Islam	<1%	1	5491
Gbazantche	Benin	Gbazantche	9,000	Islam	0%	3	447
Gberi	Sudan	Gberi	600	Islam	0%	1	5473
Gedaged	Papua New Guinea	Gedaged	3,000	Animism	0%	1	6056
Gedeo	Ethiopia	Gedeo	250,000	Animism	<1%	1	3206
Geishas in Osaka	Japan	Japanese		nr Secularism	<1%	5 82	5025
Geji	Nigeria	Geji	3,000	Islam	<1%	1	2385
Genagane	Papua New Guinea	Genagane	1,000	Animism	<1%	1	6057
Gende	Papua New Guinea	Gende	8,000	Animism	<1%	1	6058
Gera	Nigeria	Gera	13,000	Islam	<1%	1	2386
Geruma	Nigeria	Geruma	5,000	Islam	<1%	1	2387
Gesa	Indonesia	Gesa	200	Animism	<1%	1	2914
Ghale Gurung	Nepal	Ghale Gurung	10,000	Buddhist-Animist	0%	1	6509
Gheko	Burma	Gheko	4,000	Buddhist-Animist	<1%	1	2577
**Ghimeera	Ethiopia	Gimira	50,000	Animism	4%	5	364
Ghol	Sudan	Ghol	2,000	Islam	0%	1	5460
Ghotuo	Nigeria	Ghotuo	3,000	Animism	<1%	1	2388
Ghulfan	Sudan	Ghulfan	3,000	Islam	0%	1	5474
Gidar	Cameroon	Gidar	50,000	Animism	<1%	1	7056
Gidar	Chad	Gidar	50,000	Islam-Animist	<1%	1	2218
Gidicho	Ethiopia	Gidicho	500	Animism	<1%	1	3207
Gidra	Papua New Guinea	Gidra	2,000	Animism	0%	1	6059
Gilaki	Iran	Gilaki	1,950,000	Islam	1%	4	2027
Gilyak	USSR	Gilyak	4,000	Unknown	0%	1	5839
Gimi	Papua New Guinea	Gimi	18,000	Animism	<1%	1	6060
Ginuman	Papua New Guinea	Ginuman	800	Animism	<1%	1	6061
Gio	Liberia	Dan (Yacouba)	92,000	Animism	5%	5	190
Gira	Papua New Guinea	Gira	400	Animism	<1%	1	6062
Girawa	Papua New Guinea	Girawa	4,000	Animism	<1%	1	6063
Giri	Papua New Guinea	Giri	2,000	Animism	<1%	1	6064
Giryana	Kenya	Giryana	340,000	Animism	9%	4	534
Gisei	Cameroon	Masa	10,000	Animism	<1%	4	504
Gisiga	Cameroon	Gisiga	30,000	Animism	11%	4	503

NAME	COUNTRY	LANGUAGE	GROUP SIZE	PRIMARY RELIGION	% CHR	VOL V	UP ID
Gitua	Papua New Guinea	Gitua	500	Animism	<1%	1	6065
Gizra	Papua New Guinea	Gizra	600	Animism	0%	1	6066
**Glavda	Nigeria	Glavda	19,000	Animism	4%	5	1174
Gobasi	Papua New Guinea	Gobasi	1,000	Animism	0%	1	6067
Gobato	Ethiopia	Gobato	1,000	Animism	<1%	1	3208
Gobeze	Ethiopia	Gobeze	22,000	Animism	<1%	1	3209
***Godie	Ivory Coast	Godie	20,000	Animism	12%	4	308
Goemai	Nigeria	Goemai	80,000	Animism	<1%	1	2389
Gogo	Tanzania	Gogo	280,000	Animism	0%	1	5542
Gogodala	Papua New Guinea	Gogodala	10,000	Animism	<1%	1	6068
Gokana	Nigeria	Gokana	54,000	Animism	<1%	1	2390
Gola	Liberia	Gola	47,000	Islam-Animist	<1%	1	5360
	Sierra Leone	Mende	1,000	Islam-Animist	0%	1	5430
Golo	Chad	Golo	3,000	Islam-Animist	<1%	1	2219
*Gonds	India	Gondi	4,000,000	Animism	1%	5	641
Gonja	Ghana	Gonja	110,000	Islam	2%	5	1102
*Gorkha	India	Napali	180,000	Hinduism	0%	4	2009
Goroa	Tanzania	Goroa	180,000	Animism	0%	1	5543
Gorontalo	Indonesia	Gorontalo	500,000	Islam	0%	1	2915
Gosha	Kenya	Gosha	3,000	Islam-Animist	0%	3	4134
Goudari	Iran	Goudari	2,000	Islam	0%	3	2059
Gouin-Turka	Upper Volta	Gouin-Turka	25,000	Islam-Animist	0%	3	5669
Goulai	Chad	Goulai	30,000	Islam-Animist	<1%	1	2220
Gourency	Ivory Coast	Gourendi	300,000	Animism	5%	4	94
**Gouro	Cameroon	Gouro	200,000	Animism	4%	4	194
Gouvar	Cameroon	Gouvar	5,000	Animism	0%	1	7057
Government officials	Thailand	Thai	100,000	Buddhism	0%	3	59
Grasia in Gujarat	India	Grasia	27,000	Hindu-Animist	0%	1	2669
**Grebo	Liberia	Grebo Dialects	65,000	Animism	8%	4	689
Greeks, Toronto	Canada:Ontario	Greek	85,000	Nominal Christian	nr%	4	9150
Grunshi	Ghana	not reported	200,000	Animism	<1%	1	526
Gu	Benin	Gu	173,000	Animism	0%	1	5167
Guaiaqui	Paraguay	Guaiaqui		Animism	<1%	1	5124
Guajajara	Brazil	Guajajara	5,000	Animism	<1%	1	2158
Guajibo	Colombia	Guajibo	15,000	Animism	<1%	1	2197
*Guajiro	Colombia	Guajiro	60,000	Animism	12%	5	177

NAME	COUNTRY	LANGUAGE	GROUP SIZE	PRIMARY RELIGION	% CHR	V	VOL UP ID
Guambiano	Colombia	Guambiano	9,000	Animism	<1%	1	2199
Guana	Paraguay	Guana	3,000	Animism	0%	1	5125
*Guanano	Colombia	Guanano	800	Christo-Paganism	1%	4 79	442
***Guarani	Bolivia	Guarani	15,000	Animism	10%	6 79	206
Guarayu	Bolivia	Guarayu	5,000	Christo-Paganism	1%	5	605
Guarojio	Mexico	Guarojio	5,000	Christo-Paganism	<1%	1	8041
Guatemalan Refugees	Mexico	Spanish	70,000	Christo-Paganism	nr%	4	9057
Guayabero	Colombia	Guayabero	600	Animism	8%	5	1169
Gude	Cameroon	Gude	100,000	Animism	1%	4	502
Gudu	Nigeria	Gude	40,000	Animism	<1%	1	7042
Guduf	Nigeria	Guduf	1,000	Animism	<1%	1	2392
Guere	Ivory Coast	Guere	21,000	Animism	<1%	1	2393
Gugu-Yalanji	Australia	Gugu-Yalanji	120,000	Islam-Aninist	<1%	1	2289
Guhu-Samane	Papua New Guinea	Guhu-Samane	5,000	Animism	1%	4	430
Guinean Refugees	Gabon	Tribal Languages	4,000	Animism	nr%	3	9047
Gujarati	United Kingdom	Gujarati	1,200,000	Islam	<1%	1	6069
Gujars of Kashmir	India	Gujari	300,000	Hinduism	1%	6 81	1239
Gujuri	Afghanistan	Gujuri	150,000	Islam-Aninist	0%	5	7012
Gula	Chad	Gula	10,000	Islam	<1%	1	2549
Gulfe	Cameroon	Gulfe	3,000	Islam-Aninist	<1%	1	2221
Gumasi	Papua New Guinea	Gumasi	36,300	Animism	0%	1	7058
Gumine	Papua New Guinea	Gumine	30,000	Animism	<1%	1	6070
Gumuz	Ethiopia	Gumuz	53,000	Animism	<1%	1	6071
Gumuz	Sudan	Gumuz	40,000	Islam	<1%	1	3210
Gurage	Ethiopia	Gurage Dialects	750,000	Islam-Aninist	0%	1	5475
Gure-Kahugu	Nigeria	Gure-Kahugu	5,000	Islam	3%	6 80	274
Gurensi	Ghana	Gurenne	250,000	Animism	1%	4	2394
Gurma	Upper Volta	Gurma	250,000	Islam-Aninist	1%	1	527
Gurung	Nepal	Gurung	172,000	Hinduism	<1%	1	5670
Guruntum-Mbaaru	Nigeria	Guruntum-Mbaaru	10,000	Islam	0%	5	1208
Gusap	Papua New Guinea	Gusap	400	Animism	<1%	1	2395
Guwot	Papua New Guinea	Guwot	1,000	Islam-Aninism	<1%	1	6072
Gwa	Ivory Coast	Gwa	8,000	Animism	<1%	1	6073
Gwandara	Nigeria	Gwandara	25,000	Animism	<1%	5	2290
Gwari Matai	Nigeria	Gwari Matai	200,000	Islam	<1%	1	2397

NAME	COUNTRY	LANGUAGE	GROUP SIZE	PRIMARY RELIGION	% CHR	V	VOL	UP ID
Gwedena	Papua New Guinea	Gwedena	2,000	Animism	<1%	1		6074
Gwere	Uganda	Gwere	162,000	Animism	0%	1		5642
Gypsies	Brazil	Portuguese	10,000	Nominal Christian	nr%	3		4821
Gypsies	USSR	not reported	175,300	Christo-Paganism	0%	5		5810
Gypsies in Jerusalem	Israel	Romany Dialect		Islam	0%	1	82	5042
*Gypsies in Spain	Spain	Romany	200,300	Folk Religion	3%	6	79	393
Gypsies in Yugoslavia	Yugoslavia	Romany (Serbian Kaldnash)	800,000	Islam	17%	4		4038
Ha	Tanzania	Ha	286,000	Animism	0%	1		5544
Hadiyya	Ethiopia	Hadiyya	700,000	Animism	<1%	1		3211
**Hadrami	Yemen, Democratic	Arabic	151,000	Islam	0%	3		4065
Hahon	Papua New Guinea	Hahon	1,000	Animism	<1%	1		6075
Haitian Refugees	United States of America	Creole	40,000	Folk Religion	nr%	4	83	9044
Haitians, Montreal	Canada:Quebec	Creole	32,000	Folk Religion	nr%	2		9111
***Hajong	Bangladesh	Bengali	17,000	Hindu-Animist	1%	5		61
***Halam in Tripura	India	Tribal dialects	20,000	Animism	3%	5		4062
Halbi in Madhya Pradesh	India	Halbi	350,000	Hindu-Animist	<1%	1		2671
Halia	Papua New Guinea	Halia	13,000	Animism	<1%	1		6076
Hallam	Burma	Hallam	11,000	Buddhist-Animist	<1%	1		2578
Hantai	Papua New Guinea	Hantai	32,000	Animism	<1%	1		6077
Hangaza	Tanzania	Hangaza	54,000	Animism	0%	1		5545
Hani	China	Hani	138,000	Traditional Chinese	<1%	1		2818
Hanonoo	Philippines	Hanonoo	6,000	Christo-Paganism	<1%	1		3253
Harari	Ethiopia	Harari	13,000	Islam	<1%	1		3212
Harauti in Rajasthan	India	Harauti	334,000	Hindu-Animist	<1%	1		2673
Hatsa	Tanzania	Hatsa	2,000	Animism	0%	1		5546
*Havasupai	United States of America	English	2,300	Unknown	3%	4		4083
Havu	Zaire	Havu	262,000	Animism	0%	1		5710
Havunese	Indonesia	Havunese	40,000	Animism	<1%	1		2916
Haya	Tanzania	Haya	276,000	Animism	0%	1		5547
**Hazara in Kabul	Afghanistan	Hazaragi	300,000	Islam	0%	6	82	5021
Hehe	Tanzania	Hehe	192,000	Islam	0%	1		5548
Heiban	Sudan	Heiban	25,000	Islam	<1%	1		5476
Helong	Indonesia	Helong	5,000	Animism	<1%	1		2917
Herero	Botswana	Herero	10,000	Animism	<1%	1		5175
Herero	Namibia	Dhimba	40,000	Animism	<1%	1		5400
Heso	Zaire	Heso	6,000	Animism	0%	1		5767

NAME	COUNTRY	LANGUAGE	GROUP SIZE	PRIMARY RELIGION	% CHR	V	VOL	UP ID
**Hewa	Papua New Guinea	Hewa	2,000	Animism	5%	6	79	1238
Hezareh	Iran	Hezareh'i	nr	Islam	<1%	3		2068
**High School Students	Hong Kong	Cantonese	453,000	Traditional Chinese	7%	4		2113
***Higi	Nigeria	Higi	150,000	Animism	7%	5		1118
Hikkaryana	Brazil	Hikkaryana	200	Animism	<1%	1		2160
Hkun	Burma	Shan	20,000	Buddhism	0%	2		4144
****Hmong Refugee Women, Ban Vinai	Thailand	Miao	12,000	Buddhist-Animist	0%	4	83	9003
***Hmong Refugees	United States of America	Miao	35,000	Buddhist-Animist	<1%	4	83	9055
Hmong, Twin Cities	United States of America	Miao	11,000	Nominal Christian	nr%	4		9034
Ho in Bihar	India	Ho	750,000	Hindu-Animist	<1%	1		2674
Hohodene	Brazil	Hohodene	1,000	Animism	<1%	1		2161
Holiya in Madhya Pradesh	India	Holiya	3,000	Hindu-Animist	<1%	1		2675
Holoholo	Tanzania	Holoholo	5,000	Animism	0%	1		5549
Holu	Angola	Holu	12,000	Animism	0%	1		5149
Homosexuals, Toronto	Canada:Ontario	English	60,000	Secularism	nr%	1		9203
Hopi	United States of America	Hopi	6,000	Animism	4%	5		382
Hote	Papua New Guinea	Hote	3,000	Animism	<1%	1		6078
**Hotel Workers in Manila	Philippines	Pilipino	11,000	Nominal Christian	13%	5	81	7036
Hrangkhol	Burma	Hrangkhol	9,000	Buddhist-Animist	<1%	1		2579
Huachipaire	Peru	Huachipaire	200	Animism	<1%	1		3172
Huambisa	Peru	Huambisa	5,000	Animism	<1%	1		3173
Huasteco	Mexico	Huasteco	80,000	Christo-Paganism	<1%	1		8042
**Huave	Mexico	Huave	18,000	Christo-Paganism	5%	5		113
Hui	China	Hui-hui-yu	5,200,000	Islam	0%	6	80	4006
Huichol	Mexico	Huichol	8,000	Christo-Paganism	0%	6		8043
**Huila	Angola	Hula	200,000	Animism	1%	4		682
Huistan Tzotzil	Mexico	Tzotzil, Huistan	11,000	Christo-Paganism	5%	2		5104
Huitoto, Meneca	Colombia	Huitoto, Meneca	600	Animism	<1%	1		3142
Huitoto, Murui	Peru	Huitoto, Murui	800	Animism	<1%	1		3174
Hukwe	Angola	Hukwe	9,000	Animism	3%	4		511
Hula	Papua New Guinea	Hula	3,000	Animism	<1%	1		6079
Huli	Papua New Guinea	Huli	54,000	Animism	<1%	1		6080
Humene	Papua New Guinea	Humene	400	Animism	<1%	1		6081
Hunde	Zaire	Hunde	34,000	Animism	0%	1		5711
Hunjara	Papua New Guinea	Hunjara	4,000	Animism	<1%	1		6082
**Hunzakut	Pakistan	Burushaski	10,000	Islam	0%	6	79	1236

NAME	COUNTRY	LANGUAGE	GROUP SIZE	PRIMARY RELIGION	% CHR	VOL V	UP ID
Hupda Maku	Colombia	Hupda Maku	200	Animism	<1%	1	2202
Huana	Nigeria	Huana	20,000	Islam	<1%	1	7043
Huela-Numu	Ivory Coast	Huela-Numu	50,000	Islam-Aninist	<1%	1	2291
Hyam	Nigeria	Hyam	60,000	Islam	<1%	1	2398
Iatmul	Papua New Guinea	Iatmul	8,000	Animism	<1%	1	6083
Ibaji	Nigeria	Ibaji	20,000	Animism	<1%	4	544
**Iban	Malaysia	Iban	30,000	Animism	nr%	6 81	7024
Ibanag	Philippines	Ibanag	300	Animism	<1%	1	3254
*Ibataan	Philippines	Ibataan	500	Christo-Paganism	0%	4	4056
Ibibio	Nigeria	Ibibio	2,000,000	Animism	0%	1	2399
Ica	Colombia	Ica	3,000	Animism	2%	5	280
Icen	Nigeria	Icen	7,000	Islam-Aninist	<1%	1	2400
Idi	Papua New Guinea	Idi	900	Animism	0%	1	6084
Idoma	Nigeria	Idoma	300,000	Animism	<1%	1	2402
Idoma, North	Nigeria	Idoma, North	56,000	Animism	<1%	1	2403
*Ifugao (Kalangoya)	Philippines	Ifugao	95,000	Animism	6%	5	210
**Ifugao in Cababuyan	Philippines	Kalangoya	35,000	Animism	5%	4	697
Ifugao, Ambanad	Philippines	Ifugao Ambanad	4,000	Animism	14%	4	2104
Ifugao, Antipolo	Philippines	Ifugao:	15,000	Animism	<1%	1	3255
Ifugao, Kiangan	Philippines	Keley-i	5,000	Animism	6%	5	1047
Ifunu	Congo	Ifugao, Kiangan	25,000	Animism	<1%	1	3256
Igala	Nigeria	Ifunu	200	Animism	0%	1	5294
Igbirra	Nigeria	Igala	350,000	Animism	<1%	1	2404
Igede	Nigeria	Igbirra	400,000	Islam-Aninist	14%	6 80	543
Ignaciano	Bolivia	Igede	70,000	Animism	<1%	1	2405
Igora	Papua New Guinea	Ignaciano	5,000	Animism	<1%	1	2135
Igorot	Philippines	Igora	800	Animism	<1%	1	6085
Iha	Indonesia	Igorot	20,000	Animism	<1%	1	3247
Ihceve	Nigeria	Iha	6,000	Animism	<1%	1	2918
Ijo, Central-Western	Nigeria	Icheve	5,000	Animism	<1%	1	7044
Ijo, Northeast	Nigeria	Ijo	340,000	Animism	<1%	1	2406
Ijo, Northeast Central	Nigeria	Ijo	400,000	Animism	<1%	1	2407
**Ikalahan	Philippines	Ijo	8,000	Animism	<1%	1	2408
Ikizu	Tanzania	Ikalahan	40,000	Animism	6%	6	7037
Ikobi-Mena	Papua New Guinea	Swahili	9,000	Animism	0%	1	6086
Ikulu	Nigeria	Ikobi-Mena	6,000	Islam	<1%	1	2409
		Ikulu					

REGISTRY OF THE UNREACHED

NAME	COUNTRY	LANGUAGE	GROUP SIZE	PRIMARY RELIGION	% CHR	VOL	V	UP ID
Ikundun	Papua New Guinea	Ikundun	900	Animism	<1%	1		6087
Ikwere	Nigeria	Ikwere	200,000	Animism	<1%	1		7045
Ila	Zambia	Ila	39,000	Animism	0%	3		5783
Ilanun	Philippines	Ilanun	12,041	Islam	0%	3		4833
Ilongot	Philippines	Ilongot	8,000	Animism	<1%	1		3257
Inallu	Iran	Afshari	5,000	Islam	0%	3		2048
Inanwatan	Indonesia	Inanwatan	1,000	Animism	<1%	1		2920
**Indian Tamils - Colombo	Sri Lanka	Tamil	nr	Hindu-Animist	<1%	5	82	5004
*Indians in Rhodesia	Zimbabwe	Gujarati	10,000	Hinduism	9%	4		182
Indians in Dubai	United Arab Emirates	Malayalam	24,000	Hinduism	6%	5	82	5047
Indians in Fiji	Fiji	Hindustani	265,000	Hinduism	2%	6	79	131
Indians, CN Rail Lines	Canada:Ontario	English	20,000	Nominal Christian	nr%	1		9267
Indians, Cold Lake	Canada:Alberta	English	1,250	Nominal Christian	nr%	1		9266
**Indians, East Reserve	Trinidad and Tobago	English with Hindi	400,000	Hinduism	5%	6	79	1221
Indians, Eden Valley	Canada:Alberta	English	300	Nominal Christian	nr%	1		9258
Indians, Edmonton	Canada:Alberta	English	30,000	Folk Religion	nr%	1		9251
Indians, Interlake Region	Canada:Manitoba	English	10,000	Nominal Christian	nr%	1		9169
Indians, Kinistino Reserve	Canada:Saskatchewan	English	250	Animism	0%	1		9256
Indians, London	Canada:Ontario	English	8,000	Nominal Christian	5%	1		9264
Indians, Lower Mainland	Canada:British Columbia	English	2,500	Nominal Christian	nr%	1		9260
Indians, Northern Sask.	Canada:Saskatchewan	Various dialects	100,000	Nominal Christian	nr%	1		9254
Indians, Northwestern Ontario	Canada:Ontario	English	250,000	Nominal Christian	nr%	1		9261
Indians, Regina	Canada:Saskatchewan	English	33,000	Nominal Christian	nr%	1		9265
Indians, Saskatoon	Canada:Saskatchewan	English	10,000	Nominal Christian	nr%	1		9268
Indians, Thunder Bay	Canada:Ontario	English	10,000	Nominal Christian	nr%	1		9257
Indians, Vancouver	Canada:British Columbia	English	40,000	Nominal Christian	nr%	1		9262
Indians, White Bear Reserve	Canada:Saskatchewan	English	500	Nominal Christian	nr%	1		9259
**Indians, Winnipeg	Canada:Manitoba	Various dialects	70,000	Nominal Christian	nr%	1		9170
Indingosina	Papua New Guinea	Indinogosina	4,000	Animism	0%	3	84	6088
Indo-Canadians, Vancouver	Canada:British Columbia	Urdu	70,000	Sikhism	6%	4		9127
Indust.Workers Yongdungpo	Korea, Republic of	Korean	140,000	Folk Religion	0%	1		387
*Industrial Workers	Taiwan	Taiwanese (Hoklo)	500,000	Secularism	2%	5	81	4121
Inga	Colombia	Inga	6,000	Christo-Paganism	<1%	3		3143
Ingassana	Sudan	Tabi	35,000	Animism	0%	5		581

NAME	COUNTRY	LANGUAGE	GROUP SIZE	PRIMARY RELIGION	% CHR	V	UP	VOL ID
Inguhes	USSR	Ingush	158,000	Islam	0%	1		5840
*Inland Sea Island Peoples	Japan	Japanese	1,000,000	Traditional Japanese	1%	4		708
Insinai	Philippines	Insinai	10,000	Animism	<1%	1		3258
Intha	Burma	Intha	80,000	Buddhist-Animist	<1%	1		2580
Ipiko	Papua New Guinea	Ipiko	200	Animism	<1%	1		6089
Ipili	Papua New Guinea	Ipili	6,000	Animism	<1%	1		6090
Iquito	Peru	Spanish	200	Animism	<1%	1		3175
Irahutu	Indonesia	Irahutu	4,000	Animism	<1%	1		2921
**Iranian Bahai Refugees	Pakistan	Farsi	5,000	Bahai	<1%	4	83	9024
Iranians, Montreal	Canada:Quebec	Farsi	1,500	Islam	0%	1		9208
Iraqi Kurd Refugees	Iran	Kurmanji	300,000	Islam	<1%	4	83	9028
Iraqw	Tanzania	Iraqw	218,000	Animism	11%	4		492
Iravas in Kerala	India	Malayalam	3,700,000	Hinduism	1%	4		4068
Iraya	Philippines	Iraya	6,000	Christo-Paganism	<1%	1		3259
Iresim	Indonesia	Iresim	100	Animism	<1%	1		2922
Iria	Indonesia	Iria	900	Animism	<1%	1		2923
Irigwe	Nigeria	Irigwe	15,000	Animism	<1%	1		7046
***Irulas in Kerala	India	Irula	10,000	Hinduism	0%	4		2012
Irumu	Papua New Guinea	Irumu	2,000	Animism	<1%	1		6091
Isanzu	Tanzania	Isanzu	12,000	Animism	0%	1		5552
Isebe	Papua New Guinea	Isebe	800	Animism	<1%	1		6092
Isekiri	Nigeria	Isekiri	33,000	Animism	<1%	1		2412
**Ishans	Nigeria	Esan	25,000	Nominal Christian	16%	5		4033
Isneg, Dibagat-Kabugao	Philippines	Isneg, Dibagat-Kabugao	10,000	Animism	<1%	1		3260
Isneg, Karagawan	Philippines	Isneg, Karagawan	8,000	Animism	<1%	1		3261
Isoko	Nigeria	Isoko	20,000	Animism	<1%	1		2413
Itawit	Philippines	Itawit	15,000	Christo-Paganism	<1%	1		3262
Itelmen	USSR	Itelmen	1,100	Unknown	0%	1		5841
Itik	Indonesia	Itik	100	Animism	<1%	1		2924
Itneg, Adasen	Philippines	Itneg, Adasen	4,000	Christo-Paganism	<1%	1		3263
Itneg, Binongan	Philippines	Itneg, Binongan	7,000	Christo-Paganism	<1%	1		3264
Itneg, Masadiit	Philippines	Itneg, Masadiit	8,000	Christo-Paganism	<1%	1		3265
Itonama	Bolivia	Itonama	100	Animism	<1%	1		2136
Ivbie North-Okpela-Atte	Nigeria	Ivbie North-Okpela-Atte	20,000	Animism	<1%	1		2414
*Iwa	Zambia	Iwa	15,000	Animism	0%	1		5800
*Iwaidja	Australia	Iwaidja	150	Animism	7%	4		390
Iwal	Papua New Guinea	Iwal	2,000	Animism	<1%	1		6093

NAME	COUNTRY	LANGUAGE	GROUP SIZE	PRIMARY RELIGION	% CHR	V	UP ID
Iwan	Papua New Guinea	Iwan	2,000	Animism	<1%	1	6094
Iwan, Sepik	Papua New Guinea	Iwan, Sepik	4,000	Animism	<1%	1	6095
Iwur	Indonesia	Iwur	1,000	Animism	0%	1	2925
Ixil	Guatemala	Cuyolbal	45,000	Christo-Paganism	1%	4	646
Iyon	Cameroon	Iyon	4,000	Animism	0%	1	7059
	Nigeria	Iyon	2,000	Animism	<1%	1	2415
Izarek	Nigeria	Izarek	30,000	Animism	<1%	1	2416
Iznor	USSR	Iznor	1,000	Unknown	0%	1	5842
**Izi	Nigeria	Izi	200,000	Animism	11%	4	89
Jaba	Nigeria	Jaba	60,000	Animism	<1%	4	542
Jabem	Papua New Guinea	Jabem	3,000	Animism	<1%	1	6096
Jacalteco	Guatemala	Jacalteco	12,000	Animism	<1%	1	8006
Jagannathi in A.P.	India	Jagannathi	1,000	Hindu-Animist	<1%	1	2677
Jains	India	Hindi	2,000,000	Jain	1%	4	2005
Jana Mapun	Philippines	Cagayan	15,000	Islam-Animist	<1%	5 80	1149
**Jamaican Elite	Jamaica	Jamaican Patois	800,000	Secularism	0%	4	4117
Jananadi	Brazil	Jananadi	1,000	Animism	<1%	1	2162
Janbi	Indonesia	Indonesian	850,000	Islam-Animist	0%	3	4088
Janden	Indonesia	Janden	14,000	Animism	<1%	1	2926
Janshidis	Iran	Janshidi	1,000	Islam	<1%	3	2063
Jangali	Nepal	Jangali	9,000	Buddhist-Animist	0%	1	6510
Jangero	Ethiopia	Janjero	1,000	Animism	0%	1	3213
Janjo	Nigeria	Janjo	6,000	Animism	<1%	1	2417
**Japanese Students In USA	United States of America	Japanese	nr	Secularism	<1%	4	54
*Japanese in Brazil	Brazil	Japanese	750,000	Buddhism	8%	8 79	1
*Japanese in Korea	Korea, Republic of	Japanese	5,000	Traditional Japanese	1%	3	710
*Japanese, Toronto	Canada:Ontario	Japanese	20,000	Buddhism	nr%	1	9151
Jaqaru	Peru	Jaqaru	2,000	Animism	<1%	1	3176
Jara	Nigeria	Jara	40,000	Islam	<1%	1	2418
**Jarawa	Nigeria	Jaranchi	150,000	Animism	6%	5	541
Jatapu in Andhra Pradesh	India	Jatapu	36,000	Hindu-Animist	<1%	1	2678
Jati	Afghanistan	Jati	1,000	Islam	<1%	1	2550
Jaunsari in Uttar Pradesh	India	Jaunsari	60,000	Hindu-Animist	<1%	1	2679
**Javanese of Pejompongan	Indonesia	Bahasa Jawa	5,000	Islam	7%	4	319
Jebero	Peru	Spanish	3,000	Animism	<1%	1	3177
*Jeepney Drivers in Manila	Philippines	Pilipino	20,000	Nominal Christian	nr%	5 81	7018

NAME	COUNTRY	LANGUAGE	GROUP SIZE	PRIMARY RELIGION	% CHR	V UP	VOL ID
Jemez Pueblo	United States of America	Tewa (Jenez)	2,000	Christo-Paganism	5%	4	401
Jeng	Laos	Jeng	500	Animism	0%	4	110
Jera	Nigeria	Jera	23,000	Islam	<1%	1	2419
Jerawa	Nigeria	not reported	70,000	Animism	<1%	4	540
*Jewish Imgrnts.-American	Israel	Hebrew	30,000	Judaism	0%	3	327
*Jewish Imgrnts.-Argentine	Israel	Hebrew	20,000	Judaism	0%	3	323
*Jewish Imgrnts.-Australia	Israel	Hebrew	1,000	Judaism	0%	3	322
*Jewish Imgrnts.-Brazilian	Israel	Hebrew	4,000	Judaism	0%	3	325
*Jewish Imgrnts.-Mexican	Israel	Hebrew	1,000	Judaism	0%	3	326
*Jewish Imgrnts.-Uruguayan	Israel	Hebrew	3,000	Judaism	0%	3	324
*Jewish Immigrants, Other	Israel	Hebrew	6,000	Judaism	0%	3	321
***Jewish Refugees from USSR	Israel	Yiddish	170,000	Secularism	<1%	4	9013
Jews (Non-Sephardic), Montreal	Canada:Quebec	English	120,000	Judaism	1%	5	384
Jews (Sephardic), Montreal	Canada:Quebec	French	26,000	Judaism	1%	3	724
Jews in Venice	Italy	Italian	700	Judaism	0%	5	5046
Jews of Iran	Iran	Farsi	93,000	Judaism	1%	4	2042
Jews, Toronto	Canada:Ontario	English	120,000	Judaism	0%	2	9118
Jews, Vancouver	Canada:British Columbia	English	12,000	Judaism	0%	1	9108
Jews, Winnipeg	Canada:Manitoba	Yiddish	20,000	Judaism	0%	2	9121
Jharia in Orissa	India	Jharia	2,000	Hinduism	<1%	5	2680
*Jibu	Nigeria	Jibu, Jibanci	20,000	Animism	1%	5	1172
Jiji	Tanzania	Jiji	3,000	Animism	0%	1	5553
Jimajima	Papua New Guinea	Jimajima	500	Animism	<1%	1	6097
Jimbin	Nigeria	Jimbin	2,000	Islam	<1%	1	2420
**Jimini	Ivory Coast	Jimini	42,000	Islam	14%	5	4124
Jinja	Tanzania	Jinja	66,000	Animism	0%	1	5554
Jinuos	China	Tibeto-Burman	10,000	Animism	0%	5	7021
Jirel	Nepal	Jirel	3,000	Buddhist-Animist	0%	1	6511
Jita	Tanzania	Jita	71,000	Animism	0%	1	5555
**Jivaro (Achuara)	Venezuela	Jivaro	20,000	Christo-Paganism	6%	4	385
*Jiye	Sudan	Jiye (Karanojong)	7,000	Animism	0%	5	1129
Jiye	Uganda	Jiye	34,000	Animism	<1%	4	494
Jongor	Chad	Jongor	16,000	Islam-Animist	<1%	1	2223
Juang in Orissa	India	Juang	12,000	Hinduism	<1%	1	2681
Juhai	Malaysia	Juhai	400	Animism	0%	2	4112
Jukun	Nigeria	not reported	20,000	Animism	<1%	4	539

391

NAME	COUNTRY	LANGUAGE	GROUP SIZE	PRIMARY RELIGION	% CHR	V	VOL	UP ID
Jyarung	China	Jyarung	70,000	Traditional Chinese	<1%			2819
K'anjobal of Los Angeles	United States of America	K'anjobal	5,000	Christo-Paganism	5%	2		8500
**K'anjobal of San Miguel	Guatemala	K'anjobal	18,000	Ancestor Worship	10%	5		1207
Kaagan	Philippines	Kaagan	20,000	Christo-Paganism	<1%	1		3266
Kaalong	Cameroon	Kaalong	50,000	Animism	0%	1		7060
Kaba	Central African Republic	Kaba	11,000	Animism	0%	1		5181
Kaba Dunjo	Central African Republic	Kaba Dunjo	17,000	Animism	0%	1		5182
Kabadi	Papua New Guinea	Kabadi	2,000	Animism	<1%	1		6098
Kabixi	Brazil	Kabixi	100	Animism	<1%	1		2163
Kabre	Benin	Kabre	35,000	Animism	0%	1		5168
Kabre	Togo	Kabre	273,000	Animism	9%	5		192
Kabyle	Algeria	Kabyle	1,000,500	Islam	1%	6	79	145
Kachana	Ethiopia	Kachana		Animism	<1%	1		3214
Kachchi in Andhra Pradesh	India	Kachchi	471,000	Hinduism	<1%	1		2682
Kachin in Shan State	Burma	Burmese	80,000	Buddhism	0%	2		4154
Kadaklan-Barlig Bontoc	Philippines	Kadaklan-Barlig Bontoc	4,000	Animism	<1%	1		3248
Kadar in Andhra Pradesh	India	Kadar	800	Hindu-Animist	<1%	1		2683
Kadara	Nigeria	Kadara	40,000	Animism	<1%	2		538
Kadazans	Malaysia	Kadazans	110,000	Animism	9%	5		4095
Kadiweu	Brazil	Kadiweu	600	Animism	<1%	1		2164
Kadugli	Sudan	Kadugli	19,000	Islam	0%	1		5477
Kae Sung' Natives in Seoul	Korea, Republic of	Korean	20,000	Buddhism	1%	5	82	5015
Kaeti	Indonesia	Kaeti	4,000	Animism	<1%	1		2927
*Kaffa	Ethiopia	Kaffenya (Kefa)	320,000	Christo-Paganism	2%	6	80	363
**Kafirs	Pakistan	Kafiristani (Bashgali)	3,000	Animism	<1%	6	79	1233
Kagoma	Nigeria	Kagoma	6,000	Islam	<1%	1		2421
Kagoro	Mali	Logoro (Bambara)	30,000	Animism	4%	1		552
Kagulu	Tanzania	Kagulu	59,000	Animism	0%	1		5556
Kahluri in Andamans	India	Kahluri	66,000	Hindu-Animist	<1%	1		2684
Kaian	Papua New Guinea	Kaian	200	Animism	0%	1		6099
Kaibu	Nigeria	Kaibu	700	Islam	<1%	1		2422
Kaiep	Papua New Guinea	Kaiep	300	Animism	0%	1		6100
Kaikadi in Maharashtra	India	Kaikadi	12,000	Hindu-Animist	<1%	1		2685
Kaili	Indonesia	Kaili	300,000	Animism	<1%	1		2928
Kaingang	Brazil	Kaingang	7,000	Christo-Paganism	<1%	1		2165
Kairi	Papua New Guinea	Kairi	700	Animism	<1%	1		6101

NAME	LANGUAGE	COUNTRY	GROUP SIZE	PRIMARY RELIGION	% CHR	VOL V	UP	ID
Kairiru	Kairiru	Papua New Guinea	3,000	Animism	0%	1		6102
Kaiwai	Kaiwai	Indonesia	600	Animism	<1%	1		2929
Kajang	Kajang	Indonesia	50,000	Animism	<1%	1		2930
Kaka	Kaka	Cameroon	2,000	Animism	<1%	1		5241
	Kaka	Central African Republic	37,000	Animism	0%	1		5183
Kakoa	Kaka	Nigeria	2,000	Islam	<1%	1		2423
Kakuna-Manusi	Kakoa	Papua New Guinea	7,000	Animism	0%	1		6103
**Kalagan	Kakuna-Manusi	Papua New Guinea	3,000	Animism	<1%	1		6104
*Kalagan	Kalagan	Philippines	19,000	Animism	1%	5		630
Kalanga	Chikalanga	Botswana	150,000	Animism	1%	5		1163
Kalanga	Kalanga	Zimbabwe	87,000	Animism	2%	5		5410
Kalinga, Kalagua	Kalinga, Kalagua	Philippines	4,000	Animism	<1%	1		3268
Kalinga, Limus-Linan	Kalinga, Limus-Linan	Philippines	20,000	Animism	<1%	1		3269
Kalinga, Quinaang	Kalinga, Quinaang	Philippines	41,000	Animism	<1%	1		3267
*Kalinga, Southern	Kalinga, Sunadel-Tinglayan	Philippines	11,000	Animism	4%	5		1147
**Kalinga, Tanudan	Kalinga	Philippines	8,000	Nominal Christian	5%	4		4054
**Kalinga, Northern	Kalinga	Philippines	20,000	Christo-Paganism	3%	5	81	1146
Kalnytz	Kalnytz	China	70,000	Traditional Chinese	<1%	1		2820
	Kalnytz	USSR	137,700	Buddhism	0%	1		5844
Kalokalo	Kalokalo	Papua New Guinea	700	Animism	<1%	1		6105
Kan	Kan	China	830,000	Traditional Chinese	<1%	1		2821
Kamano	Kamano	Papua New Guinea	47,000	Animism	<1%	1		6106
Kamantan	Kadara	Nigeria	5,000	Animism	<1%	4		537
Kamar in Madhya Pradesh	Kamar	India	10,000	Hindu-Animist	<1%	1		2686
Kanayura	Kanayura	Brazil	100	Animism	<1%	1		2166
*Kanbari	Kambarci	Nigeria	100,000	Animism	6%	6	80	1173
Kambera	Kambera	Indonesia	200,000	Animism	<1%	1		2931
Kanberataro	Kamberataro	Papua New Guinea	1,000	Animism	<1%	1		2932
	Kamberataro	Papua New Guinea	700	Animism	<1%	1		6107
Kanbot	Kanbot	Papua New Guinea	4,000	Animism	<1%	1		6108
Kani	Kani	Tanzania	180,000	Animism	0%	1		5557
Kankam	Kankam	Cameroon	800	Animism	0%	1		5242
Kanrum	Kamrum	Papua New Guinea	400	Animism	<1%	1		6109
Kano	Kano	Nigeria	3,000	Islam	<1%	1		2424
Kanoro	Kanoro	Indonesia	8,000	Animism	<1%	1		2933
Kanpuchean Refugees	Khmer	Laos	10,400	Buddhist-Animist	0%	4		9049

REGISTRY OF THE UNREACHED

NAME	COUNTRY	LANGUAGE	GROUP SIZE	PRIMARY RELIGION	% CHR	V	UP	VOL ID
**Kampuchean Refugees, Ontario	Canada:Ontario	Khmer	600	Buddhist-Animist	0%	4	83	9046
Kampung Baru	Indonesia	Kampung Baru	400	Animism	<1%	1		2934
Kantuk-Gresi	Indonesia	Kantuk-Gresi	5,000	Animism	<1%	1		2935
*Kamuku	Nigeria	Kamuku	20,000	Animism	3%	6	80	536
Kana	Nigeria	Kana	90,000	Animism	<1%	1		2425
Kanauri in Uttar Pradesh	India	Kanauri	30,000	Hindu-Buddhist	<1%	1		2687
Kandas	Papua New Guinea	Kandas	500	Animism	<1%	1		6110
Kanembu	Chad	Kanembu	2,000	Islam-Animist	<1%	1		2224
Kanembu	Niger	Kanembu	2,000	Islam-Animist	<1%	1		5407
Kanga	Sudan	Kanga	6,000	Islam	0%	1		5479
Kanikkaran in Kerala	India	Kanikkaran	10,000	Hindu-Animist	<1%	1		2688
Kaningra	Papua New Guinea	Kaningra	300	Animism	<1%	1		6111
Kanite	Papua New Guinea	Kanite	16,000	Animism	<1%	1		6112
Kanjari in Andhra Pradesh	India	Kanjari	60,000	Hindu-Animist	<1%	1		2689
**Kankanay, Central	Philippines	Kankanay	40,000	Animism	2%	5		1200
Kankanay, Northern	Philippines	Northern Kankanay	40,000	Animism	2%	5		4057
Kanu	Zaire	Kanu	4,300	Animism	0%	1		5714
Kanum	Indonesia	Kanum	300	Animism	<1%	1		2936
Kanum	Papua New Guinea	Kanum	300	Animism	1%	6		6113
Kanuri	Nigeria	Kanuri Dialects	3,000,000	Islam	1%	6	80	4007
Kao	Ethiopia	Karo	600	Animism	<1%	1		3215
Kaonde	Zambia	Kaonde	20,000	Animism	<1%	1		5715
Kapin	Papua New Guinea	Kapin	116,000	Animism	<1%	1		5784
Kapore	Papua New Guinea	Kapore	2,600	Animism	<1%	1		6114
Kapori	Indonesia	Kapori	100	Animism	0%	1		6115
Kapriman	Papua New Guinea	Kapriman	1,000	Animism	<1%	1		2937
Kapuchin	USSR	Kapuchin	3,000	Unknown	<1%	1		5845
Kara	Papua New Guinea	Kara	2,000	Animism	<1%	1		6116
Kara	Tanzania	Kara	32,000	Animism	0%	1		5558
*Karaboro	Upper Volta	Karaboro	40,000	Animism	1%	4		4139
Karachay	USSR	Karachay-Balkan	173,000	Islam-Animist	0%	5		4042
Karagas	USSR	Karagas	600	Unknown	0%	1		5846
Karaim	USSR	Karaim	1,000	Unknown	0%	1		5847
Karakalpak	USSR	Karakalpak	277,000	Islam	0%	6	80	4011
Karam	Papua New Guinea	Karam	11,000	Animism	<1%	1		6118

Index by Group Name

NAME	COUNTRY	LANGUAGE	GROUP SIZE	PRIMARY RELIGION	% CHR	VOL V	UP ID
Karanga	Chad	Karanga	57,000	Islam-Animist	<1%	1	2225
Karangi	Papua New Guinea	Karangi	200	Animism	<1%	1	6119
Karas	Indonesia	Karas	200	Animism	<1%	1	2938
Karatin	USSR	Karatin	6,000	Unknown	0%	1	5849
**Karbis	India	Mikir	300,000	Hindu-Animist	5%	5	2120
Kare	Papua New Guinea	Kare		Animism	<1%	1	6120
Karekare	Nigeria	Karekare	39,000	Islam	<1%	1	2427
Karen, Pwo	Thailand	Sgaw Karen	80,000	Animism	1%	6	613
Karen, Pwo	Thailand	Pwo Karen	40,000	Animism	1%	5	30
Kari	Central African Republic	Kari	4,000	Animism	0%	1	5185
	Chad	Kari	40,000	Islam-Animist	<1%	1	2226
	Zaire	Kari	1,000	Animism	0%	1	5716
Karipuna Creole	Brazil	Karipuna Creole	500	Animism	<1%	1	2168
Karipuna Do Guapore	Brazil	Karipuna Do Guapore	200	Animism	<1%	1	2169
Kariya	Nigeria	Kariya	2,000	Islam	<1%	1	2428
Karkar	Papua New Guinea	Karkar	1,000	Animism	<1%	1	6121
Karko	Sudan	Karko	2,000	Islam	0%	1	5480
Karmali in Dihar	India	Karmali	70,000	Hindu-Animist	<1%	1	2690
Karon Dori	Indonesia	Karon Dori	5,000	Animism	<1%	1	2939
Karon Pantai	Indonesia	Karon Pantai	3,000	Animism	<1%	1	2940
Karre	Central African Republic	Karre	40,000	Animism	0%	1	5184
Karua	Papua New Guinea	Karua	900	Animism	<1%	1	6122
Kasanga	Guinea-Bissau	Kasanga	400	Islam-Animist	0%	1	5351
Kasele	Togo	Kasele	20,000	Islam-Animist	0%	1	5629
Kasem	Upper Volta	Kasem	28,000	Islam-Animist	0%	1	5671
**Kasena	Ghana	Kasem	70,000	Animism	11%	4	657
**Kashmiri Muslims	India	Kashmiri	3,100,000	Islam	1%	6	1231
Kasseng	Laos	Kasseng	15,000	Animism	0%	5	109
Kasua	Papua New Guinea	Kasua	1,000	Animism	<1%	1	6123
Kasuweri	Indonesia	Kasuweri	1,000	Animism	<1%	1	2941
Katab	Nigeria	Katab	30,000	Islam	<1%	1	2429
Katakari in Gujarat	India	Katakari	5,000	Hindu-Animist	<1%	1	2691
Katcha	Sudan	Katcha	6,000	Islam	0%	1	5481
Kate	Papua New Guinea	Kate	6,000	Islam	<1%	1	6124
Kati, Northern	Indonesia	Kati, Northern	8,000	Animism	<1%	1	2942
Kati, Southern	Indonesia	Kati, Southern	4,000	Animism	<1%	1	2943

395

NAME	COUNTRY	LANGUAGE	GROUP SIZE	PRIMARY RELIGION	% CHR	VOL V	UP ID
Katiati	Papua New Guinea	Katiati	2,000	Animism	<1%	1	6125
Katla	Sudan	Katla	9,000	Islam	0%	1	5482
Katukina, Panoan	Brazil	Katukina, Panoan	1,200	Animism	<1%	1	2170
Kaugat	Indonesia	Kaugat	1,000	Animism	<1%	1	2944
Kaugel	Papua New Guinea	Kaugel	35,000	Animism	<1%	1	6126
**Kaur	Indonesia	Kaur	50,000	Islam-Animist	0%	3	4084
Kaure	Indonesia	Kaure	800	Animism	<1%	1	2945
Kavwol	Indonesia	Kavwol	500	Animism	<1%	1	2946
Kavwol	Papua New Guinea	Kavwol	500	Animism	0%	1	6127
Kaw	Burma	Kaw	30,000	Animism	nr%	2	4152
Kawar in Madhya Pradesh	India	Kawar	34,000	Hindu-Animist	<1%	1	2692
Kawe	Indonesia	Kawe	300	Animism	<1%	1	2947
Kayabi	Brazil	Kayabi	300	Animism	8%	4	2171
Kayagar	Indonesia	Kayagar	9,000	Animism	0%	2	233
Kayan	Burma	Padaung	18,000	Animism	0%	3	4156
Kayan	Malaysia	Kayan	12,000	Animism	0%	4	4102
Kayapo	Brazil	Kayapo	600	Animism	0%	4	1158
Kaygir	Indonesia	Kaygir	4,000	Animism	<1%	1	2948
Kayupulau	Indonesia	Kayupulau	600	Animism	<1%	1	2949
Kazakhs	China	Kazakh	700,000	Islam-Animist	<1%	6 81	7013
Kazakhs	Iran	Kazakhi	3,000	Islam	0%	6 80	2055
Kebu	Togo	Kebu	20,000	Islam-Animist	0%	1	5630
Kebumtamp	Bhutan	Kebumtamp	400,000	Buddhist-Animist	0%	1	2566
Kedayanas	Malaysia	Kedayanas	25,000	Animism	0%	2	4094
Keer in Madhya Pradesh	India	Keer	3,000	Hindu-Animist	<1%	1	2693
Kei	Indonesia	Kei	30,000	Animism	<1%	1	2950
Keiga Jirru	Sudan	Keiga Jirru	1,000	Islam	0%	1	5483
**Kekchi	Guatemala	Kekchi	270,000	Christo-Paganism	3%	4	4034
Kela	Papua New Guinea	Kela	2,000	Animism	<1%	1	6128
Kelabit	Malaysia	Kelabit	17,000	Animism	nr%	6 81	7025
Kelah	India	Kelah	100,000	Animism	0%	1	5717
Kelao	China	Kelao	23,000	Traditional Chinese	<1%	1	2822
Kele	Gabon	Kele	13,000	Animism	<1%	1	5308
Kemak	Indonesia	Kemak	50,000	Animism	<1%	1	2951
Kembata	Ethiopia	Kembata	250,000	Animism	<1%	1	3216

NAME	COUNTRY	LANGUAGE	GROUP SIZE	PRIMARY RELIGION	% CHR	V	VOL UP	ID
Kemok	Malaysia	Kemok	400	Animism	0%	2		4115
Kenati	Papua New Guinea	Kenati	600	Animism	<1%	1		6129
Kendari	Indonesia	Kendari	500,000	Islam-Animist	1%	1		2952
Kenga	Chad	Kenga	25,000	Islam-Animist	<1%	1		2227
Kenyah	Indonesia	Kenyah	40,000	Animism	1%	1		2953
Keopara	Papua New Guinea	Keopara	20,000	Animism	1%	1		6130
*Kepas	Papua New Guinea	Kewa	5,000	Animism	1%	3		130
Kera	Cameroon	Kera	15,000	Animism	<1%	1		5243
	Chad	Kera	5,000	Islam-Animist	<1%	1		2228
Kerewe	Tanzania	Kikerewe	35,000	Animism	1%	4		243
Kerewo	Papua New Guinea	Kerewo	2,000	Animism	<1%	1		6131
Keriaka	Papua New Guinea	Keriaka	2,000	Animism	<1%	1		6132
Kerinchi	Indonesia	Kerinchi	170,000	Islam-Animist	<1%	1		2954
Ket	USSR	Ket	1,000	Unknown	0%	1		5850
Kewa, East	Papua New Guinea	Kewa, East	20,000	Animism	<1%	1		6133
Kewa, South	Papua New Guinea	Kewa, South	5,000	Animism	<1%	1		6134
Kewa, West	Papua New Guinea	Kewa, West	20,000	Animism	<1%	1		6135
Khakas	USSR	Khakas	67,000	Unknown	0%	1		5851
Khalaj	Iran	Khalaj	20,000	Islam	<1%	1		2535
Khalka	China	Khalka	68,000	Traditional Chinese	<1%	1		2823
Khan	China	Kham	11,000	Traditional Chinese	<1%	1		2824
	Nepal	Kham	40,000	Buddhist-Animist	0%	1		6512
Khanti in Assam	India	Khanti	300	Hindu-Buddhist	<1%	1		2694
*Khamu	Thailand	Khamu	6,000	Animism	0%	4		2087
Khana	Nigeria	Khana	90,000	Unknown	1%	5		1122
Khandesi	India	Khandesi	20,000	Hindu-Animist	1%	1		2695
Khanti	USSR	Khanti	21,000	Unknown	0%	1		5852
Kharia in Bihar	India	Kharia	90,000	Hindu-Animist	1%	1		2696
Khasi in Assam	India	Khasi	384,000	Hinduism	<1%	1		2697
Khasonke	Mali	Khasonke	71,000	Islam	<1%	1		5378
Khinalug	USSR	Khinalug	2,000	Unknown	0%	1		5853
Khirwar in Madhya Pradesh	India	Khirwar	34,000	Hindu-Animist	<1%	1		2698
**Khmer Refugees	Thailand	Canbodia	30,000	Buddhist-Animist	1%	4		2094
Khmer Refugees, Montreal	Canada:Quebec	Khmer	3,000	Buddhism	0%	2		9122
Khmer Refugees, Toronto	Canada:Ontario	Khmer	300	Buddhism	0%	2		9123
Khmer Refugees, Unaccd. Minors	Thailand	Khmer	3,000	Buddhist-Animist	0%	3	83	9050

REGISTRY OF THE UNREACHED

NAME	COUNTRY	LANGUAGE	GROUP SIZE	PRIMARY RELIGION	% CHR	V	VOL UP ID
Khmer, Ottawa	Canada:Ontario	French	400	Buddhism	0%	2	9124
Khojas, Agha Khani	India	Gujarati	175,000	Islam	0%	1	2006
Khowar	India	Khowar	7,000	Hindu-Animist	<1%	1	2699
Khvarshin	USSR	Khvarshin	2,000	Unknown	0%	1	5854
Kiari	Papua New Guinea	Kiari	1,000	Animism	<1%	1	6136
Kibet	Chad	Kibet	22,000	Islam-Animist	<1%	1	2229
Kibiri	Papua New Guinea	Kibiri	1,000	Animism	<1%	1	6137
Kichepo	Sudan	Kichepo	16,000	Animism	0%	3	704
Kikapoo	Mexico	Kikapoo	5,000	Christo-Paganism	<1%	1	8044
Kilba	Nigeria	Kilba	80,000	Islam	<1%	1	2430
Kilmera	Papua New Guinea	Kilmera	2,000	Animism	0%	1	6138
Kin	Central African Republic	Kin	5,000	Islam-Animist	0%	1	5186
Kinaghana	Chad	Kinaghana	5,000	Animism	<1%	1	2230
Kimbu	Indonesia	Kimbu	3,000	Animism	<1%	1	2955
*Kinyal	Tanzania	Kinyal	15,000	Animism	0%	4	5559
Kinalakna	Indonesia	Kinalakna	7,000	Animism	2%	4	228
Kinaray-A	Papua New Guinea	Kinaray-A	200	Animism	<1%	1	6139
Kinga	Philippines	Kinga	288,000	Christo-Paganism	<1%	1	3270
Kirghiz Afghan Refugees	Tanzania	Kirghiz	57,000	Animism	0%	4	5560
Kirgiz	Turkey	Kirghiz	1,300	Islam	<1%	4	83	9060
Kirgiz	Afghanistan	Kirgiz	45,000	Islam	<1%	5	2551
Kirgiz	China	Kirgiz	90,000	Islam	0%	5	4039
Kirifi	USSR	Kirgiz	1,700,000	Islam-Animist	0%	6	80	4016
Kiriwina	Nigeria	Krifi	14,000	Islam	<1%	1	2431
Kis	Papua New Guinea	Kiriwina	14,000	Animism	<1%	1	6140
Kisan in Bihar	Papua New Guinea	Kis	200	Animism	0%	1	6141
Kisankasa	India	Kisan	74,000	Hindu-Animist	<1%	1	2700
Kishanganjia in Bihar	Tanzania	Kisankasa	4,000	Animism	0%	1	5561
Kishtwari in Jammu	India	Kishanganjia	57,000	Hindu-Animist	<1%	1	2701
Kisi	India	Kishtwari	12,000	Hindu-Animist	<1%	1	2702
Kissi	Tanzania	Kisi	4,000	Animism	0%	1	5562
Kissi	Guinea	Kissi	266,000	Animism	2%	4	478
*Kissi	Liberia	Kissi	35,000	Animism	3%	4	691
Kita	Sierra Leone	Kissi, Southern	48,000	Animism	12%	4	271
Kiwai, Northeast	Mali	not reported	150,000	Islam	2%	3	553
	Papua New Guinea	Kiwai, Northeast	4,000	Animism	<1%	1	6142

398

NAME	COUNTRY	LANGUAGE	GROUP SIZE	PRIMARY RELIGION	% CHR	V	UP	VOL ID
Kiwai, Southern	Papua New Guinea	Kiwai, Southern	10,000	Animism	<1%	1		6143
Kiwai, Wabuda	Papua New Guinea	Kiwai, Wabuda	2,000	Animism	0%	1		6144
Klaoh	Liberia	Klaoh	81,000	Islam-Animist	<1%	6		5361
Koalib	Sudan	Koalib (Nuba)	320,000	Animism	6%	6	79	580
Kobiana	Guinea	Kobiana	300	Islam-Animist	0%	1		5352
Kobon	Papua New Guinea	Kobon	7,000	Animism	<1%	1		6145
**Koch	Bangladesh	Bengali	35,000	Hindu-Animist	1%	5		62
Koda in Bihar	India	Koda	14,000	Hindu-Animist	1%	1		2703
Kodi	Indonesia	Kodi	25,000	Animism	<1%	1		2956
Koenoem	Nigeria	Koenoem	3,000	Animism	<1%	1		2432
Kofyar	Nigeria	Kofyar	40,000	Animism	<1%	1		2433
**Kohli, Kutchi	Pakistan	Gujarati, Koli	50,000	Hinduism	4%	4		258
**Kohli, Parkari	Pakistan	Gujarati, Koli	100,000	Hinduism	5%	4		261
**Kohli, Tharadari	Pakistan	Gujarati, Koli	40,000	Hinduism	1%	5		259
**Kohli, Wadiara	Pakistan	Gujarati, Koli	40,000	Hindu-Animist	1%	5		260
Kohoroxitari	Brazil	Kohoroxitari	600	Animism	<1%	1		2172
Kohumono	Nigeria	Kohumono	12,000	Animism	<1%	1		2434
Koiari, Grass	Papua New Guinea	Koiari, Grass	2,000	Animism	<1%	1		6146
Koiari, Mountain	Papua New Guinea	Koiari, Mountain	2,000	Animism	<1%	1		6147
Koita	Papua New Guinea	Koita	2,000	Animism	<1%	1		6148
Kokant	Burma	Kokant	50,000	Buddhist-Animist	0%	2		4150
Koke	Chad	Koke	1,000	Islam-Animist	<1%	1		2231
Kol	Papua New Guinea	Kol	2,000	Animism	<1%	1		6149
Kol in Assan	India	Kol	80,000	Hindu-Animist	<1%	1		2704
**Kolam	India	Kolami	60,000	Hindu-Animist	1%	5		1040
Kolbila	Cameroon	Kolbila	1,000	Islam-Animist	1%	5		1155
Kole	Cameroon	Kole	300	Animism	0%	1		5244
Koliku	Papua New Guinea	Koliku	300	Animism	0%	1		6150
Kolom	Papua New Guinea	Kolom	100	Animism	0%	1		6151
Kom in Manipur	India	Kom	7,000	Hindu-Animist	<1%	1		2705
Kona	Cameroon	Kona	1,000	Animism	0%	5		5245
	Ghana	Koma	15,000	Animism	0%	1		1078
Koma, Central	Nigeria	Koma, Central	15,000	Animism	<1%	1		2435
Komba	Sudan	Komba	3,000	Islam	0%	1		5489
Komba	Papua New Guinea	Komba	10,000	Animism	<1%	1		6152
Kombio	Papua New Guinea	Kombio	2,000	Animism	0%	1		6153

REGISTRY OF THE UNREACHED

NAME	COUNTRY	LANGUAGE	GROUP SIZE	PRIMARY RELIGION	% CHR	V	VOL	UP ID
Komering	Indonesia	Komering	400,000	Islam-Animist	0%	3		4086
Komi-Permyat	USSR	Komi-Permyat	153,000	Christo-Paganism	<1%	1		5855
Komi-Zyrian	USSR	Komi-Zyrian	322,000	Christo-Paganism	<1%	1		5856
*Kono	Ethiopia	Kono	20,000	Animism	<1%	4		678
Komono	Upper Volta	Komono	6,000	Islam-Animist	0%	1		5672
Komutu	Papua New Guinea	Komutu	500	Animism	<1%	1		6154
Konaben	Cameroon	Konaben	3,000	Animism	0%	1		7061
***Kond	India	Kui	900,000	Animism	3%	5		294
Konda-Dora (Andra Pradesh)	India	Konda-Dora	16,000	Hindu-Animist	<1%	1		2706
Koneraw	Indonesia	Koneraw	300	Animism	<1%	1		2957
Kongo	Angola	Kongo	756,000	Unknown	0%	1		5150
Konkani in Gujarat	India	Konkani	1,523,000	Hindu-Animist	<1%	1		2707
Konkomba	Ghana	Konkomba	175,000	Animism	9%	5		528
*Konkomba	Togo	Kom Komba	25,000	Animism	1%	4		253
Kono	Nigeria	Kono	2,000	Islam	<1%	1		2436
**Kono	Sierra Leone	Kono	133,000	Animism	5%	5		203
Konomala	Papua New Guinea	Konomala	600	Animism	<1%	1		6155
Konongo	Tanzania	Konongo	20,000	Animism	0%	1		5563
Konso	Ethiopia	Konso	30,000	Animism	<1%	5		517
Konyagi	Guinea	Konyagi	85,000	Islam-Animist	0%	1		5342
Koraga in Kerala	India	Koraga	2,000	Hindu-Animist	<1%	1		2709
Korak	Papua New Guinea	Korak	200	Animism	<1%	1		6156
**Koranko	Sierra Leone	Kuranko (Maninka)	100,000	Islam-Animist	<1%	5		201
Korape	Papua New Guinea	Korape	4,000	Animism	<1%	1		6157
Korapun	Indonesia	Korapun	4,000	Animism	<1%	1		2958
Koreans	Canada	Korean	40,000	Buddhism	nr%	1		9167
***Koreans in Germany	German Federal Rep.	Korean	10,000	Unknown	4%	4		686
Koreans in Manchuria	China	Korean	3,000,000	Secularism	nr%	5	81	7007
*Koreans of Japan	Japan	Korean	600,000	Folk Religion	6%	5		57
Korku in Madhya Pradesh	India	Korku	250,000	Animism	1%	5		198
Koro	Nigeria	Koro	35,000	Animism	1%	5		572
Koroma	Sudan	Koroma	30,000	Animism	0%	3		706
Korop	Cameroon	Korop	10,000	Animism	0%	1		5247
Korop	Nigeria	Korop	10,000	Animism	<1%	1		2710
Korwa in Bihar	India	Korwa	10,000	Hindu-Animist	<1%	1		2437
Koryak	USSR	Koryak	8,000	Unknown	0%	1		5857

NAME	COUNTRY	LANGUAGE	GROUP SIZE	PRIMARY RELIGION	% CHR	V	UP ID
Kosorong	Papua New Guinea	Kosorong	1,000	Animism	<1%	1	6158
Kota	Gabon	Kota	nr	Animism	<1%	1	5309
Kota in Tamil Nadu	India	Kota	900	Hindu-Animist	<1%	1	2711
Kotia in Andhra Pradesh	India	Kotia	15,000	Hindu-Animist	<1%	1	2768
Kotogut	Indonesia	Kotogut	1,000	Animism	<1%	1	2959
Kotoko	Cameroon	Kotoko	31,000	Animism	0%	1	5248
	Chad	Kotoko	31,000	Islam-Animist	<1%	1	2232
Kotokoli	Benin	Kotokoli	75,000	Islam	0%	3	448
	Togo	Kotokoli	150,000	Islam-Animist	0%	4	5631
Kotopo	Cameroon	Kotopo	10,000	Animism	0%	4	501
Kotta	India	Kota	1,000	Animism	0%	5	1098
Kouya	Ivory Coast	Kouya	6,000	Islam-Animist	<1%	1	2292
Kovai	Papua New Guinea	Kovai	3,000	Animism	0%	1	6159
Kove	Papua New Guinea	Kove	3,000	Animism	0%	1	6160
**Kowaao	Liberia	Kowaao	7,000	Animism	3%	4	692
Koya in Andhra Pradesh	India	Koya	212,000	Hindu-Animist	<1%	1	2712
Kpa	Ethiopia	Koyra	5,000	Animism	<1%	1	3217
Kpelle	Cameroon	Kpa	17,000	Animism	0%	1	5249
	Guinea	Kpelle	250,000	Islam-Animist	<1%	1	5343
	Liberia	Kpelle	200,000	Animism	6%	5	556
Kposo	Togo	Kposo	45,000	Islam-Animist	0%	1	5632
*Krachi	Ghana	Krachi	22,000	Islam-Animist	0%	1	5325
***Krahn	Ivory Coast	Guere	250,000	Islam-Animist	3%	4	687
	Liberia	Krahn	55,000	Animism	7%	4	83
Kreen-Akakore	Brazil	Kreen-Akakore	100	Animism	<1%	1	2173
Krin	Sierra Leone	Mende	3,000	Islam-Animist	0%	1	5432
Krio	Gambia	Krio	3,000	Islam-Animist	<1%	1	2269
Krisa	Papua New Guinea	Krisa	500	Animism	0%	1	6161
Krobou	Ivory Coast	Krobou	3,000	Islam-Animist	<1%	1	2293
Krongo	Sudan	Krongo	121,000	Animism	1%	4	579
Krumen	Ivory Coast	Krumen	17,000	Animism	2%	4	4137
Kryz	USSR	Kryz	6,000	Unknown	0%	1	5858
Kuatinena	Brazil	Asurini	100	Animism	0%	5	1159
Kube	Papua New Guinea	Kube	4,000	Animism	<1%	1	6162
Kubu	Indonesia	Kubu	25,000	Islam-Animist	nr%	6 81	7026
Kubu	Indonesia	Local dialects	6,000	Animism	1%	6 80	1093

401

NAME	COUNTRY	LANGUAGE	GROUP SIZE	PRIMARY RELIGION	% CHR	V	VOL	UP ID
Kuda-Chano	Nigeria	Kuda-Chano	4,000	Islam	<1%	1		2438
*Kudisai Vagh Makkal	India	Tamil	1,000,000	Hinduism	2%	3		695
Kudiya	India	Kudiya	100	Hindu-Aninist	<1%	1		2713
Kugbo	Nigeria	Kugbo	2,000	Aninism	<1%	1		2439
*Kui	Thailand	Kui	160,000	Buddhist-Aninist	1%	5		607
Kuikuro	Brazil	Kuikuro	100	Aninism	<1%	1		2174
Kuka	Chad	Kuka	38,000	Islam-Aninist	<1%	1		2233
Kukele	Cameroon	Kukele	33,000	Aninism	<1%	1		5250
Kukele	Nigeria	Kukele	32,000	Aninism	<1%	1		2440
*Kuknas	India	Kukni	125,000	Hindu-Aninist	<1%	4		701
Kukuwy	Papua New Guinea	Kukuya	1,000	Aninism	<1%	1		6163
Kukwa	Congo	Kukwa	11,000	Aninism	0%	1		5295
Kulango	Ivory Coast	Kulango	60,000	Aninism	3%	4		481
Kulele	Ivory Coast	Kulele	15,000	Islam-Aninist	<1%	1		2294
Kulere	Nigeria	Kulere	8,000	Aninism	<1%	1		2441
Kullo	Ethiopia	Kullo	82,000	Islam-Aninist	1%	3		3218
**Kuluis in Himachal Pradesh	India	Kului	200,000	Hinduism	1%	5	81	2015
Kulung	Nigeria	Kulung	15,000	Islam-Aninist	<1%	1		2442
Kunal	Papua New Guinea	Kumai	4,000	Aninism	0%	1		6164
Kuman	Uganda	Kuman	100,000	Aninism	0%	1		5644
Kuman	Papua New Guinea	Kuman	66,000	Aninism	<1%	1		6165
Kumauni in Assam	India	Kumauni	1,240,000	Hindu-Aninist	<1%	1		2714
Kumdauron	Papua New Guinea	Kumdauron	400	Aninism	<1%	1		6166
Kumu	Zaire	Kumu	60,000	Aninism	<1%	1		5718
Kumukio	Papua New Guinea	Kumukio	60,300	Aninism	<1%	1		6167
Kunana	Ethiopia	Kunana	70,000	Islam	<1%	1		3219
Kunante	Guinea-Bissau	Kunante	6,000	Islam-Aninist	0%	1		5353
Kunda	Mozambique	Kunda	60,000	Aninism	0%	1		5391
	Zambia	Lala-Bisa	21,000	Aninism	0%	1		5790
	Zambia	Nyanja	8,000	Aninism	0%	1		5805
	Zinbabwe	Kunda	40,000	Aninism	0%	1		5411
Kuni	Papua New Guinea	Kuni	2,000	Aninism	<1%	1		6168
**Kunimaipa	Papua New Guinea	Kunimaipa	9,000	Christo-Paganism	6%	5		1202
Kunua	Papua New Guinea	Kunua	1,000	Aninism	<1%	1		6169
Kuot	Papua New Guinea	Kuot	900	Aninism	<1%	1		6170
Kupia in Andhra Pradesh	India	Kupia	4,000	Hindu-Aninist	<1%	1		2715

NAME	COUNTRY	LANGUAGE	GROUP SIZE	PRIMARY RELIGION	% CHR	VOL V	UP	ID
Kupsabiny	Uganda	Kupsabiny	60,000	Animism	0%	1		5645
Kurada	Papua New Guinea	Kurada	900	Animism	<1%	1		6171
Kurds in Iran	Iran	Kurdish Dialects	2,000,000	Islam	1%	6	80	2036
Kurds in Kuwait	Kuwait	Kurdish	145,000	Islam	0%	3		4136
*Kurds of Turkey	Turkey	Kurdish (Kirmancho)	1,900,000	Islam	<1%	6	79	180
Kurfei	Niger	Hausa	50,000	Animism	<1%	4		561
Kuria	Tanzania	Kuria	75,000	Animism	0%	1		5564
Kurichiya in Kerala	India	Kurichiya	12,000	Nominal Christian	<1%	5	81	2716
Kuruba in Tamil Nadu	India	Kuruba	8,000	Hindu-Animist	<1%	1		2717
Kurudu	Indonesia	Kurudu	1,000	Animism	<1%	1		2960
Kurumba	Upper Volta	Kurumba	86,000	Islam-Animist	<1%	1		5673
Kurux in Bihar	India	Kurux	1,240,000	Hindu-Animist	<1%	1		2718
**Kusaasi	Ghana	Kusaal	150,000	Animism	3%	5		1183
Kushi	Nigeria	Kushi	4,000	Islam	<1%	1		2443
Kusu	Zaire	Kusu	26,000	Animism	0%	1		5719
Kuteb	Nigeria	Kuteb	26,000	Islam	<1%	1		2444
Kutin	Cameroon	Kutin	400	Animism	<1%	1		5251
Kutu	Tanzania	Kutu	17,000	Islam	<1%	1		5565
Kuturmi	Nigeria	Kuturmi	3,000	Animism	0%	1		2445
Kuvi in Orissa	India	Kuvi	190,000	Hindu-Animist	<1%	1		2719
Kuwaa	Liberia	Kuwaa	6,000	Animism	<1%	1		5362
Kuzamani	Nigeria	Kuzamani	1,000	Islam	<1%	1		2446
Kvanadin	USSR	Kvanadin	6,000	Unknown	0%	1		5859
Kwa	Nigeria	Kwa	15,000	Islam	<1%	1		2447
Kwadi	Angola	Kwadi	3,700	Animism	0%	1		5151
Kwakum	Cameroon	Kwakum	30,000	Animism	0%	1		5252
Kwale	Papua New Guinea	Kwale	5,000	Animism	<1%	1		6172
Kwanbi	Namibia	Kwanbi	25,000	Animism	<1%	1		5401
Kwanga	Papua New Guinea	Kwanga	400	Animism	<1%	1		6173
Kwangali	Angola	Kwangali	100,000	Animism	0%	1		5152
Kwansu	Indonesia	Kwansu	150,000	Animism	0%	1		2961
Kwanyana	Angola	Kwanyana	35,000	Animism	<1%	1		5153
Kuaya	Namibia	Kwanyana	3,000	Animism	<1%	1		5402
Kwe-etshori	Tanzania	Kwaya	2,000	Animism	<1%	1		5566
	Botswana	Kwe-etshori			0%	1		5176
	Zimbabwe	Kwe-etshori						5412

NAME	COUNTRY	LANGUAGE	GROUP SIZE	PRIMARY RELIGION	% CHR	VOL V	UP ID
Kwerba	Indonesia	Kwerba	2,000	Animism	<1%	1	2962
Kwere	Tanzania	Kwere	63,000	Animism	10%	5	491
Kwese	Zaire	Kwese	60,000	Animism	<1%	1	5720
Kwesten	Indonesia	Kwesten	3,000	Animism	<1%	1	2963
Kwoma	Papua New Guinea	Kwoma	2,000	Animism	0%	1	6174
Kwontari	Papua New Guinea	Kwontari	800	Animism	<1%	1	6175
Kyibaku	Nigeria	Kyibaku	20,000	Islam	<1%	1	2448
Laanang	Nigeria	Laanang	40,000	Islam	<1%	1	2449
Labans	India	Labaani	nr	Hindu-Buddhist	<1%	3	1041
Labbai	India	Tamil	nr	Islam	<1%	1	4045
Labhani in Andhra Pradesh	India	Labhani	1,200,000	Hindu-Buddhist	<1%	1	2722
*Labourers of Jhoparpatti	India	Marathi	2,000	Hinduism	10%	4	2001
Labu	Papua New Guinea	Labu	800	Animism	<1%	1	6176
Lacandon	Mexico	Lacandon	200	Christo-Paganism	<1%	1	8045
Ladakhi in Jammu	India	Ladakhi	60,000	Hindu-Buddhist	<1%	1	2720
Ladinos	Lebanon	Ladinos	7,000	Judaism	<1%	1	2538
Laewomba	Papua New Guinea	Laewomba	2,000	Animism	<1%	1	6177
Lafofa	Sudan	Lafofa	2,000	Islam	0%	1	5494
*Lahaulis in Punjab	India	Lahouli	18,000	Buddhism	<1%	4	2016
*Lahu	Thailand	Lahu	23,000	Animism	7%	5	2088
Lahul	China	Lahul	2,000	Traditional Chinese	<1%	1	2826
Laka	Cameroon	Laka	10,000	Animism	0%	4	500
	Central African Republic	Lakal	40,000	Animism	<1%	1	5187
	Chad	Lakal	40,000	Islam-Animist	<1%	1	2234
	China	Laka	6,000	Traditional Chinese	<1%	1	2827
Lakians	USSR	Lakian	86,500	Islam	0%	1	5812
Lakka	Nigeria	Lakka	500	Islam	<1%	1	2450
Lala	Zambia	Lala	125,000	Animism	0%	1	5785
Lalia	Zaire	Lalia	30,000	Animism	0%	1	5721
Lalung in Assam	India	Lalung	11,000	Hindu-Buddhist	<1%	1	2721
Lana	Burma	Lana	3,000	Buddhist-Animist	<1%	1	2581
Lamba	Benin	Lanba	29,000	Animism	0%	1	5169
	Togo	Lamba	29,000	Animism	3%	4	425
	Zaire	Lanba	80,000	Animism	<1%	1	5722
	Zambia	Lanba	89,000	Animism	0%	1	5791
**Lambadi in Andhra Pradesh	India	Lambadi	1,300,000	Animism	nr%	5	2018

NAME	LANGUAGE	COUNTRY	GROUP SIZE	PRIMARY RELIGION	% CHR	V	VOL UP ID
Lambi	Lambi	Cameroon	1,000	Animism	<1%	1	5253
Lanbya	Lanbya	Malawi	20,000	Animism	0%	1	5366
Lanbya	Lanbya	Tanzania	7,000	Animism	0%	1	5567
Lane	Lane	Nigeria	2,000	Islam	0%	1	2451
Lanogai	Lanogai	Papua New Guinea	1,000	Animism	<1%	1	6178
Lanpung	Komering	Indonesia	1,500,000	Islam-Animist	0%	5 80	1134
Landoma	Landoma	Guinea	4,000	Islam-Animist	0%	1	5344
	Landoma	Guinea-Bissau	5,000	Islam-Animist	0%	1	5354
Langi	Langi	Tanzania	95,000	Animism	0%	1	5568
*Lango	Lango	Ethiopia	8,000	Animism	0%	3	680
Lango	Lango	Uganda	560,000	Animism	0%	1	5646
Lanoh	Lanoh	Malaysia	400	Animism	0%	3	4111
*Lao	Lao	Laos	1,910,000	Buddhism	1%	7 79	121
Lao Refugees	Lao	Argentina	1,500	Ancestor Worship	<1%	3 83	9037
*Lao Refugees	Lao	Spain	1,000	Buddhist-Animist	<1%	3 83	9056
Lao-Chinese Refugees, Edmonton	Lao	Canada:Alberta	20,000	Buddhist-Animist	<1%	4	2090
	Lao	Thailand	2,000	Buddhism	0%	1	9207
Lara	Lara	Indonesia	12,000	Animism	<1%	1	2964
Laro	Laro	Sudan	3,000	Islam	0%	1	5495
Laru	Laru	Nigeria	1,000	Islam	<1%	1	2452
Latdwalan	Latdwalan	Indonesia	900	Animism	<1%	1	2965
Lati	Lati	China	500	Traditional Chinese	<1%	1	2829
Laudje	Laudje	Indonesia	125,000	Animism	<1%	1	2966
Lavatbura-Lamusong	Lavatbura-Lamusong	Papua New Guinea	1,000	Animism	<1%	1	6179
Lavongai	Lavongai	Papua New Guinea	10,000	Animism	<1%	1	6180
Lawa, Eastern	Tibeto-Burman Dialect	Thailand	3,000	Buddhist-Animist	<1%	5 81	7039
Lawa, Mountain	Lawa	Thailand	10,000	Buddhist-Animist	4%	5	612
Lebanese, Beanington	French	Canada:Ontario	1,500	Animism	nr%	1	9269
Lebgo	Lebgo	Nigeria	30,000	Islam	<1%	1	2453
Lebong	Redjang-Lebong	Indonesia	nr	Islam	<1%	5	1090
Leco	Leco	Bolivia	200	Animism	<1%	1	2137
Lega	Lega	Zaire	150,000	Animism	<1%	1	5723
Lelemi	Lelemi	Ghana	15,000	Islam-Animist	0%	1	5326
Lengua, Northern	Lengua, Northern	Paraguay	95,000	Animism	<1%	1	5126
Lenje	Lenje	Zambia	79,000	Animism	0%	1	5793
**Lepcha	Lepcha	India	18,000	Hindu-Buddhist	10%	4	2127

NAME	COUNTRY	LANGUAGE	GROUP SIZE	PRIMARY RELIGION	% CHR	V	VOL UP	ID
**Lepers of Cen. Thailand	Thailand	Thai	20,000	Buddhist-Animist	1%	6	81	7003
**Lepers of N.E. Thailand	Thailand	Northeast Thai	200,000	Buddhism	1%	4		236
Leron	Papua New Guinea	Leron	500	Animism	1%	1		6181
Letti	Indonesia	Letti	6,000	Animism	<1%	1		2967
Lhomi	Nepal	Lhomi	10,000	Buddhist-Animist	0%	1		6513
Li	China	Li	1,000,000	Traditional Chinese	<1%	1		2830
Ligbi	Ghana	Ligbi	6,000	Islam	0%	5		1071
	Ivory Coast	Ligbi	20,000	Islam	<1%	4		482
Liguri	Sudan	Liguri	2,000	Islam-Animist	0%	1		5496
Lihir	Papua New Guinea	Lihir	5,000	Animism	0%	1		6182
Liko	Zaire	Liko	26,000	Animism	0%	1		5727
Lina	Zambia	Lina	12,000	Animism	0%	1		5792
Linba	Sierra Leone	Lima	233,000	Animism	4%	4		587
Lionese	Indonesia	Lio	100,000	Christo-Paganism	<1%	5	81	2968
Lisu	China	Lisu	470,000	Animism	6%	4		7009
Lisu	Thailand	Lisu	13,000	Animism	0%	4		2089
Liv	USSR	Liv	2,000	Unknown	5%	4		5860
*Llaneros	Colombia	Spanish	25,000	Christo-Paganism	5%	4	84	4807
Lo	Nigeria	Lo	2,000	Animism	<1%	1		2454
Lobi	Ivory Coast	Lobi	40,000	Animism	1%	4		483
Lodhi in Bihar	India	Lodhi	44,000	Hindu-Animist	<1%	1		2723
Logba	Ghana	Logba	3,900	Islam-Animist	0%	1		5327
Lohiki	Papua New Guinea	Lohiki		Animism	0%	1		6183
**Loho Loho	Indonesia	Kolaka	10,000	Animism	0%	3		137
Loinang	Indonesia	Loinang	100,000	Animism	nr%	5	81	2969
Loko	Guinea	Loko	16,000	Islam-Animist	0%	1		5345
	Sierra Leone	Loko	80,000	Animism	1%	4		586
*Lokoro	Sudan	Lokoro	22,000	Christo-Paganism	5%	4		1128
Lolo	China	Yi	4,800,000	Animism	0%	5	81	7006
Loma	Guinea	Loma	180,000	Animism	3%	4		479
	Liberia	Loma	60,000	Animism	12%	4		601
Lombi	Zaire	Lomi	8,000	Animism	0%	1		5729
Lombo	Zaire	Lombo	10,000	Animism	0%	1		5730
Lomwe	Mozambique	not reported	1,000,000	Animism	9%	4		565
Longuda	Nigeria	Longuda	32,000	Islam	<1%	1		2455
Lore	Indonesia	Lore	140,000	Animism	<1%	1		2970

NAME	COUNTRY	LANGUAGE	GROUP SIZE	PRIMARY RELIGION	% CHR	V	VOL UP ID
Lori	Sudan	Lori	1,000	Islam	0%	1		5447
Lors	Iran	Luri	600,000	Islam	0%	5	80	2028
Lotsu-Piri	Nigeria	Lotsu-Piri	2,000	Islam	<1%	1		2456
**Lotuka	Sudan	Latuka	150,000	Other	6%	5		200
Lou-Baluan-Pan	Papua New Guinea	Lou-Baluan-Pan	1,000	Animism	<1%	1		6184
Loven	Laos	Loven	25,000	Buddhist-Aninist	1%	5	81	107
Lozi	Zambia	Lozi	215,000	Aninism	0%	1		5794
Lozi	Zimbabwe	Lozi	8,000	Aninism	0%	1		5413
Lu	China	Lu	400,000	Buddhist-Aninist	<1%	1		2831
Luac	Sudan	Luac	700	Islam	0%	1		5466
Luano	Zambia	Luano	4,000	Animism	0%	1		5787
Lubang Islanders	Philippines	Pilipino	18,000	Christo-Paganism	0%	5	81	7016
Lubu	Indonesia	Lubu	1,000,000	Islam	0%	1		2971
Luchazi	Angola	Luchazi	60,000	Animism	<1%	1		5154
Luchazi	Zambia	Luchazi	34,000	Animism	<1%	1		5795
Lue	Cameroon	Lue	4,000	Animism	<1%	1		5255
Lugitana	Papua New Guinea	Lugitana	500	Animism	0%	1		6185
Luimbi	Angola	Luimbi	20,000	Animism	<1%	1		5155
Lukep	Papua New Guinea	Lukep	600	Animism	<1%	1		6186
Lumbu	Gabon	Lumbu	12,000	Animism	<1%	1		5310
Luna	Zaire	Luna	50,000	Animism	<1%	1		5732
Lunda	Angola	Lunda	50,000	Animism	<1%	1		5156
Lunda, Ndembu	Zambia	Lunda, Ndembu	100,000	not reported	nr%	1		5796
Lundu	Cameroon	Lundu	24,000	Animism	0%	1		5254
Lungu	Nigeria	Lungu	10,000	Animism	<1%	4		571
Luo	Tanzania	Luo	1,522,000	Animism	0%	1		5569
Lushai in Assam from	India	Lushai	270,000	Hindu-Animist	<1%	1		2724
Luvale Refugees from Angola	Zambia	Luvale	11,000	Aninism	nr%	4	83	9061
Luwu	Indonesia	Luwu	500,000	Islam	<1%	1		2972
Luxemburgois	Luxembourg	letzburgesch	276,000	Nominal Christian	nr%	2		6561
Luyana	Angola	Luyana	4,000	Animism	0%	1		5157
Luyana	Zambia	Luyana	50,000	Animism	0%	1		5797
Lwalu	Zaire	Lwalu	21,000	Animism	0%	1		5733
Lwena	Angola	Lwena	90,000	Animism	<1%	1		5158
Lwo	Sudan	Lwo	20,000	Islam	<1%	1		5497
Ma	Zaire	Ma	5,000	Animism	0%	1		5734

NAME	COUNTRY	LANGUAGE	GROUP SIZE	PRIMARY RELIGION	% CHR	V	VOL UP ID
Maanyan	Indonesia	Maanyan	15,000	Animism	<1%	1	2973
**Maasai	Kenya	Masai	100,000	Animism	5%	6 79	489
Maba	Chad	Maba	56,000	Islam-Animist	<1%	1	2236
	Sudan	Maba	9,000	Islam	0%	1	5498
Maban-Junjun	Sudan	Maban-Junjun	20,000	Islam	<1%	1	5499
Maca	Paraguay	Maca	600	Animism	<1%	1	5127
Machiguenga	Peru	Machiguenga	10,000	Animism	<1%	1	3178
Macu	Colombia	Macu	1,000	Animism	<1%	3	242
Macuna	Colombia	Macuna		Animism	<1%	1	3144
**Macuxi	Brazil	Macuxi	6,000	Animism	5%	3	719
Madak	Papua New Guinea	Madak	3,000	Animism	0%	1	6187
Madda	Nigeria	Madda	30,000	Animism	<1%	1	2457
Madi	Sudan	Madi	6,000	Islam	0%	1	5500
	Uganda	Madi	114,000	Animism	<1%	1	5647
Madik	Indonesia	Madik	1,000	Animism	<1%	1	2974
**Magar	Nepal	Magar	300,000	Hindu-Animist	1%	4	395
Maghi	Burma	Maghi	310,200	Buddhist-Animist	<1%	1	2582
Magori	Papua New Guinea	Magori		Animism	<1%	1	6188
Maguindanao	Philippines	Maguindanao	700,000	Islam	1%	6 80	629
**Maguzawa	Nigeria	Hausa	100,000	Animism	1%	6 79	202
Mahali in Assam	India	Mahali	14,000	Hindu-Animist	0%	1	2725
**Mahrah	Yemen, Democratic	Local dialects	50,000	Islam	<1%	3	4066
Mahri	Oman	Mahri	50,000	Islam	0%	3	2539
Mai	Papua New Guinea	Mai	200	Animism	0%	1	6189
Mailu	Papua New Guinea	Mailu	5,000	Animism	<1%	1	6190
Maiongong	Brazil	Maiongong	100	Animism	<1%	3	718
Mairasi	Indonesia	Mairasi	1,000	Animism	<1%	1	2975
Maisan	Papua New Guinea	Maisan	2,000	Hindu-Animist	0%	4	398
Maithili	Nepal	Maithili	1,000,000	Animism	<1%	1	6191
Maiwa	Papua New Guinea	Maiwa	1,000	Animism	0%	1	6192
Majhi	Nepal	Majhi	6,000	Buddhist-Animist	<1%	1	6514
Majhwar in Madhya Pradesh	India	Majhwar	28,000	Hindu-Animist	0%	1	2726
Maj	Ethiopia	Maji	15,000	Animism	<1%	4	518
Majingai-Ngana	Chad	Majingai-Ngana	47,000	Islam-Animist	<1%	1	2237
Majingai-ngana	Central African Republic	Majingai-ngana	47,000	Animism	<1%	1	5188
Maka	Cameroon	Maka	51,000	Animism	0%	1	5256

NAME	COUNTRY	LANGUAGE	GROUP SIZE	PRIMARY RELIGION	% CHR	V	UP	VOL ID
Makarin	Papua New Guinea	Makarin	2,000	Animism	0%	1		6193
Makasai	Indonesia	Makasai	70,000	Animism	<1%	1		2976
Makere	Uganda	Makere	18,000	Animism	0%	1		5648
Makian, West	Indonesia	Makian, West	12,000	Animism	<1%	1		2977
Maklew	Indonesia	Maklew	100	Animism	<1%	1		2978
Makonde	Tanzania	not reported	550,000	Islam	6%	5		144
Makua	Mozambique	Makua	1,200,000	Animism	10%	4		564
Malakkaras of Kerala	India	Malaanutha	1,000	Hindu-Animist	0%	5	81	2019
Malalanai	Papua New Guinea	Malalanai	300	Animism	<1%	1		6194
Malankuravan in Kerala	India	Malankuravan	5,000	Hindu-Animist	<1%	1		2727
Malapandaram in Kerala	India	Malapandaram	500	Hindu-Animist	<1%	1		2728
Malappanackers	India	Malappanackan	1,000	Animism	0%	4		2021
Malaryan in Kerala	India	Malaryan	5,000	Hindu-Animist	<1%	1		2729
Malas	Papua New Guinea	Malas	200	Animism	<1%	1		6195
Malasanga	Papua New Guinea	Malasanga	400	Animism	<1%	1		6196
Malavedan in Kerala	India	Malavedan	2,000	Hinduism	<1%	1		2730
*Malayalars	India	Malayalam	nr	Animism	0%	4		2020
Malayo	Colombia	Malayo	1,000	Animism	6%	4		696
Malays of Singapore	Singapore	Malay	300,000	Islam	1%	6	79	120
Male	Ethiopia	Male	12,000	Animism	<1%	1		3221
Malek	Papua New Guinea	Malek	1,000	Animism	0%	1		6197
Maleu	Papua New Guinea	Maleu	4,000	Animism	<1%	1		6198
Mali in Andhra Pradesh	India	Mali	1,000	Hindu-Animist	<1%	1		2731
Malila	Tanzania	Malila	175,000	Animism	0%	1		5570
Malki in Bihar	India	Malki	89,000	Hindu-Animist	<1%	1		2733
Malon	Papua New Guinea	Malon	3,000	Animism	0%	1		6199
Malpaharia in Assam	India	Malpaharia	9,000	Hindu-Animist	<1%	1		2732
*Maltese	Malta	Maltese	330,000	Nominal Christian	nr%	2		6560
Malvi in Madhya Pradesh	India	Malvi	644,000	Hindu-Animist	7%	5		2734
**Man Indian	Guatemala	Man	470,000	Christo-Paganism	7%	5		1124
Mana	Nigeria	Mana	20,000	Animism	<1%	1		2458
Manaa	Papua New Guinea	Manaa	200	Animism	<1%	1		6200
**Mananwa	Philippines	Minananwa	1,000	Christo-Paganism	3%	6	81	628
Manasani	Iran	Luri	110,000	Islam	0%	4		2039
Manbai	Indonesia	Manbai	80,000	Animism	<1%	1		2979
Manbila	Cameroon	Manbila	40,000	Animism	<1%	4		499

REGISTRY OF THE UNREACHED

NAME	COUNTRY	LANGUAGE	GROUP SIZE	PRIMARY RELIGION	% CHR	V	VOL	UP ID
Manbue-Lungu	Tanzania	Manbue-Lungu	16,000	Animism	0%	1		5571
	Zambia	Manbue-Lungu	121,000	Animism	<1%	1		5798
Manprusi	Ghana	Manpruli	80,000	Animism	<1%	4		529
	Ghana	Manpruli	91,000	Islam-Animist	<1%	1		5328
Manvu-Efe	Zaire	Manvu-Efe	40,000	Animism	0%	1		5735
Managalasi	Papua New Guinea	Managalasi	4,000	Animism	<1%	1		6201
Mananbu	Papua New Guinea	Mananbu	2,000	Animism	<1%	1		6202
Mancang	Senegal	Mankanya	40,000	Animism	0%	3		1141
Manchu	China	Manchu	200,000	Traditional Chinese	<1%	5	81	2832
Manda	Tanzania	Manda	10,000	Animism	0%	1		5572
Mandar	Indonesia	Mandar	300,000	Islam	<1%	1		2980
Mandara	Nigeria	Mandara	20,000	Islam	<1%	1		2459
Mandaya	Philippines	Mandaya	3,000	Animism	<1%	1		3293
Mandaya, Mansaka	Philippines	Mandaya, Mansaka	40,000	Animism	<1%	1		3271
Mander	Indonesia	Mander	100	Animism	<1%	1		2981
Manding	Senegal	Malinke, Senegalese	210,000	Islam-Animist	0%	3		1138
Mandingo	Liberia	Mandingo	30,000	Islam	<1%	6	79	622
Mandyak	Gambia	Mandyak	85,000	Islam-Animist	<1%	1		2270
Manem	Indonesia	Manem	400	Animism	0%	3		2982
Mangap	Papua New Guinea	Mangap	2,000	Animism	<1%	1		6203
Mangbai	Chad	Mangbai	2,000	Animism	<1%	1		2238
Mangbutu	Zaire	Mangbutu	8,000	Animism	0%	1		5736
Mangarai Muslim	Indonesia	Mangarai	25,000	Islam	0%	5	81	7029
Manglsa	Cameroon	Manglsa	14,000	Animism	<1%	1		5257
Mangs in Maharashtra	India	Marathi	nr	Hinduism	<1%	3		1043
***Mangyan	Philippines	Various Dialects	60,000	Animism	6%	3		231
**Manikion	Indonesia	Sough	8,000	Animism	<1%	5		1165
Maninka	Guinea-Bissau	Maninka	65,000	Islam-Animist	0%	1		5355
	Sierra Leone	Maninka	64,000	Islam-Animist	<1%	1		5434
Manjack	Senegal	Mandyale	44,000	Islam-Animist	0%	3		1140
**Manjaco	Guinea-Bissau	Mandyako	80,000	Animism	7%	4		589
Mankanya	Guinea-Bissau	Mankanya	35,000	Islam-Animist	0%	1		5356
	Senegal	Mankanya	16,000	Islam-Animist	0%	1		5425
Manna-Dora in A.P.	India	Manna-Dora	9,000	Hindu-Animist	<1%	1		2735
Mannan in Kerala	India	Mannan	5,000	Hindu-Animist	<1%	1		2736
Mano	Liberia	Mano	65,000	Animism	4%	4		602

NAME	COUNTRY	LANGUAGE	GROUP SIZE	PRIMARY RELIGION	% CHR	VOL V	UP ID
Manobo, Agusan	Philippines	Manobo, Agusan	15,000	Animism	<1%	1	3272
Manobo, Ata	Philippines	Manobo, Ata	7,000	Animism	<1%	1	3273
Manobo, Binokid	Philippines	Manobo, Binokid	41,000	Animism	<1%	4	3274
**Manobo, Cotabato	Philippines	Cotabato Manobo	10,000	Animism	<1%	1	626
Manobo, Dibabawon	Philippines	Manobo, Dibabawon	2,000	Animism	<1%	1	3275
*Manobo, Ilianen	Philippines	Ilianen Manobo	5,000	Animism	3%	5	625
Manobo, Obo	Philippines	Manobo, Obo	4,000	Animism	<1%	1	3276
Manobo, Salug	Philippines	Manobo, Tigwa	4,000	Animism	4%	5	639
**Manobo, Sarangani	Philippines	Manobo, Sarangani	15,000	Animism	<1%	1	3277
Manobo, Tagabawa	Philippines	Manobo, Tagabawa	10,000	Animism	<1%	1	3278
Manobo, Tigwa	Philippines	Manobo, Tigwa	4,000	Animism	3%	5	640
**Manobo, Western Bukidnon	Philippines	Manobo, Binokid	12,000	Animism	6%	5	618
**Manobo, Pulangi	Philippines	Manobo, Pulangi	5,000	Animism	1%	4	1171
**Mansaka	Philippines	Mansaka	25,000	Christo-Paganism	10%	5	1035
Mansi	USSR	Mansi	8,000	Unknown	0%	2	5861
Mantera	Malaysia	Mantera	4,000	Animism	<1%	1	4097
Mantion	Indonesia	Mantion	12,000	Animism	<1%	1	2984
Manu Park Panoan	Peru	Manu Park Panoan	200	Animism	<1%	1	3179
Manyika	Zimbabwe	Manyika	350,000	Animism	<1%	1	5414
Mao, Northern	Ethiopia	Mao, Northern	13,000	Animism	<1%	1	3222
Maou	Ivory Coast	Maou	80,000	Islam-Animist	<1%	1	2295
Mape	Papua New Guinea	Mape	5,000	Animism	<1%	1	6204
Mapena	Papua New Guinea	Mapena	300	Animism	<1%	1	6205
Mapoyo	Venezuela	Mapoyo	200	Animism	0%	5	5136
Mappilas	India	Malayalan	4,500,000	Islam	<1%	5	4026
Mapuche	Chile	Mapuche	300,000	Christo-Paganism	1%	5	48
Maquiritari	Venezuela	Maquiritari	12,000	Animism	1%	1	5137
Mara in Assam	India	Mara	12,000	Hindu-Animist	<1%	1	2737
Maralango	Papua New Guinea	Maralango	2,000	Animism	<1%	1	6206
Maralinan	Papua New Guinea	Maralinan	2,000	Animism	<1%	1	6207
Maranao	Philippines	Maranao	500,000	Islam	2%	6 79	638
Maranao, Lanad	Philippines	Maranao, Lanad	500,000	Islam-Animist	<1%	1	3279
Mararit	Chad	Mararit	42,000	Islam-Animist	<1%	1	2239
Marau	Indonesia	Marau	1,000	Animism	<1%	1	2985
Marba	Chad	Marba	30,000	Islam-Animist	<1%	1	2240
Marghi Central	Nigeria	Marghi Central	135,000	Islam	<1%	1	2460

411

NAME	COUNTRY	LANGUAGE	GROUP SIZE	PRIMARY RELIGION	% CHR V	VOL UP ID
Mari	Papua New Guinea	Mari	300	Animism	<1% 1	6208
Maria	USSR	Mari	599,000	Christo-Paganism	<1% 1	5862
Maria in Andhra Pradesh	Papua New Guinea	Maria	2,000	Animism	<1% 1	6209
**Mariellto Refugees in	India	Maria	80,000	Hindu-Animist	<1% 1	2738
Florida	United States of America	Spanish	125,000	Secularism	14% 4 83	6565
Marind	Indonesia	Marind	7,000	Animism	<1% 1	2986
Marind, Bian	Indonesia	Marind, Bian	900	Animism	<1% 1	2987
Maring	Papua New Guinea	Maring	8,000	Animism	<1% 1	6210
Marka	Upper Volta	Marka	39,000	Islam	0% 1	5675
Marubo	Brazil	Marubo	400	Animism	0% 1	2175
Marwari in Gujarat	India	Marwari	6,810,000	Hindu-Animist	<1% 1	2739
Masa	Chad	Masa	80,000	Animism	6% 4	514
Masaba	Uganda	Masaba	110,000	Animism	<1% 1	5650
Masakin	Sudan	Masakin	16,000	Islam	0% 1	5501
Masalit	Chad	Masalit	74,000	Islam-Animist	<1% 1	2241
	Sudan	Arabic	27,000	Islam	0% 1	5502
Masegi	Papua New Guinea	Masegi	2,000	Animism	<1% 1	6211
*Masengo	Ethiopia	Majangilir	7,000	Animism	1% 5	428
Masenrempulu	Indonesia	Masenrempulu	250,000	Islam	<1% 1	2988
Mashi	Zambia	Mashi	21,000	Animism	0% 1	5799
Massalat	Chad	Massalat	23,000	Islam-Animist	<1% 1	2242
Matakam	Cameroon	Matakam	140,000	Animism	2% 4	498
	Nigeria	Matakam	2,000	Islam	<1% 1	2461
Matawari	Surinam	Matawari	1,600	Animism	0% 1	5130
Matbat	Indonesia	Matbat	600	Animism	<1% 1	2989
Matengo	Tanzania	Matengo	58,000	Animism	0% 1	5573
***Matharis	India	Telugu	200,000	Hinduism	2% 5	4069
Matipuhy-Nahukua	Brazil	Matipuhy-Nahukua	100	Animism	<1% 1	2176
Matlatzinca, Atzingo	Mexico	Matlatzinca, Atzingo	2,000	Christo-Paganism	0% 1	8046
Matumbi	Tanzania	Matumbi	72,000	Islam	8% 4	488
Maure	Mali	Maure	58,000	Islam-Animist	0% 1	5379
Maures	Senegal	Arabic	57,000	Islam	0% 3	723
Mauri	Niger	Hausa	100,000	Animism	<1% 4	560
Maviha	Mozambique	Maviha	70,000	Animism	0% 1	5392
Mawak	Papua New Guinea	Mawak	1,000	Animism	<1% 1	6212
Mawan	Papua New Guinea	Mawan	200	Animism	<1% 1	6213

NAME	COUNTRY	LANGUAGE	GROUP SIZE	PRIMARY RELIGION	% CHR Y	VOL UP ID
**Mawchis	India	Mawchi	300,000	Hindu-Animist	3% 5	4061
Mawes	Indonesia	Mawes	700	Animism	<1% 1	2990
Maxakali	Brazil	Maxakali	400	Animism	<1% 1	2177
Mayo	Mexico	Mayo	30,000	Animism	<1% 1	8047
Mayoruna	Peru	Mayoruna	1,000	Animism	<1% 1	3180
**Mazahua	Mexico	Mazahua	150,000	Christo-Paganism	6% 4	377
Mazandaranis	Iran	Mazandarani	1,620,000	Islam	0% 4	2029
Mba	Zaire	Mba	20,000	Animism	<1% 1	5737
Mbaana	Gabon	Mbaana	12,000	Animism	0% 1	5311
Mbai	Central African Republic	Mbai	73,000	Animism	<1% 1	5189
	Chad	Mbai	73,000	Islam-Animist	<1% 1	2243
Mbala	Zaire	Mbala	200,000	Animism	0% 1	5738
Mbangwe	Zaire	Mbangwe	2,000	Animism	0% 1	5739
Mbanja	Zaire	Mbanja	81,000	Animism	0% 1	5740
Mbati	Central African Republic	Mbati	15,000	Animism	0% 1	5190
Mbe	Nigeria	Mbe	14,000	Animism	<1% 1	2462
Mbede	Gabon	Mbede	45,000	Animism	0% 1	5312
Mbembe	Cameroon	Mbembe	25,000	Animism	0% 1	5258
Mbembe (Tigong)	Nigeria	Mbembe	60,000	Animism	<1% 1	2464
Mbimu	Nigeria	Mbembe	3,000	Animism	<1% 1	2463
Mbo	Cameroon	Mbimu	nr	Animism	<1% 1	5259
	Cameroon	Mbo	23,000	Animism	0% 1	5260
	Zaire	Mbo	2,000	Animism	<1% 1	5741
Mboi	Nigeria	Mboi	3,000	Islam	<1% 1	2465
Mbole	Zaire	Mbole	100,000	Animism	0% 1	5742
Mbugwe	Tanzania	Mbugwe	8,000	Animism	0% 1	5574
Mbukushu	Angola	Kusso	6,000	Animism	6% 4	510
Mbula-Bwazza	Nigeria	Mbula-Bwazza	8,000	Islam	<1% 1	2466
Mbum	Chad	Mbum	20,000	Islam-Animist	<1% 1	2244
Mbunda	Angola	Mbunda	59,000	Animism	0% 1	5159
Mbunga	Tanzania	Mbunga	10,000	Animism	0% 1	5575
Mbwela	Angola	Mbwela	100,000	Animism	<1% 1	5160
Me'en	Ethiopia	Me'en	38,000	Animism	<1% 1	3223
Meax	Indonesia	Meax	10,000	Animism	<1% 1	2991
Meban	Sudan	Maban-Jumjum	130,000	Animism	1% 4	578
Medipa	Papua New Guinea	Medipa	60,000	Animism	<1% 1	6214

REGISTRY OF THE UNREACHED

NAME	COUNTRY	LANGUAGE	GROUP SIZE	PRIMARY RELIGION	% CHR	V	VOL UP ID
**Meghwar	Pakistan	Marwari	100,000	Hinduism	1%	6 79	262
*Mehek	Papua New Guinea	Mehek	4,000	Animism	<1%	1	6215
*Meitei	India	Manipuri	700,000	Hinduism	1%	6 79	293
**Mejah	India	Mejah	6,000	Animism	1%	4	1033
*Meje	Uganda	Meje	13,000	Animism	0%	1	5649
Mekeo	Papua New Guinea	Mekeo	7,000	Animism	<1%	1	6216
Mekwei	Indonesia	Mekwei	1,000	Animism	<1%	1	2992
**Melanau of Sarawak	Malaysia	Melanau	61,000	Animism	1%	6 80	2122
Mende	Liberia	Mende	5,000	Islam-Animist	<1%	1	5363
Mende	Sierra Leone	Mende	600,000	Animism	13%	5	585
Menemo-Mogano	Cameroon	Menemo-Mogamo	35,000	Animism	<1%	1	5261
Mengen	Papua New Guinea	Mengen	6,000	Animism	<1%	1	6217
Menka	Cameroon	Menka	10,000	Animism	0%	1	5262
Menri	Malaysia	Menri	400	Animism	0%	2	4113
Menye	Papua New Guinea	Menye	13,000	Animism	<1%	1	6218
**Meo	Thailand	Meo	30,000	Animism	9%	5	610
Meos of Rajasthan	India	Rajasthani	500,000	Islam	0%	5 80	4017
Mera Mera	Papua New Guinea	Mera Mera	1,000	Animism	<1%	1	6219
Mesengo	Ethiopia	Mesengo	28,000	Islam-Animist	<1%	1	3224
Mesme	Chad	Mesme	28,000	Islam-Animist	<1%	1	2245
Mesmedje	Chad	Mesmedje	11,000	Islam-Animist	<1%	1	2246
***Mestizos in La Paz	Bolivia	Spanish	400,000	Christo-Paganism	4%	5 82	5001
Metis, Elizabeth Settlement	Canada:Alberta	Cree	1,000	Animism	0%	1	9130
Miarmin	Papua New Guinea	Miarmin	2,000	Animism	<1%	1	6220
Miao	China	Miao	2,800,000	Animism	<1%	5 81	7000
***Miching Indians	India	Miching	300,000	Hindu-Animist	1%	4	2002
***Micmac Indians, New Brunswick	Canada:New Brunswick	English	10,000	Nominal Christian	nr%	1	9286
***Micmac Indians, Eskasoni	Canada:Nova Scotia	English	2,000	Nominal Christian	nr%	1	9285
**Middle Class-Mexico City Rev.	Mexico	Spanish	nr	Nominal Christian	nr%	5 82	5014
Midob	Sudan	Midob	2,900	Islam	0%	1	5503
Midsivindi	Papua New Guinea	Midsivindi	900	Animism	<1%	1	6221
Mien	China	Mien	740,000	Animism	<1%	6 81	7001
Migabac	Papua New Guinea	Migabac	10,000	Animism	<1%	1	6222
Migili	Nigeria	Migili	10,000	Animism	<1%	1	2467
Mikarew	Papua New Guinea	Mikarew	6,000	Animism	<1%	1	6223
*Military Officers	Ecuador	Spanish	1,000	Nominal Christian	5%	3 84	4817

NAME	COUNTRY	LANGUAGE	GROUP SIZE	PRIMARY RELIGION	% CHR	V	UP ID	VOL
**Military Personnel	Ecuador	Spanish	80,000	Nominal Christian	15%	3		4119
*Mimi	Chad	Mimi	15,000	Islam-Animist	<1%			2247
*Minika	Indonesia	Mimika	10,000	Christo-Paganism	3%	5		1049
Mina in Madhya Pradesh	India	Mina	765,000	Hindu-Animist	<1%			2741
Minangkabau	Indonesia	Minangkabau	5,000,000	Islam	1%	6	80	212
Minanibai	Papua New Guinea	Minanibai	300	Animism	<1%	1		6224
Mindik	Papua New Guinea	Mindik	2,000	Animism	<1%	1		6225
Minduumo	Gabon	Minduumo	4,000	Animism	0%	1		5313
Mingat	USSR	Mingat	4,000	Unknown	0%	1		5863
Minianka	Mali	Suppire	300,000	Animism	0%	4		554
Mirdha in Orissa	India	Mirdha	6,000	Hindu-Animist	<1%	1		2742
Miri	Sudan	Miri	8,700	Islam	0%	1		5504
Miriam	India	Miriam	12,000	Animism	<1%	1		6226
Mirung	Papua New Guinea	Mirung		Animism	1%	4		650
Mishmi in Assam	India	Mishmi	5,000	Hindu-Animist	<1%	1		2743
Miskito	Nicaragua	Miskito	20,000	Christo-Paganism	<1%	1		5110
Mitang	Papua New Guinea	Mitang	500	Animism	<1%	1		6227
Mitmit	Papua New Guinea	Mitmit	100	Animism	<1%	1		6228
**Mixes	Mexico	Mixe	60,000	Christo-Paganism	2%	5		1005
Mixteco, Amoltepec	Mexico	Mixteco, Amoltepec	6,000	Christo-Paganism	0%	1		8048
Mixteco, Apoala	Mexico	Mixteco, Apoala	6,000	Christo-Paganism	<1%	1		8049
Mixteco, Central Puebla	Mexico	Spanish	3,000	Christo-Paganism	0%	1		5050
Mixteco, Eastern	Mexico	Mixteco, Eastern	15,000	Christo-Paganism	<1%	1		5051
Mixteco, Eastern Putla	Mexico	Mixteco, Eastern Putla	7,000	Christo-Paganism	0%	1		5052
Mixteco, Huajuapan	Mexico	Mixteco, Huajuapan	3,000	Christo-Paganism	0%	1		5053
Mixteco, Silacayoapan	Mexico	Mixteco, Silacayoapan	15,000	Christo-Paganism	<1%	1		5054
Mixteco, Southern Puebla	Mexico	Mixteco, Southern Puebla	12,000	Christo-Paganism	0%	1		5055
Mixteco, Southern Putla	Mexico	Mixteco, Southern Putla	3,000	Christo-Paganism	0%	1		5056
Mixteco, Tututepec	Mexico	Mixteco, Tututepec	2,000	Christo-Paganism	<1%	1		5057
Mixteco, Yosondua	Mexico	Mixteco, Yosondua	15,000	Christo-Paganism	0%	1		5058
*Mixteco,San Juan Mixtepic	Mexico	Miya	15,000	Christo-Paganism	<1%	1		409
Miya	Nigeria	Mo (Degha)	5,000	Animism	1%	4		1175
Mo	Ivory Coast	Mo	13,000	Animism	1%	5		1100
Moba	Ghana	Binoba	800	Islam-Animist	<1%	1		2296
	Ghana	Binoba	80,000	Animism	<1%	4		530
	Togo		70,000	Animism	8%	4		597

REGISTRY OF THE UNREACHED

NAME	COUNTRY	LANGUAGE	GROUP SIZE	PRIMARY RELIGION	% CHR	V	VOL UP ID
Mober	Nigeria	Mober	45,000	Islam	<1%	1	2468
***Mocha	Ethiopia	Mocha	170,000	Animism	4%	4	429
Modo	Sudan	Modo	2,000	Islam	0%	1	5448
Moewehafen	Papua New Guinea	Moewehafen	2,000	Animism	<1%	1	6229
Mofu	Cameroon	Mofu	33,000	Animism	0%	1	5263
Mogholi	Afghanistan	Mogholi	2,000	Islam	<1%	1	2552
Mogum	Chad	Mogum	6,000	Islam-Animist	<1%	1	2248
Moi	Indonesia	Moi	4,000	Animism	<1%	1	2994
Mokareng	Papua New Guinea	Mokareng	1,000	Animism	<1%	1	6230
Moken	Burma	Moken	5,000	Animism	1%	6 79	157
Moken of Thailand	Thailand	Local dialects	3,000	Animism	<1%	3	2092
*Mokole	Benin	Mokole	7,000	Animism	0%	3	449
*Molbog	Philippines	Molbog	5,000	Islam-Animist	0%	7	1039
Molof	Indonesia	Molof	200	Animism	<1%	1	2995
Monare	Papua New Guinea	Monare	400	Animism	<1%	1	6231
Mombun	Indonesia	Mombun	300	Animism	<1%	1	2996
Momoguns	Malaysia	Momoguns	110,000	Animism	<1%	2	4096
Momolili	Papua New Guinea	Momolili	2,000	Animism	<1%	1	6232
Mon	Burma	Mon	350,000	Buddhist-Animist	<1%	5 81	2583
Mona	Ivory Coast	Mona	6,000	Islam-Animist	<1%	1	2297
Mongondow	Indonesia	Mongondow	400,000	Animism	<1%	5 81	2997
Mongour	China	Mongour	50,000	Traditional Chinese	<1%	1	2833
Moni	Indonesia	Moni	20,000	Animism	<1%	1	2998
Monjombo	Central African Republic	Monjombo	11,000	Animism	0%	1	5191
Mono	Zaire	Mono	30,000	Animism	0%	1	5690
Monpa	India	Monpa	22,000	Buddhist-Animist	0%	3	1037
**Montagnais Indians	Canada:Quebec	English	12,000	Nominal Christian	nr%	1	9263
Montol	Nigeria	Montol	20,000	Islam	<1%	1	2469
Moor & Malays	Sri Lanka	Tamil	900,000	Islam	<1%	6 79	309
Moors in Mauritania	Mauritania	Arabic (Hassani)	1,000,000	Islam	<1%	1	4043
**Mopan Maya	Belize	Mopan Maya	4,000	Christo-Paganism	15%	5	1206
**Mopan Maya	Guatemala	Mopan Maya	2,000	Christo-Paganism	15%	5	1205
Moqaddan	Iran	Moqaddan	1,000	Islam	0%	3	2069
Mor	Indonesia	Mor	1,000	Animism	<1%	1	2999
Morawa	Papua New Guinea	Morawa	800	Animism	<1%	1	6233
Moreb	Sudan	Moreb	600	Islam	0%	1	5520

NAME	COUNTRY	LANGUAGE	GROUP SIZE	PRIMARY RELIGION	% CHR	V	VOL	UP ID
Moresada	Papua New Guinea	Moresada	200	Animism	0%	1		6234
Mori	Indonesia	Mori	200,000	Islam	0%	5	81	3000
Morigi	Papua New Guinea	Morigi	700	Animism	0%	1		6235
Morina	Papua New Guinea	Morina	3,000	Animism	<1%	1		6236
Moroccan Jews	Canada:Quebec	French	10,000	Judaism	0%	3		9103
*Mororata	Bolivia	Aymara	500	Animism	<1%	4		6568
Moru	Ivory Coast	Moru	10,000	Islam-Animist	<1%	1		2298
	Sudan	Moru	23,000	Islam	0%	1		5511
Morunahua	Peru	Morunahua	200	Animism	<1%	1		3181
Morwap	Indonesia	Morwap	300	Animism	<1%	1		3001
Mosi	Tanzania	Mosi	240,000	Animism	0%	1		5576
Mossi	Upper Volta	Mole	3,300,000	Animism	7%	6	80	4009
Motilon	Colombia	Motilon	2,000	Animism	<1%	1		3145
	Venezuela	Motilon	3,000	Animism	<1%	1		5138
Movina	Bolivia	Movina	1,700	Animism	<1%	1		2139
Moxodi	Papua New Guinea	Moxodi	22,000	Animism	<1%	1		6237
Mpoto	Malawi	Mpoto	36,000	Animism	0%	1		5367
	Tanzania	Mpoto	50,000	Animism	0%	1		5577
Mru	Bangladesh	Murung	2,000	Animism	1%	5		3
Mualthuan	India	Mualthuan	36,000	Islam-Animist	5%	4		647
Mubi	Chad	Mubi	2,200	Animism	<1%	1		2249
Mugil	Papua New Guinea	Mugil	200	Animism	<1%	1		6238
Muinane	Colombia	Muinane	1,000	Animism	<1%	1		3146
Mukawa	Papua New Guinea	Mukawa	3,000	Animism	<1%	1		6239
Mulimba	Cameroon	Mulimba	16,000	Unknown	0%	1		5264
Multani in Punjab	India	Multani	10,000	Hindu-Animist	<1%	1		2744
Mumbake	Nigeria	Mumbake	200,000	Islam	<1%	1		2470
Mumuye	Nigeria	Munuye	10,000	Animism	<1%	5		570
Mun	Burma	Mun	200,000	Buddhist-Animist	<1%	1		2584
Muna	Indonesia	Muna	200,000	Islam	<1%	1		3002
Mundang	Chad	Mundang	100,000	Islam-Animist	<1%	1		2250
Mundari in Assam	India	Mundari	771,000	Hindu-Animist	<1%	1		2745
**Mundas in Bihar	India	Munda	25,000	Animism	0%	4		2010
Mundu	Zaire	Mundu	5,000	Animism	0%	1		5743
Munduruku	Brazil	Munduruku	2,000	Animism	<1%	1		3107
Mungaka	Cameroon	Mungaka	14,000	Animism	<1%	1		5265

REGISTRY OF THE UNREACHED

NAME	COUNTRY	LANGUAGE	GROUP SIZE	PRIMARY RELIGION	% CHR	VOL V	UP ID
Munggui	Indonesia	Munggui	700	Animism	<1%	1	3003
Munji-Yidgha	Afghanistan	Munji-Yidgha	14,000	Islam	<1%	1	2553
Munkip	Papua New Guinea	Munkip	100	Animism	<1%	1	6240
Mup	Papua New Guinea	Mup	100	Animism	<1%	1	6241
Mura-Piraha	Brazil	Mura-Piraha	100	Animism	<1%	1	3108
Muria in Andhra Pradesh	India	Muria	13,000	Hindu-Animist	<1%	1	2746
Murik	Papua New Guinea	Murik	2,000	Animism	<1%	4	6242
Murle	Sudan	Murle	40,000	Animism	1%	4	577
*Murngin (Wulamba)	Australia	Dhuwal	6,000	Animism	1%	4	213
Mursi	Ethiopia	Mursi	6,000	Animism	<1%	1	3225
Murut	Malaysia	Murut	38,000	Animism	0%	3	4105
Musak	Papua New Guinea	Musak	200	Animism	<1%	1	6243
Musar	Papua New Guinea	Musar	500	Animism	<1%	1	6244
Musei	Chad	Musei	60,000	Islam-Animist	<1%	1	2251
Musgu	Chad	Musgu	75,000	Islam-Animist	<1%	1	2252
Musi	Indonesia	Indonesian	400,000	Islam-Animist	0%	3	4087
Muslim Community of Bawku	Ghana	Hausa, Ghana	20,000	Islam	0%	5	1083
Muslim Gypsies in Skopije	Yugoslavia	Romany Dialects	23,000	Islam	0%	5 82	5026
**Muslim Immigrants in U.K.	United Kingdom	not reported	500,000	Islam	0%	4 83	1099
Muslim Lebanese Refugees	Canada	French	29,000	Islam	0%	4	9025
Muslim Malays	Malaysia	Bahasa Malaysia	5,500,000	Islam	<1%	6 80	50
Muslims	United Arab Emirates	Arabic	752,000	Islam	1%	6 79	365
Muslims (West Nile Dist.)	Uganda	Lugbara	45,000	Islam	1%	4	238
Muslims of Jordan	Jordan	Arabic	2,430,500	Islam	<1%	4	220
Musom	Papua New Guinea	Musom		Animism	<1%	1	6245
Muthuvan (Andra Pradesh)	India	Muthuvan	7,000	Hindu-Animist	0%	1	2747
Mutu	Venezuela	Spanish	300	Christo-Paganism	0%	1	5139
Mutum	Papua New Guinea	Mutum	400	Animism	0%	1	6246
Muwasi in Madhya Pradesh	India	Muwasi	21,000	Hindu-Animist	<1%	1	2748
Muyuw	Papua New Guinea	Muyuw	3,000	Animism	0%	1	6247
Mwanga	Tanzania	Mwanga	27,200	Animism	<1%	1	6248
Mwatebu	Papua New Guinea	Mwatebu		Animism	<1%	1	5578
Mwera	Tanzania	Mwera	110,000	Animism	<1%	1	5579
Myaung-Ze	Burma	Myaung-Ze	7,000	Animism	0%	2	4153
Nabak	Papua New Guinea	Nabak	12,000	Animism	<1%	1	6249
Nabi	Indonesia	Nabi	600	Animism	<1%	1	3004

418

NAME	COUNTRY	LANGUAGE	GROUP PRIMARY SIZE RELIGION		% CHR	VOL V	UP ID
Nadeb Maku	Brazil	Nadeb Maku	200	Animism	<1%	1	3109
**Nafaara	Ghana	Mafaara	40,000	Animism	15%	6 79	654
Nafar	Iran	Turkish	4,000	Islam	0%	3	2047
Nafri	Indonesia	Nafri	2,000	Animism	<1%	1	3005
Naga, Kalyokengnyu	India	Naga, Kalyokengnyu	14,000	Hindu-Animist	<1%	1	2751
Naga, Mao	India	Naga, Mao	20,000	Hindu-Buddhist	<1%	1	2755
Naga, Nruangmei	India	Naga, Nruangmei	49,000	Hindu-Buddhist	<1%	1	2756
Naga, Sangtam	India	Naga, Sangtam	20,000	Hindu-Buddhist	<1%	1	2757
Naga, Sema	India	Naga, Sema	70,000	Unknown	<1%	1	2758
Naga, Tangkhul	India	Naga, Tangkhul	58,000	Hindu-Buddhist	<1%	1	2759
Naga, Wancho	India	Naga, Wancho	29,000	Hindu-Buddhist	<1%	1	2760
Nagar in Madhya Pradesh	India	Nagar	7,000	Hindu-Animist	<1%	1	2761
Nagarige	Papua New Guinea	Nagarige	600	Animism	0%	1	6250
Nagatman	Papua New Guinea	Nagatman	500	Animism	0%	1	6251
Nagovisi	Papua New Guinea	Nagovisi	5,000	Animism	<1%	1	6252
Nahsi	China	Nahsi	160,000	Traditional Chinese	<1%	1	2834
Nahu	Papua New Guinea	Nahu	5,000	Animism	<1%	1	6253
*Nahua, North Puebla	Mexico	Nahua	55,000	Christo-Paganism	9%	4	435
Naka	Sudan	Naka	4,000	Islam	0%	1	5492
Nakana	Papua New Guinea	Nakana	900	Animism	<1%	1	6254
Nakanai	Papua New Guinea	Nakanai	8,000	Animism	<1%	1	6255
Nalik	Papua New Guinea	Nalik	3,000	Animism	<1%	1	6256
Naltya	Indonesia	Naltya	7,000	Animism	<1%	1	3006
Nalu	Guinea	Nalu	10,000	Islam-Animist	0%	1	5346
Nama	Namibia	Nana	10,000	Animism	<1%	1	5403
Nana	South Africa	Nana	15,000	Animism	0%	1	5437
Nambikuara	Brazil	Nambikuara	400	Animism	3%	5	379
Nambis	Papua New Guinea	Nanbis	1,000	Animism	<1%	1	6257
Nambu	Papua New Guinea	Nambu	700	Animism	0%	1	6258
**Nambya	Zimbabwe	Nambya	40,000	Animism	8%	5	1161
Namuni	Papua New Guinea	Namuni	100	Animism	0%	1	6259
Nanai	China	Nanai	1,000	Traditional Chinese	<1%	1	2835
Nanai	USSR	Nanai	12,000	Unknown	0%	1	5864
Nancere	Chad	Nancere	35,000	Islam-Animist	<1%	1	2253
Nandi	Zaire	Nandi	310,000	Animism	<1%	1	5744
Nandu-Tari	Nigeria	Nandu-Tari	4,000	Islam	<1%	1	2471

REGISTRY OF THE UNREACHED

NAME	COUNTRY	LANGUAGE	GROUP SIZE	PRIMARY RELIGION	% CHR V	VOL UP ID
Nankina	Papua New Guinea	Nankina	2,000	Animism	<1% 1	6260
Nao	Ethiopia	Naouden	5,000	Animism	<1% 1	3226
Naouden	Togo	Naouden	90,000	Islam-Animist	<1% 1	5633
Nara	Ethiopia	Nara	25,000	Islam-Animist	<1% 1	3227
	Papua New Guinea	Nara		Animism	<1% 1	6261
Naraguta	Nigeria	Naraguta	3,000	Animism	<1% 1	2472
Narak	Papua New Guinea	Narak	4,000	Animism	<1% 1	6262
Nasioi	Papua New Guinea	Nasioi	13,000	Animism	<1% 1	6263
Nata	Tanzania	Nata	10,000	Animism	0% 1	5580
Natemba	Togo	Natemba	17,000	Islam-Animist	0% 1	5634
Natioro	Upper Volta	Natioro	1,000	Islam-Animist	0% 1	5676
Nauna	Papua New Guinea	Nauna	100	Animism	0% 1	6264
Nawuri	Ghana	Nawuri	10,000	Animism	1% 5	1068
Nchinburu	Ghana	Nchunburu	7,000	Animism	7% 5	1069
Nchunbulu	Ghana	Nchunbulu	1,000	Islam-Animist	0% 1	5329
Nchumuru	Ghana	Nchumuru	8,000	Islam-Animist	0% 1	5330
Ndaaka	Zaire	Ndaaka	5,000	Animism	0% 1	5745
Ndali	Tanzania	Ndali	57,000	Animism	0% 1	5581
Ndam	Central African Republic	Ndam	700	Animism	0% 1	5192
Ndamba	Tanzania	Ndamba	19,000	Animism	0% 1	5582
Ndaomese	Indonesia	Ndao	2,000	Animism	<1% 1	3007
Ndau	Zimbabwe	Ndau	178,000	Animism	<1% 1	5415
Nde-Nsele-Nta	Nigeria	Nde-Nsele-Nta	10,000	Animism	<1% 1	2473
**Ndebele	Zimbabwe	Sindebele	1,000,000	Animism	7% 6 79	1235
Ndengereko	Tanzania	Ndengereko	53,000	Animism	0% 1	5583
Ndjem	Cameroon	Ndjem	25,000	Animism	<1% 1	5266
Ndo	Zaire	Ndo	13,000	Animism	<1% 1	5746
Ndoe	Nigeria	Ndoe	3,000	Animism	<1% 1	2474
Ndogo	Central African Republic	Ndogo	4,000	Animism	0% 1	5193
	Sudan	Ndogo	4,000	Unknown	0% 1	5512
Ndom	Indonesia	Ndom	500	Animism	<1% 1	3008
Ndomde	Tanzania	Ndomde	12,000	Animism	0% 1	5584
Ndoolo	Zaire	Ndoolo	5,000	Animism	0% 1	5747
Ndop-Baneesing	Cameroon	Ndop-Baneesing	17,000	Animism	0% 1	5267
Ndoro	Cameroon	Ndoro	10,000	Animism	0% 1	5268
**Ndoro	Nigeria	Ndoro	10,000	Animism	6% 5	1176

420

NAME	COUNTRY	LANGUAGE	GROUP SIZE	PRIMARY RELIGION	% CHR	V	VOL	UP ID
Nduga	Indonesia	Nduga	10,000	Animism	<1%	1		3009
Ndunga	Zaire	Ndunga	3,000	Animism	0%	1		5748
Ndunpa Duupa	Cameroon	Ndunpa Duupa	1,000	Islam-Animist	1%	4		1156
Negira	Papua New Guinea	Negira	1,400	Animism	0%	1		6265
Nek	Papua New Guinea	Nek	1,000	Animism	<1%	1		6266
Nekgini	Papua New Guinea	Nekgini	500	Animism	<1%	1		6267
Neko	Papua New Guinea	Neko	200	Animism	<1%	1		6268
Nengaya	Papua New Guinea	Nengaya	600	Animism	<1%	1		6269
Nentsy	USSR	Nentsy	29,000	Unknown	0%	1		5815
**Nepalese in India	India	Nepali	90,000	Hinduism	12%	4		4060
Newar in Kathmandu	Nepal	Newari	100,000	Buddhism	<1%	5	82	5030
*Newari	Nepal	Newari	500,000	Hindu-Buddhist	0%	3		660
Nevo	Ivory Coast	Nevo	5,000	Animism	0%	3		1131
Ngada	Indonesia	Ngada	40,900	Christo-Paganism	<1%	1		3010
Ngaing	Papua New Guinea	Ngaing	900	Animism	<1%	1		6270
Ngalik, North	Indonesia	Ngalik, North	35,000	Animism	<1%	1		3011
Ngalik, Southern	Indonesia	Ngalik, Southern	5,000	Animism	<1%	1		3012
Ngalum	Indonesia	Ngalum	10,000	Animism	<1%	1		3013
**Ngano	Nigeria	Ngano	18,000	Animism	8%	4		569
Nganasan	USSR	Nganasan	1,000	Unknown	0%	1		5865
Ngando	Central African Republic	Ngando	2,000	Animism	0%	1		5194
Ngando	Zaire	Ngando	121,000	Animism	0%	1		5749
Ngasa	Tanzania	Ngasa	1,000	Animism	0%	1		5585
Ngayaba	Cameroon	Ngayaba	1,000	Animism	0%	1		5269
Ngbaka	Zaire	Ngbaka	700,000	Animism	<1%	1		5750
Ngbaka Ma'bo	Central African Republic	Ngbaka Ma'bo	17,000	Animism	0%	1		5195
Ngbaka Ma'bo	Zaire	Ngbaka Ma'bo	17,000	Animism	0%	1		5751
Ngbandi	Zaire	Ngbandi	137,000	Animism	0%	1		5752
Ngbee	Zaire	Ngbee	30,000	Animism	0%	1		5753
Ngemba	Cameroon	Ngemba	34,000	Animism	<1%	1		5270
*Ngen	Ivory Coast	Ngen	20,000	Animism	2%	4		698
Ngeq	Laos	Ngeq	50,000	Animism	5%	5		105
Ngere	Ivory Coast	not reported	150,000	Animism	<1%	4		484
Ngi	Cameroon	Ngi	10,000	Animism	0%	1		5271
Ngindo	Tanzania	Ngindo	85,000	Animism	0%	1		5586
Nginyukwur	Sudan	Nginyukwur	4,000	Islam	0%	1		5485

NAME	COUNTRY	LANGUAGE	GROUP SIZE	PRIMARY RELIGION	% CHR	VOL V	UP ID
Ngirere	Sudan	Ngirere	4,000	Islam	0%	1	5486
Ngiri	Zaire	Ngiri	6,000	Animism	0%	1	5754
Ngizin	Nigeria	Ngizin	40,000	Islam	<1%	1	2475
Ngok	Sudan	Ngok	21,000	Islam	0%	1	5467
**Ngombe	Zaire	Ngombe	5,000	Animism	3%	5	4080
Ngoni	Tanzania	Ngoni	85,000	Animism	0%	1	5587
	Zambia	Ngoni	257,000	Animism	0%	1	5804
	Malawi	Ngoni	476,000	Animism	0%	1	5368
Ngulu	Tanzania	Ngulu	13,000	Animism	0%	1	5588
	Cameroon	Ngulu	10,000	Animism	<1%	1	5272
Ngumba	Cameroon	Ngumba	4,000	Animism	0%	1	5305
Ngumbi	Equatorial Guinea	Ngumbi	9,000	Islam	0%	1	5487
Ngurduna	Sudan	Ngurduna	8,000	Islam	0%	1	5488
Nguquurang	Tanzania	Nguquurang	12,000	Animism	0%	1	5589
Ngurini	Tanzania	Ngurini	46,000	Animism	0%	1	5590
Nguu	Cameroon	Nguu	10,000	Animism	0%	1	5273
Nguoi	Nigeria	Nguoi	1,000	Islam	<1%	1	2476
Nharon	Botswana	Nharon	3,000	Animism	0%	1	5177
Nhengatu	Brazil	Nhengatu	3,000	Animism	<1%	1	3110
Nias	Indonesia	Nias	230,000	Animism	<1%	1	3014
Nicaraguan Refugees	Costa Rica	Spanish	55,000	Nominal Christian	nr%	3	9053
Nielim	Chad	Nielim	2,000	Islam-Aninist	<1%	1	2254
Nihali in Madhya Pradesh	India	Nihali	1,000	Hindu-Aninist	<1%	1	2762
Nii	Papua New Guinea	Nii	9,000	Animism	<1%	1	6271
Nilamba	Tanzania	Nilamba	210,000	Animism	0%	1	5591
Ninadi in Madhya Pradesh	India	Ninadi	794,000	Hindu-Buddhist	<1%	1	2763
Ninboran	Indonesia	Ninboran	4,000	Animism	<1%	1	3015
Ninowa	Papua New Guinea	Ninowa	1,000	Animism	<1%	1	6272
Ninan	Brazil	Ninan	500	Animism	<1%	4	3111
*Ningerun	Papua New Guinea	Ningerun	3,000	Animism	<1%	1	41
Ninggrun	Indonesia	Ninggrun	4,000	Animism	<1%	1	3016
Niningo	Papua New Guinea	Niningo	500	Animism	0%	1	6273
Ninzam	Nigeria	Ninzam	35,300	Islam	<1%	1	2477
Nisa	Indonesia	Nisa	300	Animism	<1%	1	3017
Nissan	Papua New Guinea	Nissan	2,000	Animism	<1%	1	6274
Nivkhi	USSR	Nivkhi	4,000	Unknown	0%	1	5817

NAME	COUNTRY	LANGUAGE	GROUP SIZE	PRIMARY RELIGION	% CHR	VOL V	UP ID
Njadu	Indonesia	Njadu	9,000	Animism	<1%	1	3018
Njalguigule	Sudan	Njalguigule	900	Islam	0%	1	5513
Njemps	Kenya	Njemps Maasai	10,000	Animism	<1%	2	8501
Nkem-Nkum	Nigeria	Nkem-Nkum	16,700	Animism	<1%	1	2478
Nkom	Cameroon	Nkom	30,000	Animism	0%	1	5274
Nkonya	Ghana	Nkonya	17,000	Islam-Animist	0%	1	5331
*Nkoya	Zambia	Shinkoya	nr	Animism	X	4	413
Nkutu	Zaire	Nkutu	40,000	Animism	<1%	1	5755
***Nocte	India	Nocte	20,000	Animism	0%	3	1030
Nohu	Cameroon	Nohu	7,000	Animism	0%	1	5275
Nomane	Papua New Guinea	Nomane	3,000	Animism	<1%	1	6275
Nonu	Papua New Guinea	Nonu	800	Animism	<1%	1	6276
Nondiri	Papua New Guinea	Nondiri		Animism	<1%	1	6277
Norra	Burma	Norra	2,000	Animism	<1%	1	2585
North Africans in Belgium	Belgium	Arabic	90,000	Islam	<1%	6 80	4019
Northern Cagayan Negrito	Philippines	Northern Cagayan Negrito	1,000	Christo-Paganism	<1%	1	3292
Nosu	China	Nosu	556,000	Traditional Chinese	<1%	1	2837
Notsi	Papua New Guinea	Notsi	1,000	Animism	<1%	1	6278
*Nouni	Upper Volta	Nouni	50,000	Animism	3%	4	4129
Nsenga	Zambia	Nsenga	191,000	Animism	<1%	1	5802
	Zimbabwe	Nsenga	16,000	Animism	0%	1	5416
Nso	Cameroon	Nso	100,000	Animism	<1%	1	5276
Nsongo	Angola	Nsongo	15,000	Animism	<1%	1	5161
Ntomba	Zaire	Ntomba	50,000	Animism	0%	1	5756
Ntrubo	Ghana	Ntrubo	5,000	Animism	1%	5	1065
*Nuer	Togo	Ntrubo	3,000	Islam-Animist	0%	1	5635
	Ethiopia	Nuer	844,000	Animism	1%	4	519
	Sudan	Nuer		Animism	1%	6 79	576
Nuk	Papua New Guinea	Nuk	2,000	Animism	<1%	1	6279
Numana-Nunku-Gwantu	Nigeria	Numana-Nunku-Gwantu	15,000	Islam	<1%	1	2479
Numanggang	Papua New Guinea	Numanggang	2,000	Animism	<1%	1	6280
Nung	China	Nung	100,000	Traditional Chinese	<1%	1	2838
Nungu	Nigeria	Nungu	25,000	Animism	<1%	1	2480
Numuna	Upper Volta	Numuna	43,000	Islam-Animist	<1%	1	5677
**Nupe	Nigeria	Nupe	600,000	Islam	2%	5	17
Nuristani	Afghanistan	Local dialects	67,000	Islam	0%	5 80	4015

REGISTRY OF THE UNREACHED

NAME	COUNTRY	LANGUAGE	GROUP SIZE	PRIMARY RELIGION	% CHR	V	VOL UP ID
Nurses in St. Louis	United States of America	English	3,000	Secularism	<1%	5 82	5031
**Nyabwa	Ivory Coast	Nyabwa	30,000	Animism	3%	5	4125
Nyaheun	Laos	Nyaheun	15,000	Animism	2%	4	103
Nyakyusa	Malawi	Nyakyusa	34,000	Animism	<1%	1	5369
	Tanzania	Nyakyusa	193,000	Animism	0%	1	5592
Nyali	Zaire	Nyali	12,000	Animism	0%	1	5757
Nyambo	Tanzania	Nyambo	4,000	Animism	0%	1	5593
Nyamusa	Sudan	Nyamusa	1,000	Islam	0%	1	5510
Nyamwezi	Tanzania	Nyamwezi	590,000	Animism	9%	6 80	487
Nyaneka	Angola	Nyaneka	40,000	Animism	0%	1	5162
Nyang	Cameroon	Nyang	10,000	Animism	<1%	1	5277
Nyanga-Li	Zaire	Nyanga-Li	25,000	Animism	0%	1	5758
Nyangbo	Ghana	Nyangbo	3,000	Islam-Animist	0%	1	5333
Nyanja	Zimbabwe	Nyanja	252,000	Animism	0%	1	5417
Nyankole	Uganda	Nyankole	810,000	Animism	<1%	1	5651
*Nyantruku	Benin	Aledjo	4,000	Animism	0%	3	450
Nyarueng	Sudan	Nyarueng	2,000	Islam	0%	1	5461
Nyemba	Angola	Nyemba	100,000	Animism	<1%	1	5163
Nyengo	Angola	Nyengo	5,000	Animism	0%	1	5164
Nyiha	Tanzania	Nyiha	64,000	Animism	0%	1	5594
	Zambia	Nyiha	59,000	Animism	0%	1	5806
Nyoro	Uganda	Nyoro	620,000	Animism	<1%	1	5652
Nyuli	Uganda	Nyuli	140,000	Animism	0%	1	5653
Nyungue	Mozambique	Nyungue	700,000	Animism	<1%	1	5393
Nyzatom	Sudan	Toposa, Donyiro	80,000	Animism	0%	3	705
Nzakara	Central African Republic	Nzakara	3,000	Animism	0%	1	5196
Nzanyi	Nigeria	Nzanyi	14,000	Islam	<1%	1	2481
Nzebi	Congo	Nzebi	40,000	Animism	0%	1	5296
Nzema	Ghana	Nzema	275,000	Islam-Animist	<1%	1	5334
	Ivory Coast	Nzema	24,000	Islam-Animist	<1%	1	2300
O'ung	Angola	O'ung	5,000	Animism	0%	1	5148
Obanliku	Nigeria	Obanliku	20,000	Animism	<1%	1	2482
Obolo	Nigeria	Obolo	70,000	Animism	<1%	1	2483
Ocaina	Peru	Ocaina	300	Animism	<1%	1	3182
Od	Pakistan	Odki	40,000	Hinduism	1%	4	265
Odual	Nigeria	Odual	9,000	Animism	<1%	1	2484

NAME	COUNTRY	LANGUAGE	GROUP SIZE	PRIMARY RELIGION	% CHR	VOL V	UP ID
Odut	Nigeria	Odut	700	Animism	<1%	1	2485
Ogan	Indonesia	Indonesian	200,000	Islam-Animist	0%	3	4085
Ogbia	Nigeria	Ogbia	22,000	Animism	<1%	1	2486
Oi	Laos	Oi	10,000	Animism	1%	5	104
Oil Executives, Calgary	Canada:Alberta	English	5,000	Secularism	0%	1	9206
Oirat	China	Oirat	60,000	Traditional Chinese	0%	1	2839
Ojhi in Madhya Pradesh	India	Ojhi	1,000	Hindu-Animist	<1%	1	2764
Okobo	Nigeria	Okobo	11,000	Animism	<1%	1	2487
Okpanheri	Nigeria	Okpanheri	30,000	Animism	<1%	1	2488
Oksapmin	Papua New Guinea	Oksapmin	5,000	Animism	<1%	1	6281
Ollari in Orissa	India	Ollari	800	Hindu-Animist	<1%	1	2765
Olo	Papua New Guinea	Olo	9,000	Animism	<1%	1	6282
Olulumo-Ikom	Nigeria	Olulumo-Ikom	10,000	Animism	<1%	1	2489
Omati	Papua New Guinea	Omati	800	Animism	<1%	1	6283
Omie	Papua New Guinea	Omie	1,000	Animism	<1%	1	6284
Onank	Papua New Guinea	Onank	100	Animism	<1%	1	6285
Ong in Andamans	India	Ong	200	Hindu-Animist	<1%	1	2766
Onin	Indonesia	Onin	600	Animism	<1%	1	3019
Onjab	Papua New Guinea	Onjab	100	Animism	<1%	1	6286
Ono	Papua New Guinea	Ono	5,000	Animism	<1%	1	6287
Orang Kanak	Malaysia	Orang Kanak	4,000	Animism	0%	2	4100
Orang Laut	Malaysia	Orang Laut	4,000	Animism	0%	2	4101
Orang Ulu	Malaysia	Orang Ulu	4,000	Animism	0%	2	4099
Orejon	Peru	Orejon	300	Animism	<1%	1	3183
Oring	Nigeria	Oring	25,000	Animism	<1%	1	2490
Ormu	Indonesia	Ormu	800	Animism	<1%	1	3020
Oroch	USSR	Oroch	1,000	Unknown	0%	1	5867
Orok	USSR	Orok	400	Unknown	0%	1	5866
Orokaiva	Papua New Guinea	Orokaiva	25,000	Animism	<1%	1	6288
Orokolo	Papua New Guinea	Orokolo	13,000	Animism	<1%	1	6289
Oron	Nigeria	Oron	50,000	Animism	<1%	1	2491
Oronchon	China	Oronchon	2,000	Traditional Chinese	0%	1	2840
Oso	Cameroon	Oso	25,000	Animism	0%	1	5278
Osum	Papua New Guinea	Osum	600	Animism	<1%	1	6290
Ot Danum	Indonesia	Ot Danum	30,000	Animism	<1%	1	3021
Otank	Nigeria	Otank	3,000	Animism	<1%	1	2492

425

NAME	COUNTRY	LANGUAGE	GROUP SIZE	PRIMARY RELIGION	% CHR	V	VOL	UP ID
Otomi, Eastern	Mexico	Otomi, Eastern	20,000	Christo-Paganism	<1%	1		5059
Otomi, Mezquital	Mexico	Otomi, Mezquital	100,000	Christo-Paganism	<1%	1		5060
Otomi, Northwestern	Mexico	Otomi, Northwestern	40,000	Christo-Paganism	0%	1		5061
Otomi, Southeastern	Mexico	Otomi, Southeastern	2,000	Christo-Paganism	0%	1		5062
Otomi, State of Mexico	Mexico	Otomi	70,000	Christo-Paganism	<1%	1		5063
Otomi, Tenango	Mexico	Otomi, Tenango	10,000	Christo-Paganism	<1%	1		5064
Otomi, Texcatepec	Mexico	Otomi, Texcatepec	8,000	Christo-Paganism	0%	1		5065
Otoro	Sudan	Otoro	28,000	Islam	<1%	1		5514
Ouaddai	Chad	Maba	320,000	Islam	<1%	4		310
Oubi	Ivory Coast	Oubi	1,000	Islam-Animist	<1%	1		2301
Oyampipuku	Brazil	Oyampipuku	100	Animism	<1%	1		3112
Oyda	Ethiopia	Oyda	3,000	Animism	<1%	1		3228
Pacu	Brazil	Tucano	100	Animism	<1%	1		3113
***Paez	Colombia	Paez	40,000	Christo-Paganism	11%	5		1196
Pahari Garhwali (Uttar Pradesh	India	Pahari Garhwali	1,300,000	Hindu-Animist	<1%	1		2667
Pai	China	Yi	1,000,000	Buddhist-Animist	<1%	5	81	7008
Paipai	Nigeria	Pai	2,000	Animism	<1%	1		2493
Paipai	Mexico	Spanish	300	Christo-Paganism	0%	1		5066
Paite in Assam	India	Paite	28,000	Hindu-Animist	3%	4		2769
Paiute, Northern	United States of America	Paiute, Northern	5,000	Peyote Religion	3%	4		391
Paiwa	Papua New Guinea	Paiwa	2,000	Animism	<1%	1		6291
Pak-Tong	Papua New Guinea	Pak-Tong	1,000	Animism	<1%	1		6292
*Pakaasnovos	Brazil	Pakaasnovos	800	Animism	<1%	1		3114
***Pakabeti of Equator	Zaire	Pakabeti	3,000	Animism	3%	4		1007
*Pala'wan	Philippines	Pala'wan	50,000	Animism	<1%	5	81	4162
Palara	Ivory Coast	Palara	10,000	Islam-Animist	<1%	1		2302
Palaung	Burma	Palaung	150,000	Buddhism	<1%	5	79	156
Palawano	Philippines	Palawano	3,000	Animism	<1%	1		3280
Palawano, Central	Philippines	Palawano, Central	3,000	Animism	<1%	1		3281
Palembang	Indonesia	Palembang	500,000	Islam	<1%	1		3022
Palenquero	Colombia	Spanish	3,000	Animism	<1%	4	83	3147
Palestinian Refugees	Jordan	Arabic	1,160,800	Islam	<1%	4	83	9020
	Lebanon	Arabic	240,000	Islam	<1%	4		9016
Palikur	Brazil	Palikur	500	Animism	<1%	1		3115
Paloc	Sudan	Arabic	14,000	Islam	0%	1		5468
Palpa	Nepal	Palpa	3,000	Buddhist-Animist	0%	1		6515

NAME	COUNTRY	LANGUAGE	GROUP SIZE	PRIMARY RELIGION	% CHR	V	VOL	UP ID
Panbia	Central African Republic	Panbia	2,000	Animism	0%	1		5197
Pane, Central Chichimeca	Mexico	Pane, Central Chichimeca	3,000	Christo-Paganism	<1%	1		5067
Pane, Chichimeca-Jonaz	Mexico	Spanish	1,000	Christo-Paganism	0%	1		5068
Pane, Northern	Mexico	Pane, Northern	2,000	Christo-Paganism	0%	1		5069
Pana	Central African Republic	Pana	20,000	Animism	0%	1		5198
Panare	Venezuela	Panare	1,000	Animism	<1%	1		5140
Pande	Congo	Pande	1,000	Animism	0%	1		5297
Pangua	Tanzania	Pangua	26,000	Animism	0%	1		5595
Panika	India	Panika	31,000	Hindu-Animist	<1%	1		2770
Panika	India	Panika	31,000	Hindu-Animist	<1%	1		7066
**Paniyan of Kerala	India	Paniyan	6,000	Animism	<1%	5	81	2772
Pankararu	Brazil	Portuguese	2,000	Animism	<1%	1		3116
Pankhu	Bangladesh	Pankhu	600	Islam	<1%	1		2563
Pantu	Indonesia	Pantu	9,000	Animism	<1%	1		3023
Pao	Burma	Pao	100,000	Buddhism	0%	2		4149
Pao in Madhya Pradesh	India	Pao	16,000	Hindu-Buddhist	<1%	1		2773
Paongan	China	Paongan	8,000	Traditional Chinese	<1%	1		2841
Papapana	Papua New Guinea	Papapana	200	Animism	<1%	1		6293
Pape	Cameroon	Pape	1,000	Animism	0%	1		5279
Papel	Guinea-Bissau	Papel	36,000	Islam-Animist	<1%	1		5357
Papuma	Indonesia	Papuma	700	Animism	<1%	1		3024
Parakanan	Brazil	Parakanan	500	Animism	<1%	1		3117
Paranan	Philippines	Paranan	6,000	Christo-Paganism	<1%	1		3282
Parawen	Papua New Guinea	Parawen	500	Hindu-Animist	<1%	1		6294
Pardhan in Andhra Pradesh	India	Pardhan	500	Animism	<1%	1		2774
Pare	Papua New Guinea	Pare	1,000	Animism	<1%	1		6295
Pare	Tanzania	Pare	99,000	Animism	0%	1		5596
Parengi in Orissa	India	Parengi	3,000	Hindu-Animist	<1%	1		2776
Paresi	Brazil	Paresi	400	Animism	<1%	1		3118
Parintintin	Brazil	Parintintin	200	Animism	<1%	1		3119
*Parsees	India	Gujarati	120,000	Secularism	<1%	5	81	2121
*Parsis in Bombay	India	Parsi	80,000	Zorcastrianism	0%	6	82	5039
Pashayi	Afghanistan	Pashayi	96,000	Islam-Animist	<1%	1		2554
Pashtuns	Iran	Pashtu	3,000	Islam	0%	6	80	2054
Pasismanua	Papua New Guinea	Pasismanua	6,000	Animism	<1%	1		6296
Patamona	Guyana	Patamona	1,000	Christo-Paganism	<1%	1		5117

NAME	COUNTRY	LANGUAGE	GROUP SIZE	PRIMARY RELIGION	% CHR	V	UP ID
Patelia in Gujarat	India	Patelia	23,000	Hindu-Animist	<1%	1	2778
Patep	Papua New Guinea	Patep	7,000	Animism	<1%	1	6297
Pato Tapuia	Brazil	Pato Tapuia	100	Animism	<1%	1	3120
Patpatar	Papua New Guinea	Patpatar	5,000	Animism	<1%	1	6298
Paumari	Brazil	Paumari	300	Animism	<1%	1	3121
Pawaia	Papua New Guinea	Pawaia	2,000	Animism	<1%	1	6299
Pay	Papua New Guinea	Pay	600	Animism	<1%	1	6300
Paya	Honduras	Spanish	300	Animism	<1%	1	8013
Paynamar	Papua New Guinea	Paynamar	200	Animism	0%	1	6301
Penan, Western	Malaysia	Penan	200,000	Animism	nr%	6 81	7027
Pende	Zaire	Pende	3,000	Animism	0%	1	5759
Pengo in Orissa	India	Pengo	1,000	Hindu-Animist	<1%	1	2779
Pension Students-Madrid	Spain	Italian	2,000	Secularism	nr%	5 82	5032
Peremka	Papua New Guinea	Peremka	200	Animism	0%	1	6302
Peri	Nigeria	Peri	40,000	Animism	0%	1	5760
Pero	Nigeria	Pero	20,000	Islam	<1%	1	2494
Persians of Iran	Iran	Persian	2,000,000	Islam	<1%	1	4010
Phu Thai	Laos	Phu Thai	100,000	Buddhist-Animist	<1%	6 80	102
Phu Thai	Thailand	Phu Thai	80,000	Buddhist-Animist	1%	5	4809
Piapoco	Colombia	Piapoco	3,000	Animism	<1%	4 84	3148
Piaroa	Venezuela	Piaroa	12,000	Animism	<1%	1	5141
**Pila	Benin	Pila-Pila	50,000	Animism	<1%	4	237
Pila	Papua New Guinea	Pila	600	Animism	<1%	1	6303
Pilaga	Argentina	Pilaga	4,000	Animism	<1%	1	2130
Pina Bajo	Mexico	Pina Bajo	1,000	Christo-Paganism	0%	1	5070
Pimbwe	Tanzania	Pimbwe	13,000	Animism	0%	1	5597
Piratapuyo	Brazil	Tucano	800	Animism	0%	1	3122
Piro	Peru	Maniteneri	3,000	Animism	<1%	1	3184
Pisa	Indonesia	Pisa	4,000	Animism	<1%	1	3025
Pishagchi	Iran	Pishagchi	1,000	Islam	0%	3	2064
Piti	Nigeria	Piti	2,000	Islam	<1%	1	2495
Pitu Uluna Salu	Indonesia	Pitu Uluna Salu	175,000	Animism	<1%	1	3026
Piu	Nigeria	Piu	100	Islam	<1%	1	6304
Piya	Papua New Guinea	Piya	3,000	Animism	6%	5	2496
**Plantation Workers	Papua New Guinea	Local dialects	5,000	Christo-Paganism	<1%	5	4031
Pnar in Assam	India	Pnar	83,000	Hindu-Animist	<1%	1	2780

NAME	COUNTRY	LANGUAGE	GROUP SIZE	PRIMARY RELIGION	% CHR	V	VOL UP ID
Pocoman, Central	Guatemala	Pocoman, Central	15,000	Christo-Paganism	<1%	1	8007
Pocomchi, Eastern	Guatemala	Pocomchi, Eastern	20,000	Christo-Paganism	<1%	1	8008
Pocomchi, Western	Guatemala	Pocomchi, Western	25,000	Christo-Paganism	<1%	1	8009
Podokwo	Cameroon	Podokwo	25,000	Animism	<1%	4	496
Podopa	Papua New Guinea	Podopa	3,000	Animism	<1%	1	6305
Podzo	Mozambique	Podzo	45,000	Animism	0%	1	5394
Pogolo	Tanzania	Pogolo	65,000	Animism	0%	1	5598
Poke	Zaire	Poke	46,000	Animism	0%	1	5761
Pokot	Uganda	Pokot	170,000	Animism	<1%	1	5654
Pol	Congo	Pol	2,000	Animism	0%	1	5298
Polci	Nigeria	Polci	6,000	Islam	<1%	1	2497
Pom	Indonesia	Pom	2,000	Animism	<1%	1	3027
Ponan-Andra-Hus	Papua New Guinea	Ponan-Andra-Hus	1,000	Animism	<1%	1	6306
Pondoma	Nigeria	Pondoma	300	Animism	<1%	1	6307
Pongu	India	Poochi	4,000	Islam	<1%	1	2498
Poouch in Kashmir		Spanish	500,000	Islam	0%	4	4079
Popoloca, Ahuatempan	Mexico	Spanish	6,000	Christo-Paganism	0%	1	5071
Popoloca, Coyotepec	Mexico	Popoloca, Eastern	500	Christo-Paganism	0%	1	5072
Popoloca, Eastern	Mexico	Popoloca, Northern	2,000	Christo-Paganism	<1%	1	5073
Popoloca, Northern	Mexico	Spanish	6,000	Christo-Paganism	0%	1	5074
Popoloca, Southern	Mexico	Popoloca, Western	1,000	Christo-Paganism	<1%	1	5075
Popoloca, Western	Mexico	Spanish	8,000	Christo-Paganism	<1%	1	5076
Popoluca, Oluta	Mexico	Popoluca, Sayula	200	Christo-Paganism	0%	1	5077
Popoluca, Sayula	Mexico	Popoluca, Sierra	6,000	Christo-Paganism	0%	1	5079
Popoluca, Sierra	Mexico	Spanish	18,000	Christo-Paganism	<1%	1	5078
Popoluca, Texistepec	Mexico	Porapora	2,000	Christo-Paganism	0%	1	5080
Porapora	Papua New Guinea	Porohanon	400	Animism	0%	1	6308
Porohanon	Philippines	Portuguese	23,000	Animism	<1%	1	3283
**Portuguese in France	France	Portuguese	150,000	Secularism	10%	4	1186
Portuguese, Cambridge	Canada:Ontario	Portuguese	15,000	Nominal Christian	nr%	1	9154
Portuguese, London/Strathroy	Canada:Ontario		14,000	Nominal Christian	nr%	1	9155
Portuguese, Metro Toronto	Canada:Ontario	Portuguese	150,000	Nominal Christian	nr%	1	9158
Portuguese, Vancouver	Canada:British Columbia	Portuguese	15,000	Nominal Christian	nr%	1	9157
Portuguese, West Lorne Village	Canada:Ontario	Portuguese	250	Nominal Christian	nr%	1	9156
Prang	Ghana	Prang	5,000	Islam-Animist	0%	1	5335
***Prasuni	Afghanistan	Prasuni	2,000	Islam	<1%	1	2555

NAME	COUNTRY	LANGUAGE	GROUP SIZE	PRIMARY RELIGION	% CHR	V	VOL UP	ID
**Prisoners	Korea, Republic of	Korean	45,000	Secularism	10%	4		300
**Prisoners in Antananarivo	Madagascar	Malagasy	10,000	Folk Religion	2%	5	82	5012
**Pro Hockey Players	United States of America	English	600	Secularism	5%	6	82	5020
Pu-I	China	Pu-I	1,311,000	Traditional Chinese	<1%	1		2842
Puguli	Upper Volta	Puguli	5,000	Islam-Animist	0%	1		5678
Puku-Geeri-Keri-Wipsi	Nigeria	Puku-Geeri-Keri-Wipsi	15,000	Animism	<1%	1		2499
Pular	Senegal	Fouta Toro	300,000	Animism	0%	1		1136
Pulie	Papua New Guinea	Pulie	300,200	Animism	<1%	1		6309
Punu	China	Punu	220,000	Traditional Chinese	<1%	1		2843
Punu	Congo	Punu	46,000	Animism	0%	1		5299
Puragi	Indonesia	Puragi	6,900	Animism	<1%	1		3028
Purari	Papua New Guinea	Purari	900	Animism	1%	1		6310
Purig-Pa of Kashmir	India	Purig-Skad	300	Islam	1%	1		7010
Purum	Burma	Purum	7,000	Buddhist-Animist	<1%	5	81	2587
**Puyuma	Taiwan	Puyuma	6,000	Christo-Paganism	nr%	5		7033
Pye	Ivory Coast	Pye	30,000	Islam-Animist	<1%	5		508
Pygmy (Binga)	Burundi	Local dialects	2,000	Animism	0%	5		512
Pygmy (Binga)	Central African Republic	Local dialects	2,000	Animism	1%	5		396
*Pygmy (Mbuti)	Zaire	local languages	40,000	Animism	<1%	5	79	3029
Pyu	Indonesia	Pyu	100	Animism	0%	1		2056
Qajars	Iran	Qajar	3,000	Islam	0%	3		2058
Qara'i	Iran	Qara'i	2,000	Islam	0%	3		2060
Qaragozlu	Iran	Qaragozlu	2,000	Islam	0%	3		2038
Qashqa'i	Iran	Qashqa'i	350,000	Islam	0%	5	80	3149
Quaiquer	Colombia	Quaiquer	5,000	Animism	<1%	1		2159
Quarequena	Brazil	Tucano	300	Animism	4%	4		10
**Quechua	Bolivia	Quechua	1,000,000	Christo-Paganism	2%	5		1080
**Quechua, Huancayo	Peru	Quechua, Huancayo	3,000,000	Christo-Paganism	6%	5	79	152
**Quiche	Guatemala	Quiche	500,000	Animism	5%	6		4070
**Quichua	Ecuador	Quichua	2,000,000	Christo-Paganism	6%	5		676
Rabha in Assam	India	Rabha	10,000	Hindu-Animist	3%	4		400
Rabinal-Achi	Guatemala	Rabinal Achi	21,000	Christo-Paganism	4%	4		
**Racetrack Residents	United States of America	Spanish	50,000	Secularism	10%	5	79	
Rai	Nepal	Rai	232,000	Hindu-Buddhist	0%	3		663
*Rai, Danuwar	Nepal	Danuwar Rai	12,000	Hindu-Animist	0%	3		661

NAME	COUNTRY	LANGUAGE	GROUP SIZE	PRIMARY RELIGION	% CHR	VOL V	UP ID
Raj, Khaling	Nepal	Rai, Khaling	10,000	Buddhist-Animist	0%	1	6516
Raj, Kulunge	Nepal	Rai, Kulunge	10,000	Buddhist-Animist	0%	1	6524
Raj, Thulunge	Nepal	Rai, Thulunge	25,000	Buddhist-Animist	0%	1	6517
Rajasthani Muslims-Jaipur	India	Jaipuri	4,000	Islam	0%	6 82	5033
Rajbansi	Nepal	Rajbansi	15,000	Hindu-Animist	0%	3	659
Rajneeshees of Oregon	United States of America	English	1,000	New Eastern	0%	4	4806
Ralte	Burma	Ralte	17,000	Buddhist-Animist	<1%	1	2588
Ranbutyo	Papua New Guinea	Rambutyo	1,000	Animism	0%	4	6311
*Rankanhaeng Un. Students	Thailand	Thai	200,000	Buddhism	<1%	4	4053
Rangkas	Nepal	Rangkas	600	Buddhist-Animist	<1%	1	6518
Rao	Papua New Guinea	Rao	3,000	Animism	0%	1	6312
Rastafarians, Edmonton	Canada:Alberta	English	100	Other	0%	1	9205
Ratahan	Indonesia	Ratahan	150,000	Animism	<1%	1	3030
Rataning	Chad	Rataning	10,000	Islam-Animist	<1%	1	2255
*Rauto	Papua New Guinea	Rauto	200	Animism	<1%	1	6313
*Rava in Assam	India	Rava	45,000	Hinduism	<1%	5	295
Rawa	Papua New Guinea	Rawa	6,000	Animism	<1%	1	6314
Rawang	China	Rawang	60,000	Traditional Chinese	<1%	1	2844
Redjang	Indonesia	Rejang	300,000	Islam	<1%	6 80	694
Refugee Doctors	Hong Kong	Cantonese	2,000	Traditional Chinese	<1%	3	9039
Renpi	Papua New Guinea	Rempi	500	Animism	<1%	1	6315
Rendille	Kenya	Rendille	20,000	Islam-Animist	0%	3	4131
Reshe	Nigeria	Reshe	30,000	Animism	<1%		2500
Reshiat	Ethiopia	not reported	10,000	Animism	<1%	3	520
Reyesano	Bolivia	Reyesano	1,000	Animism	<1%	1	2140
Riang in Assam	India	Riang-Lang	75,000	Hindu-Buddhist	<1%	1	2782
Riang-Lang	Burma	Riang-Lang	20,000	Buddhist-Animist	<1%	1	2590
Riantana	Indonesia	Riantana	1,200	Animism	<1%	1	3031
Rikbaktsa	Brazil	Rikbaktsa			<1%	1	3123
Roba	Nigeria	Roba	30,000	Islam	<1%	1	2501
Roinji	Papua New Guinea	Roinji	300	Animism	<1%	1	6316
Romany	Turkey	Romany	20,000	Folk Religion	<1%	1	2542
Ronkun	Papua New Guinea	Ronkun	400	Animism	<1%	1	6317
	Papua New Guinea	Ronkun			<1%	1	7064
Ronga	Mozambique	Ronga	400,000	Animism	0%	1	5395
	South Africa	Ronga	600,000	Animism	0%	1	5438

NAME	COUNTRY	LANGUAGE	GROUP SIZE	PRIMARY RELIGION	% CHR	VOL	V	UP ID
Roro	Papua New Guinea	Roro	8,000	Animism	<1%	1		6318
Rotokas	Papua New Guinea	Rotokas	4,000	Animism	<1%	1		6319
Ruihi	Tanzania	Ruihi	71,000	Animism	0%	1		5599
Rukuba	Nigeria	Rukuba	50,000	Islam	<1%	1		2502
Runaya	Nigeria	Runaya	2,000	Islam	<1%	1		2503
Runga	Central African Republic	Runga	13,000	Animism	0%	1		5199
Runga	Chad	Runga	13,000	Islam-Animist	<1%	1		2256
Rungi	Tanzania	Rungi	95,000	Animism	0%	1		5600
Rungwa	Tanzania	Rungwa		Animism	0%	1		5601
Rural Refugees from Eritrea	Sudan	Tigre	300,000	Islam	0%	4	83	9008
**Rural Vodun Believers	Haiti	Creole	5,400,000	Animism	nr%	4	84	4819
Ruruma	Nigeria	Ruruma	2,000	Islam	<1%	1		2504
Rusha	Tanzania	Rusha	54,000	Islam	<1%	1		5602
Rut	Sudan	Rut	500	Islam	0%	1		5469
Rutul	USSR	Rutul	12,000	Animism	0%	1		5868
Rwanba	Uganda	Rwanba	60,000	Animism	0%	1		5655
Rwanba	Zaire	Rwanba	48,000	Animism	nr%	1		5762
***Rwandan Tutsi Refugees	Burundi	Kirundi	49,000	Animism	4%	4	83	65
*Ryukyuan	Japan	Ryukyuan	1,000,000	Traditional Japanese	0%	1		5656
Saania	Uganda	Saania	124,000	Animism	0%	1		5819
Saans	USSR	Saans	2,000	Unknown	15%	3		4078
Sabbra	Kenya	Boran	18,000	Animism	<1%	1		3033
Saberi	Indonesia	Saberi	2,000	Animism	<1%	1		2783
Sadan in Andamans	India	Sadan	810,000	Hindu-Animist	<1%	1		3034
Sadang	Indonesia	Sadang	50,000	Animism	<1%	1		6320
Saep	Papua New Guinea	Saep	500	Animism	<1%	1		5336
Safaliba	Ghana	Safaliba	3,000	Islam-Animist	3%	4		486
Safva	Tanzania	Safva	100,000	Animism	0%	1		5603
Sagala	Tanzania	Sagala	20,000	Animism	0%	1		714
**Saguye	Kenya	Galla	30,000	Islam	<1%	3		3150
Saija	Colombia	Saija	3,000	Animism	<1%	1		7034
Saisiat	Taiwan	Saisiat	3,000	Animism	nr%	5	81	
**Saiva Vellala	India	Tamil	1,500,000	Hinduism	2%	4		2000
Sakam	Papua New Guinea	Sakam	400	Animism	<1%	1		6321
Sakata	Zaire	Sakata	75,000	Animism	<1%	1		5763
Saki	Papua New Guinea	Saki	2,000	Animism	<1%	1		6322

NAME	COUNTRY	LANGUAGE	GROUP SIZE	PRIMARY RELIGION	% CHR	V UP	VOL ID
Sakuye	Kenya	Sakuye	8,000	Islam-Animist	0%	3	4132
Sala	Zambia	Sala	11,000	Animism	0%	1	5807
Salampasu	Zaire	Salaanpasu	60,000	Animism	0%	1	5764
Salar	China	Salar	31,000	Traditional Chinese	<1%	1	2845
Saliba	Colombia	Saliba	900	Animism	<1%	1	3151
Salt	Papua New Guinea	Salt	6,000	Animism	<1%	1	6323
Salvadoran Refugees	Belize	Spanish	2,000	Nominal Christian	nr%	3	9059
	Honduras	Spanish	30,000	Nominal Christian	nr%	3	9058
Sana Bangingi	Philippines	Sinama Bangini	70,000	Islam-Animist	<1%	6 80	1148
Sana Pangutaran	Philippines	Sana Pangutaran	15,000	Islam	<1%	6 80	1150
Sana, Mapun	Philippines	Sana, Mapun	20,000	Animism	<1%	1	3284
Sana, Siasi	Philippines	Sana, Siasi	100,000	Islam-Animist	<1%	1	3285
Sana, Sibuku	Philippines	Sana, Sibuku	11,000	Islam-Animist	<1%	1	3286
Sana-Badjaw	Philippines	Sanal dialects	120,000	Islam-Animist	1%	5 79	389
Samarkena	Indonesia	Samarkena	800	Animism	<1%	1	3035
**Sanburu	Kenya	Maasai, Sanburu	74,000	Animism	3%	4 84	535
Sano, Northern	Mali	Sano, Northern	50,000	Animism	0%	1	5380
	Upper Volta	Sano, Northern	70,000	Islam-Animist	<1%	1	5679
Sano, Southern	Upper Volta	Sano, Southern	8,000	Islam-Animist	0%	1	5680
*Sano-Kubo	Papua New Guinea	Sano	2,000	Animism	1%	4	386
Sanogho	Mali	Sanogho	10,000	Animism	0%	1	5381
San	Namibia	San	4,000	Animism	0%	1	5404
Sanapana	Paraguay	Sanapana	4,000	Animism	0%	1	5128
Sandawe	Tanzania	Sandawe	38,000	Animism	0%	1	5604
Sanga	Nigeria	Sanga	5,000	Islam	<1%	1	2505
**Sanga	Zaire	Sanga	35,000	Nominal Christian	nr%	4 84	5765
Sangil	Philippines	Sangil	8,000	Islam	1%	5	637
Sangir	Indonesia	Sangir	145,000	Animism	<1%	1	3036
Sangke	Indonesia	Sangke	300	Animism	<1%	1	3037
Sangu	Gabon	Sangu	18,000	Animism	<1%	1	5314
Sangu	Tanzania	Sangu	30,000	Animism	0%	1	5605
Sanio	Papua New Guinea	Sanio	600	Animism	<1%	1	6324
Santa	China	Santa	200,000	Traditional Chinese	<1%	1	2846
**Santhali	Nepal	Santhali	nr	Animism	3%	4	669
Santrokofi	Ghana	Sele	5,000	Islam-Animist	0%	1	5337
*Saruma	Brazil	Saruma	300	Animism	1%	3	720

NAME	COUNTRY	LANGUAGE	GROUP SIZE	PRIMARY RELIGION	% CHR	VOL	V	UP ID
Sanuma	Venezuela	Sanuma	4,000	Animism	<1%	1		5142
Sanza	Zaire	Sanza	15,000	Animism	0%	4		5766
Sapo	Liberia	not reported	30,000	Animism	12%	4		603
Saposa	Papua New Guinea	Saposa	1,000	Animism	<1%	1		6325
Sarakole	Senegal	Soninke	68,000	Islam	0%	6	80	1139
Saranaccan	Surinam	Saranaccan	20,000	Christo-Paganism	<1%	1		5131
Sarua	Chad	Sarua	400	Islam-Animist	<1%	1		2257
Sasak	Indonesia	Sasak	1,600,000	Islam-Animist	1%	6	80	1095
Sasanis	Iran	Sasani		Islam	0%	3		2072
Sasaru-Enwan Igwe	Nigeria	Sasaru-Enwan Igwe	4,000	Animism	<1%	1		2506
Saseng	Papua New Guinea	Saseng	200	Animism	<1%	1		6326
Satere	Brazil	Satere	3,000	Animism	<1%	1		3124
Satnamis (Madhya Pradesh)	India	Chhattisgarhi	30,000	Animism	2%	4		4076
Sau	Afghanistan	Sau	1,000	Islam	<1%	1		2556
Sau	Papua New Guinea	Sau	3,000	Animism	0%	1		6327
Sauk	Papua New Guinea	Sauk	300	Animism	<1%	1		6328
Sauria Pahari	India	Malto	53,500	Animism	<1%	2		4801
Sause	Indonesia	Sause	500	Animism	<1%	4		3038
**Save	Benin	Save (Yoruba)	15,000	Animism	16%	5		451
**Sawi	Indonesia	Sawi	3,000	Animism	0%	1		1180
Sawos	Papua New Guinea	Sawos	2,000	Animism	<1%	1		6329
Saya	Nigeria	Saya	50,000	Islam	0%	1		2507
Sayyids	Yemen, Arab Republic	Arabic	nr	Islam	<1%	1		4067
Secoya	Ecuador	Secoya	400	Animism	<1%	1		3161
Sekar	Indonesia	Sekar	500	Animism	<1%	1		3039
Sekayu	Indonesia	Indonesian	200,000	Islam-Animist	0%	3		4090
Seko	Indonesia	Seko	275,000	Animism	<1%	1		3040
Sekpele	Ghana	Sekpele	11,000	Islam-Animist	0%	1		5338
**Selakau of Sarawak	Malaysia	Selakau	5,000	Animism	7%	4		2124
Selepet	Papua New Guinea	Selepet	5,000	Animism	<1%	1		6330
Selkup	USSR	Selkup	4,000	Unknown	0%	1		5869
Semelai	Malaysia	Semelai	3,000	Animism	0%	2		4110
Sempan	Indonesia	Sempan	2,000	Animism	<1%	1		3041
Sena	Malawi	Sena	115,000	Animism	0%	1		5370
Sena	Mozambique	Sena	85,100	Animism	0%	1		5396
Senggi	Indonesia	Senggi	100	Animism	<1%	1		3042

NAME	COUNTRY	LANGUAGE	GROUP SIZE	PRIMARY RELIGION	% CHR	V	UP	ID
**Senoi	Malaysia	Native Senoi	340,000	Animism	2%	5	81	1009
Sentani	Indonesia	Sentani	10,000	Animism	1%	1		3043
Senthang	Burma	Senthang	10,000	Buddhist-Animist	<1%	1		2591
Senufo	Ivory Coast	Senari	300,900	Animism	2%	6	80	181
Sepen	Papua New Guinea	Sepen		Animism	0%	1		6331
**Serawai	Indonesia	Serawai (Pasemah)	60,000	Islam-Animist	1%	5	81	1091
Sere	Sudan	Sere	4,000	Islam	0%	1		5515
Serere	Senegal	Serere	700,000	Animism	9%	6	79	215
Serere-Non	Senegal	Serere-Non	70,000	Islam-Animist	0%	1		5426
Serere-Sine	Senegal	Serere-Sine	315,000	Islam-Animist	<1%	1		5427
Seri	Mexico	Seri	400	Christo-Paganism	<1%	1		5081
Serki	Papua New Guinea	Serki	200	Animism	<1%	1		6332
Serui-Laut	Indonesia	Serui-Laut	1,000	Animism	<1%	1		3044
Setaui Keriwa	Papua New Guinea	Setaui Keriwa	400	Animism	<1%	1		6333
Setiali	Papua New Guinea	Setiali	200	Animism	0%	1		6334
Seuci	Brazil	Tucano	400	Animism	<1%	1		3125
Seychellois	Seychelles	Creole	51,000	Secularism	10%	4		1199
Sha	Nigeria	Sha	500	Animism	<1%	1		2508
Shahsavans	Iran	Azerbaijani (Shahsavani)	180,000	Islam	0%	6	80	2043
Shambala	Tanzania	Shambala	152,000	Animism	0%	2		5606
Shan	Burma	Shan	800,000	Buddhism	0%	2		4143
Shan Chinese	Thailand	Shan	300,000	Buddhist-Animist	<1%	4		2086
Shanga	Burma	Shan	20,000	Buddhist-Animist	0%	2		4157
***Shankilla (Kazza)	Nigeria	Shanga	5,000	Animism	0%	4		568
Sharanahua	Ethiopia	Shankilla (Kazza)	2,000	Christo-Paganism	1%	5		116
Sharchagpakha	Peru	Sharanahua	20,000	Animism	<1%	1		3185
Shatt	Bhutan	Sharchagpakha	400,000	Buddhist-Animist	1%	1		2567
Shawiya	Sudan	Shatt	9,000	Islam	0%	1		5516
Sheko	Algeria	Shawiya	150,000	Islam	<1%	1		2207
*Sherpa	Ethiopia	Sheko	23,000	Animism	<1%	1		3229
**Shihu	Nepal	Sherpa	20,000	Buddhism	0%	3		671
Shilha	United Arab Emirates	Shihu	10,000	Islam	<1%	1		2543
Shilluk	Morocco	Shilha	3,000,000	Islam-Animist	0%	1		5388
Shina	Sudan	Shilluk	110,000	Islam	0%	1		5517
Shinasha	Afghanistan	Shina	50,000	Islam-Animist	<1%	1		2557
	Ethiopia	Shinasha	4,000	Animism	<1%	1		3230

REGISTRY OF THE UNREACHED

NAME	COUNTRY	LANGUAGE	GROUP SIZE	PRIMARY RELIGION	% CHR	V	VOL UP	ID
Shipibo	Peru	Shipibo	15,000	Animism	<1%	1		3186
**Shirishana	Brazil	Shirishana	200	Animism	5%	3		721
**Shluh Berbers	Morocco	Tashilhait	2,000,000	Islam-Animist	0%	5		4028
Shopping Bag Women, Toronto	Canada:Ontario	English	500	Secularism	nr%	1		9165
Shor	USSR	Shor	16,000	Unknown	0%	1		5870
*Shourastra in Tamil Nadu	India	Shourastra	200,000	Hinduism	<1%	4		2023
Shua	Botswana	Shua	400	Animism	0%	1		5178
Shughni	Afghanistan	Shughni	3,000	Islam	<1%	1		2558
Shuwa Arabic	Nigeria	Shuwa Arabic	100,000	Islam	<1%	1		2509
Shwai	Sudan	Shwai	3,000	Islam	0%	1		5518
Siagha-Yeninu	Indonesia	Siagha-Yeninu	3,000	Animism	<1%	1		3045
Sialum	Papua New Guinea	Sialum	600	Animism	<1%	1		6335
Siane	Papua New Guinea	Siane	16,000	Animism	<1%	1		6336
Siar	Papua New Guinea	Siar	2,000	Animism	<1%	1		6337
Sibo	China	Sibo	21,000	Traditional Chinese	<1%	1		2847
Sidamo	Ethiopia	Sidano	857,000	Islam-Animist	<1%	1		3231
Sikanese	Indonesia	Sikka	100,000	Animism	<1%	2		3047
Sikhs, Toronto	Canada:Ontario	Punjabi	20,000	Sikhism	0%	2		9119
Sikhule	Indonesia	Sikhule	20,000	Animism	<1%	1		3046
Sikkinese	India	Sikkineee	37,000	Hindu-Buddhist	<1%	1		2786
Sinaa	Zambia	Simaa	40,000	Animism	0%	1		5808
Sinba	Bolivia	Guarani	400	Animism	0%	4		6569
Simog	Papua New Guinea	Simog	100	Animism	<1%	1		6338
Sinagen	Papua New Guinea	Sinagen	200	Animism	0%	1		6339
Sinagoro	Papua New Guinea	Sinagoro	12,000	Animism	<1%	1		6340
Sinaki	Papua New Guinea	Sinaki	300	Animism	<1%	1		6341
Sinasina	Papua New Guinea	Sinasina	20,000	Animism	<1%	1		6342
Sindamon	Papua New Guinea	Sindamon	200	Animism	<1%	1		6343
*Sindhi Muslims in Karachi	Pakistan	Sindhi	350,000	Islam-Animist	0%	6	82	5036
*Sindhis of India	India	Sindhi	3,000,000	Hinduism	1%	5		13
Sinhalese	Sri Lanka	Sinhala	9,200,000	Buddhism	6%	5		286
Sinsauru	Papua New Guinea	Sinsauru	2,000	Animism	0%	1		6344
Sio	Papua New Guinea	Sio	2,000	Animism	<1%	1		6345
Siona	Colombia	Siona	300	Animism	<1%	1		3152
Sipoma	Papua New Guinea	Sipoma	300	Animism	<1%	1		6346
Sira	Gabon	Sira	17,000	Animism	0%	1		5315

Index by Group Name

NAME	COUNTRY	LANGUAGE	GROUP SIZE	PRIMARY RELIGION	% CHR	V	VOL UP	ID
Sirak	Papua New Guinea	Sirak	200	Animism	<1%	1		6347
Sirasira	Papua New Guinea	Sirasira	300	Animism	<1%	1		6350
Siri	Nigeria	Siri	2,000	Islam	<1%	1		2510
Siriano	Colombia	Siriano	600	Animism	<1%	1		3153
Siriono	Bolivia	Siriono	500	Animism	<1%	1		2141
Siroi	Papua New Guinea	Siroi	700	Animism	<1%	1		6348
**Sisaala	Ghana	Isaalin	60,000	Animism	1%	4		658
Sisala	Upper Volta	Sisala	4,000	Islam-Animist	0%	1		5681
Siwai	Papua New Guinea	Siwai	6,000	Animism	<1%	1		6349
Siwu	Ghana	Siwu	5,000	Islam-Animist	0%	1		5339
*Slum Dwellers of Bangkok	Thailand	Thai	45,000	Buddhism	<1%	4		4052
So	Cameroon	So	6,000	Animism	0%	1		5280
Sobei	Indonesia	Sobei	1,000	Animism	<1%	1		3048
Sochi	Pakistan	Sindhi	nr	Hinduism	1%	3		255
Soga	Uganda	Soga	780,000	Animism	0%	1		5657
*Soh	Laos	Soh	15,000	Animism	<1%	5		98
Soka Gakkai Believers	Japan	Japanese	8,000	Buddhism	<1%	5	81	2091
Sokorok	Papua New Guinea	Sokorok	6,500,000	Buddhism	0%	3		20
Soli	Zambia	Soli	300	Animism	0%	1		6351
Solorese Muslims	Indonesia	Solor	32,000	Islam	0%	1		5809
Solos	Papua New Guinea	Solos	131,000	Animism	0%	5	81	3049
Som	Papua New Guinea	Som	3,000	Animism	<1%	1		6352
*Sonagai	Indonesia	Sonagai	100	Animism	<1%	1		6353
Sonahai	Indonesia	Sonahai	3,000	Animism	0%	3		226
Sonali	Ethiopia	Somali	2,000	Animism	<1%	1		3050
Somali; Ajuran	Kenya	Somali (Ajuran)	1,000,000	Islam	1%	5		90
Somali; Degodia	Kenya	Somali	25,000	Islam	1%	6	79	467
Somali; Gurreh	Kenya	Somali	70,000	Islam	1%	5		464
Somali; Ogadenya	Kenya	Somali	54,000	Islam	1%	5		465
**Somba	Benin	Somba (Detammari)	100,000	Islam	1%	5		466
Sonrai	Central African Republic	Sonrai	60,000	Animism	1%	4		452
	Chad	Sonrai	50,000	Islam-Animist	<1%	1		5200
Sona	Papua New Guinea	Sona	2,000	Animism	<1%	1		2258
Sondwari in M.P.	India	Sondwari	32,000	Hindu-Animist	<1%	1		6354
Songe	Zaire	Songe	500,000	Animism	0%	1		2787
								5768

437

REGISTRY OF THE UNREACHED

NAME	COUNTRY	LANGUAGE	GROUP SIZE	PRIMARY RELIGION	% CHR	V	UP	VOL ID
Songhai	Mali	Songhai	130,000	Animism	<1%	1		5382
	Niger	Songhai	93,000	Islam-Animist	<1%	1		5408
	Upper Volta	Songhai	35,000	Islam-Animist	0%	1		5682
Songomeno	Zaire	Songomeno	40,000	Animism	0%	1		5769
Songoora	Gambia	Songoora	1,000	Animism	0%	1		5770
Soninke	Mali	Soninke	10,000	Islam	<1%	1		2271
	Mauritania	Soninke	283,000	Islam	0%	1		5383
	Tanzania	Soninke	22,000	Islam	0%	1		5386
Sonjo	Sudan	Sonjo	2,000	Animism	5%	5		217
Sopi	India	Sopi	2,000	Islam	0%	1		5449
Sora in Orissa	Papua New Guinea	Sora	222,000	Hinduism	<1%	1		2788
Sori-Harengan	Benin	Sori-Harengan	600	Animism	0%	1		6355
Soruba	Lesotho	Soruba	5,000	Animism	0%	3		453
South African Refugee Students		English	11,500	Nominal Christian	nr%	4	83	9014
Sowanda	Indonesia	Sowanda	1,000	Animism	<1%	1		3051
	Papua New Guinea	Sowanda	900	Animism	<1%	1		6356
Street People, Thunder Bay	Canada:Ontario	Various dialects	10,000	Secularism	nr%	1		9253
Street People, Victoria	Canada:British Columbia	English	1,900	Secularism	0%	2		9126
Street Vendors in Saigon	Viet Nam	Vietnamese	nr	Buddhist-Animist	nr%	5	82	5035
*Students in Cuiaba	German Federal Rep.	German	850,000	Secularism	10%	6	79	1106
	Brazil	Portuguese	20,000	Secularism	1%	3		712
Su	Cameroon	Su	4,000	Animism	<1%	1		5281
Suain	Papua New Guinea	Suain	900	Animism	<1%	1		6357
Suba	Papua New Guinea	Suba	17,000	Animism	0%	1		6358
**Subanen (Tuboy)	Tanzania	Subanen, Tuboy	20,000	Animism	2%	5		5607
**Subanen, Sindangan	Philippines	Subanun	80,000	Animism	<1%	6	80	1062
Subanun,Lapuyan	Philippines	Subanun, Lapuyan	25,000	Islam-Animist	<1%	1		3287
Subi	Tanzania	Subi	74,000	Animism	0%	1		5608
Sudanese Repatriates	Sudan	Tribal Languages	1,000,000	Animism	<1%	4	83	9009
**Suena	Papua New Guinea	Suena	2,000	Christo-Paganism	4%	4		431
Suga	Cameroon	Suga	10,000	Animism	0%	1		5282
Suganga	Papua New Guinea	Suganga	500	Animism	<1%	1		6359
**Sugut	Malaysia	Dusun	10,000	Animism	0%	4		2118
Sui	China	Traditional Chinese	160,000	Traditional Chinese	<1%	1		2848
Sui	Papua New Guinea	Sui	1,000	Animism	0%	1		6360

Index by Group Name

NAME	COUNTRY	LANGUAGE	GROUP SIZE	PRIMARY RELIGION	% CHR	V	UP	VOL ID
Suk	Kenya	not reported	133,000	Animism	8%	5		600
Suki	Papua New Guinea	Suki	1,000	Animism	<1%	1		6361
Suku	Zaire	Suku	74,000	Animism	0%	1		5771
Sukur	Nigeria	Sukur	10,000	Islam	<1%	1		2511
Sukurum	Papua New Guinea	Sukurum	400	Animism	<1%	1		6362
Sulka	Papua New Guinea	Sulka	1,000	Animism	<1%	1		6363
Sulung	India	Sulung	nr	Hindu-Buddhist	<1%	1		2789
Sunau	Papua New Guinea	Sunau	800	Animism	<1%	1		6364
Sunba	Indonesia	Sunba	400,000	Animism	<1%	1		1097
Sumbawa	Indonesia	Sumbawa	114,000	Islam	<1%	5		3052
Sumbwa	Tanzania	Sumbwa	64,000	Animism	0%	1		5609
Sumu	Nicaragua	Sumu	2,000	Christo-Paganism	0%	1		5111
**Sundanese	Indonesia	Sundanese	20,000,000	Islam-Animist	<1%	6	84	273
Sungor	Chad	Sungor	39,000	Islam-Animist	<1%	1		2259
Sunwar	Nepal	Sunwar	20,000	Buddhist-Animist	0%	1		6519
Suppire	Mali	Suppire	300,000	Animism	<1%	1		5384
Sura	Nigeria	Sura	40,000	Islam	<1%	1		2512
**Suri	Ethiopia	Suri	30,000	Animism	1%	4		521
***Suriguenos	Philippines	Surigueno	23,000	Secularism	7%	4		1191
Sursurunga	Papua New Guinea	Sursurunga	2,000	Animism	<1%	1		6365
Surubu	Nigeria	Surubu	2,000	Islam	<1%	1		2513
Surui	Brazil	Surui	2,300	Animism	<1%	1		3126
Susu	Guinea	Susu	815,000	Islam	nr%	1		6562
Susu	Guinea-Bissau	Susu	2,000	Islam-Animist	<1%	1		5358
Susu	Sierra Leone	Susu	90,000	Islam-Animist	<1%	1		5435
Svan	USSR	Svan	35,000	Unknown	0%	1		5871
Swaga	Zaire	Swaga	121,000	Animism	0%	1		5772
Swaka	Zambia	Swaka	33,000	Animism	0%	1		5788
Swatis	Pakistan	Swati	600,000	Islam	0%	6	79	1232
**Swazi	South Africa	siSwati	500,000	Animism	9%	5		4037
Sylhetti	United Kingdom	Sylhetti	150,000	Islam	0%	4		6566
Sywua	Nepal	Sywua	4,000	Buddhist-Animist	0%	1		6520
**T'boli	Philippines	Tboli	150,000	Animism	3%	5	81	624
T'in	Thailand	T'in	25,000	Animism	<1%	5	81	81
Ta-Oi	Laos	Ta-Oi	15,000	Animism	1%	5		99
Tabar	Papua New Guinea	Tabar	2,000	Animism	<1%	1		6366

REGISTRY OF THE UNREACHED

NAME	COUNTRY	LANGUAGE	GROUP SIZE	PRIMARY RELIGION	% CHR	V	VOL	UP ID
Tabasaran	USSR	Tabasaran	55,000	Islam	0%	1		5872
Tabi	Sudan	Tabi	10,000	Animism	0%	1		5519
Tabriak	Papua New Guinea	Tabriak	1,000	Animism	<1%	1		6367
Tacana	Bolivia	Tacana	4,000	Animism	<1%	1		2142
Tadjio	Indonesia	Tadjio	100,000	Animism	<1%	1		3053
Tadyawan	Philippines	Tadyawan	1,000	Animism	<1%	1		3288
Tafi	Togo	Tafi	1,000	Islam-Animist	0%	1		5636
Tagal	Malaysia	Tagal	19,000	Animism	nr%	6	81	7028
**Tagbanwa, Aborlan	Philippines	Tagbanwa	10,000	Animism	1%	5		1153
Tagbanwa, Kalamian	Philippines	Tagbanwa, Kalamian	5,000	Christo-Paganism	1%	5		636
***Tagin	India	Tagin	25,000	Animism	1%	3		1045
Tagula	Papua New Guinea	Tagula	2,000	Animism	<1%	1		6368
Tagwana	Ivory Coast	Tagwana	43,000	Islam-Animist	<1%	1		2304
Tehit	Indonesia	Tehit	6,000	Animism	<1%	1		3063
Taikat	Indonesia	Taikat	600	Animism	<1%	1		3054
Tairora	Papua New Guinea	Tairora	8,000	Animism	<1%	1		6369
Taiwan-Chinese Un. Stud.	Taiwan	Mandarin	310,000	Secularism	nr%	6		7038
Tajik	Afghanistan	Paniri	3,600,000	Islam	0%	5		4040
	Iran	Dari	15,000	Islam	0%	5	80	2053
	USSR	Persian (Tajiki)	2,500,000	Islam	0%	5		4041
Takalubi	Papua New Guinea	Takalubi	400	Animism	0%	1		6370
Takankar	India	Takankar	11,000	Hindu-Animist	<1%	1		2775
Takemba	Benin	Takemba	10,000	Animism	0%	1		5170
Takestani	Iran	Takestani	220,000	Islam	<1%	1		2536
Takia	Papua New Guinea	Takia	11,000	Animism	<1%	1		6371
Tal	Nigeria	Tal	10,000	Islam	<1%	1		2514
Talish	Iran	Talish	20,000	Islam	0%	3		2050
*Talo	Indonesia	Talo	90,000	Islam-Animist	<1%	3		4089
Talodi	Sudan	Talodi	1,000	Islam	0%	1		5522
Tana	Chad	Tana	60,000	Islam-Animist	<1%	1		2260
Tanagario	Indonesia	Tanagario	4,000	Animism	<1%	1		3055
Taman	Burma	Taman	10,000	Buddhist-Animist	<1%	1		2592
	Papua New Guinea	Taman	600	Animism	<1%	1		6372
*Tanang	Nepal	Tanang	nr	Hindu-Buddhist	<1%	3		666
Tanaria in Bihar	India	Tanaria	5,000	Hindu-Buddhist	<1%	1		2790
Tamazight	Morocco	Tamazight	1,800,000	Islam-Animist	0%	1		5389

NAME	LANGUAGE	COUNTRY	GROUP SIZE	PRIMARY RELIGION	% CHR	V	VOL	UP ID
Tambas	Tambas	Nigeria	3,000	Animism	<1%	1		2515
Tambo	Tambo	Zambia	7,000	Animism	0%	1		5801
Tani	Tani	Papua New Guinea	400	Animism	<1%	1		6373
Tani (Ceylonese)	Tani	Sri Lanka	1,420,000	Hinduism	5%	5		287
**Tamil Laborers in Bombay	Tamil	India	3,000	Hinduism	<1%	5	82	5017
**Tamil Muslims in Madras	Tamil	India	50,000	Islam	0%	6	82	5028
***Tamil Plantation Workers	Tamil	Malaysia	140,000	Hinduism	1%	4		1109
*Tamil in Yellagiri Hills	Tamil	India	4,000	Hinduism	2%	5		4025
**Tamils (Indian)	Tamil	Malaysia	600,000	Hinduism	7%	5		4
**Tamils (Indian)	Tamil	Sri Lanka	1,200,000	Hinduism	5%	4	79	313
Taupulna	Taupulensi	Ghana	8,000	Animism	2%	5		1077
Tana	Tana	Central African Republic	35,000	Animism	0%	1		5201
Tana	Tana	Chad	35,000	Islam-Animist	<1%	3		2261
Tanahmerah	Tanahmerah	Indonesia	3,000	Animism	<1%	1		3056
Tandanke	Tandanke	Senegal	1,000	Animism	0%	3		1145
Tandia	Tandia	Indonesia	400	Animism	<1%	1		3057
Tangale	Tangale	Nigeria	100,000	Islam	<1%	1		2516
Tangchangya	Tangchangya	Bangladesh	8,000	Animism	<1%	1		2564
Tangga	Tangga	Papua New Guinea	11,000	Animism	0%	1		6374
**Tangsa	Tangsa	India	2,000	Animism	0%	3		1031
Tangu	Tangu	Papua New Guinea	600	Animism	<1%	1		6375
Tanguat	Tanguat	Papua New Guinea	2,000	Animism	<1%	1		6376
Tani	Tani	Papua New Guinea	2,000	Animism	<1%	1		6378
Taninuca-Retuana	Taninuca-Retuana	Colombia	300	Animism	<1%	1		3154
Tao't Bato	not reported	Philippines	200	Animism	0%	4		2106
Tao-Suane	Tao-Suane	Papua New Guinea	700	Animism	0%	1		6377
Taori-Kei	Taori-Kei	Indonesia	100	Animism	<1%	1		3058
Tara	Tara	Indonesia	125,000	Animism	<1%	1		3059
Tarahumara, Northern	Tarahumara, Northern	Mexico	500	Christo-Paganism	0%	1		5082
Tarahumara, Rocoroibo	Tarahumara, Rocoroibo	Mexico	12,000	Christo-Paganism	<1%	1		5083
Tarahumara, Samachique	Tarahumara, Samachique	Mexico	40,000	Christo-Paganism	<1%	1		5084
Taran	Taran	Cameroon	3,000	Animism	0%	1		5283
Tarasco	Tarasco	Mexico	60,000	Christo-Paganism	<1%	1		5085
Targum	Targun	Israel	5,000	Judaism	<1%	1		2537
Tarof	Tarof	Indonesia	600	Animism	<1%	1		3060
Tarok	Tarok	Nigeria	60,000	Animism	<1%	1		2517

NAME	LANGUAGE	COUNTRY	GROUP SIZE	PRIMARY RELIGION	% CHR	V	VOL UP ID
Tarpia	Tarpia	Indonesia	600	Animism	<1%	1	3061
Tat	Tat	USSR	17,000	Islam	0%	1	5873
Tatars	Tatar dialects	USSR	6,000,000	Islam	1%	6 80	4008
Tate	Tate	Papua New Guinea	300	Animism	1%	1	6379
Tatoga	Tatoga	Tanzania	22,000	Animism	<1%	1	5610
**Tatuyo	Tatuyo	Colombia	300	Animism	1%	5	621
Tauade	Tauade	Papua New Guinea	11,000	Animism	<1%	1	6380
Taucouleur	Taucouleur	Senegal	500,000	Islam	0%	5 80	1137
Taungyo	Taungyo	Burma	200,000	Buddhist-Animist	<1%	1	2593
Taungyoe	Burmese	Burma	18,000	Buddhism	0%	2	4147
Taupota	Taupota	Papua New Guinea	3,000	Animism	<1%	1	6381
Taurap	Taurap	Indonesia	200	Animism	<1%	1	3062
Tausug	Tausug	Philippines	500,000	Islam	1%	6 80	635
Tavara	Tavara	Papua New Guinea	9,000	Animism	<1%	1	6382
Tawi-Pau	Tawi-Pau	Papua New Guinea	300	Animism	0%	1	6383
Tawr	Tawr	Burma	700	Buddhist-Animist	<1%	1	2594
Tayaku	Tayaku	Benin	10,000	Animism	0%	1	5171
Tchang	Tchang	Cameroon	100,000	Animism	0%	1	5284
Teda	Teda	Chad	10,000	Islam	0%	6 80	4012
Teda	Teda	Libya	16,000	Islam	<1%	1	5364
Teda	Teda	Niger	120,000	Islam-Animist	<1%	1	5409
*Teenbu	Lorhon	Ivory Coast	5,000	Animism	1%	4	311
Tegali	Tegali	Sudan	16,000	Islam	0%	1	5523
Teimuri	Teimuri	Iran	10,000	Islam	0%	3	2051
Teimurtash	Teimurtash	Iran	7,000	Islam	0%	3	2052
Teke, Eastern	Teke, Eastern	Zaire	71,000	Animism	0%	1	5773
Teke, Northern	Teke, Northern	Congo	24,000	Animism	<1%	1	5300
Teke, Southwestern	Teke, Southwestern	Congo	32,000	Animism	<1%	1	5301
Telefol	Telefol	Papua New Guinea	4,000	Animism	<1%	1	6384
Ten	Kotokoli	Togo	100,000	Islam	5%	4	596
Tembe	Tembe	Brazil	300	Animism	<1%	1	3127
Tembo	Tembo	Zaire	30,000	Animism	0%	1	5774
Temein	Temein	Sudan	2,000	Islam	0%	1	5524
Temira	Temira	Malaysia	7,000	Animism	0%	2	4108
**Temne	Temne	Sierra Leone	1,000,000	Animism	6%	6 80	123
Tenger	Tenggerese	Indonesia	400,000	Hindu-Animist	1%	5	296

NAME	LANGUAGE	COUNTRY	GROUP SIZE	PRIMARY RELIGION	% CHR	V	VOL UP ID
*Tense	Teen	Ivory Coast	5,000	Animism	<1%	5	4122
Teop	Teop	Papua New Guinea	5,000	Animism	<1%	1	6385
Tepehua, Huehuetla	Tepehua, Huehuetla	Mexico	2,000	Christo-Paganism	<1%	1	5086
Tepehua, Pisa Flores	Tepehua, Pisa Flores	Mexico	300	Christo-Paganism	0%	1	5087
Tepehua, Veracruz	Tepehua, Veracruz	Mexico	900	Christo-Paganism	<1%	1	5088
Tepehuan, Northern	Tepehuan, Northern	Mexico	5,000	Christo-Paganism	<1%	1	5089
Tepehuan, Southeastern	Tepehuan, Southeastern	Mexico	8,000	Christo-Paganism	<1%	1	5090
Tepehuan, Southwestern	Tepehuan, Southwestern	Mexico	6,000	Christo-Paganism	0%	1	5091
Tepeth	Tepeth	Uganda	4,000	Animism	0%	1	5658
Tepo	Tepo	Ivory Coast	20,000	Islam-Animist	<1%	1	2305
Tera	Tera	Nigeria	46,000	Islam	<1%	1	2518
Terebu	Terebu	Papua New Guinea	4,000	Animism	0%	1	6386
Terena	Terena	Brazil	5,000	Animism	<1%	1	3128
**Teribe	Teribe	Panama	1,000	Christo-Paganism	15%	5	1203
Ternatans	Ternate	Indonesia	42,000	Islam	<1%	1	3064
*Tertiary Level Youth	Persian	Iran	nr	Islam	1%	4	4074
**Teso	Luteso	Kenya	110,000	Animism	8%	5	4071
Teso	Teso	Uganda	830,000	Animism	<1%	1	5659
*Thado in Assam	Thado	India	42,000	Hindu-Buddhist	<1%	1	2791
*Thai Immigrants, Los Angeles	Central Thai	United States of America	60,000	Buddhism	1%	4	84	4813
*Thai Islam (Malay)	Mala, Pattani	Thailand	1,700,000	Islam-Animist	1%	6	80	39
*Thai Islam (Thai)	Thai, Southern	Thailand	600,000	Islam-Animist	0%	4	2093
*Thai University Students	Thai	Thailand	nr	Buddhism	nr%	5	81	7015
Thai-Ney	Shan	Burma	5,000	Buddhist-Animist	0%	2	4158
Thakali	Thakali	Nepal	4,000	Buddhist-Animist	0%	1	6521
Thakur	Thakur	India	99,000	Hindu-Animist	<1%	1	2792
Thami	Thami	Nepal	9,000	Buddhist-Animist	0%	1	6522
Thar in Bihar	Thar	India	9,000	Hindu-Animist	<1%	1	2793
Tharu	Bhojpuri	Nepal	44,000	Hindu-Animist	nr%	2	4800
Tharu	Bhojpuri	India	495,000	Hinduism	<1%	5	1064
Theater Arts Performers	English	Canada	6,400	Secularism	0%	2	9114
Thoi	Thoi	Sudan	400	Islam	0%	1	5470
Thuri	Thuri	Sudan	154,000	Islam	0%	1	5525
Tiang	Tiang	Papua New Guinea	800	Animism	<1%	1	6387
*Tibetan Refugees	Tibetan	Canada	400	Buddhism	0%	1	9160
*Tibetan Refugees	Tibetan	India	100,000	Buddhism	1%	4	83	2033

NAME	COUNTRY	LANGUAGE	GROUP SIZE	PRIMARY RELIGION	% CHR	V	VOL UP ID
Tibetan Refugees	Switzerland	Tibetan	1,000	Buddhism	0%	4 83	9015
Tibetans in Bhutan	Bhutan	Tibetan	5,000	Buddhism	<1%	5 81	7017
Ticuna	Brazil	Ticuna	8,000	Animism	<1%	1	3129
Tidi	Papua New Guinea	Tidi		Animism	0%	1	6388
Tidorese	Indonesia	Tidore	26,000	Islam-Animist	<1%	1	3065
Tiefo	Upper Volta	Tiefo	7,000	Islam-Animist	0%	1	5683
Tiene	Zaire	Tiene	25,000	Animism	<1%	1	5775
Tifai	Papua New Guinea	Tifai	3,000	Animism	<1%	1	6389
Tigak	Papua New Guinea	Tigak	4,000	Animism	<1%	1	6390
Tigon	Cameroon	Tigon	25,000	Animism	<1%	4	495
Tikar	Cameroon	Tikar	13,000	Animism	<1%	1	5285
Timbe	Papua New Guinea	Timbe	11,000	Animism	<1%	1	6391
Timorese	Indonesia	Timorese	300,000	Animism	<1%	1	3066
Tindin	USSR	Tat	5,000	Unknown	0%	1	5874
Tinputz	Papua New Guinea	Tinputz	2,000	Animism	<1%	1	6392
Tippera	Bangladesh	Tippera	38,000	Islam	<1%	1	2565
Tira	Sudan	Tira	10,000	Islam	0%	1	5526
Tirio	Papua New Guinea	Tirio		Animism	0%	1	6393
Tirma	Sudan	Tirma	9,000	Islam	0%	1	5527
Tiro	Indonesia	Tiro	75,000	Animism	<1%	1	3667
Tiruray	Philippines	Tiruray	30,000	Animism	<1%	1	3290
Tlapaneco, Malinaltepec	Mexico	Tlapaneco, Malinaltepec	40,000	Christo-Paganism	<1%	1	5092
Toala	Indonesia	Toala	100	Animism	<1%	1	3068
Toaripi	Papua New Guinea	Toaripi	23,000	Animism	<1%	1	6394
Tobo	Papua New Guinea	Tobo	3,000	Animism	<1%	1	6395
Toda in Tamil Nadu	India	Toda	800	Hindu-Animist	<1%	1	2794
*Tofi	Benin	Tofi		Animism	3%	4	422
Togbo	Zaire	Togbo	33,000	Animism	0%	1	5691
Tojolabal	Mexico	Tojolabal	6,000	Christo-Paganism	<1%	1	5093
Tokkaru in Tamil Nadu	India	Tokkaru	14,000	Hindu-Animist	<1%	1	2660
Tol	Honduras	Tol	1,300,000	Animism	<1%	1	8014
Tombulu	Indonesia	Tombulu	200	Animism	<1%	1	3069
Tomini	Indonesia	Tomini	40,000	Animism	<1%	1	3070
Tonda	Papua New Guinea	Tonda	50,000	Animism	<1%	1	6396
Tondanou	Indonesia	Tondanou	600	Animism	0%	1	3071
Tonga	Botswana	Tonga	35,000	Animism	<1%	1	5179
			6,000				

Index by Group Name

NAME	COUNTRY	LANGUAGE	GROUP SIZE	PRIMARY RELIGION	% CHR	V	VOL	UP ID
*Tonga	Malawi	Tonga	62,000	Animism	<1%	1		5371
	Mozambique	Tonga	10,000	Animism	<1%	1		5397
Tonga, Gwembe Valley	Zimbabwe	ChiTonga	90,000	Animism	2%	5	79	1160
	Zambia	ChiTonga	86,000	Animism	2%	7	79	188
Tongwe	Tanzania	Tongwe	8,000	Animism	0%	1		5611
Tonsea	Indonesia	Tonsea	90,000	Animism	<1%	1		3072
*Tontemboa	Indonesia	Tontemboa	140,000	Animism	<1%	1		3073
Topotha	Sudan	Toposa	60,000	Animism	2%	4		575
Toraja, Southern	Indonesia	Tae'	250,000	Animism	nr%	5	81	3074
Torau	Papua New Guinea	Torau	600	Animism	<1%	1		6397
Torricelli	Papua New Guinea	Torricelli	700	Animism	<1%	1		6398
Totis	India	Gondi	nr	Hinduism	<1%	3		1044
Totonaco, Northern	Mexico	Totonaco, Northern	15,000	Christo-Paganism	<1%	1		5094
Totonaco, Oxumatlan	Mexico	Totonaco, Oxumatlan	1,000	Christo-Paganism	0%	1		5095
Totonaco, Papantla	Mexico	Totonaco, Papantla	50,000	Christo-Paganism	<1%	1		5096
Totonaco, Sierra	Mexico	Totonaco, Sierra	100,000	Christo-Paganism	<1%	1		5097
Totonaco, Yecuatla	Mexico	Spanish	500	Christo-Paganism	0%	1		5098
*Toussian	Upper Volta	Toussian	20,100	Islam	8%	4		4123
Towei	Indonesia	Towei		Animism	<1%	1		3075
Trepo	Ivory Coast	Trepo	3,000	Islam-Animist	<1%	1		2306
Trio	Surinam	Trio	800	Animism	<1%	1		5132
Trique, San Juan Copala	Mexico	Trique, San Juan Copala	8,000	Christo-Paganism	<1%	1		5099
Tsaangi	Congo	Tsaangi	10,000	Unknown	0%	1		5302
**Tsachila	Ecuador	Colorado	1,000	Christo-Paganism	8%	5		1197
Tsakhur	USSR	Tsakhur	11,000	Islam	0%	1		5875
Tsanai	Ethiopia	Tsanai	7,000	Animism	<1%	1		3232
Tsimane	Bolivia	Tsimane	6,000	Animism	<1%	1		2143
Tsogo	Gabon	Tsogo	15,000	Animism	0%	1		5316
Tsonga	Mozambique	Tsonga	1,500,000	Animism	<1%	1		5398
Tsou	Taiwan	Tsou	4,000	Animism	0%	5	81	7035
Tswa	Mozambique	Tswa	200,000	Animism	0%	1		5399
Tswa	Zimbabwe	Tswa	300,000	Animism	0%	1		5418
Tswana	Namibia	Tswana	11,000	Animism	<1%	1		5405
Tswana	Zimbabwe	Tswana	30,000	Animism	<1%	1		5419
Tuam	Papua New Guinea	Tuam	600	Animism	<1%	1		6399
Tuareg	Niger	Tamachek	200,000	Islam	<1%	6	79	46

REGISTRY OF THE UNREACHED

NAME	COUNTRY	LANGUAGE	GROUP SIZE	PRIMARY RELIGION	% CHR	VOL	V	UP ID
Tubar	Mexico	Tubar	100	Christo-Paganism	0%	1		5100
Tubetube	Papua New Guinea	Tubetube	1,000	Animism	1%	1		6400
Tucano	Brazil	Tucano	2,000	Animism	<1%	1		3130
Tugara	India	Tugara	44,000	Hindu-Animist	<1%	1		2777
Tukude	Indonesia	Tukude	45,000	Christo-Paganism	<1%	1		3076
Tula	Nigeria	Tula	19,000	Islam	<1%	1		2519
Tulishi	Sudan	Tulishi	9,000	Islam	0%	1		5528
Tumale	Sudan	Tumale	1,000	Islam	<1%	1		5521
Tumawo	Indonesia	Tumawo	400	Animism	<1%	1		3077
Tumma	Sudan	Tumna	5,000	Islam	0%	1		5529
Tumtum	Sudan	Tumtum	7,000	Islam	0%	1		5530
Tunebo, Cobaria	Colombia	Tunebo, Cobaria	2,000	Animism	<1%	1		3155
Tung-Chia	China	Tung	1,100,000	Animism	0%	5	81	7031
Tunya	Central African Republic	Tunya	800	Islam-Animist	0%	1		5202
Tunya	Chad	Tunya	800	Animism	<1%	1		2263
Tupuri	Cameroon	Tupuri	70,000	Animism	<1%	1		5286
Tupuri	Chad	Tupuri	60,000	Islam-Animist	<1%	1		2264
Tura	Ivory Coast	Tura	20,000	Islam-Animist	<1%	1		2307
Turkana	Kenya	Turkana	224,000	Animism	4%	5	79	219
**Turkana Fishing Community	Kenya	Turkana	20,000	Animism	4%	5	79	475
Turkish Immigrant Workers	German Federal Rep.	Turkish	1,200,000	Islam	1%	6	80	134
Turkish Workers	Belgium	Kurdish	60,000	Islam	1%	6	80	4020
Turkomans	Iran	Turkomani	550,000	Islam	0%	6	80	2032
Turks in Basel	Switzerland	Kurdish	3,000	Islam	nr%	6	82	5011
Turks, Anatolian	Turkey	Turkish, Osmanli	31,000,000	Islam	<1%	6	82	4022
Turkwam	Nigeria	Turkwam	6,000	Islam	<1%	1		2520
Turu	Indonesia	Turu	800	Animism	10%	1		3078
Turu	Tanzania	Nyaturu	320,000	Animism	10%	4		485
Tuvinian	USSR	Tuvin	139,000	Buddhist-Animist	0%	1		5876
Tuyuca	Brazil	Tuyuca	500	Animism	<1%	1		3131
Twi	Sudan	Twi	9,000	Islam	0%	1		5462
Tzeltal, Bachajon	Mexico	Tzeltal, Bachajon	20,000	Christo-Paganism	<1%	1		5101
Tzeltal, Highland	Mexico	Tzeltal, Highland	25,000	Christo-Paganism	<1%	1		5102
Izutujil	Guatemala	Izutujil	5,000	Christo-Paganism	0%	4	83	8010
USSR Kirghiz Refugee Shepherds	Pakistan	Turkic	1,200	Islam	0%	4		9042
Udegeis	USSR	Udegeis	2,000	Unknown	0%	1		5877

Index by Group Name

NAME	COUNTRY	LANGUAGE	GROUP SIZE	PRIMARY RELIGION	% CHR	V	VOL	UP ID
Udin	USSR	Udin	4,000	Unknown	0%	1		5878
Udmurt	USSR	Udmurt	700,000	Animism	0%	1		5879
Uduk	Sudan	Uduk	7,000	Animism	9%	4		574
Ugandan Asian Refugees	Canada:British Columbia	Gujarati	7,000	Islam	0%	3	83	9011
Ugandan Asian Refugees, Tor.	Canada:Ontario	Various dialects	15,000	Islam	0%	1		9164
Ugandan Refugees	Sudan	Swahili	100,000	Animism	<1%	4	83	9048
	United Kingdom	English	27,000	Islam	0%	4	83	9021
Uhunduni	Indonesia	Uhunduni	14,000	Animism	<1%	1		3079
Uiguir	Afghanistan	Uigur	3,000	Islam	<1%	1		2559
	China	Uigur	4,800,000	Islam	0%	5	80	4013
Ukaan	Nigeria	Ukaan	18,000	Animism	<1%	1		2544
Ukpe-Bayobiri	Nigeria	Ukpe-Bayobiri	12,000	Animism	<1%	1		2522
**Ukrainians,Toronto	Canada:Ontario	Ukrainian	100,000	Nominal Christian	nr%	1		9152
Ukuani-Aboh	Nigeria	Ukuani-Aboh	150,000	Animism	<1%	1		2523
Ulchi	USSR	Ulchi	2,000	Unknown	0%	1		5818
Ulithi-Mall	Pacific Trust Islands	Ulithi	2,000	Christo-Paganism	<1%	4		1004
Ulatan in Kerala	India	Ullatan	2,000	Hindu-Animist	<1%	1		2796
Umm Dorein	Sudan	Umm Dorein	500	Islam	0%	1		5507
Umm Gabralla	Sudan	Umm Gabralla	9,000	Islam	0%	1		5508
**Univ. Students of Japan	Japan	Japanese	2,000,000	Traditional Japanese	1%	4		2125
*Universitarios - Rosario	Argentina	Spanish	10,000	Nominal Christian	2%	6	82	5003
*University Students	France	French	800,000	Secularism	2%	6	79	702
**University Students, Chin	China	Mandarin	600,000	Secularism	<1%	4		6567
University Students, Edmonton	Canada:Alberta	English	20,000	Secularism	1%	3		9101
Urali in Kerala	India	Urali	1,000	Hindu-Aninist	<1%	1		2797
Urarina	Peru	Urarina	4,000	Animism	<1%	1		3187
Urban Elite Vietnamese	United States of America	Vietnamese	90,000	Ancestor Worship	nr%	4		9035
**Urban Mestizos	Ecuador	Spanish	600,000	Nominal Christian	11%	5		4032
Urban Refugees in Lusaka	Zambia	Bantu Dialects	800	Animism	nr%	4	83	9038
Urban Street Women/Los Angeles	United States of America	Spanish	100	Secularism	nr%	4	84	4826
Urhobo	Nigeria	Urhobo	340,000	Animism	<1%	1		2524
Uria	Indonesia	Uria	300	Animism	<1%	1		3080
Uruangnirin	Indonesia	Uruangnirin	300	Animism	<1%	1		3081
Urubu	Brazil	Urubu	500	Animism	<1%	1		3132

NAME	COUNTRY	LANGUAGE	GROUP SIZE	PRIMARY RELIGION	% CHR	V	VOL	UP ID
Urupa	Brazil	Urupa	300	Animism	<1%	1		3133
Uspanteco	Guatemala	Uspanteco	15,000	Animism	<1%	1		8011
Utuguang	Nigeria	Utuguang	12,000	Animism	<1%	1		2525
Uvbie	Nigeria	Uvbie	6,000	Animism	<1%	1		2526
**Uzbeks	Afghanistan	Uzbeki, Turkic	1,000,000	Islam-Animist	0%	6	79	1229
Uzekwe	Nigeria	Uzekwe	5,000	Animism	<1%	1		2527
Vagala	Ghana	Vagala	3,000	Animism	<1%	4		531
Vagari	Pakistan	Gujarati Dialect	30,000	Hinduism	<1%	5		267
Vagla	Ghana	Vagla	6,000	Islam-Animist	<1%	3		5340
*Vai	Liberia	Vai	30,000	Islam	1%	6	80	688
Vai	Sierra Leone	Vai	3,000	Islam-Animist	1%	1		5436
Vaikino	Indonesia	Vaikino	14,000	Animism	<1%	1		3082
Vaiphei in Assam	India	Vaiphei	12,000	Hindu-Buddhist	<1%	1		2798
Vale	Central African Republic	Vale	1,000	Animism	0%	1		5203
Venda	Zimbabwe	Venda	38,000	Animism	0%	1		5420
Veps	USSR	Veps	16,000	Unknown	0%	1		5880
Vere	Cameroon	Vere	20,000	Animism	0%	1		5287
**Vere	Nigeria	Vere	20,000	Animism	9%	5		1177
Vidunda	Tanzania	Vidunda	11,000	Animism	0%	1		5612
Vietnamese	Laos	Vietnamese	20,000	Buddhism	1%	4		100
**Vietnamese Fishermen, Biloxi	United States of America	Vietnamese	1,300	Nominal Christian	nr%	3		4835
**Vietnamese Refugees	Australia	Vietnamese	8,000	Folk Religion	7%	4		2126
Vietnamese Refugees	China	Cantonese	2,000	Traditional Chinese	0%	4	83	9000
**Vietnamese Refugees	Korea, Republic of	Vietnamese	500	Buddhism	nr%	4		9045
	Thailand	Vietnamese	140,000	Buddhism	4%	4		2083
**Vietnamese Refugees	United States of America	Vietnamese	2,700,000	Buddhism	7%	4		1222
Vietnamese Refugees, Regina	Canada:Saskatchewan	Vietnamese	500	Buddhism	nr%	2		9105
Vietnamese, Edmonton	Canada:Alberta	Chinese	8,000	Buddhism	nr%	2		9125
Vige	Upper Volta	Vige	4,000	Islam-Animist	0%	1		5684
Vinza	Tanzania	Vinza	4,000	Animism	0%	1		5613
Vishavan in Kerala	India	Vishavan	200	Hindu-Animist	<1%	4		2799
**Vohras of Yavatnal	India	Gujarati	10,000	Islam	0%	4		2008
Voko	Cameroon	Woko	1,000	Islam-Animist	1%	4		1154
Vute	Nigeria	Vute	1,000	Animism	<1%	1		2528
Wa	Burma	Wa	50,000	Animism	0%	2		4155
Wa	China	Wa	300,000	Traditional Chinese	<1%	1		2849

NAME	COUNTRY	LANGUAGE	GROUP SIZE	PRIMARY RELIGION	% CHR	V	VOL	UP ID
Wabo	Indonesia	Wabo	900	Animism	<1%	1		3083
Waddar in Andhra Pradesh	India	Waddar	40,000	Hindu-Animist	<1%	1		2800
Wagdi in Rajasthan	India	Wagdi	800,000	Hindu-Animist	<1%	1		2801
Waimiri	Brazil	Waimiri	1,000	Animism	<1%	1		3134
Waiwai	Brazil	Waiwai	1,000	Animism	<1%	1		3135
	Guyana	Waiwai	1,000	Christo-Paganism	<1%	1		5118
*Waja	Nigeria	Waja	30,000	Islam	<1%	1		2529
**Wajita	Tanzania	Kijita	65,000	Animism	1%	4		244
Wala	Ghana	Wala	60,000	Islam	1%	4		1076
Walamo	Ethiopia	Walamo	910,000	Animism	2%	5		3233
Wambon	Indonesia	Wambon	2,000	Islam	<1%	1		3084
**Wanchoo	India	Wanchoo	nr	Animism	<1%	3		1029
Wanda	Tanzania	Wanda	8,000	Animism	0%	4		5614
Wandamen	Indonesia	Wandamen	4,000	Animism	<1%	1		3085
Wandering Homeless	United States of America	English	15,000	Secularism	nr%	4	84	4804
Wandji	Gabon	Wandji	6,000	Animism	0%	1		5317
Wanggom	Indonesia	Wanggom	1,000	Animism	<1%	1		3086
Wanji	Tanzania	Wanji	19,000	Animism	0%	1		5615
Wano	Indonesia	Wano	2,000	Animism	<1%	1		3087
Wapishana	Brazil	Wapishana	2,000	Animism	<1%	1		3136
	Guyana	Wapishana	4,000	Christo-Paganism	<1%	1		5119
	Venezuela	Wapishana	20,000	Animism	<1%	1		5143
Wara	Venezuela	Wara	15,000	Islam-Animist	0%	1		5685
Warao	Venezuela	Warao	2,000	Animism	<1%	1		5144
Ware	Upper Volta	Ware	2,400	Animism	0%	1		5385
Warembori	Mali	Warembori	2,000	Animism	<1%	1		3088
Waris	Indonesia	Waris	2,000	Animism	<1%	1		3089
*Warjawa	Nigeria	Warji	70,000	Animism	1%	4		595
*Warkay-Bipin	Indonesia	Warkay-Bipin	300	Animism	<1%	1		3090
Waropen	Indonesia	Waropen	6,000	Animism	<1%	1		3091
Wasi	Tanzania	Wasi	13,000	Animism	0%	1		5616
Watchi	Togo	Ge	1,000,000	Animism	5%	4		424
Water Surface People	Hong Kong	Cantonese dialects	11,000	Islam-Animist	0%	3	84	4822
Waura	Brazil	Uaura	100	Animism	<1%	1		3137
Wayana	Surinam	Wayana	600	Animism	<1%	1		5133
*Wazinza	Tanzania	Kizinza	2,000	Animism	7%	4		1210
Weda	Indonesia	Weda	900	Islam	<1%	1		3092

NAME	COUNTRY	LANGUAGE	GROUP SIZE	PRIMARY RELIGION	% CHR	V	UP	ID
West Indian Migrant Workers	Canada:Ontario	English	400	Hinduism	nr%	3		9102
***West Indians, Toronto	Canada:Ontario	English	200,000	Nominal Christian	nr%	1		9166
Western Sahara Refugees	Algeria	Arabic	70,000	Islam	0%	3	83	9012
Wetawit	Ethiopia	Wetawit	28,000	Animism	<1%	1		3234
Wewewa	Indonesia	Wewewa	55,000	Animism	<1%	4		3093
*White Moors	Mauritania	Hassaniya (Arabic)	nr	Islam	0%	4		6570
Widekum	Cameroon	Widekum	10,000	Animism	<1%	1		5288
**Winbun	Cameroon	Linbum	50,000	Animism	1%	5		388
Win	Upper Volta	Win	20,000	Islam-Animist	<1%	1		5686
Winji-Winji	Benin	Winji-Winji	5,000	Islam	0%	3		454
Wobe	Ivory Coast	Wobe	40,000	Animism	12%	4		532
Wodani	Indonesia	Wodani	3,000	Animism	<1%	1		3094
Woi	Indonesia	Woi	1,000	Animism	<1%	1		3095
Woleat	Pacific Trust Islands	Woleat	1,000	Christo-Paganism	<1%	4		1003
Wolio	Indonesia	Wolio	25,000	Islam-Animist	<1%	1		3096
Wolof	Senegal	Wolof	2,000,000	Islam-Animist	1%	6	80	96
Wolof, Gambian	Gambia	Wolof, Ganbian	10,000	Islam-Animist	<1%	1		2272
Wom	Nigeria	Wom	10,000	Islam-Animist	<1%	1		2530
*Women Laborers	Taiwan	Amoy	1,200,000	Traditional Chinese	2%	4		2115
Wongo	Zaire	Wongo	8,000	Animism	0%	1		5776
Woro	Sudan	Woro	400	Islam	0%	1		5493
Wumbvu	Gabon	Wumbvu	100	Animism	0%	1		5318
Wungu	Tanzania	Wungu	8,000	Animism	0%	1		5617
Xavante	Brazil	Xavante	2,000	Animism	<1%	1		3138
Xerente	Brazil	Xerente	500	Animism	<1%	1		3139
Xokleng	Brazil	Xokleng	300	Animism	<1%	1		3140
Xu	Namibia	Xu	8,000	Animism	<1%	1		5406
Yafi	Indonesia	Yafi	200	Animism	<1%	1		3097
Yaghan	Chile	Yaghan	50	Christo-Paganism	0%	1		5114
Yagnobi	USSR	Yagnobi	2,000	Unknown	0%	1		5881
Yagua	Peru	Yagua	4,000	Animism	<1%	1		3188
Yahadian	Indonesia	Yahadian	4,700	Animism	<1%	1		3098
Yaka	Zaire	Yaka	200,000	Animism	<1%	1		5777
Yakan	Philippines	Yakan	97,000	Islam-Animist	1%	6	80	25
Yakha	Nepal	Yakha	1,000	Buddhist-Animist	0%	1		6523

NAME	LANGUAGE	COUNTRY	GROUP SIZE	PRIMARY RELIGION	% CHR	V	UP	ID
Yakoma	Yakoma	Central African Republic	5,000	Animism	0%	1		5204
**Yala	Yala	Nigeria	60,000	Animism	5%	4		1011
*Yalunka	Yalunka	Sierra Leone	25,000	Islam-Animist	1%	6	80	455
Yaly	Yaly	Indonesia	12,000	Animism	1%	1		3099
Yambasa	Yambasa	Cameroon	26,000	Animism	<1%	1		5289
Yani of Orchid Island	Yani	Indonesia	2,200	Nominal Christian	nr%	4	84	4805
Yaninahua	Yaninahua	Peru	1,000	Animism	<1%	1		3189
Yanadi in Andhra Pradesh	Yanadi	India	210,000	Hindu-Animist	<1%	1		2802
Yandang	Yandang	Nigeria	10,000	Islam-Animist	<1%	1		2531
Yanga	Yanga	Togo	nr	Islam-Animist	<1%	1		5637
Yangbye	Yangbye	Burma	330,000	Buddhist-Animist	<1%	1		2596
*Yanomamo	Yanoman (Waica)	Brazil	3,000	Animism	1%	6	79	1059
Yanomamo	Shanatali	Venezuela	nr	Animism	<1%	5		2024
Yans	Yans	Zaire	165,000	Animism	0%	1		5778
**Yanyula	Yanyula (Yanjula)	Australia	150	Other	15%	4	84	230
Yao	Chiyao	Malawi	600,000	Islam-Animist	2%	4	84	1006
Yao	Islam	Mozambique	220,000	Islam	1%	5		143
**Yao	Yao (Mien Wa)	Thailand	20,000	Animism	2%	6	79	611
*Yao Refugees from Laos	Yao	Thailand	7,000	Animism	4%	4		2097
Yaoure	Yaoure	Ivory Coast	14,000	Animism	<1%	5		4120
Yaquis	Yaqui	Mexico	14,000	Christo-Paganism	<1%	5		317
Yaruro	Yaruro	Venezuela	5,000	Animism	<1%	1		5145
Yasing	Yasing	Cameroon	25,000	Animism	0%	1		5290
Yaur	Yaur	Indonesia	400	Animism	<1%	1		3100
Yava	Yava	Indonesia	5,000	Animism	<1%	1		3101
Yazgulyan	Yazgulyan	USSR	2,000	Unknown	0%	1		5882
**Yei	Yei	Botswana	10,000	Animism	1%	5		1162
Yei	Yei	Indonesia	1,000	Animism	1%	1		3102
Yela	Yela	Zaire	33,000	Animism	0%	1		5779
Yellow Uiguir	Yellow Uiguir	China	4,000	Traditional Chinese	1%	1		2850
Yelmek	Yelmek	Indonesia	400	Animism	1%	1		3103
Yemenis	Arabic (Eastern)	Yemen, Arab Republic	5,600,000	Islam	1%	5	79	1061
Yerava in Karnataka	Yerava	India	11,000	Hindu-Animist	<1%	1		2803
Yeretuar	Yeretuar	Indonesia	300	Animism	<1%	1		3104
Yerukala in A.P.	Yerukala	India	70,000	Hindu-Animist	<1%	1		2804
Yeskwa	Yeskwa	Nigeria	13,000	Islam	<1%	1		2532

NAME	COUNTRY	LANGUAGE	GROUP SIZE	PRIMARY RELIGION	% CHR	V	VOL	UP ID
Yidinit	Ethiopia	Yidinit	600	Animism	<1%	1		3236
Yin-Kyar	Burma	Shan Dialects	2,000	Animism	0%	2		4146
Yin-Nett	Burma	Shan Dialects	2,000	Animism	0%	2		4145
Yinchia	Burma	Yinchia	4,000	Buddhist-Animist	<1%	1		2597
Yinga	Cameroon	Yinga	300	Animism	1%	4		1157
Yoabu	Benin	Yoabu	8,300	Animism	0%	1		5172
Yogad	Philippines	Yogad	7,000	Animism	<1%	1		3291
Yonggom	Indonesia	Yonggom	7,000	Animism	<1%	1		3105
Yoruk	Turkey	Turkish (Danubian)	600,000	Islam	0%	5		4048
Yos	Burma	Yos	5,000	Buddhist-Animist	<1%	1		2598
Yotafa	Indonesia	Yotafa	3,000	Animism	<1%	1		3106
***Youth, Toronto Peanut District	Canada:Ontario	English	3,500	Secularism	nr%	1		9163
Yuana	Venezuela	Yuana	300	Animism	<1%	1		5146
Yucateco	Guatemala	Yucateco	3,000	Animism	<1%	1		8012
Yucateco	Mexico	Yucateco	500,000	Christo-Paganism	1%	5		5105
*Yucuna	Colombia	Yucuna	500	Christo-Paganism	1%	5		1185
Yukagirs	USSR	Yukagir	nr	Unknown	0%	1		5820
Yukpa	Colombia	Yukpa	3,000	Animism	<1%	1		3156
Yukpa	Venezuela	Yukpa	3,000	Animism	0%	1		5147
Yuku	China	Yuku	4,000	Traditional Chinese	<1%	1		2851
Yulu	Sudan	Yulu	2,000	Islam	0%	1		5531
Yungur	Nigeria	Yungur	44,000	Islam	<1%	1		2533
Yuracare	Bolivia	Yuracare	3,000	Animism	<1%	1		2144
Yurak	USSR	Yurak	29,200	Unknown	0%	1		5883
Yuruti	Colombia	Yuruti	200	Animism	<1%	1		3157
Zaghawa	Chad	Zaghawa	61,000	Islam-Animist	<1%	1		2265
Zaghawa	Libya	Zaghawa	nr	Islam	<1%	1		5365
Zaghawa	Sudan	Zaghawa	nr	Islam	<1%	1		5532
Zanaki	Tanzania	Zanaki	23,000	Animism	<1%	1		5618
Zangskari in Kashmir	India	Zangskari	5,000	Hindu-Animist	<1%	1		2805
Zanskari	India	Zanskari	8,000	Buddhism	0%	3	84	4834
Zapoteco, C Sola De Vega	Mexico	Zapoteco, C Sola De Vega	3,400	Christo-Paganism	<1%	1		6525
Zapoteco, Choapan	Mexico	Zapoteco, Choapan	10,000	Christo-Paganism	<1%	1		6528
Zapoteco, E Miahuatlan	Mexico	Zapoteco, E Miahuatlan	9,000	Christo-Paganism	<1%	1		6529
Zapoteco, E Ocotlan	Mexico	Zapoteco, E Ocotlan	7,000	Christo-Paganism	<1%	1		6530
Zapoteco, E Tlacolula	Mexico	Zapoteco, E Tlacolula	5,000	Christo-Paganism	0%	1		6531

NAME	COUNTRY	LANGUAGE	GROUP SIZE	PRIMARY RELIGION	% CHR	VOL V	UP ID
Zapoteco, E Zimatlan	Mexico	Zapoteco, E Zimatlan	5,000	Christo-Paganism	<1%	1	6532
Zapoteco, Isthmus	Mexico	Zapoteco, Isthmus	90,000	Christo-Paganism	<1%	1	6533
Zapoteco, Mazaltepec	Mexico	Zapoteco, Mazaltepec	nr	Christo-Paganism	<1%	1	6535
Zapoteco, Miahuatlan	Mexico	Zapoteco, Miahuatlan	10,000	Christo-Paganism	<1%	1	6534
Zapoteco, Mitla	Mexico	Zapoteco, Mitla	15,000	Christo-Paganism	<1%	1	6526
Zapoteco, N Isthmus	Mexico	Zapoteco, N Isthmus	7,000	Christo-Paganism	<1%	1	6538
Zapoteco, N Ocotlan	Mexico	Zapoteco, N Ocotlan	6,000	Christo-Paganism	0%	1	6539
Zapoteco, N Villa Alta	Mexico	Zapoteco, N Villa Alta	15,000	Christo-Paganism	<1%	1	6540
Zapoteco, NE Miahuatlan	Mexico	Zapoteco, NE Miahuatlan	2,000	Christo-Paganism	0%	1	6536
Zapoteco, NE Yautepec	Mexico	Zapoteco, NE Yautepec	2,000	Christo-Paganism	0%	1	6537
Zapoteco, NW Tehuantepec	Mexico	Zapoteco, NW Tehuantepec	5,000	Christo-Paganism	0%	1	6541
Zapoteco, Pochutla	Mexico	Zapoteco, Pochutla	2,000	Christo-Paganism	0%	1	6542
Zapoteco, S Ejutla	Mexico	Zapoteco, S Ejutla	2,000	Christo-Paganism	0%	1	6548
Zapoteco, S Villa Alta	Mexico	Zapoteco, S Villa Alta	8,000	Christo-Paganism	<1%	1	6549
Zapoteco, SC Zimatlan	Mexico	Zapoteco, SC Zimatlan	nr	Christo-Paganism	0%	1	6546
Zapoteco, SE Miahuatlan	Mexico	Zapoteco, SE Miahuatlan	4,000	Christo-Paganism	0%	1	6547
Zapoteco, SW Ixtlan	Mexico	Zapoteco, SW Ixtlan	10,000	Christo-Paganism	0%	1	6550
Zapoteco, Srra De Juarez	Mexico	Zapoteco, Srra De Juarez	8,000	Christo-Paganism	<1%	1	6545
Zapoteco, Stgo Xanica	Mexico	Zapoteco, Stgo Xanica	4,000	Christo-Paganism	0%	1	6543
Zapoteco, Sto Dom Albarr	Mexico	Zapoteco, Sto Dom Albarr	2,000	Christo-Paganism	0%	1	6544
Zapoteco, Tabaa	Mexico	Zapoteco, Tabaa	5,000	Christo-Paganism	<1%	1	6527
Zapoteco, Villa Alta	Mexico	Zapoteco, Villa Alta	3,000	Christo-Paganism	<1%	1	6551
Zapoteco, W Miahuatlan	Mexico	Zapoteco, W Miahuatlan	3,000	Christo-Paganism	0%	1	6552
Zapoteco, W Ocotlan	Mexico	Zapoteco, W Ocotlan	20,000	Christo-Paganism	<1%	1	6553
Zapoteco, W Sola de Vega	Mexico	Zapoteco, W Sola de Vega	2,000	Christo-Paganism	0%	1	6554
Zapoteco, W Tlacolula	Mexico	Zapoteco, W Tlacolula	32,000	Christo-Paganism	<1%	1	6555
Zapoteco, W Yautepec	Mexico	Zapoteco, W Yautepec	2,000	Christo-Paganism	0%	1	6556
Zapoteco, W Zimatlan	Mexico	Zapoteco, W Zimatlan	2,000	Christo-Paganism	0%	1	6557
Zapoteco, Yalalag	Mexico	Zapoteco, Yalalag	6,000	Christo-Paganism	0%	1	6558
Zarano	Tanzania	Zarano	300,000	Islam-Animist	2%	5	147
**Zaranda Hill Peoples	Nigeria	local languages	10,000	Animism	2%	4	1178
Zari	Nigeria	Zari	4,000	Islam	<1%	1	2534
Zayse	Ethiopia	Zayse	21,000	Animism	<1%	1	3237
Zeni Naga of Assam	India	Jeme	16,000	Animism	nr%	6 81	7002
Zenaga	Mauritania	Zenaga	16,000	Islam	0%	1	5387
Zigua	Tanzania	Zigua	112,000	Animism	0%	1	5619

453

REGISTRY OF THE UNREACHED

NAME	COUNTRY	LANGUAGE	GROUP SIZE	PRIMARY RELIGION	% CHR V	VOL UP ID
Zilmanu	Ethiopia	Zilmanu	3,000	Animism	<1% 1	3238
Zimba	Zaire	Zimba	50,000	Animism	0% 1	5781
Zimbabwean Refugees	Mozambique	Tribal Languages	170,000	Animism	nr% 4 83	9032
	Zambia	Tribal Languages	45,000	Christo-Paganism	nr% 4 83	9029
Zimbabwean Repatriates	Zimbabwe	Tribal Languages	300,000	Christo-Paganism	<1% 4 83	9019
Zinacantecos	Mexico	Tzotzil, Zinacanteco	10,000	Christo-Paganism	3% 7 79	95
Zoliang	India	Naga, Zoliang	50,000	Animism	0% 3	1085
Zome	Burma	Zome	30,000	Buddhist-Animist	<1% 1	2599
Zome in Manipur	India	Zome	30,000	Hindu-Buddhist	<1% 1	2806
Zoque, Chinalapa	Mexico	Zoque, Chinalapa	6,000	Christo-Paganism	<1% 1	5106
Zoque, Copainala	Mexico	Zoque, Copainala	10,000	Christo-Paganism	<1% 1	5107
Zoque, Francisco Leon	Mexico	Zoque, Francisco Leon	12,000	Christo-Paganism	<1% 1	5108
Zoque, Tabasco	Mexico	Zoque, Tabasco	400	Christo-Paganism	<1% 1	5109
Zowla	Ghana	Ewe	800,000	Animism	2% 5	1101
Zulu	Malawi	Zulu	40,000	Animism	<1% 1	5372
Zuni	United States of America	English	6,000	Animism	1% 4	410

454

Index by Receptivity

This index lists groups by their reported attitude toward the gospel. The judgment of receptivity or resistance to the gospel is a subjective and difficult question. Oftentimes what appears to be resistance to the gospel turns out to be a rejection of the Western or foreign cultural trappings with which the gospel is offered. Or perhaps it is a resistance to the agents who bear witness because they come from a country or people not respected by those who are being asked to hear the gospel. Nonetheless, this index gives the considered judgment of those who have reported these unreached peoples. Within each category (very receptive, receptive, indifferent, reluctant, very reluctant and unknown) peoples are listed alphabetically by group name. Their country or location is also listed.

REGISTRY OF THE UNREACHED

Very Receptive

Adi, India
Akhdam, Yemen, Arab Republic
Azteca, Mexico (79)
Bagobo, Philippines
Banaro, Papua New Guinea
Banyarwanda, Rwanda
Baoule, Ivory Coast
Basotho, Mountain, Lesotho (79)
Bipim, Indonesia
Bolinao, Philippines
Cebu, Middle-Class, Philippines
Ch'ol Sabanilla, Mexico
Citak, Indonesia
Copacabana Apt. Dwellers, Brazil
Dan, Ivory Coast
Godie, Ivory Coast
Guarani, Bolivia (79)
Halam in Tripura, India
Higi, Nigeria
Hmong Refugee Women, Ban Vinai,
    Thailand (83)
Hmong Refugees, United States of
    America (83)
Irulas in Kerala, India
Jewish Refugees from USSR, Israel
    (83)
Kond, India
Koreans in Germany, German Federal
    Rep.
Krahn, Liberia
Maguzawa, Nigeria (79)
Matharis, India
Mestizos in La Paz, Bolivia (82)
Micmac Indians, Canada:New Brunswick
Micmac Indians, Eskasoni Rsv. ,
    Canada:Nova Scotia
Mocha, Ethiopia
Nocte, India
Paez, Colombia
Pakabeti of Equator, Zaire
Prasuni, Afghanistan
Rwandan Tutsi Refugees, Burundi (83)
Sanga, Zaire (84)
Shankilla (Kazza), Ethiopia
Tagin, India
Tamil Plantation Workers, Malaysia
Vere, Nigeria
West Indians, Toronto, Canada:Ontario
Youth, Toronto Peanut District,
    Canada:Ontario

Receptive

Adja, Benin
Afghan Refugees (NWFP), Pakistan

Afo, Nigeria (80)
African Students in Cairo, Egypt
Ahl-i-Haqq in Iran, Iran (79)
Akha, Thailand (79)
Ampeeli, Papua New Guinea
Apartment Residents-Seoul, Korea,
    Republic of
Apatani in Assam, India
Apayao, Philippines
Arabs in New Orleans, United States
    of America (82)
Aymara, Bolivia
Azerbaijani, Afghanistan
Babur Thali, Nigeria (80)
Bachelors in Lagos, Nigeria (82)
Bakuba, Zaire
Balangao, Philippines
Balti, Pakistan
Banai, Bangladesh
Bassa, Nigeria
Batangeno, Philippines
Bengali Sufis, Bangladesh (84)
Bengali, Los Angeles area, United
    States of America (84)
Bhil, Pakistan
Bhils, India (79)
Bidayuh of Sarawak, Malaysia (81)
Bijogo, Guinea-Bissau
Bilan, Philippines
Black Caribs, Belize, Belize (79)
Black Caribs, Guatemala, Guatemala
Bodo Kachari, India
Boko, Benin
Bontoc, Central, Philippines (81)
Bontoc, Southern, Philippines
Boran, Kenya
Bukidnon, Philippines
Bus Drivers, South Korea, Korea,
    Republic of
Bus Girls in Seoul, Korea, Republic
    of (82)
Busanse, Ghana
Buwid, Philippines (81)
Chayahuita, Peru
Chicanos in Denver, United States of
    America (82)
Chinese Hakka of Taiwan, Taiwan (79)
Chinese Refugees, France, France (79)
Chinese Stud., Australia, Australia
Chinese Students, United Kingdom
Chinese in Australia, Australia
Chinese in Boston, United States of
    America (82)
Chinese in Brazil, Brazil
Chinese in Indonesia, Indonesia
Chinese in Panama, Panama
Chinese in Sabah, Malaysia
Chinese in Sarawak, Malaysia
Chinese in United Kingdom, United
    Kingdom
Chinese in United States, United
    States of America
Chinese, Mauritius (84)
Chinese, Vancouver, Canada:British
    Columbia
Chiriguano, Argentina

Chrau, Viet Nam
Coreguaje, Colombia
Dagomba, Ghana
Dhodias, India
Dida, Ivory Coast
Djandeau, Zaire
Doohwaayo, Cameroon
Dubla, India
Duka, Nigeria
Eritrean Refugees, Djibouti (83)
Ethiopian Refugees, Somalia (83)
Ex-Mental Patients in NYC, United
    States of America (82)
Fakai, Nigeria
Falasha, Ethiopia (79)
Fali, Nigeria
Filipino Migrant Workers, Saudi
    Arabia (84)
Gagre, Pakistan
Ghimeera, Ethiopia
Glavda, Nigeria
Gouro, Ivory Coast
Grebo, Liberia
Hadrami, Yemen, Democratic
Hajong, Bangladesh
Hazara in Kabul, Afghanistan (82)
Hewa, Papua New Guinea (79)
High School Students, Hong Kong
Hotel Workers in Manila, Philippines
    (81)
Huave, Mexico
Huila, Angola
Hunzakut, Pakistan (79)
Iban, Malaysia (81)
Ifugao (Kalangoya), Philippines
Ikalahan, Philippines
Indian Tamils - Colombo, Sri Lanka
    (82)
Indians, East, Trinidad and Tobago
    (79)
Indians, Winnipeg, Canada:Manitoba
Iranian Bahai Refugees, Pakistan (83)
Ishans, Nigeria
Izi, Nigeria
Jamaican Elite, Jamaica
Japanese Students In USA, United
    States of America
Jarawa, Nigeria
Javanese of Pejompongan, Indonesia
Jimini, Ivory Coast
Jivaro (Achuara), Venezuela
K'anjobal of San Miguel, Guatemala
Kafirs, Pakistan (79)
Kalagan, Philippines
Kalinga, Tanudan, Philippines
Kalinga,Northern, Philippines (81)
Kampuchean Refugees, Ontario,
    Canada:Ontario (83)
Kankanay, Central, Philippines
Karbis, India
Kasena, Ghana
Kashmiri Muslims, India (79)
Kaur, Indonesia
Kekchi, Guatemala
Khmer Refugees, Thailand
Koch, Bangladesh

Kohli, Kutchi, Pakistan
Kohli, Parkari, Pakistan
Kohli, Tharadari, Pakistan
Kohli, Wadiara, Pakistan
Kolam, India
Kono, Sierra Leone
Koranko, Sierra Leone
Kowaao, Liberia
Kuluis in Himachal Pradesh, India
    (81)
Kunimaipa, Papua New Guinea
Kusaasi, Ghana
Lahaulis in Punjab, India
Lambadi in Andhra Pradesh, India (81)
Lepcha, India
Lepers of Cen. Thailand, Thailand
    (81)
Lepers of N.E. Thailand, Thailand
Loho Loho, Indonesia
Lotuka, Sudan
Maasai, Kenya (79)
Macuxi, Brazil
Magar, Nepal
Mam Indian, Guatemala
Mamanua, Philippines (81)
Mangyan, Philippines
Manikion, Indonesia
Manjaco, Guinea-Bissau
Manobo, Cotabato, Philippines
Manobo, Salug, Philippines
Manobo, Tigwa, Philippines
Manobo, Western Bukidnon, Philippines
Mansaka, Philippines
Marielito Refugees in Florida
    United States of America (83)
Mawchis, India
Mazahua, Mexico
Meghwar, Pakistan (79)
Mejah, India
Melanau of Sarawak, Malaysia (80)
Meo, Thailand
Miching, India
Middle Class-Mexico City, Mexico (82)
Military Personnel, Ecuador
Mixes, Mexico
Montagnais Indians, Canada:Quebec
Mopan Maya, Belize
Mopan Maya, Guatemala
Mundas in Bihar, India
Muslim Immigrants in U.K   United
    Kingdom
Nafaara, Ghana (79)
Nambya, Zimbabwe
Ndebele, Zimbabwe (79)
Ndoro, Nigeria
Nepalese in India, India
Ngamo, Nigeria
Ngombe, Zaire
Nupe, Nigeria
Nyabwa, Ivory Coast
Paniyan of Kerala, India (81)
Pila, Benin
Plantation Workers, Papua New Guinea
Portuguese in France, France
Prisoners, Korea, Republic of
Pro Hockey Players, United States of
    America (82)

REGISTRY OF THE UNREACHED

Puyuma, Taiwan (81)
Quechua, Bolivia
Quechua, Huancayo, Peru
Quechua, Peru
Quiche, Guatemala (79)
Quichua, Ecuador
Racetrack Residents, United States of
    America (79)
Rural Vodun Believers, Haiti (84)
Saguye, Kenya
Saiva Vellala, India
Samburu, Kenya (84)
Santhali, Nepal
Save, Benin
Sawi, Indonesia
Selakau of Sarawak, Malaysia
Senoi, Malaysia (81)
Serawai, Indonesia (81)
Shihu, United Arab Emirates
Shirishana, Brazil
Shluh Berbers, Morocco
Sisaala, Ghana
Somba, Benin
Subanen (Tuboy), Philippines
Subanen, Sindangan, Philippines (80)
Suena, Papua New Guinea
Sugut, Malaysia
Sundanese, Indonesia (84)
Suri, Ethiopia
Suriguenos, Philippines
Swazi, South Africa
T'boli, Philippines (81)
Tagbanwa, Aborlan, Philippines
Tamil Laborers in Bombay, India (82)
Tamils (Indian), Sri Lanka (79)
Tangsa, India
Tatuyo, Colombia
Temne, Sierra Leone (80)
Teribe, Panama
Teso, Kenya
Tsachila, Ecuador
Turkana Fishing Community, Kenya (79)
Ukrainians, Toronto, Canada:Ontario
Univ. Students of Japan, Japan
University Students, Chin, China
Urban Mestizos, Ecuador
Uzbeks, Afghanistan (79)
Vietnamese Refugees, United States of
    America
Vietnamese Refugees, Thailand
Vietnamese Refugees, Australia
Vohras of Yavatmal, India
Wajita, Tanzania
Wanchoo, India
Wimbum, Cameroon
Yala, Nigeria
Yao, Malawi (84)
Yao, Thailand (79)
Yei, Botswana
Zaranda Hill Peoples, Nigeria

Indifferent

Afawa, Nigeria (80)
Alars, India
Alawites, Syria (79)
Albanian Muslims, Albania (80)
Albanians in Yugoslavia, Yugoslavia
Americans in Geneva, Switzerland
Ami, Taiwan (81)
Anatolian Turks-Istanbul, Turkey (82)
Arnatas, India
Asian Students, Philippines
Asmat, Indonesia (79)
Ata of Davao, Philippines
Atta, Philippines
Atye, Ivory Coast
Barbers in Tokyo, Japan (82)
Bariba, Benin (80)
Bassa, Liberia
Batak, Angkola, Indonesia (80)
Bete, Ivory Coast
Bhojpuri, Nepal
Black Caribs, Honduras, Honduras (84)
Bororo, Brazil
Bosnian, Yugoslavia (80)
Bushmen (Hiechware), Zimbabwe
Bushmen (Kung), Namibia (79)
Cambodians, Thailand
Caribs, Dominican Republic (84)
Casiguranin, Philippines
Casual Laborers-Atlanta, United
    States of America (82)
Central Thailand Farmers, Thailand
    (81)
Chakmas of Mizoram, India (81)
Cham Refugees from Kampuchea,
    Kampuchea, Democratic (83)
Chang-Pa of Kashmir, India (81)
Cherkess, Jordan (84)
Chilean Refugees, Toronto,
    Canada:Ontario (83)
Chinese Mainlanders, Taiwan
Chinese Refugees in Macau, Macau (81)
Chinese Restaurant Wrkrs., France
Chinese in Amsterdam, Netherlands
Chinese in Austria, Austria
Chinese in Holland, Netherlands
Chinese in Japan, Japan
Chinese in Korea, Korea, Republic of
Chinese in Laos, Laos
Chinese in Malaysia, Malaysia
Chinese in New Zealand, New Zealand
Chinese in South Africa, South Africa
Chinese in Thailand, Thailand
Chinese in West Germany, German
    Federal Rep.
Chinese of W. Malaysia, Malaysia
Coloureds in Eersterust, South Africa
    (82)
Cuna, Colombia (79)
Daka, Nigeria

Danchi Dwellers in Tokyo, Japan (82)
Dani, Baliem, Indonesia (79)
Dentists, Fukuoka, Japan
Deviant Youth in Taipei, Taiwan (82)
Dewein, Liberia
Dghwede, Nigeria
Dog-Pa of Ladakh, India (81)
Dogon, Mali (79)
Drug Addicts in Sao Paulo, Brazil
     (82)
Dumagat, Casiguran, Philippines (81)
English speakers, Guadalajara ,
     Mexico (84)
Expatriates in Riyadh, Saudi Arabia
     (82)
Factory Workers, Hong Kong
Favelados-Rio de Janeiro, Brazil (82)
Fulani, Benin
Fulbe, Ghana
Gabbra, Ethiopia
Galla (Bale), Ethiopia
Gonds, India
Gorkha, India
Guajiro, Colombia
Guanano, Colombia (79)
Gypsies in Spain, Spain (79)
Havasupai, United States of America
Ibataan, Philippines
Ifugao, Philippines
Indians In Rhodesia, Zimbabwe
Industrial Workers, Taiwan (81)
Inland Sea Island Peoples, Japan
Iwaidja, Australia
Japanese in Korea, Korea, Republic of
Jeepney Drivers in Manila,
     Philippines (81)
Jewish Imgrnts.-American, Israel
Jewish Imgrnts.-Argentine, Israel
Jewish Imgrnts.-Australia, Israel
Jewish Imgrnts.-Brazilian, Israel
Jewish Imgrnts.-Mexican, Israel
Jewish Imgrnts.-Uruguayan, Israel
Jewish Immigrants, Other, Israel
Jibu, Nigeria
Jiye, Sudan
Kaffa, Ethiopia (80)
Kalanga, Botswana
Kalinga, Southern, Philippines
Kambari, Nigeria (80)
Kamuku, Nigeria (80)
Karaboro, Upper Volta
Kepas, Papua New Guinea
Khamu, Thailand
Kimyal, Indonesia
Kissi, Liberia
Kissi, Sierra Leone
Komo, Ethiopia
Konkomba, Togo
Koreans of Japan, Japan
Korku in Madhya Pradesh, India
Krahn, Ivory Coast
Kudisai Vagh Makkal, India
Kui, Thailand
Kuknas, India
Kurds of Turkey, Turkey (79)
Labourers of Jhoparpatti, India

Lahu, Thailand (81)
Lango, Ethiopia
Lao Refugees, Spain (83)
Lao Refugees, Thailand
Lao, Laos (79)
Lisu, Thailand
Llaneros, Colombia (84)
Lokoro, Sudan
Mahrah, Yemen, Democratic
Malayalars, India
Maltese, Malta
Manobo, Ilianen, Philippines
Masengo, Ethiopia
Meitei, India (79)
Military Officers, Ecuador (84)
Mimika, Indonesia
Mixteco,San Juan Mixtepic, Mexico
Mokole, Benin
Molbog, Philippines
Mororata, Bolivia
Murngin (Wulamba), Australia
Nahua, North Puebla, Mexico
Newari, Nepal
Ngen, Ivory Coast
Ningerum, Papua New Guinea
Nkoya, Zambia
Nouni, Upper Volta
Nuer, Ethiopia
Nuer, Sudan (79)
Nyantruku, Benin
Pala'wan, Philippines (81)
Parsees, India (81)
Parsis in Bombay, India (82)
Prisoners in Antananarivo, Madagascar
     (82)
Pygmy (Mbuti), Zaire (79)
Rai, Danuwar, Nepal
Ramkamhaeng Un. Students, Thailand
Rava in Assam, India
Ryukyuan, Japan
Samo-Kubo, Papua New Guinea
Sanuma, Brazil
Sherpa, Nepal
Shourastra in Tamil Nadu, India
Sindhis of India, India
Slum Dwellers of Bangkok, Thailand
Soh, Thailand (81)
Somagai, Indonesia
Students, German Federal Rep. (79)
Talo, Indonesia
Tamang, Nepal
Tamil in Yellagiri Hills, India
Tamils (Indian), Malaysia
Teenbu, Ivory Coast
Tense, Ivory Coast
Tertiary Level Youth, Iran
Thai Immigrants, Los Angeles, United
     States of America (84)
Thai Islam (Thai), Thailand
Thai University Students, Thailand
     (81)
Tibetan Refugees, India (83)
Tofi, Benin
Tonga, Zimbabwe
Topotha, Sudan
Toussian, Upper Volta

REGISTRY OF THE UNREACHED

Universitarios - Rosario, Argentina
(82)
University Students, France (79)
Vai, Liberia (80)
Warjawa, Nigeria
Wazinza, Tanzania
White Moors, Mauritania
Women Laborers, Taiwan
Yalunka, Sierra Leone (80)
Yanomamo, Brazil (79)
Yanyula, Australia
Yao Refugees from Laos, Thailand
Yucuna, Colombia

Reluctant

Aborigines in Brisbane, Australia
(82)
Afar, Ethiopia (79)
Ahmadis in Lahore, Pakistan (82)
Alaba, Ethiopia
Alago, Nigeria
Arabs of Khuzestan, Iran
Barasano, Southern, Colombia
Bawoyo, Zaire
Bengalis in London, United Kingdom
(82)
Bengkulu, Indonesia
Blind, N.E. Thailand, Thailand (84)
Busa, Nigeria (80)
Butawa, Nigeria
Bwa, Upper Volta (80)
Cape Malays in Cape Town, South
Africa (82)
Chinese Fishermen, Malaysia
Chitralis, Pakistan (79)
Chola Naickans, India
Circassians in Amman, Jordan (82)
Dead-End Kids - Amsterdam,
Netherlands (82)
Deccani Muslims-Hyderabad, India (82)
Digo, Kenya (84)
Druzes, Israel (79)
Fishing Village People, Taiwan
Fra-Fra, Ghana
Fulani, Cameroon (79)
Ga-Dang, Philippines
Galla, Harar, Ethiopia
Gilakis, Iran
Gourency, Upper Volta
Government officials, Thailand
Guarayu, Bolivia
Gujarati, United Kingdom
Gujars of Kashmir, India (81)
Gypsies in Jerusalem, Israel (82)
Haitian Refugees, United States of
America (83)
Hopi, United States of America
Ica, Colombia
Ifugao in Cababuyan, Philippines
Igbira, Nigeria (80)
Indians in Fiji, Fiji (79)

Indust.Workers Yongdungpo, Korea,
Republic of
Iravas in Kerala, India
Ixil, Guatemala
Jama Mapun, Philippines (80)
Japanese in Brazil, Brazil (79)
Jews (Non-Sephardic), Montreal,
Canada:Quebec (79)
Jews (Sephardic), Montreal,
Canada:Quebec
Jews of Iran, Iran
Kankanay, Northern, Philippines
Karen, Pwo, Thailand
Kayagar, Indonesia
Kerewe, Tanzania
Khmer Refugees, Toronto,
Canada:Ontario
Komering, Indonesia
Kotokoli, Benin
Krumen, Ivory Coast
Lamba, Togo
Lawa, Eastern, Thailand (81)
Lawa, Mountain, Thailand
Lubang Islanders, Philippines (81)
Luvale Refugees from Angola, Zambia
(83)
Maithili, Nepal
Malappanackers, India
Malays of Singapore, Singapore (79)
Mappillas, India
Mapuche, Chile
Mazandaranis, Iran
Miya, Nigeria
Moken of Thailand, Thailand
Moken, Burma (79)
Monpa, India
Mru, Bangladesh
Mualthuam, India
Musi, Indonesia
Muslim Gypsies in Skoplje, Yugoslavia
(82)
Muslim Lebanese Refugees, Canada (83)
Nambikuara, Brazil
Nurses in St. Louis, United States of
America (82)
Ogan, Indonesia
Palaung, Burma (79)
Pension Students-Madrid, Spain (82)
Phu Thai, Thailand (84)
Poouch in Kashmir, India
Purig-Pa of Kashmir, India (81)
Rabinal-Achi, Guatemala
Rajasthani Muslims-Jaipur, India (82)
Rajbansi, Nepal
Rajneeshees of Oregon, United States
of America
Sabbra, Kenya
Sama Bangingi, Philippines (80)
Sama Pangutaran, Philippines (80)
Sama-Badjaw, Philippines (79)
Sangil, Philippines
Satnamis (Madhya Pradesh), India
Sayyids, Yemen, Arab Republic
Senufo, Ivory Coast (80)
Simba, Bolivia
Sindhi Muslims in Karachi, Pakistan
(82)

Sinhalese, Sri Lanka
Solorese Muslims, Indonesia (81)
Somali, Ajuran, Kenya (79)
Somali, Degodia, Kenya
Somali, Gurreh, Kenya
Somali, Ogadenya, Kenya
Street Vendors in Saigon, Viet Nam (82)
Swatis, Pakistan (79)
Sylhetti, United Kingdom
T'in, Thailand (81)
Tagbanwa, Kalamian, Philippines
Tamil (Ceylonese), Sri Lanka
Tengger, Indonesia
Tibetans in Bhutan, Bhutan (81)
Tonga, Gwembe Valley, Zambia (79)
Turkana, Kenya
Turkish Immigrant Workers, German Federal Rep. (79)
Urban Street Women/Los Angeles, United States of America (84)
Vagla, Ghana
Vietnamese Refugees, Korea, Republic of
Wala, Ghana
Watchi, Togo
Winji-Winji, Benin
Woleat, Pacific Trust Islands
Yakan, Philippines (80)
Yanomamo, Venezuela
Zowla, Ghana
Zuni, United States of America

Khojas, Agha Khani, India
Kotta, India
Kreen-Akakore, Brazil
Kurds in Iran, Iran (80)
Macu, Colombia
Maguindanao, Philippines (80)
Malakkaras of Kerala, India (81)
Malayo, Colombia
Mandingo, Liberia (79)
Maranao, Philippines (79)
Maures, Senegal
Minangkabau, Indonesia (80)
Mirung, Bangladesh
Moor & Malays, Sri Lanka (79)
Mumuye, Nigeria
Muslim Malays, Malaysia (80)
Muslims (West Nile Dist.), Uganda
Muslims of Jordan, Jordan
Muslims, United Arab Emirates (79)
North Africans in Belgium, Belgium (80)
Ouaddai, Chad
Paiute, Northern, United States of America
Redjang, Indonesia (80)
Shan, Thailand
Soka Gakkai Believers, Japan
Somali, Ethiopia
Tausug, Philippines (80)
Tem, Togo
Tepehuan, Southwestern, Mexico
Thai Islam (Malay), Thailand (80)
Tuareg, Niger (79)
Turkomans, Iran (80)
Turks in Basel, Switzerland (82)
Turks, Anatolian, Turkey
Ugandan Asian Refugees, Tor., Canada:Ontario
Ulithi-Mall, Pacific Trust Islands
Wolof, Senegal (80)
Yaoure, Ivory Coast
Yaquis, Mexico
Yemenis, Yemen, Arab Republic (79)
Zemi Naga of Assam, India (81)

Very Reluctant

Achehnese, Indonesia (80)
Arab Immigrants in Bangui, Central African Republic (82)
Arawa, Nigeria
Azerbaijani Turks, Iran (80)
Badui, Indonesia (84)
Balinese, Indonesia
Baluchi, Iran (80)
Bhutias, Bhutan
Bugis, Indonesia (80)
Chamula, Mexico (79)
Dawoodi Muslims, India
Dendi, Benin
Divehi, Maldives (80)
Fula, Guinea
Fula, Sierra Leone
Fulah, Upper Volta
Gays in San Francisco, United States of America (82)
Guaiaqui, Paraguay
Gugu-Yalanji, Australia
Gwandara, Nigeria
Jains, India
Jemez Pueblo, United States of America
Kabyle, Algeria (79)
Kae Sung Natives in Seoul, Korea, Republic of (82)

Not Reported

Abaknon, Philippines
Abanyom, Nigeria
Abau, Indonesia
Abau, Papua New Guinea
Abazin, USSR
Abe, Ivory Coast
Abialang, Sudan
Abidji, Ivory Coast
Abie, Papua New Guinea
Abkhaz, Turkey
Abkhaz, USSR
Abong, Nigeria
Abou Charib, Chad
Abu Leila, Sudan
Abua, Nigeria

REGISTRY OF THE UNREACHED

Abujmaria (Madhya Pradesh), India
Abulas, Papua New Guinea
Abure, Ivory Coast
Ach'ang, China
Achagua, Colombia
Acheron, Sudan
Achi, Cubulco, Guatemala
Achi, Rabinal, Guatemala
Achipa, Nigeria
Achode, Ghana
Acholi, Uganda
Achual, Peru
Adamawa, Cameroon
Adele, Togo
Adhola, Uganda
Adiyan in Kerala, India
Adjora, Papua New Guinea
Adygei, USSR
Adyukru, Ivory Coast
Aeka, Papua New Guinea
Aeta, Philippines
Afitti, Sudan
Afshars, Iran
Agajanis, Iran
Agarabi, Papua New Guinea
Agariya in Bihar, India
Age, Cameroon
Aghem, Cameroon
Aghu, Indonesia
Agob, Papua New Guinea
Agoi, Nigeria
Aguacateco, Guatemala
Aguaruna, Peru
Agul, USSR
Agutaynon, Philippines
Agwagwune, Nigeria
Ahir in Maharashtra, India
Ahlo, Togo
Aibondeni, Indonesia
Aiku, Papua New Guinea
Aikwakai, Indonesia
Aimol in Assam, India
Aiome, Papua New Guinea
Aion, Papua New Guinea
Airo-Sumaghaghe, Indonesia
Airoran, Indonesia
Aja, Sudan
Ajmeri in Rajasthan, India
Aka, India
Akan, Brong, Ivory Coast
Akawaio, Guyana
Ake, Nigeria
Akhavakh, USSR
Akpa-Yache, Nigeria
Akpafu, Ghana
Akrukay, Papua New Guinea
Aladian, Ivory Coast
Alak, Laos
Alamblak, Papua New Guinea
Alangan, Philippines
Alas, Indonesia
Alatil, Papua New Guinea
Alauagat, Papua New Guinea
Alege, Nigeria
Algerian Arabs in France, France
Alor, Kolana, Indonesia (81)

Alutor, USSR
Ama, Papua New Guinea
Amahuaca, Peru
Amaimon, Papua New Guinea
Amanab, Indonesia
Amanab, Papua New Guinea
Amar, Ethiopia
Amarakaeri, Peru
Amasi, Cameroon
Ambai, Indonesia
Ambasi, Papua New Guinea
Amber, Indonesia
Amberbaken, Indonesia
Ambo, Zambia
Ambonese, Indonesia
Ambonese, Netherlands
Amo, Nigeria
Amsterdam Boat Dwellers, Netherlands
Amto, Papua New Guinea
Amuesha, Peru
Amuzgo, Guerrero, Mexico
Amuzgo, Oaxaca, Mexico
Ana, Togo
Anaang, Nigeria
Anal in Manipur, India
Andarum, Papua New Guinea
Andha in Andhra Pradesh, India
Andi, USSR
Andoque, Colombia
Anem, Papua New Guinea
Anga in Bihar, India
Angaataha, Papua New Guinea
Angal Heneng, South, Papua New Guinea
Angal Heneng, West, Papua New Guinea
Angal, East, Papua New Guinea
Angas, Nigeria
Angaua, Papua New Guinea
Anggor, Papua New Guinea
Angoram, Papua New Guinea
Animere, Togo
Ankave, Papua New Guinea
Ankwe, Nigeria
Anor, Papua New Guinea
Ansar Sudanese Refugees, Ethiopia
  (83)
Ansus, Indonesia
Anuak, Ethiopia
Anuak, Sudan
Anuki, Papua New Guinea
Anyanga, Togo
Apalai, Brazil
Apinaye, Brazil
Apurina, Brazil
Ara, Indonesia
Arab-Jabbari (Kamesh), Iran
Arab-Shaibani (Kamesh), Iran
Arabela, Peru
Arafundi, Papua New Guinea
Aranadan in Tamil Nadu, India
Arandai, Indonesia
Arapaco, Brazil
Arapesh, Bumbita, Papua New Guinea
Arapesh, Mountain, Papua New Guinea
Arapesh, Muhiang, Papua New Guinea
Arawak, Guyana
Arawe, Papua New Guinea

462

Arbore, Ethiopia
Archin, USSR
Arecuna, Venezuela
Argobba, Ethiopia
Arguni, Indonesia
Arifama-Miniafia, Papua New Guinea
Arigibi, Papua New Guinea
Arinua, Papua New Guinea
Arop, Papua New Guinea
Aruop, Papua New Guinea
Arusha, Tanzania
Arutani, Venezuela
Arya in Andhra Pradesh, India
Asaro, Papua New Guinea
Asat, Papua New Guinea
Asienara, Indonesia
Assumbo, Cameroon
Asu, Tanzania
Asuri in Bihar, India
Ata, Papua New Guinea
Aten, Nigeria
Ati, Philippines
Atoc, Sudan
Atruahi, Brazil
Atsi, China
Attie, Ivory Coast
Atuot, Sudan
Au ei, Botswana
Au, Papua New Guinea
Aunalei, Papua New Guinea
Auyana, Papua New Guinea
Avatime, Ghana
Avikam, Ivory Coast
Avukaya, Sudan
Awa, Papua New Guinea
Awadhi, Nepal
Awar, Papua New Guinea
Awara, Papua New Guinea
Awin, Papua New Guinea
Awngi, Ethiopia
Awutu, Ghana
Awyi, Indonesia
Awyu, Indonesia
Ayana, Kenya
Aymara, Carangas, Chile
Ayoreo, Paraguay
Ayu, Nigeria
Azera, Papua New Guinea
Baali, Zaire
Babajou, Cameroon
Babri, India
Baburiwa, Indonesia
Bachama, Nigeria
Bada, Nigeria
Badagu in Nilgiri, India
Bade, Nigeria
Badjao, Philippines
Badyara, Guinea-Bissau
Bafut, Cameroon
Bagelkhandi in M.P., India
Baghati in H.P., India
Bagirmi, Chad
Bagri, Pakistan
Baguio Area Miners, Philippines (81)
Bahais in Teheran, Iran (82)
Baham, Indonesia

Baharlu (Kamesh), Iran
Bahawalpuri in M.P., India
Bahinemo, Papua New Guinea
Bai, Sudan
Baibai, Papua New Guinea
Baiga in Bihar, India
Baining, Papua New Guinea
Bajania, Pakistan (79)
Bajau, Indonesian, Indonesia
Bajau, Land, Malaysia
Baka, Cameroon
Baka, Zaire
Bakairi, Brazil
Bakhtiaris, Iran (80)
Bakongo Angolan Refugees, Zaire (83)
Bakwe, Ivory Coast
Bakwele, Congo
Balangaw, Philippines
Balanta Refugees, Senegal
Balanta, Senegal
Balantak, Indonesia
Balante, Guinea-Bissau
Bali, Nigeria
Bali-Vitu, Papua New Guinea
Balkars, USSR
Balmiki, Pakistan
Balong, Cameroon
Balti in Jammu, India
Bam, Papua New Guinea
Bambara, Ivory Coast
Bambara, Mali
Bambuka, Nigeria
Bamougoun-Bamenjou, Cameroon
Bamum, Cameroon
Bandawa-Minda, Nigeria
Bandi, Liberia
Bandjoun, Cameroon
Banen, Cameroon
Banga, Nigeria
Bangangte, Cameroon
Bangaru in Punjab, India
Bangba, Zaire
Banggai, Indonesia
Baniwa, Brazil
Banoni, Papua New Guinea
Bantuanon, Philippines
Banyum, Senegal
Banyun, Guinea-Bissau
Barabaig, Tanzania (79)
Barai, Papua New Guinea
Barambu, Sudan
Barasano, Colombia
Barasano, Northern, Colombia
Barau, Indonesia
Bare'e, Indonesia
Bareli in Madhya Pradesh, India
Bari, Sudan
Bariai, Papua New Guinea
Bariba, Nigeria
Bariji, Papua New Guinea
Barim, Papua New Guinea
Barok, Papua New Guinea
Baruga, Papua New Guinea
Baruya, Papua New Guinea
Basaa, Cameroon
Basakomo, Nigeria

REGISTRY OF THE UNREACHED

Basari, Guinea
Basari, Senegal
Basari, Togo
Bashar, Nigeria
Bashgali, Afghanistan
Bashkir, USSR (80)
Basila, Togo
Basketo, Ethiopia
Bata, Nigeria
Batak, Karo, Indonesia
Batak, Palawan, Philippines
Batak, Simalungun, Indonesia
Batak, Toba, Indonesia
Batanga-Ngolo, Cameroon
Bateg, Malaysia
Bathudi in Bihar, India
Batsi, USSR
Batu, Nigeria
Bau, Papua New Guinea
Baushi, Nigeria
Bauwaki, Papua New Guinea
Bavenda, South Africa
Bawm, Bangladesh
Bayats, Iran
Bayot, Gambia
Bayot, Guinea-Bissau
Bayot, Senegal
Bazigar in Gujarat, India
Bebeli, Papua New Guinea
Bediya in Bihar, India
Bedoanas, Indonesia
Beja, Ethiopia
Beja, Sudan
Bekwarra, Nigeria
Bembe, Zaire
Bembi, Papua New Guinea
Bena, Tanzania
Benabena, Papua New Guinea
Bencho, Ethiopia
Bende, Tanzania
Bene, Cameroon
Benga, Gabon
Bengali Refugees, Assam, India
Berba, Benin
Berik, Indonesia
Berom, Nigeria
Besisi, Malaysia
Bete, India
Bethen, Cameroon
Betsinga, Cameroon
Bette-Bende, Nigeria
Bhakta, India
Bharia in Madhya Pradesh, India
Bhatneri, India
Bhattri, India
Bhilala, India
Bhoyari in Maharashtra, India
Bhuiya in Bihar, India
Bhumij in Assam, India
Bhunjia in Madhya Pradesh, India
Biafada, Guinea-Bissau
Biak, Indonesia
Biaka, Papua New Guinea
Biangai, Papua New Guinea
Bibling, Papua New Guinea
Biduanda, Malaysia

Bijori in Bihar, India
Biksi, Indonesia
Bilala, Chad
Bile, Nigeria
Bilen, Ethiopia
Biliau, Papua New Guinea
Bimanese, Indonesia
Bimin, Papua New Guinea
Bimoba, Ghana
Bimoba, Togo
Binahari, Papua New Guinea
Binandere, Papua New Guinea
Binawa, Nigeria
Bine, Papua New Guinea
Binga, Sudan
Bingkokak, Indonesia
Binjhwari in Bihar, India
Binji, Zaire
Binumarien, Papua New Guinea
Bira, Indonesia
Birhor in Bihar, India
Birifor, Ghana
Birifor, Upper Volta
Bisa, Zambia
Bisaya, Malaysia (81)
Bisis, Papua New Guinea
Bitara, Papua New Guinea
Bitare, Cameroon
Bitare, Nigeria
Biti, Sudan
Biyom, Papua New Guinea
Boanaki, Papua New Guinea
Boat People, Japan
Bobe, Cameroon
Bobo Fing, Mali
Bobo Wule, Mali
Bodo in Assam, India
Boghom, Nigeria
Bohutu, Papua New Guinea
Boikin, Papua New Guinea
Bokyi, Cameroon
Bokyi, Nigeria
Bola, Papua New Guinea
Bole, Nigeria
Bolon, Upper Volta
Bolondo, Zaire
Bom, Papua New Guinea
Boma, Zaire
Bomboko, Cameroon
Bomou, Chad
Bondei, Tanzania
Bondo in Orissa, India
Bonerif, Indonesia
Bonggo, Indonesia
Bongili, Congo
Bongo, Sudan
Bongu, Papua New Guinea
Boni of Lamu, Kenya (84)
Bonkeng-Pendia, Cameroon
Bonkiman, Papua New Guinea
Bor Gok, Sudan
Bora, Colombia
Borai, Indonesia
Boran, Ethiopia
Bosavi, Papua New Guinea
Bosilewa, Papua New Guinea

Bosngun, Papua New Guinea
Bote-Majhi, Nepal
Botlikh, USSR
Bousansi, Upper Volta
Bovir-Ahmadi, Iran
Bowili, Togo
Boya, Sudan
Bozo, Mali
Brahui, Pakistan
Braj in Uttar Pradesh, India
Brao, Laos (79)
Brat, Indonesia
Breri, Papua New Guinea
Bruneis, Malaysia
Bua, Chad
Bual, Indonesia
Buang, Central, Papua New Guinea
Buang, Mangga, Papua New Guinea
Bube, Equatorial Guinea
Budibud, Papua New Guinea
Budug, USSR
Budugum, Cameroon
Buduma, Nigeria
Buglere, Panama
Bugombe, Zaire
Buhid, Philippines
Builsa, Ghana
Buin, Papua New Guinea
Buja, Zaire
Buka-khwe, Botswana
Bukaua, Papua New Guinea
Buli, Indonesia
Buli, Upper Volta
Bulia, Zaire
Bullom, Northern, Sierra Leone
Bullom, Southern, Sierra Leone
Bulu, Papua New Guinea
Buna, Papua New Guinea
Bunabun, Papua New Guinea
Bunak, Indonesia
Bunama, Papua New Guinea
Bunann in Kashmir, India
Bungku, Indonesia
Bunu, Nigeria
Bura, Cameroon
Burak, Nigeria
Buraka-Gbanziri, Congo
Buriat, China
Buriat, USSR
Burig in Kashmir, India
Burig, China
Burji, Ethiopia
Burmese Muslim Refugees, Bangladesh (83)
Buru, Indonesia
Burum, Papua New Guinea
Burun, Sudan
Burundian Hutu Refugees, Tanzania (83)
Burungi, Tanzania
Busah, Papua New Guinea
Busami, Indonesia
Bushmen (Heikum), Namibia
Bushmen in Botswana, Botswana
Bushoong, Zaire
Bussa, Ethiopia

Butung, Indonesia
Bviri, Sudan
Bwa, Zaire
Bwaidoga, Papua New Guinea
Bwisi, Zaire
Byangsi, Nepal
Cacua, Colombia
Caiwa, Brazil
Cakchiquel, Central, Guatemala
Caluyanhon, Philippines
Campa, Peru
Camsa, Colombia
Candoshi, Peru
Canela, Brazil
Capanahua, Peru
Carapana, Colombia
Cashibo, Peru
Cayapa, Ecuador
Cewa, Zambia
Ch'iang, China
Ch'ol Tila, Mexico
Chacobo, Bolivia
Chad's Refugees from N'Djamena, Cameroon (83)
Chadian Refugees, Nigeria (83)
Chagga, Tanzania
Chaghatai, Afghanistan
Chakfem-Mushere, Nigeria
Chakossi in Ghana, Ghana
Chakossi in Togo, Togo
Chala, Ghana
Cham, Viet Nam
Chamacoco, Bahia Negra, Paraguay
Chamalin, USSR
Chamari in Madhya Pradesh, India
Chamba Daka, Nigeria
Chamba Leko, Nigeria
Chambri, Papua New Guinea
Chameali in H.P., India
Chami, Colombia
Chamicuro, Peru
Chamorro, Pacific Trust Islands
Chara, Ethiopia
Chatino, Nopala, Mexico
Chatino, Panixtlahuaca, Mexico
Chatino, Tataltepec, Mexico
Chatino, Yaitepec, Mexico
Chatino, Zacatepec, Mexico
Chatino, Zenzontepec, Mexico
Chaudangsi, Nepal
Chaungtha, Burma
Chawai, Nigeria
Chenapian, Papua New Guinea
Chenchu in Andhra Pradesh, India
Chepang, Nepal
Cherkess, USSR
Chero in Bihar, India
Chiga, Uganda
Chik-Barik in Bihar, India
Chilean Refugees, Argentina (83)
Chin, China
Chin, Falam, Burma
Chin, Haka, Burma
Chin, Khumi, Burma
Chin, Ngawn, Burma
Chin, Tiddim, Burma

REGISTRY OF THE UNREACHED

Chinanteco, Ayotzintepec, Mexico
Chinanteco, Chiltepec, Mexico
Chinanteco, Comaltepec, Mexico
Chinanteco, Lalana, Mexico
Chinanteco, Lealao, Mexico
Chinanteco, Ojitlan, Mexico
Chinanteco, Palantla, Mexico
Chinanteco, Quiotepec, Mexico
Chinanteco, Sochiapan, Mexico
Chinanteco, Tepetotutla, Mexico
Chinanteco, Usila, Mexico
Chinanteco,, Mexico
Chinbok, Burma
Chinese Businessmen, Hong Kong (81)
Chinese Factory Workers, Hong Kong
Chinese Muslims, Taiwan (81)
Chinese Students, Thunder Bay ,
     Canada:Ontario
Chinese Villagers, Hong Kong
Chinese in Burma, Burma
Chinese in Costa Rica, Costa Rica
Chinese in Costa Rica, Costa Rica
Chinese in Puerto Rico, Puerto Rico
Chinese in Saudi Arabia, Saudi Arabia
Chinese, Calgary, Canada:Alberta
Chinese, Halifax, Canada:Nova Scotia
Chinese, Metro Toronto,
     Canada:Ontario
Chinese, Thunder Bay, Canada:Ontario
Chinga, Cameroon
Chingp'o, China
Chip, Nigeria
Chipaya, Bolivia
Chiquitano, Bolivia
Chocho, Mexico
Chodhari in Gujarat, India
Chokobo, Nigeria
Chokwe (Lunda), Angola
Chokwe, Zambia
Chopi, Mozambique
Chorote, Paraguay
Chorti, Guatemala
Chuabo, Mozambique
Chuang, China (81)
Chuave, Papua New Guinea
Chuj, Guatemala
Chuj, San Mateo Ixtatan, Mexico
Chukot, USSR
Chulupe, Paraguay
Chungchia, China
Churahi in H.P., India
Chwang, China
Cinta Larga, Brazil
Circassian, Turkey
Cirebon, Indonesia
Cocama, Peru
Cocopa, Mexico
Cofan, Colombia
Cogui, Colombia
Cora, Mexico
Cubeo, Colombia
Cuiba, Colombia
Cuicateco, Tepeuxila, Mexico
Cuicateco, Teutila, Mexico
Cujareno, Peru
Culina, Brazil

Curipaco, Colombia
Cuyonon, Philippines
Daba, Cameroon
Dabra, Indonesia
Dadibi, Papua New Guinea
Dadiya, Nigeria
Daga, Papua New Guinea
Dagada, Indonesia
Dagari, Ghana
Dagari, Upper Volta
Dagur, China
Dahating, Papua New Guinea
Dai, Burma
Dair, Sudan
Daju of Dar Dadju, Chad
Daju of Dar Fur, Sudan
Daju of Dar Sila, Chad
Daju of West Kordofan, Sudan
Dami, Papua New Guinea
Dan, Liberia
Dangaleat, Chad
Danu, Burma
Daonda, Papua New Guinea
Darai, Nepal
Dargin, USSR
Darmiya, Nepal
Dass, Nigeria
Dathanik, Ethiopia
Davaweno, Philippines
Dawawa, Papua New Guinea
Day, Central African Republic
Daza, Chad
Deccani Muslims, India
Dedua, Papua New Guinea
Degema, Nigeria
Degenan, Papua New Guinea
Dem, Indonesia
Demta, Indonesia
Dengese, Zaire
Deno, Nigeria
Deori in Assam, India
Dera, Nigeria
Desano, Brazil
Dghwede, Cameroon
Dhaiso, Tanzania
Dhanka in Gujarat, India
Dhanwar in Madhya Pradesh, India
Dhimal, Nepal
Dhurwa, India
Dia, Papua New Guinea
Didinga, Sudan
Didoi, USSR
Digo, Tanzania
Dimasa in Cachar, India
Dime, Ethiopia
Dimir, Papua New Guinea
Dinka, Agar, Sudan
Dinka, Sudan
Diodio, Papua New Guinea
Diola, Guinea-Bissau (80)
Diola, Senegal
Dirim, Nigeria
Dirya, Nigeria
Djuka, Surinam
Dobu, Papua New Guinea
Doe, Tanzania

466

Doga, Papua New Guinea
Doghosie, Upper Volta
Dogoro, Papua New Guinea
Dolgans, USSR
Dom, Papua New Guinea
Dompago, Benin
Domu, Papua New Guinea
Domung, Papua New Guinea
Dongjoi, Sudan
Dongo, Sudan
Dongo, Zaire
Dorlin in Andhra Pradesh, India
Dorobo, Kenya
Dorobo, Tanzania
Doromu, Papua New Guinea
Dorze, Ethiopia
Doura, Papua New Guinea
Duau, Papua New Guinea
Dubu, Indonesia
Duguir, Nigeria
Duguza, Nigeria
Dukwe Refugee Camp Residents,
    Botswana (83)
Duma, Gabon
Duna, Papua New Guinea
Dungan, USSR
Duru, Cameroon
Dusun, Malaysia (81)
Duvele, Indonesia
Dyan, Upper Volta
Dyerma, Niger (80)
Dyerma, Nigeria
Dyola, Gambia
Ebira, Nigeria
Ebrie, Ivory Coast
Edawapi, Papua New Guinea
Edo, Nigeria
Efik, Nigeria
Efutop, Nigeria
Eggon, Nigeria
Eivo, Papua New Guinea
Ejagham, Nigeria
Ekagi, Indonesia
Ekajuk, Nigeria
Eket, Nigeria
Ekpeye, Nigeria
El Molo, Kenya
Eleme, Nigeria
Elkei, Papua New Guinea
Emai-Iuleha-Ora, Nigeria
Embera, Northern, Colombia
Emerum, Papua New Guinea
Emira, Papua New Guinea
Emumu, Indonesia
Endangen, Papua New Guinea
Enga, Papua New Guinea
Engenni, Nigeria
Enya, Zaire
Eotile, Ivory Coast
Epie, Nigeria
Equatorial Guin. Refugees, Gabon (83)
Eritrean Refugees, Sudan (83)
Erokwanas, Indonesia
Esan, Nigeria
Ethiopian Refugees, Yemen, Yemen,
    Arab Republic

Eton, Cameroon
Etulo, Nigeria
Evant, Nigeria
Evenki, China
Evenks, USSR
Ewage-Notu, Papua New Guinea
Ewenkis, China (81)
Ex-Mental Patients, Hamilton,
    Canada:Ontario
Fa D'Ambu, Equatorial Guinea
Fagululu, Papua New Guinea
Faiwol, Papua New Guinea
Fali, Cameroon
Fas, Papua New Guinea
Fasu, Papua New Guinea
Feroge, Sudan
Finungwan, Papua New Guinea
Fipa, Tanzania
Foau, Indonesia
Foi, Papua New Guinea
Foran, Papua New Guinea
Fordat, Indonesia
Fore, Papua New Guinea
French, St. Pierre & Miquelon ,
    Canada:Newfoundland
Fula, Cunda, Gambia
Fula, Macina, Mali
Fula, Peuhala, Mali
Fula, Upper Volta
Fuliro, Zaire
Fulnio, Brazil
Fungom, Northern, Cameroon
Fungor, Sudan
Fur Trappers, Canada:Ontario
Furu, Zaire
Fuyuge, Papua New Guinea
Fyam, Nigeria
Fyer, Nigeria
Gaanda, Nigeria
Gabbra, Kenya
Gabri, Chad
Gadaban in Andhra Pradesh, India
Gaddi in Himachal Pradesh, India
Gade, Nigeria
Gadsup, Papua New Guinea
Gagauzes, USSR
Gagu, Ivory Coast
Gahuku, Papua New Guinea
Gaikundi, Papua New Guinea
Gaina, Papua New Guinea
Gal, Papua New Guinea
Galambi, Nigeria
Galeshis, Iran
Galla of Bucho, Ethiopia
Galler, Laos
Galong in Assam, India
Gambai, Chad
Gamei, Papua New Guinea
Gamti in Gujarat, India
Gan, Upper Volta
Gane, Indonesia
Gangam, Togo
Ganglau, Papua New Guinea
Gangte in Assam, India
Garuh, Papua New Guinea
Garus, Papua New Guinea

REGISTRY OF THE UNREACHED

Garuwahi, Papua New Guinea
Gawar-Bati, Afghanistan
Gawari in Andhra Pradesh, India
Gawwada, Ethiopia
Gayo, Indonesia (80)
Gbande, Guinea
Gbari, Nigeria (80)
Gbaya, Nigeria
Gbaya-Ndogo, Sudan
Gbazantche, Benin
Gberi, Sudan
Gedaged, Papua New Guinea
Gedeo, Ethiopia
Geishas in Osaka, Japan (82)
Geji, Nigeria
Genagane, Papua New Guinea
Gende, Papua New Guinea
Gera, Nigeria
Geruma, Nigeria
Gesa, Indonesia
Ghale Gurung, Nepal
Gheko, Burma
Ghol, Sudan
Ghotuo, Nigeria
Ghulfan, Sudan
Gidar, Cameroon
Gidar, Chad
Gidicho, Ethiopia
Gidra, Papua New Guinea
Gilyak, USSR
Gimi, Papua New Guinea
Ginuman, Papua New Guinea
Gio, Liberia
Gira, Papua New Guinea
Girawa, Papua New Guinea
Giri, Papua New Guinea
Giryama, Kenya
Gisei, Cameroon
Cʼiga, Cameroon
Giʼua, Papua New Guinea
Gizra, Papua New Guinea
Gobasi, Papua New Guinea
Gobato, Ethiopia
Gobeze, Ethiopia
Goemai, Nigeria
Gogo, Tanzania
Gogodala, Papua New Guinea
Gokana, Nigeria
Gola, Liberia
Gola, Sierra Leone
Golo, Chad
Gonja, Ghana
Goroa, Tanzania
Gorontalo, Indonesia
Gosha, Kenya
Goudari, Iran
Gouin-Turka, Upper Volta
Goulai, Chad
Gouwar, Cameroon
Grasia in Gujarat, India
Greeks, Toronto, Canada:Ontario
Grunshi, Ghana
Gu, Benin
Guajajara, Brazil
Guajibo, Colombia
Guambiano, Colombia

Guana, Paraguay
Guarojio, Mexico
Guatemalan Refugees, Mexico
Guayabero, Colombia
Gude, Cameroon
Gude, Nigeria
Gudu, Nigeria
Guduf, Nigeria
Guere, Ivory Coast
Guhu-Samane, Papua New Guinea
Guinean Refugees, Gabon
Gujuri, Afghanistan
Gula, Chad
Gulfe, Cameroon
Gumasi, Papua New Guinea
Gumine, Papua New Guinea
Gumuz, Ethiopia
Gumuz, Sudan
Gurage, Ethiopia (80)
Gure-Kahugu, Nigeria
Gurensi, Ghana
Gurma, Upper Volta
Gurung, Nepal
Guruntum-Mbaaru, Nigeria
Gusap, Papua New Guinea
Guwot, Papua New Guinea
Gwa, Ivory Coast
Gwari Matai, Nigeria
Gwedena, Papua New Guinea
Gwere, Uganda
Gypsies in Yugoslavia, Yugoslavia
Gypsies, Brazil
Gypsies, USSR
Ha, Tanzania
Hadiyya, Ethiopia
Hahon, Papua New Guinea
Haitians, Montreal, Canada:Quebec
Halbi in Madhya Pradesh, India
Halia, Papua New Guinea
Hallam, Burma
Hamtai, Papua New Guinea
Hangaza, Tanzania
Hani, China
Hanonoo, Philippines
Harari, Ethiopia
Harauti in Rajasthan, India
Hatsa, Tanzania
Havu, Zaire
Havunese, Indonesia
Haya, Tanzania
Hehe, Tanzania
Heiban, Sudan
Helong, Indonesia
Herero, Botswana
Herero, Namibia
Heso, Zaire
Hezareh, Iran
Hixkaryana, Brazil
Hkun, Burma
Hmong, Twin Cities, United States of
   America
Ho in Bihar, India
Hohodene, Brazil
Holiya in Madhya Pradesh, India
Holoholo, Tanzania
Holu, Angola

468

Homosexuals, Toronto, Canada:Ontario
Hote, Papua New Guinea
Hrangkhol, Burma
Huachipaire, Peru
Huambisa, Peru
Huasteco, Mexico
Hui, China (80)
Huichol, Mexico
Huistan Tzotzil, Mexico
Huitoto, Meneca, Colombia
Huitoto, Murui, Peru
Hukwe, Angola
Hula, Papua New Guinea
Huli, Papua New Guinea
Humene, Papua New Guinea
Hunde, Zaire
Hunjara, Papua New Guinea
Hupda Maku, Colombia
Hwana, Nigeria
Hwela-Numu, Ivory Coast
Hyam, Nigeria
Iatmul, Papua New Guinea
Ibaji, Nigeria
Ibanag, Philippines
Ibibio, Nigeria
Icen, Nigeria
Idi, Papua New Guinea
Idoma, Nigeria
Idoma, North, Nigeria
Ifugao, Ambanad, Philippines
Ifugao, Antipolo, Philippines
Ifugao, Kiangan, Philippines
Ifumu, Congo
Igala, Nigeria
Igede, Nigeria
Ignaciano, Bolivia
Igora, Papua New Guinea
Igorot, Philippines
Iha, Indonesia
Ihceve, Nigeria
Ijo, Central-Western, Nigeria
Ijo, Northeast Central, Nigeria
Ijo, Northeast, Nigeria
Ikizu, Tanzania
Ikobi-Mena, Papua New Guinea
Ikulu, Nigeria
Ikundun, Papua New Guinea
Ikwere, Nigeria
Ila, Zambia
Ilanon, Philippines
Ilongot, Philippines
Inallu, Iran
Inanwatan, Indonesia
Indians in Dubai, United Arab
    Emirates (82)
Indians, CN Rail Lines,
    Canada:Ontario
Indians, Cold Lake Reserve,
    Canada:Alberta
Indians, Eden Valley, Canada:Alberta
Indians, Edmonton, Canada:Alberta
Indians, Interlake Region,
    Canada:Manitoba
Indians, Kinistino Reserve,
    Canada:Saskatchewan
Indians, London, Canada:Ontario
Indians, Lower Mainland,
    Canada:British Columbia
Indians, Northern Sask.,
    Canada:Saskatchewan
Indians, Northwestern Ontario ,
    Canada:Ontario
Indians, Regina, Canada:Saskatchewan
Indians, Saskatoon,
    Canada:Saskatchewan
Indians, Thunder Bay, Canada:Ontario
Indians, Vancouver, Canada:British
    Columbia
Indians, White Bear Reserve,
    Canada:Saskatchewan
Indinogosima, Papua New Guinea
Indo-Canadians, Vancouver,
    Canada:British Columbia (84)
Inga, Colombia
Ingassana, Sudan
Ingushes, USSR
Insinai, Philippines
Intha, Burma
Ipiko, Papua New Guinea
Ipili, Papua New Guinea
Iquito, Peru
Irahutu, Indonesia
Iranians, Montreal, Canada:Quebec
Iraqi Kurd Refugees, Iran (83)
Iraqw, Tanzania
Iraya, Philippines
Iresim, Indonesia
Iria, Indonesia
Irigwe, Nigeria
Irumu, Papua New Guinea
Isanzu, Tanzania
Isebe, Papua New Guinea
Isekiri, Nigeria
Isneg, Dibagat-Kabugao, Philippines
Isneg, Karagawan, Philippines
Isoko, Nigeria
Itawit, Philippines
Itelmen, USSR
Itik, Indonesia
Itneg, Adasen, Philippines
Itneg, Binongan, Philippines
Itneg, Masadiit, Philippines
Itonama, Bolivia
Ivbie North-Okpela-Atte, Nigeria
Iwa, Zambia
Iwal, Papua New Guinea
Iwam, Papua New Guinea
Iwam, Sepik, Papua New Guinea
Iwur, Indonesia
Iyon, Cameroon
Iyon, Nigeria
Izarek, Nigeria
Izhor, USSR
Jaba, Nigeria
Jabem, Papua New Guinea
Jacalteco, Guatemala
Jagannathi in A.P., India
Jamamadi, Brazil
Jambi, Indonesia
Jamden, Indonesia
Jamshidis, Iran
Janggali, Nepal

REGISTRY OF THE UNREACHED

Janjero, Ethiopia
Janjo, Nigeria
Japanese, Toronto, Canada:Ontario
Jaqaru, Peru
Jara, Nigeria
Jatapu in Andhra Pradesh, India
Jati, Afghanistan
Jaunsari in Uttar Pradesh, India
Jebero, Peru
Jeng, Laos
Jera, Nigeria
Jerawa, Nigeria
Jews in Venice, Italy (82)
Jews, Toronto, Canada:Ontario
Jews, Vancouver, Canada:British
    Columbia
Jews, Winnipeg, Canada:Manitoba
Jharia in Orissa, India
Jiji, Tanzania
Jimajima, Papua New Guinea
Jimbin, Nigeria
Jinja, Tanzania
Jinuos, China (81)
Jirel, Nepal
Jita, Tanzania
Jiye, Uganda
Jongor, Chad
Juang in Orissa, India
Juhai, Malaysia
Jukun, Nigeria
Jyarung, China
K'anjobal of Los Angeles, United
    States of America
Kaagan, Philippines
Kaalong, Cameroon
Kaba Dunjo, Central African Republic
Kaba, Central African Republic
Kabadi, Papua New Guinea
Kabixi, Brazil
Kabre, Benin
Kabre, Togo
Kachama, Ethiopia
Kachchi in Andhra Pradesh, India
Kachin in Shan State, Burma
Kadaklan-Barlig Bontoc, Philippines
Kadar in Andhra Pradesh, India
Kadara, Nigeria
Kadazans, Malaysia
Kadiweu, Brazil
Kadugli, Sudan
Kaeti, Indonesia
Kagoma, Nigeria
Kagoro, Mali
Kagulu, Tanzania
Kahluri in Andamans, India
Kaian, Papua New Guinea
Kaibu, Nigeria
Kaiep, Papua New Guinea
Kaikadi in Maharashtra, India
Kaili, Indonesia
Kaingang, Brazil
Kairi, Papua New Guinea
Kairiru, Papua New Guinea
Kaiwai, Indonesia
Kajang, Indonesia
Kaka, Cameroon

Kaka, Central African Republic
Kaka, Nigeria
Kakoa, Papua New Guinea
Kakuna-Mamusi, Papua New Guinea
Kalanga, Zimbabwe
Kalinga, Kalagua, Philippines
Kalinga, Limus-Linan, Philippines
Kalinga, Quinaang, Philippines
Kalmytz, China
Kalmytz, USSR
Kalokalo, Papua New Guinea
Kam, China
Kamano, Papua New Guinea
Kamantan, Nigeria
Kamar in Madhya Pradesh, India
Kamayura, Brazil
Kambera, Indonesia
Kamberataro, Indonesia
Kamberataro, Papua New Guinea
Kambot, Papua New Guinea
Kami, Tanzania
Kamkam, Cameroon
Kamnum, Papua New Guinea
Kamo, Nigeria
Kamoro, Indonesia
Kampuchean Refugees, Laos
Kampung Baru, Indonesia
Kamtuk-Gresi, Indonesia
Kana, Nigeria
Kanauri in Uttar Pradesh, India
Kandas, Papua New Guinea
Kanembu, Chad
Kanembu, Niger
Kanga, Sudan
Kanikkaran in Kerala, India
Kaningra, Papua New Guinea
Kanite, Papua New Guinea
Kanjari in Andhra Pradesh, India
Kanu, Zaire
Kanum, Indonesia
Kanum, Papua New Guinea
Kanuri, Nigeria (80)
Kao, Ethiopia
Kaonde, Zaire
Kaonde, Zambia
Kapin, Papua New Guinea
Kapore, Papua New Guinea
Kapori, Indonesia
Kapriman, Papua New Guinea
Kapuchin, USSR
Kara, Papua New Guinea
Kara, Tanzania
Karachay, USSR
Karagas, USSR
Karaim, USSR
Karakalpak, USSR (80)
Karam, Papua New Guinea
Karanga, Chad
Karangi, Papua New Guinea
Karas, Indonesia
Karatin, USSR
Kare, Papua New Guinea
Karekare, Nigeria
Karen, Thailand (79)
Kari, Central African Republic
Kari, Chad

470

Kari, Zaire
Karipuna Creole, Brazil
Karipuna Do Guapore, Brazil
Kariya, Nigeria
Karkar, Papua New Guinea
Karko, Sudan
Karmali in Dihar, India
Karon Dori, Indonesia
Karon Pantai, Indonesia
Karre, Central African Republic
Karua, Papua New Guinea
Kasanga, Guinea-Bissau
Kasele, Togo
Kasem, Upper Volta
Kasseng, Laos
Kasua, Papua New Guinea
Kasuweri, Indonesia
Katab, Nigeria
Katakari in Gujarat, India
Katcha, Sudan
Kate, Papua New Guinea
Kati, Northern, Indonesia
Kati, Southern, Indonesia
Katiati, Papua New Guinea
Katla, Sudan
Katukina, Panoan, Brazil
Kaugat, Indonesia
Kaugel, Papua New Guinea
Kaure, Indonesia
Kavwol, Indonesia
Kavwol, Papua New Guinea
Kaw, Burma
Kawar in Madhya Pradesh, India
Kawe, Indonesia
Kayabi, Brazil
Kayan, Burma
Kayan, Malaysia
Kayapo, Brazil
Kaygir, Indonesia
Kayupulau, Indonesia
Kazakhs, China (81)
Kazakhs, Iran (80)
Kebu, Togo
Kebumtamp, Bhutan
Kedayanas, Malaysia
Keer in Madhya Pradesh, India
Kei, Indonesia
Keiga Jirru, Sudan
Keiga, Sudan
Kela, Papua New Guinea
Kelabit, Malaysia (81)
Kelah, Zaire
Kelao, China
Kele, Gabon
Kemak, Indonesia
Kembata, Ethiopia
Kemok, Malaysia
Kenati, Papua New Guinea
Kendari, Indonesia
Kenga, Chad
Kenyah, Indonesia
Keopara, Papua New Guinea
Kera, Cameroon
Kera, Chad
Kerewo, Papua New Guinea
Keriaka, Papua New Guinea

Kerinchi, Indonesia
Ket, USSR
Kewa, East, Papua New Guinea
Kewa, South, Papua New Guinea
Kewa, West, Papua New Guinea
Khakas, USSR
Khalaj, Iran
Khalka, China
Kham, China
Kham, Nepal
Khamti in Assam, India
Khana, Nigeria
Khandesi, India
Khanti, USSR
Kharia in Bihar, India
Khasi in Assam, India
Khasonke, Mali
Khinalug, USSR
Khirwar in Madhya Pradesh, India
Khmer Refugees, Montreal,
      Canada:Quebec
Khmer Refugees, Unaccd. Minors,
      Thailand (83)
Khmer, Ottawa, Canada:Ontario
Khowar, India
Khvarshin, USSR
Kiari, Papua New Guinea
Kibet, Chad
Kibiri, Papua New Guinea
Kichepo, Sudan
Kikapoo, Mexico
Kilba, Nigeria
Kilmera, Papua New Guinea
Kim, Central African Republic
Kim, Chad
Kimaghama, Indonesia
Kimbu, Tanzania
Kinalakna, Papua New Guinea
Kinaray-A, Philippines
Kinga, Tanzania
Kirghiz Afghan Refugees, Turkey (83)
Kirgiz, Afghanistan
Kirgiz, China
Kirgiz, USSR (80)
Kirifi, Nigeria
Kiriwina, Papua New Guinea
Kis, Papua New Guinea
Kisan in Bihar, India
Kisankasa, Tanzania
Kishanganjia in Bihar, India
Kishtwari in Jammu, India
Kisi, Tanzania
Kissi, Guinea
Kita, Mali
Kiwai, Northeast, Papua New Guinea
Kiwai, Southern, Papua New Guinea
Kiwai, Wabuda, Papua New Guinea
Klaoh, Liberia
Koalib, Sudan (79)
Kobiana, Guinea
Kobon, Papua New Guinea
Koda in Bihar, India
Kodi, Indonesia
Koenoem, Nigeria
Kofyar, Nigeria
Kohoroxitari, Brazil

REGISTRY OF THE UNREACHED

Kohumono, Nigeria
Koiari, Grass, Papua New Guinea
Koiari, Mountain, Papua New Guinea
Koita, Papua New Guinea
Kokant, Burma
Koke, Chad
Kol in Assam, India
Kol, Papua New Guinea
Kolbila, Cameroon
Kole, Cameroon
Koliku, Papua New Guinea
Kolom, Papua New Guinea
Kom in Manipur, India
Koma, Cameroon
Koma, Central, Sudan
Koma, Ghana
Koma, Nigeria
Komba, Papua New Guinea
Kombio, Papua New Guinea
Komi-Permyat, USSR
Komi-Zyrian, USSR
Komono, Upper Volta
Komutu, Papua New Guinea
Konabem, Cameroon
Konda-Dora (Andra Pradesh), India
Koneraw, Indonesia
Kongo, Angola
Konkani in Gujarat, India
Konkomba, Ghana
Kono, Nigeria
Konomala, Papua New Guinea
Konongo, Tanzania
Konso, Ethiopia
Konyagi, Guinea
Koraga in Kerala, India
Korak, Papua New Guinea
Korape, Papua New Guinea
Korapun, Indonesia
Koreans in Manchuria, China (81)
Koreans, Canada
Koro, Nigeria
Koroma, Sudan
Korop, Cameroon
Korop, Nigeria
Korwa in Bihar, India
Koryak, USSR
Kosorong, Papua New Guinea
Kota in Tamil Nadu, India
Kota, Gabon
Kotia in Andhra Pradesh, India
Kotogut, Indonesia
Kotoko, Cameroon
Kotoko, Chad
Kotokoli, Togo
Kotopo, Cameroon
Kouya, Ivory Coast
Kovai, Papua New Guinea
Kove, Papua New Guinea
Koya in Andhra Pradesh, India
Koyra, Ethiopia
Kpa, Cameroon
Kpelle, Guinea
Kpelle, Liberia
Kposo, Togo
Krachi, Ghana
Krim, Sierra Leone

Krio, Gambia
Krisa, Papua New Guinea
Krobou, Ivory Coast
Krongo, Sudan
Kryz, USSR
Kuatinema, Brazil
Kube, Papua New Guinea
Kubu, Indonesia (80)
Kubu, Indonesia (81)
Kuda-Chamo, Nigeria
Kudiya, India
Kugbo, Nigeria
Kuikuro, Brazil
Kuka, Chad
Kukele, Cameroon
Kukele, Nigeria
Kukuwy, Papua New Guinea
Kukwa, Congo
Kulango, Ivory Coast
Kulele, Ivory Coast
Kulere, Nigeria
Kullo, Ethiopia
Kulung, Nigeria
Kumai, Papua New Guinea
Kumam, Uganda
Kuman, Papua New Guinea
Kumauni in Assam, India
Kumdauron, Papua New Guinea
Kumu, Zaire
Kumukio, Papua New Guinea
Kunama, Ethiopia
Kunante, Guinea-Bissau
Kunda, Mozambique
Kunda, Zambia
Kunda, Zambia
Kunda, Zimbabwe
Kuni, Papua New Guinea
Kunua, Papua New Guinea
Kuot, Papua New Guinea
Kupia in Andhra Pradesh, India
Kupsabiny, Uganda
Kurada, Papua New Guinea
Kurds in Kuwait, Kuwait
Kurfei, Niger
Kuria, Tanzania
Kurichiya in Kerala, India (81)
Kuruba in Tamil Nadu, India
Kurudu, Indonesia
Kurumba, Upper Volta
Kurux in Bihar, India
Kushi, Nigeria
Kusu, Zaire
Kuteb, Nigeria
Kutin, Cameroon
Kutu, Tanzania
Kuturmi, Nigeria
Kuvi in Orissa, India
Kuwaa, Liberia
Kuzamani, Nigeria
Kvanadin, USSR
Kwa, Nigeria
Kwadi, Angola
Kwakum, Cameroon
Kwale, Papua New Guinea
Kwambi, Namibia
Kwanga, Papua New Guinea

Kwangali, Angola
Kwansu, Indonesia
Kwanyama, Angola
Kwanyama, Namibia
Kwaya, Tanzania
Kwe-etshori, Botswana
Kwe-etshori, Zimbabwe
Kwerba, Indonesia
Kwere, Tanzania
Kwese, Zaire
Kwesten, Indonesia
Kwoma, Papua New Guinea
Kwomtari, Papua New Guinea
Kyibaku, Nigeria
Laamang, Nigeria
Labans, India
Labbai, India
Labhani in Andhra Pradesh, India
Labu, Papua New Guinea
Lacandon, Mexico
Ladakhi in Jammu, India
Ladinos, Lebanon
Laewomba, Papua New Guinea
Lafofa, Sudan
Lahul, China
Laka, Cameroon
Laka, Central African Republic
Laka, Chad
Laka, China
Lakians, USSR
Lakka, Nigeria
Lala, Zambia
Lalia, Zaire
Lalung in Assam, India
Lama, Burma
Lamba, Benin
Lamba, Zaire
Lamba, Zambia
Lambi, Cameroon
Lambya, Malawi
Lambya, Tanzania
Lame, Nigeria
Lamogai, Papua New Guinea
Lampung, Indonesia (80)
Landoma, Guinea
Landoma, Guinea-Bissau
Langi, Tanzania
Lango, Uganda
Lanoh, Malaysia
Lao Refugees, Argentina (83)
Lao-Chinese Refugees, Edmonton,
    Canada:Alberta
Lara, Indonesia
Laro, Sudan
Laru, Nigeria
Latdwalam, Indonesia
Lati, China
Laudje, Indonesia
Lavatbura-Lamusong, Papua New Guinea
Lavongai, Papua New Guinea
Lebanese, Beamington, Canada:Ontario
Lebgo, Nigeria
Lebong, Indonesia
Leco, Bolivia
Lega, Zaire
Lelemi, Ghana

Lengua, Northern, Paraguay
Lenje, Zambia
Leron, Papua New Guinea
Letti, Indonesia
Lhomi, Nepal
Li, China
Ligbi, Ghana
Ligbi, Ivory Coast
Liguri, Sudan
Lihir, Papua New Guinea
Liko, Zaire
Lima, Zambia
Limba, Sierra Leone
Lionese, Indonesia
Lisu, China (81)
Liv, USSR
Lo, Nigeria
Lobi, Ivory Coast
Lodhi in Bihar, India
Logba, Ghana
Lohiki, Papua New Guinea
Loinang, Indonesia (81)
Loko, Guinea
Loko, Sierra Leone
Lolo, China (81)
Loma, Guinea
Loma, Liberia
Lombi, Zaire
Lombo, Zaire
Lomwe, Mozambique
Longuda, Nigeria
Lore, Indonesia
Lori, Sudan
Lors, Iran (80)
Lotsu-Piri, Nigeria
Lou-Baluan-Pam, Papua New Guinea
Loven, Laos (81)
Lozi, Zambia
Lozi, Zimbabwe
Lu, China
Luac, Sudan
Luano, Zambia
Lubu, Indonesia
Luchazi, Angola
Luchazi, Zambia
Lue, Cameroon
Lugitama, Papua New Guinea
Luimbi, Angola
Lukep, Papua New Guinea
Lumbu, Gabon
Luna, Zaire
Lunda, Angola
Lunda, Ndembu, Zambia
Lundu, Cameroon
Lungu, Nigeria
Luo, Tanzania
Lushai in Assam, India
Luwu, Indonesia
Luxemburgois, Luxembourg
Luyana, Angola
Luyana, Zambia
Lwalu, Zaire
Lwena, Angola
Lwo, Sudan
Ma, Zaire
Maanyan, Indonesia

REGISTRY OF THE UNREACHED

Maba, Chad
Maba, Sudan
Maban-Jumjum, Sudan
Maca, Paraguay
Machiguenga, Peru
Macuna, Colombia
Madak, Papua New Guinea
Madda, Nigeria
Madi, Sudan
Madi, Uganda
Madik, Indonesia
Maghi, Burma
Magori, Papua New Guinea
Mahali in Assam, India
Mahri, Oman
Mai, Papua New Guinea
Mailu, Papua New Guinea
Maiongong, Brazil
Mairasi, Indonesia
Maisan, Papua New Guinea
Maiwa, Papua New Guinea
Majhi, Nepal
Majhwar in Madhya Pradesh, India
Maji, Ethiopia
Majingai-Ngama, Chad
Majingai-ngama, Central African
    Republic
Maka, Cameroon
Makarim, Papua New Guinea
Makasai, Indonesia
Makere, Uganda
Makian, West, Indonesia
Maklew, Indonesia
Makonde, Tanzania
Makua, Mozambique
Malalamai, Papua New Guinea
Malankuravan in Kerala, India
Malapandaram in Kerala, India
Malaryan in Kerala, India
Malas, Papua New Guinea
Malasanga, Papua New Guinea
Malavedan in Kerala, India
Male, Ethiopia
Malek, Papua New Guinea
Maleu, Papua New Guinea
Mali in Andhra Pradesh, India
Malila, Tanzania
Malki in Bihar, India
Malon, Papua New Guinea
Malpaharia in Assam, India
Malvi in Madhya Pradesh, India
Mama, Nigeria
Mamaa, Papua New Guinea
Mamasani, Iran
Mambai, Indonesia
Mambila, Cameroon
Mambwe-Lungu, Tanzania
Mambwe-Lungu, Zambia
Mamprusi, Ghana
Mamprusi, Ghana
Mamvu-Efe, Zaire
Managalasi, Papua New Guinea
Manambu, Papua New Guinea
Mancang, Senegal
Manchu, China (81)
Manda, Tanzania

Mandar, Indonesia
Mandara, Nigeria
Mandaya, Mansaka, Philippines
Mandaya, Philippines
Mander, Indonesia
Manding, Senegal
Mandyak, Gambia
Manem, Indonesia
Mangap, Papua New Guinea
Mangbai, Chad
Mangbutu, Zaire
Manggarai Muslims, Indonesia (81)
Mangisa, Cameroon
Mangs in Maharashtra, India
Maninka, Guinea-Bissau
Maninka, Sierra Leone
Manjack, Senegal
Mankanya, Guinea-Bissau
Mankanya, Senegal
Manna-Dora in A.P., India
Mannan in Kerala, India
Mano, Liberia
Manobo, Agusan, Philippines
Manobo, Ata, Philippines
Manobo, Binokid, Philippines
Manobo, Dibabawon, Philippines
Manobo, Obo, Philippines
Manobo, Sarangani, Philippines
Manobo, Tagabawa, Philippines
Manobos, Pulangi, Philippines
Mansi, USSR
Mantera, Malaysia
Mantion, Indonesia
Manu Park Panoan, Peru
Manyika, Zimbabwe
Mao, Northern, Ethiopia
Maou, Ivory Coast
Mape, Papua New Guinea
Mapena, Papua New Guinea
Mapoyo, Venezuela
Maquiritari, Venezuela
Mara in Assam, India
Maralango, Papua New Guinea
Maraliinan, Papua New Guinea
Maranao, Lanad, Philippines
Mararit, Chad
Marau, Indonesia
Marba, Chad
Marghi Central, Nigeria
Mari, Papua New Guinea
Mari, USSR
Maria in Andhra Pradesh, India
Maria, Papua New Guinea
Marind, Bian, Indonesia
Marind, Indonesia
Maring, Papua New Guinea
Marka, Upper Volta
Marubo, Brazil
Marwari in Gujarat, India
Masa, Chad
Masaba, Uganda
Masakin, Sudan
Masalit, Chad
Masalit, Sudan
Masegi, Papua New Guinea
Masenrempulu, Indonesia

474

Mashi, Zambia
Massalat, Chad
Matakam, Cameroon
Matakam, Nigeria
Matawari, Surinam
Matbat, Indonesia
Matengo, Tanzania
Matipuhy-Nahukua, Brazil
Matlatzinca, Atzingo, Mexico
Matumbi, Tanzania
Maure, Mali
Mauri, Niger
Maviha, Mozambique
Mawak, Papua New Guinea
Mawan, Papua New Guinea
Mawes, Indonesia
Maxakali, Brazil
Mayo, Mexico
Mayoruna, Peru
Mba, Zaire
Mbaama, Gabon
Mbai, Central African Republic
Mbai, Chad
Mbala, Zaire
Mbangwe, Zaire
Mbanja, Zaire
Mbati, Central African Republic
Mbe, Nigeria
Mbede, Gabon
Mbembe (Tigong), Nigeria
Mbembe, Cameroon
Mbembe, Nigeria
Mbimu, Cameroon
Mbo, Cameroon
Mbo, Zaire
Mboi, Nigeria
Mbole, Zaire
Mbugwe, Tanzania
Mbukushu, Angola
Mbula-Bwazza, Nigeria
Mbum, Chad
Mbunda, Angola
Mbunga, Tanzania
Mbwela, Angola
Me'en, Ethiopia
Meax, Indonesia
Meban, Sudan
Medlpa, Papua New Guinea
Mehek, Papua New Guinea
Meje, Uganda
Mekeo, Papua New Guinea
Mekwei, Indonesia
Mende, Liberia
Mende, Sierra Leone
Menemo-Mogamo, Cameroon
Mengen, Papua New Guinea
Menka, Cameroon
Menri, Malaysia
Menye, Papua New Guinea
Meos of Rajasthan, India (80)
Mera Mera, Papua New Guinea
Mesengo, Ethiopia
Mesme, Chad
Mesmedje, Chad
Metis, Elizabeth Settlement,
    Canada:Alberta

Mianmin, Papua New Guinea
Miao, China (81)
Midob, Sudan
Midsivindi, Papua New Guinea
Mien, China (81)
Migabac, Papua New Guinea
Migili, Nigeria
Mikarew, Papua New Guinea
Mimi, Chad
Mina in Madhya Pradesh, India
Minanibai, Papua New Guinea
Mindik, Papua New Guinea
Minduumo, Gabon
Mingat, USSR
Minianka, Mali
Mirdha in Orissa, India
Miri, Sudan
Miriam, Papua New Guinea
Mishmi in Assam, India
Miskito, Nicaragua
Mitang, Papua New Guinea
Mitmit, Papua New Guinea
Mixteco, Amoltepec, Mexico
Mixteco, Apoala, Mexico
Mixteco, Central Puebla, Mexico
Mixteco, Eastern Putla, Mexico
Mixteco, Eastern, Mexico
Mixteco, Huajuapan, Mexico
Mixteco, Silacayoapan, Mexico
Mixteco, Southern Puebla, Mexico
Mixteco, Southern Putla, Mexico
Mixteco, Tututepec, Mexico
Mixteco, Yosondua, Mexico
Mo, Ghana
Mo, Ivory Coast
Moba, Ghana
Moba, Togo
Mober, Nigeria
Modo, Sudan
Moewehafen, Papua New Guinea
Mofu, Cameroon
Mogholi, Afghanistan
Mogum, Chad
Moi, Indonesia
Mokareng, Papua New Guinea
Molof, Indonesia
Momare, Papua New Guinea
Mombum, Indonesia
Momoguns, Malaysia
Momolili, Papua New Guinea
Mon, Burma (81)
Mona, Ivory Coast
Mongondow, Indonesia (81)
Mongour, China
Moni, Indonesia
Monjombo, Central African Republic
Mono, Zaire
Montol, Nigeria
Moors in Mauritania, Mauritania
Moqaddam, Iran
Mor, Indonesia
Morawa, Papua New Guinea
Moreb, Sudan
Moresada, Papua New Guinea
Mori, Indonesia (81)
Morigi, Papua New Guinea

REGISTRY OF THE UNREACHED

Morima, Papua New Guinea
Moroccan Jews, Canada:Quebec
Moru, Ivory Coast
Moru, Sudan
Morunahua, Peru
Morwap, Indonesia
Mosi, Tanzania
Mossi, Upper Volta (80)
Motilon, Colombia
Motilon, Venezuela
Movima, Bolivia
Moxodi, Papua New Guinea
Mpoto, Malawi
Mpoto, Tanzania
Mubi, Chad
Mugil, Papua New Guinea
Muinane, Colombia
Mukawa, Papua New Guinea
Mulimba, Cameroon
Multani in Punjab, India
Mumbake, Nigeria
Mun, Burma
Muna, Indonesia
Mundang, Chad
Mundari in Assam, India
Mundu, Zaire
Munduruku, Brazil
Mungaka, Cameroon
Munggui, Indonesia
Munji-Yidgha, Afghanistan
Munkip, Papua New Guinea
Mup, Papua New Guinea
Mura-Piraha, Brazil
Muria in Andhra Pradesh, India
Murik, Papua New Guinea
Murle, Sudan
Mursi, Ethiopia
Murut, Malaysia
Musak, Papua New Guinea
Musar, Papua New Guinea
Musei, Chad
Musgu, Chad
Muslim Community of Bawku, Ghana
Musom, Papua New Guinea
Muthuvan (Andra Pradesh), India
Mutu, Venezuela
Mutum, Papua New Guinea
Muwasi in Madhya Pradesh, India
Muyuw, Papua New Guinea
Mwanga, Tanzania
Mwatebu, Papua New Guinea
Mwera, Tanzania
Myaung-Ze, Burma
Nabak, Papua New Guinea
Nabi, Indonesia
Nadeb Maku, Brazil
Nafar, Iran
Nafri, Indonesia
Naga, Kalyokengnyu, India
Naga, Mao, India
Naga, Nruanghmei, India
Naga, Sangtam, India
Naga, Sema, India
Naga, Tangkhul, India
Naga, Wancho, India
Nagar in Madhya Pradesh, India

Nagarige, Papua New Guinea
Nagatman, Papua New Guinea
Nagovisi, Papua New Guinea
Nahsi, China
Nahu, Papua New Guinea
Naka, Sudan
Nakama, Papua New Guinea
Nakanai, Papua New Guinea
Nalik, Papua New Guinea
Naltya, Indonesia
Nalu, Guinea
Nama, Namibia
Nama, South Africa
Nambis, Papua New Guinea
Nambu, Papua New Guinea
Namuni, Papua New Guinea
Nanai, China
Nanai, USSR
Nancere, Chad
Nandi, Zaire
Nandu-Tari, Nigeria
Nankina, Papua New Guinea
Nao, Ethiopia
Naoudem, Togo
Nara, Ethiopia
Nara, Papua New Guinea
Naraguta, Nigeria
Narak, Papua New Guinea
Nasioi, Papua New Guinea
Nata, Tanzania
Natemba, Togo
Natioro, Upper Volta
Nauna, Papua New Guinea
Nawuri, Ghana
Nchimburu, Ghana
Nchumbulu, Ghana
Nchumunu, Ghana
Ndaaka, Zaire
Ndali, Tanzania
Ndam, Central African Republic
Ndamba, Tanzania
Ndaonese, Indonesia
Ndau, Zimbabwe
Nde-Nsele-Nta, Nigeria
Ndengereko, Tanzania
Ndjem, Cameroon
Ndo, Zaire
Ndoe, Nigeria
Ndogo, Central African Republic
Ndogo, Sudan
Ndom, Indonesia
Ndomde, Tanzania
Ndoolo, Zaire
Ndop-Bamessing, Cameroon
Ndoro, Cameroon
Nduga, Indonesia
Ndunga, Zaire
Ndunpa Duupa, Cameroon
Negira, Papua New Guinea
Nek, Papua New Guinea
Nekgini, Papua New Guinea
Neko, Papua New Guinea
Nengaya, Papua New Guinea
Nentsy, USSR
Newar in Kathmandu, Nepal (82)
Neyo, Ivory Coast

476

Ngada, Indonesia
Ngaing, Papua New Guinea
Ngalik, North, Indonesia
Ngalik, Southern, Indonesia
Ngalum, Indonesia
Nganasan, USSR
Ngando, Central African Republic
Ngando, Zaire
Ngasa, Tanzania
Ngayaba, Cameroon
Ngbaka Ma'bo, Central African
    Republic
Ngbaka Ma'bo, Zaire
Ngbaka, Zaire
Ngbandi, Zaire
Ngbee, Zaire
Ngemba, Cameroon
Ngeq, Laos
Ngere, Ivory Coast
Ngi, Cameroon
Ngindo, Tanzania
Nginyukwur, Sudan
Ngirere, Sudan
Ngiri, Zaire
Ngizim, Nigeria
Ngok, Sudan
Ngoni, Tanzania
Ngoni, Zambia
Ngulu, Malawi
Ngulu, Tanzania
Ngumba, Cameroon
Ngumbi, Equatorial Guinea
Ngunduna, Sudan
Nguqwurang, Sudan
Ngurimi, Tanzania
Nguu, Tanzania
Ngwo, Cameroon
Ngwoi, Nigeria
Nharon, Botswana
Nhengatu, Brazil
Nias, Indonesia
Nicaraguan Refugees, Costa Rica
Nielim, Chad
Nihali in Madhya Pradesh, India
Nii, Papua New Guinea
Nilamba, Tanzania
Nimadi in Madhya Pradesh, India
Nimboran, Indonesia
Nimowa, Papua New Guinea
Ninam, Brazil
Ninggrum, Indonesia
Niningo, Papua New Guinea
Ninzam, Nigeria
Nisa, Indonesia
Nissan, Papua New Guinea
Nivkhi, USSR
Njadu, Indonesia
Njalgulgule, Sudan
Njemps, Kenya
Nkem-Nkum, Nigeria
Nkom, Cameroon
Nkonya, Ghana
Nkutu, Zaire
Nohu, Cameroon
Nomane, Papua New Guinea
Nomu, Papua New Guinea

Nondiri, Papua New Guinea
Norra, Burma
Northern Cagayan Negrito, Philippines
Nosu, China
Notsi, Papua New Guinea
Nsenga, Zambia
Nsenga, Zimbabwe
Nso, Cameroon
Nsongo, Angola
Ntomba, Zaire
Ntrubo, Ghana
Ntrubo, Togo
Nuk, Papua New Guinea
Numana-Nunku-Gwantu, Nigeria
Numanggang, Papua New Guinea
Nung, China
Nungu, Nigeria
Nunuma, Upper Volta
Nuristani, Afghanistan (80)
Nyaheun, Laos
Nyakyusa, Malawi
Nyakyusa, Tanzania
Nyali, Zaire
Nyambo, Tanzania
Nyamusa, Sudan
Nyamwezi, Tanzania (80)
Nyaneka, Angola
Nyang, Cameroon
Nyanga-Li, Zaire
Nyangbo, Ghana
Nyanja, Zimbabwe
Nyankole, Uganda
Nyarueng, Sudan
Nyemba, Angola
Nyengo, Angola
Nyiha, Tanzania
Nyiha, Zambia
Nyoro, Uganda
Nyuli, Uganda
Nyungwe, Mozambique
Nyzatom, Sudan
Nzakara, Central African Republic
Nzanyi, Nigeria
Nzebi, Congo
Nzema, Ghana
Nzema, Ivory Coast
O'ung, Angola
Obanliku, Nigeria
Obolo, Nigeria
Ocaina, Peru
Od, Pakistan
Odual, Nigeria
Odut, Nigeria
Ogbia, Nigeria
Oi, Laos
Oil Executives, Calgary,
    Canada:Alberta
Oirat, China
Ojhi in Madhya Pradesh, India
Okobo, Nigeria
Okpamheri, Nigeria
Oksapmin, Papua New Guinea
Ollari in Orissa, India
Olo, Papua New Guinea
Olulumo-Ikom, Nigeria
Omati, Papua New Guinea

REGISTRY OF THE UNREACHED

Omie, Papua New Guinea
Onank, Papua New Guinea
Ong in Andamans, India
Onin, Indonesia
Onjab, Papua New Guinea
Ono, Papua New Guinea
Orang Kanak, Malaysia
Orang Laut, Malaysia
Orang Ulu, Malaysia
Orejon, Peru
Oring, Nigeria
Ormu, Indonesia
Oroch, USSR
Orok, USSR
Orokaiva, Papua New Guinea
Orokolo, Papua New Guinea
Oron, Nigeria
Oronchon, China
Oso, Cameroon
Osum, Papua New Guinea
Ot Danum, Indonesia
Otank, Nigeria
Otomi, Eastern, Mexico
Otomi, Mezquital, Mexico
Otomi, Northwestern, Mexico
Otomi, Southeastern, Mexico
Otomi, State of Mexico, Mexico
Otomi, Tenango, Mexico
Otomi, Texcatepec, Mexico
Otoro, Sudan
Oubi, Ivory Coast
Oyampipuku, Brazil
Oyda, Ethiopia
Pacu, Brazil
Pahari Garhwali (Uttar Pradesh, India
Pai, China (81)
Pai, Nigeria
Paipai, Mexico
Paite in Assam, India
Paiwa, Papua New Guinea
Pak-Tong, Papua New Guinea
Pakaasnovos, Brazil
Palara, Ivory Coast
Palawano, Central, Philippines
Palawano, Philippines
Palembang, Indonesia
Palenquero, Colombia
Palestinian Refugees, Jordan (83)
Palestinian Refugees, Lebanon (83)
Palikur, Brazil
Paloc, Sudan
Palpa, Nepal
Pambia, Central African Republic
Pame, Central Chichimeca, Mexico
Pame, Chichimeca-Jonaz, Mexico
Pame, Northern, Mexico
Pana, Central African Republic
Panare, Venezuela
Pande, Congo
Pangwa, Tanzania
Panika, India
Panika, India
Pankararu, Brazil
Pankhu, Bangladesh
Pantu, Indonesia
Pao in Madhya Pradesh, India

Pao, Burma
Paongan, China
Papapana, Papua New Guinea
Pape, Cameroon
Papel, Guinea-Bissau
Papuma, Indonesia
Parakanan, Brazil
Paranan, Philippines
Parawen, Papua New Guinea
Pardhan in Andhra Pradesh, India
Pare, Papua New Guinea
Pare, Tanzania
Parengi in Orissa, India
Paresi, Brazil
Parintintin, Brazil
Pashayi, Afghanistan
Pashtuns, Iran (80)
Pasismanua, Papua New Guinea
Patamona, Guyana
Patelia in Gujarat, India
Patep, Papua New Guinea
Pato Tapuia, Brazil
Patpatar, Papua New Guinea
Paumari, Brazil
Pawaia, Papua New Guinea
Pay, Papua New Guinea
Paya, Honduras
Paynamar, Papua New Guinea
Penan, Western, Malaysia (81)
Pende, Zaire
Pengo in Orissa, India
Peremka, Papua New Guinea
Peri, Zaire
Pero, Nigeria
Persians of Iran, Iran (80)
Phu Thai, Laos
Piapoco, Colombia
Piaroa, Venezuela
Pila, Papua New Guinea
Pilaga, Argentina
Pima Bajo, Mexico
Pimbwe, Tanzania
Piratapuyo, Brazil
Piro, Peru
Pisa, Indonesia
Pishagchi, Iran
Piti, Nigeria
Pitu Uluna Salu, Indonesia
Piu, Papua New Guinea
Piya, Nigeria
Pnar in Assam, India
Pocomam, Central, Guatemala
Pocomchi, Eastern, Guatemala
Pocomchi, Western, Guatemala
Podokwo, Cameroon
Podopa, Papua New Guinea
Podzo, Mozambique
Pogolo, Tanzania
Poke, Zaire
Pokot, Uganda
Pol, Congo
Polci, Nigeria
Pom, Indonesia
Ponam-Andra-Hus, Papua New Guinea
Pondoma, Papua New Guinea
Pongu, Nigeria

Popoloca, Ahuatempan, Mexico
Popoloca, Coyotepec, Mexico
Popoloca, Eastern, Mexico
Popoloca, Northern, Mexico
Popoloca, Southern, Mexico
Popoloca, Western, Mexico
Popoluca, Oluta, Mexico
Popoluca, Sayula, Mexico
Popoluca, Sierra, Mexico
Popoluca, Texistepec, Mexico
Porapora, Papua New Guinea
Porohanon, Philippines
Portuguese, Cambridge, Canada:Ontario
Portuguese, London/Strathroy,
    Canada:Ontario
Portuguese, Metro Toronto,
    Canada:Ontario
Portuguese, Vancouver, Canada:British
    Columbia
Portuguese, West Lorne Village,
    Canada:Ontario
Prang, Ghana
Pu-I, China
Puguli, Upper Volta
Puku-Geeri-Keri-Wipsi, Nigeria
Pular, Senegal
Pulie, Papua New Guinea
Punu, China
Punu, Congo
Puragi, Indonesia
Purari, Papua New Guinea
Purum, Burma
Pye, Ivory Coast
Pygmy (Binga), Burundi
Pygmy (Binga), Central African
    Republic
Pyu, Indonesia
Qajars, Iran
Qara'i, Iran
Qaragozlu, Iran
Qashqa'i, Iran (80)
Quaiquer, Colombia
Quarequena, Brazil
Rabha in Assam, India
Rai, Khaling, Nepal
Rai, Kulunge, Nepal
Rai, Nepal
Rai, Thulunge, Nepal
Ralte, Burma
Rambutyo, Papua New Guinea
Rangkas, Nepal
Rao, Papua New Guinea
Rastafarians, Edmonton,
    Canada:Alberta
Ratahan, Indonesia
Rataning, Chad
Rauto, Papua New Guinea
Rawa, Papua New Guinea
Rawang, China
Refugee Doctors, Hong Kong
Rempi, Papua New Guinea
Rendille, Kenya
Reshe, Nigeria
Reshiat, Ethiopia
Reyesano, Bolivia
Riang in Assam, India

Riang-Lang, Burma
Riantana, Indonesia
Rikbaktsa, Brazil
Roba, Nigeria
Roinji, Papua New Guinea
Romany, Turkey
Romkun, Papua New Guinea
Romkun, Papua New Guinea
Ronga, Mozambique
Ronga, South Africa
Roro, Papua New Guinea
Rotokas, Papua New Guinea
Ruihi, Tanzania
Rukuba, Nigeria
Rumaya, Nigeria
Runga, Central African Republic
Runga, Chad
Rungi, Tanzania
Rungwa, Tanzania
Rural Refugees from Eritrea, Sudan
    (83)
Ruruma, Nigeria
Rusha, Tanzania
Rut, Sudan
Rutul, USSR
Rwamba, Uganda
Rwamba, Zaire
Saamia, Uganda
Saams, USSR
Saberi, Indonesia
Sadan in Andamans, India
Sadang, Indonesia
Saep, Papua New Guinea
Safaliba, Ghana
Safwa, Tanzania
Sagala, Tanzania
Saija, Colombia
Saisiat, Taiwan (81)
Sakam, Papua New Guinea
Sakata, Zaire
Saki, Papua New Guinea
Sakuye, Kenya
Sala, Zambia
Salampasu, Zaire
Salar, China
Saliba, Colombia
Salt, Papua New Guinea
Salvadoran Refugees, Honduras
Salvadoran Refugees, Belize
Sama, Mapun, Philippines
Sama, Siasi, Philippines
Sama, Sibuku, Philippines
Samarkena, Indonesia
Samo, Northern, Mali
Samo, Northern, Upper Volta
Samo, Southern, Upper Volta
Samogho, Mali
San, Namibia
Sanapana, Paraguay
Sandawe, Tanzania
Sanga, Nigeria
Sangir, Indonesia
Sangke, Indonesia
Sangu, Gabon
Sangu, Tanzania
Sanio, Papua New Guinea

REGISTRY OF THE UNREACHED

Santa, China
Santrokofi, Ghana
Sanuma, Venezuela
Sanza, Zaire
Sapo, Liberia
Saposa, Papua New Guinea
Sarakole, Senegal (80)
Saramaccan, Surinam
Sarwa, Chad
Sasak, Indonesia (80)
Sasanis, Iran
Sasaru-Enwan Igwe, Nigeria
Saseng, Papua New Guinea
Satere, Brazil
Sau, Afghanistan
Sau, Papua New Guinea
Sauk, Papua New Guinea
Sauria Pahari, India
Sause, Indonesia
Sawos, Papua New Guinea
Saya, Nigeria
Secoya, Ecuador
Sekar, Indonesia
Sekayu, Indonesia
Seko, Indonesia
Sekpele, Ghana
Selepet, Papua New Guinea
Selkup, USSR
Semelai, Malaysia
Sempan, Indonesia
Sena, Malawi
Sena, Mozambique
Senggi, Indonesia
Sentani, Indonesia
Senthang, Burma
Sepen, Papua New Guinea
Sere, Sudan
Serere, Senegal (79)
Serere-Non, Senegal
Serere-Sine, Senegal
Seri, Mexico
Serki, Papua New Guinea
Serui-Laut, Indonesia
Setaui Keriwa, Papua New Guinea
Setiali, Papua New Guinea
Seuci, Brazil
Seychellois, Seychelles
Sha, Nigeria
Shahsavans, Iran (80)
Shambala, Tanzania
Shan Chinese, Burma
Shan, Burma
Shanga, Nigeria
Sharanahua, Peru
Sharchagpakha, Bhutan
Shatt, Sudan
Shawiya, Algeria
Sheko, Ethiopia
Shilha, Morocco
Shilluk, Sudan
Shina, Afghanistan
Shinasha, Ethiopia
Shipibo, Peru
Shopping Bag Women, Toronto,
   Canada:Ontario
Shor, USSR

Shua, Botswana
Shughni, Afghanistan
Shuwa Arabic, Nigeria
Shwai, Sudan
Siagha-Yenimu, Indonesia
Sialum, Papua New Guinea
Siane, Papua New Guinea
Siar, Papua New Guinea
Sibo, China
Sidamo, Ethiopia
Sikanese, Indonesia
Sikhs, Toronto, Canada:Ontario
Sikhule, Indonesia
Sikkimese, India
Simaa, Zambia
Simog, Papua New Guinea
Sinagen, Papua New Guinea
Sinagoro, Papua New Guinea
Sinaki, Papua New Guinea
Sinasina, Papua New Guinea
Sindamon, Papua New Guinea
Sinsauru, Papua New Guinea
Sio, Papua New Guinea
Siona, Colombia
Sipoma, Papua New Guinea
Sira, Gabon
Sirak, Papua New Guinea
Sirasira, Papua New Guinea
Siri, Nigeria
Siriano, Colombia
Siriono, Bolivia
Siroi, Papua New Guinea
Sisala, Upper Volta
Siwai, Papua New Guinea
Siwu, Ghana
So, Cameroon
Sobei, Indonesia
Sochi, Pakistan
Soga, Uganda
Soh, Laos
Sokorok, Papua New Guinea
Soli, Zambia
Solos, Papua New Guinea
Som, Papua New Guinea
Somahai, Indonesia
Somrai, Central African Republic
Somrai, Chad
Sona, Papua New Guinea
Sondwari in M.P., India
Songe, Zaire
Songhai, Mali
Songhai, Niger
Songhai, Upper Volta
Songomeno, Zaire
Songoora, Zaire
Soninke, Gambia
Soninke, Mali
Soninke, Mauritania
Sonjo, Tanzania
Sopi, Sudan
Sora in Orissa, India
Sori-Harengan, Papua New Guinea
Soruba, Benin
South African Refugee Students,
   Lesotho (83)
Sowanda, Indonesia

480

Sowanda, Papua New Guinea
Street People, Thunder Bay,
      Canada:Ontario
Street People, Victoria,
      Canada:British Columbia
Students in Cuiaba, Brazil
Su, Cameroon
Sua, Papua New Guinea
Suain, Papua New Guinea
Suba, Tanzania
Subanun,Lapuyan, Philippines
Subi, Tanzania
Sudanese Repatriates, Sudan (83)
Suga, Cameroon
Suganga, Papua New Guinea
Sui, China
Sui, Papua New Guinea
Suk, Kenya
Suki, Papua New Guinea
Suku, Zaire
Sukur, Nigeria
Sukurum, Papua New Guinea
Sulka, Papua New Guinea
Sulung, India
Sumau, Papua New Guinea
Sumba, Indonesia
Sumbawa, Indonesia
Sumbwa, Tanzania
Sumu, Nicaragua
Sungor, Chad
Sunwar, Nepal
Suppire, Mali
Sura, Nigeria
Sursurunga, Papua New Guinea
Surubu, Nigeria
Surui, Brazil
Susu, Guinea
Susu, Guinea-Bissau
Susu, Sierra Leone
Svan, USSR
Swaga, Zaire
Swaka, Zambia
Syuwa, Nepal
Ta-Oi, Laos
Tabar, Papua New Guinea
Tabasaran, USSR
Tabi, Sudan
Tabriak, Papua New Guinea
Tacana, Bolivia
Tadjio, Indonesia
Tadyawan, Philippines
Tafi, Togo
Tagal, Malaysia (81)
Tagula, Papua New Guinea
Tagwana, Ivory Coast
Tahit, Indonesia
Taikat, Indonesia
Tairora, Papua New Guinea
Taiwan-Chinese Un. Stud., Taiwan
Tajik, Afghanistan
Tajik, Iran (80)
Tajik, USSR
Takalubi, Papua New Guinea
Takankar, India
Takemba, Benin
Takestani, Iran

Takia, Papua New Guinea
Tal, Nigeria
Talish, Iran
Talodi, Sudan
Tama, Chad
Tamagario, Indonesia
Taman, Burma
Taman, Papua New Guinea
Tamaria in Bihar, India
Tamazight, Morocco
Tambas, Nigeria
Tambo, Zambia
Tami, Papua New Guinea
Tamil Muslims in Madras, India (82)
Tampulma, Ghana
Tana, Central African Republic
Tana, Chad
Tanahmerah, Indonesia
Tandanke, Senegal
Tandia, Indonesia
Tangale, Nigeria
Tangchangya, Bangladesh
Tangga, Papua New Guinea
Tangu, Papua New Guinea
Tanguat, Papua New Guinea
Tani, Papua New Guinea
Tanimuca-Retuama, Colombia
Tao't Bato, Philippines
Tao-Suame, Papua New Guinea
Taori-Kei, Indonesia
Tara, Indonesia
Tarahumara, Northern, Mexico
Tarahumara, Rocoroibo, Mexico
Tarahumara, Samachique, Mexico
Taram, Cameroon
Tarasco, Mexico
Targum, Israel
Tarof, Indonesia
Tarok, Nigeria
Tarpia, Indonesia
Tat, USSR
Tatars, USSR (80)
Tate, Papua New Guinea
Tatoga, Tanzania
Tauade, Papua New Guinea
Taucouleur, Senegal (80)
Taungyo, Burma
Taungyoe, Burma
Taupota, Papua New Guinea
Taurap, Indonesia
Tavara, Papua New Guinea
Tawi-Pau, Papua New Guinea
Tawr, Burma
Tayaku, Benin
Tchang, Cameroon
Teda, Chad (80)
Teda, Libya
Teda, Niger
Tegali, Sudan
Teimuri, Iran
Teimurtash, Iran
Teke, Eastern, Zaire
Teke, Northern, Congo
Teke, Southwestern, Congo
Telefol, Papua New Guinea
Tembe, Brazil

REGISTRY OF THE UNREACHED

Tembo, Zaire
Temein, Sudan
Temira, Malaysia
Teop, Papua New Guinea
Tepehua, Huehuetla, Mexico
Tepehua, Pisa Flores, Mexico
Tepehua, Veracruz, Mexico
Tepehuan, Northern, Mexico
Tepehuan, Southeastern, Mexico
Tepeth, Uganda
Tepo, Ivory Coast
Tera, Nigeria
Terebu, Papua New Guinea
Terena, Brazil
Ternatans, Indonesia
Teso, Uganda
Thado in Assam, India
Thai-Ney, Burma
Thakali, Nepal
Thakur, India
Thami, Nepal
Thar in Bihar, India
Tharu, India
Tharu, Nepal
Theater Arts Performers, Canada
Thoi, Sudan
Thuri, Sudan
Tiang, Papua New Guinea
Tibetan Refugees, Canada
Tibetan Refugees, Switzerland (83)
Ticuna, Brazil
Tidi, Papua New Guinea
Tidorese, Indonesia
Tiefo, Upper Volta
Tiene, Zaire
Tifai, Papua New Guinea
Tigak, Papua New Guinea
Tigon, Cameroon
Tikar, Cameroon
Timbe, Papua New Guinea
Timorese, Indonesia
Tindin, USSR
Tinputz, Papua New Guinea
Tippera, Bangladesh
Tira, Sudan
Tirio, Papua New Guinea
Tirma, Sudan
Tiro, Indonesia
Tiruray, Philippines
Tlapaneco, Malinaltepec, Mexico
Toala, Indonesia
Toaripi, Papua New Guinea
Tobo, Papua New Guinea
Toda in Tamil Nadu, India
Togbo, Zaire
Tojolabal, Mexico
Tokkaru in Tamil Nadu, India
Tol, Honduras
Tombulu, Indonesia
Tomini, Indonesia
Tonda, Papua New Guinea
Tondanou, Indonesia
Tonga, Botswana
Tonga, Malawi
Tonga, Mozambique
Tongwe, Tanzania

Tonsea, Indonesia
Tontemboa, Indonesia
Toraja, Southern, Indonesia (81)
Torau, Papua New Guinea
Torricelli, Papua New Guinea
Totis, India
Totonaco, Northern, Mexico
Totonaco, Oxumatlan, Mexico
Totonaco, Papantla, Mexico
Totonaco, Sierra, Mexico
Totonaco, Yecuatla, Mexico
Towei, Indonesia
Trepo, Ivory Coast
Trio, Surinam
Trique, San Juan Copala, Mexico
Tsaangi, Congo
Tsakhur, USSR
Tsamai, Ethiopia
Tsimane, Bolivia
Tsogo, Gabon
Tsonga, Mozambique
Tsou, Taiwan (81)
Tswa, Mozambique
Tswa, Zimbabwe
Tswana, Namibia
Tswana, Zimbabwe
Tuam, Papua New Guinea
Tubar, Mexico
Tubetube, Papua New Guinea
Tucano, Brazil
Tugara, India
Tukude, Indonesia
Tula, Nigeria
Tulishi, Sudan
Tumale, Sudan
Tumawo, Indonesia
Tumma, Sudan
Tumtum, Sudan
Tunebo, Cobaria, Colombia
Tung-Chia, China (81)
Tunya, Central African Republic
Tunya, Chad
Tupuri, Cameroon
Tupuri, Chad
Tura, Ivory Coast
Turkish Workers, Belgium (80)
Turkwam, Nigeria
Turu, Indonesia
Turu, Tanzania
Tuvinian, USSR
Tuyuca, Brazil
Twi, Sudan
Tzeltal, Bachajon, Mexico
Tzeltal, Highland, Mexico
Tzutujil, Guatemala
USSR Kirghiz Refugee Shepherds,
    Pakistan (83)
Udegeis, USSR
Udin, USSR
Udmurt, USSR
Uduk, Sudan
Ugandan Asian Refugees,
    Canada:British Columbia (83)
Ugandan Refugees, Sudan (83)
Ugandan Refugees, United Kingdom (83)
Uhunduni, Indonesia

482

Uiguir, Afghanistan
Uiguir, China (80)
Ukaan, Nigeria
Ukpe-Bayobiri, Nigeria
Ukwuani-Aboh, Nigeria
Ulchi, USSR
Ullatan in Kerala, India
Umm Dorein, Sudan
Umm Gabralla, Sudan
University Students, Edmonton ,
    Canada:Alberta
Urali in Kerala, India
Urarina, Peru
Urban Elite Vietnamese, United States
    of America
Urban Refugees in Lusaka, Zambia (83)
Urhobo, Nigeria
Uria, Indonesia
Uruangnirin, Indonesia
Urubu, Brazil
Urupa, Brazil
Uspanteco, Guatemala
Utugwang, Nigeria
Uvbie, Nigeria
Uzekwe, Nigeria
Vagala, Ghana
Vagari, Pakistan
Vai, Sierra Leone
Vaikino, Indonesia
Vaiphei in Assam, India
Vale, Central African Republic
Venda, Zimbabwe
Veps, USSR
Vere, Cameroon
Vidunda, Tanzania
Vietnamese Fishermen, Biloxi, United
    States of America
Vietnamese Refugees, Regina,
    Canada:Saskatchewan
Vietnamese Refugees, China (83)
Vietnamese, Edmonton, Canada:Alberta
Vietnamese, Laos
Vige, Upper Volta
Vinza, Tanzania
Vishavan in Kerala, India
Voko, Cameroon
Vute, Nigeria
Wa, Burma
Wa, China
Wabo, Indonesia
Waddar in Andhra Pradesh, India
Wagdi in Rajasthan, India
Waimiri, Brazil
Waiwai, Brazil
Waiwai, Guyana
Waja, Nigeria
Walamo, Ethiopia
Wambon, Indonesia
Wanda, Tanzania
Wandamen, Indonesia
Wandering Homeless, United States of
    America (84)
Wandji, Gabon
Wanggom, Indonesia
Wanji, Tanzania
Wano, Indonesia

Wapishana, Brazil
Wapishana, Guyana
Wapishana, Venezuela
Wara, Upper Volta
Warao, Venezuela
Ware, Mali
Warembori, Indonesia
Waris, Indonesia
Warkay-Bipim, Indonesia
Waropen, Indonesia
Wasi, Tanzania
Water Surface People, Hong Kong (84)
Waura, Brazil
Wayana, Surinam
Weda, Indonesia
West Indian Migrant Workers,
    Canada:Ontario
Western Sahara Refugees, Algeria (83)
Wetawit, Ethiopia
Wewewa, Indonesia
Widekum, Cameroon
Win, Upper Volta
Wobe, Ivory Coast
Wodani, Indonesia
Woi, Indonesia
Wolio, Indonesia
Wolof, Gambian, Gambia
Wom, Nigeria
Wongo, Zaire
Woro, Sudan
Wumbvu, Gabon
Wungu, Tanzania
Xavante, Brazil
Xerente, Brazil
Xokleng, Brazil
Xu, Namibia
Yafi, Indonesia
Yaghan, Chile
Yagnobi, USSR
Yagua, Peru
Yahadian, Indonesia
Yaka, Zaire
Yakha, Nepal
Yakoma, Central African Republic
Yaly, Indonesia
Yambasa, Cameroon
Yami of Orchid Island, Indonesia (84)
Yaminahua, Peru
Yanadi in Andhra Pradesh, India
Yandang, Nigeria
Yanga, Togo
Yangbye, Burma
Yans, Zaire
Yao, Mozambique
Yaruro, Venezuela
Yasing, Cameroon
Yaur, Indonesia
Yava, Indonesia
Yazgulyam, USSR
Yei, Indonesia
Yela, Zaire
Yellow Uiguir, China
Yelmek, Indonesia
Yerava in Karnataka, India
Yeretuar, Indonesia
Yerukala in A.P., India

REGISTRY OF THE UNREACHED

Yeskwa, Nigeria
Yidinit, Ethiopia
Yin-Kyar, Burma
Yin-Nett, Burma
Yinchia, Burma
Yinga, Cameroon
Yoabu, Benin
Yogad, Philippines
Yonggom, Indonesia
Yoruk, Turkey
Yos, Burma
Yotafa, Indonesia
Yuana, Venezuela
Yucateco, Guatemala
Yucateco, Mexico
Yukagirs, USSR
Yukpa, Colombia
Yukpa, Venezuela
Yuku, China
Yulu, Sudan
Yungur, Nigeria
Yuracare, Bolivia
Yurak, USSR
Yuruti, Colombia
Zaghawa, Chad
Zaghawa, Libya
Zaghawa, Sudan
Zanaki, Tanzania
Zangskari in Kashmir, India
Zanskari, India (84)
Zapoteco, C Sola De Vega, Mexico
Zapoteco, Choapan, Mexico
Zapoteco, E Miahuatlan, Mexico
Zapoteco, E Ocotlan, Mexico
Zapoteco, E Tlacolula, Mexico
Zapoteco, E Zimatlan, Mexico
Zapoteco, Isthmus, Mexico
Zapoteco, Mazaltepec, Mexico
Zapoteco, Miahuatlan, Mexico
Zapoteco, Mitla, Mexico
Zapoteco, N Isthmus, Mexico
Zapoteco, N Ocotlan, Mexico
Zapoteco, N Villa Alta, Mexico
Zapoteco, NE Miahuatlan, Mexico
Zapoteco, NE Yautepec, Mexico
Zapoteco, NW Tehuantepec, Mexico
Zapoteco, Pochutla, Mexico
Zapoteco, S Ejutla, Mexico
Zapoteco, S Villa Alta, Mexico
Zapoteco, SC Zimatlan, Mexico
Zapoteco, SE Miahuatlan, Mexico
Zapoteco, SW Ixtlan, Mexico
Zapoteco, Srra De Juarez, Mexico
Zapoteco, Stgo Xanica, Mexico
Zapoteco, Sto Dom Albarr, Mexico
Zapoteco, Tabaa, Mexico
Zapoteco, Villa Alta, Mexico
Zapoteco, W Miahuatlan, Mexico
Zapoteco, W Ocotlan, Mexico
Zapoteco, W Sola de Vega, Mexico
Zapoteco, W Tlacolula, Mexico
Zapoteco, W Yautepec, Mexico
Zapoteco, W Zimatlan, Mexico
Zapoteco, Yalalag, Mexico
Zaramo, Tanzania
Zari, Nigeria

Zayse, Ethiopia
Zenaga, Mauritania
Zigwa, Tanzania
Zilmamu, Ethiopia
Zimba, Zaire
Zimbabwean Refugees, Zambia
Zimbabwean Refugees, Mozambique (83)
Zimbabwean Repatriates, Zimbabwe (83)
Zinacantecos, Mexico (79)
Zoliang, India
Zome in Manipur, India
Zome, Burma
Zoque, Chimalapa, Mexico
Zoque, Copainala, Mexico
Zoque, Francisco Leon, Mexico
Zoque, Tabasco, Mexico
Zulu, Malawi

Index by Religion

This list indicates predominant professed religion, whether or not a majority of those who profess the religion are active practitioners. Many of the groups have more than one professed religion present, but only the one with the largest percentage of followers is indicated in this section.

REGISTRY OF THE UNREACHED

African Independent

**Dida, Ivory Coast

Ancestor Worship

**Akha, Thailand (79)
Boat People, Japan
**K'anjobal of San Miguel, Guatemala
Lao Refugees, Argentina (83)
Urban Elite Vietnamese, United
States of America

Animism

Abanyom, Nigeria
Abau, Indonesia
Abau, Papua New Guinea
Abie, Papua New Guinea
Abua, Nigeria
Abulas, Papua New Guinea
Achagua, Colombia
Achi, Cubulco, Guatemala
Achi, Rabinal, Guatemala
Acholi, Uganda
Achual, Peru
Adamawa, Cameroon
Adhola, Uganda
***Adi, India
**Adja, Benin
Adjora, Papua New Guinea
Aeka, Papua New Guinea
*Afawa, Nigeria (80)
**Afo, Nigeria (80)
Agarabi, Papua New Guinea
Age, Cameroon
Aghem, Cameroon
Aghu, Indonesia
Agob, Papua New Guinea
Agoi, Nigeria
Aguacateco, Guatemala
Aguaruna, Peru
Agwagwune, Nigeria
Aibondeni, Indonesia
Aiku, Papua New Guinea
Aikwakai, Indonesia
Aiome, Papua New Guinea
Aion, Papua New Guinea
Airo-Sumaghaghe, Indonesia
Airoran, Indonesia
Aka, India
Ake, Nigeria
Akpa-Yache, Nigeria

Akrukay, Papua New Guinea
Alago, Nigeria
Alak, Laos
Alamblak, Papua New Guinea
Alatil, Papua New Guinea
Alauagat, Papua New Guinea
Alege, Nigeria
Alor, Kolana, Indonesia (81)
Ama, Papua New Guinea
Amahuaca, Peru
Amaimon, Papua New Guinea
Amanab, Indonesia
Amanab, Papua New Guinea
Amar, Ethiopia
Amarakaeri, Peru
Amasi, Cameroon
Ambai, Indonesia
Ambasi, Papua New Guinea
Amber, Indonesia
Amberbaken, Indonesia
Ambo, Zambia
Ambonese, Indonesia
Ambonese, Netherlands
Amo, Nigeria
Amto, Papua New Guinea
Amuesha, Peru
Anaang, Nigeria
Anal in Manipur, India
Andarum, Papua New Guinea
Andha in Andhra Pradesh, India
Andoque, Colombia
Anem, Papua New Guinea
Angaataha, Papua New Guinea
Angal Heneng, South, Papua New
Guinea
Angal Heneng, West, Papua New
Guinea
Angal, East, Papua New Guinea
Angas, Nigeria
Angaua, Papua New Guinea
Anggor, Papua New Guinea
Angoram, Papua New Guinea
Ankave, Papua New Guinea
Ankwe, Nigeria
Anor, Papua New Guinea
Ansus, Indonesia
Anuak, Ethiopia
Anuak, Sudan
Anuki, Papua New Guinea
Apalai, Brazil
**Apatani in Assam, India
Apinaye, Brazil
Apurina, Brazil
Arabela, Peru
Arafundi, Papua New Guinea
Arandai, Indonesia
Arapaco, Brazil
Arapesh, Bumbita, Papua New Guinea
Arapesh, Mountain, Papua New
Guinea
Arapesh, Muhiang, Papua New Guinea
Arawe, Papua New Guinea
Arbore, Ethiopia
Arecuna, Venezuela
Argobba, Ethiopia
Arguni, Indonesia

Arifama-Miniafia, Papua New Guinea
Arigibi, Papua New Guinea
Arinua, Papua New Guinea
*Arnatas, India
Arop, Papua New Guinea
Aruop, Papua New Guinea
Arusha, Tanzania
Arutani, Venezuela
Asaro, Papua New Guinea
Asat, Papua New Guinea
Asienara, Indonesia
*Asmat, Indonesia (79)
Assumbo, Cameroon
Asu, Tanzania
Asuri in Bihar, India
*Ata of Davao, Philippines
Ata, Papua New Guinea
Atruahi, Brazil
*Atta, Philippines
*Atye, Ivory Coast
Au el, Botswana
Au, Papua New Guinea
Aunalei, Papua New Guinea
Auyana, Papua New Guinea
Awa, Papua New Guinea
Awar, Papua New Guinea
Awara, Papua New Guinea
Awin, Papua New Guinea
Awyi, Indonesia
Awyu, Indonesia
**Aymara, Bolivia
Ayoreo, Paraguay
Azera, Papua New Guinea
Baali, Zaire
Babajou, Cameroon
**Babur Thali, Nigeria (80)
Baburiwa, Indonesia
Bada, Nigeria
Badagu in Nilgiri, India
Badui, Indonesia (84)
Bafut, Cameroon
Baghati in H.P., India
Baham, Indonesia
Bahawalpuri in M.P., India
Bahinemo, Papua New Guinea
Baibai, Papua New Guinea
Baiga in Bihar, India
Baining, Papua New Guinea
Baka, Cameroon
Baka, Zaire
Bakairi, Brazil
Bakongo Angolan Refugees, Zaire
   (83)
**Bakuba, Zaire
Bakwele, Congo
Balangaw, Philippines
Balanta Refugees, Senegal
Balanta, Senegal
Balante, Guinea-Bissau
Bali-Vitu, Papua New Guinea
Balong, Cameroon
Balti in Jammu, India
Bam, Papua New Guinea
Bamougoun-Bamenjou, Cameroon
***Banaro, Papua New Guinea
Bandi, Liberia

Bandjoun, Cameroon
Banen, Cameroon
Bangba, Zaire
Baniwa, Brazil
Banoni, Papua New Guinea
***Banyarwanda, Rwanda
Banyun, Guinea-Bissau
***Baoule, Ivory Coast
Barabaig, Tanzania (79)
Barai, Papua New Guinea
Barasano, Colombia
Barasano, Northern, Colombia
Barasano, Southern, Colombia
Barau, Indonesia
Bare'e, Indonesia
Bariai, Papua New Guinea
*Bariba, Benin (80)
Bariji, Papua New Guinea
Barim, Papua New Guinea
Barok, Papua New Guinea
Baruga, Papua New Guinea
Baruya, Papua New Guinea
Basakomo, Nigeria
Basari, Guinea
Basari, Senegal
Basari, Togo
Bashar, Nigeria
Basketo, Ethiopia
***Basotho, Mountain, Lesotho (79)
*Bassa, Liberia
**Bassa, Nigeria
Batak, Karo, Indonesia
Batak, Simalungun, Indonesia
Batak, Toba, Indonesia
Batanga-Ngolo, Cameroon
Bateg, Malaysia
Bau, Papua New Guinea
Bauwaki, Papua New Guinea
Bavenda, South Africa
Bazigar in Gujarat, India
Bebeli, Papua New Guinea
Bediya in Bihar, India
Bedoanas, Indonesia
Bekwarra, Nigeria
Bembe, Zaire
Bembi, Papua New Guinea
Bena, Tanzania
Benabena, Papua New Guinea
Bencho, Ethiopia
Bende, Tanzania
Bene, Cameroon
Benga, Gabon
Berba, Benin
Berik, Indonesia
Berom, Nigeria
Besisi, Malaysia
Bete, India
*Bete, Ivory Coast
Bethen, Cameroon
Betsinga, Cameroon
Bette-Bende, Nigeria
Bharia in Madhya Pradesh, India
**Bhils, India (79)
Bhuiya in Bihar, India
Biafada, Guinea-Bissau
Biak, Indonesia

REGISTRY OF THE UNREACHED

Biaka, Papua New Guinea
Biangai, Papua New Guinea
Bibling, Papua New Guinea
Biduanda, Malaysia
Biksi, Indonesia
**Bilan, Philippines
Biliau, Papua New Guinea
Bimin, Papua New Guinea
Binahari, Papua New Guinea
Binandere, Papua New Guinea
Bine, Papua New Guinea
Binji, Zaire
Binumarien, Papua New Guinea
Birifor, Ghana
Bisa, Zambia
Bisaya, Malaysia (81)
Bisis, Papua New Guinea
Bitara, Papua New Guinea
Bitare, Cameroon
Biyom, Papua New Guinea
Boanaki, Papua New Guinea
Bobe, Cameroon
Bobo Fing, Mali
Bobo Wule, Mali
Bodo in Assam, India
Boghom, Nigeria
Bohutu, Papua New Guinea
Boikin, Papua New Guinea
**Boko, Benin
Bokyi, Cameroon
Bokyi, Nigeria
Bola, Papua New Guinea
Bolondo, Zaire
Bom, Papua New Guinea
Boma, Zaire
Bomboko, Cameroon
Bonerif, Indonesia
Bonggo, Indonesia
Bongili, Congo
Bongu, Papua New Guinea
Bonkeng-Pendia, Cameroon
Bonkiman, Papua New Guinea
**Bontoc, Central, Philippines (81)
Bora, Colombia
Borai, Indonesia
*Bororo, Brazil
Bosavi, Papua New Guinea
Bosilewa, Papua New Guinea
Bosngun, Papua New Guinea
Boya, Sudan
Bozo, Mali
Braj in Uttar Pradesh, India
Brao, Laos (79)
Brat, Indonesia
Breri, Papua New Guinea
Bruneis, Malaysia
Bua, Chad
Buang, Central, Papua New Guinea
Buang, Mangga, Papua New Guinea
Bube, Equatorial Guinea
Budibud, Papua New Guinea
Budugum, Cameroon
Bugombe, Zaire
Builsa, Ghana
Buin, Papua New Guinea
Buja, Zaire

Buka-khwe, Botswana
Bukaua, Papua New Guinea
**Bukidnon, Philippines
Bulia, Zaire
Bulu, Papua New Guinea
Buna, Papua New Guinea
Bunabun, Papua New Guinea
Bunak, Indonesia
Bunama, Papua New Guinea
Bunann in Kashmir, India
Bungku, Indonesia
Bunu, Nigeria
Bura, Cameroon
Buraka-Gbanziri, Congo
Burig in Kashmir, India
Burji, Ethiopia
Buru, Indonesia
Burum, Papua New Guinea
Burundian Hutu Refugees, Tanzania
  (83)
Burungi, Tanzania
Busah, Papua New Guinea
Busami, Indonesia
**Busanse, Ghana
Bushmen (Heikum), Namibia
*Bushmen (Hiechware), Zimbabwe
*Bushmen (Kung), Namibia (79)
Bushmen in Botswana, Botswana
Bushoong, Zaire
Bussa, Ethiopia
**Buwid, Philippines (81)
Bwa, Upper Volta (80)
Bwa, Zaire
Bwaidoga, Papua New Guinea
Bwisi, Zaire
Cacua, Colombia
Caiwa, Brazil
Cakchiquel, Central, Guatemala
Campa, Peru
Camsa, Colombia
Candoshi, Peru
Canela, Brazil
Capanahua, Peru
Carapana, Colombia
*Caribs, Dominican Republic (84)
Cashibo, Peru
Cayapa, Ecuador
Cewa, Zambia
Ch'ol Tila, Mexico
Chacobo, Bolivia
Chagga, Tanzania
Chakfem-Mushere, Nigeria
Chakossi in Ghana, Ghana
Chakossi in Togo, Togo
Chamacoco, Bahia Negra, Paraguay
Chambri, Papua New Guinea
Chami, Colombia
Chamicuro, Peru
Chara, Ethiopia
Chawai, Nigeria
Chenapian, Papua New Guinea
Chero in Bihar, India
Chiga, Uganda
Chik-Barik in Bihar, India
Chinga, Cameroon
Chip, Nigeria

Chipaya, Bolivia
Chiquitano, Bolivia
**Chiriguano, Argentina
Chokobo, Nigeria
Chokwe (Lunda), Angola
Chokwe, Zambia
Chola Naickans, India
Chopi, Mozambique
Chorote, Paraguay
Chorti, Guatemala
**Chrau, Viet Nam
Chuabo, Mozambique
Chuang, China (81)
Chuave, Papua New Guinea
Chuj, Guatemala
Cinta Larga, Brazil
***Citak, Indonesia
Cocama, Peru
Cofan, Colombia
Cogui, Colombia
**Coreguaje, Colombia
Cubeo, Colombia
Cuiba, Colombia
Cujareno, Peru
Culina, Brazil
*Cuna, Colombia (79)
Curipaco, Colombia
Daba, Cameroon
Dabra, Indonesia
Dadibi, Papua New Guinea
Daga, Papua New Guinea
Dagada, Indonesia
Dagari, Ghana
Dahating, Papua New Guinea
Daju of Dar Fur, Sudan
*Daka, Nigeria
Dami, Papua New Guinea
***Dan, Ivory Coast
*Dani, Baliem, Indonesia (79)
Daonda, Papua New Guinea
Dathanik, Ethiopia
Dawawa, Papua New Guinea
Day, Central African Republic
Dedua, Papua New Guinea
Degema, Nigeria
Degenan, Papua New Guinea
Dem, Indonesia
Demta, Indonesia
Dengese, Zaire
Deori in Assam, India
Desano, Brazil
Dghwede, Cameroon
*Dghwede, Nigeria
Dhaiso, Tanzania
Dhanka in Gujarat, India
Dhanwar in Madhya Pradesh, India
Dia, Papua New Guinea
Didinga, Sudan
Digo, Tanzania
Dimasa in Cachar, India
Dime, Ethiopia
Dimir, Papua New Guinea
Dinka, Sudan
Diodio, Papua New Guinea
**Djandeau, Zaire
Dobu, Papua New Guinea

Doe, Tanzania
*Dog-Pa of Ladakh, India (81)
Doga, Papua New Guinea
*Dogon, Mali (79)
Dogoro, Papua New Guinea
Dom, Papua New Guinea
Dompago, Benin
Domu, Papua New Guinea
Domung, Papua New Guinea
Dongo, Zaire
**Doohwaayo, Cameroon
Dorobo, Kenya
Dorobo, Tanzania
Doromu, Papua New Guinea
Dorze, Ethiopia
Doura, Papua New Guinea
Duau, Papua New Guinea
Dubu, Indonesia
**Duka, Nigeria
Dukwe Refugee Camp Residents,
  Botswana (83)
Duma, Gabon
*Dumagat, Casiguran, Philippines
  (81)
Duna, Papua New Guinea
Duru, Cameroon
Dusun, Malaysia (81)
Duvele, Indonesia
Edawapi, Papua New Guinea
Edo, Nigeria
Efik, Nigeria
Efutop, Nigeria
Eggon, Nigeria
Eivo, Papua New Guinea
Ejagham, Nigeria
Ekagi, Indonesia
Ekajuk, Nigeria
Eket, Nigeria
Ekpeye, Nigeria
El Molo, Kenya
Eleme, Nigeria
Elkei, Papua New Guinea
Emai-Iuleha-Ora, Nigeria
Embera, Northern, Colombia
Emerum, Papua New Guinea
Emira, Papua New Guinea
Emumu, Indonesia
Endangen, Papua New Guinea
Enga, Papua New Guinea
Engenni, Nigeria
Enya, Zaire
Epie, Nigeria
Erokwanas, Indonesia
Esan, Nigeria
Eton, Cameroon
Etulo, Nigeria
Evant, Nigeria
Ewage-Notu, Papua New Guinea
Ewenkis, China (81)
Fa D'Ambu, Equatorial Guinea
Fagululu, Papua New Guinea
Faiwol, Papua New Guinea
**Fakai, Nigeria
**Fali, Nigeria
Fas, Papua New Guinea
Fasu, Papua New Guinea

REGISTRY OF THE UNREACHED

Finungwan, Papua New Guinea
Fipa, Tanzania
Foau, Indonesia
Foi, Papua New Guinea
Foran, Papua New Guinea
Fordat, Indonesia
Fore, Papua New Guinea
Fra-Fra, Ghana
Fula, Macina, Mali
Fula, Peuhala, Mali
Fuliro, Zaire
Fulnio, Brazil
Fungom, Northern, Cameroon
Furu, Zaire
Fuyuge, Papua New Guinea
Fyam, Nigeria
Fyer, Nigeria
Ga-Dang, Philippines
Gade, Nigeria
Gadsup, Papua New Guinea
**Gagre, Pakistan
Gagu, Ivory Coast
Gahuku, Papua New Guinea
Gaikundi, Papua New Guinea
Gaina, Papua New Guinea
Gal, Papua New Guinea
Galler, Laos
Gam..i, Papua New Guinea
Gane, Indonesia
Ganglau, Papua New Guinea
Garuh, Papua New Guinea
Garus, Papua New Guinea
Garuwahi, Papua New Guinea
Gawwada, Ethiopia
Gbande, Guinea
Gbari, Nigeria (80)
Gedaged, Papua New Guinea
Gedeo, Ethiopia
Genagane, Papua New Guinea
Gende, Papua New Guinea
Gesa, Indonesia
**Ghimeera, Ethiopia
Ghotuo, Nigeria
Gidar, Cameroon
Gidicho, Ethiopia
Gidra, Papua New Guinea
Gimi, Papua New Guinea
Ginuman, Papua New Guinea
Gio, Liberia
Gira, Papua New Guinea
Girawa, Papua New Guinea
Giri, Papua New Guinea
Giryama, Kenya
Gisei, Cameroon
Gisiga, Cameroon
Gitua, Papua New Guinea
Gizra, Papua New Guinea
**Glavda, Nigeria
Gobasi, Papua New Guinea
Gobato, Ethiopia
Gobeze, Ethiopia
***Godie, Ivory Coast
Goemai, Nigeria
Gogo, Tanzania
Gogodala, Papua New Guinea
Gokana, Nigeria

*Gonds, India
Goroa, Tanzania
Gourency, Upper Volta
**Gouro, Ivory Coast
Gouwar, Cameroon
**Grebo, Liberia
Grunshi, Ghana
Gu, Benin
Guaiaqui, Paraguay
Guajajara, Brazil
Guajibo, Colombia
*Guajiro, Colombia
Guambiano, Colombia
Guana, Paraguay
***Guarani, Bolivia (79)
Guayabero, Colombia
Gude, Cameroon
Gude, Nigeria
Gudu, Nigeria
Guduf, Nigeria
Gugu-Yalanji, Australia
Guhu-Samane, Papua New Guinea
Gulfe, Cameroon
Gumasi, Papua New Guinea
Gumine, Papua New Guinea
Gumuz, Ethiopia
Gurensi, Ghana
Gusap, Papua New Guinea
Guwot, Papua New Guinea
Gwandara, Nigeria
Gwedena, Papua New Guinea
Gwere, Uganda
Ha, Tanzania
Hadiyya, Ethiopia
Hahon, Papua New Guinea
***Halam in Tripura, India
Halia, Papua New Guinea
Hamtai, Papua New Guinea
Hangaza, Tanzania
Hatsa, Tanzania
Havu, Zaire
Havunese, Indonesia
Haya, Tanzania
Hehe, Tanzania
Helong, Indonesia
Herero, Botswana
Herero, Namibia
Heso, Zaire
**Hewa, Papua New Guinea (79)
***Higi, Nigeria
Hixkaryana, Brazil
Hohodene, Brazil
Holoholo, Tanzania
Holu, Angola
Hopi, United States of America
Hote, Papua New Guinea
Huachipaire, Peru
Huambisa, Peru
**Huila, Angola
Huitoto, Meneca, Colombia
Huitoto, Murui, Peru
Hukwe, Angola
Hula, Papua New Guinea
Huli, Papua New Guinea
Humene, Papua New Guinea
Hunde, Zaire

Hunjara, Papua New Guinea
Hupda Maku, Colombia
Iatmul, Papua New Guinea
Ibaji, Nigeria
**Iban, Malaysia (81)
Ibanag, Philippines
Ibibio, Nigeria
Ica, Colombia
Idi, Papua New Guinea
Idoma, Nigeria
Idoma, North, Nigeria
**Ifugao (Kalangoya), Philippines
Ifugao in Cababuyan, Philippines
Ifugao, Ambanad, Philippines
Ifugao, Antipolo, Philippines
Ifugao, Kiangan, Philippines
*Ifugao, Philippines
Ifumu, Congo
Igala, Nigeria
Igede, Nigeria
Ignaciano, Bolivia
Igora, Papua New Guinea
Igorot, Philippines
Iha, Indonesia
Ihceve, Nigeria
Ijo, Central-Western, Nigeria
Ijo, Northeast Central, Nigeria
Ijo, Northeast, Nigeria
**Ikalahan, Philippines
Ikizu, Tanzania
Ikobi-Mena, Papua New Guinea
Ikundun, Papua New Guinea
Ikwere, Nigeria
Ila, Zambia
Ilongot, Philippines
Inanwatan, Indonesia
Indians, Kinistino Reserve,
  Canada:Saskatchewan
Indinogosima, Papua New Guinea
Ingassana, Sudan
Insinai, Philippines
Ipiko, Papua New Guinea
Ipili, Papua New Guinea
Iquito, Peru
Irahutu, Indonesia
Iraqw, Tanzania
Iresim, Indonesia
Iria, Indonesia
Irigwe, Nigeria
Irumu, Papua New Guinea
Isanzu, Tanzania
Isebe, Papua New Guinea
Isekiri, Nigeria
Isneg, Dibagat-Kabugao,
  Philippines
Isneg, Karagawan, Philippines
Isoko, Nigeria
Itik, Indonesia
Itonama, Bolivia
Ivbie North-Okpela-Atte, Nigeria
Iwa, Zambia
*Iwaidja, Australia
Iwal, Papua New Guinea
Iwam, Papua New Guinea
Iwam, Sepik, Papua New Guinea
Iwur, Indonesia

Iyon, Cameroon
Iyon, Nigeria
Izarek, Nigeria
**Izi, Nigeria
Jaba, Nigeria
Jabem, Papua New Guinea
Jacalteco, Guatemala
Jamamadi, Brazil
Jamden, Indonesia
Janjero, Ethiopia
Janjo, Nigeria
Jaqaru, Peru
**Jarawa, Nigeria
Jebero, Peru
Jeng, Laos
Jerawa, Nigeria
*Jibu, Nigeria
Jiji, Tanzania
Jimajima, Papua New Guinea
Jinja, Tanzania
Jinuos, China (81)
Jita, Tanzania
*Jiye, Sudan
Jiye, Uganda
Juhai, Malaysia
Jukun, Nigeria
Kaalong, Cameroon
Kaba Dunjo, Central African
  Republic
Kaba, Central African Republic
Kabadi, Papua New Guinea
Kabixi, Brazil
Kabre, Benin
Kabre, Togo
Kachama, Ethiopia
Kadaklan-Barlig Bontoc,
  Philippines
Kadara, Nigeria
Kadazans, Malaysia
Kadiweu, Brazil
Kaeti, Indonesia
**Kafirs, Pakistan (79)
Kagoro, Mali
Kagulu, Tanzania
Kaian, Papua New Guinea
Kaiep, Papua New Guinea
Kaili, Indonesia
Kairi, Papua New Guinea
Kairiru, Papua New Guinea
Kaiwai, Indonesia
Kajang, Indonesia
Kaka, Cameroon
Kaka, Central African Republic
Kakoa, Papua New Guinea
Kakuna-Mamusi, Papua New Guinea
**Kalagan, Philippines
*Kalanga, Botswana
Kalanga, Zimbabwe
Kalinga, Kalagua, Philippines
Kalinga, Limus-Linan, Philippines
Kalinga, Quinaang, Philippines
*Kalinga, Southern, Philippines
Kalokalo, Papua New Guinea
Kamano, Papua New Guinea
Kamantan, Nigeria
Kamayura, Brazil

REGISTRY OF THE UNREACHED

*Kambari, Nigeria (80)
Kambera, Indonesia
Kamberataro, Indonesia
Kamberataro, Papua New Guinea
Kambot, Papua New Guinea
Kami, Tanzania
Kamkam, Cameroon
Kamnum, Papua New Guinea
Kamoro, Indonesia
Kampung Baru, Indonesia
Kamtuk-Gresi, Indonesia
*Kamuku, Nigeria (80)
Kana, Nigeria
Kandas, Papua New Guinea
Kaningra, Papua New Guinea
Kanite, Papua New Guinea
**Kankanay, Central, Philippines
Kankanay, Northern, Philippines
Kanu, Zaire
Kanum, Indonesia
Kanum, Papua New Guinea
Kao, Ethiopia
Kaonde, Zaire
Kaonde, Zambia
Kapin, Papua New Guinea
Kapore, Papua New Guinea
Kapori, Indonesia
Kapriman, Papua New Guinea
Kara, Papua New Guinea
Kara, Tanzania
*Karaboro, Upper Volta
Karam, Papua New Guinea
Karangi, Papua New Guinea
Karas, Indonesia
Kare, Papua New Guinea
Karen, Pwo, Thailand
Karen, Thailand (79)
Kari, Central African Republic
Kari, Zaire
Karipuna Creole, Brazil
Karipuna Do Guapore, Brazil
Karkar, Papua New Guinea
Karon Dori, Indonesia
Karon Pantai, Indonesia
Karre, Central African Republic
Karua, Papua New Guinea
**Kasena, Ghana
Kasseng, Laos
Kasua, Papua New Guinea
Kasuweri, Indonesia
Kate, Papua New Guinea
Kati, Northern, Indonesia
Kati, Southern, Indonesia
Katiati, Papua New Guinea
Katukina, Panoan, Brazil
Kaugat, Indonesia
Kaugel, Papua New Guinea
Kaure, Indonesia
Kavwol, Indonesia
Kavwol, Papua New Guinea
Kaw, Burma
Kawe, Indonesia
Kayabi, Brazil
Kayagar, Indonesia
Kayan, Burma
Kayan, Malaysia

Kayapo, Brazil
Kaygir, Indonesia
Kayupulau, Indonesia
Kedayanas, Malaysia
Kei, Indonesia
Kela, Papua New Guinea
Kelabit, Malaysia (81)
Kelah, Zaire
Kele, Gabon
Kemak, Indonesia
Kembata, Ethiopia
Kemok, Malaysia
Kenati, Papua New Guinea
Kenyah, Indonesia
Keopara, Papua New Guinea
*Kepas, Papua New Guinea
Kera, Cameroon
Kerewe, Tanzania
Kerewo, Papua New Guinea
Keriaka, Papua New Guinea
Kewa, East, Papua New Guinea
Kewa, South, Papua New Guinea
Kewa, West, Papua New Guinea
*Khamu, Thailand
Kiari, Papua New Guinea
Kibiri, Papua New Guinea
Kichepo, Sudan
Kilmera, Papua New Guinea
Kim, Central African Republic
Kimaghama, Indonesia
Kimbu, Tanzania
*Kimyal, Indonesia
Kinalakna, Papua New Guinea
Kinga, Tanzania
Kiriwina, Papua New Guinea
Kis, Papua New Guinea
Kisankasa, Tanzania
Kisi, Tanzania
Kissi, Guinea
*Kissi, Liberia
*Kissi, Sierra Leone
Kiwai, Northeast, Papua New Guinea
Kiwai, Southern, Papua New Guinea
Kiwai, Wabuda, Papua New Guinea
Koalib, Sudan (79)
Kobon, Papua New Guinea
Kodi, Indonesia
Koenoem, Nigeria
Kofyar, Nigeria
Kohoroxitari, Brazil
Kohumono, Nigeria
Koiari, Grass, Papua New Guinea
Koiari, Mountain, Papua New Guinea
Koita, Papua New Guinea
Kol, Papua New Guinea
Kole, Cameroon
Koliku, Papua New Guinea
Kolom, Papua New Guinea
Koma, Cameroon
Koma, Ghana
Koma, Nigeria
Komba, Papua New Guinea
Kombio, Papua New Guinea
*Komo, Ethiopia
Komutu, Papua New Guinea
Konabem, Cameroon

***Kond, India
Koneraw, Indonesia
Konkomba, Ghana
*Konkomba, Togo
**Kono, Sierra Leone
Konomala, Papua New Guinea
Konongo, Tanzania
Konso, Ethiopia
Korak, Papua New Guinea
Korape, Papua New Guinea
Korapun, Indonesia
*Korku in Madhya Pradesh, India
Koro, Nigeria
Koroma, Sudan
Korop, Cameroon
Korop, Nigeria
Kosorong, Papua New Guinea
Kota, Gabon
Kotogut, Indonesia
Kotoko, Cameroon
Kotopo, Cameroon
Kotta, India
Kovai, Papua New Guinea
Kove, Papua New Guinea
**Kowaao, Liberia
Koyra, Ethiopia
Kpa, Cameroon
Kpelle, Liberia
*Krahn, Ivory Coast
***Krahn, Liberia
Kreen-Akakore, Brazil
Krisa, Papua New Guinea
Krongo, Sudan
Krumen, Ivory Coast
Kuatinema, Brazil
Kube, Papua New Guinea
Kubu, Indonesia (80)
Kugbo, Nigeria
Kuikuro, Brazil
Kukele, Cameroon
Kukele, Nigeria
Kukuwy, Papua New Guinea
Kukwa, Congo
Kulango, Ivory Coast
Kulere, Nigeria
Kumai, Papua New Guinea
Kumam, Uganda
Kuman, Papua New Guinea
Kumdauron, Papua New Guinea
Kumu, Zaire
Kumukio, Papua New Guinea
Kunda, Mozambique
Kunda, Zambia
Kunda, Zambia
Kunda, Zimbabwe
Kuni, Papua New Guinea
Kunua, Papua New Guinea
Kuot, Papua New Guinea
Kupsabiny, Uganda
Kurada, Papua New Guinea
Kurfei, Niger
Kuria, Tanzania
Kurudu, Indonesia
**Kusaasi, Ghana
Kusu, Zaire
Kutin, Cameroon

Kutu, Tanzania
Kwadi, Angola
Kwakum, Cameroon
Kwale, Papua New Guinea
Kwambi, Namibia
Kwanga, Papua New Guinea
Kwangali, Angola
Kwansu, Indonesia
Kwanyama, Angola
Kwanyama, Namibia
Kwaya, Tanzania
Kwe-etshori, Botswana
Kwe-etshori, Zimbabwe
Kwerba, Indonesia
Kwere, Tanzania
Kwese, Zaire
Kwesten, Indonesia
Kwoma, Papua New Guinea
Kwomtari, Papua New Guinea
Labu, Papua New Guinea
Laewomba, Papua New Guinea
*Lahu, Thailand (81)
Laka, Cameroon
Laka, Central African Republic
Lala, Zambia
Lalia, Zaire
Lamba, Benin
Lamba, Togo
Lamba, Zaire
Lamba, Zambia
**Lambadi in Andhra Pradesh, India
    (81)
Lambi, Cameroon
Lambya, Malawi
Lambya, Tanzania
Lamogai, Papua New Guinea
Langi, Tanzania
*Lango, Ethiopia
Lango, Uganda
Lanoh, Malaysia
Lara, Indonesia
Latdwalam, Indonesia
Laudje, Indonesia
Lavatbura-Lamusong, Papua New
    Guinea
Lavongai, Papua New Guinea
Lebgo, Nigeria
Leco, Bolivia
Lega, Zaire
Lengua, Northern, Paraguay
Lenje, Zambia
Leron, Papua New Guinea
Letti, Indonesia
Lihir, Papua New Guinea
Liko, Zaire
Lima, Zambia
Limba, Sierra Leone
Lisu, China (81)
*Lisu, Thailand
Lo, Nigeria
Lobi, Ivory Coast
Lohiki, Papua New Guinea
**Loho Loho, Indonesia
Loinang, Indonesia (81)
Loko, Sierra Leone
Lolo, China (81)

REGISTRY OF THE UNREACHED

Loma, Guinea
Loma, Liberia
Lombi, Zaire
Lombo, Zaire
Lomwe, Mozambique
Lore, Indonesia
Lou-Baluan-Pam, Papua New Guinea
Lozi, Zambia
Lozi, Zimbabwe
Luano, Zambia
Luchazi, Angola
Luchazi, Zambia
Lue, Cameroon
Lugitama, Papua New Guinea
Luimbi, Angola
Lukep, Papua New Guinea
Lumbu, Gabon
Luna, Zaire
Lunda, Angola
Lundu, Cameroon
Lungu, Nigeria
Luo, Tanzania
Luvale Refugees from Angola,
  Zambia (83)
Luyana, Angola
Luyana, Zambia
Lwalu, Zaire
Lwena, Angola
Ma, Zaire
Maanyan, Indonesia
**Maasai, Kenya (79)
Maca, Paraguay
Machiguenga, Peru
Macu, Colombia
Macuna, Colombia
**Macuxi, Brazil
Madak, Papua New Guinea
Madda, Nigeria
Madi, Uganda
Madik, Indonesia
Magori, Papua New Guinea
***Maguzawa, Nigeria (79)
Mahri, Oman
Mai, Papua New Guinea
Mailu, Papua New Guinea
Maiongong, Brazil
Mairasi, Indonesia
Maisan, Papua New Guinea
Maiwa, Papua New Guinea
Maji, Ethiopia
Majingai-ngama, Central African
  Republic
Maka, Cameroon
Makarim, Papua New Guinea
Makasai, Indonesia
Makere, Uganda
Makian, West, Indonesia
Maklew, Indonesia
Makua, Mozambique
Malalamai, Papua New Guinea
Malappanackers, India
Malas, Papua New Guinea
Malasanga, Papua New Guinea
*Malayalars, India
Malayo, Colombia
Male, Ethiopia

Malek, Papua New Guinea
Maleu, Papua New Guinea
Malila, Tanzania
Malon, Papua New Guinea
Mama, Nigeria
Mamaa, Papua New Guinea
Mambai, Indonesia
Mambila, Cameroon
Mambwe-Lungu, Tanzania
Mambwe-Lungu, Zambia
Mamprusi, Ghana
Mamvu-Efe, Zaire
Managalasi, Papua New Guinea
Manambu, Papua New Guinea
Mancang, Senegal
Manda, Tanzania
Mandaya, Mansaka, Philippines
Mandaya, Philippines
Mander, Indonesia
Manem, Indonesia
Mangap, Papua New Guinea
Mangbutu, Zaire
Mangisa, Cameroon
**Mangyan, Philippines
**Manikion, Indonesia
**Manjaco, Guinea-Bissau
Mano, Liberia
Manobo, Agusan, Philippines
Manobo, Ata, Philippines
Manobo, Binokid, Philippines
**Manobo, Cotabato, Philippines
Manobo, Dibabawon, Philippines
*Manobo, Ilianen, Philippines
Manobo, Obo, Philippines
**Manobo, Salug, Philippines
Manobo, Sarangani, Philippines
Manobo, Tagabawa, Philippines
**Manobo, Tigwa, Philippines
**Manobo, Western Bukidnon,
  Philippines
Manobos, Pulangi, Philippines
Mantera, Malaysia
Mantion, Indonesia
Manu Park Panoan, Peru
Manyika, Zimbabwe
Mao, Northern, Ethiopia
Mape, Papua New Guinea
Mapena, Papua New Guinea
Mapoyo, Venezuela
Maquiritari, Venezuela
Maralango, Papua New Guinea
Maraliinan, Papua New Guinea
Marau, Indonesia
Mari, Papua New Guinea
Maria, Papua New Guinea
Marind, Bian, Indonesia
Marind, Indonesia
Maring, Papua New Guinea
Marubo, Brazil
Masa, Chad
Masaba, Uganda
Masegi, Papua New Guinea
*Masengo, Ethiopia
Mashi, Zambia
Matakam, Cameroon
Matawari, Surinam

Matbat, Indonesia
Matengo, Tanzania
Matipuhy-Nahukua, Brazil
Mauri, Niger
Maviha, Mozambique
Mawak, Papua New Guinea
Mawan, Papua New Guinea
Mawes, Indonesia
Maxakali, Brazil
Mayoruna, Peru
Mba, Zaire
Mbaama, Gabon
Mbai, Central African Republic
Mbala, Zaire
Mbangwe, Zaire
Mbanja, Zaire
Mbati, Central African Republic
Mbe, Nigeria
Mbede, Gabon
Mbembe (Tigong), Nigeria
Mbembe, Cameroon
Mbembe, Nigeria
Mbinu, Cameroon
Mbo, Cameroon
Mbo, Zaire
Mbole, Zaire
Mbugwe, Tanzania
Mbukushu, Angola
Mbunda, Angola
Mbunga, Tanzania
Mbwela, Angola
Me'en, Ethiopia
Meax, Indonesia
Meban, Sudan
Medlpa, Papua New Guinea
Mehek, Papua New Guinea
**Mejah, India
Meje, Uganda
Mekeo, Papua New Guinea
Mekwei, Indonesia
**Melanau of Sarawak, Malaysia (80)
Mende, Sierra Leone
Menemo-Mogamo, Cameroon
Mengen, Papua New Guinea
Menka, Cameroon
Menri, Malaysia
Menye, Papua New Guinea
**Meo, Thailand
Mera Mera, Papua New Guinea
Metis, Elizabeth Settlement,
    Canada:Alberta
Mianmin, Papua New Guinea
Miao, China (81)
Midsivindi, Papua New Guinea
Mien, China (81)
Migabac, Papua New Guinea
Migili, Nigeria
Mikarew, Papua New Guinea
Minanibai, Papua New Guinea
Mindik, Papua New Guinea
Minduumo, Gabon
Minianka, Mali
Miriam, Papua New Guinea
Mirung, Bangladesh
Mitang, Papua New Guinea
Mitmit, Papua New Guinea

Miya, Nigeria
Mo, Ghana
Moba, Ghana
Moba, Togo
***Mocha, Ethiopia
Moewehafen, Papua New Guinea
Mofu, Cameroon
Moi, Indonesia
Mokareng, Papua New Guinea
Moken of Thailand, Thailand
Moken, Burma (79)
*Mokole, Benin
Molof, Indonesia
Momare, Papua New Guinea
Mombum, Indonesia
Momoguns, Malaysia
Momolili, Papua New Guinea
Mongondow, Indonesia (81)
Moni, Indonesia
Monjombo, Central African Republic
Mono, Zaire
Mor, Indonesia
Morawa, Papua New Guinea
Moresada, Papua New Guinea
Morigi, Papua New Guinea
Morima, Papua New Guinea
*Mororata, Bolivia
Morunahua, Peru
Morwap, Indonesia
Mosi, Tanzania
Mossi, Upper Volta (80)
Motilon, Colombia
Motilon, Venezuela
Movima, Bolivia
Moxodi, Papua New Guinea
Mpoto, Malawi
Mpoto, Tanzania
Mru, Bangladesh
Mualthuam, India
Mugil, Papua New Guinea
Muinane, Colombia
Mukawa, Papua New Guinea
Mumuye, Nigeria
**Mundas in Bihar, India
Mundu, Zaire
Munduruku, Brazil
Mungaka, Cameroon
Munggui, Indonesia
Munkip, Papua New Guinea
Mup, Papua New Guinea
Mura-Piraha, Brazil
Murik, Papua New Guinea
Murle, Sudan
*Murngin (Wulamba), Australia
Mursi, Ethiopia
Murut, Malaysia
Musak, Papua New Guinea
Musar, Papua New Guinea
Musom, Papua New Guinea
Mutum, Papua New Guinea
Muyuw, Papua New Guinea
Mwanga, Tanzania
Mwatebu, Papua New Guinea
Mwera, Tanzania
Myaung-Ze, Burma
Nabak, Papua New Guinea

495

REGISTRY OF THE UNREACHED

Nabi, Indonesia
Nadeb Maku, Brazil
**Nafaara, Ghana (79)
Nafri, Indonesia
Nagarige, Papua New Guinea
Nagatman, Papua New Guinea
Nagovisi, Papua New Guinea
Nahu, Papua New Guinea
Nakama, Papua New Guinea
Nakanai, Papua New Guinea
Nalik, Papua New Guinea
Naltya, Indonesia
Nama, Namibia
Nama, South Africa
Nambikuara, Brazil
Nambis, Papua New Guinea
Nambu, Papua New Guinea
**Nambya, Zimbabwe
Namuni, Papua New Guinea
Nandi, Zaire
Nankina, Papua New Guinea
Nao, Ethiopia
Nara, Papua New Guinea
Naraguta, Nigeria
Narak, Papua New Guinea
Nasioi, Papua New Guinea
Nata, Tanzania
Nauna, Papua New Guinea
Nawuri, Ghana
Nchimburu, Ghana
Ndaaka, Zaire
Ndali, Tanzania
Ndam, Central African Republic
Ndamba, Tanzania
Ndaonese, Indonesia
Ndau, Zimbabwe
Nde-Nsele-Nta, Nigeria
**Ndebele, Zimbabwe (79)
Ndengereko, Tanzania
Ndjem, Cameroon
Ndo, Zaire
Ndoe, Nigeria
Ndogo, Central African Republic
Ndom, Indonesia
Ndomde, Tanzania
Ndoolo, Zaire
Ndop-Bamessing, Cameroon
Ndoro, Cameroon
**Ndoro, Nigeria
Nduga, Indonesia
Ndunga, Zaire
Negira, Papua New Guinea
Nek, Papua New Guinea
Nekgini, Papua New Guinea
Neko, Papua New Guinea
Nengaya, Papua New Guinea
Neyo, Ivory Coast
Ngaing, Papua New Guinea
Ngalik, North, Indonesia
Ngalik, Southern, Indonesia
Ngalum, Indonesia
**Ngamo, Nigeria
Ngando, Central African Republic
Ngando, Zaire
Ngasa, Tanzania
Ngayaba, Cameroon

Ngbaka Ma'bo, Central African
  Republic
Ngbaka Ma'bo, Zaire
Ngbaka, Zaire
Ngbandi, Zaire
Ngbee, Zaire
Ngemba, Cameroon
*Ngen, Ivory Coast
Ngeq, Laos
Ngere, Ivory Coast
Ngi, Cameroon
Ngindo, Tanzania
Ngiri, Zaire
**Ngombe, Zaire
Ngoni, Tanzania
Ngoni, Zambia
Ngulu, Malawi
Ngulu, Tanzania
Ngumba, Cameroon
Ngumbi, Equatorial Guinea
Ngurimi, Tanzania
Nguu, Tanzania
Ngwo, Cameroon
Nharon, Botswana
Nhengatu, Brazil
Nias, Indonesia
Nii, Papua New Guinea
Nilamba, Tanzania
Nimboran, Indonesia
Nimowa, Papua New Guinea
Ninam, Brazil
*Ningerum, Papua New Guinea
Ninggrum, Indonesia
Niningo, Papua New Guinea
Nisa, Indonesia
Nissan, Papua New Guinea
Njadu, Indonesia
Njemps, Kenya
Nkem-Nkum, Nigeria
Nkom, Cameroon
*Nkoya, Zambia
Nkutu, Zaire
***Nocte, India
Nohu, Cameroon
Nomane, Papua New Guinea
Nomu, Papua New Guinea
Nondiri, Papua New Guinea
Notsi, Papua New Guinea
*Nouni, Upper Volta
Nsenga, Zambia
Nsenga, Zimbabwe
Nso, Cameroon
Nsongo, Angola
Ntomba, Zaire
Ntrubo, Ghana
*Nuer, Ethiopia
*Nuer, Sudan (79)
Nuk, Papua New Guinea
Numanggang, Papua New Guinea
Nungu, Nigeria
**Nyabwa, Ivory Coast
Nyaheun, Laos
Nyakyusa, Malawi
Nyakyusa, Tanzania
Nyali, Zaire
Nyambo, Tanzania

Nyamwezi, Tanzania (80)
Nyaneka, Angola
Nyang, Cameroon
Nyanga-Li, Zaire
Nyanja, Zimbabwe
Nyankole, Uganda
*Nyantruku, Benin
Nyemba, Angola
Nyengo, Angola
Nyiha, Tanzania
Nyiha, Zambia
Nyoro, Uganda
Nyuli, Uganda
Nyungwe, Mozambique
Nyzatom, Sudan
Nzakara, Central African Republic
Nzebi, Congo
O'ung, Angola
Obanliku, Nigeria
Obolo, Nigeria
Ocaina, Peru
Odual, Nigeria
Odut, Nigeria
Ogbia, Nigeria
Oi, Laos
Okobo, Nigeria
Okpamheri, Nigeria
Oksapmin, Papua New Guinea
Olo, Papua New Guinea
Olulumo-Ikom, Nigeria
Omati, Papua New Guinea
Omie, Papua New Guinea
Onank, Papua New Guinea
Onin, Indonesia
Onjab, Papua New Guinea
Ono, Papua New Guinea
Orang Kanak, Malaysia
Orang Laut, Malaysia
Orang Ulu, Malaysia
Orejon, Peru
Oring, Nigeria
Ormu, Indonesia
Orokaiva, Papua New Guinea
Orokolo, Papua New Guinea
Oron, Nigeria
Oso, Cameroon
Osum, Papua New Guinea
Ot Danum, Indonesia
Otank, Nigeria
Oyampipuku, Brazil
Oyda, Ethiopia
Pacu, Brazil
Pai, Nigeria
Paiwa, Papua New Guinea
Pak-Tong, Papua New Guinea
Pakaasnovos, Brazil
***Pakabeti of Equator, Zaire
*Pala'wan, Philippines (81)
Palawano, Central, Philippines
Palawano, Philippines
Palenquero, Colombia
Palikur, Brazil
Pambia, Central African Republic
Pana, Central African Republic
Panare, Venezuela
Pande, Congo

Pangwa, Tanzania
**Paniyan of Kerala, India (81)
Pankararu, Brazil
Pantu, Indonesia
Papapana, Papua New Guinea
Pape, Cameroon
Papuma, Indonesia
Parakanan, Brazil
Parawen, Papua New Guinea
Pare, Papua New Guinea
Pare, Tanzania
Paresi, Brazil
Parintintin, Brazil
Pasismanua, Papua New Guinea
Patep, Papua New Guinea
Pato Tapuia, Brazil
Patpatar, Papua New Guinea
Paumari, Brazil
Pawaia, Papua New Guinea
Pay, Papua New Guinea
Paya, Honduras
Paynamar, Papua New Guinea
Penan, Western, Malaysia (81)
Pende, Zaire
Peremka, Papua New Guinea
Peri, Zaire
Piapoco, Colombia
Piaroa, Venezuela
**Pila, Benin
Pila, Papua New Guinea
Pilaga, Argentina
Pimbwe, Tanzania
Piratapuyo, Brazil
Piro, Peru
Pisa, Indonesia
Pitu Uluna Salu, Indonesia
Piu, Papua New Guinea
Podokwo, Cameroon
Podopa, Papua New Guinea
Podzo, Mozambique
Pogolo, Tanzania
Poke, Zaire
Pokot, Uganda
Pol, Congo
Pom, Indonesia
Ponam-Andra-Hus, Papua New Guinea
Pondoma, Papua New Guinea
Porapora, Papua New Guinea
Porohanon, Philippines
Pular, Senegal
Pulie, Papua New Guinea
Punu, Congo
Puragi, Indonesia
Purari, Papua New Guinea
Pygmy (Binga), Burundi
Pygmy (Binga), Central African
   Republic
*Pygmy (Mbuti), Zaire (79)
Pyu, Indonesia
Quaiquer, Colombia
Quarequena, Brazil
**Quechua, Huancayo, Peru
Rambutyo, Papua New Guinea
Rao, Papua New Guinea
Ratahan, Indonesia
Rauto, Papua New Guinea

REGISTRY OF THE UNREACHED

Rawa, Papua New Guinea
Rempi, Papua New Guinea
Reshe, Nigeria
Reshiat, Ethiopia
Reyesano, Bolivia
Riantana, Indonesia
Rikbaktsa, Brazil
Roinji, Papua New Guinea
Romkun, Papua New Guinea
Romkun, Papua New Guinea
Ronga, Mozambique
Ronga, South Africa
Roro, Papua New Guinea
Rotokas, Papua New Guinea
Ruihi, Tanzania
Runga, Central African Republic
Rungi, Tanzania
Rungwa, Tanzania
**Rural Vodun Believers, Haiti (84)
Rusha, Tanzania
Rwamba, Uganda
Rwamba, Zaire
***Rwandan Tutsi Refugees, Burundi
    (83)
Saamia, Uganda
Sabbra, Kenya
Saberi, Indonesia
Sadang, Indonesia
Saep, Papua New Guinea
Safwa, Tanzania
Sagala, Tanzania
Saija, Colombia
Saisiat, Taiwan (81)
Sakam, Papua New Guinea
Sakata, Zaire
Saki, Papua New Guinea
Sala, Zambia
Salampasu, Zaire
Saliba, Colombia
Salt, Papua New Guinea
Sama, Mapun, Philippines
Samarkena, Indonesia
**Samburu, Kenya (84)
Samo, Northern, Mali
*Samo-Kubo, Papua New Guinea
Samogho, Mali
San, Namibia
Sanapana, Paraguay
Sandawe, Tanzania
Sangir, Indonesia
Sangke, Indonesia
Sangu, Gabon
Sangu, Tanzania
Sanio, Papua New Guinea
**Santhali, Nepal
*Sanuma, Brazil
Sanuma, Venezuela
Sanza, Zaire
Sapo, Liberia
Saposa, Papua New Guinea
Sasaru-Enwan Igwe, Nigeria
Saseng, Papua New Guinea
Satere, Brazil
Satnamis (Madhya Pradesh), India
Sau, Papua New Guinea
Sauk, Papua New Guinea

Sauria Pahari, India
Sause, Indonesia
**Save, Benin
**Sawi, Indonesia
Sawos, Papua New Guinea
Secoya, Ecuador
Sekar, Indonesia
Seko, Indonesia
**Selakau of Sarawak, Malaysia
Selepet, Papua New Guinea
Semelai, Malaysia
Sempan, Indonesia
Sena, Malawi
Sena, Mozambique
Senggi, Indonesia
**Senoi, Malaysia (81)
Sentani, Indonesia
Senufo, Ivory Coast (80)
Sepen, Papua New Guinea
Serere, Senegal (79)
Serki, Papua New Guinea
Serui-Laut, Indonesia
Setaui Keriwa, Papua New Guinea
Setiali, Papua New Guinea
Seuci, Brazil
Sha, Nigeria
Shambala, Tanzania
Shanga, Nigeria
Sharanahua, Peru
Sheko, Ethiopia
Shinasha, Ethiopia
Shipibo, Peru
**Shirishana, Brazil
Shua, Botswana
Siagha-Yenimu, Indonesia
Sialum, Papua New Guinea
Siane, Papua New Guinea
Siar, Papua New Guinea
Sikanese, Indonesia
Sikhule, Indonesia
Simaa, Zambia
Simba, Bolivia
Simog, Papua New Guinea
Sinagen, Papua New Guinea
Sinagoro, Papua New Guinea
Sinaki, Papua New Guinea
Sinasina, Papua New Guinea
Sindamon, Papua New Guinea
Sinsauru, Papua New Guinea
Sio, Papua New Guinea
Siona, Colombia
Sipoma, Papua New Guinea
Sira, Gabon
Sirak, Papua New Guinea
Sirasira, Papua New Guinea
Siriano, Colombia
Siriono, Bolivia
Siroi, Papua New Guinea
**Sisaala, Ghana
Siwai, Papua New Guinea
So, Cameroon
Sobei, Indonesia
Soga, Uganda
Soh, Laos
*Soh, Thailand (81)
Sokorok, Papua New Guinea

Index by Religion

Soli, Zambia
Solos, Papua New Guinea
Som, Papua New Guinea
*Somagai, Indonesia
Somahai, Indonesia
**Somba, Benin
Somrai, Central African Republic
Sona, Papua New Guinea
Songe, Zaire
Songhai, Mali
Songomeno, Zaire
Songoora, Zaire
Sonjo, Tanzania
Sori-Harengan, Papua New Guinea
Soruba, Benin
Sowanda, Indonesia
Sowanda, Papua New Guinea
Su, Cameroon
Sua, Papua New Guinea
Suain, Papua New Guinea
Suba, Tanzania
**Subanen (Tuboy), Philippines
**Subanen, Sindangan, Philippines
  (80)
Subi, Tanzania
Sudanese Repatriates, Sudan (83)
Suga, Cameroon
Suganga, Papua New Guinea
**Sugut, Malaysia
Sui, Papua New Guinea
Suk, Kenya
Suki, Papua New Guinea
Suku, Zaire
Sukurum, Papua New Guinea
Sulka, Papua New Guinea
Sumau, Papua New Guinea
Sumba, Indonesia
Sumbwa, Tanzania
Suppire, Mali
**Suri, Ethiopia
Sursurunga, Papua New Guinea
Surui, Brazil
Swaga, Zaire
Swaka, Zambia
**Swazi, South Africa
**T'boli, Philippines (81)
T'in, Thailand (81)
Ta-Oi, Laos
Tabar, Papua New Guinea
Tabi, Sudan
Tabriak, Papua New Guinea
Tacana, Bolivia
Tadjio, Indonesia
Tadyawan, Philippines
Tagal, Malaysia (81)
**Tagbanwa, Aborlan, Philippines
***Tagin, India
Tagula, Papua New Guinea
Tahit, Indonesia
Taikat, Indonesia
Tairora, Papua New Guinea
Takalubi, Papua New Guinea
Takemba, Benin
Takia, Papua New Guinea
Tamagario, Indonesia
Taman, Papua New Guinea

Tambas, Nigeria
Tambo, Zambia
Tani, Papua New Guinea
Tampulma, Ghana
Tana, Central African Republic
Tanahmerah, Indonesia
Tandanke, Senegal
Tandia, Indonesia
Tangga, Papua New Guinea
**Tangsa, India
Tangu, Papua New Guinea
Tanguat, Papua New Guinea
Tani, Papua New Guinea
Tanimuca-Retuama, Colombia
Tao't Bato, Philippines
Tao-Suame, Papua New Guinea
Taori-Kei, Indonesia
Tara, Indonesia
Taram, Cameroon
Tarof, Indonesia
Tarok, Nigeria
Tarpia, Indonesia
Tate, Papua New Guinea
Tatoga, Tanzania
**Tatuyo, Colombia
Tauade, Papua New Guinea
Taupota, Papua New Guinea
Taurap, Indonesia
Tavara, Papua New Guinea
Tawi-Pau, Papua New Guinea
Tayaku, Benin
Tchang, Cameroon
*Teenbu, Ivory Coast
Teke, Eastern, Zaire
Teke, Northern, Congo
Teke, Southwestern, Congo
Telefol, Papua New Guinea
Tembe, Brazil
Tembo, Zaire
Temira, Malaysia
**Temne, Sierra Leone (80)
*Tense, Ivory Coast
Teop, Papua New Guinea
Tepeth, Uganda
Terebu, Papua New Guinea
Terena, Brazil
**Teso, Kenya
Teso, Uganda
Tiang, Papua New Guinea
Tiana, Brazil
Tioi, Papua New Guinea
Tiene, Zaire
Tifai, Papua New Guinea
Tigak, Papua New Guinea
Tigon, Cameroon
Tikar, Cameroon
Timbe, Papua New Guinea
Timorese, Indonesia
Tinputz, Papua New Guinea
Tirio, Papua New Guinea
Tiro, Indonesia
Tiruray, Philippines
Toala, Indonesia
Toaripi, Papua New Guinea
Tobo, Papua New Guinea
*Tofi, Benin

REGISTRY OF THE UNREACHED

Togbo, Zaire
Tol, Honduras
Tombulu, Indonesia
Tomini, Indonesia
Tonda, Papua New Guinea
Tondanou, Indonesia
Tonga, Botswana
Tonga, Gwembe Valley, Zambia (79)
Tonga, Malawi
Tonga, Mozambique
*Tonga, Zimbabwe
Tongwe, Tanzania
Tonsea, Indonesia
Tontemboa, Indonesia
*Topotha, Sudan
Toraja, Southern, Indonesia (81)
Torau, Papua New Guinea
Torricelli, Papua New Guinea
Towei, Indonesia
Trio, Surinam
Tsamai, Ethiopia
Tsimane, Bolivia
Tsogo, Gabon
Tsonga, Mozambique
Tsou, Taiwan (81)
Tswa, Mozambique
Tswa, Zimbabwe
Tswana, Namibia
Tswana, Zimbabwe
Tuam, Papua New Guinea
Tubetube, Papua New Guinea
Tucano, Brazil
Tunawo, Indonesia
Tunebo, Cobaria, Colombia
Tung-Chia, China (81)
Tunya, Central African Republic
Tupuri, Cameroon
**Turkana Fishing Community, Kenya (79)
Turkana, Kenya
Turu, Indonesia
Turu, Tanzania
Tuyuca, Brazil
Udmurt, USSR
Uduk, Sudan
Ugandan Refugees, Sudan (83)
Uhunduni, Indonesia
Ukaan, Nigeria
Ukpe-Bayobiri, Nigeria
Ukwuani-Aboh, Nigeria
Urarina, Peru
Urban Refugees in Lusaka, Zambia (83)
Urhobo, Nigeria
Uria, Indonesia
Uruangnirin, Indonesia
Urubu, Brazil
Urupa, Brazil
Uspanteco, Guatemala
Utugwang, Nigeria
Uvbie, Nigeria
Uzekwe, Nigeria
Vagala, Ghana
Vaikino, Indonesia
Vale, Central African Republic
Venda, Zimbabwe

Vere, Cameroon
***Vere, Nigeria
Vidunda, Tanzania
Vinza, Tanzania
Vute, Nigeria
Wa, Burma
Wabo, Indonesia
Waimiri, Brazil
Waiwai, Brazil
**Wajita, Tanzania
Walamo, Ethiopia
Wambon, Indonesia
**Wanchoo, India
Wanda, Tanzania
Wandamen, Indonesia
Wandji, Gabon
Wanggom, Indonesia
Wanji, Tanzania
Wano, Indonesia
Wapishana, Brazil
Wapishana, Venezuela
Warao, Venezuela
Ware, Mali
Warembori, Indonesia
Waris, Indonesia
*Warjawa, Nigeria
Warkay-Bipim, Indonesia
Waropen, Indonesia
Wasi, Tanzania
Watchi, Togo
Waura, Brazil
Wayana, Surinam
*Wazinza, Tanzania
Wetawit, Ethiopia
Wewewa, Indonesia
Widekum, Cameroon
**Wimbum, Cameroon
Wobe, Ivory Coast
Wodani, Indonesia
Woi, Indonesia
Wongo, Zaire
Wumbvu, Gabon
Wungu, Tanzania
Xavante, Brazil
Xerente, Brazil
Xokleng, Brazil
Xu, Namibia
Yafi, Indonesia
Yagua, Peru
Yahadian, Indonesia
Yaka, Zaire
Yakoma, Central African Republic
**Yala, Nigeria
Yaly, Indonesia
Yambasa, Cameroon
Yaminahua, Peru
*Yanomamo, Brazil (79)
Yanomamo, Venezuela
Yans, Zaire
*Yao Refugees from Laos, Thailand
**Yao, Thailand (79)
Yaoure, Ivory Coast
Yaruro, Venezuela
Yasing, Cameroon
Yaur, Indonesia
Yava, Indonesia

**Yei, Botswana
Yei, Indonesia
Yela, Zaire
Yelmek, Indonesia
Yeretuar, Indonesia
Yidinit, Ethiopia
Yin-Kyar, Burma
Yin-Nett, Burma
Yinga, Cameroon
Yoabu, Benin
Yogad, Philippines
Yonggom, Indonesia
Yotafa, Indonesia
Yuana, Venezuela
Yucateco, Guatemala
Yukpa, Colombia
Yukpa, Venezuela
Yuracare, Bolivia
Yuruti, Colombia
Zanaki, Tanzania
**Zaranda Hill Peoples, Nigeria
Zayse, Ethiopia
Zemi Naga of Assam, India (81)
Zigwa, Tanzania
Zilmamu, Ethiopia
Zimba, Zaire
Zimbabwean Refugees, Mozambique
   (83)
Zoliang, India
Zowla, Ghana
Zulu, Malawi
Zuni, United States of America

Bahaism

Bahais in Teheran, Iran (82)
**Iranian Bahai Refugees, Pakistan
   (83)

Buddhism

*Barbers in Tokyo, Japan (82)
Bhutias, Bhutan
Chinese, Halifax, Canada:Nova
   Scotia
Chinese, Metro Toronto,
   Canada:Ontario
Chinese, Thunder Bay,
   Canada:Ontario
Danu, Burma
Government officials, Thailand
Hkun, Burma
Japanese in Brazil, Brazil (79)
Japanese, Toronto, Canada:Ontario
Kachin in Shan State, Burma
Kae Sung Natives in Seoul, Korea,
   Republic of (82)
Kalmytz, USSR

Khmer Refugees, Montreal,
   Canada:Quebec
Khmer Refugees, Toronto,
   Canada:Ontario
Khmer, Ottawa, Canada:Ontario
Koreans, Canada
**Lahaulis in Punjab, India
*Lao, Laos (79)
Lao-Chinese Refugees, Edmonton,
   Canada:Alberta
**Lepers of N.E. Thailand, Thailand
Newar in Kathmandu, Nepal (82)
Palaung, Burma (79)
Pao, Burma
*Ramkamhaeng Un. Students, Thailand
Shan, Burma
*Sherpa, Nepal
Sinhalese, Sri Lanka
*Slum Dwellers of Bangkok, Thailand
Soka Gakkai Believers, Japan
Taungyoe, Burma
*Thai Immigrants, Los Angeles,
   United States of America (84)
*Thai University Students, Thailand
   (81)
Tibetan Refugees, Canada
*Tibetan Refugees, India (83)
Tibetan Refugees, Switzerland (83)
Tibetans in Bhutan, Bhutan (81)
Vietnamese Refugees, Regina,
   Canada:Saskatchewan
**Vietnamese Refugees, United States
   of America
**Vietnamese Refugees, Thailand
Vietnamese Refugees, Korea,
   Republic of
Vietnamese, Edmonton,
   Canada:Alberta
Vietnamese, Laos
Zanskari, India (84)

Buddhist-Animist

*Ami, Taiwan (81)
**Banai, Bangladesh
Blind, N.E. Thailand, Thailand
   (84)
Bote-Majhi, Nepal
Buriat, USSR
Byangsi, Nepal
*Cambodians, Thailand
*Central Thailand Farmers, Thailand
   (81)
*Chakmas of Mizoram, India (81)
*Chang-Pa of Kashmir, India (81)
Chaudangsi, Nepal
Chaungtha, Burma
Chepang, Nepal
Chin, Falam, Burma
Chin, Haka, Burma
Chin, Khumi, Burma
Chin, Ngawn, Burma

REGISTRY OF THE UNREACHED

Chin, Tiddim, Burma
Chinbok, Burma
**Chinese, Mauritius (84)
Dai, Burma
Darai, Nepal
Darmiya, Nepal
Dhimal, Nepal
Evenks, USSR
Ghale Gurung, Nepal
Gheko, Burma
Hallam, Burma
***Hmong Refugee Women, Ban Vinai, Thailand (83)
***Hmong Refugees, United States of America (83)
Hrangkhol, Burma
Intha, Burma
Janggali, Nepal
Jirel, Nepal
**Kampuchean Refugees, Ontario, Canada:Ontario (83)
Kampuchean Refugees, Laos
Kebumtamp, Bhutan
Kham, Nepal
**Khmer Refugees, Thailand
Khmer Refugees, Unaccd. Minors, Thailand (83)
Kokant, Burma
*Kui, Thailand
Lama, Burma
*Lao Refugees, Spain (83)
*Lao Refugees, Thailand
Lawa, Eastern, Thailand (81)
Lawa, Mountain, Thailand
**Lepers of Cen. Thailand, Thailand (81)
Lhomi, Nepal
Loven, Laos (81)
Lu, China
Maghi, Burma
Majhi, Nepal
Mon, Burma (81)
Monpa, India
Mun, Burma
Norra, Burma
Pai, China (81)
Palpa, Nepal
Phu Thai, Laos
Phu Thai, Thailand (84)
Purum, Burma
Rai, Khaling, Nepal
Rai, Kulunge, Nepal
Rai, Thulunge, Nepal
Ralte, Burma
Rangkas, Nepal
Riang-Lang, Burma
Senthang, Burma
Shan Chinese, Burma
Shan, Thailand
Sharchagpakha, Bhutan
Street Vendors in Saigon, Viet Nam (82)
Sunwar, Nepal
Syuwa, Nepal
Taman, Burma
Taungyo, Burma

Tawr, Burma
Thai-Ney, Burma
Thakali, Nepal
Thami, Nepal
Tuvinian, USSR
Yakha, Nepal
Yangbye, Burma
Yinchia, Burma
Yos, Burma
Zome, Burma

Christo-Paganism

Abaknon, Philippines
Aeta, Philippines
Akawaio, Guyana
Alangan, Philippines
**Ampeeli, Papua New Guinea
Amuzgo, Guerrero, Mexico
Amuzgo, Oaxaca, Mexico
*Apayao, Philippines
Arawak, Guyana
Ati, Philippines
Aymara, Carangas, Chile
***Azteca, Mexico (79)
***Bagobo, Philippines
**Balangao, Philippines
Bantuanon, Philippines
Batak, Palawan, Philippines
**Bidayuh of Sarawak, Malaysia (81)
***Bipim, Indonesia
**Black Caribs, Belize, Belize (79)
**Black Caribs, Guatemala, Guatemala
*Black Caribs, Honduras, Honduras (84)
**Bontoc, Southern, Philippines
Buglere, Panama
Buhid, Philippines
Caluyanhon, Philippines
***Cebu, Middle-Class, Philippines
***Ch'ol Sabanilla, Mexico
Chamorro, Pacific Trust Islands
Chamula, Mexico (79)
Chatino, Nopala, Mexico
Chatino, Panixtlahuaca, Mexico
Chatino, Tataltepec, Mexico
Chatino, Yaitepec, Mexico
Chatino, Zacatepec, Mexico
Chatino, Zenzontepec, Mexico
**Chayahuita, Peru
Chinanteco, Ayotzintepec, Mexico
Chinanteco, Chiltepec, Mexico
Chinanteco, Comaltepec, Mexico
Chinanteco, Lalana, Mexico
Chinanteco, Lealao, Mexico
Chinanteco, Ojitlan, Mexico
Chinanteco, Palantla, Mexico
Chinanteco, Quiotepec, Mexico
Chinanteco, Sochiapan, Mexico
Chinanteco, Tepetotutla, Mexico
Chinanteco, Usila, Mexico
Chinanteco, , Mexico

502

Chocho, Mexico
Chuj, San Mateo Ixtatan, Mexico
Chulupe, Paraguay
Cocopa, Mexico
Cora, Mexico
Cuicateco, Tepeuxila, Mexico
Cuicateco, Teutila, Mexico
Cuyonon, Philippines
Davaweno, Philippines
Djuka, Surinam
*Favelados-Rio de Janeiro, Brazil (82)
Gagauzes, USSR
Galla of Bucho, Ethiopia
*Guanano, Colombia (79)
Guarayu, Bolivia
Guarojio, Mexico
Guatemalan Refugees, Mexico
Gypsies, USSR
Hanonoo, Philippines
Huasteco, Mexico
**Huave, Mexico
Huichol, Mexico
Huistan Tzotzil, Mexico
*Ibataan, Philippines
Inga, Colombia
Iraya, Philippines
Itawit, Philippines
Itneg, Adasen, Philippines
Itneg, Binongan, Philippines
Itneg, Masadiit, Philippines
Ixil, Guatemala
Jemez Pueblo, United States of America
**Jivaro (Achuara), Venezuela
K'anjobal of Los Angeles, United States of America
Kaagan, Philippines
*Kaffa, Ethiopia (80)
Kaingang, Brazil
**Kalinga,Northern, Philippines (81)
**Kekchi, Guatemala
Kikapoo, Mexico
Kinaray-A, Philippines
Komi-Permyat, USSR
Komi-Zyrian, USSR
**Kunimaipa, Papua New Guinea
Lacandon, Mexico
Lionese, Indonesia
*Llaneros, Colombia (84)
*Lokoro, Sudan
Lubang Islanders, Philippines (81)
**Mam Indian, Guatemala
**Mamanua, Philippines (81)
**Mansaka, Philippines
Mapuche, Chile
Mari, USSR
Matlatzinca, Atzingo, Mexico
Mayo, Mexico
**Mazahua, Mexico
***Mestizos in La Paz, Bolivia (82)
*Mimika, Indonesia
Miskito, Nicaragua
**Mixes, Mexico
Mixteco, Amoltepec, Mexico
Mixteco, Apoala, Mexico

Mixteco, Central Puebla, Mexico
Mixteco, Eastern Putla, Mexico
Mixteco, Eastern, Mexico
Mixteco, Huajuapan, Mexico
Mixteco, Silacayoapan, Mexico
Mixteco, Southern Puebla, Mexico
Mixteco, Southern Putla, Mexico
Mixteco, Tututepec, Mexico
Mixteco, Yosondua, Mexico
*Mixteco,San Juan Mixtepic, Mexico
**Mopan Maya, Belize
**Mopan Maya, Guatemala
Mutu, Venezuela
*Nahua, North Puebla, Mexico
Ngada, Indonesia
Northern Cagayan Negrito, Philippines
Otomi, Eastern, Mexico
Otomi, Mezquital, Mexico
Otomi, Northwestern, Mexico
Otomi, Southeastern, Mexico
Otomi, State of Mexico, Mexico
Otomi, Tenango, Mexico
Otomi, Texcatepec, Mexico
***Paez, Colombia
Paipai, Mexico
Pame, Central Chichimeca, Mexico
Pame, Chichimeca-Jonaz, Mexico
Pame, Northern, Mexico
Paranan, Philippines
Patamona, Guyana
Pima Bajo, Mexico
**Plantation Workers, Papua New Guinea
Pocomam, Central, Guatemala
Pocomchi, Eastern, Guatemala
Pocomchi, Western, Guatemala
Popoloca, Ahuatempan, Mexico
Popoloca, Coyotepec, Mexico
Popoloca, Eastern, Mexico
Popoloca, Northern, Mexico
Popoloca, Southern, Mexico
Popoloca, Western, Mexico
Popoluca, Oluta, Mexico
Popoluca, Sayula, Mexico
Popoluca, Sierra, Mexico
Popoluca, Texistepec, Mexico
**Puyuma, Taiwan (81)
**Quechua, Bolivia
**Quechua, Peru
**Quiche, Guatemala (79)
**Quichua, Ecuador
Rabinal-Achi, Guatemala
Saramaccan, Surinam
Seri, Mexico
***Shankilla (Kazza), Ethiopia
**Suena, Papua New Guinea
Sumu, Nicaragua
Tagbanwa, Kalamian, Philippines
Tarahumara, Northern, Mexico
Tarahumara, Rocoroibo, Mexico
Tarahumara, Samachique, Mexico
Tarasco, Mexico
Tepehua, Huehuetla, Mexico
Tepehua, Pisa Flores, Mexico
Tepehua, Veracruz, Mexico

Tepehuan, Northern, Mexico
Tepehuan, Southeastern, Mexico
Tepehuan, Southwestern, Mexico
**Teribe, Panama
Tlapaneco, Malinaltepec, Mexico
Tojolabal, Mexico
Totonaco, Northern, Mexico
Totonaco, Oxumatlan, Mexico
Totonaco, Papantla, Mexico
Totonaco, Sierra, Mexico
Totonaco, Yecuatla, Mexico
Trique, San Juan Copala, Mexico
**Tsachila, Ecuador
Tubar, Mexico
Tukude, Indonesia
Tzeltal, Bachajon, Mexico
Tzeltal, Highland, Mexico
Tzutujil, Guatemala
Ulithi-Mall, Pacific Trust Islands
Waiwai, Guyana
Wapishana, Guyana
Woleat, Pacific Trust Islands
Yaghan, Chile
Yaquis, Mexico
Yucateco, Mexico
*Yucuna, Colombia
Zapoteco, C Sola De Vega, Mexico
Zapoteco, Choapan, Mexico
Zapoteco, E Miahuatlan, Mexico
Zapoteco, E Ocotlan, Mexico
Zapoteco, E Tlacolula, Mexico
Zapoteco, E Zimatlan, Mexico
Zapoteco, Isthmus, Mexico
Zapoteco, Mazaltepec, Mexico
Zapoteco, Miamuatlan, Mexico
Zapoteco, Mitla, Mexico
Zapoteco, N Isthmus, Mexico
Zapoteco, N Ocotlan, Mexico
Zapoteco, N Villa Alta, Mexico
Zapoteco, NE Miahuatlan, Mexico
Zapoteco, NE Yautepec, Mexico
Zapoteco, NW Tehuantepec, Mexico
Zapoteco, Pochutla, Mexico
Zapoteco, S Ejutla, Mexico
Zapoteco, S Villa Alta, Mexico
Zapoteco, SC Zimatlan, Mexico
Zapoteco, SE Miahuatlan, Mexico
Zapoteco, SW Ixtlan, Mexico
Zapoteco, Srra De Juarez, Mexico
Zapoteco, Stgo Xanica, Mexico
Zapoteco, Sto Dom Albarr, Mexico
Zapoteco, Tabaa, Mexico
Zapoteco, Villa Alta, Mexico
Zapoteco, W Miahuatlan, Mexico
Zapoteco, W Ocotlan, Mexico
Zapoteco, W Sola de Vega, Mexico
Zapoteco, W Tlacolula, Mexico
Zapoteco, W Yautepec, Mexico
Zapoteco, W Zimatlan, Mexico
Zapoteco, Yalalag, Mexico
Zimbabwean Refugees, Zambia
Zimbabwean Repatriates, Zimbabwe
  (83)
Zinacantecos, Mexico (79)
Zoque, Chimalapa, Mexico
Zoque, Copainala, Mexico

Zoque, Francisco Leon, Mexico
Zoque, Tabasco, Mexico

Folk Religion

*Alars, India
**Apartment Residents-Seoul, Korea,
  Republic of
*Deviant Youth in Taipei, Taiwan
  (82)
Druzes, Israel (79)
*Gabbra, Ethiopia
Gabbra, Kenya
*Gypsies in Spain, Spain (79)
Haitian Refugees, United States of
  America (83)
Haitians, Montreal, Canada:Quebec
Indians, Edmonton, Canada:Alberta
Indust.Workers Yongdungpo, Korea,
  Republic of
*Koreans of Japan, Japan
*Prisoners in Antananarivo,
  Madagascar (82)
Romany, Turkey
**Vietnamese Refugees, Australia

Hindu—Animist

Abujmaria (Madhya Pradesh), India
Aimol in Assam, India
Ajmeri in Rajasthan, India
Aranadan in Tamil Nadu, India
Bagelkhandi in M.P., India
Balinese, Indonesia
Bangaru in Punjab, India
Bhakta, India
Bhattri, India
Bhilala, India
Bhoyari in Maharashtra, India
Bhumij in Assam, India
Bhunjia in Madhya Pradesh, India
Bijori in Bihar, India
Binjhwari in Bihar, India
Birhor in Bihar, India
**Bodo Kachari, India
Cham, Viet Nam
Chamari in Madhya Pradesh, India
Chameali in H.P., India
Chenchu in Andhra Pradesh, India
Chodhari in Gujarat, India
Churahi in H.P., India
**Dhodias, India
Dhurwa, India
Dorlin in Andhra Pradesh, India
**Dubla, India
Gadaban in Andhra Pradesh, India
Gaddi in Himachal Pradesh, India
Galong in Assam, India

Gamti in Gujarat, India
Gangte in Assam, India
Gawari in Andhra Pradesh, India
Grasia in Gujarat, India
**Hajong, Bangladesh
Halbi in Madhya Pradesh, India
Harauti in Rajasthan, India
Ho in Bihar, India
Holiya in Madhya Pradesh, India
**Indian Tamils - Colombo, Sri Lanka
  (82)
Jagannathi in A.P., India
Jatapu in Andhra Pradesh, India
Jaunsari in Uttar Pradesh, India
Kadar in Andhra Pradesh, India
Kahluri in Andamans, India
Kaikadi in Maharashtra, India
Kamar in Madhya Pradesh, India
Kanikkaran in Kerala, India
Kanjari in Andhra Pradesh, India
**Karbis, India
Karmali in Dihar, India
Katakari in Gujarat, India
Kawar in Madhya Pradesh, India
Keer in Madhya Pradesh, India
Khandesi, India
Kharia in Bihar, India
Khirwar in Madhya Pradesh, India
Khowar, India
Kisan in Bihar, India
Kishanganjia in Bihar, India
Kishtwari in Jammu, India
**Koch, Bangladesh
Koda in Bihar, India
**Kohli, Wadiara, Pakistan
Kol in Assam, India
**Kolam, India
Kom in Manipur, India
Konda-Dora (Andra Pradesh), India
Konkani in Gujarat, India
Koraga in Kerala, India
Korwa in Bihar, India
Kota in Tamil Nadu, India
Kotia in Andhra Pradesh, India
Koya in Andhra Pradesh, India
Kudiya, India
*Kuknas, India
Kumauni in Assam, India
Kupia in Andhra Pradesh, India
Kuruba in Tamil Nadu, India
Kurux in Bihar, India
Kuvi in Orissa, India
Lodhi in Bihar, India
Lushai in Assam, India
**Magar, Nepal
Mahali in Assam, India
Maithili, Nepal
Majhwar in Madhya Pradesh, India
Malakkaras of Kerala, India (81)
Malankuravan in Kerala, India
Malapandaram in Kerala, India
Malaryan in Kerala, India
Mali in Andhra Pradesh, India
Malki in Bihar, India
Malpaharia in Assam, India
Malvi in Madhya Pradesh, India

Manna-Dora in A.P., India
Mannan in Kerala, India
Mara in Assam, India
Maria in Andhra Pradesh, India
Marwari in Gujarat, India
**Mawchis, India
**Miching, India
Mina in Madhya Pradesh, India
Mirdha in Orissa, India
Mishmi in Assam, India
Multani in Punjab, India
Mundari in Assam, India
Muria in Andhra Pradesh, India
Muthuvan (Andra Pradesh), India
Muwasi in Madhya Pradesh, India
Naga, Kalyokengnyu, India
Nagar in Madhya Pradesh, India
Nihali in Madhya Pradesh, India
Ojhi in Madhya Pradesh, India
Ollari in Orissa, India
Ong in Andamans, India
Pahari Garhwali (Uttar Pradesh,
  India
Paite in Assam, India
Panika, India
Panika, India
Pardhan in Andhra Pradesh, India
Parengi in Orissa, India
Patelia in Gujarat, India
Pengo in Orissa, India
Pnar in Assam, India
Rabha in Assam, India
*Rai, Danuwar, Nepal
Rajbansi, Nepal
Sadan in Andamans, India
Sondwari in M.P., India
Takankar, India
Tengger, Indonesia
Thakur, India
Thar in Bihar, India
Tharu, India
Toda in Tamil Nadu, India
Tokkaru in Tamil Nadu, India
Tugara, India
Ullatan in Kerala, India
Urali in Kerala, India
Vishavan in Kerala, India
Waddar in Andhra Pradesh, India
Wagdi in Rajasthan, India
Yanadi in Andhra Pradesh, India
Yerava in Karnataka, India
Yerukala in A.P., India
Zangskari in Kashmir, India

Hindu—Buddhist

Awadhi, Nepal
Kanauri in Uttar Pradesh, India
Khamti in Assam, India
Labans, India
Labhani in Andhra Pradesh, India
Ladakhi in Jammu, India

REGISTRY OF THE UNREACHED

Lalung in Assam, India
**Lepcha, India
Naga, Mao, India
Naga, Nruanghmei, India
Naga, Sangtam, India
Naga, Tangkhul, India
Naga, Wancho, India
*Newari, Nepal
Nimadi in Madhya Pradesh, India
Pao in Madhya Pradesh, India
Rai, Nepal
Riang in Assam, India
Sikkimese, India
Sulung, India
*Tamang, Nepal
Tamaria in Bihar, India
Thado in Assam, India
Vaiphei in Assam, India
Zome in Manipur, India

**Nepalese in India, India
Od, Pakistan
*Rava in Assam, India
**Saiva Vellala, India
*Shourastra in Tamil Nadu, India
*Sindhis of India, India
Sochi, Pakistan
Sora in Orissa, India
Tamil (Ceylonese), Sri Lanka
**Tamil Laborers in Bombay, India
  (82)
***Tamil Plantation Workers, Malaysia
*Tamil in Yellagiri Hills, India
*Tamils (Indian), Malaysia
**Tamils (Indian), Sri Lanka (79)
Tharu, Nepal
Totis, India
Vagari, Pakistan
West Indian Migrant Workers,
  Canada:Ontario

Hinduism

Adiyan in Kerala, India
Agariya in Bihar, India
Anga in Bihar, India
Arya in Andhra Pradesh, India
Babri, India
Bagri, Pakistan
Bajania, Pakistan (79)
Balmiki, Pakistan
Bareli in Madhya Pradesh, India
Bathudi in Bihar, India
**Bhil, Pakistan
*Bhojpuri, Nepal
Bondo in Orissa, India
*Gorkha, India
Gujarati, United Kingdom
Gurung, Nepal
*Indians In Rhodesia, Zimbabwe
Indians in Dubai, United Arab
  Emirates (82)
Indians in Fiji, Fiji (79)
**Indians, East, Trinidad and Tobago
  (79)
Iravas in Kerala, India
***Irulas in Kerala, India
Jharia in Orissa, India
Juang in Orissa, India
Kachchi in Andhra Pradesh, India
Khasi in Assam, India
**Kohli, Kutchi, Pakistan
**Kohli, Parkari, Pakistan
**Kohli, Tharadari, Pakistan
*Kudisai Vagh Makkal, India
**Kuluis in Himachal Pradesh, India
  (81)
*Labourers of Jhoparpatti, India
Malavedan in Kerala, India
Mangs in Maharashtra, India
***Matharis, India
**Meghwar, Pakistan (79)
*Meitei, India (79)

Islam

Abazin, USSR
Abialang, Sudan
Abkhaz, Turkey
Abong, Nigeria
Abu Leila, Sudan
Achehnese, Indonesia (80)
Acheron, Sudan
Achipa, Nigeria
Adygei, USSR
**Afghan Refugees (NWFP), Pakistan
Afitti, Sudan
**African Students in Cairo, Egypt
Afshars, Iran
Agajanis, Iran
Agul, USSR
Ahir in Maharashtra, India
**Ahl-i-Haqq in Iran, Iran (79)
Ahmadis in Lahore, Pakistan (82)
Aja, Sudan
Alaba, Ethiopia
*Alawites, Syria (79)
*Albanian Muslims, Albania (80)
*Albanians in Yugoslavia,
  Yugoslavia
Algerian Arabs in France, France
*Anatolian Turks-Istanbul, Turkey
  (82)
Ansar Sudanese Refugees, Ethiopia
  (83)
Ara, Indonesia
Arab Immigrants in Bangui, Central
  African Republic (82)
Arab-Jabbari (Kamesh), Iran
Arab-Shaibani (Kamesh), Iran
**Arabs in New Orleans, United
  States of America (82)
Arabs of Khuzestan, Iran
Arawa, Nigeria
*Asian Students, Philippines

Index by Religion

Aten, Nigeria
Atoc, Sudan
Atuot, Sudan
Avukaya, Sudan
Awngi, Ethiopia
Ayu, Nigeria
Azerbaijani Turks, Iran (80)
**Azerbaijani, Afghanistan
Bachama, Nigeria
Bade, Nigeria
Badjao, Philippines
Badyara, Guinea-Bissau
Baharlu (Kamesh), Iran
Bai, Sudan
Bajau, Indonesian, Indonesia
Bakhtiaris, Iran (80)
Balkars, USSR
**Balti, Pakistan
Baluchi, Iran (80)
Bambara, Mali
Bambuka, Nigeria
Bandawa-Minda, Nigeria
Banga, Nigeria
Banggai, Indonesia
Barambu, Sudan
Bari, Sudan
Bashgali, Afghanistan
Bashkir, USSR (80)
*Batak, Angkola, Indonesia (80)
Batu, Nigeria
Baushi, Nigeria
Bawm, Bangladesh
Bayats, Iran
Beja, Ethiopia
Beja, Sudan
Bengali Refugees, Assam, India
**Bengali Sufis, Bangladesh (84)
**Bengali, Los Angeles area, United
  States of America (84)
Bengalis in London, United Kingdom
  (82)
Bengkulu, Indonesia
Bhatneri, India
**Bijogo, Guinea-Bissau
Bilen, Ethiopia
Bimanese, Indonesia
Binawa, Nigeria
Binga, Sudan
Bingkokak, Indonesia
Biti, Sudan
Bole, Nigeria
Bondei, Tanzania
Bongo, Sudan
Bor Gok, Sudan
*Bosnian, Yugoslavia (80)
Bovir-Ahmadi, Iran
Brahui, Pakistan
Bual, Indonesia
Buduma, Nigeria
Burak, Nigeria
Burmese Muslim Refugees,
  Bangladesh (83)
Burun, Sudan
Busa, Nigeria (80)
Butawa, Nigeria
Bviri, Sudan

Cape Malays in Cape Town, South
  Africa (82)
Chad's Refugees from N'Djamena,
  Cameroon (83)
Chadian Refugees, Nigeria (83)
Chaghatai, Afghanistan
*Cham Refugees from Kampuchea,
  Kampuchea, Democratic (83)
Cherkess, USSR
Chinese Muslims, Taiwan (81)
Chinese in Saudi Arabia, Saudi
  Arabia
Chitralis, Pakistan (79)
Circassian, Turkey
Circassians in Amman, Jordan (82)
Dadiya, Nigeria
Dair, Sudan
Daju of West Kordofan, Sudan
Dargin, USSR
Dawoodi Muslims, India
Daza, Chad
Deccani Muslims, India
Deccani Muslims-Hyderabad, India
  (82)
Dendi, Benin
Deno, Nigeria
Dera, Nigeria
*Dewein, Liberia
Digo, Kenya (84)
Dinka, Agar, Sudan
Diola, Guinea-Bissau (80)
Dirya, Nigeria
Divehi, Maldives (80)
Dongjoi, Sudan
Dongo, Sudan
Duguir, Nigeria
Duguza, Nigeria
Dungan, USSR
Dyerma, Nigeria
**Eritrean Refugees, Djibouti (83)
Eritrean Refugees, Sudan (83)
**Ethiopian Refugees, Somalia (83)
Fali, Cameroon
Feroge, Sudan
Fula, Guinea
Fula, Sierra Leone
Fulah, Upper Volta
Fungor, Sudan
Galambi, Nigeria
Galeshis, Iran
Galla, Harar, Ethiopia
Gawar-Bati, Afghanistan
Gbaya, Nigeria
Gbaya-Ndogo, Sudan
Gbazantche, Benin
Gberi, Sudan
Geji, Nigeria
Gera, Nigeria
Geruma, Nigeria
Ghol, Sudan
Ghulfan, Sudan
Gilakis, Iran
Gonja, Ghana
Gorontalo, Indonesia
Goudari, Iran
Guinean Refugees, Gabon

507

REGISTRY OF THE UNREACHED

Gujuri, Afghanistan
Gumuz, Sudan
Gure-Kahugu, Nigeria
Guruntum-Mbaaru, Nigeria
Gwari Matai, Nigeria
Gypsies in Jerusalem, Israel (82)
Gypsies in Yugoslavia, Yugoslavia
**Hadrami, Yemen, Democratic
Harari, Ethiopia
**Hazara in Kabul, Afghanistan (82)
Heiban, Sudan
Hezareh, Iran
Hui, China (80)
**Hunzakut, Pakistan (79)
Hwana, Nigeria
Hyam, Nigeria
Ikulu, Nigeria
Ilanon, Philippines
Inallu, Iran
Ingushes, USSR
Iranians, Montreal, Canada:Quebec
Iraqi Kurd Refugees, Iran (83)
Jamshidis, Iran
Jara, Nigeria
Jati, Afghanistan
**Javanese of Pejompongan, Indonesia
Jera, Nigeria
Jimbin, Nigeria
**Jimini, Ivory Coast
Kabyle, Algeria (79)
Kadugli, Sudan
Kagoma, Nigeria
Kaibu, Nigeria
Kaka, Nigeria
Kamo, Nigeria
Kanga, Sudan
Kanuri, Nigeria (80)
Karakalpak, USSR (80)
Karekare, Nigeria
Kariya, Nigeria
Karko, Sudan
**Kashmiri Muslims, India (79)
Katab, Nigeria
Katcha, Sudan
Katla, Sudan
Kazakhs, Iran (80)
Keiga Jirru, Sudan
Keiga, Sudan
Khalaj, Iran
Khasonke, Mali
Khojas, Agha Khani, India
Kilba, Nigeria
Kirghiz Afghan Refugees, Turkey
  (83)
Kirgiz, Afghanistan
Kirgiz, China
Kirifi, Nigeria
Kita, Mali
Koma, Central, Sudan
Kono, Nigeria
Kotokoli, Benin
Kuda-Chamo, Nigeria
Kunama, Ethiopia
Kurds in Iran, Iran (80)
Kurds in Kuwait, Kuwait
*Kurds of Turkey, Turkey (79)

Kushi, Nigeria
Kuteb, Nigeria
Kuturmi, Nigeria
Kuzamani, Nigeria
Kwa, Nigeria
Kyibaku, Nigeria
Laamang, Nigeria
Labbai, India
Lafofa, Sudan
Lakians, USSR
Lakka, Nigeria
Lame, Nigeria
Laro, Sudan
Laru, Nigeria
Lebanese, Beamington,
  Canada:Ontario
Lebong, Indonesia
Ligbi, Ghana
Ligbi, Ivory Coast
Longuda, Nigeria
Lori, Sudan
Lors, Iran (80)
Lotsu-Piri, Nigeria
Luac, Sudan
Lubu, Indonesia
Luwu, Indonesia
Lwo, Sudan
Maba, Sudan
Maban-Jumjum, Sudan
Madi, Sudan
Maguindanao, Philippines (80)
*Mahrah, Yemen, Democratic
Makonde, Tanzania
Malays of Singapore, Singapore
  (79)
Mamasani, Iran
Mandar, Indonesia
Mandara, Nigeria
Mandingo, Liberia (79)
Manggarai Muslims, Indonesia (81)
Mappillas, India
Maranao, Philippines (79)
Marghi Central, Nigeria
Marka, Upper Volta
Masakin, Sudan
Masalit, Sudan
Masenrempulu, Indonesia
Matakam, Nigeria
Matumbi, Tanzania
Maures, Senegal
Mazandaranis, Iran
Mboi, Nigeria
Mbula-Bwazza, Nigeria
Meos of Rajasthan, India (80)
Midob, Sudan
Minangkabau, Indonesia (80)
Miri, Sudan
Mober, Nigeria
Modo, Sudan
Mogholi, Afghanistan
Montol, Nigeria
Moor & Malays, Sri Lanka (79)
Moors in Mauritania, Mauritania
Moqaddam, Iran
Moreb, Sudan
Mori, Indonesia (81)

Moru, Sudan
Mumbake, Nigeria
Munji-Yidgha, Afghanistan
Muslim Community of Bawku, Ghana
Muslim Gypsies in Skoplje,
  Yugoslavia (82)
**Muslim Immigrants in U.K., United
  Kingdom
Muslim Lebanese Refugees, Canada
  (83)
Muslim Malays, Malaysia (80)
Muslims (West Nile Dist.), Uganda
Muslims of Jordan, Jordan
Muslims, United Arab Emirates (79)
Nafar, Iran
Naka, Sudan
Nandu-Tari, Nigeria
Nginyukwur, Sudan
Ngirere, Sudan
Ngizim, Nigeria
Ngok, Sudan
Ngunduna, Sudan
Nguqwurang, Sudan
Ngwoi, Nigeria
Ninzam, Nigeria
Njalgulgule, Sudan
North Africans in Belgium, Belgium
  (80)
Numana-Nunku-Gwantu, Nigeria
**Nupe, Nigeria
Nuristani, Afghanistan (80)
Nyamusa, Sudan
Nyarueng, Sudan
Nzanyi, Nigeria
Otoro, Sudan
Ouaddai, Chad
Palembang, Indonesia
Palestinian Refugees, Jordan (83)
Palestinian Refugees, Lebanon (83)
Paloc, Sudan
Pankhu, Bangladesh
Pashtuns, Iran (80)
Pero, Nigeria
Persians of Iran, Iran (80)
Pishagchi, Iran
Piti, Nigeria
Piya, Nigeria
Polci, Nigeria
Pongu, Nigeria
Poouch in Kashmir, India
***Prasuni, Afghanistan
Puku-Geeri-Keri-Wipsi, Nigeria
Purig-Pa of Kashmir, India (81)
Qajars, Iran
Qara'i, Iran
Qaragozlu, Iran
Qashqa'i, Iran (80)
Rajasthani Muslims-Jaipur, India
  (82)
Redjang, Indonesia (80)
Roba, Nigeria
Rukuba, Nigeria
Rumaya, Nigeria
Rural Refugees from Eritrea, Sudan
  (83)
Ruruma, Nigeria

Rut, Sudan
Rutul, USSR
**Saguye, Kenya
Sama Pangutaran, Philippines (80)
Sanga, Nigeria
Sangil, Philippines
Sarakole, Senegal (80)
Sasanis, Iran
Sau, Afghanistan
Saya, Nigeria
Sayyids, Yemen, Arab Republic
Sere, Sudan
Shahsavans, Iran (80)
Shatt, Sudan
Shawiya, Algeria
**Shihu, United Arab Emirates
Shilluk, Sudan
Shughni, Afghanistan
Shuwa Arabic, Nigeria
Shwai, Sudan
Siri, Nigeria
Solorese Muslims, Indonesia (81)
Somali, Ajuran, Kenya (79)
Somali, Degodia, Kenya
Somali, Ethiopia
Somali, Gurreh, Kenya
Somali, Ogadenya, Kenya
Soninke, Gambia
Soninke, Mali
Soninke, Mauritania
Sopi, Sudan
Sukur, Nigeria
Sumbawa, Indonesia
Sura, Nigeria
Surubu, Nigeria
Susu, Guinea
Swatis, Pakistan (79)
Sylhetti, United Kingdom
Tabasaran, USSR
Tajik, Afghanistan
Tajik, Iran (80)
Tajik, USSR
Takestani, Iran
Tal, Nigeria
Talish, Iran
Talodi, Sudan
Tamil Muslims in Madras, India
  (82)
Tangale, Nigeria
Tangchangya, Bangladesh
Tat, USSR
Tatars, USSR (80)
Taucouleur, Senegal (80)
Tausug, Philippines (80)
Teda, Chad (80)
Teda, Libya
Tegali, Sudan
Teimuri, Iran
Teimurtash, Iran
Tem, Togo
Temein, Sudan
Tera, Nigeria
Ternatans, Indonesia
*Tertiary Level Youth, Iran
Thoi, Sudan
Thuri, Sudan

REGISTRY OF THE UNREACHED

Tippera, Bangladesh
Tira, Sudan
Tirma, Sudan
*Toussian, Upper Volta
Tsakhur, USSR
Tuareg, Niger (79)
Tula, Nigeria
Tulishi, Sudan
Tumale, Sudan
Tumma, Sudan
Tumtum, Sudan
Turkish Immigrant Workers, German
 Federal Rep. (79)
Turkish Workers, Belgium (80)
Turkomans, Iran (80)
Turks in Basel, Switzerland (82)
Turks, Anatolian, Turkey
Turkwam, Nigeria
Twi, Sudan
USSR Kirghiz Refugee Shepherds,
 Pakistan (83)
Ugandan Asian Refugees, Tor.,
 Canada:Ontario
Ugandan Asian Refugees,
 Canada:British Columbia (83)
Ugandan Refugees, United Kingdom
 (83)
Uiguir, Afghanistan
Uiguir, China (80)
Umm Dorein, Sudan
Umm Gabralla, Sudan
*Vai, Liberia (80)
**Vohras of Yavatmal, India
Waja, Nigeria
Wala, Ghana
Weda, Indonesia
Western Sahara Refugees, Algeria
 (83)
*White Moors, Mauritania
Winji-Winji, Benin
Woro, Sudan
Yao, Mozambique
Yemenis, Yemen, Arab Republic (79)
Yeskwa, Nigeria
Yoruk, Turkey
Yulu, Sudan
Yungur, Nigeria
Zaghawa, Libya
Zaghawa, Sudan
Zari, Nigeria
Zenaga, Mauritania

Islam-Animist

Abe, Ivory Coast
Abidji, Ivory Coast
Abou Charib, Chad
Abure, Ivory Coast
Achode, Ghana
Adele, Togo
Adyukru, Ivory Coast
Afar, Ethiopia (79)

Agutaynon, Philippines
Ahlo, Togo
Akan, Brong, Ivory Coast
***Akhdam, Yemen, Arab Republic
Akpafu, Ghana
Aladian, Ivory Coast
Alas, Indonesia
Ana, Togo
Animere, Togo
Anyanga, Togo
Attie, Ivory Coast
Avatime, Ghana
Avikam, Ivory Coast
Awutu, Ghana
Ayana, Kenya
Bagirmi, Chad
Bajau, Land, Malaysia
Bakwe, Ivory Coast
Balantak, Indonesia
Bali, Nigeria
Bambara, Ivory Coast
Banyum, Senegal
Bariba, Nigeria
Basila, Togo
Bata, Nigeria
Bayot, Gambia
Bayot, Guinea-Bissau
Bayot, Senegal
Bilala, Chad
Bile, Nigeria
Bimoba, Ghana
Bimoba, Togo
Bira, Indonesia
Birifor, Upper Volta
Bitare, Nigeria
Bolon, Upper Volta
Bomou, Chad
Boni of Lamu, Kenya (84)
Boran, Ethiopia
**Boran, Kenya
Bousansi, Upper Volta
Bowili, Togo
Bugis, Indonesia (80)
Buli, Indonesia
Buli, Upper Volta
Bullom, Northern, Sierra Leone
Bullom, Southern, Sierra Leone
Butung, Indonesia
Chala, Ghana
Chamba Daka, Nigeria
Chamba Leko, Nigeria
Cirebon, Indonesia
Dagari, Upper Volta
**Dagomba, Ghana
Daju of Dar Dadju, Chad
Daju of Dar Sila, Chad
Dan, Liberia
Dangaleat, Chad
Dass, Nigeria
Diola, Senegal
Dirim, Nigeria
Doghosie, Upper Volta
Dyan, Upper Volta
Dyerma, Niger (80)
Dyola, Gambia
Ebira, Nigeria

Ebrie, Ivory Coast
Eotile, Ivory Coast
Fula, Cunda, Gambia
Fula, Upper Volta
*Fulani, Benin
Fulani, Cameroon (79)
*Fulbe, Ghana
Gabri, Chad
*Galla (Bale), Ethiopia
Gambai, Chad
Gan, Upper Volta
Gangam, Togo
Gayo, Indonesia (80)
Gidar, Chad
Gola, Liberia
Gola, Sierra Leone
Golo, Chad
Gosha, Kenya
Gouin-Turka, Upper Volta
Goulai, Chad
Guere, Ivory Coast
Gujars of Kashmir, India (81)
Gula, Chad
Gurage, Ethiopia (80)
Gurma, Upper Volta
Gwa, Ivory Coast
Hwela-Numu, Ivory Coast
Icen, Nigeria
Igbira, Nigeria (80)
Jama Mapun, Philippines (80)
Jambi, Indonesia
Jongor, Chad
Kanembu, Chad
Kanembu, Niger
Karachay, USSR
Karanga, Chad
Kari, Chad
Kasanga, Guinea-Bissau
Kasele, Togo
Kasem, Upper Volta
**Kaur, Indonesia
Kazakhs, China (81)
Kebu, Togo
Kendari, Indonesia
Kenga, Chad
Kera, Chad
Kerinchi, Indonesia
Kibet, Chad
Kim, Chad
Kirgiz, USSR (80)
Klaoh, Liberia
Kobiana, Guinea
Koke, Chad
Kolbila, Cameroon
Komering, Indonesia
Komono, Upper Volta
Konyagi, Guinea
**Koranko, Sierra Leone
Kotoko, Chad
Kotokoli, Togo
Kouya, Ivory Coast
Kpelle, Guinea
Kposo, Togo
Krachi, Ghana
Krim, Sierra Leone
Krio, Gambia

Krobou, Ivory Coast
Kubu, Indonesia (81)
Kuka, Chad
Kulele, Ivory Coast
Kullo, Ethiopia
Kulung, Nigeria
Kunante, Guinea-Bissau
Kurumba, Upper Volta
Kuwaa, Liberia
Laka, Chad
Lampung, Indonesia (80)
Landoma, Guinea
Landoma, Guinea-Bissau
Lelemi, Ghana
Liguri, Sudan
Logba, Ghana
Loko, Guinea
Maba, Chad
Majingai-Ngama, Chad
Mamprusi, Ghana
Manding, Senegal
Mandyak, Gambia
Mangbai, Chad
Maninka, Guinea-Bissau
Maninka, Sierra Leone
Manjack, Senegal
Mankanya, Guinea-Bissau
Mankanya, Senegal
Maou, Ivory Coast
Maranao, Lanad, Philippines
Mararit, Chad
Marba, Chad
Masalit, Chad
Massalat, Chad
Maure, Mali
Mbai, Chad
Mbum, Chad
Mende, Liberia
Mesengo, Ethiopia
Mesme, Chad
Mesmedje, Chad
Mimi, Chad
Mo, Ivory Coast
Mogum, Chad
*Molbog, Philippines
Mona, Ivory Coast
Moru, Ivory Coast
Mubi, Chad
Muna, Indonesia
Mundang, Chad
Musei, Chad
Musgu, Chad
Musi, Indonesia
Nalu, Guinea
Nancere, Chad
Naoudem, Togo
Nara, Ethiopia
Natemba, Togo
Natioro, Upper Volta
Nchumbulu, Ghana
Nchumunu, Ghana
Ndunpa Duupa, Cameroon
Nielim, Chad
Nkonya, Ghana
Ntrubo, Togo
Nunuma, Upper Volta

REGISTRY OF THE UNREACHED

Nyangbo, Ghana
Nzema, Ghana
Nzema, Ivory Coast
Ogan, Indonesia
Oubi, Ivory Coast
Palara, Ivory Coast
Papel, Guinea-Bissau
Pashayi, Afghanistan
Prang, Ghana
Puguli, Upper Volta
Pye, Ivory Coast
Rataning, Chad
Rendille, Kenya
Runga, Chad
Safaliba, Ghana
Sakuye, Kenya
Sama Bangingi, Philippines (80)
Sama, Siasi, Philippines
Sama, Sibuku, Philippines
Sama-Badjaw, Philippines (79)
Samo, Northern, Upper Volta
Samo, Southern, Upper Volta
Santrokofi, Ghana
Sarwa, Chad
Sasak, Indonesia (80)
Sekayu, Indonesia
Sekpele, Ghana
**Serawai, Indonesia (81)
Serere-Non, Senegal
Serere-Sine, Senegal
Shilha, Morocco
Shina, Afghanistan
**Shluh Berbers, Morocco
Sidamo, Ethiopia
Sindhi Muslims in Karachi,
   Pakistan (82)
Sisala, Upper Volta
Siwu, Ghana
Somrai, Chad
Songhai, Niger
Songhai, Upper Volta
Subanun,Lapuyan, Philippines
**Sundanese, Indonesia (84)
Sungor, Chad
Susu, Guinea-Bissau
Susu, Sierra Leone
Tafi, Togo
Tagwana, Ivory Coast
*Talo, Indonesia
Tama, Chad
Tamazight, Morocco
Tana, Chad
Teda, Niger
Tepo, Ivory Coast
Thai Islam (Malay), Thailand (80)
*Thai Islam (Thai), Thailand
Tidorese, Indonesia
Tiefo, Upper Volta
Trepo, Ivory Coast
Tunya, Chad
Tupuri, Chad
Tura, Ivory Coast
**Uzbeks, Afghanistan (79)
Vagla, Ghana
Vai, Sierra Leone
Vige, Upper Volta

Voko, Cameroon
Wara, Upper Volta
Water Surface People, Hong Kong
   (84)
Win, Upper Volta
Wolio, Indonesia
Wolof, Gambian, Gambia
Wolof, Senegal (80)
Wom, Nigeria
Yakan, Philippines (80)
*Yalunka, Sierra Leone (80)
Yandang, Nigeria
Yanga, Togo
**Yao, Malawi (84)
Zaghawa, Chad
Zaramo, Tanzania

Jain

Jains, India

Judaism

**Falasha, Ethiopia (79)
*Jewish Imgrnts.-American, Israel
*Jewish Imgrnts.-Argentine, Israel
*Jewish Imgrnts.-Australia, Israel
*Jewish Imgrnts.-Brazilian, Israel
*Jewish Imgrnts.-Mexican, Israel
*Jewish Imgrnts.-Uruguayan, Israel
*Jewish Immigrants, Other, Israel
Jews (Non-Sephardic), Montreal,
   Canada:Quebec (79)
Jews (Sephardic), Montreal,
   Canada:Quebec
Jews in Venice, Italy (82)
Jews of Iran, Iran
Jews, Toronto, Canada:Ontario
Jews, Vancouver, Canada:British
   Columbia
Jews, Winnipeg, Canada:Manitoba
Ladinos, Lebanon
Moroccan Jews, Canada:Quebec
Targum, Israel

New Eastern

Rajneeshees of Oregon, United
   States of America

512

Nominal Christian

Baguio Area Miners, Philippines (81)
**Batangeno, Philippines
Bawoyo, Zaire
***Bolinao, Philippines
*Casiguranin, Philippines
*Cherkess, Jordan (84)
**Chicanos in Denver, United States of America (82)
Chilean Refugees, Argentina (83)
*Chilean Refugees, Toronto, Canada:Ontario (83)
***Copacabana Apt. Dwellers, Brazil
*Drug Addicts in Sao Paulo, Brazil (82)
Equatorial Guin. Refugees, Gabon (83)
**Filipino Migrant Workers, Saudi Arabia (84)
French, St. Pierre & Miquelon , Canada:Newfoundland
Gaanda, Nigeria
Greeks, Toronto, Canada:Ontario
Gypsies, Brazil
Hmong, Twin Cities, United States of America
**Hotel Workers in Manila, Philippines (81)
Indians, CN Rail Lines, Canada:Ontario
Indians, Cold Lake Reserve, Canada:Alberta
Indians, Eden Valley, Canada:Alberta
Indians, Interlake Region, Canada:Manitoba
Indians, London, Canada:Ontario
Indians, Lower Mainland, Canada:British Columbia
Indians, Northern Sask., Canada:Saskatchewan
Indians, Northwestern Ontario , Canada:Ontario
Indians, Regina, Canada:Saskatchewan
Indians, Saskatoon, Canada:Saskatchewan
Indians, Thunder Bay, Canada:Ontario
Indians, Vancouver, Canada:British Columbia
Indians, White Bear Reserve, Canada:Saskatchewan
**Indians, Winnipeg, Canada:Manitoba
**Ishans, Nigeria
*Jeepney Drivers in Manila, Philippines (81)
**Kalinga, Tanudan, Philippines
Kurichiya in Kerala, India (81)

Luxemburgois, Luxembourg
*Maltese, Malta
***Micmac Indians, Canada:New Brunswick
***Micmac Indians, Eskasoni Rsv. , Canada:Nova Scotia
**Middle Class-Mexico City, Mexico (82)
*Military Officers, Ecuador (84)
*Military Personnel, Ecuador
**Montagnais Indians, Canada:Quebec
Nicaraguan Refugees, Costa Rica
Portuguese, Cambridge, Canada:Ontario
Portuguese, London/Strathroy, Canada:Ontario
Portuguese, Metro Toronto, Canada:Ontario
Portuguese, Vancouver, Canada:British Columbia
Portuguese, West Lorne Village, Canada:Ontario
Salvadoran Refugees, Honduras
Salvadoran Refugees, Belize
***Sanga, Zaire (84)
South African Refugee Students, Lesotho (83)
**Ukrainians, Toronto, Canada:Ontario
*Universitarios - Rosario, Argentina (82)
**Urban Mestizos, Ecuador
Vietnamese Fishermen, Biloxi, United States of America
***West Indians, Toronto, Canada:Ontario
Yami of Orchid Island, Indonesia (84)

Peyote Religion

Paiute, Northern, United States of America

Secularism

Aborigines in Brisbane, Australia (82)
*Americans in Geneva, Switzerland
Amsterdam Boat Dwellers, Netherlands
**Bachelors in Lagos, Nigeria (82)
**Bus Girls in Seoul, Korea, Republic of (82)
*Casual Laborers-Atlanta, United States of America (82)
**Chinese Stud., Australia, Australia

REGISTRY OF THE UNREACHED

Chinese Students, Thunder Bay ,
 Canada:Ontario
**Chinese in Boston, United States
 of America (82)
Chinese in Costa Rica, Costa Rica
*Chinese in Korea, Korea, Republic
 of
*Chinese in West Germany, German
 Federal Rep.
*Coloureds in Eersterust, South
 Africa (82)
*Danchi Dwellers in Tokyo, Japan
 (82)
Dead-End Kids - Amsterdam,
 Netherlands (82)
*Dentists, Fukuoka, Japan
*English speakers, Guadalajara ,
 Mexico (84)
**Ex-Mental Patients in NYC, United
 States of America (82)
Ex-Mental Patients, Hamilton,
 Canada:Ontario
*Expatriates in Riyadh, Saudi
 Arabia (82)
Fur Trappers, Canada:Ontario
Gays in San Francisco, United
 States of America (82)
Geishas in Osaka, Japan (82)
Homosexuals, Toronto,
 Canada:Ontario
*Industrial Workers, Taiwan (81)
**Jamaican Elite, Jamaica
**Japanese Students In USA, United
 States of America
***Jewish Refugees from USSR, Israel
 (83)
Koreans in Manchuria, China (81)
**Marielito Refugees in Florida
 United States of America (83)
Nurses in St. Louis, United States
 of America (82)
Oil Executives, Calgary,
 Canada:Alberta
*Parsees, India (81)
Pension Students-Madrid, Spain
 (82)
**Portuguese in France, France
**Prisoners, Korea, Republic of
**Pro Hockey Players, United States
 of America (82)
**Racetrack Residents, United States
 of America (79)
Seychellois, Seychelles
Shopping Bag Women, Toronto,
 Canada:Ontario
Street People, Thunder Bay,
 Canada:Ontario
Street People, Victoria,
 Canada:British Columbia
Students in Cuiaba, Brazil
*Students, German Federal Rep. (79)
**Suriguenos, Philippines
Taiwan-Chinese Un. Stud., Taiwan
Theater Arts Performers, Canada
*University Students, France (79)
**University Students, Chin, China

University Students, Edmonton ,
 Canada:Alberta
Urban Street Women/Los Angeles,
 United States of America (84)
Wandering Homeless, United States
 of America (84)
***Youth, Toronto Peanut District,
 Canada:Ontario

Sikhism

Indo-Canadians, Vancouver,
 Canada:British Columbia (84)
Sikhs, Toronto, Canada:Ontario

Traditional Chinese

Ach'ang, China
Atsi, China
Buriat, China
Burig, China
Ch'iang, China
Chin, China
Chinese Businessmen, Hong Kong
 (81)
Chinese Factory Workers, Hong Kong
Chinese Fishermen, Malaysia
**Chinese Hakka of Taiwan, Taiwan
 (79)
*Chinese Mainlanders, Taiwan
*Chinese Refugees in Macau, Macau
 (81)
**Chinese Refugees, France, France
 (79)
*Chinese Restaurant Wrkrs., France
**Chinese Students, United Kingdom
Chinese Villagers, Hong Kong
**Chinese in Australia, Australia
*Chinese in Austria, Austria
**Chinese in Brazil, Brazil
Chinese in Burma, Burma
**Chinese in Indonesia, Indonesia
*Chinese in Japan, Japan
*Chinese in Laos, Laos
*Chinese in Malaysia, Malaysia
*Chinese in New Zealand, New
 Zealand
**Chinese in Panama, Panama
Chinese in Puerto Rico, Puerto
 Rico
**Chinese in Sabah, Malaysia
**Chinese in Sarawak, Malaysia
*Chinese in South Africa, South
 Africa
*Chinese in Thailand, Thailand
**Chinese in United Kingdom, United
 Kingdom
**Chinese in United States, United
 States of America

*Chinese of W. Malaysia, Malaysia
Chinese, Calgary, Canada:Alberta
**Chinese, Vancouver, Canada:British
  Columbia
Chingp'o, China
Chungchia, China
Chwang, China
Dagur, China
Evenki, China
Fishing Village People, Taiwan
Hani, China
**High School Students, Hong Kong
Jyarung, China
Kalmytz, China
Kam, China
Kelao, China
Khalka, China
Kham, China
Lahul, China
Laka, China
Lati, China
Li, China
Manchu, China (81)
Mongour, China
Nahsi, China
Nanai, China
Nosu, China
Nung, China
Oirat, China
Oronchon, China
Paongan, China
Pu-I, China
Puru, China
Rawang, China
Refugee Doctors, Hong Kong
Salar, China
Santa, China
Sibo, China
Sui, China
Vietnamese Refugees, China (83)
Wa, China
*Women Laborers, Taiwan
Yellow Uiguir, China
Yuku, China

Traditional Japanese

*Inland Sea Island Peoples, Japan
*Japanese in Korea, Korea, Republic
  of
*Ryukyuan, Japan
**Univ. Students of Japan, Japan

Zoroastrianism

*Parsis in Bombay, India (82)

Other

**Lotuka, Sudan
Rastafarians, Edmonton,
  Canada:Alberta
*Yanyula, Australia

Unknown

Abkhaz, USSR
Akhavakh, USSR
Alutor, USSR
Andi, USSR
Archin, USSR
Bangangte, Cameroon
Basaa, Cameroon
Batsi, USSR
Botlikh, USSR
Budug, USSR
**Bus Drivers, South Korea, Korea,
  Republic of
Chamalin, USSR
*Chinese in Amsterdam, Netherlands
Chinese in Costa Rica, Costa Rica
*Chinese in Holland, Netherlands
Chukot, USSR
Didoi, USSR
Dolgans, USSR
*Factory Workers, Hong Kong
Gilyak, USSR
*Havasupai, United States of
  America
Itelmen, USSR
Izhor, USSR
Kapuchin, USSR
Karagas, USSR
Karaim, USSR
Karatin, USSR
Ket, USSR
Khakas, USSR
Khana, Nigeria
Khanti, USSR
Khinalug, USSR
Khvarshin, USSR
Kongo, Angola
***Koreans in Germany, German Federal
  Rep.
Koryak, USSR
Kryz, USSR
Kvanadin, USSR
Liv, USSR
Mansi, USSR
Mingat, USSR
Mulimba, Cameroon
Naga, Sema, India
Nanai, USSR
Ndogo, Sudan

REGISTRY OF THE UNREACHED

Nentsy, USSR
Nganasan, USSR
Nivkhi, USSR
Oroch, USSR
Orok, USSR
Saams, USSR
Selkup, USSR
Shor, USSR
Svan, USSR
Tindin, USSR
Tsaangi, Congo
Udegeis, USSR
Udin, USSR
Ulchi, USSR
Veps, USSR
Yagnobi, USSR
Yazgulyam, USSR
Yukagirs, USSR
Yurak, USSR

Not Reported

Bamum, Cameroon
Ethiopian Refugees, Yemen, Yemen,
  Arab Republic
Lunda, Ndembu, Zambia

Index by Language

Groups are listed according to their primary vernacular language. In many cases, groups are bilingual or trilingual, speaking several languages including a more commonly known trade language.

REGISTRY OF THE UNREACHED

Abaknon	Abaknon, Philippines
Abanyom	Abanyom, Nigeria
Abau	Abau, Indonesia
	Abau, Papua New Guinea
Abazin	Abazin, USSR
Abe	Abe, Ivory Coast
Abialang	Abialang, Sudan
Abie	Abie, Papua New Guinea
Abkhaz	Abkhaz, Turkey
	Abkhaz, USSR
Abong	Abong, Nigeria
Abou Charib	Abou Charib, Chad
Abu Leila	Abu Leila, Sudan
Abua	Abua, Nigeria
Abujmaria	Abujmaria (Madhya Pradesh), India
Abulas	Abulas, Papua New Guinea
Abure	Abure, Ivory Coast
Ach'ang	Ach'ang, China
Achagua	Achagua, Colombia
Achehnese	Achehnese, Indonesia (80)
Acheron	Acheron, Sudan
Achi, Cubulco	Achi, Cubulco, Guatemala
Achi, Rabinal	Achi, Rabinal, Guatemala
Achipa	Achipa, Nigeria
Achode	Achode, Ghana
Acholi	Acholi, Uganda
Achual	Achual, Peru
Adele	Adele, Togo
Adhola	Adhola, Uganda
Adi	***Adi, India
Adidji	Abidji, Ivory Coast
Adiyan	Adiyan in Kerala, India
Adjora	Adjora, Papua New Guinea
Adygei	Adygei, USSR
Adyukru	Adyukru, Ivory Coast
Aeka	Aeka, Papua New Guinea
Aeta	Aeta, Philippines
Afanci	*Afawa, Nigeria (80)
Afar	Afar, Ethiopia (79)
Afitti	Afitti, Sudan
Afrikaans	Cape Malays in Cape Town, South Africa (82)
	*Coloureds in Eersterust, South Africa (82)
Afshari	Afshars, Iran
	Inallu, Iran
Agajanis	Agajanis, Iran
Agarabi	Agarabi, Papua New Guinea
Agariya	Agariya in Bihar, India
Agau	**Falasha, Ethiopia (79)
Age	Age, Cameroon
Aghem	Aghem, Cameroon
Aghu	Aghu, Indonesia
Agob	Agob, Papua New Guinea
Agoi	Agoi, Nigeria
Aguacateco	Aguacateco, Guatemala
Aguaruna	Aguaruna, Peru
Agul	Agul, USSR
Agutaynon	Agutaynon, Philippines
Agwagwune	Agwagwune, Nigeria
Ahir	Ahir in Maharashtra, India
Ahlo	Ahlo, Togo
Aibondeni	Aibondeni, Indonesia
Aiku	Aiku, Papua New Guinea
Aikwakai	Aikwakai, Indonesia
Aimol	Aimol in Assam, India

Aiome — Aiome, Papua New Guinea
Aion — Aion, Papua New Guinea
Airo-Sumaghaghe — Airo-Sumaghaghe, Indonesia
Airoran — Airoran, Indonesia
Aja — Aja, Sudan
Ajmeri — Ajmeri in Rajasthan, India
Aka — Aka, India
Akan, Brong — Akan, Brong, Ivory Coast
Akawaio — Akawaio, Guyana
Ake — Ake, Nigeria
Akha — **Akha, Thailand (79)
Akhavakh — Akhavakh, USSR
Akpa-Yache — Akpa-Yache, Nigeria
Akpafu — Akpafu, Ghana
Akrukay — Akrukay, Papua New Guinea
Alaban — Alaba, Ethiopia
Aladian — Aladian, Ivory Coast
Alago — Alago, Nigeria
Alak — Alak, Laos
Alamblak — Alamblak, Papua New Guinea
Alangan — Alangan, Philippines
Alatil — Alatil, Papua New Guinea
Alauagat — Alauagat, Papua New Guinea
Albanian (Gheg) — *Albanians in Yugoslavia, Yugoslavia
Albanian Tosk — *Albanian Muslims, Albania (80)
Aledjo — *Nyantruku, Benin
Alege — Alege, Nigeria
Allar — *Alars, India
Alor, Kolana — Alor, Kolana, Indonesia (81)
Altaic — Ewenkis, China (81)
Alutor — Alutor, USSR
Ama — Ama, Papua New Guinea
Amahuaca — Amahuaca, Peru
Amaimon — Amaimon, Papua New Guinea
Amanab — Amanab, Indonesia
Amanab, Papua New Guinea
Amar — Amar, Ethiopia
Amarakaeri — Amarakaeri, Peru
Amasi — Amasi, Cameroon
Ambai — Ambai, Indonesia
Ambasi — Ambasi, Papua New Guinea
Amber — Amber, Indonesia
Amberbaken — Amberbaken, Indonesia
Ambo — Ambo, Zambia
Ambonese — Ambonese, Indonesia
Ambonese, Netherlands
Ami — *Ami, Taiwan (81)
Amo — Amo, Nigeria
Amoy — Fishing Village People, Taiwan
*Women Laborers, Taiwan
Ampale — **Ampeeli, Papua New Guinea
Amto — Amto, Papua New Guinea
Amuesha — Amuesha, Peru
Amuzgo, Guerrero — Amuzgo, Guerrero, Mexico
Amuzgo, Oaxaca — Amuzgo, Oaxaca, Mexico
Ana — Ana, Togo
Anaang — Anaang, Nigeria
Anal — Anal in Manipur, India
Andarum — Andarum, Papua New Guinea
Andha — Andha in Andhra Pradesh, India
Andi — Andi, USSR
Andoque — Andoque, Colombia
Anem — Anem, Papua New Guinea
Anga — Anga in Bihar, India
Angaataha — Angaataha, Papua New Guinea

REGISTRY OF THE UNREACHED

Angal Heneng, South	Angal Heneng, South, Papua New Guinea
Angal Heneng, West	Angal Heneng, West, Papua New Guinea
Angal, East	Angal, East, Papua New Guinea
Angas	Angas, Nigeria
Angaua	Angaua, Papua New Guinea
Anggor	Anggor, Papua New Guinea
Angoram	Angoram, Papua New Guinea
Animere	Animere, Togo
Ankave	Ankave, Papua New Guinea
Ankwai	Ankwe, Nigeria
Anor	Anor, Papua New Guinea
Ansus	Ansus, Indonesia
Anuak	Anuak, Ethiopia
	Anuak, Sudan
Anuki	Anuki, Papua New Guinea
Anyanga	Anyanga, Togo
Apalai	Apalai, Brazil
Apartani	**Apatani in Assam, India
Apinaye	Apinaye, Brazil
Apurina	Apurina, Brazil
Ara	Ara, Indonesia
Arabela	Arabela, Peru
Arabic	***Akhdam, Yemen, Arab Republic
	*Alawites, Syria (79)
	Algerian Arabs in France, France
	Ansar Sudanese Refugees, Ethiopia (83)
	Arab Immigrants in Bangui, Central African Republic (82)
	Arab-Jabbari (Kamesh), Iran
	Arab-Shaibani (Kamesh), Iran
	**Arabs in New Orleans, United States of America (82)
	Arabs of Khuzestan, Iran
	Chadian Refugees, Nigeria (83)
	Chinese in Saudi Arabia, Saudi Arabia
	Circassians in Amman, Jordan (82)
	Druzes, Israel (79)
	**Hadrami, Yemen, Democratic
	Masalit, Sudan
	Maures, Senegal
	Muslims of Jordan, Jordan
	Muslims, United Arab Emirates (79)
	North Africans in Belgium, Belgium (80)
	Palestinian Refugees, Jordan (83)
	Palestinian Refugees, Lebanon (83)
	Sayyids, Yemen, Arab Republic
	Western Sahara Refugees, Algeria (83)
Arabic (Eastern)	Yemenis, Yemen, Arab Republic (79)
Arabic (Hassani)	Moors in Mauritania, Mauritania
Arafundi	Arafundi, Papua New Guinea
Aranadan	Aranadan in Tamil Nadu, India
Aranatan	*Arnatas, India
Arandai	Arandai, Indonesia
Arapesh, Bumbita	Arapesh, Bumbita, Papua New Guinea
Arapesh, Mountain	Arapesh, Mountain, Papua New Guinea
Arapesh, Muhiang	Arapesh, Muhiang, Papua New Guinea
Arawak	Arawak, Guyana
Arawe	Arawe, Papua New Guinea
Arbore	Arbore, Ethiopia

Archin	Archin, USSR
Arecuna	Arecuna, Venezuela
Argobba	Argobba, Ethiopia
Arguni	Arguni, Indonesia
Arifama-Miniafia	Arifama-Miniafia, Papua New Guinea
Arigibi	Arigibi, Papua New Guinea
Arinua	Arinua, Papua New Guinea
Arop	Arop, Papua New Guinea
Aruop	Aruop, Papua New Guinea
Arusha	Arusha, Tanzania
Arya	Arya in Andhra Pradesh, India
Asaro	Asaro, Papua New Guinea
Asat	Asat, Papua New Guinea
Asienara	Asienara, Indonesia
Asmat	*Asmat, Indonesia (79)
Assumbo	Assumbo, Cameroon
Asu	Asu, Tanzania
Asuri	Asuri in Bihar, India
Asurini	Kuatinema, Brazil
Ata	Ata, Papua New Guinea
Aten	Aten, Nigeria
Ati	Ati, Philippines
Atoc	Atoc, Sudan
Atruahi	Atruahi, Brazil
Atsi	Atsi, China
Atta	*Atta, Philippines
Attie	Attie, Ivory Coast
Atuot	Atuot, Sudan
Atye	*Atye, Ivory Coast
Au	Au, Papua New Guinea
Au ei	Au ei, Botswana
Aunalei	Aunalei, Papua New Guinea
Auyana	Auyana, Papua New Guinea
Avatime	Avatime, Ghana
Avikam	Avikam, Ivory Coast
Avukaya	Avukaya, Sudan
Awa	Awa, Papua New Guinea
Awadhi	Awadhi, Nepal
Awar	Awar, Papua New Guinea
Awara	Awara, Papua New Guinea
Awin	Awin, Papua New Guinea
Awngi	Awngi, Ethiopia
Awutu	Awutu, Ghana
Awyi	Awyi, Indonesia
Awyu	Awyu, Indonesia
Ayana	Ayana, Kenya
Aymara	**Aymara, Bolivia
	*Mororata, Bolivia
Aymara, Carangas	Aymara, Carangas, Chile
Ayoreo	Ayoreo, Paraguay
Ayu	Ayu, Nigeria
Azera	Azera, Papua New Guinea
Azerbaijani	**Azerbaijani, Afghanistan
Azerbaijani (Shahsavani)	Shahsavans, Iran (80)
Azerbaijani Turkish	Azerbaijani Turks, Iran (80)
Baali	Baali, Zaire
Babajou	Babajou, Cameroon
Babri	Babri, India
Baburiwa	Baburiwa, Indonesia
Bachama	Bachama, Nigeria
Bada	Bada, Nigeria
Badagu	Badagu in Nilgiri, India
Bade	Bade, Nigeria
Badjao	Badjao, Philippines
Badui	Badui, Indonesia (84)
Badyara	Badyara, Guinea-Bissau

REGISTRY OF THE UNREACHED

Bafut	Bafut, Cameroon
Bagelkhandi	Bagelkhandi in M.P., India
Baghati	Baghati in H.P., India
Bagirmi	Bagirmi, Chad
Bagobo	***Bagobo, Philippines
Bagri	Bagri, Pakistan
Baham	Baham, Indonesia
Bahasa Jawa	**Javanese of Pejompongan, Indonesia
Bahasa Malaysia	Muslim Malays, Malaysia (80)
Bahawalpuri	Bahawalpuri in M.P., India
Bahinemo	Bahinemo, Papua New Guinea
Bai	Bai, Sudan
Baibai	Baibai, Papua New Guinea
Baiga	Baiga in Bihar, India
Baining	Baining, Papua New Guinea
Bajau, Indonesian	Bajau, Indonesian, Indonesia
Bajaus	Bajau, Land, Malaysia
Baka	Baka, Cameroon
	Baka, Zaire
Bakairi	Bakairi, Brazil
Bakhtiaris	Bakhtiaris, Iran (80)
Bakwe	Bakwe, Ivory Coast
Bakwele	Bakwele, Congo
Balangao	**Balangao, Philippines
Balangaw	Balangaw, Philippines
Balanta	Balanta Refugees, Senegal
	Balanta, Senegal
	Balante, Guinea-Bissau
Balantak	Balantak, Indonesia
Bali	Bali, Nigeria
Bali-Vitu	Bali-Vitu, Papua New Guinea
Balinese	Balinese, Indonesia
Balkar	Balkars, USSR
Balti	Balti in Jammu, India
	**Balti, Pakistan
Baluchi	Baluchi, Iran (80)
Bam	Bam, Papua New Guinea
Bambara	Bambara, Ivory Coast
	Bambara, Mali
Bambuka	Bambuka, Nigeria
Bamougoun-Bamenjou	Bamougoun-Bamenjou, Cameroon
Bamum	Bamum, Cameroon
Banaro	***Banaro, Papua New Guinea
Bandawa-Minda	Bandawa-Minda, Nigeria
Bandi	Bandi, Liberia
	Gbande, Guinea
Bandjoun	Bandjoun, Cameroon
Banen	Banen, Cameroon
Banga	Banga, Nigeria
Bangba	Bangba, Zaire
Banggai	Banggai, Indonesia
Bangri	Bangaru in Punjab, India
Baniwa	Baniwa, Brazil
Banoni	Banoni, Papua New Guinea
Bantu Dialects	Urban Refugees in Lusaka, Zambia (83)
Bantuanon	Bantuanon, Philippines
Banyum	Banyum, Senegal
Banyun	Banyun, Guinea-Bissau
Barai	Barai, Papua New Guinea
Barambu	Barambu, Sudan
Barasano	Barasano, Colombia
Barasano, Northern	Barasano, Northern, Colombia
Barau	Barau, Indonesia
Bare'e	Bare'e, Indonesia
Bareli	Bareli in Madhya Pradesh, India

Bari   Bari, Sudan
Bariai   Bariai, Papua New Guinea
Bariba   *Bariba, Benin (80)
    Bariba, Nigeria
Bariji   Bariji, Papua New Guinea
Barim   Barim, Papua New Guinea
Barok   Barok, Papua New Guinea
Baruga   Baruga, Papua New Guinea
Baruya   Baruya, Papua New Guinea
Basaa   Basaa, Cameroon
Basari   Basari, Guinea
    Basari, Senegal
    Basari, Togo
Bashar   Bashar, Nigeria
Bashgali   Bashgali, Afghanistan
Basila   Basila, Togo
Basketo   Basketo, Ethiopia
Bassa   *Bassa, Liberia
    **Bassa, Nigeria
Bata   Bata, Nigeria
Batak, Angkola   *Batak, Angkola, Indonesia (80)
Batak, Karo   Batak, Karo, Indonesia
Batak, Palawan   Batak, Palawan, Philippines
Batak, Simalungun   Batak, Simalungun, Indonesia
Batak, Toba   Batak, Toba, Indonesia
Batanga-Ngolo   Batanga-Ngolo, Cameroon
Bateg   Bateg, Malaysia
Bathudi   Bathudi in Bihar, India
Batsi   Batsi, USSR
Batu   Batu, Nigeria
Bau   Bau, Papua New Guinea
Baule   ***Baoule, Ivory Coast
Baushi   Baushi, Nigeria
Bauwaki   Bauwaki, Papua New Guinea
Bawm   Bawm, Bangladesh
Bayat   Bayats, Iran
Bayot   Bayot, Gambia
    Bayot, Guinea-Bissau
    Bayot, Senegal
Bazigar   Bazigar in Gujarat, India
Bebeli   Bebeli, Papua New Guinea
Bediya   Bediya in Bihar, India
Bedoanas   Bedoanas, Indonesia
Beja   Beja, Ethiopia
    Beja, Sudan
Bekwarra   Bekwarra, Nigeria
Bembe   Bembe, Zaire
Bembi   Bembi, Papua New Guinea
Bena   Bena, Tanzania
Benabena   Benabena, Papua New Guinea
Bencho   Bencho, Ethiopia
Bende   Bende, Tanzania
Bene   Bene, Cameroon
Benga   Benga, Gabon
Bengali   **Banai, Bangladesh
    Bengali Refugees, Assam, India
    **Bengali Sufis, Bangladesh (84)
    Bengalis in London, United Kingdom (82)
    Burmese Muslim Refugees, Bangladesh (83)
    **Hajong, Bangladesh
    **Koch, Bangladesh
Bengkulu   Bengkulu, Indonesia
Berba   Berba, Benin
Berik   Berik, Indonesia

523

REGISTRY OF THE UNREACHED

Berom	Berom, Nigeria
Besisi	Besisi, Malaysia
Bete	Bete, India
	*Bete, Ivory Coast
Bethen	Bethen, Cameroon
Betsinga	Betsinga, Cameroon
Bette-Bende	Bette-Bende, Nigeria
Bhakta	Bhakta, India
Bharia	Bharia in Madhya Pradesh, India
Bhatneri	Bhatneri, India
Bhattri	Bhattri, India
Bhilala	Bhilala, India
Bhojpuri	.*Bhojpuri, Nepal
	Tharu, India
	Tharu, Nepal
Bhoyari	Bhoyari in Maharashtra, India
Bhuiya	Bhuiya in Bihar, India
Bhumij	Bhumij in Assam, India
Bhunjia	Bhunjia in Madhya Pradesh, India
Biafada	Biafada, Guinea-Bissau
Biak	Biak, Indonesia
Biaka	Biaka, Papua New Guinea
Biangai	Biangai, Papua New Guinea
Biatah	**Bidayuh of Sarawak, Malaysia (81)
Bibling	Bibling, Papua New Guinea
Biduanda	Biduanda, Malaysia
Bidyogo	**Bijogo, Guinea-Bissau
Bijori	Bijori in Bihar, India
Biksi	Biksi, Indonesia
Bilaan	**Bilan, Philippines
Bilala	Bilala, Chad
Bile	Bile, Nigeria
Bilen	Bilen, Ethiopia
Biliau	Biliau, Papua New Guinea
Bima	Bimanese, Indonesia
Bimin	Bimin, Papua New Guinea
Bimoba	Bimoba, Ghana
	Bimoba, Togo
	Moba, Ghana
	Moba, Togo
Binahari	Binahari, Papua New Guinea
Binandere	Binandere, Papua New Guinea
Binawa	Binawa, Nigeria
Bine	Bine, Papua New Guinea
Binga	Binga, Sudan
Bingkokak	Bingkokak, Indonesia
Binjhwari	Binjhwari in Bihar, India
Binji	Binji, Zaire
Binumarien	Binumarien, Papua New Guinea
Bipim	***Bipim, Indonesia
Bira	Bira, Indonesia
Birhor	Birhor in Bihar, India
Birifor	Birifor, Ghana
	Birifor, Upper Volta
Bisa	Bisa, Zambia
	Bousansi, Upper Volta
Bisa (Busanga)	**Busanse, Ghana
Bisaya	Bisaya, Malaysia (81)
Bisis	Bisis, Papua New Guinea
Bitara	Bitara, Papua New Guinea
Bitare	Bitare, Cameroon
	Bitare, Nigeria
Biti	Biti, Sudan
Biyom	Biyom, Papua New Guinea
Boanaki	Boanaki, Papua New Guinea
Bobe	Bobe, Cameroon

Bobo Fing   Bobo Fing, Mali
Bobo Wule   Bobo Wule, Mali
Bodo   **Bodo Kachari, India
                    Bodo in Assam, India
Boghom   Boghom, Nigeria
Bohutu   Bohutu, Papua New Guinea
Boikin   Boikin, Papua New Guinea
Boko (Busa)   **Boko, Benin
Bokyi   Bokyi, Cameroon
                    Bokyi, Nigeria
Bola   Bola, Papua New Guinea
Bole   Bole, Nigeria
Bolinao   ***Bolinao, Philippines
Bolon   Bolon, Upper Volta
Bolondo   Bolondo, Zaire
Bom   Bom, Papua New Guinea
Boma   Boma, Zaire
Bomboko   Bomboko, Cameroon
Bomou   Bomou, Chad
Bondei   Bondei, Tanzania
Bondo   Bondo in Orissa, India
Bonerif   Bonerif, Indonesia
Bonggo   Bonggo, Indonesia
Bongili   Bongili, Congo
Bongo   Bongo, Sudan
Bongu   Bongu, Papua New Guinea
Boni   Boni of Lamu, Kenya (84)
Bonkeng-Pendia Bonkeng-Pendia, Cameroon
Bonkiman   Bonkiman, Papua New Guinea
Bontoc, Central **Bontoc, Central, Philippines (81)
Bor Gok   Bor Gok, Sudan
Bora   Bora, Colombia
Borai   Borai, Indonesia
Boran   Boran, Ethiopia
                    **Boran, Kenya
                    Sabbra, Kenya
Bororo   *Bororo, Brazil
Bosavi   Bosavi, Papua New Guinea
Bosilewa   Bosilewa, Papua New Guinea
Bosngun   Bosngun, Papua New Guinea
Bote-Majhi   Bote-Majhi, Nepal
Botlikh   Botlikh, USSR
Bowili   Bowili, Togo
Boya   Boya, Sudan
Bozo   Bozo, Mali
Brahui   Brahui, Pakistan
Braj   Braj in Uttar Pradesh, India
Brao   Brao, Laos (79)
Brat   Brat, Indonesia
Breri   Breri, Papua New Guinea
Bruneis   Bruneis, Malaysia
Bua   Bua, Chad
Bual   Bual, Indonesia
Buamu (Bobo Wule) Bwa, Upper Volta (80)
Buang, Central   Buang, Central, Papua New Guinea
Buang, Mangga   Buang, Mangga, Papua New Guinea
Bube   Bube, Equatorial Guinea
Budibud   Budibud, Papua New Guinea
Budug   Budug, USSR
Buduma   Buduma, Nigeria
Bugis   Bugis, Indonesia (80)
Buglere   Buglere, Panama
Bugombe   Bugombe, Zaire
Buhid   Buhid, Philippines
Buin   Buin, Papua New Guinea
Buja   Buja, Zaire

REGISTRY OF THE UNREACHED

Buka-khwe	Bushmen in Botswana, Botswana
Bukaua	Bukaua, Papua New Guinea
Buli	Builsa, Ghana
	Buli, Indonesia
	Buli, Upper Volta
Bulia	Bulia, Zaire
Bullom, Northern	Bullom, Northern, Sierra Leone
Bullom, Southern	Bullom, Southern, Sierra Leone
Bulu	Bulu, Papua New Guinea
Buna	Buna, Papua New Guinea
Bunabun	Bunabun, Papua New Guinea
Bunak	Bunak, Indonesia
Bunama	Bunama, Papua New Guinea
Bunan	Bunann in Kashmir, India
Bungku	Bungku, Indonesia
Bunu	Bunu, Nigeria
Bura	Bura, Cameroon
Bura (Babur)	**Babur Thali, Nigeria (80)
Burak	Burak, Nigeria
Buraka-Gbanziri	Buraka-Gbanziri, Congo
Buriat	Buriat, China
	Buriat, USSR
Burig	Burig in Kashmir, India
	Burig, China
Burji	Burji, Ethiopia
Burmese	Danu, Burma
	Kachin in Shan State, Burma
	Taungyoe, Burma
Buru	Buru, Indonesia
Burum	Burum, Papua New Guinea
Burun	Burun, Sudan
Burungi	Burungi, Tanzania
Burushaski	**Hunzakut, Pakistan (79)
Busa (Bokobarn Akiba)	Busa, Nigeria (80)
Busah	Busah, Papua New Guinea
Busami	Busami, Indonesia
Bushoong	Bushoong, Zaire
Bussa	Bussa, Ethiopia
Buta	Butawa, Nigeria
Butung	Butung, Indonesia
Buwid	**Buwid, Philippines (81)
Bviri	Bviri, Sudan
Bwa	Bwa, Zaire
Bwaidoga	Bwaidoga, Papua New Guinea
Bwisi	Bwisi, Zaire
Byangsi	Byangsi, Nepal
Cacua	Cacua, Colombia
Cagayan	Jama Mapun, Philippines (80)
Caiwa	Caiwa, Brazil
Cakchiquel, Central	Cakchiquel, Central, Guatemala
Caluyanhon	Caluyanhon, Philippines
Cambodia	**Khmer Refugees, Thailand
Campa	Campa, Peru
Camsa	Camsa, Colombia
Canarese	Chola Naickans, India
Candoshi	Candoshi, Peru
Canela	Canela, Brazil
Cantonese	Chinese Businessmen, Hong Kong (81)
	Chinese Factory Workers, Hong Kong
	*Chinese Refugees in Macau, Macau (81)
	Chinese Villagers, Hong Kong
	*Chinese in Amsterdam, Netherlands
	**Chinese in Australia, Australia
	Chinese in Costa Rica, Costa Rica

	*Chinese in New Zealand, New Zealand
	*Chinese in South Africa, South Africa
	*Chinese of W. Malaysia, Malaysia
	**Chinese, Vancouver, Canada:British Columbia
	*Factory Workers, Hong Kong
	**High School Students, Hong Kong
	Refugee Doctors, Hong Kong
	Vietnamese Refugees, China (83)
Cantonese dialects	Water Surface People, Hong Kong (84)
Capanahua	Capanahua, Peru
Carapana	Carapana, Colombia
Cashibo	Cashibo, Peru
Casiguranin	*Casiguranin, Philippines
Cayapa	Cayapa, Ecuador
Cebuano	***Cebu, Middle-Class, Philippines
Central Thai	*Thai Immigrants, Los Angeles, United States of America (84)
Cewa	Cewa, Zambia
Ch'iang	Ch'iang, China
Ch'ol	***Ch'ol Sabanilla, Mexico
Chacobo	Chacobo, Bolivia
Chagga	Chagga, Tanzania
Chaghatai	Chaghatai, Afghanistan
Chakfem-Mushere	Chakfem-Mushere, Nigeria
Chakma	*Chakmas of Mizoram, India (81)
Chakossi	Chakossi in Ghana, Ghana
	Chakossi in Togo, Togo
Chala	Chala, Ghana
Cham	*Cham Refugees from Kampuchea, Kampuchea, Democratic (83)
	Cham, Viet Nam
Chamacoco, Bahia Negra	Chamacoco, Bahia Negra, Paraguay
Chamalin	Chamalin, USSR
Chamari	Chamari in Madhya Pradesh, India
Chamba Daka	Chamba Daka, Nigeria
Chamba Leko	Chamba Leko, Nigeria
Chambri	Chambri, Papua New Guinea
Chameali	Chameali in H.P., India
Chami	Chami, Colombia
Chamicuro	Chamicuro, Peru
Chamorro	Chamorro, Pacific Trust Islands
Chara	Chara, Ethiopia
Chatino, Nopala	Chatino, Nopala, Mexico
Chatino, Panixtlahuaca	Chatino, Panixtlahuaca, Mexico
Chatino, Tataltepec	Chatino, Tataltepec, Mexico
Chatino, Zacatepec	Chatino, Zacatepec, Mexico
Chatino, Zenzontepec	Chatino, Zenzontepec, Mexico
Chaudangsi	Chaudangsi, Nepal
Chaungtha	Chaungtha, Burma
Chawai	Chawai, Nigeria
Chayawita	**Chayahuita, Peru
Chenapian	Chenapian, Papua New Guinea
Chenchu	Chenchu in Andhra Pradesh, India
Chepang	Chepang, Nepal
Cherkes	Cherkess, USSR
Chero	Chero in Bihar, India
Chhattisgarhi	Satnamis (Madhya Pradesh), India
ChiTonga	Tonga, Gwembe Valley, Zambia (79)
	*Tonga, Zimbabwe
Chiga	Chiga, Uganda
Chik-Barik	Chik-Barik in Bihar, India
Chikalanga	*Kalanga, Botswana

REGISTRY OF THE UNREACHED

Chin	Chin, China
Chin, Falam	Chin, Falam, Burma
Chin, Haka	Chin, Haka, Burma
Chin, Khumi	Chin, Khumi, Burma
Chin, Ngawn	Chin, Ngawn, Burma
Chin, Tiddim	Chin, Tiddim, Burma
Chinanteco, Ayotzintepec	Chinanteco, Ayotzintepec, Mexico
Chinanteco, Chiltepec	Chinanteco, Chiltepec, Mexico
Chinanteco, Comaltepec	Chinanteco, Comaltepec, Mexico
Chinanteco, Lalana	Chinanteco, Lalana, Mexico
Chinanteco, Lealao	Chinanteco, Lealao, Mexico
Chinanteco, Ojitlan	Chinanteco, Ojitlan, Mexico
Chinanteco, Palantla	Chinanteco, Palantla, Mexico
Chinanteco, Quiotepec	Chinanteco, Quiotepec, Mexico
Chinanteco, Sochiapan	Chinanteco, Sochiapan, Mexico
Chinanteco, Tepetotutla	Chinanteco, Tepetotutla, Mexico
Chinanteco, Tepinapa	Chinanteco,, Mexico
Chinanteco, Usila	Chinanteco, Usila, Mexico
Chinbok	Chinbok, Burma
Chinese	Vietnamese, Edmonton, Canada:Alberta
Chinese Dialects	**Chinese Stud., Australia, Australia
Chinese dialects	*Chinese in Malaysia, Malaysia
Chinese, Min-Nan	*Deviant Youth in Taipei, Taiwan (82)
Chinga	Chinga, Cameroon
Chingp'o	Chingp'o, China
Chip	Chip, Nigeria
Chipaya	Chipaya, Bolivia
Chiquitano	Chiquitano, Bolivia
Chiyao	**Yao, Malawi (84)
Chodhari	Chodhari in Gujarat, India
Chokobo	Chokobo, Nigeria
Chokwe	Chokwe (Lunda), Angola
	Chokwe, Zambia
Chopi	Chopi, Mozambique
Chorote	Chorote, Paraguay
Chorti	Chorti, Guatemala
Chuang	Chuang, China (81)
Chuave	Chuave, Papua New Guinea
Chuj	Chuj, Guatemala
Chuj, San Mateo Ixtatan	Chuj, San Mateo Ixtatan, Mexico
Chukot	Chukot, USSR
Chulupe	Chulupe, Paraguay
Chungchia	Chungchia, China
Churahi	Churahi in H.P., India
Chwabo	Chwabo, Mozambique
Chwang	Chwang, China
Cinta Larga	Cinta Larga, Brazil
Circassian	Circassian, Turkey
Citak (Asmat)	***Citak, Indonesia
Cocama	Cocama, Peru
Cocopa	Cocopa, Mexico
Cofan	Cofan, Colombia
Cogui	Cogui, Colombia
Colorado	**Tsachila, Ecuador
Cora	Cora, Mexico
Coreguaje	**Coreguaje, Colombia
Cotabato Manobo	**Manobo, Cotabato, Philippines
Cree	Metis, Elizabeth Settlement, Canada:Alberta
Creole	Haitian Refugees, United States of America (83)
	Haitians, Montreal, Canada:Quebec
	**Rural Vodun Believers, Haiti (84)

	Seychellois, Seychelles
Cubeo	Cubeo, Colombia
Cuiba	Cuiba, Colombia
Cuicateco, Tepeuxila	Cuicateco, Tepeuxila, Mexico
Cuicateco, Teutila	Cuicateco, Teutila, Mexico
Cujareno	Cujareno, Peru
Culina	Culina, Brazil
Cuna	*Cuna, Colombia (79)
Curipaco	Curipaco, Colombia
Cuyolbal	Ixil, Guatemala
Cuyonon	Cuyonon, Philippines
Daba	Daba, Cameroon
Dabra	Dabra, Indonesia
Dadibi	Dadibi, Papua New Guinea
Dadiya	Dadiya, Nigeria
Daga	Daga, Papua New Guinea
Dagada	Dagada, Indonesia
Dagari	Dagari, Ghana
	Dagari, Upper Volta
Dagbanli	**Dagomba, Ghana
Dagur	Dagur, China
Dahating	Dahating, Papua New Guinea
Dai	Dai, Burma
Dair	Dair, Sudan
Daju	Daju of Dar Fur, Sudan
	Daju of West Kordofan, Sudan
Daju of Dar Dadju	Daju of Dar Dadju, Chad
Daju of Dar Sila	Daju of Dar Sila, Chad
Dakanci	*Daka, Nigeria
Dakhni	Deccani Muslims-Hyderabad, India (82)
Dakhni (Urdu)	Deccani Muslims, India
Dami	Dami, Papua New Guinea
Dan	***Dan, Ivory Coast
	Dan, Liberia
Dan (Yacouba)	Gio, Liberia
Dangaleat	Dangaleat, Chad
Dangi	**Bhils, India (79)
Dani, Grand Valley	*Dani, Baliem, Indonesia (79)
Danuwar Rai	*Rai, Danuwar, Nepal
Daonda	Daonda, Papua New Guinea
Darai	Darai, Nepal
Dargin	Dargin, USSR
Dari	**Afghan Refugees (NWFP), Pakistan
	Tajik, Iran (80)
Darmiya	Darmiya, Nepal
Dass	Dass, Nigeria
Dathanik	Dathanik, Ethiopia
Davaweno	Davaweno, Philippines
Dawawa	Dawawa, Papua New Guinea
Day	Day, Central African Republic
Dazaga	Daza, Chad
De	*Dewein, Liberia
Dedua	Dedua, Papua New Guinea
Degeme	Degema, Nigeria
Degenan	Degenan, Papua New Guinea
Dem	Dem, Indonesia
Demta	Demta, Indonesia
Dendi	Dendi, Benin
Dengese	Dengese, Zaire
Deno	Deno, Nigeria
Deori	Deori in Assam, India
Dera	Dera, Nigeria
Desano	Desano, Brazil
Dghwede	Dghwede, Cameroon
Dhaiso	Dhaiso, Tanzania

REGISTRY OF THE UNREACHED

Dhanka	Dhanka in Gujarat, India
Dhanwar	Dhanwar in Madhya Pradesh, India
Dhimal	Dhimal, Nepal
Dhimba	Herero, Namibia
Dhodia Dialects	**Dhodias, India
Dhuwal	*Murngin (Wulamba), Australia
Dia	Dia, Papua New Guinea
Dida	**Dida, Ivory Coast
Didinga	Didinga, Sudan
Didoi	Didoi, USSR
Digo	Digo, Kenya (84)
	Digo, Tanzania
Dimasa	Dimasa in Cachar, India
Dime	Dime, Ethiopia
Dimir	Dimir, Papua New Guinea
Dinka	Dinka, Sudan
Dinka, Agar	Dinka, Agar, Sudan
Diodio	Diodio, Papua New Guinea
Diola	Diola, Guinea-Bissau (80)
	Diola, Senegal
Dirim	Dirim, Nigeria
Dirya	Dirya, Nigeria
Divehi	Divehi, Maldives (80)
Djuka	Djuka, Surinam
Dobu	Dobu, Papua New Guinea
Doe	Doe, Tanzania
Doga	Doga, Papua New Guinea
Doghosie	Doghosie, Upper Volta
Dogon	*Dogon, Mali (79)
Dogoro	Dogoro, Papua New Guinea
Dolgan	Dolgans, USSR
Dom	Dom, Papua New Guinea
Dompago	Dompago, Benin
Domu	Domu, Papua New Guinea
Domung	Domung, Papua New Guinea
Dongjoi	Dongjoi, Sudan
Dongo	Dongo, Sudan
	Dongo, Zaire
Doohyaayo	**Doohwaayo, Cameroon
Dorli	Dorlin in Andhra Pradesh, India
Doromu	Doromu, Papua New Guinea
Dorze	Dorze, Ethiopia
Doura	Doura, Papua New Guinea
Duala	Balong, Cameroon
Duan	Duna, Papua New Guinea
Duau	Duau, Papua New Guinea
Dubu	Dubu, Indonesia
Duguri	Duguir, Nigeria
Duguza	Duguza, Nigeria
Dukanci	**Duka, Nigeria
Duma	Duma, Gabon
Dumagat	*Dumagat, Casiguran, Philippines (81)
Dungan	Dungan, USSR
Duru	Duru, Cameroon
Dusun	**Sugut, Malaysia
Dutch	Amsterdam Boat Dwellers, Netherlands
	Dead-End Kids - Amsterdam, Netherlands (82)
Duvele	Duvele, Indonesia
Dyan	Dyan, Upper Volta
Dyerma	Dyerma, Niger (80)
	Dyerma, Nigeria
Dyola	Dyola, Gambia
Ebira	Ebira, Nigeria

Index by Language

Ebrie   Ebrie, Ivory Coast
Edawapi   Edawapi, Papua New Guinea
Edo   Edo, Nigeria
Efik   Efik, Nigeria
Efutop   Efutop, Nigeria
Eggon   Eggon, Nigeria
Eivo   Eivo, Papua New Guinea
Ejagham   Ejagham, Nigeria
Ekagi   Ekagi, Indonesia
Ekajuk   Ekajuk, Nigeria
Eket   Eket, Nigeria
Ekpeye   Ekpeye, Nigeria
Eleme   Eleme, Nigeria
Elkei   Elkei, Papua New Guinea
Eloyi   **Afo, Nigeria (80)
Emai-Iuleha-Ora   Emai-Iuleha-Ora, Nigeria
Embera   Embera, Northern, Colombia
Emerum   Emerum, Papua New Guinea
Emira   Emira, Papua New Guinea
Emumu   Emumu, Indonesia
Endangen   Endangen, Papua New Guinea
Enga   Enga, Papua New Guinea
Engenni   Engenni, Nigeria
English   Aborigines in Brisbane, Australia
(82)
*Americans in Geneva, Switzerland
*Asian Students, Philippines
**Bengali, Los Angeles area, United
States of America (84)
*Caribs, Dominican Republic (84)
*Casual Laborers-Atlanta, United
States of America (82)
Chinese, Calgary, Canada:Alberta
Chinese, Metro Toronto,
Canada:Ontario
*English speakers, Guadalajara ,
Mexico (84)
Ex-Mental Patients, Hamilton,
Canada:Ontario
*Expatriates in Riyadh, Saudi
Arabia (82)
Gays in San Francisco, United
States of America (82)
*Havasupai, United States of
America
Homosexuals, Toronto,
Canada:Ontario
Indians, CN Rail Lines,
Canada:Ontario
Indians, Cold Lake Reserve,
Canada:Alberta
Indians, Eden Valley,
Canada:Alberta
Indians, Edmonton, Canada:Alberta
Indians, Interlake Region,
Canada:Manitoba
Indians, Kinistino Reserve,
Canada:Saskatchewan
Indians, London, Canada:Ontario
Indians, Lower Mainland,
Canada:British Columbia
Indians, Northwestern Ontario ,
Canada:Ontario
Indians, Regina,
Canada:Saskatchewan
Indians, Saskatoon,
Canada:Saskatchewan

REGISTRY OF THE UNREACHED

Indians, Thunder Bay,
  Canada:Ontario
Indians, Vancouver, Canada:British
  Columbia
Indians, White Bear Reserve,
  Canada:Saskatchewan
Jews (Non-Sephardic), Montreal,
  Canada:Quebec (79)
Jews, Toronto, Canada:Ontario
Jews, Vancouver, Canada:British
  Columbia
***Micmac Indians, Canada:New
  Brunswick
***Micmac Indians, Eskasoni Rsv. ,
  Canada:Nova Scotia
 **Montagnais Indians, Canada:Quebec
Nurses in St. Louis, United States
  of America (82)
Oil Executives, Calgary,
  Canada:Alberta
 **Pro Hockey Players, United States
  of America (82)
Rajneeshees of Oregon, United
  States of America
Rastafarians, Edmonton,
  Canada:Alberta
Shopping Bag Women, Toronto,
  Canada:Ontario
South African Refugee Students,
  Lesotho (83)
Street People, Victoria,
  Canada:British Columbia
Theater Arts Performers, Canada
Ugandan Refugees, United Kingdom
  (83)
University Students, Edmonton ,
  Canada:Alberta
Wandering Homeless, United States
  of America (84)
West Indian Migrant Workers,
  Canada:Ontario
***West Indians, Toronto,
  Canada:Ontario
***Youth, Toronto Peanut District,
  Canada:Ontario
Zuni, United States of America

English with Hindi	**Indians, East, Trinidad and Tobago (79)
Enya	Enya, Zaire
Eotile	Eotile, Ivory Coast
Epie	Epie, Nigeria
Erokwanas	Erokwanas, Indonesia
Esan	Esan, Nigeria
	**Ishans, Nigeria
Eton	Eton, Cameroon
Etulo	Etulo, Nigeria
Evant	Evant, Nigeria
Evenk	Evenks, USSR
Evenki	Evenki, China
Ewage-Notu	Ewage-Notu, Papua New Guinea
Ewe	Zowla, Ghana
Fa D'Ambu	Fa D'Ambu, Equatorial Guinea
Fagululu	Fagululu, Papua New Guinea
Faiwol	Faiwol, Papua New Guinea
Faka	**Fakai, Nigeria
Fali	Fali, Cameroon

	**Fali, Nigeria
Farsi	Bahais in Teheran, Iran (82)
	**Iranian Bahai Refugees, Pakistan (83)
	Iranians, Montreal, Canada:Quebec
	Jews of Iran, Iran
Fas	Fas, Papua New Guinea
Fasu	Fasu, Papua New Guinea
Feroge	Feroge, Sudan
Finungwan	Finungwan, Papua New Guinea
Fipa	Fipa, Tanzania
Foau	Foau, Indonesia
Foi	Foi, Papua New Guinea
Foran	Foran, Papua New Guinea
Fordat	Fordat, Indonesia
Fore	Fore, Papua New Guinea
Fouta Toro	Pular, Senegal
Fra-Fra	Fra-Fra, Ghana
French	French, St. Pierre & Miquelon , Canada:Newfoundland
	Fur Trappers, Canada:Ontario
	Jews (Sephardic), Montreal, Canada:Quebec
	Khmer, Ottawa, Canada:Ontario
	Lebanese, Beamington, Canada:Ontario
	Moroccan Jews, Canada:Quebec
	Muslim Lebanese Refugees, Canada (83)
	*University Students, France (79)
Fula	Fula, Cunda, Gambia
	Fula, Guinea
	Fula, Sierra Leone
	Fula, Upper Volta
Fula, Macina	Fula, Macina, Mali
Fula, Peuhala	Fula, Peuhala, Mali
Fulani	Adamawa, Cameroon
	Fulah, Upper Volta
	*Fulani, Benin
	Fulani, Cameroon (79)
	*Fulbe, Ghana
Fuliro	Fuliro, Zaire
Fulnio	Fulnio, Brazil
Fungom, Northern	Fungom, Northern, Cameroon
Fungor	Fungor, Sudan
Furu	Furu, Zaire
Fuyuge	Fuyuge, Papua New Guinea
Fyam	Fyam, Nigeria
Fyer	Fyer, Nigeria
Ga-Dang	Ga-Dang, Philippines
Gabri	Gabri, Chad
Gabrinja	*Gabbra, Ethiopia
Gadaba	Gadaban in Andhra Pradesh, India
Gaddi	Gaddi in Himachal Pradesh, India
Gade	Gade, Nigeria
Gadsup	Gadsup, Papua New Guinea
Gagou	Gagu, Ivory Coast
Gaguaz	Gagauzes, USSR
Gahuku	Gahuku, Papua New Guinea
Gaikundi	Gaikundi, Papua New Guinea
Gaina	Gaina, Papua New Guinea
Gal	Gal, Papua New Guinea
Galambi	Galambi, Nigeria
Galeshi	Galeshis, Iran
Galla	Eritrean Refugees, Sudan (83)
	Gabbra, Kenya

REGISTRY OF THE UNREACHED

	*Galla (Bale), Ethiopia
	**Saguye, Kenya
Galler	Galler, Laos
Gallinya	Galla, Harar, Ethiopia
Gallinya (Oromo)	Galla of Bucho, Ethiopia
Galong	Galong in Assam, India
Gambai	Gambai, Chad
Gamei	Gamei, Papua New Guinea
Gamti	Gamti in Gujarat, India
Gan	Gan, Upper Volta
Gane	Gane, Indonesia
Gangam	Gangam, Togo
Ganglau	Ganglau, Papua New Guinea
Gangte	Gangte in Assam, India
Garifuna	**Black Caribs, Belize, Belize (79)
	**Black Caribs, Guatemala, Guatemala
	*Black Caribs, Honduras, Honduras (84)
Garuh	Garuh, Papua New Guinea
Garus	Garus, Papua New Guinea
Garuwahi	Garuwahi, Papua New Guinea
Gawar-Bati	Gawar-Bati, Afghanistan
Gawari	Gawari in Andhra Pradesh, India
Gawwada	Gawwada, Ethiopia
Gayo	Alas, Indonesia
	Gayo, Indonesia (80)
Gbari	Gbari, Nigeria (80)
Gbaya	Gbaya, Nigeria
Gbaya-Ndogo	Gbaya-Ndogo, Sudan
Gbazantche	Gbazantche, Benin
Gberi	Gberi, Sudan
Ge	**Adja, Benin
	Watchi, Togo
Gedaged	Gedaged, Papua New Guinea
Gedeo	Gedeo, Ethiopia
Geji	Geji, Nigeria
Genagane	Genagane, Papua New Guinea
Gende	Gende, Papua New Guinea
Gera	Gera, Nigeria
German	*Students, German Federal Rep. (79)
Geruma	Geruma, Nigeria
Gesa	Gesa, Indonesia
Ghale Gurung	Ghale Gurung, Nepal
Gheko	Gheko, Burma
Ghol	Ghol, Sudan
Ghotuo	Ghotuo, Nigeria
Ghulfan	Ghulfan, Sudan
Gidar	Gidar, Cameroon
	Gidar, Chad
Gidicho	Gidicho, Ethiopia
Gidra	Gidra, Papua New Guinea
Gilaki	Gilakis, Iran
Gilyak	Gilyak, USSR
Gimi	Gimi, Papua New Guinea
Gimira	**Ghimeera, Ethiopia
Ginuman	Ginuman, Papua New Guinea
Gira	Gira, Papua New Guinea
Girawa	Girawa, Papua New Guinea
Giri	Giri, Papua New Guinea
Giryama	Giryama, Kenya
Gisiga	Gisiga, Cameroon
Gitua	Gitua, Papua New Guinea
Gizra	Gizra, Papua New Guinea
Glavda	**Glavda, Nigeria
Gobasi	Gobasi, Papua New Guinea
Gobato	Gobato, Ethiopia

534

Gobeze	Gobeze, Ethiopia
Godie	***Godie, Ivory Coast
Goemai	Goemai, Nigeria
Gogo	Gogo, Tanzania
Gogodala	Gogodala, Papua New Guinea
Gokana	Gokana, Nigeria
Gola	Gola, Liberia
Golo	Golo, Chad
Gondi	*Gonds, India
	Totis, India
Gonja	Gonja, Ghana
Goroa	Goroa, Tanzania
Gorontalo	Gorontalo, Indonesia
Gosha	Gosha, Kenya
Goudari	Goudari, Iran
Gouin-Turka	Gouin-Turka, Upper Volta
Goulai	Goulai, Chad
Gourendi	Gourency, Upper Volta
Gouro	**Gouro, Ivory Coast
Gouwar	Gouwar, Cameroon
Grasia	Grasia in Gujarat, India
Grebo Dialects	**Grebo, Liberia
Greek	Greeks, Toronto, Canada:Ontario
Gu	Gu, Benin
Guaiaqui	Guaiaqui, Paraguay
Guajajara	Guajajara, Brazil
Guajibo	Guajibo, Colombia
Guajiro	*Guajiro, Colombia
Guambiano	Guambiano, Colombia
Guana	Guana, Paraguay
Guanano	*Guanano, Colombia (79)
Guarani	***Guarani, Bolivia (79)
	Simba, Bolivia
Guarani (Bolivian)	**Chiriguano, Argentina
Guarayu	Guarayu, Bolivia
Guarojio	Guarojio, Mexico
Guayabero	Guayabero, Colombia
Gude	Gude, Cameroon
	Gude, Nigeria
Gudu	Gudu, Nigeria
Guduf	Guduf, Nigeria
Guere	Guere, Ivory Coast
	*Krahn, Ivory Coast
Gugu-Yalanji	Gugu-Yalanji, Australia
Guhu-Samane	Guhu-Samane, Papua New Guinea
Gujarati	Dawoodi Muslims, India
	**Dubla, India
	Gujarati, United Kingdom
	*Indians in Rhodesia, Zimbabwe
	Khojas, Agha Khani, India
	*Parsees, India (81)
	Ugandan Asian Refugees, Canada:British Columbia (83)
	**Vohras of Yavatmal, India
Gujarati Dialect	Bajania, Pakistan (79)
	Vagari, Pakistan
Gujarati, Koli	**Kohli, Kutchi, Pakistan
	**Kohli, Parkari, Pakistan
	**Kohli, Tharadari, Pakistan
	**Kohli, Wadiara, Pakistan
Gujari	Gujars of Kashmir, India (81)
Gujuri	Gujuri, Afghanistan
Gula	Gula, Chad
Gulfe	Gulfe, Cameroon
Gumasi	Gumasi, Papua New Guinea
Gumine	Gumine, Papua New Guinea

REGISTRY OF THE UNREACHED

Gumuz	Gumuz, Ethiopia
	Gumuz, Sudan
Gurage Dialects	Gurage, Ethiopia (80)
Gure-Kahugu	Gure-Kahugu, Nigeria
Gurenne	Gurensi, Ghana
Gurma	Gurma, Upper Volta
Gurung	Gurung, Nepal
Guruntum-Mbaaru	Guruntum-Mbaaru, Nigeria
Gusap	Gusap, Papua New Guinea
Guwot	Guwot, Papua New Guinea
Gwa	Gwa, Ivory Coast
Gwandara	Gwandara, Nigeria
Gwari Matai	Gwari Matai, Nigeria
Gwedena	Gwedena, Papua New Guinea
Gwere	Gwere, Uganda
Ha	Ha, Tanzania
Hadiyya	Hadiyya, Ethiopia
Hadza	Dorobo, Tanzania
Hahon	Hahon, Papua New Guinea
Hakka	**Chinese Hakka of Taiwan, Taiwan (79)
	**Chinese in Brazil, Brazil
	Chinese in Puerto Rico, Puerto Rico
	**Chinese in Sabah, Malaysia
	*Chinese in Thailand, Thailand
	**Chinese, Mauritius (84)
Halbi	Halbi in Madhya Pradesh, India
Halia	Halia, Papua New Guinea
Hallam	Hallam, Burma
Hamtai	Hamtai, Papua New Guinea
Hangaza	Hangaza, Tanzania
Hani	Hani, China
Hanonoo	Hanonoo, Philippines
Harari	Harari, Ethiopia
Harauti	Harauti in Rajasthan, India
Hassaniya (Arabic)	*White Moors, Mauritania
Hatsa	Hatsa, Tanzania
Hausa	Arawa, Nigeria
	Kurfei, Niger
	***Maguzawa, Nigeria (79)
	Mauri, Niger
	Muslim Community of Bawku, Ghana
Hausa, Ghana	Havu, Zaire
Havu	
Havunese	Havunese, Indonesia
Haya	Haya, Tanzania
Hazaragi	**Hazara in Kabul, Afghanistan (82)
Hebrew	*Jewish Imgrnts.-American, Israel
	*Jewish Imgrnts.-Argentine, Israel
	*Jewish Imgrnts.-Australia, Israel
	*Jewish Imgrnts.-Brazilian, Israel
	*Jewish Imgrnts.-Mexican, Israel
	*Jewish Imgrnts.-Uruguayan, Israel
	*Jewish Immigrants, Other, Israel
Hehe	Hehe, Tanzania
Heiban	Heiban, Sudan
Heikum	Bushmen (Heikum), Namibia
Helong	Helong, Indonesia
Herero	Herero, Botswana
Heso	Heso, Zaire
Hewa	**Hewa, Papua New Guinea (79)
Hezara'i	Hezareh, Iran
Higi	***Higi, Nigeria
Hindi	Jains, India
Hindustani	Balmiki, Pakistan
	Indians in Fiji, Fiji (79)

Hixkaryana — Hixkaryana, Brazil
Ho — Ho in Bihar, India
Hohodene — Hohodene, Brazil
Hokkien — Chinese Fishermen, Malaysia
Holiya — Holiya in Madhya Pradesh, India
Holoholo — Holoholo, Tanzania
Holu — Holu, Angola
Hopi — Hopi, United States of America
Hote — Hote, Papua New Guinea
Hrangkhol — Hrangkhol, Burma
Huachipaire — Huachipaire, Peru
Huambisa — Huambisa, Peru
Huasteco — Huasteco, Mexico
Huave — **Huave, Mexico
Hui-hui-yu — Hui, China (80)
Huichol — Huichol, Mexico
Huila — **Huila, Angola
Huitoto, Meneca — Huitoto, Meneca, Colombia
Huitoto, Murui — Huitoto, Murui, Peru
Hukwe — Hukwe, Angola
Hula — Hula, Papua New Guinea
Huli — Huli, Papua New Guinea
Humene — Humene, Papua New Guinea
Hunde — Hunde, Zaire
Hunjara — Hunjara, Papua New Guinea
Hupda Maku — Hupda Maku, Colombia
Hwana — Hwana, Nigeria
Hwela-Numu — Hwela-Numu, Ivory Coast
Hyam — Hyam, Nigeria
Iatmul — Iatmul, Papua New Guinea
Ibaji — Ibaji, Nigeria
Iban — **Iban, Malaysia (81)
Ibanag — Ibanag, Philippines
Ibataan — *Ibataan, Philippines
Ibibio — Ibibio, Nigeria
Ica — Ica, Colombia
Icen — Icen, Nigeria
Icheve — Iheve, Nigeria
Idi — Idi, Papua New Guinea
Idoma — Idoma, Nigeria
Idoma, North — Idoma, North, Nigeria
Ifugao — Ifugao in Cababuyan, Philippines
— *Ifugao, Philippines
Ifugao, Ambanad — Ifugao, Ambanad, Philippines
Ifugao, Kiangan — Ifugao, Kiangan, Philippines
Ifumu — Ifumu, Congo
Igala — Igala, Nigeria
Igbirra — Igbira, Nigeria (80)
Igede — Igede, Nigeria
Ignaciano — Ignaciano, Bolivia
Igora — Igora, Papua New Guinea
Igorot — Igorot, Philippines
Iha — Iha, Indonesia
Ijo — Ijo, Central-Western, Nigeria
— Ijo, Northeast Central, Nigeria
— Ijo, Northeast, Nigeria
Ikalahan — **Ikalahan, Philippines
Ikobi-Mena — Ikobi-Mena, Papua New Guinea
Ikulu — Ikulu, Nigeria
Ikundun — Ikundun, Papua New Guinea
Ikwere — Ikwere, Nigeria
Ila — Ila, Zambia
Ilanun — Ilanon, Philippines
Ilianen Manobo — *Manobo, Ilianen, Philippines
Ilocano — Baguio Area Miners, Philippines (81)

REGISTRY OF THE UNREACHED

Ilongot	Ilongot, Philippines
Inanwatan	Inanwatan, Indonesia
Indinogosima	Indinogosima, Papua New Guinea
Indonesian	**Chinese in Indonesia, Indonesia
	Jambi, Indonesia
	Musi, Indonesia
	Ogan, Indonesia
	Sekayu, Indonesia
Inga	Inga, Colombia
Ingush	Ingushes, USSR
Insinai	Insinai, Philippines
Intha	Intha, Burma
Ipiko	Ipiko, Papua New Guinea
Ipili	Ipili, Papua New Guinea
Irahutu	Irahutu, Indonesia
Iraqw	Iraqw, Tanzania
Iraya	Iraya, Philippines
Iresim	Iresim, Indonesia
Iria	Iria, Indonesia
Irigwe	Irigwe, Nigeria
Irula	***Irulas in Kerala, India
Irumu	Irumu, Papua New Guinea
Isaalin	**Sisaala, Ghana
Isanzu	Isanzu, Tanzania
Isebe	Isebe, Papua New Guinea
Isekiri	Isekiri, Nigeria
Isneg	**Apayao, Philippines
Isneg, Dibagat-Kabugao	Isneg, Dibagat-Kabugao, Philippines
Isneg, Karagawan	Isneg, Karagawan, Philippines
Isoko	Isoko, Nigeria
Italian	Jews in Venice, Italy (82)
	Pension Students-Madrid, Spain (82)
Itawit	Itawit, Philippines
Itelmen	Itelmen, USSR
Itik	Itik, Indonesia
Itneg, Adasen	Itneg, Adasen, Philippines
Itneg, Binongan	Itneg, Binongan, Philippines
Itneg, Masadiit	Itneg, Masadiit, Philippines
Itonama	Itonama, Bolivia
Ivbie North-Okpela-Atte	Ivbie North-Okpela-Atte, Nigeria
Iwa	Iwa, Zambia
Iwaidja	*Iwaidja, Australia
Iwal	Iwal, Papua New Guinea
Iwam	Iwam, Papua New Guinea
Iwam, Sepik	Iwam, Sepik, Papua New Guinea
Iwur	Iwur, Indonesia
Iyon	Iyon, Cameroon
	Iyon, Nigeria
Izarek	Izarek, Nigeria
Izhor	Izhor, USSR
Izi	**Izi, Nigeria
Jaba	Jaba, Nigeria
Jabem	Jabem, Papua New Guinea
Jacalteco	Jacalteco, Guatemala
Jagannathi	Jagannathi in A.P., India
Jaipuri	Rajasthani Muslims-Jaipur, India (82)
Jamaican Patois	**Jamaican Elite, Jamaica
Jamamadi	Jamamadi, Brazil
Jamden	Jamden, Indonesia
Jamshidi	Jamshidis, Iran
Janena	Barasano, Southern, Colombia
Janggali	Janggali, Nepal
Janjero	Janjero, Ethiopia

538

Janjo   Janjo, Nigeria
Japanese   *Barbers in Tokyo, Japan (82)
    *Danchi Dwellers in Tokyo, Japan (82)
    *Dentists, Fukuoka, Japan
    Geishas in Osaka, Japan (82)
    *Inland Sea Island Peoples, Japan
    **Japanese Students In USA, United States of America
    Japanese in Brazil, Brazil (79)
    *Japanese in Korea, Korea, Republic of
    Japanese, Toronto, Canada:Ontario
    Soka Gakkai Believers, Japan
    **Univ. Students of Japan, Japan
Jaqaru   Jaqaru, Peru
Jara   Jara, Nigeria
Jaranchi   **Jarawa, Nigeria
Jatapu   Jatapu in Andhra Pradesh, India
Jati   Jati, Afghanistan
Jaunsari   Jaunsari in Uttar Pradesh, India
Javanese, Tjirebon   Cirebon, Indonesia
Jeme   Zemi Naga of Assam, India (81)
Jeng   Jeng, Laos
Jera   Jera, Nigeria
Jharia   Jharia in Orissa, India
Jibu, Jibanci   *Jibu, Nigeria
Jiji   Jiji, Tanzania
Jimajima   Jimajima, Papua New Guinea
Jimbin   Jimbin, Nigeria
Jimini   **Jimini, Ivory Coast
Jinja   Jinja, Tanzania
Jirel   Jirel, Nepal
Jita   Jita, Tanzania
Jivaro   **Jivaro (Achuara), Venezuela
Jiye   Jiye, Uganda
Jiye (Karamojong)   *Jiye, Sudan
Jongor   Jongor, Chad
Jro   **Chrau, Viet Nam
Juang   Juang in Orissa, India
Juhai   Juhai, Malaysia
Jyarung   Jyarung, China
K'anjobal   K'anjobal of Los Angeles, United States of America
    **K'anjobal of San Miguel, Guatemala
Kaagan   Kaagan, Philippines
Kaalong   Kaalong, Cameroon
Kaba   Kaba, Central African Republic
Kaba Dunjo   Kaba Dunjo, Central African Republic
Kabadi   Kabadi, Papua New Guinea
Kabixi   Kabixi, Brazil
Kabre   Kabre, Benin
    Kabre, Togo
Kabyle   Kabyle, Algeria (79)
Kachama   Kachama, Ethiopia
Kachchi   Kachchi in Andhra Pradesh, India
Kadaklan-Barlig Bontoc   Kadaklan-Barlig Bontoc, Philippines
Kadar   Kadar in Andhra Pradesh, India
Kadara   Kadara, Nigeria
    Kamantan, Nigeria
Kadazan   Dusun, Malaysia (81)
Kadazans   Kadazans, Malaysia
Kadiweu   Kadiweu, Brazil
Kadugli   Kadugli, Sudan

REGISTRY OF THE UNREACHED

Kaeti	Kaeti, Indonesia
Kaffenya (Kefa)	*Kaffa, Ethiopia (80)
Kafiristani (Bashgali)	**Kafirs, Pakistan (79)
Kagoma	Kagoma, Nigeria
Kagulu	Kagulu, Tanzania
Kahluri	Kahluri in Andamans, India
Kaian	Kaian, Papua New Guinea
Kaibu	Kaibu, Nigeria
Kaiep	Kaiep, Papua New Guinea
Kaikadi	Kaikadi in Maharashtra, India
Kaili	Kaili, Indonesia
Kaingang	Kaingang, Brazil
Kairi	Kairi, Papua New Guinea
Kairiru	Kairiru, Papua New Guinea
Kaiwai	Kaiwai, Indonesia
Kajang	Kajang, Indonesia
Kaka	Kaka, Cameroon
	Kaka, Central African Republic
	Kaka, Nigeria
Kakoa	Kakoa, Papua New Guinea
Kakuna-Mamusi	Kakuna-Mamusi, Papua New Guinea
Kalagan	**Kalagan, Philippines
Kalanga	Kalanga, Zimbabwe
Kalangoya	**Ifugao (Kalangoya), Philippines
Kalinga,Sumadel-Tinglayan	*Kalinga, Southern, Philippines
Kalinga	**Kalinga, Tanudan, Philippines
	**Kalinga,Northern, Philippines (81)
Kalinga, Kalagua	Kalinga, Kalagua, Philippines
Kalinga, Limus-Linan	Kalinga, Limus-Linan, Philippines
Kalinga, Quinaang	Kalinga, Quinaang, Philippines
Kalmytz	Kalmytz, China
	Kalmytz, USSR
Kalokalo	Kalokalo, Papua New Guinea
Kam	Kam, China
Kamano	Kamano, Papua New Guinea
Kamar	Kamar in Madhya Pradesh, India
Kamayura	Kamayura, Brazil
Kambarci	*Kambari, Nigeria (80)
Kambera	Kambera, Indonesia
Kamberataro	Kamberataro, Indonesia
	Kamberataro, Papua New Guinea
Kambot	Kambot, Papua New Guinea
Kami	Kami, Tanzania
Kamkam	Kamkam, Cameroon
Kamnum	Kamnum, Papua New Guinea
Kamo	Kamo, Nigeria
Kamoro	Kamoro, Indonesia
Kampung Baru	Kampung Baru, Indonesia
Kamtuk-Gresi	Kamtuk-Gresi, Indonesia
Kamuku	*Kamuku, Nigeria (80)
Kana	Kana, Nigeria
Kanauri	Kanauri in Uttar Pradesh, India
Kandas	Kandas, Papua New Guinea
Kanembu	Kanembu, Chad
	Kanembu, Niger
Kanga	Kanga, Sudan
Kanikkaran	Kanikkaran in Kerala, India
Kaningra	Kaningra, Papua New Guinea
Kanite	Kanite, Papua New Guinea
Kanjari	Kanjari in Andhra Pradesh, India
Kankanay	**Kankanay, Central, Philippines
Kanu	Kanu, Zaire
Kanum	Kanum, Indonesia
	Kanum, Papua New Guinea
Kanuri Dialects	Kanuri, Nigeria (80)
Kaonde	Kaonde, Zaire

Kaonde, Zambia
Kapin — Kapin, Papua New Guinea
Kapore — Kapore, Papua New Guinea
Kapori — Kapori, Indonesia
Kapriman — Kapriman, Papua New Guinea
Kapuchin — Kapuchin, USSR
Kara — Kara, Papua New Guinea
Kara — Kara, Tanzania
Karaboro — *Karaboro, Upper Volta
Karachay-Balkan — Karachay, USSR
Karagas — Karagas, USSR
Karaim — Karaim, USSR
Karakalpak — Karakalpak, USSR (80)
Karam — Karam, Papua New Guinea
Karanga — Karanga, Chad
Karangi — Karangi, Papua New Guinea
Karas — Karas, Indonesia
Karatin — Karatin, USSR
Kare — Kare, Papua New Guinea
Karekare — Karekare, Nigeria
Kari — Kari, Central African Republic
Kari, Chad
Kari, Zaire
Karipuna Creole — Karipuna Creole, Brazil
Karipuna Do Guapore — Karipuna Do Guapore, Brazil
Kariya — Kariya, Nigeria
Karkar — Karkar, Papua New Guinea
Karko — Karko, Sudan
Karmali — Karmali in Dihar, India
Karo — Kao, Ethiopia
Karon Dori — Karon Dori, Indonesia
Karon Pantai — Karon Pantai, Indonesia
Karre — Karre, Central African Republic
Karua — Karua, Papua New Guinea
Kasanga — Kasanga, Guinea-Bissau
Kasele — Kasele, Togo
Kasem — Kasem, Upper Volta
**Kasena, Ghana
Kashmiri — **Kashmiri Muslims, India (79)
Kasseng — Kasseng, Laos
Kasua — Kasua, Papua New Guinea
Kasuweri — Kasuweri, Indonesia
Katab — Katab, Nigeria
Katakari — Katakari in Gujarat, India
Katcha — Katcha, Sudan
Kate — Kate, Papua New Guinea
Kati, Northern — Kati, Northern, Indonesia
Kati, Southern — Kati, Southern, Indonesia
Katiati — Katiati, Papua New Guinea
Katla — Katla, Sudan
Katukina, Panoan — Katukina, Panoan, Brazil
Kaugat — Kaugat, Indonesia
Kaugel — Kaugel, Papua New Guinea
Kaur — **Kaur, Indonesia
Kaure — Kaure, Indonesia
Kavwol — Kavwol, Indonesia
Kavwol, Papua New Guinea
Kaw — Kaw, Burma
Kawar — Kawar in Madhya Pradesh, India
Kawe — Kawe, Indonesia
Kayabi — Kayabi, Brazil
Kayagar — Kayagar, Indonesia
Kayan — Kayan, Malaysia
Kayapo — Kayapo, Brazil
Kaygir — Kaygir, Indonesia
Kayupulau — Kayupulau, Indonesia

REGISTRY OF THE UNREACHED

Kazakh	Kazakhs, China (81)
Kazakhi	Kazakhs, Iran (80)
Kebu	Kebu, Togo
Kebumtamp	Kebumtamp, Bhutan
Kedayanas	Kedayanas, Malaysia
Keer	Keer in Madhya Pradesh, India
Kei	Kei, Indonesia
Keiga	Keiga, Sudan
Keiga Jirru	Keiga Jirru, Sudan
Kekchi	**Kekchi, Guatemala
Kela	Kela, Papua New Guinea
	Kelah, Zaire
Kelabit	Kelabit, Malaysia (81)
Kelao	Kelao, China
Kele	Kele, Gabon
Keley-i	Ifugao, Antipolo, Philippines
Kemak	Kemak, Indonesia
Kembata	Kembata, Ethiopia
Kemok	Kemok, Malaysia
Kenati	Kenati, Papua New Guinea
Kendari	Kendari, Indonesia
Kenga	Kenga, Chad
Kenyah	Kenyah, Indonesia
Keopara	Keopara, Papua New Guinea
Kera	Kera, Cameroon
	Kera, Chad
Kerewo	Kerewo, Papua New Guinea
Keriaka	Keriaka, Papua New Guinea
Kerinchi	Kerinchi, Indonesia
Ket	Ket, USSR
Kewa	*Kepas, Papua New Guinea
Kewa, East	Kewa, East, Papua New Guinea
Kewa, South	Kewa, South, Papua New Guinea
Kewa, West	Kewa, West, Papua New Guinea
Khakas	Khakas, USSR
Khalaj	Khalaj, Iran
Khalka	Khalka, China
Kham	Kham, China
	Kham, Nepal
Khamti	Khamti in Assam, India
Khamu	*Khamu, Thailand
Khana	Khana, Nigeria
Khandesi	Khandesi, India
Khanti	Khanti, USSR
Kharia	Kharia in Bihar, India
Khasi	Khasi in Assam, India
Khasonke	Khasonke, Mali
Khinalug	Khinalug, USSR
Khirwar	Khirwar in Madhya Pradesh, India
Khmer	**Kampuchean Refugees, Ontario, Canada:Ontario (83)
	Kampuchean Refugees, Laos
	Khmer Refugees, Montreal, Canada:Quebec
	Khmer Refugees, Toronto, Canada:Ontario
	Khmer Refugees, Unaccd. Minors, Thailand (83)
Khowar	Khowar, India
Khuwar	Chitralis, Pakistan (79)
Khvarshin	Khvarshin, USSR
Kiari	Kiari, Papua New Guinea
Kibet	Kibet, Chad
Kibiri	Kibiri, Papua New Guinea
Kichepo	Kichepo, Sudan
Kijita	**Wajita, Tanzania

542

Kikapoo	Kikapoo, Mexico
Kikerewe	Kerewe, Tanzania
Kikongo	Bakongo Angolan Refugees, Zaire (83)
Kilba	Kilba, Nigeria
Kilmera	Kilmera, Papua New Guinea
Kim	Kim, Central African Republic
	Kim, Chad
Kimaghama	Kimaghama, Indonesia
Kimbu	Kimbu, Tanzania
Kimyal	*Kimyal, Indonesia
Kinalakna	Kinalakna, Papua New Guinea
Kinaray-A	Kinaray-A, Philippines
Kinga	Kinga, Tanzania
Kinyarwanda	***Banyarwanda, Rwanda
Kirghiz	Kirghiz Afghan Refugees, Turkey (83)
Kirgiz	Kirgiz, Afghanistan
	Kirgiz, China
	Kirgiz, USSR (80)
Kiriwina	Kiriwina, Papua New Guinea
Kirundi	Burundian Hutu Refugees, Tanzania (83)
	***Rwandan Tutsi Refugees, Burundi (83)
Kis	Kis, Papua New Guinea
Kisan	Kisan in Bihar, India
Kisankasa	Kisankasa, Tanzania
Kishanganjia	Kishanganjia in Bihar, India
Kishtwari	Kishtwari in Jammu, India
Kisi	Kisi, Tanzania
Kissi	Kissi, Guinea
	*Kissi, Liberia
Kissi, Southern	*Kissi, Sierra Leone
Kiwai, Northeast	Kiwai, Northeast, Papua New Guinea
Kiwai, Southern	Kiwai, Southern, Papua New Guinea
Kiwai, Wabuda	Kiwai, Wabuda, Papua New Guinea
Kiwoyo	Bawoyo, Zaire
Kizinza	*Wazinza, Tanzania
Klaoh	Klaoh, Liberia
Koalib (Nuba)	Koalib, Sudan (79)
Kobiana	Kobiana, Guinea
Kobon	Kobon, Papua New Guinea
Koda	Koda in Bihar, India
Kodi	Kodi, Indonesia
Koenoem	Koenoem, Nigeria
Kofyar	Kofyar, Nigeria
Kohoroxitari	Kohoroxitari, Brazil
Kohumono	Kohumono, Nigeria
Koiari, Grass	Koiari, Grass, Papua New Guinea
Koiari, Mountain	Koiari, Mountain, Papua New Guinea
Koita	Koita, Papua New Guinea
Kokant	Kokant, Burma
Koke	Koke, Chad
Kol	Kol in Assam, India
	Kol, Papua New Guinea
Kolaka	**Loho Loho, Indonesia
Kolami	**Kolam, India
Kolbila	Kolbila, Cameroon
Kole	Kole, Cameroon
Koliku	Koliku, Papua New Guinea
Kolom	Kolom, Papua New Guinea
Kom	Kom in Manipur, India
Kom Komba	*Konkomba, Togo
Koma	Koma, Cameroon
	Koma, Ghana

	Koma, Nigeria
Koma, Central	Koma, Central, Sudan
Komba	Komba, Papua New Guinea
Kombio	Kombio, Papua New Guinea
Komering	Komering, Indonesia
	Lampung, Indonesia (80)
Komi-Permyat	Komi-Permyat, USSR
Komi-Zyrian	Komi-Zyrian, USSR
Komo	*Komo, Ethiopia
Komono	Komono, Upper Volta
Komutu	Komutu, Papua New Guinea
Konabem	Konabem, Cameroon
Konda-Dora	Konda-Dora (Andra Pradesh), India
Koneraw	Koneraw, Indonesia
Kongo	Kongo, Angola
Konkani	Konkani in Gujarat, India
Konkomba	Konkomba, Ghana
Kono	Kono, Nigeria
	**Kono, Sierra Leone
Konomala	Konomala, Papua New Guinea
Konongo	Konongo, Tanzania
Konso	Konso, Ethiopia
Konyagi	Konyagi, Guinea
Koraga	Koraga in Kerala, India
Korak	Korak, Papua New Guinea
Korape	Korape, Papua New Guinea
Korapun	Korapun, Indonesia
Korean	**Apartment Residents-Seoul, Korea, Republic of
	**Bus Drivers, South Korea, Korea, Republic of
	**Bus Girls in Seoul, Korea, Republic of (82)
	Indust.Workers Yongdungpo, Korea, Republic of
	Kae Sung Natives in Seoul, Korea, Republic of (82)
	***Koreans in Germany, German Federal Rep.
	Koreans in Manchuria, China (81)
	*Koreans of Japan, Japan
	Koreans, Canada
	**Prisoners, Korea, Republic of
Korku	*Korku in Madhya Pradesh, India
Koro	Koro, Nigeria
Koroma	Koroma, Sudan
Korop	Korop, Cameroon
	Korop, Nigeria
Korwa	Korwa in Bihar, India
Koryak	Koryak, USSR
Kosorong	Kosorong, Papua New Guinea
Kota	Kota in Tamil Nadu, India
	Kota, Gabon
	Kotta, India
Kotia	Kotia in Andhra Pradesh, India
Kotogut	Kotogut, Indonesia
Kotoko	Kotoko, Cameroon
	Kotoko, Chad
Kotokoli	Kotokoli, Benin
	Kotokoli, Togo
	Tem, Togo
Kotopo	Kotopo, Cameroon
Kouya	Kouya, Ivory Coast
Kovai	Kovai, Papua New Guinea
Kove	Kove, Papua New Guinea
Kowaao	**Kowaao, Liberia

Koya	Koya in Andhra Pradesh, India
Koyra	Koyra, Ethiopia
Kpa	Kpa, Cameroon
Kpelle	Kpelle, Guinea
	Kpelle, Liberia
Kposo	Kposo, Togo
Krachi	Krachi, Ghana
Krahn	***Krahn, Liberia
Kreen-Akakore	Kreen-Akakore, Brazil
Krifi	Kirifi, Nigeria
Krio	Krio, Gambia
Krisa	Krisa, Papua New Guinea
Krobou	Krobou, Ivory Coast
Krongo	Krongo, Sudan
Krumen	Krumen, Ivory Coast
Kryz	Kryz, USSR
Kube	Kube, Papua New Guinea
Kubu	Kubu, Indonesia (81)
Kuda-Chamo	Kuda-Chamo, Nigeria
Kudiya	Kudiya, India
Kugbo	Kugbo, Nigeria
Kui	***Kond, India
	*Kui, Thailand
Kuikuro	Kuikuro, Brazil
Kuka	Kuka, Chad
Kukele	Kukele, Cameroon
	Kukele, Nigeria
Kukni	*Kuknas, India
Kukuya	Kukuwy, Papua New Guinea
Kukwa	Kukwa, Congo
Kulango	Kulango, Ivory Coast
Kulele	Kulele, Ivory Coast
Kulere	Kulere, Nigeria
Kullo	Kullo, Ethiopia
Kului	**Kuluis in Himachal Pradesh, India (81)
Kulung	Kulung, Nigeria
Kumai	Kumai, Papua New Guinea
Kumam	Kumam, Uganda
Kuman	Kuman, Papua New Guinea
Kumauni	Kumauni in Assam, India
Kumdauron	Kumdauron, Papua New Guinea
Kumu	Kumu, Zaire
Kumukio	Kumukio, Papua New Guinea
Kunama	Kunama, Ethiopia
Kunante	Kunante, Guinea-Bissau
Kunda	Kunda, Mozambique
	Kunda, Zimbabwe
Kuni	Kuni, Papua New Guinea
Kunimaipa	**Kunimaipa, Papua New Guinea
Kunua	Kunua, Papua New Guinea
Kuot	Kuot, Papua New Guinea
Kupia	Kupia in Andhra Pradesh, India
Kupsabiny	Kupsabiny, Uganda
Kurada	Kurada, Papua New Guinea
Kuranko (Maninka)	**Koranko, Sierra Leone
Kurdish	Kurds in Kuwait, Kuwait
	Turkish Workers, Belgium (80)
	Turks in Basel, Switzerland (82)
Kurdish (Kirmancho)	*Kurds of Turkey, Turkey (79)
Kurdish Dialects	Kurds in Iran, Iran (80)
Kurdish dialects	**Ahl-i-Haqq in Iran, Iran (79)
Kuria	Kuria, Tanzania
Kurichiya	Kurichiya in Kerala, India (81)
Kurmanji	Iraqi Kurd Refugees, Iran (83)
Kuruba	Kuruba in Tamil Nadu, India

Kurudu	Kurudu, Indonesia
Kurumba	Kurumba, Upper Volta
Kurux	Kurux in Bihar, India
Kusaal	**Kusaasi, Ghana
Kushi	Kushi, Nigeria
Kusso	Mbukushu, Angola
Kusu	Kusu, Zaire
Kuteb	Kuteb, Nigeria
Kutin	Kutin, Cameroon
Kutu	Kutu, Tanzania
Kuturmi	Kuturmi, Nigeria
Kuvi	Kuvi in Orissa, India
Kuwaa	Kuwaa, Liberia
Kuzamani	Kuzamani, Nigeria
Kvanadin	Kvanadin, USSR
Kwa	Kwa, Nigeria
Kwadi	Kwadi, Angola
Kwakum	Kwakum, Cameroon
Kwale	Kwale, Papua New Guinea
Kwambi	Kwambi, Namibia
Kwanga	Kwanga, Papua New Guinea
Kwangali	Kwangali, Angola
Kwansu	Kwansu, Indonesia
Kwanyama	Kwanyama, Angola
	Kwanyama, Namibia
Kwaya	Kwaya, Tanzania
Kwe-Etshari	*Bushmen (Hiechware), Zimbabwe
Kwe-etshori	Kwe-etshori, Botswana
	Kwe-etshori, Zimbabwe
Kwerba	Kwerba, Indonesia
Kwere	Kwere, Tanzania
Kwese	Kwese, Zaire
Kwesten	Kwesten, Indonesia
Kwoma	Kwoma, Papua New Guinea
Kwomtari	Kwomtari, Papua New Guinea
Kyibaku	Kyibaku, Nigeria
LaLa-Bisa	Kunda, Zambia
Laamang	Laamang, Nigeria
Labaani	Labans, India
Labhani	Labhani in Andhra Pradesh, India
Labu	Labu, Papua New Guinea
Lacandon	Lacandon, Mexico
Ladakhi	Ladakhi in Jammu, India
Ladinos	Ladinos, Lebanon
Laewomba	Laewomba, Papua New Guinea
Lafofa	Lafofa, Sudan
Lahouli	**Lahaulis in Punjab, India
Lahu	*Lahu, Thailand (81)
Lahul	Lahul, China
Laka	Laka, Cameroon
	Laka, Central African Republic
	Laka, China
Lakal	Laka, Chad
Lakian	Lakians, USSR
Lakka	Lakka, Nigeria
Lala	Lala, Zambia
Lalia	Lalia, Zaire
Lalung	Lalung in Assam, India
Lama	Lama, Burma
Lamba	Lamba, Benin
	Lamba, Togo
	Lamba, Zaire
	Lamba, Zambia
Lambadi	**Lambadi in Andhra Pradesh, India (81)
Lambi	Lambi, Cameroon

Lambya	Lambya, Malawi
	Lambya, Tanzania
Lame	Lame, Nigeria
Lamogai	Lamogai, Papua New Guinea
Landoma	Landoma, Guinea
	Landoma, Guinea-Bissau
Langi	Langi, Tanzania
Lango	*Lango, Ethiopia
	Lango, Uganda
Lanoh	Lanoh, Malaysia
Lao	Lao Refugees, Argentina (83)
	*Lao Refugees, Spain (83)
	*Lao Refugees, Thailand
	*Lao, Laos (79)
	Lao-Chinese Refugees, Edmonton, Canada:Alberta
Lara	Lara, Indonesia
Laro	Laro, Sudan
Laru	Laru, Nigeria
Latdwalam	Latdwalam, Indonesia
Lati	Lati, China
Latuka	**Lotuka, Sudan
Laudje	Laudje, Indonesia
Lavatbura-Lamusong	Lavatbura-Lamusong, Papua New Guinea
Lavongai	Lavongai, Papua New Guinea
Lawa	Lawa, Mountain, Thailand
Lebgo	Lebgo, Nigeria
Leco	Leco, Bolivia
Lega	Lega, Zaire
Lelemi	Lelemi, Ghana
Lengua, Northern	Lengua, Northern, Paraguay
Lenje	Lenje, Zambia
Lepcha	**Lepcha, India
Leron	Leron, Papua New Guinea
Letti	Letti, Indonesia
Lhomi	Lhomi, Nepal
Li	Li, China
Ligbi	Ligbi, Ghana
	Ligbi, Ivory Coast
Liguri	Liguri, Sudan
Lihir	Lihir, Papua New Guinea
Liko	Liko, Zaire
Lima	Lima, Zambia
Limba	Limba, Sierra Leone
Limbum	**Wimbum, Cameroon
Lio	Lionese, Indonesia
Lisu	*Lisu, Thailand
Liv	Liv, USSR
Lo	Lo, Nigeria
Lobi	Lobi, Ivory Coast
Local Dialects	Bangangte, Cameroon
Local dialects	Buka-khwe, Botswana
	Kubu, Indonesia (80)
	*Mahrah, Yemen, Democratic
	Moken of Thailand, Thailand
	Nuristani, Afghanistan (80)
	**Plantation Workers, Papua New Guinea
	Pygmy (Binga), Burundi
	Pygmy (Binga), Central African Republic
Lodhi	Lodhi in Bihar, India
Logba	Logba, Ghana
Logoro (Bambara)	Kagoro, Mali
Lohiki	Lohiki, Papua New Guinea

REGISTRY OF THE UNREACHED

Loinang	Loinang, Indonesia (81)
Loko	Loko, Guinea
	Loko, Sierra Leone
Lokoro	*Lokoro, Sudan
Loma	Loma, Guinea
	Loma, Liberia
Lombi	Lombi, Zaire
Lombo	Lombo, Zaire
Longuda	Longuda, Nigeria
Lore	Lore, Indonesia
Lorhon	*Teenbu, Ivory Coast
Lori	Bovir-Ahmadi, Iran
	Lori, Sudan
Lotsu-Piri	Lotsu-Piri, Nigeria
Lou-Baluan-Pam	Lou-Baluan-Pam, Papua New Guinea
Loven	Loven, Laos (81)
Lozi	Lozi, Zambia
	Lozi, Zimbabwe
Lu	Lu, China
Luac	Luac, Sudan
Luano	Luano, Zambia
Lubu	Lubu, Indonesia
Luchazi	Luchazi, Angola
	Luchazi, Zambia
Lue	Lue, Cameroon
Lugbara	Muslims (West Nile Dist.), Uganda
Lugitama	Lugitama, Papua New Guinea
Luimbi	Luimbi, Angola
Lukep	Lukep, Papua New Guinea
Lumbu	Lumbu, Gabon
Luna	Luna, Zaire
Lunda	Lunda, Angola
Lunda, Ndembu	Lunda, Ndembu, Zambia
Lundu	Lundu, Cameroon
Lungu	Lungu, Nigeria
Luo	Luo, Tanzania
Luri	Lors, Iran (80)
	Mamasani, Iran
Lushai	Lushai in Assam, India
Luteso	**Teso, Kenya
Luvale	Luvale Refugees from Angola, Zambia (83)
Luwu	Luwu, Indonesia
Luyana	Luyana, Angola
	Luyana, Zambia
Lwalu	Lwalu, Zaire
Lwena	Lwena, Angola
Lwo	Lwo, Sudan
Ma	Ma, Zaire
Maanyan	Maanyan, Indonesia
Maasai, Samburu	**Samburu, Kenya (84)
Maba	Maba, Chad
	Maba, Sudan
	Ouaddai, Chad
Maban-Jumjum	Maban-Jumjum, Sudan
	Meban, Sudan
Maca	Maca, Paraguay
Machiguenga	Machiguenga, Peru
Macu	Macu, Colombia
Macuna	Macuna, Colombia
Macuxi	**Macuxi, Brazil
Madak	Madak, Papua New Guinea
Madda	Madda, Nigeria
Madi	Madi, Sudan
	Madi, Uganda
Madik	Madik, Indonesia

Mafaara · **Nafaara, Ghana (79)
Magar · **Magar, Nepal
Maghi · Maghi, Burma
Magori · Magori, Papua New Guinea
Maguindanao · Maguindanao, Philippines (80)
Mahali · Mahali in Assam, India
Mahri · Mahri, Oman
Mai · Mai, Papua New Guinea
Mailu · Mailu, Papua New Guinea
Maiongong · Maiongong, Brazil
Mairasi · Mairasi, Indonesia
Maisan · Maisan, Papua New Guinea
Maithili · Maithili, Nepal
Maiwa · Maiwa, Papua New Guinea
Majangiir · *Masengo, Ethiopia
Majhi · Majhi, Nepal
Majhwar · Majhwar in Madhya Pradesh, India
Maji · Maji, Ethiopia
Majingai-Ngama · Majingai-Ngama, Chad
Majingai-ngama · Majingai-ngama, Central African Republic
Maka · Maka, Cameroon
Makarim · Makarim, Papua New Guinea
Makasai · Makasai, Indonesia
Makere · Makere, Uganda
Makian, West · Makian, West, Indonesia
Maklew · Maklew, Indonesia
Makua · Makua, Mozambique
Mala, Pattani · Thai Islam (Malay), Thailand (80)
Malagasy · *Prisoners in Antananarivo, Madagascar (82)
Malalamai · Malalamai, Papua New Guinea
Malamutha · Malakkaras of Kerala, India (81)
Malankuravan · Malankuravan in Kerala, India
Malapandaram · Malapandaram in Kerala, India
Malappanackan · Malappanackers, India
Malaryan · Malaryan in Kerala, India
Malas · Malas, Papua New Guinea
Malasanga · Malasanga, Papua New Guinea
Malavedan · Malavedan in Kerala, India
Malay · Malays of Singapore, Singapore (79)
Malayalam · Indians in Dubai, United Arab Emirates (82)
Iravas in Kerala, India
*Malayalars, India
Malayalan · Mappillas, India
Malayo · Malayo, Colombia
Male · Male, Ethiopia
Malek · Malek, Papua New Guinea
Maleu · Maleu, Papua New Guinea
Mali · Mali in Andhra Pradesh, India
Malila · Malila, Tanzania
Malinke, Senegalese · Manding, Senegal
Malki · Malki in Bihar, India
Malon · Malon, Papua New Guinea
Malpaharia · Malpaharia in Assam, India
Maltese · *Maltese, Malta
Malto · Sauria Pahari, India
Malvi · Malvi in Madhya Pradesh, India
Mam · **Mam Indian, Guatemala
Mama · Mama, Nigeria
Mamaa · Mamaa, Papua New Guinea
Mambai · Mambai, Indonesia
Mambila · Mambila, Cameroon
Mambwe-Lungu · Mambwe-Lungu, Tanzania

REGISTRY OF THE UNREACHED

	Mambwe-Lungu, Zambia
Mampruli	Mamprusi, Ghana
	Mamprusi, Ghana
Mamvu-Efe	Mamvu-Efe, Zaire
Managalasi	Managalasi, Papua New Guinea
Manambu	Manambu, Papua New Guinea
Manchu	Manchu, China (81)
Manda	Manda, Tanzania
Mandar	Mandar, Indonesia
Mandara	Mandara, Nigeria
Mandarin	*Chinese Mainlanders, Taiwan
	Chinese Muslims, Taiwan (81)
	**Chinese Refugees, France, France (79)
	Chinese Students, Thunder Bay , Canada:Ontario
	**Chinese Students, United Kingdom
	*Chinese in Austria, Austria
	**Chinese in Boston, United States of America (82)
	Chinese in Costa Rica, Costa Rica
	*Chinese in Holland, Netherlands
	*Chinese in Japan, Japan
	*Chinese in Korea, Korea, Republic of
	*Chinese in Laos, Laos
	**Chinese in United Kingdom, United Kingdom
	**Chinese in United States, United States of America
	*Chinese in West Germany, German Federal Rep.
	Chinese, Halifax, Canada:Nova Scotia
	Taiwan-Chinese Un. Stud., Taiwan
	**University Students, Chin, China
Mandarin and dialects	Chinese in Burma, Burma
	**Chinese in Sarawak, Malaysia
Mandaya	Mandaya, Philippines
Mandaya, Mansaka	Mandaya, Mansaka, Philippines
Mander	Mander, Indonesia
Mandingo	Mandingo, Liberia (79)
Mandyak	Mandyak, Gambia
Mandyako	**Manjaco, Guinea-Bissau
Mandyale	Manjack, Senegal
Manem	Manem, Indonesia
Mangap	Mangap, Papua New Guinea
Mangbai	Mangbai, Chad
Mangbutu	Mangbutu, Zaire
Manggarai	Manggarai Muslims, Indonesia (81)
Mangisa	Mangisa, Cameroon
Maninka	Maninka, Guinea-Bissau
	Maninka, Sierra Leone
Manipuri	*Meitei, India (79)
Maniteneri	Piro, Peru
Mankanya	Mancang, Senegal
	Mankanya, Guinea-Bissau
	Mankanya, Senegal
Manna-Dora	Manna-Dora in A.P., India
Mannan	Mannan in Kerala, India
Mano	Mano, Liberia
Manobo	*Ata of Davao, Philippines
Manobo, Agusan	Manobo, Agusan, Philippines
Manobo, Ata	Manobo, Ata, Philippines
Manobo, Binokid	Manobo, Binokid, Philippines
	**Manobo, Western Bukidnon, Philippines

Manobo, Binukid   **Bukidnon, Philippines
Manobo, Dibabawon   Manobo, Dibabawon, Philippines
Manobo, Obo   Manobo, Obo, Philippines
Manobo, Pulangi   Manobos, Pulangi, Philippines
Manobo, Sarangani   Manobo, Sarangani, Philippines
Manobo, Tagabawa   Manobo, Tagabawa, Philippines
Manobo, Tigwa   **Manobo, Salug, Philippines
    **Manobo, Tigwa, Philippines
Mansaka   **Mansaka, Philippines
Mansi   Mansi, USSR
Mantera   Mantera, Malaysia
Mantion   Mantion, Indonesia
Manu Park Panoan   Manu Park Panoan, Peru
Manyika   Manyika, Zimbabwe
Mao, Northern   Mao, Northern, Ethiopia
Maou   Maou, Ivory Coast
Mape   Mape, Papua New Guinea
Mapena   Mapena, Papua New Guinea
Mapoyo   Mapoyo, Venezuela
Mapuche   Mapuche, Chile
Maquiritari   Maquiritari, Venezuela
Mara   Mara in Assam, India
Maralango   Maralango, Papua New Guinea
Maraliinan   Maraliinan, Papua New Guinea
Maranao   Maranao, Philippines (79)
Maranao, Lanad   Maranao, Lanad, Philippines
Mararit   Mararit, Chad
Marathi   *Labourers of Jhoparpatti, India
    Mangs in Maharashtra, India
Marau   Marau, Indonesia
Marba   Marba, Chad
Marghi Central   Marghi Central, Nigeria
Mari   Mari, Papua New Guinea
    Mari, USSR
Maria   Maria in Andhra Pradesh, India
    Maria, Papua New Guinea
Marind   Marind, Indonesia
Marind, Bian   Marind, Bian, Indonesia
Maring   Maring, Papua New Guinea
Marka   Marka, Upper Volta
Marubo   Marubo, Brazil
Marwari   **Bhil, Pakistan
    Marwari in Gujarat, India
    **Meghwar, Pakistan (79)
Masa   Budugum, Cameroon
    Gisel, Cameroon
    Masa, Chad
Masaba   Masaba, Uganda
Masai   **Maasai, Kenya (79)
Masakin   Masakin, Sudan
Masalit   Masalit, Chad
Masegi   Masegi, Papua New Guinea
Masenrempulu   Masenrempulu, Indonesia
Mashi   Mashi, Zambia
Massalat   Massalat, Chad
Matakam   Matakam, Cameroon
    Matakam, Nigeria
Matawari   Matawari, Surinam
Matbat   Matbat, Indonesia
Matengo   Matengo, Tanzania
Matipuhy-Nahukua   Matipuhy-Nahukua, Brazil
Matlatzinca, Atzingo   Matlatzinca, Atzingo, Mexico
Matumbi   Matumbi, Tanzania
Maure   Maure, Mali
Maviha   Maviha, Mozambique
Mawak   Mawak, Papua New Guinea

REGISTRY OF THE UNREACHED

Mawan	Mawan, Papua New Guinea
Mawchi	**Mawchis, India
Mawes	Mawes, Indonesia
Maxakali	Maxakali, Brazil
Mayo	Mayo, Mexico
Mayoruna	Mayoruna, Peru
Mazahua	**Mazahua, Mexico
Mazandarani	Mazandaranis, Iran
Mba	Mba, Zaire
Mbaama	Mbaama, Gabon
Mbai	Mbai, Central African Republic
	Mbai, Chad
Mbala	Mbala, Zaire
Mbangwe	Mbangwe, Zaire
Mbanja	Mbanja, Zaire
Mbati	Mbati, Central African Republic
Mbe	Mbe, Nigeria
Mbede	Mbede, Gabon
Mbembe	Mbembe (Tigong), Nigeria
	Mbembe, Cameroon
	Mbembe, Nigeria
Mbimu	Mbimu, Cameroon
Mbo	Mbo, Cameroon
	Mbo, Zaire
Mboi	Mboi, Nigeria
Mbole	Mbole, Zaire
Mbugwe	Mbugwe, Tanzania
Mbula-Bwazza	Mbula-Bwazza, Nigeria
Mbum	Mbum, Chad
Mbunda	Mbunda, Angola
Mbunga	Mbunga, Tanzania
Mbwela	Mbwela, Angola
Me'en	Me'en, Ethiopia
Meax	Meax, Indonesia
Medlpa	Medlpa, Papua New Guinea
Mehek	Mehek, Papua New Guinea
Mejah	**Mejah, India
Meje	Meje, Uganda
Mekeo	Mekeo, Papua New Guinea
Mekwei	Mekwei, Indonesia
Melanau	**Melanau of Sarawak, Malaysia (80)
Mende	Gola, Sierra Leone
	Krim, Sierra Leone
	Mende, Liberia
	Mende, Sierra Leone
Menemo-Mogamo	Menemo-Mogamo, Cameroon
Mengen	Mengen, Papua New Guinea
Menka	Menka, Cameroon
Menri	Menri, Malaysia
Menye	Menye, Papua New Guinea
Meo	**Meo, Thailand
Mera Mera	Mera Mera, Papua New Guinea
Mesengo	Mesengo, Ethiopia
Mesme	Mesme, Chad
Mesmedje	Mesmedje, Chad
Mianmin	Mianmin, Papua New Guinea
Miao	***Hmong Refugee Women, Ban Vinai, Thailand (83)
	***Hmong Refugees, United States of America (83)
	Hmong, Twin Cities, United States of America
	Miao, China (81)
Miching	**Miching, India
Midob	Midob, Sudan
Midsivindi	Midsivindi, Papua New Guinea

552

Mien   Mien, China (81)
Migabac   Migabac, Papua New Guinea
Migili   Migili, Nigeria
Mikarew   Mikarew, Papua New Guinea
Mikir   **Karbis, India
Mimi   Mimi, Chad
Mimika   *Mimika, Indonesia
Mina   Mina in Madhya Pradesh, India
Minamanwa   **Mamanua, Philippines (81)
Minangkabau   Minangkabau, Indonesia (80)
Minanibai   Minanibai, Papua New Guinea
Mindik   Mindik, Papua New Guinea
Minduumo   Minduumo, Gabon
Mingat   Mingat, USSR
Mirdha   Mirdha in Orissa, India
Miri   Miri, Sudan
Miriam   Miriam, Papua New Guinea
Mirung   Mirung, Bangladesh
Mishmi   Mishmi in Assam, India
Miskito   Miskito, Nicaragua
Mitang   Mitang, Papua New Guinea
Mitmit   Mitmit, Papua New Guinea
Mixe   **Mixes, Mexico
Mixteco   *Mixteco, San Juan Mixtepic, Mexico
Mixteco, Amoltepec   Mixteco, Amoltepec, Mexico
Mixteco, Apoala   Mixteco, Apoala, Mexico
Mixteco, Eastern   Mixteco, Eastern, Mexico
Mixteco, Eastern Putla   Mixteco, Eastern Putla, Mexico
Mixteco, Huajuapan   Mixteco, Huajuapan, Mexico
Mixteco, Silacayoapan   Mixteco, Silacayoapan, Mexico
Mixteco, Southern Puebla   Mixteco, Southern Puebla, Mexico
Mixteco, Southern Putla   Mixteco, Southern Putla, Mexico
Mixteco, Tututepec   Mixteco, Tututepec, Mexico
Mixteco, Yosondua   Mixteco, Yosondua, Mexico
Miya   Miya, Nigeria
Mo   Mo, Ivory Coast
Mo (Degha)   Mo, Ghana
Mober   Mober, Nigeria
Mocha   ***Mocha, Ethiopia
Modo   Modo, Sudan
Moewehafen   Moewehafen, Papua New Guinea
Mofu   Mofu, Cameroon
Mogholi   Mogholi, Afghanistan
Mogum   Mogum, Chad
Moi   Moi, Indonesia
Mokareng   Mokareng, Papua New Guinea
Moken   Moken, Burma (79)
Mokole   *Mokole, Benin
Molbog   *Molbog, Philippines
Mole   Mossi, Upper Volta (80)
Molof   Molof, Indonesia
Momare   Momare, Papua New Guinea
Mombum   Mombum, Indonesia
Momoguns   Momoguns, Malaysia
Momolili   Momolili, Papua New Guinea
Mon   Mon, Burma (81)
Mona   Mona, Ivory Coast
Mongondow   Mongondow, Indonesia (81)
Mongour   Mongour, China
Moni   Moni, Indonesia
Monjombo   Monjombo, Central African Republic
Mono   Mono, Zaire
Monpa   Monpa, India
Montol   Montol, Nigeria
Mopan Maya   **Mopan Maya, Belize
  **Mopan Maya, Guatemala

REGISTRY OF THE UNREACHED

Moqaddam — Moqaddam, Iran
Mor — Mor, Indonesia
Morawa — Morawa, Papua New Guinea
Moreb — Moreb, Sudan
Moresada — Moresada, Papua New Guinea
Mori — Mori, Indonesia (81)
Morigi — Morigi, Papua New Guinea
Morima — Morima, Papua New Guinea
Moru — Moru, Ivory Coast
— Moru, Sudan

Morunahua — Morunahua, Peru
Morwap — Morwap, Indonesia
Mosi — Mosi, Tanzania
Motilon — Motilon, Colombia
— Motilon, Venezuela
Movima — Movima, Bolivia
Moxodi — Moxodi, Papua New Guinea
Mpoto — Mpoto, Malawi
— Mpoto, Tanzania

Mualthuam — Mualthuam, India
Mubi — Mubi, Chad
Mugil — Mugil, Papua New Guinea
Muinane — Muinane, Colombia
Mukawa — Mukawa, Papua New Guinea
Mulimba — Mulimba, Cameroon
Multani — Multani in Punjab, India
Mumbake — Mumbake, Nigeria
Mumuye — Mumuye, Nigeria
Mun — Mun, Burma
Muna — Muna, Indonesia
Munda — **Mundas in Bihar, India
Mundang — Mundang, Chad
Mundari — Mundari in Assam, India
Mundu — Mundu, Zaire
Munduruku — Munduruku, Brazil
Mungaka — Mungaka, Cameroon
Munggui — Munggui, Indonesia
Munji-Yidgha — Munji-Yidgha, Afghanistan
Munkip — Munkip, Papua New Guinea
Mup — Mup, Papua New Guinea
Mura-Piraha — Mura-Piraha, Brazil
Muria — Muria in Andhra Pradesh, India
Murik — Murik, Papua New Guinea
Murle — Murle, Sudan
Mursi — Mursi, Ethiopia
Murung — Mru, Bangladesh
Murut — Murut, Malaysia
Musak — Musak, Papua New Guinea
Musar — Musar, Papua New Guinea
Musei — Musei, Chad
Musgu — Musgu, Chad
Musom — Musom, Papua New Guinea
Muthuvan — Muthuvan (Andra Pradesh), India
Mutum — Mutum, Papua New Guinea
Muwasi — Muwasi in Madhya Pradesh, India
Muyuw — Muyuw, Papua New Guinea
Mwanga — Mwanga, Tanzania
Mwatebu — Mwatebu, Papua New Guinea
Mwera — Mwera, Tanzania
Myaung-Ze — Myaung-Ze, Burma
Nabak — Nabak, Papua New Guinea
Nabi — Nabi, Indonesia
Nadeb Maku — Nadeb Maku, Brazil
Nafri — Nafri, Indonesia
Naga, Kalyokengnyu — Naga, Kalyokengnyu, India
Naga, Mao — Naga, Mao, India

554

Naga, Nruanghmei	Naga, Nruanghmei, India
Naga, Sangtam	Naga, Sangtam, India
Naga, Sema	Naga, Sema, India
Naga, Tangkhul	Naga, Tangkhul, India
Naga, Wancho	Naga, Wancho, India
Naga, Zoliang	Zoliang, India
Nagar	Nagar in Madhya Pradesh, India
Nagarige	Nagarige, Papua New Guinea
Nagatman	Nagatman, Papua New Guinea
Nagovisi	Nagovisi, Papua New Guinea
Nahsi	Nahsi, China
Nahu	Nahu, Papua New Guinea
Nahua	*Nahua, North Puebla, Mexico
Nahuatl, Hidalgo	***Azteca, Mexico (79)
Naka	Naka, Sudan
Nakama	Nakama, Papua New Guinea
Nakanai	Nakanai, Papua New Guinea
Nalik	Nalik, Papua New Guinea
Naltya	Naltya, Indonesia
Nalu	Nalu, Guinea
Nama	Nama, Namibia
	Nama, South Africa
Nambikuara	Nambikuara, Brazil
Nambis	Nambis, Papua New Guinea
Nambu	Nambu, Papua New Guinea
Nambya	**Nambya, Zimbabwe
Namuni	Namuni, Papua New Guinea
Nanai	Nanai, China
	Nanai, USSR
Nancere	Nancere, Chad
Nandi	Dorobo, Kenya
	Nandi, Zaire
Nandu-Tari	Nandu-Tari, Nigeria
Nankina	Nankina, Papua New Guinea
Nao	Nao, Ethiopia
Naoudem	Naoudem, Togo
Napali	*Gorkha, India
Nara	Nara, Ethiopia
	Nara, Papua New Guinea
Naraguta	Naraguta, Nigeria
Narak	Narak, Papua New Guinea
Nasioi	Nasioi, Papua New Guinea
Nata	Nata, Tanzania
Natemba	Natemba, Togo
Natioro	Natioro, Upper Volta
Native Senoi	**Senoi, Malaysia (81)
Nauna	Nauna, Papua New Guinea
Nawuri	Nawuri, Ghana
Nchumbulu	Nchumbulu, Ghana
Nchumburu	Nchimburu, Ghana
Nchumuru	Nchumuru, Ghana
Ndaaka	Ndaaka, Zaire
Ndali	Ndali, Tanzania
Ndam	Ndam, Central African Republic
Ndamba	Ndamba, Tanzania
Ndao	Ndaonese, Indonesia
Ndau	Ndau, Zimbabwe
Nde-Nsele-Nta	Nde-Nsele-Nta, Nigeria
Ndengereko	Ndengereko, Tanzania
Ndjem	Ndjem, Cameroon
Ndo	Ndo, Zaire
Ndoe	Ndoe, Nigeria
Ndogo	Ndogo, Central African Republic
	Ndogo, Sudan
Ndom	Ndom, Indonesia
Ndomde	Ndomde, Tanzania

REGISTRY OF THE UNREACHED

Ndoolo   Ndoolo, Zaire
Ndop-Bamessing   Ndop-Bamessing, Cameroon
Ndoro   Ndoro, Cameroon
     **Ndoro, Nigeria
Nduga   Nduga, Indonesia
Ndunga   Ndunga, Zaire
Ndunpa Duupa   Ndunpa Duupa, Cameroon
Negira   Negira, Papua New Guinea
Nek   Nek, Papua New Guinea
Nekgini   Nekgini, Papua New Guinea
Neko   Neko, Papua New Guinea
Nengaya   Nengaya, Papua New Guinea
Nentsy   Nentsy, USSR
Nepali   **Nepalese in India, India
Nevo   Nevo, Ivory Coast
Newari   Newar in Kathmandu, Nepal (82)
     *Newari, Nepal
Ngada   Ngada, Indonesia
Ngaing   Ngaing, Papua New Guinea
Ngalik, North   Ngalik, North, Indonesia
Ngalik, Southern   Ngalik, Southern, Indonesia
Ngalum   Ngalum, Indonesia
Ngamo   **Ngamo, Nigeria
Nganasan   Nganasan, USSR
Ngando   Ngando, Central African Republic
     Ngando, Zaire
Ngasa   Ngasa, Tanzania
Ngayaba   Ngayaba, Cameroon
Ngbaka   Ngbaka, Zaire
Ngbaka Ma'bo   Ngbaka Ma'bo, Central African
     Republic
     Ngbaka Ma'bo, Zaire
Ngbandi   Ngbandi, Zaire
Ngbee   Ngbee, Zaire
Ngemba   Ngemba, Cameroon
Ngen   *Ngen, Ivory Coast
Ngeq   Ngeq, Laos
Ngi   Ngi, Cameroon
Ngindo   Ngindo, Tanzania
Nginyukwur   Nginyukwur, Sudan
Ngirere   Ngirere, Sudan
Ngiri   Ngiri, Zaire
Ngizim   Ngizim, Nigeria
Ngok   Ngok, Sudan
Ngombe   **Ngombe, Zaire
Ngoni   Ngoni, Tanzania
     Ngoni, Zambia
Ngulu   Ngulu, Malawi
     Ngulu, Tanzania
Ngumba   Ngumba, Cameroon
Ngumbi   Ngumbi, Equatorial Guinea
Ngunduna   Ngunduna, Sudan
Nguqwurang   Nguqwurang, Sudan
Ngurimi   Ngurimi, Tanzania
Nguu   Nguu, Tanzania
Ngwo   Ngwo, Cameroon
Ngwoi   Ngwoi, Nigeria
Nharon   Nharon, Botswana
Nhengatu   Nhengatu, Brazil
Nias   Nias, Indonesia
Nielim   Nielim, Chad
Nihali   Nihali in Madhya Pradesh, India
Nii   Nii, Papua New Guinea
Nilamba   Nilamba, Tanzania
Nimadi   Nimadi in Madhya Pradesh, India
Nimboran   Nimboran, Indonesia

Nimowa	Nimowa, Papua New Guinea
Ninam	Ninam, Brazil
Ningerum	*Ningerum, Papua New Guinea
Ninggrum	Ninggrum, Indonesia
Niningo	Niningo, Papua New Guinea
Ninzam	Ninzam, Nigeria
Nisa	Nisa, Indonesia
Nissan	Nissan, Papua New Guinea
Nivkhi	Nivkhi, USSR
Njadu	Njadu, Indonesia
Njalgulgule	Njalgulgule, Sudan
Njemps Maasai	Njemps, Kenya
Nkem-Nkum	Nkem-Nkum, Nigeria
Nkom	Nkom, Cameroon
Nkonya	Nkonya, Ghana
Nkutu	Nkutu, Zaire
Nocte	***Nocte, India
Nohu	Nohu, Cameroon
Nomane	Nomane, Papua New Guinea
Nomu	Nomu, Papua New Guinea
Nondiri	Nondiri, Papua New Guinea
Norra	Norra, Burma
Northeast Thai	Blind, N.E. Thailand, Thailand (84)
	**Lepers of N.E. Thailand, Thailand
Northern Cagayan Negrito	Northern Cagayan Negrito, Philippines
Northern Kamer	*Cambodians, Thailand
Northern Kankanay	Kankanay, Northern, Philippines
Nosu	Nosu, China
Notsi	Notsi, Papua New Guinea
Nouni	*Nouni, Upper Volta
Nsenga	Nsenga, Zambia
	Nsenga, Zimbabwe
Nso	Nso, Cameroon
Nsongo	Nsongo, Angola
Ntomba	Ntomba, Zaire
Ntrubo	Ntrubo, Ghana
	Ntrubo, Togo
Nuer	*Nuer, Ethiopia
	*Nuer, Sudan (79)
Nuk	Nuk, Papua New Guinea
Numana-Nunku-Gwantu	Numana-Nunku-Gwantu, Nigeria
Numanggang	Numanggang, Papua New Guinea
Nung	Nung, China
Nungu	Nungu, Nigeria
Nunuma	Nunuma, Upper Volta
Nupe	**Nupe, Nigeria
Nyabwa	**Nyabwa, Ivory Coast
Nyaheun	Nyaheun, Laos
Nyakyusa	Nyakyusa, Malawi
	Nyakyusa, Tanzania
Nyali	Nyali, Zaire
Nyambo	Nyambo, Tanzania
Nyamusa	Nyamusa, Sudan
Nyamwezi	Nyamwezi, Tanzania (80)
Nyaneka	Nyaneka, Angola
Nyang	Nyang, Cameroon
Nyanga-Li	Nyanga-Li, Zaire
Nyangbo	Nyangbo, Ghana
Nyanja	Kunda, Zambia
	Nyanja, Zimbabwe
Nyankole	Nyankole, Uganda
Nyarueng	Nyarueng, Sudan
Nyaturu	Turu, Tanzania
Nyemba	Nyemba, Angola

REGISTRY OF THE UNREACHED

Nyengo	Nyengo, Angola
Nyiha	Nyiha, Tanzania
	Nyiha, Zambia
Nyoro	Nyoro, Uganda
Nyuli	Nyuli, Uganda
Nyungwe	Nyungwe, Mozambique
Nzakara	Nzakara, Central African Republic
Nzanyi	Nzanyi, Nigeria
Nzebi	Nzebi, Congo
Nzema	Nzema, Ghana
	Nzema, Ivory Coast
O'ung	O'ung, Angola
Obanliku	Obanliku, Nigeria
Obolo	Obolo, Nigeria
Ocaina	Ocaina, Peru
Odki	Od, Pakistan
Odual	Odual, Nigeria
Odut	Odut, Nigeria
Ogbia	Ogbia, Nigeria
Oi	Oi, Laos
Oirat	Oirat, China
Ojhi	Ojhi in Madhya Pradesh, India
Okobo	Okobo, Nigeria
Okpamheri	Okpamheri, Nigeria
Oksapmin	Oksapmin, Papua New Guinea
Ollari	Ollari in Orissa, India
Olo	Olo, Papua New Guinea
Olulumo-Ikom	Olulumo-Ikom, Nigeria
Omati	Omati, Papua New Guinea
Omie	Omie, Papua New Guinea
Onank	Onank, Papua New Guinea
Ong	Ong in Andamans, India
Onin	Onin, Indonesia
Onjab	Onjab, Papua New Guinea
Ono	Ono, Papua New Guinea
Orang Kanak	Orang Kanak, Malaysia
Orang Laut	Orang Laut, Malaysia
Orang Ulu	Orang Ulu, Malaysia
Orejon	Orejon, Peru
Oring	Oring, Nigeria
Ormu	Ormu, Indonesia
Oroch	Oroch, USSR
Orok	Orok, USSR
Orokaiva	Orokaiva, Papua New Guinea
Orokolo	Orokolo, Papua New Guinea
Oromo	**Ethiopian Refugees, Somalia (83)
Oron	Oron, Nigeria
Oronchon	Oronchon, China
Oso	Oso, Cameroon
Osum	Osum, Papua New Guinea
Ot Danum	Ot Danum, Indonesia
Otank	Otank, Nigeria
Otomi	Otomi, State of Mexico, Mexico
Otomi, Eastern	Otomi, Eastern, Mexico
Otomi, Mezquital	Otomi, Mezquital, Mexico
Otomi, Northwestern	Otomi, Northwestern, Mexico
Otomi, Southeastern	Otomi, Southeastern, Mexico
Otomi, Tenango	Otomi, Tenango, Mexico
Otomi, Texcatepec	Otomi, Texcatepec, Mexico
Otoro	Otoro, Sudan
Oubi	Oubi, Ivory Coast
Oyampipuku	Oyampipuku, Brazil
Oyda	Oyda, Ethiopia
Padaung	Kayan, Burma
Paez	***Paez, Colombia
Pahari Garhwali	Pahari Garhwali (Uttar Pradesh, India

Pai	Pai, Nigeria
Paite	Paite in Assam, India
Paiute, Northern	Paiute, Northern, United States of America
Paiwa	Paiwa, Papua New Guinea
Pak-Tong	Pak-Tong, Papua New Guinea
Pakaasnovos	Pakaasnovos, Brazil
Pakabeti	***Pakabeti of Equator, Zaire
Pala'wan	*Pala'wan, Philippines (81)
Palara	Palara, Ivory Coast
Palaung	Palaung, Burma (79)
Palawano	Palawano, Philippines
Palawano, Central	Palawano, Central, Philippines
Palembang	Palembang, Indonesia
Palikur	Palikur, Brazil
Paloc	Paloc, Sudan
Palpa	Palpa, Nepal
Pambia	Pambia, Central African Republic
Pame, Central Chichimeca	Pame, Central Chichimeca, Mexico
Pame, Northern	Pame, Northern, Mexico
Pamiri	Tajik, Afghanistan
Pana	Pana, Central African Republic
Panare	Panare, Venezuela
Pande	Pande, Congo
Pangwa	Pangwa, Tanzania
Panika	Panika, India
	Panika, India
Paniyan	**Paniyan of Kerala, India (81)
Panjabi	Ahmadis in Lahore, Pakistan (82)
Pankhu	Pankhu, Bangladesh
Pantu	Pantu, Indonesia
Pao	Pao in Madhya Pradesh, India
	Pao, Burma
Paongan	Paongan, China
Papapana	Papapana, Papua New Guinea
Pape	Pape, Cameroon
Papel	Papel, Guinea-Bissau
Papuma	Papuma, Indonesia
Parakanan	Parakanan, Brazil
Paranan	Paranan, Philippines
Parawen	Parawen, Papua New Guinea
Pardhan	Pardhan in Andhra Pradesh, India
Pare	Pare, Papua New Guinea
	Pare, Tanzania
Parengi	Parengi in Orissa, India
Paresi	Paresi, Brazil
Parintintin	Parintintin, Brazil
Parji	Dhurwa, India
Parsi	*Parsis in Bombay, India (82)
Pashayi	Pashayi, Afghanistan
Pashtu	Pashtuns, Iran (80)
Pasismanua	Pasismanua, Papua New Guinea
Patamona	Patamona, Guyana
Patelia	Patelia in Gujarat, India
Patep	Patep, Papua New Guinea
Pato Tapuia	Pato Tapuia, Brazil
Patpatar	Patpatar, Papua New Guinea
Paumari	Paumari, Brazil
Pawaia	Pawaia, Papua New Guinea
Pay	Pay, Papua New Guinea
Paynamar	Paynamar, Papua New Guinea
Penan	Penan, Western, Malaysia (81)
Pende	Pende, Zaire
Pengo	Pengo in Orissa, India
Peremka	Peremka, Papua New Guinea
Peri	Peri, Zaire

REGISTRY OF THE UNREACHED

Pero — Pero, Nigeria
Persian — Persians of Iran, Iran (80)
*Tertiary Level Youth, Iran
Persian (Tajiki) — Tajik, USSR
Phu Thai — Phu Thai, Laos
Phu Thai, Thailand (84)
Piapoco — Piapoco, Colombia
Piaroa — Piaroa, Venezuela
Pila — Pila, Papua New Guinea
Pila-Pila — **Pila, Benin
Pilaga — Pilaga, Argentina
Pilipino — **Hotel Workers in Manila,
    Philippines (81)
    *Jeepney Drivers in Manila,
    Philippines (81)
    Lubang Islanders, Philippines (81)
Pima Bajo — Pima Bajo, Mexico
Pimbwe — Pimbwe, Tanzania
Pisa — Pisa, Indonesia
Pishagchi — Pishagchi, Iran
Piti — Piti, Nigeria
Pitu Uluna Salu — Pitu Uluna Salu, Indonesia
Piu — Piu, Papua New Guinea
Piya — Piya, Nigeria
Pnar — Pnar in Assam, India
Pocomam, Central — Pocomam, Central, Guatemala
Pocomchi, Eastern — Pocomchi, Eastern, Guatemala
Pocomchi, Western — Pocomchi, Western, Guatemala
Podokwo — Podokwo, Cameroon
Podopa — Podopa, Papua New Guinea
Podzo — Podzo, Mozambique
Pogolo — Pogolo, Tanzania
Poke — Poke, Zaire
Pokot — Pokot, Uganda
Pol — Pol, Congo
Polci — Polci, Nigeria
Pom — Pom, Indonesia
Ponam-Andra-Hus — Ponam-Andra-Hus, Papua New Guinea
Pondoma — Pondoma, Papua New Guinea
Pongu — Pongu, Nigeria
Poochi — Poouch in Kashmir, India
Popoloca, Eastern — Popoloca, Eastern, Mexico
Popoloca, Northern — Popoloca, Northern, Mexico
Popoloca, Western — Popoloca, Western, Mexico
Popoluca, Sayula — Popoluca, Sayula, Mexico
Popoluca, Sierra — Popoluca, Sierra, Mexico
Porapora — Porapora, Papua New Guinea
Porohanon — Porohanon, Philippines
Portuguese — ***Copacabana Apt. Dwellers, Brazil
    *Drug Addicts in Sao Paulo, Brazil
    (82)
    *Favelados-Rio de Janeiro, Brazil
    (82)
    Gypsies, Brazil
    Pankararu, Brazil
    **Portuguese in France, France
    Portuguese, Cambridge,
    Canada:Ontario
    Portuguese, London/Strathroy,
    Canada:Ontario
    Portuguese, Metro Toronto,
    Canada:Ontario
    Portuguese, Vancouver,
    Canada:British Columbia
    Portuguese, West Lorne Village,
    Canada:Ontario

	Students in Cuiaba, Brazil
Prang	Prang, Ghana
Prasuni	***Prasuni, Afghanistan
Pu-I	Pu-I, China
Puguli	Puguli, Upper Volta
Puku-Geeri-Keri-Wipsi	Puku-Geeri-Keri-Wipsi, Nigeria
Pulie	Pulie, Papua New Guinea
Punjabi	**Gagre, Pakistan
	Sikhs, Toronto, Canada:Ontario
Punu	Punu, China
	Punu, Congo
Puragi	Puragi, Indonesia
Purari	Purari, Papua New Guinea
Purig-Skad	Purig-Pa of Kashmir, India (81)
Purum	Purum, Burma
Puyuma	**Puyuma, Taiwan (81)
Pwo Karen	Karen, Pwo, Thailand
Pye	Pye, Ivory Coast
Pyu	Pyu, Indonesia
Qajar	Qajars, Iran
Qara'i	Qara'i, Iran
Qaragozlu	Qaragozlu, Iran
Qashqa'i	Qashqa'i, Iran (80)
Quaiquer	Quaiquer, Colombia
Quechua	**Quechua, Bolivia
	**Quechua, Peru
Quechua, Huancayo	**Quechua, Huancayo, Peru
Quiche	**Quiche, Guatemala (79)
Quichua	**Quichua, Ecuador
Rabha	Rabha in Assam, India
Rabinal Achi	Rabinal-Achi, Guatemala
Rai	Rai, Nepal
Rai, Khaling	Rai, Khaling, Nepal
Rai, Kulunge	Rai, Kulunge, Nepal
Rai, Thulunge	Rai, Thulunge, Nepal
Rajasthani	Meos of Rajasthan, India (80)
Rajbansi	Rajbansi, Nepal
Ralte	Ralte, Burma
Rambutyo	Rambutyo, Papua New Guinea
Rangkas	Rangkas, Nepal
Rao	Rao, Papua New Guinea
Ratahan	Ratahan, Indonesia
Rataning	Rataning, Chad
Rauto	Rauto, Papua New Guinea
Rava	*Rava in Assam, India
Rawa	Rawa, Papua New Guinea
Rawang	Rawang, China
Redjang-Lebong	Lebong, Indonesia
Rejang	Redjang, Indonesia (80)
Rempi	Rempi, Papua New Guinea
Rendille	Rendille, Kenya
Reshe	Reshe, Nigeria
Reyesano	Reyesano, Bolivia
Riang	Riang in Assam, India
Riang-Lang	Riang-Lang, Burma
Riantana	Riantana, Indonesia
Rikbaktsa	Rikbaktsa, Brazil
Roba	Roba, Nigeria
Roinji	Roinji, Papua New Guinea
Romany	*Gypsies in Spain, Spain (79)
	Romany, Turkey
Romany (Serbian Kaldnash)	Gypsies in Yugoslavia, Yugoslavia
Romany Dialect	Gypsies in Jerusalem, Israel (82)
Romany Dialects	Muslim Gypsies in Skoplje, Yugoslavia (82)
Romkun	Romkun, Papua New Guinea

REGISTRY OF THE UNREACHED

	Romkun, Papua New Guinea
Ronga	Ronga, Mozambique
	Ronga, South Africa
Roro	Roro, Papua New Guinea
Rotokas	Rotokas, Papua New Guinea
Ruihi	Ruihi, Tanzania
Rukuba	Rukuba, Nigeria
Rumaya	Rumaya, Nigeria
Runga	Runga, Central African Republic
	Runga, Chad
Rungi	Rungi, Tanzania
Rungwa	Rungwa, Tanzania
Ruruma	Ruruma, Nigeria
Rusha	Rusha, Tanzania
Rut	Rut, Sudan
Rutul	Rutul, USSR
Rwamba	Rwamba, Uganda
	Rwamba, Zaire
Ryukyuan	*Ryukyuan, Japan
Saamia	Saamia, Uganda
Saams	Saams, USSR
Saberi	Saberi, Indonesia
Sadan	Sadan in Andamans, India
Sadang	Sadang, Indonesia
Saep	Saep, Papua New Guinea
Safaliba	Safaliba, Ghana
Safwa	Safwa, Tanzania
Sagala	Sagala, Tanzania
Saija	Saija, Colombia
Saisiat	Saisiat, Taiwan (81)
Sakam	Sakam, Papua New Guinea
Sakata	Sakata, Zaire
Saki	Saki, Papua New Guinea
Sakuye	Sakuye, Kenya
Sala	Sala, Zambia
Salampasu	Salampasu, Zaire
Salar	Salar, China
Saliba	Saliba, Colombia
Salt	Salt, Papua New Guinea
Sama Pangutaran	Sama Pangutaran, Philippines (80)
Sama, Mapun	Sama, Mapun, Philippines
Sama, Siasi	Sama, Siasi, Philippines
Sama, Sibuku	Sama, Sibuku, Philippines
Samal dialects	Sama-Badjaw, Philippines (79)
Samarkena	Samarkena, Indonesia
Samburu	El Molo, Kenya
Samo	*Samo-Kubo, Papua New Guinea
Samo, Northern	Samo, Northern, Mali
	Samo, Northern, Upper Volta
Samo, Southern	Samo, Southern, Upper Volta
Samogho	Samogho, Mali
San	San, Namibia
Sanapana	Sanapana, Paraguay
Sandawe	Sandawe, Tanzania
Sanga	Sanga, Nigeria
	***Sanga, Zaire (84)
Sangil	Sangil, Philippines
Sangir	Sangir, Indonesia
Sangke	Sangke, Indonesia
Sangu	Sangu, Gabon
	Sangu, Tanzania
Sanio	Sanio, Papua New Guinea
Santa	Santa, China
Santhali	**Santhali, Nepal
Sanuma	*Sanuma, Brazil
	Sanuma, Venezuela

Sanza	Sanza, Zaire
Saposa	Saposa, Papua New Guinea
Saramaccan	Saramaccan, Surinam
Sarwa	Sarwa, Chad
Sasak	Sasak, Indonesia (80)
Sasani	Sasanis, Iran
Sasaru-Enwan Igwe	Sasaru-Enwan Igwe, Nigeria
Saseng	Saseng, Papua New Guinea
Satere	Satere, Brazil
Sau	Sau, Afghanistan
	Sau, Papua New Guinea
Sauk	Sauk, Papua New Guinea
Sause	Sause, Indonesia
Save (Yoruba)	**Save, Benin
Sawi	**Sawi, Indonesia
Sawos	Sawos, Papua New Guinea
Saya	Saya, Nigeria
Secoya	Secoya, Ecuador
Sekar	Sekar, Indonesia
Seko	Seko, Indonesia
Sekpele	Sekpele, Ghana
Selakau	**Selakau of Sarawak, Malaysia
Sele	Santrokofi, Ghana
Selepet	Selepet, Papua New Guinea
Selkup	Selkup, USSR
Semelai	Semelai, Malaysia
Sempan	Sempan, Indonesia
Sena	Sena, Malawi
	Sena, Mozambique
Senari	Senufo, Ivory Coast (80)
Senggi	Senggi, Indonesia
Sentani	Sentani, Indonesia
Senthang	Senthang, Burma
Sepen	Sepen, Papua New Guinea
Serawai (Pasemah)	**Serawai, Indonesia (81)
Serbo-Croation	*Bosnian, Yugoslavia (80)
Sere	Sere, Sudan
Serere	Serere, Senegal (79)
Serere-Non	Serere-Non, Senegal
Serere-Sine	Serere-Sine, Senegal
Seri	Seri, Mexico
Serki	Serki, Papua New Guinea
Serui-Laut	Serui-Laut, Indonesia
Setaui Keriwa	Setaui Keriwa, Papua New Guinea
Setiali	Setiali, Papua New Guinea
Sgaw Karen	Karen, Thailand (79)
Sha	Sha, Nigeria
Shamatali	Yanomamo, Venezuela
Shambala	Shambala, Tanzania
Shan	Hkun, Burma
	Shan Chinese, Burma
	Shan, Burma
	Shan, Thailand
	Thai-Ney, Burma
Shan Dialects	Yin-Kyar, Burma
	Yin-Nett, Burma
Shanga	Shanga, Nigeria
Shankilla (Kazza)	***Shankilla (Kazza), Ethiopia
Sharanahua	Sharanahua, Peru
Sharchagpakha	Bhutias, Bhutan
	Sharchagpakha, Bhutan
Sharkas	*Cherkess, Jordan (84)
Shatt	Shatt, Sudan
Shawiya	Shawiya, Algeria
Sheko	Sheko, Ethiopia
Sherpa	*Sherpa, Nepal

REGISTRY OF THE UNREACHED

Shihu	**Shihu, United Arab Emirates
Shilha	Shilha, Morocco
Shilluk	Shilluk, Sudan
Shina	Shina, Afghanistan
Shinasha	Shinasha, Ethiopia
Shinkoya	*Nkoya, Zambia
Shipibo	Shipibo, Peru
Shirishana	**Shirishana, Brazil
Shor	Shor, USSR
Shourastra	*Shourastra in Tamil Nadu, India
Shrina	*Dog-Pa of Ladakh, India (81)
Shua	Shua, Botswana
Shughni	Shughni, Afghanistan
Shuwa Arabic	Shuwa Arabic, Nigeria
Shwai	Shwai, Sudan
Siagha-Yenimu	Siagha-Yenimu, Indonesia
Sialum	Sialum, Papua New Guinea
Siane	Siane, Papua New Guinea
Siar	Siar, Papua New Guinea
Sibo	Sibo, China
Sidamo	Sidamo, Ethiopia
Sikhule	Sikhule, Indonesia
Sikka	Sikanese, Indonesia
Sikkimese	Sikkimese, India
Simaa	Simaa, Zambia
Simog	Simog, Papua New Guinea
Sinagen	Sinagen, Papua New Guinea
Sinagoro	Sinagoro, Papua New Guinea
Sinaki	Sinaki, Papua New Guinea
Sinama Bangini	Sama Bangingi, Philippines (80)
Sinasina	Sinasina, Papua New Guinea
Sindamon	Sindamon, Papua New Guinea
Sindebele	**Ndebele, Zimbabwe (79)
Sindhi	Sindhi Muslims in Karachi, Pakistan (82)
	*Sindhis of India, India
	Sochi, Pakistan
Sinhala	Sinhalese, Sri Lanka
Sinsauru	Sinsauru, Papua New Guinea
Sio	Sio, Papua New Guinea
Siona	Siona, Colombia
Sipoma	Sipoma, Papua New Guinea
Sira	Sira, Gabon
Sirak	Sirak, Papua New Guinea
Sirasira	Sirasira, Papua New Guinea
Siri	Siri, Nigeria
Siriano	Siriano, Colombia
Siriono	Siriono, Bolivia
Siroi	Siroi, Papua New Guinea
Sisala	Sisala, Upper Volta
Siwai	Siwai, Papua New Guinea
Siwu	Siwu, Ghana
So	So, Cameroon
Sobei	Sobei, Indonesia
Soga	Soga, Uganda
Soh	Soh, Laos
	*Soh, Thailand (81)
Sokorok	Sokorok, Papua New Guinea
Soli	Soli, Zambia
Solor	Solorese Muslims, Indonesia (81)
Solos	Solos, Papua New Guinea
Som	Som, Papua New Guinea
Somagai	*Somagai, Indonesia
Somahai	Somahai, Indonesia
Somali	**Eritrean Refugees, Djibouti (83)
	Somali, Degodia, Kenya

Somali, Ethiopia
Somali, Gurreh, Kenya
Somali, Ogadenya, Kenya
Somali (Ajuran)   Somali, Ajuran, Kenya (79)
Somba (Detammari)   **Somba, Benin
Somrai   Somrai, Central African Republic
                         Somrai, Chad
Sona   Sona, Papua New Guinea
Sondwari   Sondwari in M.P., India
Songe   Songe, Zaire
Songhai   Songhai, Mali
                         Songhai, Niger
                         Songhai, Upper Volta
Songomeno   Songomeno, Zaire
Songoora   Songoora, Zaire
Soninke   Sarakole, Senegal (80)
                         Soninke, Gambia
                         Soninke, Mali
                         Soninke, Mauritania
Sonjo   Sonjo, Tanzania
Sopi   Sopi, Sudan
Sora   Sora in Orissa, India
Sori-Harengan   Sori-Harengan, Papua New Guinea
Soruba   Soruba, Benin
Sough   **Manikion, Indonesia
Southern Bontoc   **Bontoc, Southern, Philippines
Southern Sesotho   ***Basotho, Mountain, Lesotho (79)
Sowanda   Sowanda, Indonesia
                         Sowanda, Papua New Guinea
Spanish   Arutani, Venezuela
                         Chatino, Yaitepec, Mexico
                         **Chicanos in Denver, United States
                            of America (82)
                         Chilean Refugees, Argentina (83)
                         *Chilean Refugees, Toronto,
                            Canada:Ontario (83)
                         **Chinese in Panama, Panama
                         Chocho, Mexico
                         **Ex-Mental Patients in NYC, United
                            States of America (82)
                         Guatemalan Refugees, Mexico
                         Iquito, Peru
                         Jebero, Peru
                         *Llaneros, Colombia (84)
                         **Marielito Refugees in Florida,
                            United States of America (83)
                         ***Mestizos in La Paz, Bolivia (82)
                         **Middle Class-Mexico City, Mexico
                            (82)
                         *Military Officers, Ecuador (84)
                         **Military Personnel, Ecuador
                         Mixteco, Central Puebla, Mexico
                         Mutu, Venezuela
                         Nicaraguan Refugees, Costa Rica
                         Paipai, Mexico
                         Palenquero, Colombia
                         Pame, Chichimeca-Jonaz, Mexico
                         Paya, Honduras
                         Popoloca, Ahuatempan, Mexico
                         Popoloca, Coyotepec, Mexico
                         Popoloca, Southern, Mexico
                         Popoluca, Oluta, Mexico
                         Popoluca, Texistepec, Mexico
                         **Racetrack Residents, United States
                            of America (79)
                         Salvadoran Refugees, Honduras

REGISTRY OF THE UNREACHED

	Salvadoran Refugees, Belize
	Totonaco, Yecuatla, Mexico
	*Universitarios - Rosario,
	Argentina (82)
	**Urban Mestizos, Ecuador
	Urban Street Women/Los Angeles,
	United States of America (84)
Su	Su, Cameroon
Sua	Sua, Papua New Guinea
Suain	Suain, Papua New Guinea
Suba	Suba, Tanzania
Subanen, Tuboy	**Subanen (Tuboy), Philippines
Subanun	**Subanen, Sindangan, Philippines
	(80)
Subanun, Lapuyan	Subanun,Lapuyan, Philippines
Subi	Subi, Tanzania
Suena	**Suena, Papua New Guinea
Suga	Suga, Cameroon
Suganga	Suganga, Papua New Guinea
Sui	Sui, China
	Sui, Papua New Guinea
Suki	Suki, Papua New Guinea
Suku	Suku, Zaire
Sukur	Sukur, Nigeria
Sukurum	Sukurum, Papua New Guinea
Sulka	Sulka, Papua New Guinea
Sulung	Sulung, India
Sumau	Sumau, Papua New Guinea
Sumba	Sumba, Indonesia
Sumbawa	Sumbawa, Indonesia
Sumbwa	Sumbwa, Tanzania
Sumu	Sumu, Nicaragua
Sundanese	**Sundanese, Indonesia (84)
Sungor	Sungor, Chad
Sunwar	Sunwar, Nepal
Suppire	Minianka, Mali
	Suppire, Mali
Sura	Sura, Nigeria
Suri	**Suri, Ethiopia
Surigueno	Suriguenos, Philippines
Sursurunga	Sursurunga, Papua New Guinea
Surubu	Surubu, Nigeria
Surui	Surui, Brazil
Susu	Susu, Guinea
	Susu, Guinea-Bissau
	Susu, Sierra Leone
Svan	Svan, USSR
Swaga	Swaga, Zaire
Swahili	Ikizu, Tanzania
	Ugandan Refugees, Sudan (83)
Swaka	Swaka, Zambia
Swati	Swatis, Pakistan (79)
Sylhetti	Sylhetti, United Kingdom
Syuwa	Syuwa, Nepal
T'in	T'in, Thailand (81)
Ta-Oi	Ta-Oi, Laos
Tabar	Tabar, Papua New Guinea
Tabasaran	Tabasaran, USSR
Tabi	Ingassana, Sudan
	Tabi, Sudan
Tabriak	Tabriak, Papua New Guinea
Tacana	Tacana, Bolivia
Tadjio	Tadjio, Indonesia
Tadyawan	Tadyawan, Philippines
Tae'	Toraja, Southern, Indonesia (81)
Tafi	Tafi, Togo

Tagal	Tagal, Malaysia (81)
Tagalog	**Batangeno, Philippines
	**Filipino Migrant Workers, Saudi Arabia (84)
Tagbanwa	**Tagbanwa, Aborlan, Philippines
Tagbanwa, Kalamian	Tagbanwa, Kalamian, Philippines
Tagin	***Tagin, India
Tagula	Tagula, Papua New Guinea
Tagwana	Tagwana, Ivory Coast
Taikat	Taikat, Indonesia
Tairora	Tairora, Papua New Guinea
Taiwanese (Hoklo)	*Industrial Workers, Taiwan (81)
Takalubi	Takalubi, Papua New Guinea
Takankar	Takankar, India
Takemba	Takemba, Benin
Takestani	Takestani, Iran
Takia	Takia, Papua New Guinea
Tal	Tal, Nigeria
Talish	Talish, Iran
Talo	*Talo, Indonesia
Talodi	Talodi, Sudan
Tama	Tama, Chad
Tamachek	Tuareg, Niger (79)
Tamagario	Tamagario, Indonesia
Taman	Taman, Burma
	Taman, Papua New Guinea
Tamang	*Tamang, Nepal
Tamaria	Tamaria in Bihar, India
Tamazight	Tamazight, Morocco
Tambas	Tambas, Nigeria
Tambo	Tambo, Zambia
Tami	Tami, Papua New Guinea
Tamil	**Indian Tamils - Colombo, Sri Lanka (82)
	*Kudisai Vagh Makkal, India
	Labbai, India
	Moor & Malays, Sri Lanka (79)
	**Saiva Vellala, India
	Tamil (Ceylonese), Sri Lanka
	**Tamil Laborers in Bombay, India (82)
	Tamil Muslims in Madras, India (82)
	***Tamil Plantation Workers, Malaysia
	*Tamil in Yellagiri Hills, India
	*Tamils (Indian), Malaysia
	**Tamils (Indian), Sri Lanka (79)
Tampulensi	Tampulma, Ghana
Tana	Tana, Central African Republic
	Tana, Chad
Tanahmerah	Tanahmerah, Indonesia
Tancouleur	Taucouleur, Senegal (80)
Tandanke	Tandanke, Senegal
Tandia	Tandia, Indonesia
Tangale	Tangale, Nigeria
Tangchangya	Tangchangya, Bangladesh
Tangga	Tangga, Papua New Guinea
Tangsa	**Tangsa, India
Tangu	Tangu, Papua New Guinea
Tanguat	Tanguat, Papua New Guinea
Tani	Tani, Papua New Guinea
Tanimuca-Retuama	Tanimuca-Retuama, Colombia
Tao-Suame	Tao-Suame, Papua New Guinea
Taori-Kei	Taori-Kei, Indonesia
Tara	Tara, Indonesia
Tarahumara, Northern	Tarahumara, Northern, Mexico

REGISTRY OF THE UNREACHED

Tarahumara, Rocoroibo	Tarahumara, Rocoroibo, Mexico
Tarahumara, Samachique	Tarahumara, Samachique, Mexico
Taram	Taram, Cameroon
Tarasco	Tarasco, Mexico
Targum	Targum, Israel
Tarof	Tarof, Indonesia
Tarok	Tarok, Nigeria
Tarpia	Tarpia, Indonesia
Tashilhait	**Shluh Berbers, Morocco
Tat	Tat, USSR
	Tindin, USSR
Tatar	Bashkir, USSR (80)
Tatar dialects	Tatars, USSR (80)
Tate	Tate, Papua New Guinea
Tatoga	Barabaig, Tanzania (79)
	Tatoga, Tanzania
Tatuyo	**Tatuyo, Colombia
Tauade	Tauade, Papua New Guinea
Taungyo	Taungyo, Burma
Taupota	Taupota, Papua New Guinea
Taurap	Taurap, Indonesia
Tausug	Tausug, Philippines (80)
Tavara	Tavara, Papua New Guinea
Tawi-Pau	Tawi-Pau, Papua New Guinea
Tawr	Tawr, Burma
Tayaku	Tayaku, Benin
T'boli	**T'boli, Philippines (81)
Tchang	Tchang, Cameroon
Teda	Teda, Chad (80)
	Teda, Libya
	Teda, Niger
Teen	*Tense, Ivory Coast
Tegali	Tegali, Sudan
Tehit	Tahit, Indonesia
Teimuri	Teimuri, Iran
Teimurtash	Teimurtash, Iran
Teke, Eastern	Teke, Eastern, Zaire
Teke, Northern	Teke, Northern, Congo
Teke, Southwestern	Teke, Southwestern, Congo
Telefol	Telefol, Papua New Guinea
Telugu	***Matharis, India
Tembe	Tembe, Brazil
Tembo	Tembo, Zaire
Temein	Temein, Sudan
Temira	Temira, Malaysia
Temne	**Temne, Sierra Leone (80)
Tenggerese	Tengger, Indonesia
Teop	Teop, Papua New Guinea
Tepehua, Huehuetla	Tepehua, Huehuetla, Mexico
Tepehua, Pisa Flores	Tepehua, Pisa Flores, Mexico
Tepehua, Veracruz	Tepehua, Veracruz, Mexico
Tepehuan, Northern	Tepehuan, Northern, Mexico
Tepehuan, Southeastern	Tepehuan, Southeastern, Mexico
Tepehuan, Southwestern	Tepehuan, Southwestern, Mexico
Tepeth	Tepeth, Uganda
Tepo	Tepo, Ivory Coast
Tera	Tera, Nigeria
Terebu	Terebu, Papua New Guinea
Terena	Terena, Brazil
Teribe	**Teribe, Panama
Ternate	Ternatans, Indonesia
Teso	Teso, Uganda
Tewa (Jemez)	Jemez Pueblo, United States of America
Thado	Thado in Assam, India
Thai	*Central Thailand Farmers, Thailand (81)

568

Index by Language

	Government officials, Thailand
	**Lepers of Cen. Thailand, Thailand (81)
	*Ramkamhaeng Un. Students, Thailand
	*Slum Dwellers of Bangkok, Thailand
	*Thai University Students, Thailand (81)
Thai, Southern	*Thai Islam (Thai), Thailand
Thakali	Thakali, Nepal
Thakur	Thakur, India
Thami	Thami, Nepal
Thar	Thar in Bihar, India
Thoi	Thoi, Sudan
Thuri	Thuri, Sudan
Tiang	Tiang, Papua New Guinea
Tibetan	Tibetan Refugees, Canada
	*Tibetan Refugees, India (83)
	Tibetan Refugees, Switzerland (83)
	Tibetans in Bhutan, Bhutan (81)
Tibetan Dialect	*Chang-Pa of Kashmir, India (81)
Tibeto-Burman	Jinuos, China (81)
	Lisu, China (81)
Tibeto-Burman Dialect	Lawa, Eastern, Thailand (81)
Ticuna	Ticuna, Brazil
Tidi	Tidi, Papua New Guinea
Tidore	Tidorese, Indonesia
Tiefo	Tiefo, Upper Volta
Tiene	Tiene, Zaire
Tifai	Tifai, Papua New Guinea
Tigak	Tigak, Papua New Guinea
Tigon	Tigon, Cameroon
Tigre	Ethiopian Refugees, Yemen, Yemen, Arab Republic
	Rural Refugees from Eritrea, Sudan (83)
Tikar	Tikar, Cameroon
Tila Chol	Ch'ol Tila, Mexico
Timbe	Timbe, Papua New Guinea
Timorese	Timorese, Indonesia
Tinputz	Tinputz, Papua New Guinea
Tippera	Tippera, Bangladesh
Tira	Tira, Sudan
Tirio	Tirio, Papua New Guinea
Tirma	Tirma, Sudan
Tiro	Tiro, Indonesia
Tiruray	Tiruray, Philippines
Tlapaneco, Malinaltepec	Tlapaneco, Malinaltepec, Mexico
Toala	Toala, Indonesia
Toaripi	Toaripi, Papua New Guinea
Tobo	Tobo, Papua New Guinea
Toda	Toda in Tamil Nadu, India
Tofi	*Tofi, Benin
Togbo	Togbo, Zaire
Tojolabal	Tojolabal, Mexico
Tokkaru	Tokkaru in Tamil Nadu, India
Tol	Tol, Honduras
Tombulu	Tombulu, Indonesia
Tomini	Tomini, Indonesia
Tonda	Tonda, Papua New Guinea
Tondanou	Tondanou, Indonesia
Tonga	Tonga, Botswana
	Tonga, Malawi
	Tonga, Mozambique
Tongwe	Tongwe, Tanzania
Tonsea	Tonsea, Indonesia
Tontemboa	Tontemboa, Indonesia

Toposa	*Topotha, Sudan
Toposa, Donyiro	Nyzatom, Sudan
Torau	Torau, Papua New Guinea
Torricelli	Torricelli, Papua New Guinea
Totonaco, Northern	Totonaco, Northern, Mexico
Totonaco, Oxumatlan	Totonaco, Oxumatlan, Mexico
Totonaco, Papantla	Totonaco, Papantla, Mexico
Totonaco, Sierra	Totonaco, Sierra, Mexico
Toussian	*Toussian, Upper Volta
Towei	Towei, Indonesia
Trepo	Trepo, Ivory Coast
Tribal Languages	**Bachelors in Lagos, Nigeria (82)
	Chad's Refugees from N'Djamena, Cameroon (83)
	Dukwe Refugee Camp Residents, Botswana (83)
	Equatorial Guin. Refugees, Gabon (83)
	Guinean Refugees, Gabon
	Sudanese Repatriates, Sudan (83)
	Zimbabwean Refugees, Zambia
	Zimbabwean Refugees, Mozambique (83)
	Zimbabwean Repatriates, Zimbabwe (83)
Tribal dialects	**Djandeau, Zaire
	***Halam in Tripura, India
Trio	Trio, Surinam
Trique, San Juan Copala	Trique, San Juan Copala, Mexico
Tsaangi	Tsaangi, Congo
Tsakhur	Tsakhur, USSR
Tsamai	Tsamai, Ethiopia
Tschievenda	Bavenda, South Africa
Tshiluba	**Bakuba, Zaire
Tsimane	Tsimane, Bolivia
Tsogo	Tsogo, Gabon
Tsonga	Tsonga, Mozambique
Tsou	Tsou, Taiwan (81)
Tswa	Tswa, Mozambique
	Tswa, Zimbabwe
Tswana	Tswana, Namibia
	Tswana, Zimbabwe
Tuam	Tuam, Papua New Guinea
Tubar	Tubar, Mexico
Tubetube	Tubetube, Papua New Guinea
Tucano	Pacu, Brazil
	Piratapuyo, Brazil
	Quarequena, Brazil
	Seuci, Brazil
	Tucano, Brazil
Tucanoan	Arapaco, Brazil
Tugara	Tugara, India
Tukude	Tukude, Indonesia
Tula	Tula, Nigeria
Tulishi	Tulishi, Sudan
Tumale	Tumale, Sudan
Tumawo	Tumawo, Indonesia
Tumma	Tumma, Sudan
Tumtum	Tumtum, Sudan
Tunebo, Cobaria	Tunebo, Cobaria, Colombia
Tung	Tung-Chia, China (81)
Tunya	Tunya, Central African Republic
	Tunya, Chad
Tupuri	Tupuri, Cameroon
	Tupuri, Chad
Tura	Tura, Ivory Coast

Turkana	**Turkana Fishing Community, Kenya (79)
	Turkana, Kenya
Turkic	USSR Kirghiz Refugee Shepherds, Pakistan (83)
Turkish	*Anatolian Turks-Istanbul, Turkey (82)
	Baharlu (Kamesh), Iran
	Nafar, Iran
	Turkish Immigrant Workers, German Federal Rep. (79)
Turkish (Danubian)	Yoruk, Turkey
Turkish, Osmanli	Turks, Anatolian, Turkey
Turkomani	Turkomans, Iran (80)
Turkwam	Turkwam, Nigeria
Turu	Turu, Indonesia
Tuvin	Tuvinian, USSR
Tuyuca	Tuyuca, Brazil
Twi	Twi, Sudan
Tzeltal, Bachajon	Tzeltal, Bachajon, Mexico
Tzeltal, Highland	Tzeltal, Highland, Mexico
Tzotzil (Chamula)	Chamula, Mexico (79)
Tzotzil, Huistan	Huistan Tzotzil, Mexico
Tzotzil, Zinacanteco	Zinacantecos, Mexico (79)
Tzutujil	Tzutujil, Guatemala
Udegeis	Udegeis, USSR
Udin	Udin, USSR
Udmurt	Udmurt, USSR
Uduk	Uduk, Sudan
Uhunduni	Uhunduni, Indonesia
Uiguir	Uiguir, Afghanistan
	Uiguir, China (80)
Ukaan	Ukaan, Nigeria
Ukpe-Bayobiri	Ukpe-Bayobiri, Nigeria
Ukrainian	**Ukrainians, Toronto, Canada:Ontario
Ukwuani-Aboh	Ukwuani-Aboh, Nigeria
Ulchi	Ulchi, USSR
Ulithi	Ulithi-Mall, Pacific Trust Islands
Ullatan	Ullatan in Kerala, India
Umm Dorein	Umm Dorein, Sudan
Umm Gabralla	Umm Gabralla, Sudan
Urali	Urali in Kerala, India
Urarina	Urarina, Peru
Urdu	Indo-Canadians, Vancouver, Canada:British Columbia (84)
Urhobo	Urhobo, Nigeria
Uria	Uria, Indonesia
Uruangnirin	Uruangnirin, Indonesia
Urubu	Urubu, Brazil
Urupa	Urupa, Brazil
Uspanteco	Uspanteco, Guatemala
Utugwang	Utugwang, Nigeria
Uvbie	Uvbie, Nigeria
Uzbeki, Turkic	**Uzbeks, Afghanistan (79)
Uzekwe	Uzekwe, Nigeria
Vagala	Vagala, Ghana
Vagla	Vagla, Ghana
Vai	*Vai, Liberia (80)
	Vai, Sierra Leone
Vaikino	Vaikino, Indonesia
Vaiphei	Vaiphei in Assam, India
Vale	Vale, Central African Republic
Various Dialects	**Mangyan, Philippines
Various dialects	**African Students in Cairo, Egypt
	Chinese, Thunder Bay, Canada:Ontario

	Indians, Northern Sask., Canada:Saskatchewan
	**Indians, Winnipeg, Canada:Manitoba
	Street People, Thunder Bay, Canada:Ontario
	Ugandan Asian Refugees, Tor., Canada:Ontario
Venda	Venda, Zimbabwe
Veps	Veps, USSR
Vere	Vere, Cameroon
	***Vere, Nigeria
Vidunda	Vidunda, Tanzania
Vietnamese	Boat People, Japan
	Street Vendors in Saigon, Viet Nam (82)
	Urban Elite Vietnamese, United States of America
	Vietnamese Fishermen, Biloxi, United States of America
	Vietnamese Refugees, Regina, Canada:Saskatchewan
	**Vietnamese Refugees, United States of America
	**Vietnamese Refugees, Thailand
	**Vietnamese Refugees, Australia
	Vietnamese Refugees, Korea, Republic of
	Vietnamese, Laos
Vige	Vige, Upper Volta
Vinza	Vinza, Tanzania
Vishavan	Vishavan in Kerala, India
Vute	Vute, Nigeria
Wa	Wa, Burma
	Wa, China
Wabo	Wabo, Indonesia
Waddar	Waddar in Andhra Pradesh, India
Wagdi	Wagdi in Rajasthan, India
Waimiri	Waimiri, Brazil
Waiwai	Waiwai, Brazil
	Waiwai, Guyana
Waja	Waja, Nigeria
Walamo	Walamo, Ethiopia
Wali	Wala, Ghana
Wambon	Wambon, Indonesia
Wanchoo	**Wanchoo, India
Wanda	Wanda, Tanzania
Wandamen	Wandamen, Indonesia
Wandji	Wandji, Gabon
Wanggom	Wanggom, Indonesia
Wanji	Wanji, Tanzania
Wano	Wano, Indonesia
Wapishana	Wapishana, Brazil
	Wapishana, Guyana
	Wapishana, Venezuela
Wara	Wara, Upper Volta
Warao	Warao, Venezuela
Ware	Ware, Mali
Warembori	Warembori, Indonesia
Waris	Waris, Indonesia
Warji	*Warjawa, Nigeria
Warkay-Bipim	Warkay-Bipim, Indonesia
Waropen	Waropen, Indonesia
Wasi	Wasi, Tanzania
Waura	Waura, Brazil
Wayana	Wayana, Surinam
Weda	Weda, Indonesia

Wetawit	Wetawit, Ethiopia
Wewewa	Wewewa, Indonesia
Widekum	Widekum, Cameroon
Win	Win, Upper Volta
Winji-Winji	Winji-Winji, Benin
Wobe	Wobe, Ivory Coast
Wodani	Wodani, Indonesia
Woi	Woi, Indonesia
Woko	Voko, Cameroon
Woleat	Woleat, Pacific Trust Islands
Wolio	Wolio, Indonesia
Wolof	Wolof, Senegal (80)
Wolof, Gambian	Wolof, Gambian, Gambia
Wom	Wom, Nigeria
Won Chow	*Chinese Restaurant Wrkrs., France
Wongo	Wongo, Zaire
Woro	Woro, Sudan
Wumbvu	Wumbvu, Gabon
Wungu	Wungu, Tanzania
Xavante	Xavante, Brazil
Xerente	Xerente, Brazil
Xokleng	Xokleng, Brazil
Xu	*Bushmen (Kung), Namibia (79)
	Xu, Namibia
Yafi	Yafi, Indonesia
Yaghan	Yaghan, Chile
Yagnobi	Yagnobi, USSR
Yagua	Yagua, Peru
Yahadian	Yahadian, Indonesia
Yaka	Yaka, Zaire
Yakan	Yakan, Philippines (80)
Yakha	Yakha, Nepal
Yakoma	Yakoma, Central African Republic
Yala	**Yala, Nigeria
Yalunka	*Yalunka, Sierra Leone (80)
Yaly	Yaly, Indonesia
Yambasa	Yambasa, Cameroon
Yami	Yami of Orchid Island, Indonesia (84)
Yaminahua	Yaminahua, Peru
Yanadi	Yanadi in Andhra Pradesh, India
Yandang	Yandang, Nigeria
Yanga	Yanga, Togo
Yangbye	Yangbye, Burma
Yanomam (Waica)	*Yanomamo, Brazil (79)
Yans	Yans, Zaire
Yanyula (Yanjula)	*Yanyula, Australia
Yao	*Yao Refugees from Laos, Thailand
	Yao, Mozambique
Yao (Mien Wa)	**Yao, Thailand (79)
Yaoure	Yaoure, Ivory Coast
Yaqui	Yaquis, Mexico
Yaruro	Yaruro, Venezuela
Yasing	Yasing, Cameroon
Yaur	Yaur, Indonesia
Yava	Yava, Indonesia
Yazgulyam	Yazgulyam, USSR
Yei	**Yei, Botswana
	Yei, Indonesia
Yela	Yela, Zaire
Yellow Uiguir	Yellow Uiguir, China
Yelmek	Yelmek, Indonesia
Yerava	Yerava in Karnataka, India
Yeretuar	Yeretuar, Indonesia
Yerukala	Yerukala in A.P., India
Yeskwa	Yeskwa, Nigeria

Yi	Lolo, China (81)
	Pai, China (81)
Yiddish	***Jewish Refugees from USSR, Israel (83)
	Jews, Winnipeg, Canada:Manitoba
Yidinit	Yidinit, Ethiopia
Yinchia	Yinchia, Burma
Yinga	Yinga, Cameroon
Yoabu	Yoabu, Benin
Yogad	Yogad, Philippines
Yonggom	Yonggom, Indonesia
Yos	Yos, Burma
Yotafa	Yotafa, Indonesia
Yuana	Yuana, Venezuela
Yucateco	Yucateco, Guatemala
	Yucateco, Mexico
Yucuna	*Yucuna, Colombia
Yukagir	Yukagirs, USSR
Yukpa	Yukpa, Colombia
	Yukpa, Venezuela
Yuku	Yuku, China
Yulu	Yulu, Sudan
Yungur	Yungur, Nigeria
Yuracare	Yuracare, Bolivia
Yurak	Yurak, USSR
Yuruti	Yuruti, Colombia
Zaghawa	Zaghawa, Chad
	Zaghawa, Libya
	Zaghawa, Sudan
Zanaki	Zanaki, Tanzania
Zangskari	Zangskari in Kashmir, India
Zanskari	Zanskari, India (84)
Zapoteco N Villa Alta	Zapoteco, N Villa Alta, Mexico
Zapoteco, E Miahuatlan	Zapoteco, E Miahuatlan, Mexico
Zapoteco, C Sola De Vega	Zapoteco, C Sola De Vega, Mexico
Zapoteco, Choapan	Zapoteco, Choapan, Mexico
Zapoteco, E Ocotlan	Zapoteco, E Ocotlan, Mexico
Zapoteco, E Tlacolula	Zapoteco, E Tlacolula, Mexico
Zapoteco, E Zimatlan	Zapoteco, E Zimatlan, Mexico
Zapoteco, Isthmus	Zapoteco, Isthmus, Mexico
Zapoteco, Mazaltepec	Zapoteco, Mazaltepec, Mexico
Zapoteco, Miahuatlan	Zapoteco, Miahuatlan, Mexico
Zapoteco, Mitla	Zapoteco, Mitla, Mexico
Zapoteco, N Isthmus	Zapoteco, N Isthmus, Mexico
Zapoteco, N Ocotlan	Zapoteco, N Ocotlan, Mexico
Zapoteco, NE Miahuatlan	Zapoteco, NE Miahuatlan, Mexico
Zapoteco, NE Yautepec	Zapoteco, NE Yautepec, Mexico
Zapoteco, NW Tehuantepec	Zapoteco, NW Tehuantepec, Mexico
Zapoteco, Pochutla	Zapoteco, Pochutla, Mexico
Zapoteco, S Ejutla	Zapoteco, S Ejutla, Mexico
Zapoteco, S Villa Alta	Zapoteco, S Villa Alta, Mexico
Zapoteco, SC Zimatlan	Zapoteco, SC Zimatlan, Mexico
Zapoteco, SE Miahuatlan	Zapoteco, SE Miahuatlan, Mexico
Zapoteco, SW Ixtlan	Zapoteco, SW Ixtlan, Mexico
Zapoteco, Srra De Juarez	Zapoteco, Srra De Juarez, Mexico
Zapoteco, Stgo Xanica	Zapoteco, Stgo Xanica, Mexico
Zapoteco, Sto Dom Albarr	Zapoteco, Sto Dom Albarr, Mexico
Zapoteco, Tabaa	Zapoteco, Tabaa, Mexico
Zapoteco, Villa Alta	Zapoteco, Villa Alta, Mexico
Zapoteco, W Miahuatlan	Zapoteco, W Miahuatlan, Mexico
Zapoteco, W Ocotlan	Zapoteco, W Ocotlan, Mexico
Zapoteco, W Sola de Vega	Zapoteco, W Sola de Vega, Mexico
Zapoteco, W Tlacolula	Zapoteco, W Tlacolula, Mexico
Zapoteco, W Yautepec	Zapoteco, W Yautepec, Mexico
Zapoteco, W Zimatlan	Zapoteco, W Zimatlan, Mexico
Zapoteco, Yalalag	Zapoteco, Yalalag, Mexico

Zaramo	Zaramo, Tanzania
Zari	Zari, Nigeria
Zayse	Zayse, Ethiopia
Zenaga	Zenaga, Mauritania
Zighvana(Dghwede)	*Dghwede, Nigeria
Zigwa	Zigwa, Tanzania
Zilmamu	Zilmamu, Ethiopia
Zimba	Zimba, Zaire
Zome	Zome in Manipur, India
	Zome, Burma
Zoque, Chimalapa	Zoque, Chimalapa, Mexico
Zoque, Copainala	Zoque, Copainala, Mexico
Zoque, Francisco Leon	Zoque, Francisco Leon, Mexico
Zoque, Tabasco	Zoque, Tabasco, Mexico
Zulu	Zulu, Malawi
letzburgesch	Luxemburgois, Luxembourg
local languages	*Pygmy (Mbuti), Zaire (79)
	**Zaranda Hill Peoples, Nigeria
siSwati	**Swazi, South Africa

Index by Country

Groups are listed by the countries for which information has been reported by questionnaires. In most cases, this means they are listed in the country where they are primarily located. Many peoples are found in several countries. This listing is limited to the country for which the MARC files have information. Groups are listed alphabetically under each country listed.

Please note that not all countries will be found in this index. Peoples have not been reported from every country. Cambodia is listed under its new name, Kampuchea. The Republic of China is listed as Taiwan. Dahomey is listed under its current name, Benin. The French Territory of the Afars and the Issas is listed under its new name, Djibouti. The population estimate given is an indication of the size of that people in that one country. In some cases, this is only a part of a large people to be found in several other countries as well.

For an explanation of the data fields included in this listing, see the introduction to the Index by Country. The second column in the present index gives information on *Scripture* in the vernacular language of each group. Preceding this information is a character indicating the presence (+) or absence (-) of *recordings* in that language; if no character appears, that information has not been reported to the MARC data files.

Afghanistan

NAME	SCRIPTURE	LANGUAGE	GROUP SIZE	PRIMARY RELIGION	% CHR	VOL V	V	UP ID
**Azerbaijani	Bible	Azerbaijani	5,000	Islam	<1%	1		2545
Bashgali	none	Bashgali	10,000	Islam	<1%	1		2546
Chaghatai	portions	Chaghatai	300,000	Islam	<1%	1		2547
Gawar-Bati	none	Gawar-Bati	8,000	Islam	<1%	1		2548
Gujuri	none	Gujuri	10,000	Islam	<1%	1		2549
**Hazara in Kabul	+none	Hazaragi	300,000	Islam	0%	6	82	5021
Jati	none	Jati	1,000	Islam	<1%	1		2550
Kirgiz	none	Kirgiz	45,000	Islam	<1%	1		2551
Mogholi	none	Mogholi	2,000	Islam	<1%	1		2552
Munji-Yidghu	none	Munji-Yidgha	14,000	Islam	<1%	1		2553
Nuristani	stories,portions	Local dialects	67,000	Islam	0%	5	80	4015
Pashayi	none	Pashayi	96,000	Islam-Animist	<1%	1		2554
***Prasuni	none	Prasuni	2,000	Islam	<1%	1		2555
Sau	none	Sau	1,000	Islam	<1%	1		2556
Shina	portions	Shina	50,000	Islam-Animist	<1%	1		2557
Shughni	none	Shughni	3,000	Islam	<1%	1		2558
Tajik	portions	Pamiri	3,600,000	Islam	0%	5		4040
Uiguir	Bible	Uiguir	3,000	Islam	<1%	1		2559
**Uzbeks	portions	Uzbeki, Turkic	1,000,000	Islam-Animist	0%	6	79	1229

578

NAME	SCRIPTURE	LANGUAGE	GROUP SIZE	PRIMARY RELIGION	% CHR	VOL V	UP	ID

Albania

| *Albanian Muslims | New Testament | Albanian Tosk | 1,700,000 | Islam | 0% | 6 | 80 | 4000 |

Algeria

Kabyle	New Testament	Kabyle	1,000,000	Islam	1%	6	79	145
Shawiya	none	Shawiya	150,000	Islam	<1%	1		2207
Western Sahara Refugees	+Bible	Arabic	70,000	Islam	0%	3	83	9012

Angola

Chokwe (Lunda)	NT,portions,tracts,other	Chokwe	400,000	Animism	9%	5		149
Holu	portions	Holu	12,000	Animism	0%	1		5149
**Huila	portions	Huila	200,000	Animism	1%	4		682
Hukwe	none	Hukwe	9,000	Animism	3%	4		511
Kongo	Bible	Kongo	756,000	Unknown	0%	1		5150
Kuadi	none	Kuadi	15,000	Animism	0%	1		5151
Kwangali	New Testament	Kwangali	25,000	Animism	0%	1		5152
Kwanyana	New Testament	Kwanyana	100,000	Animism	0%	1		5153
Luchazi	Bible	Luchazi	60,000	Animism	<1%	1		5154
Luimbi	portions	Luimbi	20,000	Animism	<1%	1		5155

NAME	SCRIPTURE	LANGUAGE	GROUP SIZE	PRIMARY RELIGION	% CHR	VOL	V	UP ID
Lunda	Bible	Lunda	50,000	Animism	<1%	1		5156
Luyana	none	Luyana	4,000	Animism	0%	1		5157
Lwena	Bible	Lwena	90,000	Animism	<1%	1		5158
Mbukushu	none	Kusso	6,000	Animism	6%	4		510
Mbunda	portions	Mbunda	59,000	Animism	0%	1		5159
Mbwela	none	Mbwela	100,000	Animism	<1%	1		5160
Neongo	portions	Neongo	15,000	Animism	<1%	1		5161
Nyaneka	none	Nyaneka	40,000	Animism	0%	1		5162
Nyemba	portions	Nyemba	100,000	Animism	<1%	1		5163
Nyengo	none	Nyengo	5,000	Animism	0%	1		5164
O'ung	none	O'ung	5,000	Animism	0%	1		5148

Argentina

NAME	SCRIPTURE	LANGUAGE	GROUP SIZE	PRIMARY RELIGION	% CHR	VOL	V	UP ID
Chilean Refugees	+Bible	Spanish	1,850	Nominal Christian	nr%	4	83	9031
**Chiriguano	New Testament	Guarani (Bolivian)	23,000	Animism	8%	5		14
Lao Refugees	+not reported	Lao	1,500	Ancestor Worship	<1%	3	83	9037
Pilaga	portions	Pilaga	4,000	Animism	<1%	1		2130
*Universitarios - Rosario	+Bible	Spanish	10,000	Nominal Christian	2%	6	82	5003

Australia

NAME	SCRIPTURE	LANGUAGE	GROUP SIZE	PRIMARY RELIGION	% CHR	VOL	V	UP ID
Aborigines in Brisbane	+Bible	English	8,000	Secularism	6%	6	82	5000
**Chinese Stud., Australia	Bible	Chinese Dialects	6,000	Secularism	5%	4		2119
**Chinese in Australia	Bible	Cantonese	30,000	Traditional Chinese	8%	4		747
*Gugu-Yalanji	portions	Gugu-Yalanji	5,000	Animism	1%	4		430
*Iwaidja	not reported	Iwaidja	150	Animism	7%	4		390
*Murngin (Wulamba)	NT,portions	Dhuwal	4,000	Animism	1%	4		213

NAME	SCRIPTURE	LANGUAGE	GROUP SIZE	PRIMARY RELIGION	% CHR	VOL V	UP ID
**Vietnamese Refugees	Bible	Vietnamese	8,000	Folk Religion	7%	4	2126
*Yanyula	portions	Yanyula (Yanjula)	150	Other	15%	4	230

Austria

NAME	SCRIPTURE	LANGUAGE	GROUP SIZE	PRIMARY RELIGION	% CHR	VOL V	UP ID
*Chinese in Austria	Bible	Mandarin	1,000	Traditional Chinese	5%	4	753

Bangladesh

NAME	SCRIPTURE	LANGUAGE	GROUP SIZE	PRIMARY RELIGION	% CHR	VOL V	UP ID
**Banai	Bible	Bengali	2,000	Buddhist-Animist	1%	4	63
Baum	Bible	Baum	7,000	Islam	<1%	1	2561
**Bengali Sufis	not reported	Bengali	70,000	Islam	0%	4 84	4820
Burmese Muslim Refugees	+portions	Bengali	200,000	Islam	0%	3 83	9001
**Hajong	Bible	Bengali	17,000	Hindu-Animist	1%	5	61
**Koch	Bible	Bengali	35,000	Hindu-Animist	1%	5	62
Mirung	none	Mirung	12,000	Animism	1%	4	650
Mru	not reported	Murung	50,000	Animism	1%	5	3
Pankhu	none	Pankhu	600	Islam	<1%	1	2563
Tangchangya	none	Tangchangya	8,000	Islam	<1%	1	2564
Tippera	none	Tippera	38,000	Islam	<1%	1	2565

NAME	SCRIPTURE	LANGUAGE	GROUP SIZE	PRIMARY RELIGION	% CHR	V	VOL UP	ID
Belgium								
North Africans in Belgium	Bible	Arabic	90,000	Islam	<1%	6	80	4019
Turkish Workers	Bible	Kurdish	60,000	Islam	1%	6	80	4020
Belize								
**Black Caribs, Belize	New Testament	Garifuna	10,000	Christo-Paganism	1%	6	79	252
**Mopan Maya	portions	Mopan Maya	4,000	Christo-Paganism	15%	5		1206
Salvadoran Refugees	+Bible	Spanish	2,000	Nominal Christian	nr%	3		9059
Benin								
**Adja	Bible	Ge	250,000	Animism	5%	4		423
*Bariba	New Testament	Bariba	400,000	Animism	4%	6	80	246
Berba		Berba	44,000	Animism	0%	1		5165
**Boko	portions	Boko (Busa)	40,000	Animism	2%	4		444
Dendi	none	Dendi	40,000	Islam	0%	3		445
Donpago	portions	Donpago	19,000	Animism	7%	4		515
*Fulani	none	Fulani	70,000	Islam-Animist	1%	4		446
Gbazantche	none	Gbazantche	9,000	Islam	0%	3		447
Gu	Bible	Gu	173,000	Animism	0%	1		5167

NAME	SCRIPTURE	LANGUAGE	GROUP SIZE	PRIMARY RELIGION	% CHR	V	UP ID
Kabre	portions	Kabre	35,000	Animism	0%	1	5168
Kotokoli	none	Kotokoli	75,000	Islam	0%	3	448
Lamba	portions	Lamba	29,000	Animism	0%	3	5169
*Mokole	none	Mokole	7,000	Animism	0%	3	449
*Nyantruku	none	Aledjo	4,000	Animism	0%	3	450
**Pila	portions	Pila-Pila	50,000	Animism	1%	4	237
**Save	Bible	Save (Yoruba)	15,000	Animism	1%	4	451
**Somba	portions	Somba (Detammari)	60,000	Animism	1%	4	452
Soruba	none	Soruba	5,000	Animism	0%	3	453
Takemba	none	Takemba	10,000	Animism	0%	1	5170
Tayaku	none	Tayaku	10,000	Animism	0%	1	5171
*Tofi	none	Tofi	33,000	Islam	3%	4	422
Winji-Winji	none	Winji-Winji	5,000	Islam	0%	3	454
Yoabu	none	Yoabu	8,000	Animism	0%	1	5172

Bhutan

NAME	SCRIPTURE	LANGUAGE	GROUP SIZE	PRIMARY RELIGION	% CHR	V	UP ID
Bhutias	New Testament	Sharchagpakha	780,000	Buddhism	1%	6	2022
Kebuntamp	none	Kebuntamp	400,000	Buddhist-Animist	<1%	1	2566
Sharchagpakha	none	Sharchagpakha	400,000	Buddhist-Animist	<1%	1	2567
Tibetans in Bhutan	Bible	Tibetan	5,000	Buddhism	<1%	5 81	7017

Bolivia

NAME	SCRIPTURE	LANGUAGE	GROUP SIZE	PRIMARY RELIGION	% CHR	V	UP ID
**Aymara	NT,portions	Aymara	850,000	Animism	7%	5	8
Chacobo	New Testament	Chacobo	300	Animism	<1%	1	2132
Chipaya	NT,portions	Chipaya	100	Animism	<1%	1	2133
Chiquitano	NT,portions	Chiquitano	20,000	Animism	<1%	1	2134

NAME	SCRIPTURE	LANGUAGE	GROUP SIZE	PRIMARY RELIGION	% CHR	V	VOL UP ID
***Guarani	New Testament	Guarani	15,000	Animism	10%	6 79	206
Guarayu	portions	Guarayu	5,000	Christo-Paganism	1%	5	605
Ignaciano	portions,NT	Ignaciano	5,000	Animism	<1%	1	2135
Itonama	portions	Itonama	100	Animism	<1%	1	2136
Leco	none	Leco	200	Animism	<1%	1	2137
***Mestizos in La Paz	+Bible	Spanish	400,000	Christo-Paganism	4%	5 82	5001
*Mororata	New Testament	Aymara	500	Animism	<1%	4	6568
Movina	portions	Movina	1,000	Animism	<1%	1	2139
**Quechua	New Testament	Quechua	1,000,000	Christo-Paganism	4%	4	33
Reyesano	Bible	Reyesano	1,000	Animism	<1%	4	2140
Simba	New Testament	Guarani	400	Animism	0%	4	6569
Siriono	New Testament	Siriono	500	Animism	1%	1	2141
Tacana	portions	Tacana	4,000	Animism	<1%	1	2142
Tsimane	portions	Tsimane	6,000	Animism	<1%	1	2143
Yuracare	portions	Yuracare	3,000	Animism	<1%	1	2144

Botswana

NAME	SCRIPTURE	LANGUAGE	GROUP SIZE	PRIMARY RELIGION	% CHR	V	VOL UP ID
Au ei	none	Au ei	5,000	Animism	0%	1	5173
Buka-khwe	none	Local dialects	9,000	Animism	0%	1	5174
Bushmen in Botswana	none	Buka-khwe	30,000	Animism	7%	4	509
Dukwe Refugee Camp Residents	not reported	Tribal Languages	800	Animism	nr%	4 83	9022
Herero	New Testament	Herero	10,000	Animism	0%	1	5175
*Kalanga	portions	Chikalanga	150,000	Animism	2%	5	1163
Kwe-etshori	none	Kwe-etshori	3,000	Animism	<1%	1	5176
Nharon	none	Nharon	3,000	Animism	1%	1	5177
Shua	none	Shua	400	Animism	0%	1	5178
**Tonga	Bible	Tonga	6,000	Animism	0%	1	5179
**Yei	none	Yei	10,000	Animism	1%	5	1162

NAME	SCRIPTURE	LANGUAGE	GROUP SIZE	PRIMARY RELIGION	% CHR	V	UP	VOL ID
Brazil								
Apalai	portions	Apalai	100	Animism	<1%	1		2145
Apinaye	portions	Apinaye	200	Animism	<1%	1		2146
Apurina	none	Apurina	1,000	Animism	<1%	1		2147
Arapaco	none	Tucanoan	300	Animism	<1%	1		2148
Atruahi	portions	Atruahi	500	Animism	<1%	1		2149
Bakairi	none	Bakairi	300	Animism	<1%	1		2150
Baniwa	New Testament	Baniwa	3,000	Animism	<1%	1		2151
*Bororo	portions	Bororo	500	Animism	1%	5		441
Caiwa	portions	Caiwa	7,000	Animism	<1%	1		2152
Canela	none	Canela	1,000	Animism	<1%	1		2153
**Chinese in Brazil	Bible	Hakka	45,000	Traditional Chinese	8%	4		755
Cinta Larga	none	Cinta Larga	500	Animism	8%	4		2154
***Copacabana Apt. Dwellers	Bible	Portuguese	400,000	Nominal Christian	11%	4		4116
Culina	portions	Culina	800	Animism	11%	4		2155
Desano	portions	Desano	1,000	Animism	<1%	1		2156
*Drug Addicts in Sao Paulo	+Bible	Portuguese	200,000	Nominal Christian	nr%	5	82	5022
*Favelados-Rio de Janeiro	+Bible	Portuguese	600,000	Christo-Paganism	<1%	5	82	5043
Fulnio	Bible	Fulnio	2,000	Animism	<1%	1		2157
Guajajara	portions	Guajajara	5,000	Animism	<1%	1		2158
Gypsies	not reported	Portuguese	10,000	Nominal Christian	nr%	3		4821
Hixkaryana	New Testament	Hixkaryana	200	Animism	<1%	1		2160
Hohodene	not reported	Hohodene	1,000	Animism	<1%	1		2161
Jamamadi	not reported	Jamamadi	1,000	Animism	<1%	1		2162
Japanese in Brazil	Bible	Japanese	750,000	Buddhism	8%	8	79	1
Kabixi	not reported	Kabixi	100	Animism	<1%	1		2163
Kadiweu	not reported	Kadiweu	600	Animism	<1%	1		2164
Kaingang	New Testament	Kaingang	7,000	Christo-Paganism	<1%	1		2165
Kamayura	none	Kamayura	100	Animism	<1%	1		2166

NAME	SCRIPTURE	LANGUAGE	GROUP SIZE	PRIMARY RELIGION	% CHR	V	VOL UP ID
Karipuna Creole	none	Karipuna Creole	500	Animism	<1%	1	2168
Karipuna Do Guapore	not reported	Karipuna Do Guapore	200	Animism	<1%	1	2169
Katukina, Panoan	none	Katukina, Panoan	200	Animism	<1%	1	2170
Kayabi	none	Kayabi	300	Animism	<1%	1	2171
Kayapo	portions	Kayapo	600	Animism	0%	4	1158
Kohoroxitari	none	Kohoroxitari	600	Animism	<1%	1	2172
Kreen-Akakore	none	Kreen-Akakore	100	Animism	<1%	1	2173
Kuatinema	none	Asurini	100	Animism	0%	5	1159
Kuikuro	none	Kuikuro	100	Animism	<1%	1	2174
**Macuxi	portions	Macuxi	6,000	Animism	5%	3	719
Maiongong	New Testament	Maiongong	100	Animism	<1%	3	718
Marubo	none	Marubo	400	Animism	<1%	1	2175
Matipuhy-Nahukua	none	Matipuhy-Nahukua	100	Animism	<1%	1	2176
Maxakali	portions	Maxakali	400	Animism	<1%	1	2177
Munduruku	portions	Munduruku	2,000	Animism	<1%	1	3107
Mura-Piraha	none	Mura-Piraha	2,100	Animism	<1%	1	3108
Nadeb Maku	none	Nadeb Maku	200	Animism	<1%	1	3109
Nambikuara	portions	Nambikuara	400	Animism	3%	5	379
Nhengatu	New Testament	Nhengatu	3,000	Animism	<1%	1	3110
Ninam	portions	Ninam	500	Animism	<1%	1	3111
Oyampipuku	none	Oyampipuku	100	Animism	<1%	1	3112
Pacu	none	Tucano	100	Animism	<1%	1	3113
Pakaasnovos	portions	Pakaasnovos	800	Animism	<1%	1	3114
Palikur	portions	Palikur	500	Animism	<1%	1	3115
Pankararu	none	Portuguese	2,000	Animism	<1%	1	3116
Parakanan	none	Parakanan	500	Animism	<1%	1	3117
Paresi	portions	Paresi	400	Animism	<1%	1	3118
Parintintin	portions	Parintintin	200	Animism	<1%	1	3119
Pato Tapuia	none	Pato Tapuia	100	Animism	<1%	1	3120
Paumari	portions	Paumari	300	Animism	<1%	1	3121
Piratapuyo	none	Tucano	800	Animism	<1%	1	3122
Quarequena	not reported	Tucano	300	Animism	<1%	1	2159
Rikbaktsa	portions	Rikbaktsa	200	Animism	<1%	1	3123
*Sanuma	portions	Sanuma	300	Animism	1%	3	720
Satere	portions	Satere	3,000	Animism	<1%	1	3124
Seuci	none	Tucano	400	Animism	<1%	1	3125

NAME	SCRIPTURE	LANGUAGE	GROUP SIZE	PRIMARY RELIGION	% CHR	VOL V	UP ID
**Shiriahana	portions	Shiriahana	200	Animism	5%	3	721
Students in Cuiaba	not reported	Portuguese	20,000	Secularism	1%	3	712
Surui	none	Surui	300	Animism	<1%	1	3126
Tembe	none	Tembe	300	Animism	<1%	1	3127
Terena	portions	Terena	5,000	Animism	<1%	1	3128
Ticuna	portions	Ticuna	8,000	Animism	<1%	1	3129
Tucano	portions	Tucano	2,000	Animism	<1%	1	3130
Tuyuca	none	Tuyuca	500	Animism	<1%	1	3131
Urubu	portions	Urubu	500	Animism	<1%	1	3132
Urupa	none	Urupa	300	Animism	<1%	1	3133
Waimiri	none	Waimiri	1,000	Animism	<1%	1	3134
Waiwai	portions	Waiwai	1,000	Animism	<1%	1	3135
Wapishana	portions	Wapishana	2,000	Animism	<1%	1	3136
Waura	none	Waura	100	Animism	<1%	1	3137
Xavante	portions	Xavante	2,000	Animism	<1%	1	3138
Xerente	portions	Xerente	500	Animism	<1%	1	3139
Xokleng	none	Xokleng	300	Animism	<1%	1	3140
*Yanomano	portions	Yanonan (Waica)	3,000	Animism	1%	6 79	1059

Burma

NAME	SCRIPTURE	LANGUAGE	GROUP SIZE	PRIMARY RELIGION	% CHR	VOL V	UP ID
Chaungtha	none	Chaungtha	40,000	Buddhist-Animist	<1%	1	2568
Chin, Falam	New Testament	Chin, Falam	92,000	Buddhist-Animist	<1%	2	2570
Chin, Haka	New Testament	Chin, Haka	85,000	Buddhist-Animist	<1%	2	2571
Chin, Khumi	New Testament	Chin, Khumi	30,000	Buddhist-Animist	nr%	2	2572
Chin, Ngaun	portions	Chin, Ngaun	5,000	Buddhist-Animist	<1%	1	2573
Chin, Tiddim	New Testament	Chin, Tiddim	38,000	Buddhist-Animist	<1%	1	2574
Chinbok	none	Chinbok	21,000	Buddhist-Animist	<1%	1	2575
Chinese in Burma	Bible	Mandarin and dialects	600,000	Traditional Chinese	2%	4	751
Dai	none	Dai	20,000	Buddhist-Animist	<1%	3	2576
Danu	Bible	Burmese	70,000	Buddhism	0%	2	4148
Gheko	none	Gheko	4,000	Buddhist-Animist	<1%	1	2577

NAME	SCRIPTURE	LANGUAGE	GROUP SIZE	PRIMARY RELIGION	% CHR	V	VOL	UP ID
Hallam	portions	Hallam	11,000	Buddhist-Animist	<1%	1		2578
Hkun	not reported	Shan	20,000	Buddhism	0%	2		4144
Hrangkhol	none	Hrangkhol	9,000	Buddhist-Animist	<1%	1		2579
Intha	none	Intha	80,000	Buddhist-Animist	<1%	1		2580
Kachin in Shan State	Bible	Burmese	80,000	Buddhism	0%	2		4154
Kaw	not reported	Kaw	30,000	Animism	nr%	2		4152
Kayan	not reported	Padaung	18,000	Animism	0%	2		4156
Kokant	not reported	Kokant	50,000	Buddhist-Animist	0%	2		4150
Lana	none	Lana	3,000	Buddhist-Animist	<1%	1		2581
Maghi	portions	Maghi	310,000	Buddhist-Animist	<1%	1		2582
Moken	none	Moken	5,000	Animism	1%	6	79	157
Mon	Bible	Mon	350,000	Buddhist-Animist	<1%	1		2583
Mun	none	Mun	10,000	Buddhist-Animist	<1%	1		2584
Myaung-Ze	not reported	Myaung-Ze	7,000	Animism	0%	2		4153
Norra	none	Norra	10,000	Buddhist-Animist	1%	5	81	2585
Palaung	none	Palaung	150,000	Buddhism	1%	5	79	156
Pao	not reported	Pao	100,000	Buddhism	0%	2		4149
Purum	none	Purum	300	Buddhist-Animist	<1%	1		2587
Ralte	portions	Ralte	17,000	Buddhist-Animist	<1%	1		2588
Riang-Lang	none	Riang-Lang	20,000	Buddhist-Animist	<1%	1		2590
Senthang	not reported	Senthang	10,000	Buddhism	<1%	1		2591
Shan	not reported	Shan	800,000	Buddhism	0%	2		4143
Shan Chinese	none	Shan	20,000	Buddhist-Animist	0%	2		4157
Taaan	none	Taaan	10,000	Buddhist-Animist	<1%	1		2592
Taungyo	Bible	Taungyo	200,000	Buddhist-Animist	<1%	1		2593
Taungyoe	none	Burmese	18,000	Buddhist-Animist	0%	2		4147
Taurr	not reported	Taurr	700	Buddhist-Animist	<1%	1		2594
Thai-Ney	not reported	Shan	5,000	Buddhist-Animist	0%	2		4158
Wa	none	Wa	50,000	Animism	<1%	1		4155
Yangbye	none	Yangbye	330,000	Buddhist-Animist	0%	2		2596
Yin-Kyar	not reported	Shan Dialects	2,000	Animism	0%	2		4146
Yin-Nett	not reported	Shan Dialects	2,000	Animism	0%	2		4145
Yinchia	none	Yinchia	4,000	Buddhist-Animist	<1%	1		2597
Yos	none	Yos	5,000	Buddhist-Animist	<1%	1		2598
Zome	New Testament	Zome	30,000	Buddhist-Animist	<1%	1		2599

NAME	SCRIPTURE	LANGUAGE	GROUP SIZE	PRIMARY RELIGION	% CHR	VOL V	UP ID

Burundi

| Pygmy (Binga) | none | Local dialects | 30,000 | Animism | 6% | 5 | 508 |
| ***Rwandan Tutsi Refugees | +Bible | Kirundi | 49,000 | Animism | nr% | 4 83 | 9041 |

Cameroon

Adamawa	New Testament	Fulani	380,000	Animism	<1%	5	507
Age	none	Age	7,000	Animism	0%	1	5206
Aghem	none	Aghem	5,000	Animism	0%	1	5207
Amasi	none	Amasi	10,000	Animism	0%	1	5208
Assumbo	none	Assumbo	10,000	Animism	<1%	1	5209
Babajou	none	Babajou	500	Animism	0%	1	5210
Bafut	not reported	Bafut	25,000	Animism	0%	1	5211
Baka	none	Baka	15,000	Animism	<1%	1	5212
Balong	none	Duala	5,000	Animism	<1%	1	5213
Banougoun-Bamenjou	none	Banougoun-Bamenjou	31,000	Animism	0%	1	5214
Banum	New Testament	Banum	75,000	not reported	nr%	1	5215
Bandjoun	portions	Bandjoun	60,000	Animism	0%	1	5216
Banen	none	Banen	28,000	Animism	0%	1	5217
Bangangte	New Testament	Local Dialects	475,000	Unknown	<1%	1	5218
Basaa	NT portions	Basaa	170,000	Unknown	0%	1	5219
Batanga-Ngolo	portions	Batanga-Ngolo	9,000	Animism	<1%	1	5220
Bene	none	Bene	60,000	Animism	0%	1	5221
Bethen	none	Bethen	10,000	Animism	0%	1	5222
Betsinga	none	Betsinga	10,000	Animism	0%	1	5223

REGISTRY OF THE UNREACHED

NAME	SCRIPTURE	LANGUAGE	GROUP SIZE	PRIMARY RELIGION	% CHR	V	VOL	UP ID
Bitare	not reported	Bitare	50,000	Animism	0%	1		5224
Bobe	none	Bobe	600	Animism	0%	1		5225
Bokyi	New Testament	Bokyi	43,000	Animism	<1%	1		5226
Bonboko	none	Bonboko	3,000	Animism	<1%	1		5227
Bonkeng-Pendia	none	Bonkeng-Pendia	2,000	Animism	0%	1		5228
Budugun	Bible	Masa	10,000	Animism	<1%	4		506
Bura	New Testament	Bura	100,000	Animism	<1%	1		5229
Chad's Refugees from N'Djamena	not reported	Tribal Languages	100,000	Islam	<1%	4	83	9005
Chinga	none	Chinga	13,000	Animism	0%	1		7050
Daba	portions	Daba	31,000	Animism	<1%	1		7051
Dghwede	New Testament	Dghwede	13,000	Animism	<1%	1		7052
**Doohwaayo	not reported	Doohyaayo	15,000	Animism	12%	5		5
Duru	none	Duru	20,000	Animism	6%	4		7040
Eton	none	Eton	112,000	Animism	0%	1		7053
Fali	New Testament	Fali	50,000	Islam	<1%	1		7054
Fulani, Northern	not reported	Fulani	250,000	Islam-Animist	1%	5	79	37
Fungom, Northern	none	Fungom, Northern	12,000	Animism	0%	1		7055
Gidar	portions	Gidar	50,000	Animism	<1%	1		7056
Gisei	none	Masa	10,000	Animism	<1%	4		504
Gisiga	portions	Gisiga	30,000	Animism	11%	4		503
Gouwar	none	Gouwar	5,000	Animism	0%	1		7057
Gude	none	Gude	100,000	Animism	1%	4		502
Gulfe	none	Gulfe	36,000	Animism	0%	1		7058
Iyon	none	Iyon	4,000	Animism	0%	1		7059
Kaalong	none	Kaalong	50,000	Animism	0%	1		7060
Kaka	portions	Kaka	2,000	Animism	<1%	1		5241
Kankam	none	Kankam	800	Animism	1%	1		5242
Kera	none	Kera	15,000	Islam-Animist	<1%	5		5243
Kolbila	not reported	Kolbila	1,000	Animism	1%	5		1155
Kole	none	Kole	300	Animism	0%	1		5244
Koma	none	Koma	15,000	Animism	0%	1		5245
Konaben	none	Konaben	3,000	Animism	0%	1		7061
Korop	none	Korop	10,000	Animism	0%	1		5247
Kotoko	none	Kotoko	31,000	Animism	0%	1		5248
Kotopo	none	Kotopo	10,000	Animism	0%	4		501

NAME	SCRIPTURE	LANGUAGE	GROUP SIZE	PRIMARY RELIGION	% CHR	V UP	VOL ID
Kpa	portions	Kpa	17,000	Animism	0%	1	5249
Kukele	NT,portions	Kukele	33,000	Animism	<1%	1	5250
Kutin	none	Kutin	400	Animism	0%	1	5251
Kwakum	none	Kwakum	3,000	Animism	0%	1	5252
Laka	none	Laka	10,000	Animism	0%	4	500
Lambi	not reported	Lambi	1,000	Animism	<1%	1	5253
Lue	none	Lue	4,000	Animism	0%	1	5255
Lundu	none	Lundu	24,000	Animism	0%	1	5254
Maka	none	Maka	51,000	Animism	0%	1	5256
Mambila	not reported	Mambila	40,000	Animism	<1%	4	499
Mangisa	none	Mangisa	14,000	Animism	0%	1	5257
Matakam	New Testament	Matakam	140,000	Animism	2%	4	498
Mbembe	none	Mbembe	25,000	Animism	0%	1	5258
Mbinu	none	Mbinu	nr	Animism	<1%	1	5259
Mbo	none	Mbo	23,000	Animism	<1%	1	5260
Meneno-Mogano	portions	Meneno-Mogano	35,000	Animism	0%	1	5261
Menka	none	Menka	10,000	Animism	0%	1	5262
Mofu	none	Mofu	33,000	Animism	0%	1	5263
Mulimba	none	Mulimba	3,000	Unknown	0%	1	5264
Mungaka	Bible	Mungaka	14,000	Animism	<1%	1	5265
Ndjen	portions	Ndjen	25,000	Animism	<1%	1	5266
Ndop-Baneessing	none	Ndop-Baneessing	17,000	Animism	0%	1	5267
Ndoro	none	Ndoro	10,000	Animism	0%	1	5268
Ndunpa Duupa	not reported	Ndunpa Duupa	1,000	Islam-Animist	1%	4	1156
Ngayaba	none	Ngayaba	1,000	Animism	0%	1	5269
Ngemba	portions	Ngemba	34,000	Animism	<1%	1	5270
Ngi	none	Ngi	10,000	Animism	0%	1	5271
Ngunba	portions	Ngunba	10,000	Animism	0%	1	5272
Nguo	none	Nguo	10,000	Animism	<1%	1	5273
Nkom	portions	Nkom	30,000	Animism	0%	1	5274
Nohu	portions	Nohu	7,000	Animism	0%	1	5275
Nso	portions	Nso	100,000	Animism	0%	1	5276
Nyang	none	Nyang	10,000	Animism	<1%	1	5277
Oso	none	Oso	25,000	Animism	0%	1	5278
Pape	none	Pape	1,000	Animism	0%	1	5279
Podokwo	none	Podokwo	25,000	Animism	<1%	4	496

NAME	SCRIPTURE	LANGUAGE	GROUP SIZE	PRIMARY RELIGION	% CHR	V	VOL	UP ID
So	none	So	6,000	Animism	0%	1		5280
Su	portions	Su	500	Animism	<1%	1		5281
Suga	none	Suga	10,000	Animism	0%	1		5282
Taran	none	Taran	3,000	Animism	0%	1		5283
Tchang	none	Tchang	100,000	Animism	0%	1		5284
Tigon	none	Tigon	25,000	Animism	<1%	4		495
Tikar	portions	Tikar	13,000	Animism	<1%	1		5285
Tupuri	portions	Tupuri	70,000	Animism	<1%	1		5286
Vere	none	Vere	20,000	Animism	0%	1		5287
Voko	not reported	Voko	1,000	Islam-Animist	<1%	4		1154
Widekun	none	Widekun	10,000	Animism	<1%	1		5288
**Winbun	not reported	Winbun	50,000	Animism	1%	5		388
Yambasa	portions	Yambasa	26,000	Animism	<1%	1		5289
Yasing	none	Yasing	25,000	Animism	0%	1		5290
Yinga	not reported	Yinga	300	Animism	1%	4		1157

Canada

NAME	SCRIPTURE	LANGUAGE	GROUP SIZE	PRIMARY RELIGION	% CHR	V	VOL	UP ID
Koreans	+Bible	Korean	40,000	Buddhism	nr%	1		9167
Muslim Lebanese Refugees	+Bible	French	29,000	Islam	0%	4	83	9025
Theater Arts Performers	+Bible	English	6,000	Secularism	0%	2		9114
Tibetan Refugees	+portions	Tibetan	400	Buddhism	0%	1		9160

Canada:Alberta

NAME	SCRIPTURE	LANGUAGE	GROUP SIZE	PRIMARY RELIGION	% CHR	V	VOL	UP ID
Chinese, Calgary	+Bible	English	30,000	Traditional Chinese	nr%	2		9171
Indians, Cold Lake Reserve	+Bible	English	1,250	Nominal Christian	nr%	1		9266

NAME	SCRIPTURE	LANGUAGE	GROUP SIZE	PRIMARY RELIGION	% CHR V	VOL UP ID
Indians, Eden Valley	+Bible	English	300	Nominal Christian	nr% 1	9258
Indians, Edmonton	+Bible	English	30,000	Folk Religion	nr% 1	9251
Lao-Chinese Refugees, Edmonton	+Bible	Lao	2,000	Buddhism	0% 1	9207
Metis, Elizabeth Settlement	+not reported	Cree	1,000	Animism	0% 1	9130
Oil Executives, Calgary	+Bible	English	5,000	Secularism	0% 1	9206
Rastafarians, Edmonton	+Bible	English	100	Other	0% 1	9205
University Students, Edmonton	+Bible	English	20,000	Secularism	1% 3	9101
Vietnamese, Edmonton	+Bible	Chinese	8,000	Buddhism	nr% 2	9125

Canada:British Columbia

NAME	SCRIPTURE	LANGUAGE	GROUP SIZE	PRIMARY RELIGION	% CHR V	VOL UP ID
**Chinese, Vancouver	Bible	Cantonese	80,000	Traditional Chinese	6% 4	758
Indians, Lower Mainland	+Bible	English	2,500	Nominal Christian	nr% 1	9260
Indians, Vancouver	+Bible	English	40,000	Nominal Christian	nr% 1	9262
Indo-Canadians, Vancouver	+Bible	Urdu	70,000	Sikhism	0% 3 84	9127
Jews, Vancouver	+Bible	English	12,000	Judaism	0% 1	9108
Portuguese, Vancouver	+Bible	Portuguese	15,000	Nominal Christian	nr% 1	9157
Street People, Victoria	+Bible	English	1,900	Secularism	0% 2	9126
Ugandan Asian Refugees	+not reported	Gujarati	7,000	Islam	0% 3 83	9011

Canada:Manitoba

NAME	SCRIPTURE	LANGUAGE	GROUP SIZE	PRIMARY RELIGION	% CHR V	VOL UP ID
Indians, Interlake Region	+Bible	English	10,000	Nominal Christian	nr% 1	9169
**Indians, Winnipeg	+Bible	Various dialects	70,000	Nominal Christian	nr% 1	9170
Jews, Winnipeg	+Bible	Yiddish	20,000	Judaism	0% 2	9121

NAME	SCRIPTURE	LANGUAGE	GROUP SIZE	PRIMARY RELIGION	% CHR	VOL V	UP ID
Canada:New Brunswick							
***Micmac Indians	+portions	English	10,000	Nominal Christian	nr%	1	9286
Canada:Newfoundland							
French, St. Pierre & Miquelon	+Bible	French	6,000	Nominal Christian	nr%	1	9159
Canada:Nova Scotia							
Chinese, Halifax	+Bible	Mandarin	3,000	Buddhism	0%	2	9120
***Micmac Indians, Eskasoni Rsv.	+portions	English	2,000	Nominal Christian	nr%	1	9285

594

Canada:Ontario

NAME	SCRIPTURE	LANGUAGE	SIZE	RELIGION	CHR%	V	GR	
*Chilean Refugees, Toronto	+Bible	Spanish	10,000	Nominal Christian	nr%	4	83	9023
Chinese Students, Thunder Bay	+Bible	Mandarin	500	Secularism	0%	2		9113
Chinese, Metro Toronto	+Bible	English	40,000	Buddhism	nr%	4		9100
Chinese, Thunder Bay	+Bible	Various dialects	1,000	Buddhism	nr%	2		9109
Ex-Mental Patients, Hamilton	+Bible	English	800	Secularism	0%	2		9116
Fur Trappers	+Bible	French	8,000	Secularism	0%	2		9115
Greeks, Toronto	+Bible	Greek	85,000	Nominal Christian	nr%	1		9150
Homosexuals, Toronto	+Bible	English	60,000	Secularism	nr%	1		9203
Indians, CN Rail Lines	+Bible	English	20,000	Nominal Christian	nr%	1		9267
Indians, London	+Bible	English	8,000	Nominal Christian	5%	1		9264
Indians, Northwestern Ontario	+Bible	English	250,000	Nominal Christian	nr%	1		9261
Indians, Thunder Bay	+Bible	English	10,000	Nominal Christian	nr%	1		9257
Japanese, Toronto	+Bible	Japanese	20,000	Buddhism	nr%	1		9151
Jews, Toronto	+Bible	English	120,000	Judaism	0%	2		9118
**Kampuchean Refugees, Ontario	+Bible	Khmer	600	Buddhist-Animist	0%	4	83	9046
Khmer Refugees, Toronto	+Bible	Khmer	300	Buddhism	0%	2		9123
Khmer, Ottawa	+Bible	French	400	Buddhism	0%	2		9124
Lebanese, Beamington	+Bible	French	1,500	Islam	nr%	1		9269
Portuguese, Cambridge	+Bible	Portuguese	15,000	Nominal Christian	nr%	1		9154
Portuguese, London/Strathroy	+Bible	Portuguese	14,000	Nominal Christian	nr%	1		9155
Portuguese, Metro Toronto	+Bible	Portuguese	150,000	Nominal Christian	nr%	1		9158
Portuguese, West Lorne Village	+Bible	Portuguese	250	Nominal Christian	nr%	1		9156

NAME	SCRIPTURE	LANGUAGE	GROUP SIZE	PRIMARY RELIGION	% CHR	V	VOL	V	UP ID
Shopping Bag Women, Toronto	+Bible	English	500	Secularism	nr%	1			9165
Sikhs, Toronto	+Bible	Punjabi	20,000	Sikhism	0%	2			9119
Street People, Thunder Bay	+Bible	Various dialects	10,000	Secularism	nr%	1			9253
Ugandan Asian Refugees, Tor.	not reported	Various dialects	15,000	Islam	0%	1			9164
**Ukrainians, Toronto	+Bible	Ukrainian	100,000	Nominal Christian	nr%	1			9152
West Indian Migrant Workers	+Bible	English	400	Hinduism	nr%	3			9102
***West Indians, Toronto	+Bible	English	200,000	Nominal Christian	nr%	1			9166
****Youth, Toronto Peanut District	+Bible	English	3,500	Secularism	nr%	1			9163

Canada:Quebec

NAME	SCRIPTURE	LANGUAGE	GROUP SIZE	PRIMARY RELIGION	% CHR	V	VOL	V	UP ID
Haitians, Montreal	+Bible	Creole	32,000	Folk Religion	nr%	2			9111
Iranians, Montreal	+Bible	Farsi	1,500	Islam	0%	1	5	79	9208
Jews (Non-Sephardic), Montreal	Bible	English	120,000	Judaism	1%	5	79		384
Jews (Sephardic), Montreal	not reported	French	26,000	Judaism	1%	3			724
Khmer Refugees, Montreal	+Bible	Khmer	3,000	Buddhism	0%	2			9122
**Montagnais Indians	+Bible	English	12,000	Nominal Christian	nr%	1			9263
Moroccan Jews	+Bible	French	10,000	Judaism	0%	3			9103

NAME	SCRIPTURE	LANGUAGE	GROUP SIZE	PRIMARY RELIGION	% CHR	V	VOL UP ID

Canada:Saskatchewan

NAME	SCRIPTURE	LANGUAGE	GROUP SIZE	PRIMARY RELIGION	% CHR	V	VOL UP ID
Indians, Kinistino Reserve	+Bible	English	250	Animism	0%	1	9256
Indians, Northern Sask.	+Bible	Various dialects	100,000	Nominal Christian	nr%	1	9254
Indians, Regina	+Bible	English	33,000	Nominal Christian	nr%	1	9265
Indians, Saskatoon	+Bible	English	10,000	Nominal Christian	nr%	1	9268
Indians, White Bear Reserve	+Bible	English		Nominal Christian	nr%	1	9259
Vietnamese Refugees, Regina	+Bible	Vietnamese	500	Buddhism	nr%	2	9105

Central African Republic

NAME	SCRIPTURE	LANGUAGE	GROUP SIZE	PRIMARY RELIGION	% CHR	V	VOL UP ID
Arab Immigrants in Bangui	+Bible	Arabic	5,000	Islam	0%	5 82	5045
Day	none	Day	2,000	Animism	<1%	1	5180
Kaba	New Testament	Kaba	11,000	Animism	0%	1	5181
Kaba Dunjo	none	Kaba Dunjo	17,000	Animism	0%	1	5182
Kaka	portions	Kaka	37,000	Animism	0%	1	5183
Kari	none	Kari	4,000	Animism	0%	1	5185
Karre	New Testament	Karre	40,000	Animism	0%	1	5184
Kin	New Testament	Kin	5,000	Animism	0%	1	5186
Laka	New Testament	Laka	40,000	Animism	<1%	1	5187
Majingai-ngana	none	Majingai-ngana	47,000	Animism	1%	1	5188
Mbai	portions,NT	Mbai	73,000	Animism	<1%	1	5189
Mbati	none	Mbati	15,000	Animism	0%	1	5190

597

NAME	SCRIPTURE	LANGUAGE	GROUP SIZE	PRIMARY RELIGION	% CHR	VOL V	UP ID
Monjombo	none	Monjombo	11,000	Animism	0%	1	5191
Ndan	none	Ndan	700	Animism	0%	1	5192
Ndogo	none	Ndogo	4,000	Animism	0%	1	5193
Ngando	none	Ngando	2,000	Animism	0%	1	5194
Ngbaka Ma'bo	portions	Ngbaka Ma'bo	17,000	Animism	0%	1	5195
Nzakara	none	Nzakara	3,000	Animism	0%	1	5196
Pambia	none	Pambia	2,000	Animism	0%	1	5197
Pana	portions	Pana	20,000	Animism	0%	1	5198
Pygmy (Binga)	none	Local dialects	2,000	Animism	0%	4	512
Runga	none	Runga	13,000	Animism	0%	1	5199
Sonrai	none	Somrai	50,000	Animism	0%	1	5200
Tana	none	Tana	35,000	Animism	0%	1	5201
Tunya	none	Tunya	800	Animism	0%	1	5202
Vale	none	Vale	1,000	Animism	0%	1	5203
Yakoma	none	Yakoma	5,000	Animism	0%	1	5204

Chad

NAME	SCRIPTURE	LANGUAGE	GROUP SIZE	PRIMARY RELIGION	% CHR	VOL V	UP ID
Abou Charib	none	Abou Charib	25,000	Islam-Animist	<1%	1	2208
Bagirmi	none	Bagirmi	40,000	Islam-Animist	<1%	1	2209
Bilala	none	Bilala	42,000	Islam-Animist	<1%	1	2210
Bomou	none	Bomou	15,000	Islam-Animist	<1%	1	2211
Bua	portions	Bua	20,000	Animism	0%	3	513
Daju of Dar Dadju	none	Daju of Dar Dadju	27,000	Islam-Animist	<1%	1	2213
Daju of Dar Sila	none	Daju of Dar Sila	33,000	Islam-Animist	<1%	1	2214
Dangaleat	none	Dangaleat	20,000	Islam-Animist	<1%	1	2215
Daza	not reported	Dazaga	159,000	Islam	0%	5	4044
Gabri	none	Gabri	20,000	Islam-Animist	<1%	1	2216
Gambai	portions,NT	Gambai	200,000	Islam-Animist	<1%	1	2217
Gidar	none	Gidar	50,000	Islam-Animist	<1%	1	2218
Golo	none	Golo	3,000	Islam-Animist	<1%	1	2219
Goulai	portions	Goulai	30,000	Islam-Animist	<1%	1	2220

NAME	SCRIPTURE	LANGUAGE	GROUP SIZE	PRIMARY RELIGION	% CHR	VOL V	UP ID
Gula	none	Gula	3,000	Islam-Animist	<1%	1	2221
Jongor	none	Jongor	16,000	Islam-Animist	<1%	1	2223
Kanembu	none	Kanembu	57,000	Islam-Animist	<1%	1	2224
Karanga	none	Karanga	40,000	Islam-Animist	<1%	1	2225
Kari	New Testament	Kari	25,000	Islam-Animist	<1%	1	2226
Kenga	none	Kenga	5,000	Islam-Animist	<1%	1	2227
Kera	none	Kera	22,000	Islam-Animist	<1%	1	2228
Kibet	none	Kibet	5,000	Islam-Animist	<1%	1	2229
Kim	New Testament	Kim	11,000	Islam-Animist	<1%	1	2230
Koke	none	Koke	31,000	Islam-Animist	<1%	1	2231
Kotoko	none	Kotoko	38,000	Islam-Animist	<1%	1	2232
Kuka	none	Kuka	40,000	Islam-Animist	<1%	1	2233
Laka	New Testament	Lakal	56,000	Islam-Animist	<1%	1	2234
Maba	none	Maba	47,000	Islam-Animist	<1%	1	2236
Majingai-Ngana	portions	Majingai-Ngana	2,000	Islam-Animist	<1%	1	2237
Mangbai	none	Mangbai	42,000	Islam-Animist	<1%	1	2238
Mararit	none	Mararit	36,000	Islam-Animist	<1%	1	2239
Marba	portions	Marba	80,000	Islam-Animist	<1%	1	2240
Masa	New Testament	Masa	74,000	Animism	6%	4	514
Masalit	none	Masalit	23,000	Islam-Animist	<1%	1	2241
Massalat	none	Massalat	73,000	Islam-Animist	<1%	1	2242
Mbai	New Testament	Mbai	20,000	Islam-Animist	<1%	1	2243
Mbum	portions,NT	Mbum	28,000	Islam-Animist	<1%	1	2244
Mesme	none	Mesme	11,000	Islam-Animist	<1%	1	2245
Mesmedje	none	Mesmedje	15,000	Islam-Animist	<1%	1	2246
Mimi	none	Mimi	6,000	Islam-Animist	<1%	1	2247
Mogum	none	Mogum	36,000	Islam-Animist	<1%	1	2248
Mubi	portions,OT	Mubi	100,000	Islam-Animist	<1%	1	2249
Mundang	none	Mundang	60,000	Islam-Animist	<1%	1	2250
Musei	New Testament	Musei	75,000	Islam-Animist	<1%	1	2251
Musgu	New Testament	Musgu	35,000	Islam-Animist	<1%	1	2252
Nancere	none	Nancere	2,000	Islam-Animist	<1%	1	2253
Nielim	not reported	Nielim	320,000	Islam	1%	4	2254
Ouaddai	none	Maba	10,000	Islam-Animist	<1%	1	310
Rataning	none	Rataning	13,000	Islam-Animist	<1%	1	2255
Runga	none	Runga					2256

599

NAME	SCRIPTURE	LANGUAGE	GROUP PRIMARY SIZE RELIGION		% CHR	VOL V	UP ID
Sarwa	none	Sarwa	400	Islam-Animist	<1%	1	2257
Somrai	none	Somrai	50,000	Islam-Animist	<1%	1	2258
Sungor	none	Sungor	39,000	Islam-Animist	<1%	1	2259
Tana	none	Tana	60,000	Islam-Animist	<1%	1	2260
Tana	none	Tana	35,000	Islam-Animist	<1%	1	2261
Teda	not reported	Teda	10,000	Islam	0% 6	80	4012
Tunya	none	Tunya	800	Islam-Animist	<1%	1	2263
Tupuri	none	Tupuri	60,000	Islam-Animist	<1%	1	2264
Zaghawa	none	Zaghawa	61,000	Islam-Animist	<1%	1	2265

Chile

NAME	SCRIPTURE	LANGUAGE	GROUP PRIMARY SIZE RELIGION		% CHR	VOL V	UP ID
Aymara, Carangas	none	Aymara, Carangas	20,000	Christo-Paganism	0%	1	5113
Mapuche	NT,portions	Mapuche	300,000	Christo-Paganism	1%	5	48
Yaghan	none	Yaghan	50	Christo-Paganism	0%	1	5114

China

NAME	SCRIPTURE	LANGUAGE	GROUP PRIMARY SIZE RELIGION		% CHR	VOL V	UP ID
Ach'ang	none	Ach'ang	¡10,000	Traditional Chinese	<1%	1	2807
Atsi	portions	Atsi	50,000	Traditional Chinese	<1%	1	2808
Buriat	portions	Buriat	30,000	Traditional Chinese	<1%	1	2809
Burig	portions	Burig	148,000	Traditional Chinese	<1%	1	2810
Ch'iang	none	Ch'iang	77,000	Traditional Chinese	<1%	1	2811
Chin	New Testament	Chin	100,000	Traditional Chinese	<1%	1	2812
Chingp'o	Bible	Chingp'o	100,000	Traditional Chinese	<1%	1	2813
Chuang	none	Chuang	12,000,000	Animism	0% 5	81	7014
Chungchia	portions	Chungchia	1,500,000	Traditional Chinese	<1%	1	2814
Chwang	none	Chwang	7,800,000	Traditional Chinese	<1%	1	2815

NAME	SCRIPTURE	LANGUAGE	GROUP SIZE	PRIMARY RELIGION	% CHR	VOL	V	UP ID
Dagur	none	Dagur	23,000	Traditional Chinese	<1%	1		2816
Evenki	none	Evenki	7,000	Traditional Chinese	<1%	1		2817
Evenkis	not reported	Altaic	10,000	Animism	0%	5	81	7020
Hani	not reported	Hani	138,000	Traditional Chinese	<1%	1		2818
Hui	not reported	Hui-hui-yu	5,200,000	Islam	0%	6	80	4006
Jinuos	none	Tibeto-Burman	10,000	Animism	0%	5	81	7021
Jyarung	none	Jyarung	70,000	Traditional Chinese	<1%	1		2819
Kalmytz	New Testament	Kalmytz	70,000	Traditional Chinese	<1%	1		2820
Kam	none	Kam	830,000	Traditional Chinese	<1%	1		2821
Kazakhs	New Testament	Kazakh	700,000	Islam-Animist	0%	6	81	7013
Kelao	none	Kelao	23,000	Traditional Chinese	<1%	1		2822
Khalka	New Testament	Khalka	68,000	Traditional Chinese	<1%	1		2823
Khan	none	Khan	11,000	Traditional Chinese	<1%	1		2824
Kirgiz	not reported	Kirgiz	90,000	Islam	0%	5		4039
Koreans in Manchuria	none	Korean	3,000,000	Secularism	nr%	5	81	7007
Lahul	none	Lahul	2,000	Traditional Chinese	<1%	1		2826
Laka	portions	Laka	6,000	Traditional Chinese	<1%	1		2827
Lati	none	Lati	500	Traditional Chinese	<1%	1		2829
Li	none	Li	1,000,000	Animism	<1%	1		2830
Lisu	not reported	Tibeto-Burman	470,000	Animism	0%	5	81	7009
Lolo	not reported	Yi	4,800,000	Animism	0%	5	81	7006
Lu	New Testament	Lu	400,000	Buddhist-Animist	<1%	1		2831
Manchu	New Testament	Manchu	200,000	Traditional Chinese	<1%	5	81	2832
Miao	New Testament	Miao	2,800,000	Animism	<1%	5	81	7000
Mien	New Testament	Mien	740,000	Animism	<1%	6	81	7001
Mongour	none	Mongour	50,000	Traditional Chinese	<1%	1		2833
Nahsi	portions	Nahsi	160,000	Traditional Chinese	<1%	1		2834
Nanai	portions	Nanai	1,000	Traditional Chinese	<1%	1		2835
Nosu	New Testament	Nosu	556,000	Traditional Chinese	<1%	1		2837
Nung	none	Nung	100,000	Traditional Chinese	<1%	1		2838
Oirat	none	Oirat	60,000	Traditional Chinese	<1%	1		2839
Oronchon	none	Oronchon	2,000	Traditional Chinese	<1%	1		2840
Pai	none	Yi	1,000,000	Buddhist-Animist	<1%	5	81	7008
Paongan	none	Paongan	8,000	Traditional Chinese	<1%	1		2841
Pu-I	none	Pu-I	1,311,000	Traditional Chinese	<1%	1		2842
Punu	none	Punu	220,000	Traditional Chinese	<1%	1		2843

NAME	SCRIPTURE	LANGUAGE	GROUP SIZE	PRIMARY RELIGION	% CHR	V	VOL UP ID
Rawang	New Testament	Rawang	60,000	Traditional Chinese	<1%	1	2844
Salar	none	Salar	31,000	Traditional Chinese	<1%	1	2845
Santa	none	Santa	200,000	Traditional Chinese	<1%	1	2846
Sibo	none	Sibo	21,000	Traditional Chinese	<1%	1	2847
Sui	none	Sui	160,000	Traditional Chinese	<1%	1	2848
Tung-Chia	not reported	Tung	1,100,000	Animism	0%	5 81	7031
Uiguir	Bible	Uiguir	4,800,000	Islam	0%	5 80	4013
**University Students, Chin	+Bible	Mandarin	600,000	Secularism	<1%	4	6567
Vietnamese Refugees	+Bible	Cantonese	2,000	Traditional Chinese	0%	4 83	9000
Wa	New Testament	Wa	300,000	Traditional Chinese	<1%	1	2849
Yellow Uiguir	none	Yellow Uiguir	4,000	Traditional Chinese	<1%	1	2850
Yuku	none	Yuku	4,000	Traditional Chinese	<1%	1	2851

Colombia

NAME	SCRIPTURE	LANGUAGE	GROUP SIZE	PRIMARY RELIGION	% CHR	V	VOL UP ID
Achagua	none	Achagua	100	Animism	<1%	1	2178
Andoque	none	Andoque	100	Animism	<1%	1	2179
Barasano, Northern	none	Barasano	400	Animism	<1%	1	2180
Barasano, Southern	portions	Barasano, Northern	450	Animism	3%	5	474
	portions	Janena	400	Animism	2%	4	289
Bora	NT,portions	Bora	400	Animism	<1%	1	2181
Cacua	none	Cacua	200	Animism	<1%	1	2182
Cansa	portions	Cansa	2,000	Animism	<1%	1	2183
Carapana	none	Carapana	200	Animism	<1%	1	2184
Chani	none	Chani	3,000	Animism	<1%	1	2186
Cofan	portions	Cofan	300	Animism	<1%	1	2188
Cogui	none	Cogui	4,000	Animism	<1%	1	2189
**Coreguaje	none	Coreguaje	500	Animism	1%	4	397
Cubeo	portions	Cubeo	2,000	Animism	<1%	1	2191
Cuiba	portions	Cuiba	2,000	Animism	<1%	1	2192
*Cuna	not reported	Cuna	600	Animism	7%	5 79	9
Curipaco	New Testament	Curipaco	3,000	Animism	<1%	1	2194

NAME	SCRIPTURE	LANGUAGE	GROUP SIZE	PRIMARY RELIGION	% CHR	V	VOL	UP ID
Embera, Northern	New Testament	Embera	2,000	Animism	<1%	1		2196
Guajibo	portions	Guajibo	15,000	Animism	<1%	1		2197
*Guajiro	portions	Guajiro	60,000	Animism	12%	5		177
Guambiano	none	Guambiano	9,000	Animism	<1%	4		2199
*Guanano	portions	Guanano	800	Christo-Paganism	1%	4	79	442
Guayabero	New Testament	Guayabero	600	Animism	8%	5		1169
Huitoto, Meneca	NT,portions	Huitoto, Meneca	600	Animism	<1%	1		3142
Hupda Maku	none	Hupda Maku	200	Animism	<1%	1		2202
Ica	none	Ica		Animism	2%	5		280
Inga	+Bible	Inga	3,000	Christo-Paganism	<1%	1		3143
*Llaneros	portions	Spanish	6,000	Christo-Paganism	5%	4	84	4807
Macu	none	Macu	25,000	Animism	<1%	3		242
Macuna	none	Macuna	1,000	Animism	<1%	1		3144
Malayo	portions	Malayo	300	Animism	6%	4		696
Motilon	none	Motilon	1,000	Animism	<1%	1		3145
Muinane	NT,portions	Muinane	2,000	Animism	<1%	1		3146
***Paez	portions	Paez	40,000	Christo-Paganism	<1%	5		1196
Palenquero	none	Spanish	3,000	Animism	<1%	1		3147
Piapoco	New Testament	Piapoco	5,000	Animism	<1%	1		3148
Qualquer	portions	Qualquer	3,000	Animism	<1%	1		3149
Saija	none	Saija	900	Animism	<1%	1		3150
Saliba	none	Saliba		Animism	<1%	1		3151
Siona	NT,portions	Siona	300	Animism	<1%	1		3152
Siriano	none	Siriano	600	Animism	<1%	1		3153
Taninuca-Retuana	none	Taninuca-Retuana	300	Animism	<1%	1		3154
**Tatuyo	portions	Tatuyo	300	Animism	1%	5		621
Tunebo, Cobaria	portions	Tunebo, Cobaria	2,000	Animism	<1%	1		3155
*Yucuna	portions	Yucuna	500	Christo-Paganism	1%	5		1185
Yukpa	none	Yukpa	3,000	Animism	<1%	1		3156
Yuruti	none	Yuruti	200	Animism	<1%	1		3157

NAME	SCRIPTURE	LANGUAGE	GROUP SIZE	PRIMARY RELIGION	% CHR	VOL V	UP ID

Congo

NAME	SCRIPTURE	LANGUAGE	GROUP SIZE	PRIMARY RELIGION	% CHR	VOL V	UP ID
Bakwele	none	Bakwele	8,000	Animism	0%	1	5291
Bongili	New Testament	Bongili	4,000	Animism	0%	1	5292
Buraka-Gbanziri	none	Buraka-Gbanziri	1,200	Animism	0%	1	5293
Ifumu	none	Ifumu	200	Animism	0%	1	5294
Kukwa	not reported	Kukwa	11,000	Animism	0%	1	5295
Nzebi	portions	Nzebi	40,000	Animism	0%	1	5296
Pande	none	Pande	1,000	Animism	0%	1	5297
Pol	none	Pol	2,000	Animism	0%	1	5298
Punu	none	Punu	46,000	Animism	0%	1	5299
Teke, Northern	portions	Teke, Northern	24,000	Animism	<1%	1	5300
Teke, Southwestern	none	Teke, Southwestern	32,000	Animism	<1%	1	5301
Tsaangi	none	Tsaangi	10,000	Unknown	0%	1	5302

Costa Rica

NAME	SCRIPTURE	LANGUAGE	GROUP SIZE	PRIMARY RELIGION	% CHR	VOL V	UP ID
Chinese in Costa Rica	Bible	Cantonese	5,000	Unknown	1%	3	736
	not reported	Mandarin	4,000	Secularism	1%	3	4141
Nicaraguan Refugees	+Bible	Spanish	55,000	Nominal Christian	nr%	3	9053

NAME	SCRIPTURE	LANGUAGE	GROUP PRIMARY SIZE RELIGION	% CHR	VOL V	UP ID

Djibouti

| **Eritrean Refugees | +Bible | Somali | 25,000 Islam | <1% | 4 83 | 9018 |

Dominican Republic

| *Caribs | +Bible | English | 2,500 Animism | nr% | 4 84 | 4825 |

Ecuador

Cayapa	portions	Cayapa	3,000 Animism	<1%	1	3158
**Military Officers	+Bible	Spanish	1,000 Nominal Christian	5%	3 84	4817
**Military Personnel	Bible	Spanish	80,000 Nominal Christian	15%	3	4119
**Quichua	New Testament	Quichua	2,000,000 Christo-Paganism	6%	5	4070
Secoya	portions	Secoya	400 Animism	<1%	1	3161
**Tsachila	portions	Colorado	1,000 Christo-Paganism	8%	5	1197
**Urban Mestizos	Bible	Spanish	600,000 Nominal Christian	11%	5	4032

605

REGISTRY OF THE UNREACHED

NAME	SCRIPTURE	LANGUAGE	GROUP SIZE	PRIMARY RELIGION	% CHR	VOL V	UP ID

Egypt

| **African Students in Cairo | Bible | Various dialects | 700 | Islam | 9% | 4 | 2100 |

Equatorial Guinea

Bube	portions	Bube	20,000	Animism	0%	1	5303
Fa D'Ambu	none	Fa D'Ambu	2,000	Animism	0%	1	5304
Ngumbi	portions	Ngumbi	4,000	Animism	0%	1	5305

Ethiopia

Afar	not reported	Afar	300,000	Islam-Animist	1%	6 79	21
Alaba	none	Alaban	50,000	Islam	3%	4	358
Amar	none	Amar	23,000	Animism	<1%	1	3190
Ansar Sudanese Refugees	+New Testament	Arabic	11,000	Islam	<1%	4 83	9010
Anuak	New Testament	Anuak	52,000	Animism	<1%	5	516
Arbore	none	Arbore	2,000	Animism	<1%	1	3191
Argobba	none	Argobba	3,000	Animism	<1%	1	3192
Aungi	none	Aungi	50,000	Islam	<1%	1	3193
Basketo	none	Basketo	9,000	Animism	<1%	1	3194
Beja	none	Beja	39,000	Islam	<1%	1	3195

NAME	SCRIPTURE	LANGUAGE	GROUP SIZE	PRIMARY RELIGION	% CHR	VOL V	UP ID
Bencho	none	Bencho	5,000	Animism	<1%	1	3196
Bilen	portions	Bilen	32,000	Islam	<1%	1	3197
Boran	New Testament	Boran	95,000	Islam-Animist	<1%	1	3198
Burji	none	Burji	20,000	Animism	<1%	1	3199
Bussa	none	Bussa	1,000	Animism	<1%	1	3200
Chara	none	Chara	1,000	Animism	<1%	1	3201
Dathanik	none	Dathanik	18,000	Animism	<1%	1	3202
Dime	none	Dime	2,000	Animism	<1%	1	3203
Dorze	none	Dorze	3,000	Animism	<1%	1	3204
**Falasha	Bible	Agau	30,000	Judaism	7%	7 79	159
*Gabbra	portions	Gabrinja	nr	Folk Religion	7%	4	234
*Galla (Bale)	portions	Galla	750,000	Islam-Animist	7%	5	277
Galla of Bucho	Bible	Gallinya (Oromo)	2,000	Christo-Paganism	<1%	3	404
Galla, Harar	Bible	Gallinya	1,310,000	Islam	1%	5	367
Gawuada	none	Gawuada	4,000	Animism	<1%	1	3205
Gedeo	none	Gedeo	250,000	Animism	<1%	1	3206
**Ghimeera	not reported	Ginira	50,000	Animism	4%	5	364
Gidicho	none	Gidicho	500	Animism	<1%	1	3207
Gobato	none	Gobato	1,000	Animism	<1%	1	3208
Gobeze	none	Gobeze	22,000	Animism	<1%	1	3209
Gumuz	none	Gumuz	53,000	Animism	<1%	1	3210
Gurage	New Testament	Gurage Dialects	750,000	Islam-Animist	3%	6 80	274
Hadiyya	portions	Hadiyya	700,000	Animism	<1%	1	3211
Harari	none	Harari	13,000	Islam	<1%	1	3212
Janjero	none	Janjero	1,000	Animism	<1%	1	3213
Kachana	none	Kachana	500	Animism	<1%	1	3214
*Kaffa	portions	Kaffenya (Kefa)	320,000	Christo-Paganism	2%	6 80	363
Kao	none	Karo	600	Animism	<1%	1	3215
Kembata	none	Kembata	250,000	Animism	<1%	1	3216
*Komo	none	Komo	20,000	Animism	<1%	4	678
Konso	none	Konso	30,000	Animism	<1%	5	517
Koyra	none	Koyra	5,000	Animism	<1%	1	3217
Kullo	none	Kullo	82,000	Islam-Animist	<1%	1	3218
Kunana	New Testament	Kunana	70,000	Islam	<1%	1	3219
*Lango	none	Lango	8,000	Islam	0%	3	680
Maji	none	Maji	15,000	Animism	<1%	4	518

NAME	SCRIPTURE	LANGUAGE	GROUP SIZE	PRIMARY RELIGION	% CHR	VOL V	UP ID
Male	none	Male	12,000	Animism	<1%	1	3221
Mao, Northern	none	Mao, Northern	13,000	Animism	<1%	1	3222
*Masengo	none	Majangiir	7,000	Animism	<1%	5	428
Me'en	none	Me'en	38,000	Animism	<1%	1	3223
Mesengo	none	Mesengo	28,000	Islam-Animist	<1%	1	3224
***Mocha	none	Mocha	170,000	Animism	4%	4	429
Mursi	none	Mursi	6,000	Animism	<1%	1	3225
Nao	none	Nao	5,000	Animism	<1%	1	3226
Nara	none	Nara	25,000	Islam-Animist	<1%	1	3227
*Nuer	New Testament	Nuer	70,000	Animism	<1%	4	519
Oyda	none	Oyda	3,000	Animism	<1%	1	3228
Reshiat	not reported	not reported	10,000	Animism	<1%	3	520
***Shankilla (Kazza)	not reported	Shankilla (Kazza)	20,000	Christo-Paganism	1%	5	116
Sheko	none	Sheko	23,000	Animism	<1%	1	3229
Shinasha	none	Shinasha	4,000	Animism	<1%	1	3230
Sidamo	portions	Sidamo	857,000	Islam-Animist	<1%	1	3231
Somali	Bible	Somali	1,000,000	Islam	<1%	5	90
**Suri	portions	Suri	30,000	Animism	<1%	4	521
Tsamai	none	Tsamai	7,000	Animism	<1%	1	3232
Walamo	portions	Walamo	910,000	Animism	<1%	1	3233
Wetawit	none	Wetawit	28,000	Animism	<1%	1	3234
Yidinit	none	Yidinit	28,600	Animism	<1%	1	3236
Zayse	none	Zayse	21,000	Animism	<1%	1	3237
Zilmamu	none	Zilmamu	3,000	Animism	<1%	1	3238

Fiji

NAME	SCRIPTURE	LANGUAGE	GROUP SIZE	PRIMARY RELIGION	% CHR	VOL V	UP ID
Indians in Fiji	Bible	Hindustani	265,000	Hinduism	2%	6 79	131

NAME	SCRIPTURE	LANGUAGE	GROUP SIZE	PRIMARY RELIGION	% CHR	VOL V	UP	ID

France

Algerian Arabs in France	not reported	Arabic	800,000	Islam	0%	3		1086
**Chinese Refugees, France	Bible	Mandarin	100,000	Traditional Chinese	2%	4	79	1226
*Chinese Restaurant Wrkrs.	Bible	Won Chow	50,000	Traditional Chinese	2%	4		1227
**Portuguese in France	Bible	Portuguese	150,000	Secularism	10%	4		1186
*University Students	Bible	French	800,000	Secularism	2%	6	79	702

Gabon

Benga	NT,portions	Benga	nr	Animism	0%	1		5306
Duma	none	Duma	10,000	Animism	0%	1		5307
Equatorial Guin. Refugees	not reported	Tribal Languages	60,000	Nominal Christian	nr%	4	83	9033
Guinean Refugees	not reported	Tribal Languages	1,200,000	Islam	nr%	3		9047
Kele	portions	Kele	15,000	Animism	<1%	1		5308
Kota	none	Kota	nr	Animism	<1%	1		5309
Lumbu	portions	Lumbu	12,000	Animism	<1%	1		5310
Mbaana	none	Mbaana	12,000	Animism	0%	1		5311
Mbede	none	Mbede	45,000	Animism	0%	1		5312
Minduumo	none	Minduumo	4,000	Animism	0%	1		5313
Sangu	portions	Sangu	18,000	Animism	<1%	1		5314
Sira	portions	Sira	17,000	Animism	0%	1		5315
Tsogo	portions	Tsogo	13,000	Animism	0%	1		5316
Wandji	none	Wandji	6,000	Animism	0%	1		5317
Wumbvu	none	Wumbvu	6,100	Animism	0%	1		5318

NAME	SCRIPTURE	LANGUAGE	GROUP SIZE	PRIMARY RELIGION	% CHR	VOL V	UP ID

Gambia

Bayot	none	Bayot	4,000	Islam-Animist	<1%	1	2266
Dyola	portions	Dyola	216,000	Islam-Animist	<1%	1	2267
Fula, Cunda	none	Fula	70,000	Islam-Animist	<1%	1	2268
Krio	none	Krio	3,000	Islam-Animist	<1%	1	2269
Mandyak	portions	Mandyak	85,000	Islam-Animist	<1%	1	2270
Soninke	none	Soninke	10,000	Islam	<1%	1	2271
Wolof, Gambian	portions	Wolof, Gambian	70,000	Islam-Animist	<1%	1	2272

German Federal Rep.

*Chinese in West Germany	Bible	Mandarin	5,000	Secularism	2%	4	1228
***Koreans in Germany	Bible	Korean	10,000	Unknown	4%	4	686
*Students	Bible	German	850,000	Secularism	10%	6 79	1106
Turkish Immigrant Workers	Bible	Turkish	1,200,000	Islam	1%	6 79	134

Ghana

Achode	none	Achode	5,000	Islam-Animist	<1%	1	5319
Akpafu	none	Akpafu	8,000	Islam-Animist	0%	1	5320
Avatine	none	Avatine	10,000	Islam-Animist	0%	1	5321

NAME	SCRIPTURE	LANGUAGE	GROUP SIZE	PRIMARY RELIGION	% CHR	V	UP	VOL ID
Awutu	none	Awutu	85,000	Islam-Animist	0%	1		5322
Bimoba	portions	Bimoba	50,000	Islam-Animist	<1%	1		5323
Birifor	none	Birifor	40,000	Animism	3%	5		1075
Builsa	portions	Buli	97,000	Animism	<1%	4		522
**Busanse	none	Bisa (Busanga)	50,000	Animism	2%	5		1082
Chakossi in Ghana	none	Chakossi	31,000	Animism	1%	5		524
Chala	none	Chala	1,000	Islam-Animist	0%	1		5324
Dagari	none	Dagari	200,000	Animism	<1%	4		523
**Dagomba	portions	Dagbanli	350,000	Islam-Animist	1%	4		525
Fra-Fra	portions	Fra-Fra	230,000	Animism	<1%	4		656
*Fulbe	not reported	Fulani	6,000	Islam-Animist	0%	5		1081
Gonja	portions	Gonja	110,000	Islam	2%	5		1102
Grunshi	none	not reported	200,000	Animism	<1%	4		526
Gurensi	portions	Gurenne	250,000	Animism	1%	4		527
**Kasena	portions	Kasem	70,000	Animism	11%	4		657
Koma	portions	Koma	1,000	Animism	0%	5		1078
Konkomba	none	Konkomba	175,000	Animism	9%	5		528
Krachi	none	Krachi	22,000	Islam-Animist	0%	1		5325
**Kusaasi	New Testament	Kusaal	150,000	Animism	3%	5		1183
Lelemi	not reported	Lelemi	15,000	Islam-Animist	0%	1		5326
Ligbi	none	Ligbi	6,000	Islam	0%	5		1071
Logba	none	Logba	3,000	Islam-Animist	0%	1		5327
Mamprusi	portions	Mampruli	80,000	Animism	<1%	4		529
	portions	Mampruli	91,000	Islam-Animist	<1%	1		5328
Mo	none	Mo (Degha)	13,000	Animism	1%	5		1100
Moba	portions	Bimoba	80,000	Islam-Animist	<1%	4		530
Muslim Community of Bawku	portions	Hausa, Ghana	20,000	Islam	0%	3		1083
**Nafaara	portions	Mafaara	40,000	Animism	15%	6	79	654
Nawuri	none	Nawuri	10,000	Animism	1%	5		1068
Nchimburu	none	Nchumburu	7,000	Animism	7%	5		1069
Nchumbulu	none	Nchumbulu	1,000	Islam-Animist	0%	1		5329
Nchumunu	none	Nchumunu	8,000	Islam-Animist	0%	1		5330
Nkonya	none	Nkonya	17,000	Islam-Animist	0%	1		5331
Ntrubo	none	Ntrubo	5,000	Animism	1%	5		1065
Nyangbo	none	Nyangbo	3,000	Islam-Animist	0%	1		5333
Nzema	portions	Nzema	275,000	Islam-Animist	<1%	1		5334

NAME	SCRIPTURE	LANGUAGE	GROUP SIZE	PRIMARY RELIGION	% CHR	VOL V	UP	ID
Prang	none	Prang	5,000	Islam-Animist	0%	1		5335
Safaliba	none	Safaliba	3,000	Islam-Animist	<1%	1		5336
Santrokofi	none	Sele	5,000	Islam-Animist	0%	1		5337
Sekpele	none	Sekpele	11,000	Islam-Animist	0%	4		5338
**Sisaala	portions	Isaalin	60,000	Animism	1%	4		658
Siwu	none	Siwu	5,000	Islam-Animist	0%	1		5339
Tampulma	New Testament	Tampulensi	8,000	Animism	2%	5		1077
Vagla	New Testament	Vagla	3,000	Animism	<1%	4		531
Vagla	New Testament	Vagla	6,000	Islam-Animist	<1%	3		5340
Wala	New Testament	Wali	60,000	Islam	2%	5		1076
Zowla	Bible	Ewe	800,000	Animism	2%	5		1101

Guatemala

NAME	SCRIPTURE	LANGUAGE	GROUP SIZE	PRIMARY RELIGION	% CHR	VOL V	UP	ID
Achi, Cubulco	portions	Achi, Cubulco	15,000	Animism	<1%	1		8000
Achi, Rabinal	portions	Achi, Rabinal	21,000	Animism	<1%	1		8001
Aguacateco	New Testament	Aguacateco	16,000	Animism	25%	2		8002
**Black Caribs, Guatemala	New Testament	Garifuna	2,000	Christo-Paganism	1%	5		251
Cakchiquel, Central	portions	Cakchiquel, Central	300,000	Animism	<1%	1		8003
Chorti	New Testament	Chorti	25,000	Animism	<1%	1		8004
Chuj	portions	Chuj	30,000	Animism	17%	2		8005
Ixil	portions	Cuyolbal	45,000	Christo-Paganism	1%	4		646
Jacalteco	portions	Jacalteco	12,000	Animism	<1%	1		8006
**K'anjobal of San Miguel	portions	K'anjobal	18,000	Ancestor Worship	10%	5		1207
**Kekchi	New Testament	Kekchi	270,000	Christo-Paganism	3%	4		4034
**Mam Indian	New Testament	Man	470,000	Christo-Paganism	7%	5		1124
*Mopan Maya	portions	Mopan Maya	2,000	Christo-Paganism	15%	5		1205
Pocoman, Central	portions	Pocoman, Central	15,000	Christo-Paganism	<1%	1		8007
Poconchi, Eastern	portions	Poconchi, Eastern	20,000	Christo-Paganism	<1%	1		8008
Poconchi, Western	none	Poconchi, Western	25,000	Christo-Paganism	<1%	1		8009
**Quiche	New Testament	Quiche	500,000	Christo-Paganism	5%	6	79	152
Rabinal-Achi	portions	Rabinal Achi	21,000	Christo-Paganism	4%	4		400

NAME	SCRIPTURE	LANGUAGE	GROUP SIZE	PRIMARY RELIGION	% CHR	VOL V	UP ID
Tzutujil	portions	Tzutujil	5,000	Christo-Paganism	<1%	1	8010
Uspanteco	none	Uspanteco	15,000	Animism	<1%	1	8011
Yucateco	New Testament	Yucateco	3,000	Animism	<1%	1	8012

Guinea

NAME	SCRIPTURE	LANGUAGE	GROUP SIZE	PRIMARY RELIGION	% CHR	VOL V	UP ID
Basari	none	Basari	4,000	Animism	0%	1	5341
Fula	portions	Fula	1,500,000	Islam	1%	5	406
Gbande	portions	Bandi	66,000	Animism	3%	4	477
Kissi	portions	Kissi	266,000	Animism	2%	4	478
Kobiana	none	Kobiana	300	Islam-Animist	0%	1	5352
Konyagi	New Testament	Konyagi	85,000	Islam-Animist	0%	1	5342
Kpelle	none	Kpelle	250,000	Islam-Animist	<1%	1	5343
Landona	portions	Landona	4,000	Islam-Animist	0%	1	5344
Loko	portions	Loko	16,000	Islam-Animist	0%	1	5345
Loma	portions	Loma	180,000	Animism	3%	4	479
Nalu	none	Nalu	10,000	Islam-Animist	0%	1	5346
Susu	portions	Susu	815,000	Islam	nr%	1	6562

Guinea-Bissau

NAME	SCRIPTURE	LANGUAGE	GROUP SIZE	PRIMARY RELIGION	% CHR	VOL V	UP ID
Badyara	none	Badyara	10,000	Islam	0%	1	5347
Balante	portions	Balanta	100,000	Animism	7%	4	594
Banyun	none	Banyun	15,000	Animism	6%	4	593
Bayot	none	Bayot	3,000	Islam-Animist	0%	1	5348
**Biafada	none	Biafada	15,000	Animism	6%	4	592
**Bijogo	portions	Bidyogo	25,000	Islam	8%	5 80	591
Diola	portions	Diola	15,000	Islam	3%	5	590

NAME	SCRIPTURE	LANGUAGE	GROUP SIZE	PRIMARY RELIGION	% CHR	V	VOL UP ID
Kasanga	none	Kasanga	400	Islam-Animist	0%	1	5351
Kunante	none	Kunante	6,000	Islam-Animist	0%	1	5353
Landona	none	Landona	5,000	Islam-Animist	0%	1	5354
Maninka	NT portions	Maninka	65,000	Islam-Animist	0%	1	5355
**Manjaco	none	Mandyako	80,000	Animism	7%	4	589
Mankanya	none	Mankanya	35,000	Islam-Animist	0%	1	5356
Papel	not reported	Papel	36,000	Islam-Animist	<1%	1	5357
Susu	portions	Susu	2,000	Islam-Animist	<1%	1	5358

Guyana

NAME	SCRIPTURE	LANGUAGE	GROUP SIZE	PRIMARY RELIGION	% CHR	V	VOL UP ID
Akawaio	portions	Akawaio	3,000	Christo-Paganism	<1%	1	5115
Arawak	portions	Arawak	5,000	Christo-Paganism	<1%	1	5116
Patamona	New Testament	Patamona	1,000	Christo-Paganism	<1%	1	5117
Waiwai	portions	Waiwai	1,000	Christo-Paganism	<1%	1	5118
Wapishana	none	Wapishana	4,000	Christo-Paganism	<1%	1	5119

Haiti

NAME	SCRIPTURE	LANGUAGE	GROUP SIZE	PRIMARY RELIGION	% CHR	V	VOL UP ID
**Rural Vodun Believers	not reported	Creole	5,400,000	Animism	nr%	4	84 4819

NAME	SCRIPTURE	LANGUAGE	GROUP SIZE	PRIMARY RELIGION	% CHR V	VOL UP ID
Honduras						
*Black Caribs, Honduras	New Testament	Garifuna	80,000	Christo-Paganism	<1% 5 84	245
Paya	none	Spanish	300	Animism	<1% 1	8013
Salvadoran Refugees	+Bible	Spanish	30,000	Nominal Christian	nr% 3	9058
Tol	none	Tol	200	Animism	<1% 1	8014
Hong Kong						
Chinese Businessmen	Bible	Cantonese	10,000	Traditional Chinese	8% 5 81	2111
Chinese Factory Workers	Bible	Cantonese	500,000	Traditional Chinese	2% 3	744
Chinese Villagers	Bible	Cantonese	500,000	Traditional Chinese	1% 3	742
*Factory Workers	Bible	Cantonese	40,000	Unknown	5% 6	1010
**High School Students	Bible	Cantonese	453,000	Traditional Chinese	7% 4	2113
Refugee Doctors	+Bible	Cantonese	2,000	Traditional Chinese	<1% 3	9039
Water Surface People	not reported	Cantonese dialects	11,000	Islam-Animist	0% 3 84	4822
India						
Abujmaria (Madhya Pradesh)	none	Abujmaria	11,000	Hindu-Aninist	<1% 1	2600
***Adi	portions	Adi	80,000	Aninism	2% 4	1027

615

NAME	SCRIPTURE	LANGUAGE	GROUP SIZE	PRIMARY RELIGION	% CHR	VOL V	UP ID
Adiyan in Kerala	none	Adiyan	3,000	Hinduism	<1%	1	2601
Agariya in Bihar	none	Agariya	12,000	Hinduism	<1%	1	2602
Ahir in Maharashtra	none	Ahir	133,000	Islam	<1%	1	2603
Aimol in Assam	none	Aimol	100	Hindu-Animist	<1%	1	2604
Ajmeri in Rajasthan	none	Ajmeri	600	Hindu-Animist	<1%	1	2605
Aka	none	Aka	2,000	Animism	0%	3	1036
*Alars	Bible	Allar	400	Folk Religion	0%	4	2017
Anal in Manipur	portions	Anal	7,000	Animism	<1%	1	2607
Andha in Andhra Pradesh	none	Andha	65,000	Animism	<1%	1	2608
Anga in Bihar	none	Anga	424,000	Hinduism	<1%	1	2609
**Apatani in Assam	none	Apartani	11,000	Animism	<1%	4	1026
Aranadan in Tamil Nadu	none	Aranadan	600	Hindu-Animist	<1%	1	2610
*Arnatas	Bible	Aranatan	700	Animism	<1%	4	2014
Arya in Andhra Pradesh	none	Arya	3,000	Hinduism	<1%	1	2611
Asuri in Bihar	none	Asuri	5,000	Animism	<1%	1	2613
Babri	none	Babri	10,000	Hinduism	<1%	1	2624
Badagu in Nilgiri	portions	Badagu	110,000	Animism	<1%	1	2614
Bagelkhandi in M.P.	New Testament	Bagelkhandi	230,000	Hindu-Animist	<1%	1	2616
Baghati in H.P.	none	Baghati	4,000	Animism	<1%	1	2617
Bahawalpuri in M.P.	none	Bahawalpuri	600	Animism	<1%	1	2618
Baiga in Bihar	none	Baiga	11,000	Animism	<1%	1	2619
Balti in Jammu	portions	Balti	40,000	Animism	<1%	1	2620
Bangaru in Punjab	none	Bangri	4,000,000	Hindu-Animist	<1%	1	2621
Bareli in Madhya Pradesh	none	Bareli	230,000	Hinduism	<1%	1	2622
Bathudi in Bihar	none	Bathudi	74,000	Hinduism	<1%	1	2623
Baziqar in Gujarat	none	Baziqar	100	Animism	<1%	1	2626
Bediya in Bihar	none	Bediya	32,000	Animism	<1%	1	2627
Bengali Refugees, Assam	not reported	Bengali	4,000,000	Islam	<1%	3	9054
Bete	portions	Bete	3,000	Animism	<1%	1	7049
Bhakta	none	Bhakta	55,000	Hindu-Animist	<1%	1	2615
Bharia in Madhya Pradesh	none	Bharia	5,000	Animism	<1%	1	2628
Bhatneri	New Testament	Bhatneri	200	Islam	<1%	1	2629
Bhattri	none	Bhattri	100,000	Hindu-Animist	<1%	1	7047
Bhilala	none	Bhilala	247,000	Hindu-Animist	<1%	1	7048
**Bhils	Bible	Dangi	800,000	Animism	1%	6	291
Bhoyari in Maharashtra	none	Bhoyari	5,000	Hindu-Animist	<1%	1	2632

NAME	SCRIPTURE	LANGUAGE	GROUP SIZE	PRIMARY RELIGION	% CHR	VOL	V	UP ID
Bhuiya in Bihar	none	Bhuiya	5,000	Animism	<1%			2633
Bhunij in Assam	none	Bhumij	50,000	Hindu-Animist	<1%			2634
Bhunjla in Madhya Pradesh	none	Bhunjia	2,000	Hindu-Animist	<1%			2635
Bijori in Bihar	none	Bijori	3,000	Hindu-Animist	<1%			2638
Binjhwari in Bihar	none	Binjhwari	49,000	Hindu-Animist	<1%			2639
Birhor in Bihar	none	Birhor	600	Hindu-Animist	<1%			2640
**Bodo Kachari	New Testament	Bodo	610,000	Hindu-Animist	2%	4		2007
Bodo in Assam	New Testament	Bodo	510,000	Animism	<1%			2641
Bondo in Orissa	none	Bondo	2,000	Hinduism	<1%			2642
Braj in Uttar Pradesh	New Testament	Braj	6,000,000	Animism	<1%			2643
Bunann in Kashmir	portions	Bunan	2,000	Animism	<1%			2644
Burig in Kashmir	portions	Burig	132,000	Animism	<1%			2645
*Chakmas of Mizoram	New Testament	Chakma	20,000	Buddhist-Animist	<1%	5	81	2011
Chamari in Madhya Pradesh	none	Chamari	5,000	Hindu-Animist	<1%			2647
Chameali in H.P.	portions	Chameali	53,000	Hindu-Animist	<1%			2648
*Chang-Pa of Kashmir	Bible	Tibetan Dialect	7,000	Buddhist-Animist	0%	5	81	7011
Chenchu in Andhra Pradesh	none	Chenchu	18,000	Hindu-Animist	<1%			2650
Chero in Bihar	none	Chero	28,000	Animism	<1%			2649
Chik-Barik in Bihar	none	Chik-Barik	30,000	Animism	<1%			2651
Chodhari in Gujarat	none	Chodhari	139,000	Animism	<1%			2654
Chola Naickans	not reported	Canarese	100	Animism	0%	3		124
Churahi in H.P.	none	Churahi	35,000	Hindu-Animist	<1%			2655
Dawoodi Muslims	Bible	Gujarati	225,000	Islam	0%	4		2004
Deccani Muslims	Bible	Dakhni (Urdu)	nr	Islam	<1%	5		4047
Deccani Muslims-Hyderabad	not reported	Dakhni	500,000	Islam	0%	6	82	5027
Deori in Assam	none	Deori	15,000	Animism	<1%			2656
Dhanka in Gujarat	none	Dhanka	10,000	Animism	<1%			2657
Dharwar in Madhya Pradesh	none	Dharwar	21,000	Animism	<1%			2658
**Dhodias	not reported	Dhodia Dialects	300,000	Hindu-Animist	0%	4		4059
Dhurwa	none	Parji	20,000	Hindu-Animist	1%	4		700
Dinasa in Cachar	portions	Dinasa	38,000	Animism	<1%			2659
*Dog-Pa of Ladakh	none	Shrina	2,000	Animism	0%	6	81	7005
Dorlin in Andhra Pradesh	none	Dorli	24,000	Hindu-Animist	4%	4		122
**Dubla	Bible	Gujarati	200,000	Hindu-Animist	<1%			2661
Gadaban in Andhra Pradesh	none	Gadaba	20,000	Hindu-Animist	<1%			2662
Gaddi in Hinachal Pradesh	none	Gaddi	70,000	Hindu-Animist	<1%			2663

NAME	SCRIPTURE	LANGUAGE	GROUP SIZE	PRIMARY RELIGION	% CHR	VOL	V	UP ID
Galong in Assam	none	Galong	37,000	Hindu-Animist	<1%	1		2664
Ganti in Gujarat	none	Ganti	140,000	Hindu-Animist	<1%	1		2665
Gangte in Assan	New Testament	Gangte	6,000	Hindu-Animist	<1%	1		2666
Gawari in Andhra Pradesh	none	Gawari	21,000	Hindu-Animist	<1%	1		2668
*Gonds	portions	Gondi	4,000,000	Animism	1%	5		641
*Gorkha	New Testament	Napali	180,000	Hinduism	0%	4		2009
Grasia in Gujarat	none	Grasia	2,000	Hindu-Animist	<1%	1		2669
Gujars of Kashmir	New Testament	Gujari	150,000	Islam-Animist	0%	5	81	7012
***Halam in Tripura	not reported	Tribal dialects	20,000	Animism	3%	5		4062
Halbi in Madhya Pradesh	none	Halbi	350,000	Hindu-Animist	<1%	1		2671
Harauti in Rajasthan	New Testament	Harauti	334,000	Hindu-Animist	<1%	1		2673
Ho in Bihar	portions	Ho	750,000	Hindu-Animist	<1%	1		2674
Holiya in Madhya Pradesh	none	Holiya	3,000	Hindu-Animist	<1%	1		2675
Iravas in Kerala	Bible	Malayalam	3,700,000	Hinduism	1%	4		4068
***Irulas in Kerala	Bible	Irula	10,000	Hinduism	0%	4		2012
Jagannathi in A.P.	none	Jagannathi	1,000	Hindu-Animist	<1%	1		2677
Jains	Bible	Hindi	2,000,000	Jain	1%	4		2005
Jatapu in Andhra Pradesh	none	Jatapu	36,000	Hindu-Animist	<1%	1		2678
Jaunsari in Uttar Pradesh	portions	Jaunsari	60,000	Hindu-Animist	<1%	1		2679
Jharia in Orissa	none	Jharia	2,000	Hinduism	<1%	1		2680
Juang in Orissa	none	Juang	12,000	Hinduism	<1%	1		2681
Kachchi in Andhra Pradesh	portions	Kachchi	471,800	Hinduism	<1%	1		2682
Kadar in Andhra Pradesh	none	Kadar	800	Hindu-Animist	<1%	1		2683
Kahluri in Andamans	none	Kahluri	66,000	Hindu-Animist	<1%	1		2684
Kaikadi in Maharashtra	none	Kaikadi	12,000	Hindu-Animist	<1%	1		2685
Kawar in Madhya Pradesh	none	Kawar	10,000	Hindu-Animist	<1%	1		2686
Kanauri in Uttar Pradesh	portions	Kanauri	30,000	Hindu-Buddhist	<1%	1		2687
Kanikkaran in Kerala	none	Kanikkaran	10,000	Hindu-Animist	<1%	1		2688
Kanjari in Andhra Pradesh	none	Kanjari	60,000	Hindu-Animist	<1%	1		2689
**Karbis	none	Mikir	300,000	Hindu-Animist	5%	5		2120
Karmali in Dihar	none	Karmali	70,000	Hindu-Animist	<1%	1		2690
**Kashmiri Muslims	Bible	Kashmiri	3,100,000	Islam	1%	6	79	1231
Katakari in Gujarat	none	Katakari	5,000	Hindu-Animist	<1%	1		2691
Kawar in Madhya Pradesh	none	Kawar	34,000	Hindu-Animist	<1%	1		2692
Keer in Madhya Pradesh	none	Keer	3,000	Hindu-Animist	<1%	1		2693
Khanti in Assam	none	Khanti	300	Hindu-Buddhist	<1%	1		2694

NAME	SCRIPTURE	LANGUAGE	GROUP SIZE	PRIMARY RELIGION	% CHR	VOL	V	UP ID
Khandesi	none	Khandesi	20,000	Hindu-Animist	<1%	1		2695
Kharia in Bihar	portions	Kharia	90,000	Hindu-Animist	<1%	1		2696
Khasi in Assam	New Testament	Khasi	384,000	Hinduism	<1%	1		2697
Khirwar in Madhya Pradesh	none	Khirwar	34,000	Hindu-Animist	<1%	1		2698
Khojas, Agha Khani	Bible	Gujarati	175,000	Islam	0%	4		2006
Khowar	none	Khowar	7,000	Hindu-Animist	<1%	1		2699
Kisan in Bihar	none	Kisan	74,000	Hindu-Animist	<1%	1		2700
Kishanganjia in Bihar	none	Kishanganjia	57,000	Hindu-Animist	<1%	1		2701
Kishtwari in Jammu	none	Kishtwari	12,000	Hindu-Animist	<1%	1		2702
Koda in Bihar	none	Koda	14,000	Hindu-Animist	<1%	1		2703
Kol in Assam	none	Kol	80,000	Hindu-Animist	<1%	1		2704
**Kolam	portions	Kolami	60,000	Hindu-Animist	<1%	5		1040
Kom in Manipur	portions	Kom	7,000	Hindu-Animist	<1%	1		2705
***Kond	portions	Kui	900,000	Animism	3%	5		294
Konda-Dora (Andra Pradesh)	none	Konda-Dora	16,000	Hindu-Animist	<1%	1		2706
Konkani in Gujarat	New Testament	Konkani	1,523,000	Hindu-Animist	<1%	1		2707
*Koraga in Kerala	none	Koraga	2,000	Hindu-Animist	<1%	1		2709
*Korku in Madhya Pradesh	portions	Korku	250,000	Animism	<1%	5		198
Korwa in Bihar	none	Korwa	10,000	Hindu-Animist	<1%	1		2710
Kota in Tamil Nadu	none	Kota	900	Hindu-Animist	<1%	1		2711
Kotia in Andhra Pradesh	portions	Kotia	15,000	Hindu-Animist	<1%	1		2768
Kotta	none	Kotta	1,000	Animism	0%	5		1098
Koya in Andhra Pradesh	none	Koya	212,000	Hindu-Animist	<1%	1		2712
*Kudisai Vagh Makkal	Bible	Tamil	1,000,100	Hinduism	2%	3		695
Kudiya	none	Kudiya	100	Hindu-Animist	<1%	1		2713
**Kuknas	none	Kukni	125,000	Hindu-Animist	<1%	4		701
**Kuluis in Himachal Pradesh	portions	Kului	200,000	Hinduism	1%	5	81	2015
Kumauni in Assam	New Testament	Kumauni	1,240,000	Hindu-Animist	<1%	1		2714
Kupia in Andhra Pradesh	portions	Kupia	4,000	Hindu-Animist	<1%	1		2715
Kurichiya in Kerala	none	Kurichiya	12,000	Nominal Christian	<1%	5	81	2716
Kuruba in Tamil Nadu	none	Kuruba	8,000	Hindu-Animist	<1%	1		2717
Kurux in Bihar	New Testament	Kurux	1,240,000	Hindu-Animist	<1%	1		2718
Kuvi in Orissa	portions	Kuvi	190,000	Hindu-Animist	<1%	1		2719
Labans	none	Labaani		nr Hindu-Buddhist	<1%	3		1041

REGISTRY OF THE UNREACHED

NAME	SCRIPTURE	LANGUAGE	GROUP SIZE	PRIMARY RELIGION	% CHR	V	UP ID
Labbai	Bible	Tamil	nr	Islam	<1%	5	4045
Labhani in Andhra Pradesh	portions	Labhani	1,200,000	Hindu-Buddhist	<1%	1	2722
*Labourers of Jhoparpatti	Bible	Marathi	2,000	Hinduism	10%	4	2001
Ladakhi in Jammu	portions	Ladakhi	60,000	Hindu-Buddhist	<1%	1	2720
**Lahaulis in Punjab	not reported	Lahouli	18,000	Buddhism	<1%	1	2016
Lalung in Assam	none	Lalung	11,000	Hindu-Buddhist	<1%	1	2721
**Lambadi in Andhra Pradesh	portions	Lambadi	1,300,000	Animism	nr%	5 81	2018
**Lepcha	New Testament	Lepcha	18,000	Hindu-Buddhist	10%	1	2127
Lodhi in Bihar	none	Lodhi	44,000	Hindu-Animist	<1%	1	2723
Lushai in Assam	Bible	Lushai	270,000	Hindu-Animist	<1%	1	2724
Mahali in Assam	none	Mahali	14,000	Hindu-Animist	<1%	1	2725
Majhwar in Madhya Pradesh	none	Majhwar	28,000	Hindu-Animist	<1%	1 81	2726
Malakkaras of Kerala	Bible	Malanutha	1,000	Hindu-Animist	0%	5	2019
Malankuravan in Kerala	none	Malankuravan	5,000	Hindu-Animist	<1%	1	2727
Malapandaram in Kerala	none	Malapandaran	500	Hindu-Animist	<1%	1	2728
Malappanackers	Bible	Malappanackan	1,000	Animism	0%	4	2021
Malaryan in Kerala	none	Malaryan	5,000	Hindu-Animist	<1%	1	2729
Malavedan in Kerala	none	Malavedan	2,000	Hinduism	<1%	1	2730
*Malayalars	Bible	Malayalan	nr	Animism	<1%	4	2020
Malki in Andhra Pradesh	none	Mali	1,000	Hindu-Animist	<1%	1	2731
Malki in Bihar	portions	Malki	89,000	Hindu-Animist	<1%	1	2733
Malpaharia in Assam	none	Malpaharia	9,000	Hindu-Animist	<1%	1	2732
Malvi in Madhya Pradesh	New Testament	Malvi	644,000	Hinduism	<1%	3	2734
Mangs in Maharashtra	Bible	Marathi	nr	Hindu-Animist	<1%	1	1043
Manna-Dora in A.P.	none	Manna-Dora	9,000	Hindu-Animist	<1%	1	2735
Mannan in Kerala	none	Mannan	5,000	Hindu-Animist	<1%	1	2736
Mappillas	Bible,stories,tracts	Malayalan	4,500,000	Islam	<1%	5	4026
Mara in Andhra Pradesh	Bible	Mara	12,000	Hindu-Animist	<1%	1	2737
Maria in Andhra Pradesh	none	Maria	80,000	Hindu-Animist	<1%	1	2738
Marwari in Gujarat	New Testament	Marwari	6,810,000	Hindu-Animist	<1%	1	2739
**Mathakis	Bible	Telugu	200,000	Hinduism	2%	5	4069
**Mawchi	none	Mawchi	300,000	Hindu-Animist	3%	5	4061
*Meitei	New Testament	Manipuri	700,000	Hinduism	1%	6 79	293
**Mejah	portions	Mejah	6,000	Hinduism	1%	4	1033
Meos of Rajasthan	not reported	Rajasthani	500,000	Islam	0%	5 80	4017
**Miching	Bible	Miching	300,000	Hindu-Animist	1%	4	2002

NAME	SCRIPTURE	LANGUAGE	GROUP SIZE	PRIMARY RELIGION	% CHR	VOL V	UP ID
Mina in Madhya Pradesh	none	Mina	765,000	Hindu-Animist	<1%	1	2741
Mirdha in Orissa	none	Mirdha	6,000	Hindu-Animist	<1%	1	2742
Mishmi in Assam	none	Mishmi	5,000	Hindu-Animist	<1%	1	2743
Monpa	none	Monpa	22,000	Buddhist-Animist	0%	3	1037
Mualthuan	none	Mualthuan	2,000	Animism	5%	4	647
Multani in Punjab	none	Multani	16,000	Hindu-Animist	<1%	1	2744
Mundari in Assam	Bible	Mundari	771,000	Hindu-Animist	<1%	1	2745
**Mundas in Bihar	Bible	Munda	25,000	Animism	0%	4	2010
Muria in Andhra Pradesh	none	Muria	13,000	Hindu-Animist	<1%	1	2746
Muthuvan (Andhra Pradesh)	none	Muthuvan	7,000	Hindu-Animist	<1%	1	2747
Muwasi in Madhya Pradesh	none	Muwasi	21,000	Hindu-Animist	<1%	1	2748
Naga, Kalyokengnyu	none	Naga, Kalyokengnyu	14,000	Hindu-Animist	<1%	1	2751
Naga, Mao	New Testament	Naga, Mao	20,000	Hindu-Buddhist	<1%	1	2755
Naga, Nruangrmei	portions	Naga, Nruangrmei	49,000	Hindu-Buddhist	<1%	1	2756
Naga, Sangtam	New Testament	Naga, Sangtam	20,000	Hindu-Buddhist	<1%	1	2757
Naga, Sema	New Testament	Naga, Sema	70,000	Unknown	<1%	1	2758
Naga, Tangkhul	New Testament	Naga, Tangkhul	58,000	Hindu-Buddhist	<1%	1	2759
Naga, Wancho	none	Naga, Wancho	29,000	Hindu-Buddhist	<1%	1	2760
Nagar in Madhya Pradesh	none	Nagar	7,000	Hindu-Animist	<1%	1	2761
**Nepalese in India	Bible	Nepali	90,000	Hinduism	12%	4	4060
Nihali in Madhya Pradesh	none	Nihali	1,000	Hindu-Animist	<1%	1	2762
Nimadi in Madhya Pradesh	none	Ninadi	794,000	Hindu-Buddhist	<1%	1	2763
***Nocte	none	Nocte	20,000	Animism	0%	3	1030
Ojhi in Madhya Pradesh	none	Ojhi	1,000	Hindu-Animist	<1%	1	2764
Ollari in Orissa	none	Ollari	800	Hindu-Animist	<1%	1	2765
Ong in Andamans	none	Ong	200	Hindu-Animist	<1%	1	2766
Pahari Garwali (Uttar Pradesh)	New Testament	Pahari Garwali	1,300,000	Hindu-Animist	<1%	1	2667
Paite in Assam	Bible	Paite	28,000	Hindu-Animist	<1%	1	2769
Panika	none	Panika	31,000	Hindu-Animist	<1%	1	2770
Panika	none	Panika	31,000	Hindu-Animist	<1%	1	7066
**Paniyan of Kerala	none	Paniyan	6,000	Animism	<1%	5 81	2772
Pao in Madhya Pradesh	none	Pao	16,500	Hindu-Buddhist	<1%	1	2773
Pardhan in Andhra Pradesh	none	Pardhan		Hindu-Animist	<1%	1	2774
Parengi in Orissa	none	Parengi	3,000	Hindu-Animist	<1%	1	2776
*Parsees	Bible	Gujarati	120,000	Secularism	<1%	5 81	2121

REGISTRY OF THE UNREACHED

NAME	SCRIPTURE	LANGUAGE	GROUP SIZE	PRIMARY RELIGION	% CHR	V	UP	VOL ID
*Parsis in Bombay	+Bible	Parsia	80,000	Zoroastrianism	0%	6	82	5039
Patelia in Gujarat	none	Patelia	23,000	Hindu-Animist	<1%	1		2778
Pengo in Orissa	none	Pengo	1,000	Hindu-Animist	<1%	1		2779
Pnar in Assam	none	Pnar	83,000	Hindu-Animist	<1%	1		2780
Poouch in Kashmir	none	Poochi	500,000	Islam	0%	4		4079
Purig-Pa of Kashmir	none	Purig-Skad	nr	Islam	<1%	5	81	7010
Rabha in Assam	none	Rabha	10,000	Hindu-Animist	3%	4		676
Rajasthani Muslims-Jaipur	not reported	Jaipuri	4,000	Islam	0%	6	82	5033
*Rava in Assam	not reported	Rava	45,000	Hinduism	<1%	5		295
Riang in Assam	portions	Riang	75,000	Hindu-Buddhist	<1%	1		2782
Sadan in Andamans	portions	Sadan	810,000	Hindu-Animist	<1%	1		2783
**Saiva Vellala	Bible	Tamil	1,500,000	Hinduism	2%	4		2000
Satnanis (Madhya Pradesh)	+not reported	Chhattisgarhi	30,000	Hinduism	2%	4		4076
Sauria Pahari	none	Malto	53,000	Animism	<1%	2		4801
*Shourastra in Tamil Nadu	none	Shourastra	200,000	Hinduism	<1%	4		2023
Sikkimese	none	Sikkimese	37,000	Hindu-Buddhist	<1%	4		2786
*Sindhis of India	New Testament	Sindhi	3,000,000	Hinduism	<1%	5		13
Sondwari in M.P.	none	Sondwari	32,000	Hindu-Animist	<1%	1		2787
Sora in Orissa	New Testament	Sora	222,000	Hinduism	<1%	1		2788
Sulung	none	Sulung	nr	Hindu-Buddhist	<1%	1		2789
***Tagin	none	Tagin	25,000	Animism	0%	3		1045
Takankar	none	Takankar	11,000	Hindu-Animist	<1%	1		2775
Tamaria in Bihar	none	Tamaria	5,000	Hindu-Buddhist	<1%	1		2790
**Tamil Laborers in Bombay	+Bible	Tamil	3,000	Hinduism	<1%	5	82	5017
Tamil Muslims in Madras	-Bible	Tamil	50,000	Islam	0%	6	82	5028
**Tamil in Yellagiri Hills	Bible	Tamil	4,000	Hinduism	2%	5		4025
**Tangsa	none	Tangsa	11,000	Animism	0%	3		1031
Thado in Assam	portions,NT	Thado	42,000	Hindu-Buddhist	<1%	1		2791
Thakur	none	Thakur	99,000	Hindu-Animist	<1%	1		2792
Thar in Bihar	none	Thar	9,000	Hindu-Animist	<1%	1		2793
Tharu	+portions,tracts	Bhojpuri	44,000	Hindu-Animist	nr%	2		4800
*Tibetan Refugees	New Testament	Tibetan	100,800	Buddhism	1%	1	83	2033
Toda in Tamil Nadu	portions	Toda	800	Hindu-Animist	<1%	1		2794
Tokkaru in Tamil Nadu	New Testament	Tokkaru	1,300,000	Hindu-Animist	<1%	1		2660
Totis	none	Gondi	nr	Hinduism	<1%	3		1044
Tugara	none	Tugara	44,000	Hindu-Animist	<1%	1		2777

NAME	SCRIPTURE	LANGUAGE	GROUP SIZE	PRIMARY RELIGION	% CHR	VOL V	UP ID
Ullatan in Kerala	none	Ullatan	2,000	Hindu-Animist	<1%	1	2796
Urali in Kerala	none	Urali	1,000	Hindu-Animist	<1%	1	2797
Vaiphei in Assam	portions,NT	Vaiphei	12,000	Hindu-Buddhist	<1%	1	2798
Viehavan in Kerala	none	Viehavan	200	Hindu-Animist	<1%	1	2799
**Vohras of Yavatmal	New Testament	Gujarati	10,000	Islam	0%	4	2008
Waddar in Andhra Pradesh	none	Waddar	40,000	Hindu-Animist	<1%	1	2800
Wagdi in Rajasthan	none	Wagdi	800,000	Hindu-Animist	<1%	1	2801
**Wanchoo	none	Wanchoo	nr	Animism	<1%	3	1029
Yanadi in Andhra Pradesh	none	Yanadi	210,000	Hindu-Animist	<1%	1	2802
Yerava in Karnataka	none	Yerava	11,000	Hindu-Animist	<1%	1	2803
Yerukala in A.P.	none	Yerukala	70,000	Hindu-Animist	<1%	1	2804
Zangskari in Kashmir	portions	Zangskari	5,000	Hindu-Animist	<1%	1	2805
Zanskari	none	Zanskari	8,000	Buddhism	0%	3 84	4834
Zemi Naga of Assam	New Testament	Jeme	16,000	Animism	nr%	6 81	7002
Zoliang	not reported	Naga, Zoliang	50,000	Animism	0%	3	1085
Zome in Manipur	New Testament	Zome	30,000	Hindu-Buddhist	<1%	1	2806

Indonesia

NAME	SCRIPTURE	LANGUAGE	GROUP SIZE	PRIMARY RELIGION	% CHR	VOL V	UP ID
Abau	none	Abau	3,000	Animism	<1%	1	2852
Achehnese	portions	Achehnese	2,200,000	Islam	<1%	6 80	97
Aghu	none	Aghu	3,000	Animism	<1%	1	2853
Aibondeni	none	Aibondeni	200	Animism	<1%	1	2854
Aikwakai	none	Aikwakai	400	Animism	<1%	1	2855
Airo-Sumaghaghe	none	Airo-Sumaghaghe	2,000	Animism	<1%	1	2856
Airoran	none	Airoran	400	Animism	<1%	1	2857
Alas	none	Gayo	30,000	Islam-Animism	0%	5	1133
Alor, Kolana	portions	Alor, Kolana	90,000	Animism	<1%	5 81	2858
Amanab	none	Amanab	6,000	Animism	<1%	1	2859
Ambai	portions	Ambai	6,300	Animism	<1%	1	2860
Amber	none	Amber		Animism	<1%	1	2861
Amberbaken	none	Amberbaken	5,000	Animism	<1%	1	2862

NAME	SCRIPTURE	LANGUAGE	GROUP SIZE	PRIMARY RELIGION	% CHR	V	VOL	UP ID
Anbonese	none	Anbonese	80,000	Animism	<1%	1		2863
Ansus	none	Ansus	3,000	Animism	<1%	1		2864
Ara	none	Ara	75,000	Islam	<1%	1		2865
Arandai	none	Arandai	2,000	Animism	<1%	1		2866
Arguni	none	Arguni	200	Animism	<1%	1		2867
Asienara	none	Asienara	700	Animism	<1%	1		2868
*Asmat	portions	Asmat	30,000	Animism	7%	6	79	205
Auyi	none	Auyi	400	Animism	<1%	1		2870
Auyu	none	Auyu	18,000	Animism	<1%	1		2871
Baburiwa	none	Baburiwa	200	Animism	<1%	1		2872
Badui	none	Badui	5,000	Animism	<1%	4	84	4812
Bahan	none	Bahan	500	Animism	<1%	1		2873
Bajau, Indonesian	none	Bajau, Indonesian	50,000	Islam-Animist	<1%	1		2874
Balantak	none	Balantak	125,000	Islam-Animist	<1%	1		2875
Balinese	portions	Balinese	2,000,000	Hindu-Animist	1%	5		1094
Banggai	none	Banggai	200,000	Islam	<1%	1		2876
Barau	none	Barau	300	Animism	<1%	1		2877
Bare'e	New Testament	Bare'e	325,000	Animism	<1%	1		2878
*Batak, Angkola	not reported	Batak, Angkola	nr	Islam	6%	6	80	4002
Batak, Karo	New Testament	Batak, Karo	400,000	Animism	<1%	1		2879
Batak, Simalungun	New Testament	Batak, Simalungun	800,000	Animism	<1%	1		2880
Batak, Toba	Bible	Batak, Toba	1,600,000	Animism	<1%	1		2881
Bedoanas	none	Bedoanas	300	Animism	<1%	1		2882
Bengkulu	none	Bengkulu	25,000	Islam	0%	4		6563
Berik	none	Berik	800	Animism	<1%	1		2883
Biak	portions	Biak	40,000	Animism	<1%	1		2884
Biksi	none	Biksi	200	Animism	<1%	1		2885
Bimanese	none	Bina	300,000	Islam	1%	5		1096
Bingkokak	none	Bingkokak	150,000	Islam	<1%	1		2886
***Bipim	none	Bipim	500	Christo-Paganism	5%	4		1119
Bira	none	Bira	75,000	Islam-Animist	<1%	1		2887
Bonerif	none	Bonerif	100	Animism	<1%	1		2888
Bonggo	none	Bonggo	400	Animism	<1%	1		2889
Boral	none	Boral	1,000	Animism	<1%	1		2890
Brat	none	Brat	20,000	Animism	<1%	1		2891
Bual	none	Bual	150,000	Islam	<1%	1		2892

NAME	SCRIPTURE	LANGUAGE	GROUP SIZE	PRIMARY RELIGION	% CHR	V	UP	ID
Bugis	portions	Bugis	3,500,000	Islam-Animist	1%	6	80	7
Buli	none	Buli	1,000	Islam-Animist	<1%	1		2893
Bunak	none	Bunak	50,000	Animism	<1%	1		2894
Bungku	none	Bungku	180,000	Animism	<1%	1		2895
Buru	none	Buru	6,000	Animism	<1%	1		2896
Busani	none	Busani	400	Animism	<1%	1		2897
Butung	none	Butung	200,000	Islam-Animist	<1%	4		2898
**Chinese in Indonesia	Bible	Indonesian	3,600,000	Traditional Chinese	6%	4		733
Cirebon	none	Javanese, Tjirebon	2,500,000	Islam-Animist	1%	5		1135
***Citak	portions	Citak (Asmat)	7,000	Islam-Animist	<1%	5		1166
Dabra	none	Dabra	100	Animism	<1%	1		2900
Dagada	none	Dagada	30,000	Animism	<1%	1		2901
*Dani, Baliem	none	Dani, Grand Valley	50,000	Animism	3%	6	79	1219
Dem	none	Dem	2,000	Animism	<1%	1		2902
Denta	none	Denta	800	Animism	<1%	1		2903
Dubu	none	Dubu	100	Animism	<1%	1		2904
Duvele	none	Duvele	500	Animism	<1%	1		2905
Ekagi	portions,NT	Ekagi	100,000	Animism	<1%	1		2906
Emumu	none	Emumu	1,000	Animism	<1%	1		2907
Erokwanas	none	Erokwanas	300	Animism	<1%	1		2911
Foau	none	Foau	200	Animism	<1%	1		2910
Fordat	none	Fordat	10,000	Animism	<1%	1		2912
Gane	none	Gane	2,000	Animism	<1%	1		2913
Gayo	none	Gayo	200,000	Islam-Animist	<1%	4	80	1132
Gesa	none	Gesa	200	Animism	<1%	1		2914
Gorontalo	none	Gorontalo	500,000	Islam	<1%	1		2915
Havunese	portions	Havunese	40,000	Animism	<1%	1		2916
Helong	none	Helong	5,000	Animism	<1%	1		2917
Iha	none	Iha	6,000	Animism	<1%	1		2918
Inanwatan	none	Inanwatan	1,000	Animism	<1%	1		2920
Irahutu	none	Irahutu	4,000	Animism	<1%	1		2921
Iresim	none	Iresim	100	Animism	<1%	1		2922
Iria	none	Iria	900	Animism	<1%	1		2923
Itik	none	Itik	100	Animism	<1%	1		2924
Iwur	none	Iwur	1,000	Animism	0%	1		2925
Janbi	Bible	Indonesian	850,000	Islam-Animist	0%	3		4088

NAME	SCRIPTURE	LANGUAGE	GROUP SIZE	PRIMARY RELIGION	% CHR	VOL V	UP ID
Janden	none	Janden	14,000	Animism	<1%	1	2926
**Javanese of Pejompongan	Bible	Bahasa Jawa	5,000	Islam	7%	4	319
Kaeti	none	Kaeti	4,000	Animism	<1%	1	2927
Kaili	portions	Kaili	300,000	Animism	<1%	1	2928
Kaiwai	none	Kaiwai	600	Animism	<1%	1	2929
Kajang	none	Kajang	50,000	Animism	<1%	1	2930
Kambera	New Testament	Kambera	200,000	Animism	<1%	1	2931
Kamberataro	none	Kamberataro	1,000	Animism	<1%	1	2932
Kanoro	none	Kanoro	8,000	Animism	<1%	1	2933
Kampung Baru	none	Kampung Baru	400	Animism	<1%	1	2934
Kantuk-Gresi	none	Kantuk-Gresi	5,000	Animism	<1%	1	2935
Karum	none	Karum	300	Animism	<1%	1	2936
Kapori	none	Kapori	100	Animism	<1%	1	2937
Karas	none	Karas	200	Animism	<1%	1	2938
Karon Dori	none	Karon Dori	5,000	Animism	<1%	1	2939
Karon Pantai	none	Karon Pantai	3,000	Animism	<1%	1	2940
Kasuweri	none	Kasuweri	1,000	Animism	<1%	1	2941
Kati, Northern	none	Kati, Northern	8,000	Animism	<1%	1	2942
Kati, Southern	none	Kati, Southern	4,000	Animism	<1%	1	2943
Kaugat	none	Kaugat	1,000	Animism	<1%	1	2944
**Kaur	none	Kaur	50,000	Islam-Animist	0%	3	4084
Kaure	none	Kaure	800	Animism	<1%	1	2945
Kavwol	none	Kavwol	500	Animism	<1%	1	2946
Kawe	none	Kawe	300	Animism	<1%	1	2947
Kayagar	portions	Kayagar	9,000	Animism	8%	4	233
Kaygir	none	Kaygir	4,000	Animism	<1%	1	2948
Kayupulau	none	Kayupulau	600	Animism	<1%	1	2949
Kei	none	Kei	30,000	Animism	<1%	1	2950
Kemak	none	Kemak	50,000	Animism	<1%	1	2951
Kendari	portions	Kendari	500,000	Islam-Animist	<1%	1	2952
Kenyah	portions	Kenyah	40,000	Animism	<1%	1	2953
Kerinchi	none	Kerinchi	170,000	Islam-Animist	<1%	1	2954
Kinaghana	none	Kinaghana	3,000	Animism	<1%	1	2955
*Kinyal	portions	Kinyal	7,000	Animism	2%	4	228
Kodi	none	Kodi	25,000	Animism	<1%	1	2956
Komering	not reported	Komering	400,000	Islam-Animist	0%	3	4086

NAME	SCRIPTURE	LANGUAGE	GROUP SIZE	PRIMARY RELIGION	% CHR	V	UP	ID
Koneraw	none	Koneraw	300	Animism	<1%	1		2957
Korapun	none	Korapun	4,000	Animism	<1%	1		2958
Kotogut	none	Kotogut	1,000	Animism	<1%	1		2959
Kubu	not reported	Kubu	25,000	Islam-Aninist	nr%	6	81	7026
	none	Local dialects	6,000	Animism	1%	6	80	1093
Kurudu	none	Kurudu	1,000	Animism	<1%	1		2960
Kwansu	none	Kwansu	400	Animism	<1%	1		2961
Kwerba	none	Kwerba	2,000	Animism	<1%	1		2962
Kwesten	none	Kwesten	3,000	Animism	<1%	1		2963
Lampung	none	Komering	1,500,000	Islam-Animist	0%	5	80	1134
Lara	none	Lara	12,000	Animism	<1%	1		2964
Latdwalan	none	Latdwalan	900	Animism	<1%	1		2965
Laudje	none	Laudje	125,000	Islam	<1%	5		2966
Lebong	none	Redjang-Lebong	nr	Islam	<1%	1		1090
Letti	none	Letti	6,000	Animism	<1%	5		2967
**Lioneee	none	Lio	100,000	Christo-Paganism	0%	3		137
**Loho Loho	not reported	Kolaka	10,000	Animism	nr%	5	81	2968
Loinang	none	Loinang	100,000	Animism	<1%	1		2969
Lore	none	Lore	140,000	Animism	<1%	1		2970
Lubu	none	Lubu	1,000,000	Islam	<1%	1		2971
Luwu	none	Luwu	500,000	Islam	<1%	1		2972
Maanyan	portions	Maanyan	15,000	Animism	<1%	1		2973
Madik	none	Madik	1,000	Animism	<1%	1		2974
Mairasi	none	Mairasi	1,000	Animism	<1%	1		2975
Makasai	none	Makasai	70,000	Animism	<1%	1		2976
Makian, West	none	Makian, West	12,000	Animism	<1%	1		2977
Maklew	none	Maklew	100	Animism	<1%	1		2978
Manbai	portions	Manbai	80,000	Animism	<1%	1		2979
Mandar	portions	Mandar	300,100	Islam	<1%	1		2980
Mander	none	Mander	100	Animism	<1%	1		2981
Manem	none	Manem	400	Animism	<1%	1		2982
**Manggarai Muslims	none	Manggarai	25,000	Islam	0%	5		7029
**Manikion	portions	Sough	8,000	Animism	<1%	5		1165
Mantion	portions	Mantion	12,000	Animism	<1%	1		2984
Marau	none	Marau	1,000	Animism	<1%	1		2985
Marind	none	Marind	7,000	Animism	<1%	1		2986

REGISTRY OF THE UNREACHED

NAME	SCRIPTURE	LANGUAGE	GROUP SIZE	PRIMARY RELIGION	% CHR	VOL V	UP ID
Marind, Bian	none	Marind, Bian	900	Animism	<1%	1	2987
Masenrempulu	none	Masenrempulu	250,000	Islam	<1%	1	2988
Matbat	none	Matbat	600	Animism	<1%	1	2989
Mawes	none	Mawes	700	Animism	<1%	1	2990
Meax	none	Meax	10,000	Animism	<1%	1	2991
Mekwei	none	Mekwei	1,000	Animism	<1%	1	2992
*Minika	portions	Minika	10,000	Christo-Paganism	3%	5	1049
Minangkabau	none	Minangkabau	5,000,000	Islam	1%	6 80	212
Moi	none	Moi	4,000	Animism	<1%	1	2994
Molof	none	Molof	200	Animism	<1%	1	2995
Mombum	none	Mombum	300	Animism	<1%	1	2996
Mongondow	portions	Mongondow	400,000	Animism	<1%	5 81	2997
Moni	New Testament	Moni	20,000	Animism	<1%	1	2998
Mor	none	Mor	1,000	Animism	<1%	1	2999
Mori	New Testament	Mori	200,000	Islam	0%	5 81	3000
Morwap	none	Morwap	300	Animism	<1%	1	3001
Muna	none	Muna	200,000	Islam-Animist	<1%	1	3002
Munggui	none	Munggui	700	Animism	<1%	1	3003
Musi	Bible	Indonesian	400,000	Islam-Animist	0%	3	4087
Nabi	none	Nabi	600	Animism	<1%	1	3004
Nafri	none	Nafri	2,000	Animism	<1%	1	3005
Naltya	none	Naltya	7,000	Animism	<1%	1	3006
Ndaonese	none	Ndao	2,000	Animism	<1%	1	3007
Ndom	none	Ndom	500	Animism	<1%	1	3008
Nduga	New Testament	Nduga	10,000	Animism	<1%	1	3009
Ngada	none	Ngada	40,000	Christo-Paganism	<1%	1	3010
Ngalik, North	none	Ngalik, North	35,000	Animism	<1%	1	3011
Ngalik, Southern	none	Ngalik, Southern	5,000	Animism	<1%	1	3012
Ngalum	none	Ngalum	10,000	Animism	<1%	1	3013
Nias	Bible	Nias	230,000	Animism	<1%	1	3014
Nimboran	none	Nimboran	4,000	Animism	<1%	1	3015
Ninggrum	none	Ninggrum	4,000	Animism	<1%	1	3016
Nisa	none	Nisa	300	Animism	<1%	1	3017
Njadu	portions	Njadu	9,300	Animism	<1%	1	3018
Ogan	Bible	Indonesian	200,000	Islam-Animist	0%	3	4085
Onin	none	Onin	600	Animism	<1%	1	3019

NAME	SCRIPTURE	LANGUAGE	GROUP SIZE	PRIMARY RELIGION	% CHR	VOL V	UP ID
Ormu	none	Ormu	800	Animism	<1%	1	3020
Ot Danum	portions	Ot Danum	30,000	Animism	<1%	1	3021
Palembang	none	Palembang	500,000	Islam	<1%	1	3022
Pantu	none	Pantu	9,000	Islam	<1%	1	3023
Papuma	none	Papuma	700	Animism	<1%	1	3024
Pisa	none	Pisa	4,000	Animism	<1%	1	3025
Pitu Uluna Salu	none	Pitu Uluna Salu	175,000	Animism	<1%	1	3026
Pom	none	Pom	2,000	Animism	<1%	1	3027
Puragi	none	Puragi	900	Animism	<1%	1	3028
Pyu	none	Pyu	100	Animism	<1%	1	3029
Ratahan	none	Ratahan	150,000	Animism	<1%	6 80	3030
Redjang	none	Rejang	300,000	Islam	<1%	1	694
Riantana	none	Riantana	1,000	Animism	<1%	1	3031
Saberi	none	Saberi	2,000	Animism	<1%	1	3033
Sadang	Bible	Sadang	50,000	Animism	<1%	1	3034
Sanarkena	none	Sanarkena	800	Animism	<1%	1	3035
Sangir	New Testament	Sangir	145,000	Animism	<1%	1	3036
Sangke	none	Sangke		Animism	<1%	1	3037
Sasak	portions	Sasak	1,600,300	Islam-Animist	<1%	6 80	1095
Sause	none	Sause	500	Animism	<1%	1	3038
**Sawi	New Testament	Sawi	3,000	Animism	16%	5	1180
Sekar	none	Sekar	500	Animism	<1%	1	3039
Sekayu	Bible	Indonesian	200,000	Islam-Animist	0%	3	40,90
Seko	none	Seko	275,000	Animism	<1%	1	3040
Senpan	none	Senpan	2,000	Animism	<1%	1	3041
Senggi	none	Senggi	100	Animism	<1%	1	3042
Sentani	none	Sentani	10,000	Animism	<1%	1	3043
**Serawai	none	Serawai (Pasemah)	60,000	Islam-Animist	<1%	5 81	1091
Serui-Laut	none	Serui-Laut	1,000	Animism	<1%	1	3044
Siagha-Yenimu	none	Siagha-Yenimu	3,000	Animism	<1%	1	3045
Sikanese	none	Sikka	100,000	Animism	<1%	1	3046
Sikhule	none	Sikhule	20,000	Animism	<1%	1	3048
Sobei	none	Sobei		Animism	<1%	1	3049
*Soloree Muslims	none	Solor	131,000	Islam	0%	5 81	226
Somagai	none	Somagai	3,000	Animism	0%	3	3050
Somahai	none	Somahai	2,000	Animism	<1%	1	

NAME	SCRIPTURE	LANGUAGE	GROUP SIZE	PRIMARY RELIGION	% CHR V	VOL UP ID
Sowanda	none	Sowanda	1,000	Animism	<1% 1	3051
Sunba	not reported	Sunba	400,000	Animism	<1% 5	1097
Sumbawa	none	Sumbawa	114,000	Islam	<1% 5	3052
**Sundanese	Bible	Sundanese	20,000,000	Islam-Animist	<1% 6 84	273
Tadjio	none	Tadjio	100,000	Animism	<1% 1	3053
Tahit	none	Tehit	6,000	Animism	<1% 1	3063
Taikat	none	Taikat	600	Animism	<1% 1	3054
*Talo	none	Talo	90,000	Islam-Animist	<1% 3	4089
Tanagario	none	Tanagario	4,000	Animism	<1% 1	3055
Tanahmerah	none	Tanahmerah	3,000	Animism	<1% 1	3056
Tandia	none	Tandia	400	Animism	<1% 1	3057
Taori-Kei	none	Taori-Kei	100	Animism	<1% 1	3058
Tara	none	Tara	125,000	Animism	<1% 1	3059
Tarof	none	Tarof	600	Animism	<1% 1	3060
Tarpia	none	Tarpia	600	Animism	<1% 1	3061
Taurap	none	Taurap	200	Animism	<1% 1	3062
Tengger	not reported	Tenggerese	400,000	Hindu-Animist	<1% 5	296
Ternatans	none	Ternate	42,000	Islam	<1% 1	3064
Tidorese	none	Tidore	26,000	Islam-Animist	<1% 1	3065
Timorese	New Testament	Timorese	300,000	Animism	<1% 1	3066
Tiro	none	Tiro	75,000	Animism	<1% 1	3067
Toala	none	Toala	100	Animism	<1% 1	3068
Tombulu	portions	Tombulu	40,000	Animism	<1% 1	3069
Tomini	none	Tomini	50,000	Animism	<1% 1	3070
Tondanou	none	Tondanou	35,000	Animism	<1% 1	3071
Tonsea	none	Tonsea	90,000	Animism	<1% 1	3072
Tontemboa	portions	Tontemboa	140,000	Animism	<1% 1	3073
Toraja, Southern	Bible	Tae'	250,000	Animism	nr% 5 81	3074
Towei	none	Towei	100	Animism	<1% 1	3075
Tukude	none	Tukude	45,000	Christo-Paganism	<1% 1	3076
Tunawo	none	Tunawo	400	Animism	<1% 1	3077
Turu	none	Turu	800	Animism	<1% 1	3078
Uhunduni	portions	Uhunduni	14,000	Animism	<1% 1	3079
Uria	none	Uria	300	Animism	<1% 1	3080
Uruangnirin	none	Uruangnirin	300	Animism	<1% 1	3081
Vaikino	none	Vaikino	14,000	Animism	<1% 1	3082

NAME	SCRIPTURE	LANGUAGE	GROUP SIZE	PRIMARY RELIGION	% CHR	VOL V	UP ID
Uabo	none	Uabo	900	Animism	<1%	1	3083
Uanbon	none	Uanbon	2,000	Animism	<1%	1	3084
Uandanen	portions	Uandanen	4,000	Animism	<1%	1	3085
Uanggom	none	Uanggom	1,000	Animism	<1%	1	3086
Uano	none	Uano	2,000	Animism	<1%	1	3087
Uarembori	none	Uarembori	400	Animism	<1%	1	3088
Uaris	none	Uaris	2,000	Animism	<1%	1	3089
Uarkay-Bipim	none	Uarkay-Bipim	300	Animism	<1%	1	3090
Uaropen	none	Uaropen	6,000	Animism	<1%	1	3091
Ueda	portions	Ueda	900	Islam	<1%	1	3092
Uewewa	New Testament	Uewewa	55,000	Animism	<1%	1	3093
Uodani	none	Uodani	3,000	Animism	<1%	1	3094
Uoi	none	Uoi	1,000	Animism	<1%	1	3095
Uolio	none	Uolio	25,000	Islam-Animist	<1%	1	3096
Yafi	none	Yafi	200	Animism	<1%	1	3097
Yahadian	none	Yahadian	700	Animism	<1%	1	3098
Yaly of Orchid Island	none	Yaly	12,000	Animism	<1%	1	3099
Yami	portions	Yami	2,200	Nominal Christian	nr%	4	84 4805
Yaur	none	Yaur	400	Animism	<1%	1	3100
Yava	none	Yava	5,000	Animism	<1%	1	3101
Yei	none	Yei	1,000	Animism	<1%	1	3102
Yelmek	none	Yelmek	400	Animism	<1%	1	3103
Yeretuar	none	Yeretuar	300	Animism	<1%	1	3104
Yonggom	portions	Yonggom	2,000	Animism	<1%	1	3105
Yotafa	none	Yotafa	3,000	Animism	<1%	1	3106

Iran

NAME	SCRIPTURE	LANGUAGE	GROUP SIZE	PRIMARY RELIGION	% CHR	VOL V	UP ID
Afshars	portions	Afshari	290,000	Islam	0%	4	2035
Agajanis	none	Agajanis	1,000	Islam	0%	3	2065
**Ahl-i-Haqq in Iran	portions	Kurdish dialects	500,000	Islam	0%	6 79	1237
Arab-Jabbari (Kamesh)	not reported	Arabic	13,000	Islam	0%	3	2044

REGISTRY OF THE UNREACHED

NAME	SCRIPTURE	LANGUAGE	GROUP PRIMARY SIZE RELIGION	% CHR	VOL V	UP ID
Arab-Shaibani (Kamesh)	not reported	Arabic	16,000 Islam	0%	3	2045
Arabs of Khuzestan	Bible	Arabic	520,000 Islam	1%	4	2034
Azerbaijani Turks	Bible	Azerbaijani Turkish	6,000,000 Islam	0%	5 80	2026
Bahais in Teheran	+Bible	Farsi	45,000 Bahaism	0%	6 82	5037
Baharlu (Kamesh)	not reported	Turkish	8,000 Islam	0%	3	2046
Bakhtiaris	portions	Bakhtiaris	590,000 Islam	0%	5 80	2031
Baluchi	portions	Baluchi	1,100,000 Islam	0%	6 80	2030
Bayats	none	Bayat	nr Islam	<1%	3	2067
Bovir-Ahmadi	portions	Lori	110,000 Islam	0%	4	2040
Galeshis	none	Galeshi	2,000 Islam	0%	3	2057
Gilakis	none	Gilaki	1,950,000 Islam	1%	4	2027
Goudari	none	Goudari	2,000 Islam	0%	3	2059
Hezareh	none	Hezara'i	nr Islam	<1%	3	2068
Inallu	not reported	Afshari	5,000 Islam	0%	3	2048
Iraqi Kurd Refugees	+New Testament	Kurmanji	300,000 Islam	<1%	4 83	9028
Jamshidis	none	Jamshidi	1,000 Islam	0%	3	2063
Jews of Iran	Bible	Farsi	93,000 Judaism	1%	4	2042
Kazakhs	New Testament	Kazakhi	3,000 Islam	<1%	5 80	2055
Khalaj	none	Khalaj	20,000 Islam	0%	1	2535
Kurds in Iran	New Testament	Kurdish Dialects	2,000,000 Islam	1%	6 80	2036
Lors	portions	Luri	600,000 Islam	0%	5 80	2039
Manasani	portions	Luri	110,000 Islam	0%	4	2041
Mazandaranis	portions	Mazandarani	1,620,000 Islam	0%	4	2029
Moqaddan	none	Moqaddan	1,000 Islam	0%	3	2069
Nafar	not reported	Turkish	4,000 Islam	0%	3	2047
Pashtuns	Bible	Pashtu	3,000 Islam	0%	6 80	2054
Persians of Iran	Bible	Persian	2,000,000 Islam	<1%	6 80	4010
Pishagchi	none	Pishagchi	1,000 Islam	0%	3	2064
Qajars	not reported	Qajar	3,000 Islam	0%	3	2056
Qara'i	not reported	Qara'i	2,000 Islam	0%	3	2058
Qaragozlu	not reported	Qaragozlu	2,000 Islam	0%	3	2060
Qashqa'i	none	Qashqa'i	350,000 Islam	0%	5 80	2038
Sasanis	none	Sasani	1,000 Islam	0%	3	2072
Shahsavans	none	Azerbaijani (Shahsavani)	180,000 Islam	0%	6 80	2043
Tajik	portions	Dari	15,000 Islam	0%	5 80	2053
Takestani	none	Takestani	220,000 Islam	<1%	1	2536

NAME	SCRIPTURE	LANGUAGE	GROUP SIZE	PRIMARY RELIGION	% CHR	V	UP	ID
Talish	none	Talish	20,000	Islam	0%	3		2050
Teimuri	none	Teimuri	10,000	Islam	0%	3		2051
Teimurtash	none	Teimurtash	7,000	Islam	0%	3		2052
*Tertiary Level Youth	Bible	Persian	nr	Islam	1%	4		4074
Turkomans	portions	Turkomani	550,000	Islam	0%	6	80	2032

Israel

NAME	SCRIPTURE	LANGUAGE	GROUP SIZE	PRIMARY RELIGION	% CHR	V	UP	ID
Druzes	Bible	Arabic	33,000	Folk Religion	0%	6	79	1230
Gypsies in Jerusalem	+Bible	Romany Dialect	30,300	Islam	0%	5	82	5042
*Jewish Ingrnts.-American	Bible	Hebrew	30,000	Judaism	0%	3		327
*Jewish Ingrnts.-Argentine	Bible	Hebrew	20,000	Judaism	0%	3		323
*Jewish Ingrnts.-Australia	Bible	Hebrew	1,000	Judaism	0%	3		322
*Jewish Ingrnts.-Brazilian	Bible	Hebrew	4,000	Judaism	0%	3		325
*Jewish Ingrnts.-Mexican	Bible	Hebrew	1,000	Judaism	0%	3		326
*Jewish Ingrnts.-Uruguayan	Bible	Hebrew	3,000	Judaism	0%	3		324
*Jewish Immigrants,Other	Bible	Hebrew	6,000	Judaism	0%	3		321
***Jewish Refugees from USSR	+Bible	Yiddish	170,000	Secularism	<1%	4	83	9013
Targum	none	Targum	5,000	Judaism	<1%	1		2537

Italy

NAME	SCRIPTURE	LANGUAGE	GROUP SIZE	PRIMARY RELIGION	% CHR	V	UP	ID
Jews in Venice	+Bible	Italian	700	Judaism	0%	5	82	5046

Ivory Coast

NAME	SCRIPTURE	LANGUAGE	GROUP SIZE	PRIMARY RELIGION	% CHR V	VOL UP ID
Abe	portions	Abe	30,000	Islam-Animist	<1%	1	2273
Abidji	portions	Adidji	23,000	Islam-Animist	<1%	1	2274
Abure	none	Abure	25,000	Islam-Animist	<1%	1	2275
Adyukru	portions	Adyukru	51,000	Islam-Animist	<1%	1	2276
Akan, Brong	Bible	Akan; Brong	50,000	Islam-Animist	<1%	1	2277
Aladian	portions	Aladian	15,000	Islam-Animist	<1%	1	2278
Attie	portions	Attie	160,000	Islam-Animist	<1%	1	2279
*Atye	portions,NT	Atye	210,000	Animism	9%	4	4127
Avikan	none	Avikan	8,000	Islam-Animist	<1%	1	2280
Bakue	portions	Bakue	5,000	Islam-Animist	<1%	1	2281
Bambara	Bible	Bambara	1,000,000	Islam-Animist	<1%	1	2282
***Baoule	portions,NT	Baule	1,200,000	Animism	9%	4	407
Bete	portions	Bete	300,000	Animism	1%	5	4128
***Dan	portions	Dan	270,000	Animism	2%	5	4126
**Dida	portions	Dida	120,000	African Independent	7%	4	4138
Ebrie	portions	Ebrie	50,000	Islam-Animist	<1%	1	2287
Eotile	none	Eotile	4,000	Islam-Animist	<1%	1	2288
Gagou	portions	Gagou	25,000	Animism	1%	4	480
***Godie	portions	Godie	20,000	Animism	12%	4	308
**Gouro	NT,portions	Gouro	200,000	Animism	4%	4	194
Guere	none	Guere	120,000	Islam-Animist	<1%	1	2289
Gwa	none	Gwa	8,000	Islam-Animist	<1%	1	2290
Huela-Numu	none	Huela-Numu	50,000	Islam-Animist	<1%	1	2291
**Jimini	portions	Jimini	42,000	Islam	14%	5	4124
*Kouya	none	Kouya	6,000	Islam-Animist	<1%	1	2292
*Krahn	portions	Guere	250,000	Animism	3%	4	687
Krobou	none	Krobou	3,000	Islam-Animist	<1%	1	2293
Krumen	portions	Krumen	17,000	Animism	2%	4	4137

NAME	SCRIPTURE	LANGUAGE	GROUP SIZE	PRIMARY RELIGION	% CHR	V	UP ID
Kulango	New Testament	Kulango	60,000	Animism	3%	4	481
Kulele	none	Kulele	15,000	Islam-Animist	<1%	1	2294
Ligbi	none	Ligbi	20,000	Islam	<1%	1	482
Lobi	New Testament	Lobi	40,000	Animism	<1%	4	483
Maou	none	Maou	80,000	Islam-Animist	<1%	1	2295
Mo	none	Mo	800	Islam-Animist	<1%	1	2296
Mona	none	Mona	6,000	Islam-Animist	<1%	1	2297
Moru	none	Moru	10,000	Islam-Animist	<1%	1	2298
Neyo	not reported	Nevo	5,000	Animism	0%	3	1131
Ngen	not reported	Ngen	20,000	Animism	2%	4	698
*Ngere	none	Ngere	150,000	Animism	<1%	4	484
**Nyabua	portions	not reported	30,000	Animism	3%	5	4125
Nzema	portions	Nzema	24,000	Islam-Animist	<1%	1	2300
Oubi	none	Oubi	1,000	Islam-Animist	<1%	1	2301
Palara	none	Palara	10,000	Islam-Animist	<1%	1	2302
Pye	none	Pye	6,000	Islam-Animist	<1%	1	2303
Senufo	portions	Senari	300,000	Animism	2%	6 80	181
Taguana	none	Taguana	43,000	Islam-Animist	<1%	4	2304
*Teenbu	portions	Lorhon	5,000	Animism	1%	5	311
*Tense	portions	Teen	20,000	Animism	<1%	1	4122
Tepo	none	Tepo	20,000	Islam-Animist	<1%	1	2305
Trepo	none	Trepo	3,000	Islam-Animist	<1%	1	2306
Tura	New Testament	Tura	20,000	Islam-Animist	<1%	1	2307
Uobe	none	Uobe	40,000	Animism	12%	4	532
Yaoure	none	Yaoure	14,000	Animism	<1%	4	4120

Jamaica

NAME	SCRIPTURE	LANGUAGE	GROUP SIZE	PRIMARY RELIGION	% CHR	V	UP ID
**Jamaican Elite	Bible	Jamaican Patois	800,000	Secularism	0%	4	4117

NAME	SCRIPTURE	LANGUAGE	GROUP SIZE	PRIMARY RELIGION	% CHR	VOL V	UP ID
Japan							
*Barbers in Tokyo	+Bible	Japanese	220,000	Buddhism	1%	6 82	5009
Boat People	+Bible	Vietnamese	1,800	Ancestor Worship	nr%	4	9036
*Chinese in Japan	Bible	Mandarin	50,000	Traditional Chinese	1%	4	738
*Danchi Dwellers in Tokyo	+Bible	Japanese	2,500,000	Secularism	2%	5 82	5005
*Dentists, Fukuoka	Bible	Japanese	4,500	Secularism	nr%	4	4808
Geishas in Osaka	+Bible	Japanese	nr	Secularism	<1%	5 82	5025
*Inland Sea Island Peoples	Bible	Japanese	1,000,000	Traditional Japanese	1%	4	708
*Koreans of Japan	Bible	Korean	600,000	Folk Religion	6%	5	57
*Ryukyuan	not reported	Ryukyuan	1,000,000	Traditional Japanese	4%	4	65
Soka Gakkai Believers	Bible	Japanese	6,500,000	Buddhism	0%	3	20
**Univ. Students of Japan	Bible	Japanese	2,000,000	Traditional Japanese	1%	4	2125
Jordan							
*Cherkess	Bible	Sharkas	60,000	Nominal Christian	nr%	4 84	4814
Circassians in Amman	+Bible	Arabic	17,000	Islam	0%	5 82	5018
Muslims of Jordan	Bible	Arabic	2,430,000	Islam	<1%	4	220
Palestinian Refugees	+portions	Arabic	1,160,800	Islam	<1%	4 83	9020

NAME	SCRIPTURE	LANGUAGE	GROUP SIZE	PRIMARY RELIGION	% CHR	V	VOL UP	ID
Kampuchea, Democratic								
*Chan Refugees from Kampuchea	not reported	Cham	20,000	Islam	0%	6	83	91
Kenya								
Ayana	not reported	Ayana	5,000	Islam-Animist	0%	3		4133
Boni of Lamu	not reported	Boni	2,500	Islam-Animist	nr%	4	84	4803
**Boran	New Testament	Boran	37,000	Islam-Animist	3%	5		4077
Digo	not reported	Digo	168,000	Islam	<1%	4	84	4050
Dorobo	not reported	Nandi	22,000	Animism	1%	5		151
El Molo	none	Samburu	1,000	Animism	3%	4		533
Gabbra	not reported	Galla	12,000	Folk Religion	1%	4		715
Giryana	Bible	Giryama	340,000	Animism	9%	4		534
Gosha	not reported	Gosha	3,000	Islam-Animist	0%	3		4134
**Maasai	New Testament	Masai	100,000	Animism	5%	6	79	489
Njemps	+ NT,portions	Njemps Maasai	10,000	Animism	<1%	2		8501
Rendille	not reported	Rendille	20,000	Islam-Animist	0%	3		4131
Sabbra	New Testament	Boran	18,000	Animism	15%	3		4078
**Saguye	not reported	Galla	30,000	Islam	1%	3		714
Sakuye	not reported	Sakuye	8,000	Islam-Animist	0%	3		4132
**Samburu	portions	Maasai, Samburu	74,000	Animism	3%	4	84	535
Somali; Ajuran	Bible	Somali (Ajuran)	25,000	Islam	1%	6	79	467
Somali; Degodia	New Testament	Somali	70,000	Islam	1%	5		464
Somali; Gurreh	New Testament	Somali	54,000	Islam	1%	5		465

NAME	SCRIPTURE	LANGUAGE	GROUP SIZE	PRIMARY RELIGION	% CHR	VOL V	UP	ID
Somali, Ogadenya	Bible	Somali	100,000	Islam	1%	5		466
**Suk	New Testament	not reported	133,000	Animism	8%	5		600
**Teso	Bible	Luteso	110,000	Animism	8%	5		4071
*Turkana	portions	Turkana	224,000	Animism	4%	5		219
***Turkana Fishing Community	portions	Turkana	20,000	Animism	4%	5	79	475

Korea, Republic of

**Apartment Residents-Seoul	Bible	Korean	87,000	Folk Religion	11%	4		301
**Bus Drivers, South Korea	Bible	Korean	26,000	Unknown	8%	4		1195
**Bus Girls in Seoul	+Bible	Korean	50,000	Secularism	8%	6	82	5023
*Chinese in Korea	Bible	Mandarin	20,000	Secularism	5%	4		298
Indust.Workers Yongdungpo	Bible	Korean	140,000	Folk Religion	6%	4		387
*Japanese in Korea	Bible	Japanese	5,000	Traditional Japanese	1%	3		710
Kae Sung Natives in Seoul	+Bible	Korean	20,000	Buddhism	1%	5	82	5015
***Prisoners	Bible	Korean	45,000	Secularism	10%	4		300
Vietnamese Refugees	+Bible	Vietnamese	500	Buddhism	nr%	4		9045

Kuwait

Kurds in Kuwait	not reported	Kurdish	145,000	Islam	0%	3		4136

NAME	SCRIPTURE	LANGUAGE	GROUP SIZE	PRIMARY RELIGION	% CHR	V	UP	VOL ID
Laos								
Alak	not reported	Alak	8,000	Animism	1%	5		112
Brao	not reported	Brao	18,000	Animism	1%	6	79	108
*Chinese in Laos	Bible	Mandarin	25,000	Traditional Chinese	1%	4		101
Galler	New Testament	Galler	50,000	Animism	1%	4		111
Jeng	not reported	Jeng	500	Animism	0%	4		110
Kampuchean Refugees	Bible	Khmer	10,400	Buddhist-Animist	0%	5		9049
Kasseng	not reported	Kasseng	15,000	Animism	0%	5		109
*Lao	Bible	Lao	1,910,000	Buddhism	1%	7	79	121
Loven	not reported	Loven	25,000	Buddhist-Animist	1%	5	81	107
Ngeq	portions	Ngeq	50,000	Animism	5%	5		105
Nyaheun	not reported	Nyaheun	15,000	Animism	2%	4		103
Oi	not reported	Oi	10,000	Animism	1%	5		104
Phu Thai	not reported	Phu Thai	100,000	Buddhist-Animist	1%	5		102
Soh	not reported	Soh	15,000	Animism	1%	5		98
Ta-Oi	not reported	Ta-Oi	15,000	Animism	1%	5		99
Vietnamese	Bible	Vietnamese	20,000	Buddhism	1%	4		100
Lebanon								
Ladinos	Bible	Ladinos	7,000	Judaism	<1%	1		2538
Palestinian Refugees	+portions	Arabic	240,000	Islam	<1%	4	83	9016

639

REGISTRY OF THE UNREACHED

NAME	SCRIPTURE	LANGUAGE	GROUP SIZE	PRIMARY RELIGION	% CHR	V	UP	VOL ID

Lesotho

NAME	SCRIPTURE	LANGUAGE	GROUP SIZE	PRIMARY RELIGION	% CHR	V	UP	VOL ID
***Basotho, Mountain	Bible	Southern Sesotho	70,000	Animism	8%	6	79	232
South African Refugee Students	+Bible	English	11,500	Nominal Christian	nr%	4	83	9014

Liberia

NAME	SCRIPTURE	LANGUAGE	GROUP SIZE	PRIMARY RELIGION	% CHR	V	UP	VOL ID
Bandi	portions	Bandi	32,000	Animism	6%	4		555
*Bassa	NT,portions	Bassa	200,000	Animism	11%	5		366
*Dewein	none	Dan	94,000	Islam-Animist	<1%	1		5359
Gio	New Testament	De	5,000	Islam	1%	4		690
Gola	portions	Dan (Yacouba)	92,000	Animism	5%	5		190
**Grebo	portions	Gola	47,000	Islam-Animist	<1%	1		5360
*Kissi	New Testament	Grebo Dialects	65,000	Animism	8%	4		689
Klaoh	portions	Kissi	35,000	Animism	3%	4		691
**Kowaao	not reported	Klaoh	81,000	Islam-Animist	<1%	1		5361
Kpelle	New Testament	Kowaao	7,000	Animism	3%	4		692
***Krahn	portions	Kpelle	200,000	Animism	6%	5		556
Kuwaa	portions	Krahn	55,000	Animism	7%	4		83
Loma	portions	Kuwaa	6,000	Islam-Animist	<1%	1		5362
Mandingo	portions	Lona	60,000	Animism	12%	4		601
Mano	portions	Mandingo	30,000	Islam	1%	6	79	622
Mende	Bible	Mano	65,000	Animism	4%	4		602
Sapo	portions	Mende	5,000	Islam-Animist	<1%	1		5363
		not reported	30,000	Animism	12%	4		603

NAME	SCRIPTURE	LANGUAGE	GROUP PRIMARY SIZE RELIGION	% CHR	V	UP	VOL ID
*Vai	portions	Vai	30,000 Islam	1%	6	80	688

Libya

| Teda | none | Teda | 16,000 Islam | <1% | 1 | | 5364 |
| Zaghawa | none | Zaghawa | nr Islam | <1% | 1 | | 5365 |

Luxembourg

| Luxemburgois | Bible | letzburgesch | 276,000 Nominal Christian | nr% | 2 | | 6561 |

Macau

| *Chinese Refugees in Macau | Bible | Cantonese | 100,000 Traditional Chinese | 1% | 5 | 81 | 129 |

Madagascar

| *Prisoners in Antananarivo | +Bible | Malagasy | 10,000 Folk Religion | 2% | 5 | 82 | 5012 |

NAME	SCRIPTURE	LANGUAGE	GROUP SIZE	PRIMARY RELIGION	% CHR	VOL V	UP ID

Malawi

Lambya	none	Lambya	20,000	Animism	0%	1	5366
Mpoto	portions	Mpoto	22,000	Animism	0%	1	5367
Ngulu	NT,portions	Ngulu	476,000	Animism	0%	1	5368
Nyakyusa	New Testament	Nyakyusa	34,000	Animism	<1%	1	5369
Sena	New Testament	Sena	115,000	Animism	0%	1	5370
Tonga	Bible	Tonga	62,000	Animism	<1%	1	5371
**Yao	Bible	Chiyao	600,000	Islam-Animist	2%	4 84	1006
Zulu	Bible	Zulu	40,000	Animism	<1%	1	5372

Malaysia

Bajau, Land	none	Bajaus	90,000	Islam-Animist	0%	2	4091
Bateg	none	Bateg	400	Animism	0%	2	4114
Besisi	none	Besisi	7,000	Animism	0%	2	4109
**Bidayuh of Sarawak	New Testament	Biatah	110,000	Christo-Paganism	<1%	5 81	2123
Biduanda	none	Biduanda	4,000	Animism	0%	2	4098
Bisaya	portions	Bisaya	3,000	Animism	nr%	6 81	7022
Bruneis	none	Bruneis	25,000	Animism	0%	2	4092
Chinese Fishermen	not reported	Hokkien	4,000	Traditional Chinese	0%	3	4142
*Chinese in Malaysia	Bible	Chinese dialects	4,000,000	Traditional Chinese	8%	5	408
**Chinese in Sabah	Bible	Hakka	180,000	Traditional Chinese	10%	4	740
**Chinese in Sarawak	Bible	Mandarin and dialects	330,000	Traditional Chinese	7%	4	737
*Chinese of W. Malaysia	Bible	Cantonese	3,500,000	Traditional Chinese	4%	4	757
Dusun	NT,portions	Kadazan	160,000	Animism	nr%	6 81	7023

NAME	SCRIPTURE	LANGUAGE	GROUP SIZE	PRIMARY RELIGION	% CHR	VOL V	UP ID
**Iban	New Testament	Iban	30,000	Animism	nr%	6 81	7024
Juhai	none	Juhai	400	Animism	0%	2	4112
Kadazans	not reported	Kadazans	110,000	Animism	<1%	2	4095
Kayan	New Testament	Kayan	12,000	Animism	0%	3	4102
Kedayanas	none	Kedayanas	25,000	Animism	0%	2	4094
Kelabit	portions	Kelabit	17,000	Animism	nr%	6 81	7025
Kemok	none	Kemok	400	Animism	0%	2	4115
Lanoh	none	Lanoh	400	Animism	0%	2	4111
Mantera	none	Mantera	400	Animism	0%	2	4097
**Melanau of Sarawak	none	Melanau	61,000	Animism	1%	6 80	2122
Menri	none	Menri	400	Animism	0%	2	4113
Monoguns	none	Monoguns	110,000	Animism	<1%	3	4096
Murut	none	Murut	38,000	Animism	0%	3	4105
Muslim Malays	New Testament	Bahasa Malaysia	5,500,000	Islam	<1%	6 80	50
Orang Kanak	none	Orang Kanak	4,000	Animism	0%	2	4100
Orang Laut	none	Orang Laut	4,000	Animism	0%	2	4101
Orang Ulu	none	Orang Ulu	4,000	Animism	0%	2	4099
Penan, Western	portions	Penan	3,000	Animism	nr%	6 81	7027
**Selakau of Sarawak	none	Selakau	5,000	Animism	7%	4	2124
Semelai	none	Semelai	3,000	Animism	0%	2	4110
**Senoi	portions	Native Senoi	340,000	Animism	2%	5 81	1009
**Sugut	Bible	Dusun	10,000	Animism	0%	4	2118
Tagal	portions	Tagal	19,000	Animism	nr%	6 81	7028
***Tamil Plantation Workers	Bible	Tamil	140,000	Hinduism	1%	4	1109
*Tamils (Indian)	Bible	Tamil	600,000	Hinduism	7%	5	4
Tenira	none	Tenira	7,000	Animism	0%	2	4108

Maldives

NAME	SCRIPTURE	LANGUAGE	GROUP SIZE	PRIMARY RELIGION	% CHR	VOL V	UP ID
Divehi	not reported	Divehi	120,000	Islam	0%	6 80	4005

NAME	SCRIPTURE	LANGUAGE	GROUP PRIMARY SIZE RELIGION		% CHR	VOL V	UP ID

Mali

Bambara	Bible	Bambara	1,000,000	Islam	1%	5	604
Bobo Fing	portions	Bobo Fing	3,000	Animism	<1%	1	5373
Bobo Wule	New Testament	Bobo Wule	366,000	Animism	<1%	1	5374
Bozo	none	Bozo	nr	Animism	0%	1	5375
*Dogon	New Testament	Dogon	312,000	Animism	10%	6 79	150
Fula, Macina	portions	Fula, Macina	50,000	Animism	<1%	1	5376
Fula, Peuhala	none	Fula, Peuhala	450,000	Animism	0%	1	5377
Kagoro	none	Logoro (Bambara)	30,000	Animism	<1%	4	552
Khasonke	none	Khasonke	71,000	Animism	<1%	1	5378
Kita	none	not reported	150,000	Islam	2%	3	553
Maure	not reported	Maure	58,000	Islam-Animist	0%	1	5379
Minianka	portions	Suppire	300,000	Animism	<1%	4	554
Sano, Northern	none	Sano, Northern	50,000	Animism	0%	1	5380
Sanogho	none	Sanogho	10,000	Animism	0%	1	5381
Songhai	New Testament	Songhai	130,000	Islam	<1%	1	5382
Soninke	none	Soninke	283,000	Islam	0%	1	5383
Suppire	portions	Suppire	300,000	Animism	<1%	1	5384
Ware	none	Ware	2,000	Animism	0%	1	5385

Malta

| *Maltese | Bible | Maltese | 330,000 | Nominal Christian | nr% | 2 | 6560 |

NAME	SCRIPTURE	LANGUAGE	GROUP SIZE	PRIMARY RELIGION	% CHR	VOL V	UP ID

Mauritania

Moors in Mauritania	not reported	Arabic (Hassani)	1,000,000	Islam	0%	5	4043
Soninke	none	Soninke	22,000	Islam	0%	1	5386
*White Moors	none	Hassaniya (Arabic)		nr	0%	4	6570
Zenaga	none	Zenaga	16,000	Islam	0%	1	5387

Mauritius

| **Chinese | Bible | Hakka | 30,000 | Buddhist-Animist | 2% | 4 84 | 4811 |

Mexico

Amuzgo, Guerrero	New Testament	Amuzgo, Guerrero	20,000	Christo-Paganism	<1%	1	8015
Amuzgo, Oaxaca	none	Amuzgo, Oaxaca	5,000	Christo-Paganism	<1%	1	8016
***Azteca	portions	Nahuatl, Hidalgo	250,000	Christo-Paganism	2%	6 79	284
***Ch'ol Sabanilla	New Testament	Ch'ol	20,000	Christo-Paganism	5%	4	114
Ch'ol Tila	New Testament	Tila Chol	38,000	Animism	1%	5	1216
Chamula	New Testament	Tzotzil (Chamula)	50,000	Christo-Paganism	10%	6 79	162
Chatino, Nopala	none	Chatino, Nopala	8,000	Christo-Paganism	<1%	1	8017
Chatino, Panixtlahuaca	none	Chatino, Panixtlahuaca	5,000	Christo-Paganism	0%	1	8018
Chatino, Tataltepec	New Testament	Chatino, Tataltepec	2,000	Christo-Paganism	<1%	1	8019

645

NAME	SCRIPTURE	LANGUAGE	GROUP SIZE	PRIMARY RELIGION	% CHR	V	V	VOL UP ID
Chatino, Yaitepec	portions	Spanish	2,000	Christo-Paganism	<1%	1		8020
Chatino, Zacatepec	none	Chatino, Zacatepec	500	Christo-Paganism	0%	1		8021
Chatino, Zenzontepec	none	Chatino, Zenzontepec	4,000	Christo-Paganism	0%	1		8022
Chinanteco, Tepinapa	none	Chinanteco, Tepinapa	3,000	Christo-Paganism	0%	1		8033
Chinanteco, Ayotzintepec	none	Chinanteco, Ayotzintepec	2,000	Christo-Paganism	0%	1		8023
Chinanteco, Chiltepec	none	Chinanteco, Chiltepec	3,000	Christo-Paganism	0%	1		8024
Chinanteco, Comaltepec	portions	Chinanteco, Comaltepec	2,000	Christo-Paganism	<1%	1		8025
Chinanteco, Lalana	New Testament	Chinanteco, Lalana	10,000	Christo-Paganism	<1%	1		8026
Chinanteco, Lealao	portions	Chinanteco, Lealao	5,000	Christo-Paganism	<1%	1		8027
Chinanteco, Ojitlan	New Testament	Chinanteco, Ojitlan	10,000	Christo-Paganism	<1%	1		8028
Chinanteco, Palantla	New Testament	Chinanteco, Palantla	11,000	Christo-Paganism	<1%	1		8029
Chinanteco, Quiotepec	portions	Chinanteco, Quiotepec	7,000	Christo-Paganism	<1%	1		8030
Chinanteco, Sochiapan	portions	Chinanteco, Sochiapan	2,000	Christo-Paganism	<1%	1		8031
Chinanteco, Tepetotutla	portions	Chinanteco, Tepetotutla	1,000	Christo-Paganism	<1%	1		8032
Chinanteco, Usila	portions	Chinanteco, Usila	5,000	Christo-Paganism	<1%	1		8034
Chocho	none	Spanish	3,000	Christo-Paganism	<1%	2		8035
Chuj, San Mateo Ixtatan	New Testament	Chuj, San Mateo Ixtatan		Christo-Paganism	0%	1		8036
Cocopa	none	Cocopa	900	Christo-Paganism	<1%	1		8037
Cora	portions	Cora	8,000	Christo-Paganism	<1%	1		8038
Cuicateco, Tepeuxila	New Testament	Cuicateco, Tepeuxila	10,000	Christo-Paganism	<1%	1		8039
Cuicateco, Teutila	New Testament	Cuicateco, Teutila	6,000	Christo-Paganism	<1%	1		8040
*English speakers, Guadalajara	+Bible	English	25,000	Secularism	15%	3	84	4816
Guarojio	none	Guarojio	5,000	Christo-Paganism	<1%	1		8041
Guatemalan Refugees	+Bible	Spanish	70,000	Christo-Paganism	nr%	4		9057
Huasteco	New Testament	Huasteco	80,000	Christo-Paganism	<1%	1		8042
**Huave	New Testament	Huave	18,000	Christo-Paganism	5%	5		113
Huichol	portions,NT	Huichol	8,000	Christo-Paganism	<1%	1		8043
Huistan Tzotzil	NT,portions	Tzotzil, Huistan	11,000	Christo-Paganism	5%	2		5104
Kikapoo	none	Kikapoo	5,000	Christo-Paganism	<1%	1		8044
Lacandon	New Testament	Lacandon	200	Christo-Paganism	<1%	1		8045
Matlatzinca, Atzingo	none	Matlatzinca, Atzingo	2,000	Christo-Paganism	0%	1		8046
Mayo	portions	Mayo	30,000	Christo-Paganism	<1%	1		8047
***Mazahua	New Testament	Mazahua	150,000	Nominal Christian	6%	4		377
**Middle Class-Mexico City	+Bible	Spanish	nr	Christo-Paganism	nr%	5	82	5014
**Mixes	New Testament	Mixe	60,000	Christo-Paganism	2%	5		1005

NAME	SCRIPTURE	LANGUAGE	GROUP SIZE	PRIMARY RELIGION	% CHR	VOL V UP	ID
Mixteco, Amoltepec	none	Mixteco, Amoltepec	6,000	Christo-Paganism	0%	1	8048
Mixteco, Apoala	none	Mixteco, Apoala	6,000	Christo-Paganism	<1%	1	8049
Mixteco, Central Puebla	none	Spanish	3,000	Christo-Paganism	<1%	1	5050
Mixteco, Eastern	New Testament	Mixteco, Eastern	15,000	Christo-Paganism	<1%	1	5051
Mixteco, Eastern Putla	none	Mixteco, Eastern Putla	7,000	Christo-Paganism	0%	1	5052
Mixteco, Huajuapan	none	Mixteco, Huajuapan	3,000	Christo-Paganism	<1%	1	5053
Mixteco, Silacyoapan	portions	Mixteco, Silacayoapan	15,000	Christo-Paganism	<1%	1	5054
Mixteco, Southern Puebla	New Testament	Mixteco, Southern Puebla	12,000	Christo-Paganism	<1%	1	5055
Mixteco, Southern Putla	none	Mixteco, Southern Putla	3,000	Christo-Paganism	0%	1	5056
Mixteco, Tututepec	none	Mixteco, Tututepec	2,000	Christo-Paganism	0%	1	5057
Mixteco, Yosondua	portions	Mixteco, Yosondua	15,000	Christo-Paganism	<1%	1	5058
*Mixteco,San Juan Mixtepic	portions	Mixteco	15,000	Christo-Paganism	1%	4	409
*Nahua, North Puebla	portions	Nahua	55,000	Christo-Paganism	9%	4	435
Otomi, Eastern	New Testament	Otomi, Eastern	20,000	Christo-Paganism	<1%	1	5059
Otomi, Mezquital	New Testament	Otomi, Mezquital	100,000	Christo-Paganism	<1%	1	5060
Otomi, Northwestern	none	Otomi, Northwestern	40,000	Christo-Paganism	0%	1	5061
Otomi, Southeastern	none	Otomi, Southeastern	2,000	Christo-Paganism	0%	1	5062
Otomi, State of Mexico	New Testament	Otomi	70,000	Christo-Paganism	<1%	1	5063
Otomi, Tenango	New Testament	Otomi, Tenango	10,000	Christo-Paganism	<1%	1	5064
Otomi, Texcatepec	none	Otomi, Texcatepec	8,300	Christo-Paganism	<1%	1	5065
Paipai	none	Spanish	300	Christo-Paganism	0%	1	5066
Pane, Central Chichimeca	portions	Pane, Central Chichimeca	3,000	Christo-Paganism	<1%	1	5067
Pane, Chichimeca-Jonaz	none	Spanish	1,000	Christo-Paganism	0%	1	5068
Pane, Northern	none	Pane, Northern	2,000	Christo-Paganism	0%	1	5069
Pina Bajo	none	Pina Bajo	1,000	Christo-Paganism	0%	1	5070
Spanish	none	Spanish	6,000	Christo-Paganism	0%	1	5071
Popoloca, Ahuatempan	none	Spanish	500	Christo-Paganism	0%	1	5072
Popoloca, Coyotepec	none	Popoloca, Eastern	2,000	Christo-Paganism	<1%	1	5073
Popoloca, Eastern	none	Popoloca, Northern	6,000	Christo-Paganism	<1%	1	5074
Popoloca, Northern	none	Spanish	1,000	Christo-Paganism	0%	1	5075
Popoloca, Southern	none	Popoloca, Western	2,000	Christo-Paganism	0%	1	5076
Popoloca, Western	none	Spanish	8,200	Christo-Paganism	0%	1	5077
Popoloca, Ojuta	none	Popoloca, Sayula	6,000	Christo-Paganism	0%	1	5078
Popoloca, Sayula	New Testament	Popoloca, Sierra	18,000	Christo-Paganism	<1%	1	5079
Popoloca, Sierra	New Testament	Spanish	2,000	Christo-Paganism	0%	1	5080
Popoloca, Texistepec	none	Seri	400	Christo-Paganism	<1%	1	5081
Seri	New Testament						

NAME	SCRIPTURE	LANGUAGE	GROUP SIZE	PRIMARY RELIGION	% CHR	VOL V	UP ID
Tarahumara, Northern	none	Tarahumara, Northern	500	Christo-Paganism	0%	1	5082
Tarahumara, Rocoroibo	portions	Tarahumara, Rocoroibo	12,000	Christo-Paganism	<1%	1	5083
Tarahumara, Samachique	New Testament	Tarahumara, Samachique	40,000	Christo-Paganism	<1%	1	5084
Tarasco	New Testament	Tarasco	60,000	Christo-Paganism	<1%	1	5085
Tepehua, Huehuetla	New Testament	Tepehua, Huehuetla	2,000	Christo-Paganism	<1%	1	5086
Tepehua, Pisa Flores	none	Tepehua, Pisa Flores	300	Christo-Paganism	0%	1	5087
Tepehua, Veracruz	none	Tepehua, Veracruz	900	Christo-Paganism	<1%	1	5088
Tepehuan, Northern	New Testament	Tepehuan, Northern	5,000	Christo-Paganism	<1%	1	5089
Tepehuan, Southeastern	portions	Tepehuan, Southeastern	8,000	Christo-Paganism	<1%	1	5090
Tepehuan, Southwestern	none	Tepehuan, Southwestern	6,000	Christo-Paganism	0%	1	5091
Tlapaneco, Malinaltepec	New Testament	Tlapaneco, Malinaltepec	40,000	Christo-Paganism	<1%	1	5092
Tojolabal	New Testament	Tojolabal	14,000	Christo-Paganism	<1%	1	5093
Totonaco, Northern	New Testament	Totonaco, Northern	15,000	Christo-Paganism	<1%	1	5094
Totonaco, Oxumatlan		Totonaco, Oxumatlan	1,000	Christo-Paganism	0%	1	5095
Totonaco, Papantla	portions	Totonaco, Papantla	50,000	Christo-Paganism	<1%	1	5096
Totonaco, Sierra	New Testament	Totonaco, Sierra	100,000	Christo-Paganism	<1%	1	5097
Totonaco, Yecuatla	none	Spanish	500	Christo-Paganism	0%	1	5098
Trique, San Juan Copala	portions	Trique, San Juan Copala	8,000	Christo-Paganism	<1%	1	5099
Tubar	none	Tubar	100	Christo-Paganism	0%	1	5100
Tzeltal, Bachajon	New Testament	Tzeltal, Bachajon	20,000	Christo-Paganism	<1%	1	5101
Tzeltal, Highland	New Testament	Tzeltal, Highland	25,000	Christo-Paganism	<1%	1	5102
Yaquis	portions	Yaqui	14,000	Christo-Paganism	<1%	5	317
Yucateco	New Testament	Yucateco	500,000	Christo-Paganism	<1%	1	5105
Zapoteco, C Sola De Vega	portions	Zapoteco, C Sola De Vega	3,400	Christo-Paganism	<1%	1	6525
Zapoteco, Choapan	portions	Zapoteco, Choapan	10,000	Christo-Paganism	<1%	1	6528
Zapoteco, E Miahuatlan	portions	Zapoteco, E Miahuatlan	9,000	Christo-Paganism	<1%	1	6529
Zapoteco, E Ocotlan	portions	Zapoteco, E Ocotlan	7,000	Christo-Paganism	<1%	1	6530
Zapoteco, E Tlacolula	none	Zapoteco, E Tlacolula	5,000	Christo-Paganism	0%	1	6531
Zapoteco, E Zimatlan	portions	Zapoteco, E Zimatlan	5,000	Christo-Paganism	<1%	1	6532
Zapoteco, Isthmus	New Testament	Zapoteco, Isthmus	90,000	Christo-Paganism	<1%	1	6533
Zapoteco, Mazaltepec	none	Zapoteco, Mazaltepec	nr	Christo-Paganism	0%	1	6535
Zapoteco, Miahuatlan	New Testament	Zapoteco, Miahuatlan	10,000	Christo-Paganism	<1%	1	6534
Zapoteco, Mitla	New Testament	Zapoteco, Mitla	15,000	Christo-Paganism	<1%	1	6526
Zapoteco, N Isthmus	portions	Zapoteco, N Isthmus	7,000	Christo-Paganism	<1%	1	6538
Zapoteco, N Ocotlan	none	Zapoteco, N Ocotlan	6,000	Christo-Paganism	0%	1	6539
Zapoteco, N Villa Alta	New Testament	Zapoteco, N Villa Alta	15,000	Christo-Paganism	<1%	1	6540

NAME	SCRIPTURE	LANGUAGE	GROUP SIZE	PRIMARY RELIGION	% CHR	VOL V	UP	ID
Zapoteco, NE Miahuatlan	none	Zapoteco, NE Miahuatlan	2,000	Christo-Paganism	0%	1		6536
Zapoteco, NE Yautepec	none	Zapoteco, NE Yautepec	2,000	Christo-Paganism	0%	1		6537
Zapoteco, NW Tehuantepec	none	Zapoteco, NW Tehuantepec	5,000	Christo-Paganism	0%	1		6541
Zapoteco, Pochutla	none	Zapoteco, Pochutla	2,000	Christo-Paganism	0%	1		6542
Zapoteco, S Ejutla	none	Zapoteco, S Ejutla	2,000	Christo-Paganism	0%	1		6548
Zapoteco, S Villa Alta	portions	Zapoteco, S Villa Alta	8,000	Christo-Paganism	<1%	1		6549
Zapoteco, SC Zinatlan	none	Zapoteco, SC Zinatlan	nr	Christo-Paganism	0%	1		6546
Zapoteco, SE Miahuatlan	none	Zapoteco, SE Miahuatlan	4,000	Christo-Paganism	0%	1		6547
Zapoteco, SW Ixtlan	portions	Zapoteco, SW Ixtlan	10,000	Christo-Paganism	0%	1		6550
Zapoteco, Strra De Juarez	New Testament	Zapoteco, Srra De Juarez	8,000	Christo-Paganism	<1%	1		6545
Zapoteco, Stgo Xanica	none	Zapoteco, Stgo Xanica	4,000	Christo-Paganism	0%	1		6543
Zapoteco, Sto Dom Albarr	none	Zapoteco, Sto Dom Albarr	2,000	Christo-Paganism	0%	1		6544
Zapoteco, Tabaa	New Testament	Zapoteco, Tabaa	5,000	Christo-Paganism	<1%	1		6527
Zapoteco, Villa Alta	New Testament	Zapoteco, Villa Alta	3,000	Christo-Paganism	<1%	1		6551
Zapoteco, W Miahuatlan	none	Zapoteco, W Miahuatlan	3,000	Christo-Paganism	0%	1		6552
Zapoteco, W Ocotlan	portions	Zapoteco, W Ocotlan	20,000	Christo-Paganism	<1%	1		6553
Zapoteco, W Sola de Vega	none	Zapoteco, W Sola de Vega	3,000	Christo-Paganism	0%	1		6554
Zapoteco, W Tlacolula	portions	Zapoteco, W Tlacolula	32,000	Christo-Paganism	<1%	1		6555
Zapoteco, W Yautepec	none	Zapoteco, W Yautepec	2,000	Christo-Paganism	0%	1		6556
Zapoteco, W Zinatlan	none	Zapoteco, W Zinatlan	2,000	Christo-Paganism	0%	1		6557
Zapoteco, Yalalag	none	Zapoteco, Yalalag	6,000	Christo-Paganism	0%	1		6558
Zinacantecos	portions	Tzotzil, Zinacanteco		Christo-Paganism	3%	7	79	95
Zoque, Chinalapa	none	Zoque, Chinalapa	6,000	Christo-Paganism	<1%	1		5106
Zoque, Copainala	New Testament	Zoque, Copainala	6,000	Christo-Paganism	<1%	1		5107
Zoque, Francisco Leon	New Testament	Zoque, Francisco Leon	10,000	Christo-Paganism	<1%	1		5108
Zoque, Tabasco	New Testament	Zoque, Tabasco	400	Christo-Paganism	<1%	1		5109

Morocco

NAME	SCRIPTURE	LANGUAGE	GROUP SIZE	PRIMARY RELIGION	% CHR	VOL V	UP	ID
Shilha	not reported	Shilha	3,000,000	Islam-Animist	0%	1		5388
**Shluh Berbers	none	Tashilhait	2,000,000	Islam-Animist	0%	5		4028
Tamazight	portions	Tamazight	1,800,000	Islam-Animist	0%	1		5389

NAME	SCRIPTURE	LANGUAGE	GROUP SIZE	PRIMARY RELIGION	% CHR	VOL V	UP ID

Mozambique

NAME	SCRIPTURE	LANGUAGE	GROUP SIZE	PRIMARY RELIGION	% CHR	VOL V	UP ID
Chopi	portions	Chopi	400,000	Animism	<1%	1	5390
Chuabo	none	Chuabo	250,000	Animism	9%	4	566
Kunda	none	Kunda	60,000	Animism	0%	1	5391
Lomue	New Testament	not reported	1,000,000	Animism	9%	4	564
Makua	portions	Makua	1,200,000	Animism	10%	4	565
Maviha	none	Maviha	70,000	Animism	0%	1	5392
Nyungue	portions	Nyungue	700,000	Animism	<1%	1	5393
Podzo	portions	Podzo	45,000	Animism	0%	1	5394
Ronga	Bible	Ronga	400,000	Animism	0%	1	5395
Sena	portions	Sena	85,000	Animism	0%	1	5396
Tonga	NT,portions	Tonga	10,000	Animism	<1%	1	5397
Tsonga	Bible	Tsonga	1,500,000	Animism	<1%	1	5398
Tswa	Bible	Tswa	200,000	Animism	0%	1	5399
Yao	Bible	Yao	220,000	Islam	12%	5	143
Zimbabwean Refugees	+not reported	Tribal Languages	170,000	Animism	nr%	4 83	9032

Namibia

NAME	SCRIPTURE	LANGUAGE	GROUP SIZE	PRIMARY RELIGION	% CHR	VOL V	UP ID
Bushmen (Heikum)	none	Heikum	16,000	Animism	6%	4	563
*Bushmen (Kung)	none	Xu	10,000	Animism	6%	6 79	562
Herero	NT,portions	Dhimba	40,000	Animism	<1%	1	5400
Kwanbi	New Testament	Kwanbi	30,000	Animism	<1%	1	5401
Kwanyana	NT,portions	Kwanyana	150,000	Animism	<1%	1	5402
Nana	Bible	Nana	10,000	Animism	<1%	1	5403

NAME	SCRIPTURE	LANGUAGE	GROUP SIZE	PRIMARY RELIGION	% CHR	VOL V	UP ID
San	none	San	6,000	Animism	0%	1	5404
Tswana	Bible	Tswana	11,000	Animism	<1%	1	5405
Xu	portions	Xu	8,000	Animism	<1%	1	5406

Nepal

NAME	SCRIPTURE	LANGUAGE	GROUP SIZE	PRIMARY RELIGION	% CHR	VOL V	UP ID
Awadhi	none	Awadhi	317,000	Hindu-Buddhist	0%	1	6501
*Bhojpuri	portions	Bhojpuri	810,000	Hinduism	1%	4	670
Bote-Majhi	none	Bote-Majhi	6,000	Buddhist-Animist	0%	1	6502
Byangsi	none	Byangsi	2,000	Buddhist-Animist	0%	1	6503
Chaudangsi	none	Chaudangsi	2,000	Buddhist-Animist	0%	1	6504
Chepang	portions	Chepang	10,000	Buddhist-Animist	0%	1	6505
Darai	portions	Darai	3,000	Buddhist-Animist	0%	1	6506
Darmiya	none	Darmiya	2,000	Buddhist-Animist	0%	1	6507
Dhimal	none	Dhimal	8,000	Buddhist-Animist	0%	1	6508
Ghale Gurung	portions	Ghale Gurung	10,000	Buddhist-Animist	0%	1	6509
Gurung	portions	Gurung	172,000	Hinduism	0%	5	1208
Janggali	none	Janggali	9,000	Buddhist-Animist	0%	1	6510
Jirel	portions	Jirel	3,000	Buddhist-Animist	0%	1	6511
Khan	portions	Khan	40,000	Buddhist-Animist	0%	1	6512
Lhomi	portions	Lhomi	10,000	Buddhist-Animist	0%	1	6513
**Magar	none	Magar	300,000	Hindu-Animist	1%	4	395
Maithili	portions	Maithili	1,000,000	Hindu-Animist	0%	4	398
Majhi	none	Majhi	6,000	Buddhist-Animist	0%	1	6514
Newari in Kathmandu	+portions	Newari	100,000	Buddhism	<1%	5 82	5030
*Newari	portions	Newari	500,000	Hindu-Buddhist	0%	3	660
Palpa	New Testament	Paipa	3,000	Buddhist-Animist	0%	3	6515
Rai	none	Rai	232,000	Hindu-Buddhist	0%	3	663
*Rai, Danuwar	none	Danuwar Rai	12,000	Hindu-Animist	0%	3	661
Rai, Khaling	portions	Rai; Khaling	10,000	Buddhist-Animist	0%	1	6516
Rai, Kulunge	none	Rai; Kulunge	10,000	Buddhist-Animist	0%	1	6524
Rai, Thulunge	none	Rai; Thulunge	25,000	Buddhist-Animist	0%	1	6517

REGISTRY OF THE UNREACHED

NAME	SCRIPTURE	LANGUAGE	GROUP SIZE	PRIMARY RELIGION	% CHR	VOL V	UP ID
Rajbansi	none	Rajbansi	15,000	Hindu-Animist	0%	3	659
Rangkas	none	Rangkas	600	Buddhist-Animist	0%	1	6518
**Santhali	Bible	Santhali	nr	Animism	3%	4	669
*Sherpa	none	Sherpa	20,000	Buddhism	0%	3	671
Sunwar	portions	Sunwar	20,000	Buddhist-Animist	0%	1	6519
Syuwa	portions	Syuwa	4,000	Buddhist-Animist	0%	1	6520
*Tanang	none	Tanang	nr	Hindu-Buddhist	<1%	3	666
Thakali	none	Thakali	4,000	Buddhist-Animist	0%	1	6521
Thami	none	Thami	9,000	Buddhist-Animist	0%	1	6522
Tharu	portions	Bhojpuri	495,000	Hinduism	<1%	5	1064
Yakha	none	Yakha	1,000	Buddhist-Animist	0%	1	6523

Netherlands

NAME	SCRIPTURE	LANGUAGE	GROUP SIZE	PRIMARY RELIGION	% CHR	VOL V	UP ID
Ambonese	Bible	Ambonese	30,000	Animism	2%	4	67
Amsterdam Boat Dwellers	Bible	Dutch	8,000	Secularism	0%	3	4159
*Chinese in Amsterdam	Bible	Cantonese	15,000	Unknown	1%	4	735
*Chinese in Holland	Bible	Mandarin	35,000	Unknown	1%	3	734
Dead-End Kids - Amsterdam	+Bible	Dutch	30,000	Secularism	0%	6 82	5034

New Zealand

NAME	SCRIPTURE	LANGUAGE	GROUP SIZE	PRIMARY RELIGION	% CHR	VOL V	UP ID
*Chinese in New Zealand	Bible	Cantonese	13,000	Traditional Chinese	4%	4	752

NAME	SCRIPTURE	LANGUAGE	GROUP SIZE	PRIMARY RELIGION	% CHR	VOL	UP ID
Nicaragua							
Miskito	NT,portions	Miskito	20,000	Christo-Paganism	<1%	1	5110
Sumu	none	Sumu	2,000	Christo-Paganism	0%	1	5111
Niger							
Dyerma	New Testament	Dyerma	1,000,000	Islam-Animist	1%	6 80	4014
Kanembu	none	Kanembu	2,000	Islam-Animist	0%	1	5407
Kurfei	none	Hausa	50,000	Animism	<1%	4	561
Mauri	none	Hausa	100,000	Animism	<1%	4	560
Songhai	New Testament	Songhai	93,000	Islam-Animist	<1%	1	5408
Teda	none	Teda	120,000	Islam-Animist	<1%	1	5409
Tuareg	not reported	Tuanachek	200,000	Islam	<1%	6 79	46
Nigeria							
Abanyom	none	Abanyom	4,000	Animism	<1%	1	2311
Abong	none	Abong	1,000	Islam	<1%	1	2312
Abua	New Testament	Abua	24,000	Animism	<1%	1	2313
Achipa	none	Achipa	4,000	Islam	<1%	1	2314
*Afaua	none	Afanci	10,000	Animism	1%	6 80	559

653

NAME	SCRIPTURE	LANGUAGE	GROUP SIZE	PRIMARY RELIGION	% CHR	VOL V	UP ID
**Afo	none	Eloyi	25,000	Animism	1%	6	80 558
Agoi	none	Agoi	4,000	Animism	<1%	1	2315
Aguagwune	portions	Aguagwune	20,000	Animism	<1%	1	2316
Ake	none	Ake	300	Animism	<1%	1	2317
Akpa-Yache	none	Akpa-Yache	15,000	Animism	<1%	1	2318
Alago	none	Alago	35,000	Animism	2%	5	1058
Alege	none	Alege	1,000	Animism	<1%	1	2319
Amo	none	Amo	4,000	Animism	<1%	1	2320
Anaang	New Testament	Anaang	246,000	Animism	<1%	1	2321
Angas	portions	Angas	100,000	Animism	<1%	1	2322
Ankwe	Bible	Ankwai	10,000	Animism	<1%	4	557
Arawa	portions	Hausa	200,000	Islam	1%	4	644
Aten	portions	Aten	4,000	Islam	<1%	1	2323
Ayu	none	Ayu	4,000	Islam	<1%	1	2324
**Babur Thali	New Testament	Bura (Babur)	75,000	Animism	3%	6	80 1057
Bachama	portions	Bachama	20,000	Islam	<1%	1	2325
**Bachelors in Lagos	+Bible	Tribal Languages	26,000	Secularism	nr%	6	82 5013
Bada	none	Bada	10,000	Animism	<1%	1	2326
Bade	none	Bade	100,000	Islam	<1%	1	2327
Bali	none	Bali	1,000	Islam-Animist	<1%	1	2328
Bambuka	none	Bambuka	10,000	Islam	<1%	1	2329
Bandawa-Minda	none	Bandawa-Minda	10,000	Islam	<1%	1	2330
Banga	none	Banga	8,000	Islam	<1%	1	2331
Bariba	portions	Bariba	55,000	Islam-Animist	<1%	1	7041
Basakomo	portions	Basakomo	60,000	Animism	12%	4	550
Bashar	none	not reported	20,000	Islam-Animist	<1%	1	2333
**Bassa	NT,portions	Bassa	100,000	Animism	8%	5	1056
Bata	none	Bata	30,000	Islam-Animist	<1%	1	2334
Batu	none	Batu	25,000	Islam	<1%	1	2335
Baushi	none	Baushi	3,000	Islam	<1%	1	2336
Bekwarra	portions	Bekwarra	34,000	Animism	<1%	1	2337
Berom	portions	Berom	116,000	Animism	<1%	1	2338
Bette-Bende	portions	Bette-Bende	40,000	Animism	<1%	1	2339
Bile	none	Bile	1,000	Islam-Animist	<1%	1	2340
Binawa	none	Binawa	2,000	Islam	<1%	1	2341
Bitare	none	Bitare	3,000	Islam-Animist	<1%	1	2342

NAME	SCRIPTURE	LANGUAGE	GROUP SIZE	PRIMARY RELIGION	% CHR	VOL V	UP ID
Boghom	portions	Boghom	50,000	Animism	<1%	1	2343
Bokyi	New Testament	Bokyi	44,000	Animism	<1%	1	2344
Bole	none	Bole	32,000	Islam	<1%	1	2345
Buduna	none	Buduna	80,000	Islam	<1%	1	2346
Bunu	none	Bunu	150,000	Animism	<1%	4	549
Burak	portions	Burak	2,000	Islam	<1%	1	2347
Busa	+portions	Busa (Bokobarn Akiba)	50,000	Islam	1%	6 80	1055
Butawa	none	Buta	20,000	Islam	0%	5	548
Chadian Refugees		Arabic	3,000	Islam	<1%	4 83	9043
Chakfien-Mushere	none	Chakfien-Mushere	5,000	Animism	<1%	1	2348
Chamba Daka	portions	Chamba Daka	66,000	Islam-Animist	<1%	1	2349
Chamba Leko	none	Chamba Leko	30,000	Islam-Animist	<1%	1	2350
Chawai	portions	Chawai	30,000	Animism	<1%	4	547
Chip	none	Chip	6,000	Animism	<1%	1	2351
Chokobo	none	Chokobo	400	Animism	<1%	1	2352
Dadiya	none	Dadiya	2,000	Islam	<1%	1	2353
*Daka	Bible	Dakanci	10,000	Animism	3%	4	546
Dass	none	Dass	9,000	Islam-Animist	<1%	1	2354
Degena	none	Degeme	10,000	Animism	<1%	1	2355
Deno	none	Deno	10,000	Islam	<1%	1	2356
Dera	portions	Dera	20,000	Islam	<1%	1	2357
*Dghwede	portions	Zighvana(Dghwede)	13,000	Animism	1%	5	1179
Dirim	none	Dirim	11,000	Islam-Animist	<1%	1	2358
Dirya	none	Dirya	4,000	Islam	<1%	1	2359
Duguri	none	Duguri	12,000	Islam	<1%	1	2360
Duguza	none	Duguza	2,000	Islam	<1%	1	2361
**Duka	none	Dukanci	10,000	Animism	1%	5	1054
Dyerma	New Testament	Dyerma	50,000	Islam	<1%	1	2362
Ebira	portions,NT	Ebira	325,000	Islam-Animist	<1%	1	2363
Edo	Bible	Edo	430,000	Animism	<1%	1	2364
Efik	none	Efik	30,000	Animism	<1%	1	2365
Efutop	New Testament	Efutop	10,000	Animism	<1%	1	2366
Eggon	none	Eggon	80,000	Animism	12%	5	146
Ejagham	New Testament	Ejaghan	100,000	Animism	<1%	1	2368
Ekajuk	none	Ekajuk	15,000	Animism	<1%	1	2369
Eket	New Testament	Eket	22,000	Animism	<1%	1	2370

REGISTRY OF THE UNREACHED

NAME	SCRIPTURE	LANGUAGE	GROUP SIZE	PRIMARY RELIGION	% CHR	V	VOL	UP ID
Ekpeye	none	Ekpeye	30,000	Animism	<1%	1		2371
Eleme	none	Eleme	16,000	Animism	<1%	1		2372
Emai-Iuleha-Ora	portions	Emai-Iuleha-Ora	48,000	Animism	<1%	1		2373
Engenni	New Testament	Engenni	10,000	Animism	<1%	1		2374
Epie	none	Epie	12,000	Animism	<1%	1		2375
Esan	portions	Esan	200,000	Animism	<1%	1		2376
Etulo	none	Etulo	3,000	Animism	<1%	1		2377
Evant	none	Evant	5,000	Animism	<1%	1		2378
**Fakai	none	Faka	15,000	Animism	<1%	5		1053
**Fali	none	Fali	25,000	Animism	2%	1		1052
Fyam	none	Fyan	14,000	Animism	<1%	1		2379
Fyer	none	Fyer	3,000	Animism	<1%	1		2380
Gaanda	not reported	not reported	10,000	Nominal Christian	<1%	1		2381
Gade	none	Gade	25,000	Animism	<1%	4		545
Galambi	none	Galambi	1,000	Islam	<1%	1		2382
Gbari	New Testament	Gbari	500,000	Animism	2%	6	80	158
Gbaya	New Testament	Gbaya	350,000	Islam	<1%	1		2384
Geji	none	Geji	3,000	Islam	<1%	1		2385
Gera	none	Gera	13,000	Islam	<1%	1		2386
Geruma	none	Geruma	5,000	Islam	<1%	1		2387
Ghotuo	none	Ghotuo	9,000	Animism	<1%	1		2388
**Glavda	not reported	Glavda	19,000	Animism	4%	5		1174
Goemai	none	Goemai	80,000	Animism	<1%	1		2389
Gokana	none	Gokana	54,000	Animism	<1%	1		2390
Gude	portions	Gude	40,000	Animism	<1%	1		7042
Gudu	none	Gudu	1,000	Animism	<1%	1		2392
Guduf	portions	Guduf	21,000	Animism	<1%	1		2393
Gure-Kahugu	none	Gure-Kahugu	5,000	Islam	<1%	1		2394
Guruntum-Mbaaru	none	Guruntum-Mbaaru	10,000	Islam	<1%	5		1113
Gwandara	none	Gwandara	25,000	Animism	<1%	1		2395
Gwari Matai	New Testament	Gwari Matai	200,000	Islam	<1%	1		2397
***Higi	New Testament	Higi	150,000	Animism	7%	5		1118
Huana	none	Huana	20,000	Islam	<1%	1		7043
Hyan	portions	Hyan	20,000	Islam	<1%	1		2398
Ibaji	none	Ibaji	60,000	Animism	<1%	4		544
Ibibio	none	Ibibio	2,000,000	Animism	<1%	1		2399

NAME	SCRIPTURE	LANGUAGE	GROUP SIZE	PRIMARY RELIGION	% CHR	V	VOL UP ID
Icen	none	Icen	7,000	Islam-Animist	<1%	1	2400
Idoma	New Testament	Idoma	300,000	Animism	<1%	1	2402
Idoma, North	New Testament	Idoma, North	56,000	Animism	<1%	1	2403
Igala	Bible	Igala	350,000	Animism	<1%	1	2404
Igbira	portions	Igbirra	400,000	Islam-Animist	14%	6 80	543
Igede	NT,portions	Igede	70,000	Animism	<1%	1	2405
Ihceve	none	Icheve	5,000	Animism	<1%	1	7044
Ijo, Central-Western	portions	Ijo	340,000	Animism	<1%	1	2406
Ijo, Northeast	portions	Ijo	400,000	Animism	<1%	1	2407
Ijo, Northeast Central	none	Ijo	8,000	Animism	<1%	1	2408
Ikulu	none	Ikulu	6,000	Islam	<1%	1	2409
Ikwere	none	Ikwere	200,000	Animism	<1%	1	7045
Irigwe	portions	Irigwe	15,000	Animism	<1%	1	7046
Isekiri	none	Isekiri	33,000	Animism	<1%	1	2412
**Ishans	portions	Esan	25,000	Nominal Christian	16%	5	4033
Isoko	Bible	Isoko	20,000	Animism	<1%	1	2413
Ivbie North-Okpela-Atte	none	Ivbie North-Okpela-Atte	20,000	Animism	<1%	1	2414
Iyon	none	Iyon	2,000	Animism	<1%	1	2415
Izarek	portions	Izarek	30,000	Animism	<1%	1	2416
**Izi	NT,portions	Izi	200,000	Animism	11%	4	89
Jaba	portions	Jaba	60,000	Animism	<1%	4	542
Janjo	none	Janjo	6,000	Animism	<1%	1	2417
Jara	none	Jara	40,000	Islam	<1%	1	2418
**Jarawa	portions	Jaranchi	150,000	Animism	6%	5	541
Jera	none	Jera	23,000	Islam	<1%	1	2419
Jerawa	portions	not reported	70,000	Animism	<1%	4	540
*Jibu	portions	Jibu,Jibanci	20,000	Animism	1%	5	1172
Jimbin	none	Jimbin	2,000	Islam	<1%	1	2420
Jukun	portions	not reported	20,000	Animism	<1%	4	539
Kadara	Bible	Kadara	40,000	Animism	9%	5	538
Kagoma	none	Kagoma	6,000	Islam	<1%	1	2421
Kaibu	none	Kaibu	700	Islam	<1%	1	2422
Kaka	none	Kaka	2,000	Islam	<1%	1	2423
Kanantan	none	Kadara	5,000	Animism	<1%	4	537
*Kambari	portions	Kanbarci	100,000	Animism	6%	6 80	1173
Kano	none	Kano	3,000	Islam	<1%	1	2424

NAME	SCRIPTURE	LANGUAGE	GROUP SIZE	PRIMARY RELIGION	% CHR	VOL V	UP ID
*Kamuku	none	Kamuku	20,000	Animism	3%	6 80	536
Kana	Bible	Kana	90,000	Animism	<1%	1	2425
Kanuri	portions	Kanuri Dialects	3,000,000	Islam	<1%	6 80	4007
Karekare	none	Karekare	39,000	Islam	<1%	1	2427
Kariya	none	Kariya	2,000	Islam	<1%	1	2428
Katab	portions	Katab	30,000	Islam	<1%	1	2429
Khana	not reported	Khana	90,000	Unknown	1%	5	1122
Kilba	portions	Kilba	80,000	Islam	<1%	1	2430
Kirifi	none	Krifi	14,000	Islam	<1%	1	2431
Koenoem	none	Koenoem	3	Animism	<1%	1	2432
Kofyar	none	Kofyar	40,000	Animism	<1%	1	2433
Kohumono	none	Kohumono	12,000	Animism	<1%	1	2434
Koma	none	Koma	15,000	Animism	<1%	1	2435
Kono	none	Kono	2,000	Islam	<1%	1	2436
Koro	New Testament	Koro	35,000	Animism	1%	5	572
Korop	none	Korop	10,000	Animism	<1%	1	2437
Kuda-Chano	none	Kuda-Chano	4	Islam	<1%	1	2438
Kugbo	none	Kugbo	2,000	Animism	<1%	1	2439
Kukele	NT,portions	Kukele	32,000	Animism	<1%	1	2440
Kulere	none	Kulere	8,000	Animism	<1%	1	2441
Kulung	portions	Kulung	15,000	Islam-Animist	<1%	1	2442
Kushi	none	Kushi	4,000	Islam	<1%	1	2443
Kuteb	portions	Kuteb	26,000	Islam	<1%	1	2444
Kuturmi	none	Kuturmi	3,000	Islam	<1%	1	2445
Kuzamani	none	Kuzamani	1,000	Islam	<1%	1	2446
Kwa	none	Kwa	1,000	Islam	<1%	1	2447
Kyibaku	none	Kyibaku	20,000	Islam	<1%	1	2448
Laamang	none	Laamang	40,000	Islam	<1%	1	2449
Lakka	none	Lakka	500	Islam	<1%	1	2450
Lame	none	Lame	2,000	Islam	<1%	1	2451
Laru	none	Laru	1,000	Islam	<1%	1	2452
Lebgo	none	Lebgo	30,000	Animism	<1%	1	2453
Lo	none	Lo	2,000	Animism	<1%	1	2454
Longuda	New Testament	Longuda	32,000	Islam	<1%	1	2455
Lotsu-Piri	none	Lotsu-Piri	2,000	Islam	<1%	1	2456
Lungu	none	Lungu	10,000	Animism	<1%	4	571

NAME	SCRIPTURE	LANGUAGE	GROUP SIZE	PRIMARY RELIGION	% CHR	VOL V	UP	ID
Madda	none	Madda	30,000	Animism	<1%	1		2457
***Maguzawa	Bible	Hausa	100,000	Animism	1%	6	79	202
Mana	none	Mana	20,000	Animism	<1%	1		2458
Mandara	portions	Mandara	20,000	Islam	<1%	1		2459
Marghi Central	portions	Marghi Central	135,000	Islam	<1%	1		2460
Matakam	New Testament	Matakam	2,000	Islam	<1%	1		2461
Mbe	none	Mbe	14,000	Animism	<1%	1		2462
Mbembe	none	Mbembe	60,000	Animism	<1%	1		2464
Mbembe (Tigong)	none	Mbembe	3,000	Animism	<1%	1		2463
Mboi	none	Mboi	3,000	Islam	<1%	1		2465
Mbula-Buazza	none	Mbula-Buazza	8,000	Islam	<1%	1		2466
Migili	none	Migili	10,000	Animism	<1%	1		2467
Miya	none	Miya	5,000	Islam	<1%	5		1175
Mober	none	Mober	45,000	Islam	<1%	1		2468
Montol	none	Montol	10,000	Animism	<1%	1		2469
Mumbake	none	Mumbake	10,000	Islam	<1%	1		2470
Munuye	Bible	Munuye	200,000	Animism	1%	5		570
Nandu-Tari	none	Nandu-Tari	4,000	Islam	<1%	1		2471
Naraguta	none	Naraguta	3,000	Animism	<1%	1		2472
Nde-Nsele-Nta	none	Nde-Nsele-Nta	10,000	Animism	<1%	1		2473
Ndoe	none	Ndoe	3,000	Animism	<1%	1		2474
**Ndoro	none	Ndoro	10,000	Animism	6%	5		1176
**Ngano	none	Ngano	18,000	Animism	8%	4		569
Ngizim	none	Ngizim	40,000	Islam	<1%	1		2475
Nguoi	none	Nguoi	1,000	Islam	<1%	1		2476
Ninzam	none	Ninzam	35,000	Islam	<1%	1		2477
Nkem-Nkum	none	Nkem-Nkum	16,700	Animism	<1%	1		2478
Numana-Nunku-Gwantu	none	Numana-Nunku-Gwantu	15,000	Islam	<1%	1		2479
Nungu	none	Nungu	25,000	Animism	<1%	1		2480
**Nupe	Bible	Nupe	600,000	Islam	2%	5		17
Nzanyi	none	Nzanyi	14,000	Islam	<1%	1		2481
Obanliku	none	Obanliku	20,000	Animism	<1%	1		2482
Obolo	none	Obolo	70,000	Animism	<1%	1		2483
Odual	New Testament	Odual	9,000	Animism	<1%	1		2484
Odut	none	Odut	700	Animism	<1%	1		2485
Ogbia	none	Ogbia	22,000	Animism	<1%	1		2486

NAME	SCRIPTURE	LANGUAGE	GROUP SIZE	PRIMARY RELIGION	% CHR	VOL V	UP ID
Okobo	none	Okobo	11,000	Animism	<1%	1	2487
Okpamheri	none	Okpamheri	30,000	Animism	<1%	1	2488
Olulumo-Ikom	none	Olulumo-Ikom	10,000	Animism	<1%	1	2489
Oring	none	Oring	25,000	Animism	<1%	1	2490
Oron	none	Oron	50,000	Animism	<1%	1	2491
Otank	none	Otank	3,000	Animism	<1%	1	2492
Pai	none	Pai	2,000	Animism	<1%	1	2493
Pero	portions	Pero	20,000	Islam	<1%	1	2494
Piti	none	Piti	2,000	Islam	<1%	1	2495
Piya	portions	Piya	3,000	Islam	<1%	1	2496
Polci	none	Polci	6,000	Islam	<1%	1	2497
Pongu	none	Pongu	4,000	Islam	<1%	1	2498
Puku-Geeri-Keri-Wipsi	none	Puku-Geeri-Keri-Wipsi	15,000	Islam	<1%	1	2499
Reshe	none	Reshe	30,000	Animism	<1%	1	2500
Roba	none	Roba	50,000	Islam	<1%	1	2501
Rukuba	portions	Rukuba	2,000	Islam	<1%	1	2502
Rumaya	none	Rumaya	2,000	Islam	<1%	1	2503
Ruruma	none	Ruruma	2,000	Islam	<1%	1	2504
Sanga	none	Sanga	5,000	Islam	<1%	1	2505
Sasaru-Enwan Igwe	none	Sasaru-Enwan Igwe	4,000	Animism	<1%	1	2506
Saya	none	Saya	50,000	Islam	<1%	1	2507
Sha	none	Sha	500	Animism	<1%	1	2508
Shanga	none	Shanga	5,000	Animism	0%	4	568
Shuwa Arabic	none	Shuwa Arabic	100,000	Islam	<1%	1	2509
Siri	none	Siri	2,000	Islam	<1%	1	2510
Sukur	none	Sukur	10,000	Islam	<1%	1	2511
Sura	portions	Sura	40,000	Islam	<1%	1	2512
Surubu	none	Surubu	2,000	Islam	<1%	1	2513
Tal	none	Tal	10,000	Islam	<1%	1	2514
Tambas	none	Tambas	3,000	Animism	<1%	1	2515
Tangale	New Testament	Tangale	100,000	Islam	<1%	1	2516
Tarok	portions	Tarok	60,000	Animism	<1%	1	2517
Tera	portions	Tera	46,000	Islam	<1%	1	2518
Tula	portions	Tula	19,000	Islam	<1%	1	2519
Turkwam	none	Turkwam	8,000	Islam	<1%	1	2520
Ukaan	none	Ukaan	18,000	Animism	<1%	1	2544

NAME	SCRIPTURE	LANGUAGE	GROUP SIZE	PRIMARY RELIGION	% CHR	VOL V UP ID
Ukpe-Bayobiri	none	Ukpe-Bayobiri	12,000	Animism	<1% 1	2522
Ukwuani-Aboh	none	Ukwuani-Aboh	150,000	Animism	<1% 1	2523
Urhobo	New Testament	Urhobo	340,000	Animism	<1% 1	2524
Utugwang	none	Utugwang	12,000	Animism	<1% 1	2525
Uvbie	none	Uvbie	6,000	Animism	<1% 1	2526
Uzekwe	none	Uzekwe	5,000	Animism	<1% 1	2527
***Vere	none	Vere	20,000	Animism	9% 5	1177
Vute	none	Vute	1,000	Animism	<1% 1	2528
Waja	portions	Waja	30,000	Islam	<1% 1	2529
*Warjawa	none	Warji	70,000	Animism	<1% 4	595
Won	none	Won	10,000	Islam-Aninist	<1% 1	2530
**Yala	Bible	Yala	60,000	Animism	5% 4	1011
Yandang	none	Yandang	10,000	Islam-Aninist	<1% 1	2531
Yeskwa	none	Yeskwa	13,000	Islam	<1% 1	2532
Yungur	none	Yungur	43,000	Islam	<1% 1	2533
**Zaranda Hill Peoples	not reported	local languages	10,000	Animism	2% 4	1178
Zari	none	Zari	4,000	Islam	<1% 1	2534

Oman

NAME	SCRIPTURE	LANGUAGE	GROUP SIZE	PRIMARY RELIGION	% CHR	VOL V UP ID
Mahri	portions	Mahri	50,000	Animism	<1% 1	2539

Pacific Trust Islands

NAME	SCRIPTURE	LANGUAGE	GROUP SIZE	PRIMARY RELIGION	% CHR	VOL V UP ID
Chamorro	none	Chamorro	15,000	Christo-Paganism	10% 4	1001
Ulithi-Mall	none	Ulithi	2,000	Christo-Paganism	<1% 4	1004
Woleat	none	Woleat	1,000	Christo-Paganism	<1% 4	1003

Pakistan

NAME	SCRIPTURE	LANGUAGE	GROUP SIZE	PRIMARY RELIGION	% CHR	V	UP	ID
*Afghan Refugees (NWFP)	+Bible	Dari	1,835,000	Islam	<1%	4		9004
Ahmadis in Lahore	+Bible	Panjabi	60,000	Islam	0%	6	82	5016
Bagri	none	Bagri	20,000	Hinduism	1%	4		268
Bajania	none	Gujarati Dialect	20,000	Hinduism	1%	6	79	263
Balmiki	not reported	Hindustani	20,000	Hinduism	1%	5		254
**Balti	none	Balti	80,000	Islam	<1%	4		4802
**Bhil	portions	Marwari	800,000	Hinduism	1%	6		35
Brahui	portions	Brahui	745,000	Islam	<1%	5		4049
Chitralis	none	Khuwar	120,000	Islam	0%	6	79	1234
**Gagre	New Testament	Punjabi	40,000	Animism	1%	4		264
**Hunzakut	+none	Burushaski	10,000	Islam	0%	6	79	1236
*Iranian Bahai Refugees	+Bible	Farsi	5,000	Bahaism	<1%	4	83	9024
**Kafirs	none	Kafiristani (Bashgali)	3,000	Animism	<1%	6	79	1233
**Kohli, Kutchi	portions	Gujarati, Koli	50,000	Hinduism	4%	4		258
**Kohli, Parkari	portions	Gujarati, Koli	100,000	Hinduism	5%	4		261
**Kohli, Tharadari	none	Gujarati, Koli	40,000	Hinduism	1%	5		259
**Kohli, Wadiara	portions	Gujarati, Koli	40,000	Hindu-Animist	1%	5		260
**Meghwar	none	Marwari	100,000	Hinduism	1%	6	79	262
Od	none	Odki	40,000	Hinduism	1%	4		265
Sindhi Muslims in Karachi	+Bible	Sindhi	350,000	Islam-Animist	0%	6	82	5036
Sochi	not reported	Sindhi	nr	Hinduism	1%	3		255
Swatis	none	Swati	600,000	Islam	0%	6	79	1232
USSR Kirghiz Refugee Shepherds	+not reported	Turkic	1,200	Islam	0%	4	83	9042
Vagari	none	Gujarati Dialect	30,000	Hinduism	1%	5		267

NAME	SCRIPTURE	LANGUAGE	GROUP SIZE	PRIMARY RELIGION	% CHR V	VOL UP ID

Panama

NAME	SCRIPTURE	LANGUAGE	GROUP SIZE	PRIMARY RELIGION	% CHR V	VOL UP ID
Buglere	none	Buglere	2,000	Christo-Paganism	<1% 1	5112
**Chinese in Panama	Bible	Spanish	25,000	Traditional Chinese	1% 3	4140
**Teribe	portions	Teribe	1,000	Christo-Paganism	15% 5	1203

Papua New Guinea

NAME	SCRIPTURE	LANGUAGE	GROUP SIZE	PRIMARY RELIGION	% CHR V	VOL UP ID
Abau	NT,portions	Abau	3,000	Animism	<1% 1	5900
Abie	portions	Abie	600	Animism	<1% 1	5901
Abulas	portions	Abulas	33,000	Animism	<1% 1	5902
Adjora	none	Adjora	2,000	Animism	<1% 1	5903
Aeka	none	Aeka	3,000	Animism	<1% 1	5904
Agarabi	portions	Agarabi	12,000	Animism	<1% 1	5905
Agob	none	Agob	1,000	Animism	0% 1	5906
Aiku	none	Aiku	800	Animism	<1% 1	5907
Aiome	none	Aiome	900	Animism	<1% 1	5908
Aion	none	Aion	800	Animism	<1% 1	5909
Akrukay	none	Akrukay	200	Animism	<1% 1	5910
Alamblak	portions	Alamblak	2,000	Animism	<1% 1	5911
Alatil	none	Alatil	400	Animism	0% 1	5912
Alauagat	none	Alauagat	300	Animism	<1% 1	5913
Ama	portions	Ama	400	Animism	0% 1	5914
Anaimon	none	Anaimon	400	Animism	<1% 1	5915
Amanab	portions	Amanab	3,000	Animism	<1% 1	5916
Ambasi	none	Ambasi	500	Animism	<1% 1	5917

NAME	LANGUAGE	SCRIPTURE	GROUP SIZE	PRIMARY RELIGION	% CHR	VOL V	UP ID
**Ampeeli	Ampale	portions	1,000	Christo-Paganism	1%	4	411
Anto	Anto	none	200	Animism	<1%	1	5918
Andarum	Andarun	none	700	Animism	<1%	1	5919
Anem	Anem	none	1,000	Animism	<1%	1	5920
Angaataha	Angaataha	portions	800	Animism	<1%	1	5921
Angal Heneng, South	Angal Heneng, South	portions	15,000	Animism	<1%	1	5922
Angal Heneng, West	Angal Heneng, West	New Testament	25,000	Animism	<1%	1	5923
Angal, East	Angal, East	portions	10,000	Animism	<1%	1	5924
Angaua	Angaua	none	2,000	Animism	<1%	1	5925
Anggor	Anggor	portions	1,000	Animism	<1%	1	5926
Angoram	Angoram	none	4,000	Animism	0%	1	5927
Ankave	Ankave	none	2,000	Animism	0%	1	5928
Anor	Anor	none	600	Animism	<1%	1	5929
Anuki	Anuki	none	500	Animism	<1%	1	5930
Arafundi	Arafundi	none	1,000	Animism	0%	1	5931
Arapesh, Bumbita	Arapesh, Bumbita	none	2,000	Animism	<1%	1	5932
Arapesh, Mountain	Arapesh, Mountain	portions	5,000	Animism	<1%	1	5933
Arapesh, Muhiang	Arapesh, Muhiang	portions	8,000	Animism	<1%	1	5934
Arawe	Arawe	not reported	2,000	Animism	<1%	1	5935
Arifama-Miniafia	Arifama-Miniafia	portions	2,000	Animism	<1%	1	5936
Arigibi	Arigibi	none		Animism	<1%	1	5937
Arinua	Arinua	none	2,000	Animism	0%	1	5938
Arop	Arop	none	2,000	Animism	<1%	1	5939
Aruop	Aruop	none	500	Animism	0%	1	5940
Asaro	Asaro	NT,portions	12,000	Animism	<1%	1	5941
Asat	Asat	none	700	Animism	<1%	1	5942
Ata	Ata	none	1,000	Animism	<1%	1	5943
Au	Au	portions	4,000	Animism	<1%	1	5944
Aunalei	Aunalei	none	2,000	Animism	0%	1	5945
Auyana	Auyana	portions	7,000	Animism	<1%	1	5946
Awa	Awa	New Testament	2,000	Animism	<1%	1	5947
Awar	Awar	none	600	Animism	<1%	1	5948
Awara	Awara	none	900	Animism	<1%	1	5949
Awin	Awin	portions	7,000	Animism	<1%	1	5950
Azera	Azera	New Testament	400	Animism	<1%	1	5951
Bahinemo	Bahinemo	portions	300	Animism	<1%	1	5952

NAME	SCRIPTURE	LANGUAGE	GROUP SIZE	PRIMARY RELIGION	% CHR	VOL V UP ID
Baibai	none	Baibai	300	Animism	0% 1	5953
Baining	portions	Baining	5,000	Animism	<1% 1	5954
Bali-Vitu	none	Bali-Vitu	7,000	Animism	<1% 1	5955
Ban	none	Ban	600	Animism	0% 1	5956
***Banaro	none	Banaro	3,000	Animism	5% 4	195
Banoni	none	Banoni	1,000	Animism	<1% 1	5957
Barai	portions	Barai	2,000	Animism	<1% 1	5958
Barai	none	Barai	3,000	Animism	<1% 1	5959
Bariji	portions	Bariji	300	Animism	<1% 1	5960
Barim	none	Barim	600	Animism	<1% 1	5961
Barok	none	Barok	1,000	Animism	<1% 1	5962
Baruga	none	Baruga	1,000	Animism	<1% 1	5963
Baruya	portions	Baruya	4,000	Animism	<1% 1	7063
Bau	none	Bau	2,000	Animism	<1% 1	5965
Bauwaki	none	Bauwaki	400	Animism	<1% 1	5966
Bebeli	none	Bebeli	600	Animism	<1% 1	5967
Bembi	none	Bembi	400	Animism	0% 1	5968
Benabena	NT,portions	Benabena	14,000	Animism	<1% 1	5969
Biaka	none	Biaka	400	Animism	<1% 1	5970
Biangai	portions	Biangai	1,000	Animism	<1% 1	5971
Bibling	none	Bibling	2,000	Animism	<1% 1	5972
Biliau	none	Biliau	600	Animism	<1% 1	5973
Bimin	none	Bimin	400	Animism	<1% 1	5974
Binahari	none	Binahari	800	Animism	<1% 1	5975
Binandere	portions	Binandere	3,000	Animism	<1% 1	5976
Bine	portions	Bine	2,000	Animism	<1% 1	5977
Binumarien	portions	Binumarien	200	Animism	<1% 1	5978
Bisis	none	Bisis	400	Animism	0% 1	5979
Bitara	none	Bitara	100	Animism	0% 1	5980
Biyom	none	Biyom	400	Animism	0% 1	5981
Boanaki	none	Boanaki	2,000	Animism	<1% 1	5982
Bohutu	none	Bohutu	1,000	Animism	<1% 1	5983
Boikin	portions	Boikin	31,000	Animism	<1% 1	5984
Bola	New Testament	Bola	5,000	Animism	<1% 1	5985
Bom	none	Bom	1,000	Animism	<1% 1	5986
Bongu	none	Bongu	400	Animism	<1% 1	5987

NAME	SCRIPTURE	LANGUAGE	GROUP SIZE	PRIMARY RELIGION	% CHR	VOL V	UP ID
Bonkiman	none	Bonkiman	300	Animism	<1%	1	5988
Bosavi	none	Bosavi	400	Animism	0%	1	5989
Bosilewa	none	Bosilewa	400	Animism	<1%	1	5990
Bosngun	none	Bosngun	700	Animism	<1%	1	5991
Breri	none	Breri	700	Animism	0%	1	5992
Buang, Central	New Testament	Buang, Central	6,000	Animism	<1%	1	5993
Buang, Manga	New Testament	Buang, Manga	3,000	Animism	<1%	1	5994
Budibud	none	Budibud	200	Animism	<1%	1	5995
Buin	portions	Buin	9,000	Animism	<1%	1	5996
Bukaua	none	Bukaua	5,000	Animism	0%	1	5997
Bulu	none	Bulu	200	Animism	0%	1	5998
Buna	none	Buna	900	Animism	0%	1	5999
Bunabun	none	Bunabun	500	Animism	<1%	1	6000
Bunana	portions	Bunana	5,000	Animism	<1%	1	6001
Burun	none	Burun	3,000	Animism	<1%	1	6002
Busah	none	Busah	200	Animism	0%	1	6003
Buaidoga	portions	Buaidoga	5,000	Animism	<1%	1	6004
Chanbri	none	Chanbri	900	Animism	0%	1	6005
Chenapian	none	Chenapian	200	Animism	0%	1	6006
Chuave	portions	Chuave	20,000	Animism	<1%	1	6007
Dadibi	portions	Dadibi	6,000	Animism	<1%	1	6008
Daga	New Testament	Daga	6,000	Animism	<1%	1	6009
Dahating	none	Dahating	900	Animism	<1%	1	6010
Dani	portions	Dani	1,000	Animism	<1%	1	6011
Daonda	none	Daonda	100	Animism	0%	1	6012
Dawawa	none	Dawawa	2,000	Animism	<1%	1	6013
Dedua	none	Dedua	4,000	Animism	0%	1	6014
Degenan	none	Degenan	500	Animism	0%	1	6015
Dia	none	Dia	2,000	Animism	<1%	1	6016
Dimir	none	Dimir	1,000	Animism	<1%	1	6017
Diodio	none	Diodio	1,000	Animism	<1%	1	6018
Dobu	New Testament	Dobu	8,000	Animism	<1%	1	6019
Doga	none	Doga	200	Animism	<1%	1	6020
Dogoro	none	Dogoro	100	Animism	0%	1	6021
Dom	portions	Dom	9,000	Animism	<1%	1	6022
Domu	none	Domu	500	Animism	<1%	1	6023

NAME	SCRIPTURE	LANGUAGE	GROUP SIZE	PRIMARY RELIGION	% CHR V	VOL	UP ID
Domung	none	Domung	900	Animism	<1%	1	6024
Doromu	none	Doromu	800	Animism	<1%	1	6025
Doura	none	Doura	300	Animism	<1%	1	6026
Duau	none	Duau	7,000	Animism	<1%	1	6027
Duna	New Testament	Duan	11,000	Animism	<1%	1	6028
Edawapi	none	Edawapi	4,000	Animism	0%	1	6029
Eivo	none	Eivo	1,000	Animism	<1%	1	6030
Elkei	none	Elkei	1,000	Animism	<1%	1	6031
Emerun	none	Emerun	500	Animism	0%	1	6032
Emira	none	Emira	4,000	Animism	<1%	1	6033
Endangen	none	Endangen	500	Animism	0%	1	6034
Enga	New Testament	Enga	110,000	Animism	<1%	1	6035
Ewage-Notu	portions	Ewage-Notu	10,000	Animism	<1%	1	6036
Fagululu	none	Fagululu	400	Animism	<1%	1	6037
Faiwol	portions	Faiwol	3,000	Animism	<1%	1	6038
Fas	portions	Fas	2,000	Animism	<1%	1	6039
Fasu	New Testament	Fasu	900	Animism	<1%	1	6040
Finungwan	none	Finungwan	400	Animism	0%	1	6041
Foi	New Testament	Foi	3,000	Animism	<1%	1	6042
Foran	none	Foran	800	Animism	<1%	1	6043
Fore	New Testament	Fore	16,000	Animism	<1%	1	6044
Fuyuge	none	Fuyuge	13,000	Animism	<1%	1	6045
Gadsup	portions	Gadsup	7,000	Animism	<1%	1	6046
Gahuku	New Testament	Gahuku	8,000	Animism	<1%	1	6047
Gaikundi	portions	Gaikundi	700	Animism	<1%	1	6048
Gaina	none	Gaina	1,000	Animism	<1%	1	6049
Gal	none	Gal	200	Animism	<1%	1	6050
Gamei	none	Gamei	900	Animism	<1%	1	6051
Ganglau	none	Ganglau	200	Animism	<1%	1	6052
Garuh	portions	Garuh	2,000	Animism	<1%	1	6053
Garus	none	Garus	2,000	Animism	<1%	1	6054
Garuwahi	none	Garuwahi	200	Animism	<1%	1	6055
Gedaged	New Testament	Gedaged	3,000	Animism	<1%	1	6056
Genagane	none	Genagane	1,000	Animism	0%	1	6057
Gende	none	Gende	8,000	Animism	<1%	1	6058
Gidra	none	Gidra	2,000	Animism	0%	1	6059

NAME	SCRIPTURE	LANGUAGE	GROUP SIZE	PRIMARY RELIGION	% CHR	V	UP	ID
Gimi	portions	Gimi	18,000	Animism	<1%		1	6060
Ginuman	none	Ginuman	800	Animism	<1%		1	6061
Gira	none	Gira	400	Animism	<1%		1	6062
Girawa	none	Girawa	4,000	Animism	<1%		1	6063
Giri	none	Giri	2,000	Animism	<1%		1	6064
Gitua	none	Gitua	500	Animism	<1%		1	6065
Gizra	none	Gizra	600	Animism	<1%		1	6066
Gobasi	none	Gobasi	1,000	Animism	0%		1	6067
Gogodala	New Testament	Gogodala	10,000	Animism	0%		1	6068
Guhu-Samane	New Testament	Guhu-Samane	4,000	Animism	<1%		1	6069
Gumasi	none	Gumasi	300	Animism	<1%		1	6070
Gumine	portions	Gumine	30,000	Animism	<1%		1	6071
Gusap	none	Gusap	400	Animism	<1%		1	6072
Guwot	none	Guwot	1,000	Animism	<1%		1	6073
Gwedena	none	Gwedena	2,000	Animism	<1%		1	6074
Hahon	none	Hahon	2,000	Animism	<1%		1	6075
Halia	New Testament	Halia	11,000	Animism	<1%		1	6076
Hantai	New Testament	Hantai	13,000	Animism	<1%		1	6077
**Hewa	none	Hewa	32,000	Animism	5%	6	79	1238
Hote	none	Hote	2,000	Animism	<1%		1	6078
Hula	New Testament	Hula	3,000	Animism	<1%		1	6079
Huli	New Testament	Huli	54,000	Animism	<1%		1	6080
Humene	none	Humene	400	Animism	<1%		1	6081
Hunjara	New Testament	Hunjara	4,000	Animism	<1%		1	6082
Iatmul	none	Iatmul	8,000	Animism	<1%		1	6083
Idi	none	Idi	900	Animism	0%		1	6084
Igora	none	Igora	800	Animism	<1%		1	6085
Ikobi-Mena	none	Ikobi-Mena	700	Animism	<1%		1	6086
Ikundun	none	Ikundun	900	Animism	<1%		1	6087
Indinogosina	none	Indinogosina	4,000	Animism	0%		1	6088
Ipiko	none	Ipiko	200	Animism	<1%		1	6089
Ipili	not reported	Ipili	6,000	Animism	<1%		1	6090
Irumu	none	Irumu	2,000	Animism	<1%		1	6091
Isebe	none	Isebe	800	Animism	<1%		1	6092
Iwal	portions	Iwal	2,000	Animism	<1%		1	6093
Iwam	portions	Iwam	2,000	Animism	<1%		1	6094

NAME	SCRIPTURE	LANGUAGE	GROUP SIZE	PRIMARY RELIGION	% CHR	VOL v	UP ID
Iwan, Sepik	portions	Iwan, Sepik	4,000	Animism	<1%	1	6095
Jabem	New Testament	Jabem	3,000	Animism	<1%	1	6096
Jinajina	none	Jinajina	500	Animism	<1%	1	6097
Kabadi	none	Kabadi	2,000	Animism	<1%	1	6098
Kaian	none	Kaian	200	Animism	0%	1	6099
Kaiep	none	Kaiep	300	Animism	0%	1	6100
Kairi	portions	Kairi	700	Animism	<1%	1	6101
Kairiru	none	Kairiru		Animism	0%	1	6102
Kakoa	none	Kakoa	3,000	Animism	0%	1	6103
Kakuna-Mamusi	none	Kakuna-Mamusi	7,000	Animism	<1%	1	6104
Kalokalo	none	Kalokalo	3,000	Animism	<1%	1	6105
Kamano	New Testament	Kamano	700	Animism	<1%	1	6106
Kamberataro	none	Kamberataro	47,000	Animism	0%	1	6107
Kanbot	none	Kanbot	700	Animism	<1%	1	6108
Kannum	none	Kannum	4,000	Animism	<1%	1	6109
Kandas	none	Kandas	400	Animism	<1%	1	6110
Kaningra	none	Kaningra	500	Animism	<1%	1	6111
Kanite	New Testament	Kanite	300	Animism	<1%	1	6112
Kanum	none	Kanum	16,000	Animism	<1%	1	6113
Kapin	none	Kapin	300	Animism	0%	1	6114
Kapore	none	Kapore	2,000	Animism	<1%	1	6115
Kapriman	none	Kapriman	600	Animism	0%	1	6116
Kara	none	Kara	1,000	Animism	0%	1	6117
Karam	portions	Karan	2,000	Animism	<1%	1	6118
Karangi	none	Karangi	11,000	Animism	<1%	1	6119
Kare	none	Kare	200	Animism	<1%	1	6120
Karkar	portions	Karkar	300	Animism	<1%	1	6121
Karua	none	Karua	1,000	Animism	<1%	1	6122
Kasua	portions	Kasua	900	Animism	<1%	1	6123
Kate	NT,portions	Kate	1,000	Animism	<1%	1	6124
Katiati	none	Katiati	6,000	Animism	<1%	1	6125
Kaugel	portions	Kaugel	2,000	Animism	<1%	1	6126
Kavwol	none	Kavwol	35,000	Animism	<1%	1	6127
Kela	none	Kela	500	Animism	0%	1	6128
Kenati	portions	Kenati	2,000	Animism	<1%	1	6129
Keopara	portions	Keopara	20,000	Animism	<1%	1	6130

NAME	SCRIPTURE	LANGUAGE	GROUP SIZE	PRIMARY RELIGION	% CHR	VOL V	UP ID
*Kepas	not reported	Kewa	5,000	Animism	1%	3	130
Kerewo	portions	Kerewo	2,000	Animism	<1%	1	6131
Keriaka	none	Keriaka	1,000	Animism	<1%	1	6132
Kewa, East	portions	Kewa, East	20,000	Animism	<1%	1	6133
Kewa, South	portions	Kewa, South	5,000	Animism	<1%	1	6134
Kewa, West	New Testament	Kewa, West	20,000	Animism	<1%	1	6135
Kiari	none	Kiari	1,000	Animism	<1%	1	6136
Kibiri	none	Kibiri	1,000	Animism	<1%	1	6137
Kilmera	portions	Kilmera	2,000	Animism	<1%	1	6138
Kinalakna	none	Kinalakna	200	Animism	0%	1	6139
Kiriwina	New Testament	Kiriwina	14,000	Animism	<1%	1	6140
Kis	none	Kis	200	Animism	0%	1	6141
Kiwai, Northeast	portions	Kiwai, Northeast	4,000	Animism	<1%	1	6142
Kiwai, Southern	New Testament	Kiwai, Southern	10,000	Animism	<1%	1	6143
Kiwai, Wabuda	none	Kiwai, Wabuda	2,000	Animism	0%	1	6144
Kobon	portions	Kobon	7,000	Animism	<1%	1	6145
Koiari, Grass	none	Koiari, Grass	2,000	Animism	<1%	1	6146
Koiari, Mountain	New Testament	Koiari, Mountain	2,000	Animism	<1%	1	6147
Koita	none	Koita	2,000	Animism	<1%	1	6148
Kol	none	Kol	2,000	Animism	<1%	1	6149
Koliku	none	Koliku	300	Animism	0%	1	6150
Kolom	none	Kolom	100	Animism	<1%	1	6151
Komba	New Testament	Komba	10,000	Animism	<1%	1	6152
Kombio	none	Kombio	2,000	Animism	0%	1	6153
Komutu	none	Komutu	500	Animism	<1%	1	6154
Konomala	none	Konomala	600	Animism	<1%	1	6155
Korak	none	Korak	200	Animism	<1%	1	6156
Korape	portions	Korape	4,000	Animism	<1%	1	6157
Kosorong	none	Kosorong	1,000	Animism	<1%	1	6158
Kovai	none	Kovai	3,000	Animism	0%	1	6159
Kove	none	Kove	3,000	Animism	0%	1	6160
Krisa	none	Krisa	500	Animism	0%	1	6161
Kube	none	Kube	4,000	Animism	<1%	1	6162
Kukuya	none	Kukuya	1,000	Animism	<1%	1	6163
Kunai	portions	Kunai	4,000	Animism	0%	1	6164
Kuman	New Testament	Kuman	66,000	Animism	<1%	1	6165

NAME	SCRIPTURE	LANGUAGE	GROUP SIZE	PRIMARY RELIGION	% CHR	VOL V	UP ID
Kundauron	none	Kundauron	400	Animism	<1%	1	6166
Kumukio	none	Kumukio	300	Animism	<1%	1	6167
Kuni	none	Kuni	2,000	Animism	<1%	1	6168
**Kunimaipa	portions	Kunimaipa	9,000	Christo-Paganism	6%	5	1202
Kunua	none	Kunua	1,000	Animism	<1%	1	6169
Kuot	none	Kuot	900	Animism	<1%	1	6170
Kurada	none	Kurada	900	Animism	<1%	1	6171
Kwale	none	Kwale	700	Animism	<1%	1	6172
Kwanga	none	Kwanga	5,000	Animism	<1%	1	6173
Kwoma	none	Kwoma	2,000	Animism	0%	1	6174
Kwomtari	none	Kwomtari	800	Animism	<1%	1	6175
Labu	none	Labu	800	Animism	<1%	1	6176
Laewomba	portions	Laewomba	2,000	Animism	<1%	1	6177
Lanogai	none	Lanogai	1,000	Animism	<1%	1	6178
Lavatbura-Lanusong	Lavatbura-Lanusong	Lavatbura-Lanusong	1,000	Animism	<1%	1	6179
Lavongai	none	Lavongai	10,000	Animism	<1%	1	6180
Leron	none	Leron	500	Animism	<1%	1	6181
Lihir	none	Lihir	5,000	Animism	0%	1	6182
Lohiki	none	Lohiki	900	Animism	0%	1	6183
Lou-Baluan-Pam	Lou-Baluan-Pam	Lou-Baluan-Pam	1,000	Animism	<1%	1	6184
Lugitana	none	Lugitana	500	Animism	0%	1	6185
Lukep	none	Lukep	600	Animism	0%	1	6186
Madak	none	Madak	3,000	Animism	0%	1	6187
Magori	none	Magori	200	Animism	<1%	1	6188
Mai	none	Mai	200	Animism	0%	1	6189
Mailu	New Testament	Mailu	5,000	Animism	<1%	1	6190
Maisan	none	Maisan	2,000	Animism	<1%	1	6191
Maiwa	none	Maiwa	1,000	Animism	<1%	1	6192
Makarim	none	Makarim	2,000	Animism	<1%	1	6193
Malalanai	none	Malalanai	300	Animism	<1%	1	6194
Malas	none	Malas	200	Animism	<1%	1	6195
Malasanga	none	Malasanga	400	Animism	<1%	1	6196
Malek	none	Malek	1,000	Animism	0%	1	6197
Maleu	portions	Maleu	4,000	Animism	<1%	1	6198
Malon	none	Malon	3,000	Animism	0%	1	6199
Manaa	none	Manaa	200	Animism	<1%	1	6200

REGISTRY OF THE UNREACHED

NAME	SCRIPTURE	LANGUAGE	GROUP SIZE	PRIMARY RELIGION	% CHR V	VOL UP ID
Managalasi	New Testament	Managalasi	4,000	Animism	<1% 1	6201
Manambu	New Testament	Manambu	2,000	Animism	<1% 1	6202
Mangap	none	Mangap	2,000	Animism	<1% 1	6203
Mape	none	Mape	5,000	Animism	<1% 1	6204
Mapena	none	Mapena	300	Animism	<1% 1	6205
Maralango	none	Maralango	2,000	Animism	<1% 1	6206
Maralinan	none	Maralinan	2,000	Animism	<1% 1	6207
Mari	none	Mari	300	Animism	<1% 1	6208
Maria	none	Maria	2,000	Animism	<1% 1	6209
Maring	portions	Maring	8,000	Animism	<1% 1	6210
Masegi	portions	Masegi	2,000	Animism	<1% 1	6211
Mawak	portions	Mawak	1,000	Animism	<1% 1	6212
Mawan	none	Mawan	200	Animism	<1% 1	6213
Medipa	New Testament	Medipa	60,000	Animism	<1% 1	6214
Mehek	none	Mehek	4,000	Animism	<1% 1	6215
Mekeo	none	Mekeo	7,000	Animism	<1% 1	6216
Mengen	portions	Mengen	6,000	Animism	<1% 1	6217
Menye	portions	Menye	13,000	Animism	<1% 1	6218
Mera Mera	none	Mera Mera	1,000	Animism	<1% 1	6219
Miarmin	portions	Miarmin	2,000	Animism	<1% 1	6220
Midsivindi	none	Midsivindi	900	Animism	<1% 1	6221
Migabac	none	Migabac	1,000	Animism	<1% 1	6222
Mikarew	none	Mikarew	6,000	Animism	<1% 1	6223
Minanibai	none	Minanibai	300	Animism	<1% 1	6224
Mindik	portions	Mindik	2,000	Animism	<1% 1	6225
Miriam	none	Miriam	700	Animism	<1% 1	6226
Mitang	none	Mitang	500	Animism	<1% 1	6227
Mitmit	none	Mitmit	100	Animism	<1% 1	6228
Moewehafen	none	Moewehafen	2,000	Animism	<1% 1	6229
Mokareng	none	Mokareng	1,000	Animism	<1% 1	6230
Momare	none	Momare	400	Animism	<1% 1	6231
Momolili	none	Monolili	2,000	Animism	<1% 1	6232
Morawa	none	Morawa	800	Animism	<1% 1	6233
Moresada	none	Moresada	200	Animism	0% 1	6234
Morigi	none	Morigi	700	Animism	0% 1	6235
Morima	none	Morima	3,000	Animism	<1% 1	6236

NAME	SCRIPTURE	LANGUAGE	GROUP SIZE	PRIMARY RELIGION	% CHR	VOL V UP	ID
Moxodi	portions	Moxodi	700	Animism	<1%	1	6237
Mugil	none	Mugil	2,000	Animism	<1%	1	6238
Mukawa	Bible	Mukawa	1,000	Animism	<1%	1	6239
Munkip	none	Munkip	100	Animism	<1%	1	6240
Mup	none	Mup	100	Animism	<1%	1	6241
Murik	portions	Murik	2,000	Animism	<1%	1	6242
Musak	portions	Musak	200	Animism	<1%	1	6243
Musar	none	Musar	500	Animism	<1%	1	6244
Musom	none	Musom	500	Animism	<1%	1	6245
Mutum	none	Mutum	400	Animism	0%	1	6246
Muyuw	New Testament	Muyuw	3,000	Animism	<1%	1	6247
Mwatebu	none	Mwatebu	200	Animism	<1%	1	6248
Nabak	portions	Nabak	12,000	Animism	<1%	1	6249
Nagarige	none	Nagarige	600	Animism	0%	1	6250
Nagatman	none	Nagatman	500	Animism	0%	1	6251
Nagovisi	portions	Nagovisi	5,000	Animism	<1%	1	6252
Nahu	none	Nahu	5,000	Animism	<1%	1	6253
Nakama	none	Nakama	900	Animism	<1%	1	6254
Nakanai	portions	Nakanai	8,000	Animism	<1%	1	6255
Nalik	none	Nalik	3,000	Animism	<1%	1	6256
Nambis	none	Nambis	1,000	Animism	<1%	1	6257
Nambu	none	Nambu	700	Animism	0%	1	6258
Nanuni	none	Nanuni	100	Animism	0%	1	6259
Nankina	none	Nankina	2,000	Animism	<1%	1	6260
Nara	none	Nara	700	Animism	<1%	1	6261
Narak	New Testament	Narak	4,000	Animism	<1%	1	6262
Nasioi	portions	Nasioi	13,000	Animism	<1%	1	6263
Nauna	none	Nauna	100	Animism	0%	1	6264
Negira	none	Negira	400	Animism	0%	1	6265
Nek	none	Nek	1,000	Animism	<1%	1	6266
Nekgini	none	Nekgini	500	Animism	<1%	1	6267
Neko	none	Neko	200	Animism	<1%	1	6268
Nengaya	none	Nengaya	600	Animism	<1%	1	6269
Ngaing	none	Ngaing	900	Animism	<1%	1	6270
Nii	portions	Nii	9,000	Animism	<1%	1	6271
Ninowa	none	Ninowa	1,000	Animism	<1%	1	6272

NAME	SCRIPTURE	LANGUAGE	GROUP SIZE	PRIMARY RELIGION	% CHR	VOL V	UP ID
*Ningerum	not reported	Ningerum	3,000	Animism	<1%	4	41
Niningo	none	Niningo	500	Animism	0%	1	6273
Nissan	none	Nissan	2,000	Animism	<1%	1	6274
Nomane	portions	Nomane	3,000	Animism	<1%	1	6275
Nomu	none	Nomu	800	Animism	<1%	1	6276
Nondiri	none	Nondiri	2,000	Animism	<1%	1	6277
Notsi	none	Notsi	1,000	Animism	<1%	1	6278
Nuk	none	Nuk	2,000	Animism	<1%	1	6279
Numanggang	none	Numanggang	2,000	Animism	<1%	1	6280
Oksapmin	portions	Oksapmin	5,000	Animism	<1%	1	6281
Olo	portions	Olo	9,000	Animism	<1%	1	6282
Omati	none	Omati	800	Animism	<1%	1	6283
Omie	portions	Omie	1,000	Animism	<1%	1	6284
Onank	none	Onank	100	Animism	<1%	1	6285
Onjab	none	Onjab	100	Animism	<1%	1	6286
Ono	portions	Ono	5,000	Animism	<1%	1	6287
Orokaiva	portions	Orokaiva	25,000	Animism	<1%	1	6288
Orokolo	New Testament	Orokolo	13,000	Animism	<1%	1	6289
Osun	none	Osun	600	Animism	<1%	1	6290
Paiwa	none	Paiwa	2,000	Animism	<1%	1	6291
Pak-Tong	none	Pak-Tong	1,000	Animism	<1%	1	6292
Papapana	none	Papapana	200	Animism	<1%	1	6293
Parawen	none	Parawen	500	Animism	<1%	1	6294
Pare	portions	Pare	1,000	Animism	<1%	1	6295
Pasismanua	none	Pasismanua	6,000	Animism	<1%	1	6296
Patep	portions	Patep	7,000	Animism	<1%	1	6297
Patpatar	portions	Patpatar	5,000	Animism	<1%	1	6298
Pawaia	portions	Pawaia	2,000	Animism	<1%	1	6299
Pay	none	Pay	600	Animism	<1%	1	6300
Paynamar	none	Paynamar	200	Animism	0%	1	6301
Perenka	none	Perenka	200	Animism	<1%	1	6302
Pila	none	Pila	600	Animism	0%	1	6303
Piu	none	Piu	100	Animism	<1%	1	6304
**Plantation Workers	NT,portions	Local dialects	5,000	Christo-Paganism	6%	5	4031
Podopa	portions	Podopa	3,000	Animism	<1%	1	6305
Ponam-Andra-Hus	none	Ponam-Andra-Hus	1,000	Animism	<1%	1	6306

NAME	SCRIPTURE	LANGUAGE	GROUP SIZE	PRIMARY RELIGION	% CHR V	VOL UP ID
Pondoma	none	Pondoma	300	Animism	<1% 1	6307
Porapora	none	Porapora	400	Animism	0% 1	6308
Pulie	none	Pulie	200	Animism	<1% 1	6309
Purari	New Testament	Purari	6,000	Animism	<1% 1	6310
Rambutyo	none	Rambutyo	1,000	Animism	0% 1	6311
Rao	none	Rao	3,000	Animism	0% 1	6312
Rauto	none	Rauto	200	Animism	<1% 1	6313
Rawa	portions	Rawa	6,000	Animism	<1% 1	6314
Rempi	none	Rempi	500	Animism	<1% 1	6315
Roinji	none	Roinji	300	Animism	<1% 1	6316
Romkun	none	Romkun	200	Animism	<1% 1	6317
	none	Romkun	400	Animism	<1% 1	7064
Roro	portions	Roro	8,000	Animism	<1% 1	6318
Rotokas	New Testament	Rotokas	4,000	Animism	<1% 1	6319
Saep	none	Saep	500	Animism	<1% 1	6320
Sakan	none	Sakan	400	Animism	<1% 1	6321
Saki	none	Saki	2,000	Animism	<1% 1	6322
Salt	none	Salt	6,000	Animism	<1% 1	6323
*Sano-Kubo	New Testament	Sano	2,000	Animism	1% 4	386
Sanio	portions	Sanio	600	Animism	<1% 1	6324
Saposa	portions	Saposa	1,000	Animism	<1% 1	6325
Saseng	none	Saseng	200	Animism	<1% 1	6326
Sau	New Testament	Sau	3,000	Animism	0% 1	6327
Sauk	none	Sauk	300	Animism	<1% 1	6328
Sawos	none	Sawos	2,000	Animism	0% 1	6329
Selepet	portions	Selepet	6,000	Animism	<1% 1	6330
Sepen	none	Sepen	200	Animism	0% 1	6331
Serki	none	Serki	900	Animism	<1% 1	6332
Setaui Keriwa	none	Setaui Keriwa	400	Animism	<1% 1	6333
Setiali	none	Setiali	200	Animism	0% 1	6334
Sialum	none	Sialum	600	Animism	<1% 1	6335
Siane	portions	Siane	16,000	Animism	<1% 1	6336
Siar	none	Siar	2,000	Animism	<1% 1	6337
Sinog	none	Sinog	100	Animism	<1% 1	6338
Sinagen	none	Sinagen	200	Animism	0% 1	6339
Sinagoro	none	Sinagoro	12,000	Animism	<1% 1	6340

675

NAME	SCRIPTURE	LANGUAGE	GROUP SIZE	PRIMARY RELIGION	% CHR V	VOL UP ID
Sinaki	New Testament	Sinaki	300	Animism	<1%	6341
Sinasina	New Testament	Sinasina	20,000	Animism	<1%	6342
Sindamon	none	Sindamon	200	Animism	<1%	6343
Sinsauru	none	Sinsauru	400	Animism	0%	6344
Sio	none	Sio	2,000	Animism	<1%	6345
Sipoma	none	Sipoma	300	Animism	<1%	6346
Sirak	none	Sirak	200	Animism	<1%	6347
Sirasira	none	Sirasira	300	Animism	<1%	6348
Sirol	New Testament	Sirol	700	Animism	<1%	6349
Siwai	New Testament	Siwai	6,000	Animism	<1%	6350
Sokorok	none	Sokorok	300	Animism	0%	6351
Solos	none	Solos	3,000	Animism	<1%	6352
Som	none	Som	100	Animism	<1%	6353
Sona	none	Sona	2,000	Animism	<1%	6354
Sori-Harengan	none	Sori-Harengan	600	Animism	0%	6355
Sowanda	none	Sowanda	900	Animism	<1%	6356
Sua	none	Sua	4,000	Animism	<1%	6357
Suain	none	Suain	900	Animism	<1%	6358
**Suena	portions	Suena	2,000	Christo-Paganism	4%	431
Suganga	none	Suganga	500	Animism	<1%	6359
Sui	not reported	Sui	1,000	Animism	0%	6360
Suki	New Testament	Suki	1,000	Animism	<1%	6361
Sukurun	none	Sukurun	400	Animism	<1%	6362
Suika	portions	Suika	1,000	Animism	<1%	6363
Sumau	none	Sumau	800	Animism	<1%	6364
Sursurunga	portions	Sursurunga	2,000	Animism	<1%	6365
Tabar	none	Tabar	2,000	Animism	<1%	6366
Tabriak	none	Tabriak	2,000	Animism	<1%	6367
Tagula	none	Tagula	2,000	Animism	<1%	6368
Talrora	New Testament	Talrora	8,000	Animism	<1%	6369
Takalubi	none	Takalubi	400	Animism	<1%	6370
Takia	portions	Takia	11,000	Animism	<1%	6371
Tanan	none	Tanan	600	Animism	<1%	6372
Tani	none	Tani	400	Animism	<1%	6373
Tangga	portions	Tangga	5,000	Animism	<1%	6374
Tangu	none	Tangu	2,000	Animism	<1%	6375

NAME	SCRIPTURE	LANGUAGE	GROUP SIZE	PRIMARY RELIGION	% CHR	VOL V UP	ID
Tanguat	none	Tanguat	600	Animism	0%	1	6376
Tani	none	Tani	2,000	Animism	<1%	1	6378
Tao-Suame	none	Tao-Suame	700	Animism	0%	1	6377
Tate	New Testament	Tate	300	Animism	0%	1	6379
Tauade	none	Tauade	11,000	Animism	<1%	1	6380
Taupota	none	Taupota	3,000	Animism	<1%	1	6381
Tavara	portions	Tavara	9,000	Animism	<1%	1	6382
Tawi-Pau	none	Tawi-Pau	300	Animism	0%	1	6383
Telefol	portions	Telefol	4,000	Animism	<1%	1	6384
Teop	portions	Teop	5,000	Animism	<1%	1	6385
Terebu	none	Terebu	4,000	Animism	0%	1	6386
Tiang	none	Tiang	800	Animism	<1%	1	6387
Tidi	none	Tidi	500	Animism	0%	1	6388
Tifal	portions	Tifal	3,000	Animism	<1%	1	6389
Tigak	portions	Tigak	4,000	Animism	<1%	1	6390
Timbe	portions	Timbe	11,000	Animism	<1%	1	6391
Tinputz	portions	Tinputz	2,000	Animism	<1%	1	6392
Tirio	none	Tirio	300	Animism	0%	1	6393
Toaripi	New Testament	Toaripi	23,000	Animism	<1%	1	6394
Tobo	none	Tobo	3,000	Animism	<1%	1	6395
Tonda	none	Tonda	600	Animism	0%	1	6396
Torau	none	Torau	600	Animism	<1%	1	6397
Torricelli	none	Torricelli	700	Animism	<1%	1	6398
Tuam	none	Tuam	600	Animism	<1%	1	6399
Tubetube	portions	Tubetube	1,000	Animism	<1%	1	6400

Paraguay

NAME	SCRIPTURE	LANGUAGE	GROUP SIZE	PRIMARY RELIGION	% CHR	VOL V UP	ID
Ayoreo	New Testament	Ayoreo	700	Animism	<1%	1	5120
Chamacoco, Bahia Negra	none	Chamacoco, Bahia Negra	1,000	Animism	<1%	1	5121
Chorote	none	Chorote	nr	Animism	<1%	1	5122
Chulupe	New Testament	Chulupe	8,000	Christo-Paganism	<1%	1	5123

NAME	SCRIPTURE	LANGUAGE	GROUP SIZE	PRIMARY RELIGION	% CHR V	VOL UP ID
Guaiaqui	none	Guaiaqui	400	Animism	<1% 1	5124
Guana	none	Guana	3,000	Animism	0% 1	5125
Lengua, Northern	New Testament	Lengua, Northern	95,000	Animism	<1% 1	5126
Maca	none	Maca	600	Animism	<1% 1	5127
Sanapana	none	Sanapana	4,000	Animism	0% 1	5128

Peru

NAME	SCRIPTURE	LANGUAGE	GROUP SIZE	PRIMARY RELIGION	% CHR V	VOL UP ID
Achual	NT,portions	Achual	5,000	Animism	<1% 1	3162
Aguaruna	New Testament	Aguaruna	22,000	Animism	<1% 1	3163
Amahuaca	portions	Amahuaca	2,000	Animism	<1% 1	2203
Amarakaeri	portions	Amarakaeri	500	Animism	<1% 1	3164
Anuesha	New Testament	Anuesha	5,000	Animism	<1% 1	3165
Arabela	portions	Arabela	200	Animism	<1% 1	3166
Campa	portions	Campa	5,000	Animism	<1% 1	2204
Candoshi	portions	Candoshi	3,000	Animism	<1% 1	3167
Capanahua	NT,portions	Capanahua	500	Animism	<1% 1	2205
Cashibo	NT,portions	Cashibo	2,000	Animism	<1% 1	3168
Chanicuro	none	Chanicuro	200	Animism	<1% 1	3169
**Chayahuita	portions	Chayawita	6,000	Christo-Paganism	11% 4	84
Cocama	portions	Cocama	18,000	Animism	<1% 1	3170
Cujareno	none	Cujareno	100	Animism	<1% 1	3171
Huachipaire	none	Huachipaire	200	Animism	<1% 1	3172
Huambisa	New Testament	Huambisa	5,000	Animism	<1% 1	3173
Huitoto, Murui	New Testament	Huitoto, Murui	800	Animism	<1% 1	3174
Iquito	portions	Spanish	200	Animism	<1% 1	3175
Jaqaru	none	Jaqaru	2,000	Animism	<1% 1	3176
Jebero	none	Spanish	3,000	Animism	<1% 1	3177
Machiguenga	New Testament	Machiguenga	10,000	Animism	<1% 1	3178
Manu Park Panoan	none	Manu Park Panoan	200	Animism	<1% 1	3179
Mayoruna	portions	Mayoruna	1,000	Animism	<1% 1	3180
Morunahua	none	Morunahua	200	Animism	<1% 1	3181

NAME	SCRIPTURE	LANGUAGE	GROUP SIZE	PRIMARY RELIGION	% CHR V	VOL UP	ID
Ocaina	portions	Ocaina	300	Animism	<1% 1		3182
Orejon	portions	Orejon	300	Animism	<1% 1		3183
Piro	New Testament	Maniteneri	3,000	Animism	<1% 1		3184
**Quechua	not reported	Quechua	3,000,000	Christo-Paganism	2% 5		10
**Quechua, Huancayo	none	Quechua, Huancayo	275,000	Animism	6% 5		1080
Sharanahua	portions	Sharanahua	2,000	Animism	<1% 1		3185
Shipibo	portions	Shipibo	15,000	Animism	<1% 1		3186
Urarina	portions	Urarina	4,000	Animism	<1% 1		3187
Yagua	portions	Yagua	4,000	Animism	<1% 1		3188
Yaninahua	none	Yaninahua	1,000	Animism	<1% 1		3189

Philippines

NAME	SCRIPTURE	LANGUAGE	GROUP SIZE	PRIMARY RELIGION	% CHR V	VOL UP	ID
Abaknon	none	Abaknon	10,000	Christo-Paganism	<1% 1		3239
Aeta	none	Aeta	500	Christo-Paganism	<1% 1		3240
Agutaynon	none	Agutaynon	7,000	Islam-Animist	<1% 1		3241
Alangan	portions	Alangan	6,000	Christo-Paganism	<1% 1		3242
**Apayao	portions	Isneg	12,000	Christo-Paganism	9% 6		1201
*Asian Students	Bible	English	2,000	Islam	2% 4		2101
*Ata of Davao	portions	Manobo	10,000	Animism	4% 4		627
Ati	none	Ati	2,000	Christo-Paganism	<1% 1		3243
*Atta	not reported	Atta	1,000	Animism	1% 5		634
Badjao	portions	Badjao	4,900	Islam	0% 3		4832
***Bagobo	Bible	Bagobo	35,000	Christo-Paganism	14% 5		4072
Baguio Area Miners	Bible	Ilocano	40,000	Nominal Christian	15% 5	81	7004
**Balangao	portions	Balangao	5,000	Christo-Paganism	3% 4		633
Balangaw	portions	Balangaw	5,000	Animism	<1% 1		3246
Bantuanon	none	Bantuanon	50,000	Christo-Paganism	<1% 1		3244
Batak, Palawan	portions	Batak, Palawan	400	Christo-Paganism	6% 4		3245
**Batangeno	Bible	Tagalog	nr	Nominal Christian	<1% 1		4073
**Bilan	portions	Bilaan	75,000	Animism	<1% 5		1025
***Bolinao	New Testament	Bolinao	26,000	Nominal Christian	19% 4		4058

REGISTRY OF THE UNREACHED

NAME	SCRIPTURE	LANGUAGE	GROUP SIZE	PRIMARY RELIGION	% CHR	V	VOL	UP ID
**Bontoc, Central	portions	Bontoc, Central	20,000	Animism	1%	5	81	632
**Bontoc, Southern	none	Southern Bontoc	12,000	Christo-Paganism	4%	5		1060
**Bukidnon	portions	Buhid	6,000	Christo-Paganism	<1%	1		3249
**Buwid	portions	Manobo, Binukid	100,000	Animism	15%	5	81	1063
**Buwid	portions	Buwid	6,000	Animism	8%	5	81	4161
Caluyanhon	none	Caluyanhon	30,000	Christo-Paganism	<1%	1		3250
*Casiguranin	none	Casiguranin	10,000	Nominal Christian	17%	4		4055
***Cebu, Middle-Class	Bible	Cebuano	500,000	Christo-Paganism	12%	4		1079
Cuyonon	NT,portions	Cuyonon	49,000	Christo-Paganism	<1%	1		3251
Davaweno	none	Davaweno	13,000	Christo-Paganism	<1%	1		3252
*Dunagat, Casiguran	portions	Dunagat	1,000	Animism	3%	6	81	2
Ga-Dang	none	Ga-Dang	6,000	Animism	<1%	5		631
Hanonoo	portions	Hanonoo	6,000	Christo-Paganism	<1%	1		3253
**Hotel Workers in Manila	Bible	Pilipino	11,000	Nominal Christian	13%	5	81	7036
Ibanag	New Testament	Ibanag	300	Animism	<1%	1		3254
*Ibatan	none	Ibatan	500	Christo-Paganism	0%	4		4056
Ifugao	portions	Ifugao	95,000	Animism	6%	5		210
**Ifugao (Kalangoya)	portions	Kalangoya	35,000	Animism	5%	4		697
Ifugao in Cababuyan	New Testament	Ifugao	4,000	Animism	14%	1		2104
Ifugao, Ambanad	portions	Ifugao, Ambanad	15,000	Animism	<1%	1		3255
Ifugao, Antipolo	New Testament	Keley-i	25,000	Animism	6%	5		1047
Ifugao, Kiangan	portions	Ifugao, Kiangan	20,000	Animism	<1%	1		3256
Igorot	portions	Igorot	40,000	Animism	<1%	1		3247
**Ikalahan	NT,portions	Ikalahan	12,041	Animism	6%	6		7037
Ilanon	not reported	Ilanun	8,000	Islam	0%	3		4833
Ilongot	portions	Ilongot	10,000	Animism	<1%	1		3257
Insinai	portions	Insinai	6,000	Animism	<1%	1		3258
Iraya	none	Iraya	10,000	Christo-Paganism	<1%	1		3259
Isneg, Dibagat-Kabugao	portions	Isneg, Dibagat-Kabugao	10,000	Animism	<1%	1		3260
Isneg, Karagawan	portions	Isneg, Karagawan	8,000	Animism	<1%	1		3261
Itawit	none	Itawit	15,000	Christo-Paganism	<1%	1		3262
Itneg, Adasen	none	Itneg, Adasen	4,000	Christo-Paganism	<1%	1		3263
Itneg, Binongan	portions	Itneg, Binongan	7,000	Christo-Paganism	<1%	1		3264
Itneg, Masadiit	none	Itneg, Masadiit	8,000	Christo-Paganism	<1%	1		3265
Jana Mapun	portions	Cagayan	15,000	Islam-Animist	<1%	5	80	1149
*Jeepney Drivers in Manila	Bible	Pilipino	20,000	Nominal Christian	nr%	5	81	7018

NAME	SCRIPTURE	LANGUAGE	GROUP SIZE	PRIMARY RELIGION	% CHR	V	VOL	UP ID
Kaagan	none	Kaagan	20,000	Christo-Paganism	<1%	1		3266
Kadaklan-Barlig Bontoc	none	Kadaklan-Barlig Bontoc	4,000	Animism	<1%	1		3248
**kalagan	portions	Kalagan	19,000	Animism	1%	5		630
Kalinga, Kalagua	none	Kalinga, Kalagua	4,000	Animism	<1%	1		3268
Kalinga, Limus-Linan	none	Kalinga, Linus-Linan	20,000	Animism	<1%	1		3269
Kalinga, Quinaang	portions	Kalinga, Quinaang	41,000	Animism	<1%	1		3267
*kalinga, Southern	none	Kalinga, Sunadel-Tinglayan	11,000	Animism	4%	5		1147
**kalinga, Tanudan	none	Kalinga	8,000	Nominal Christian	5%	4		4054
*kalinga,Northern	none	Kalinga	20,000	Christo-Paganism	3%	5		1146
**kankanay, Central	portions	Kankanay	40,000	Animism	2%	5		1200
Kankanay, Northern	portions	Northern Kankanay	40,000	Animism	2%	5		4057
Kinaray-A	none	Kinaray-A	288,000	Christo-Paganism	<1%	1		3270
Lubang Islanders	Bible	Pilipino	18,000	Christo-Paganism	0%	5	81	7016
Maguindanao	portions	Maguindanao	700,000	Islam	1%	6	80	629
**mamanua	portions	Minamanwa	1,000	Christo-Paganism	3%	6	81	628
Mandaya	none	Mandaya	3,000	Animism	<1%	1		3293
Mandaya, Mansaka	New Testament	Mandaya, Mansaka	40,000	Animism	<1%	1		3271
*mangyan	portions	Various Dialects	60,000	Animism	6%	5		231
Manobo, Agusan	portions	Manobo, Agusan	15,000	Animism	<1%	1		3272
Manobo, Ata	portions	Manobo, Ata	7,000	Animism	<1%	1		3273
Manobo, Binokid	portions	Manobo, Binokid	41,000	Animism	<1%	1		3274
**manobo, Cotabato	New Testament	Cotabato Manobo	10,000	Animism	1%	4		626
Manobo, Dibabauon	portions	Manobo, Dibabauon	2,000	Animism	<1%	1		3275
*ilianen	portions	Ilianen Manobo	5,000	Animism	3%	5		625
Manobo, Obo	portions	Manobo, Obo	4,000	Animism	<1%	1		3276
**manobo, Salug	Bible	Manobo, Tigwa	4,000	Animism	4%	5		639
Manobo, Sarangani	portions	Manobo, Sarangani	15,000	Animism	<1%	1		3277
Manobo, Tagabawa	portions	Manobo, Tagabawa	10,000	Animism	<1%	1		3278
**manobo, Tigwa	portions	Manobo, Tigwa	4,000	Animism	3%	5		640
**manobo, Western Bukidnon	portions	Manobo, Binokid	12,000	Animism	6%	5		618
Manobos, Pulangi	portions	Manobo, Pulangi	5,000	Animism	1%	4		1171
**mansaka	portions	Mansaka	25,000	Christo-Paganism	10%	5		1035
Maranao	New Testament	Maranao, Lanad	500,000	Islam	2%	6	79	638
Maranao, Lanad	NT,portions	Maranao, Lanad	500,000	Islam-Aninist	<1%	6		3279
*molbog	portions	Molbog	5,000	Islam-Aninist	0%	7		1039
Northern Cagayan Negrito	portions	Northern Cagayan Negrito	1,000	Christo-Paganism	<1%	1		3292

REGISTRY OF THE UNREACHED

NAME	SCRIPTURE	LANGUAGE	GROUP SIZE	PRIMARY RELIGION	% CHR	V	UP	ID
*Pala'wan	New Testament	Pala'wan	50,000	Animism	<1%	5	81	4162
Palawano	none	Palawano	3,000	Animism	<1%	1		3280
Palawano, Central	New Testament	Palawano, Central	3,000	Animism	<1%	1		3281
Paranan	none	Paranan	6,000	Christo-Paganism	<1%	1		3282
Porohanon	none	Porohanon	23,000	Animism	<1%	1		3283
Sana Bangingi	none	Sinama Bangini	70,000	Islam-Animist	<1%	6	80	1148
Sana Pangutaran	none	Sana Pangutaran	15,000	Islam	<1%	6	80	1150
Sana, Mapun	none	Sana, Mapun	20,000	Animism	<1%	1		3284
Sana, Siasi	portions	Sana, Siasi	100,000	Islam-Animist	<1%	1		3285
Sana, Sibuku	none	Sana, Sibuku	11,000	Islam-Animist	<1%	1		3286
Sana-Badjaw	portions	Sanal dialects	120,000	Islam-Animist	1%	5	79	389
Sangil	none	Sangil	8,000	Islam	1%	5		637
**Subanen (Tuboy)	portions	Subanen, Tuboy	20,000	Animism	2%	5		51
**Subanen, Sindangan	portions	Subanun	80,000	Animism	<1%	6	80	1062
Subanun,Lapuyan	New Testament	Subanun, Lapuyan	25,000	Islam-Animist	<1%	1		1191
**Suriguenos	none	Surigueno	23,000	Secularism	7%	4		624
**T'boli	not reported	Tboli	150,000	Animism	3%	5	81	3288
**Tadyawan	none	Tadyawan	1,000	Animism	<1%	1		1153
**Tagbanwa, Aborlan	portions	Tagbanwa	10,000	Animism	1%	5		636
Tagbanwa, Kalamian	portions	Tagbanwa, Kalamian	5,000	Christo-Paganism	1%	5		2106
Tao't Bato	none	not reported	200	Animism	0%	4		635
Tausug	portions	Tausug	500,000	Islam	1%	6	80	3290
Tiruray	portions	Tiruray	30,000	Animism	1%	1		25
Yakan	portions	Yakan	97,000	Islam-Animist	1%	6	80	3291
Yogad	none	Yogad	7,000	Animism	<1%	1		

Puerto Rico

NAME	SCRIPTURE	LANGUAGE	GROUP SIZE	PRIMARY RELIGION	% CHR	V	UP	ID
Chinese in Puerto Rico	Bible	Hakka	200	Traditional Chinese	0%	2		748

NAME	SCRIPTURE	LANGUAGE	GROUP SIZE	PRIMARY RELIGION	% CHR	VOL V	UP ID

Rwanda

| ***Banyarwanda | Bible | Kinyarwanda | 4,000,000 | Animism | 6% | 5 | 4027 |

Saudi Arabia

Chinese in Saudi Arabia	not reported	Arabic	20,000	Islam	0%	3 82	4135
*Expatriates in Riyadh	+Bible	English	nr	Secularism	<1%	5 82	5024
**Filipino Migrant Workers	+Bible	Tagalog	132,000	Nominal Christian	50%	4 84	4815

Senegal

Balanta	none	Balanta	50,000	Animism	0%	3	1142
Balanta Refugees	+portions	Balanta	60,000	Animism	<1%	4	9030
Banyun	none	Banyun	9,000	Islam-Animist	0%	1	5421
Basari	none	Basari	8,000	Animism	0%	1	5422
Bayot	portions	Bayot	4,000	Islam-Animist	0%	1	5423
Diola	portions	Diola	266,000	Islam-Animist	1%	5	434
Mancang	none	Mankanya	40,000	Animism	0%	3	1141
Manding	portions	Malinke, Senegalese	210,000	Islam-Animist	0%	3	1138
Manjack	none	Mandyale	44,000	Islam-Animist	0%	3	1140
Mankanya	none	Mankanya	16,000	Islam-Animist	0%	1	5425

REGISTRY OF THE UNREACHED

NAME	SCRIPTURE	LANGUAGE	GROUP SIZE	PRIMARY RELIGION	% CHR	V	VOL UP	ID
Maures	not reported	Arabic	57,000	Islam	0%	3		723
Pular	portions	Fouta Toro	300,000	Animism	0%	3		1136
Sarakole	none	Soninke	68,000	Islam	0%	6	80	1139
Serere	not reported	Serere	700,000	Animism	9%	6	79	215
Serere-Non	none	Serere-Non	70,000	Islam-Animist	0%	1		5426
Serere-Sine	portions	Serere-Sine	315,000	Islam-Animist	<1%	1		5427
Tandanke	none	Tandanke	1,000	Animism	0%	3		1145
Taucouleur	portions	Tancouleur	500,000	Islam	0%	5	80	1137
Wolof	NT,portions	Wolof	2,000,000	Islam-Animist	1%	6	80	96

Seychelles

NAME	SCRIPTURE	LANGUAGE	GROUP SIZE	PRIMARY RELIGION	% CHR	V	VOL UP	ID
Seychellois	portions	Creole	51,000	Secularism	10%	4		1199

Sierra Leone

NAME	SCRIPTURE	LANGUAGE	GROUP SIZE	PRIMARY RELIGION	% CHR	V	VOL UP	ID
Bullom, Northern	portions	Bullom, Northern	167,000	Islam-Animist	<1%	1		5428
Bullom, Southern	portions	Bullom, Southern	40,000	Islam-Animist	<1%	1		5429
Fula	portions	Fula	250,000	Islam	0%	5		4035
Gola	portions		1,000	Islam-Animist	0%	1		5430
*Kissi	not reported	Kissi, Southern	48,000	Animism	12%	4		271
**Kono	portions	Kono	133,000	Animism	5%	5		203
**Koranko	NT,portions	Kuranko (Maninka)	100,000	Islam-Animist	1%	5		201
Krim	none	Mende	3,000	Islam-Animist	0%	1		5432
Limba	New Testament	Limba	233,000	Animism	4%	4		587
Loko	portions	Loko	80,000	Animism	1%	4		586
Maninka	portions,NT	Maninka	64,000	Islam-Animist	0%	1		5434
Mende	Bible	Mende	600,000	Animism	13%	5		585

NAME	SCRIPTURE	LANGUAGE	GROUP SIZE	PRIMARY RELIGION	% CHR	VOL V	UP ID
Susu	portions	Susu	90,000	Islam-Animist	<1%	1	5435
**Temne	New Testament	Temne	1,000,000	Animism	6%	6 80	123
Vai	portions	Vai	3,000	Islam-Animist	0%	1	5436
*Yalunka	New Testament	Yalunka	25,000	Islam-Animist	1%	6 80	455

Singapore

NAME	SCRIPTURE	LANGUAGE	GROUP SIZE	PRIMARY RELIGION	% CHR	VOL V	UP ID
Malays of Singapore	New Testament	Malay	300,000	Islam	1%	6 79	120

Somalia

NAME	SCRIPTURE	LANGUAGE	GROUP SIZE	PRIMARY RELIGION	% CHR	VOL V	UP ID
**Ethiopian Refugees	+Bible	Oromo	700,000	Islam	<1%	4 83	9027

South Africa

NAME	SCRIPTURE	LANGUAGE	GROUP SIZE	PRIMARY RELIGION	% CHR	VOL V	UP ID
Bavenda	not reported	Tschievenda	360,000	Animism	nr%	4	6564
Cape Malays in Cape Town	+Bible	Afrikaans	150,000	Islam	7%	6 82	5006
*Chinese in South Africa	Bible	Cantonese	9,000	Traditional Chinese	9%	4	756
*Coloureds in Eersterust	+Bible	Afrikaans	20,000	Secularism	15%	6 82	5040
Nana	Bible	Nana	15,000	Animism	0%	1	5437
Ronga	Bible	Ronga	600,000	Animism	0%	1	5438
**Swazi	portions	siSwati	500,000	Animism	9%	5	4037

685

REGISTRY OF THE UNREACHED

NAME	SCRIPTURE	LANGUAGE	GROUP PRIMARY SIZE RELIGION		% CHR V VOL V UP	ID

Spain

NAME	SCRIPTURE	LANGUAGE	GROUP SIZE	PRIMARY RELIGION	% CHR V V UP	ID
*Gypsies in Spain	Bible	Romany	200,000	Folk Religion	3% 6 79	393
*Lao Refugees	+Bible	Lao	1,000	Buddhist-Animist	<1% 3 83	9056
Pension Students-Madrid	+Bible	Italian	2,000	Secularism	nr% 5 82	5032

Sri Lanka

NAME	SCRIPTURE	LANGUAGE	GROUP SIZE	PRIMARY RELIGION	% CHR V V UP	ID
**Indian Tamils - Colombo	+Bible	Tamil	nr	Hindu-Animist	<1% 5 82	5004
Moor & Malays	Bible	Tamil	900,000	Islam	<1% 6 79	309
Sinhalese	Bible	Sinhala	9,200,000	Buddhism	6% 5	286
Tamil (Ceylonese)	Bible	Tamil	1,420,000	Hinduism	5% 5	287
**Tamils (Indian)	Bible	Tamil	1,200,000	Hinduism	5% 4 79	313

Sudan

NAME	SCRIPTURE	LANGUAGE	GROUP SIZE	PRIMARY RELIGION	% CHR V V UP	ID
Abialang	not reported	Abialang	7,000	Islam	0% 1	5464
Abu Leila	not reported	Abu Leila	4,000	Islam	0% 1	5505
Acheron	not reported	Acheron	3,000	Islam	0% 1	5506
Afitti	none	Afitti	3,000	Islam	0% 1	5439
Aja	none	Aja	1,000	Islam	0% 1	5440
Anuak	New Testament	Anuak	30,000	Animism	4% 5	584

NAME	SCRIPTURE	LANGUAGE	GROUP SIZE	PRIMARY RELIGION	% CHR	VOL V	UP ID
Atoc	not reported	Atoc	5,000	Islam	0%	1	5459
Atuot	none	Atuot	8,000	Islam	0%	1	5441
Avukaya	none	Avukaya	5,000	Islam	0%	1	5442
Bai	none	Bai	3,000	Islam	0%	1	5443
Barambu	none	Barambu	46,000	Islam	0%	1	5444
Bari	New Testament	Bari	340,000	Islam	0%	1	5445
Beja	none	Beja	91,000	Islam	0%	1	5446
Binga	none	Binga	1,000	Islam	0%	1	5450
Bitl	not reported	Bitl	300	Islam	0%	1	5509
Bongo	none	Bongo	2,000	Islam	0%	1	5451
Bor Gok	not reported	Bor Gok	6,000	Islam	0%	1	5463
Boya	none	Boya	15,000	Animism	<1%	4	703
Burun	none	Burun	5,000	Islam	0%	1	5452
Bviri	none	Bviri	16,000	Islam	0%	1	5453
Dair	none	Dair	200	Islam	0%	1	5454
Daju of Dar Fur	none	Daju	12,000	Animism	0%	1	5455
Daju of West Kordofan	none	Daju	6,000	Islam	0%	1	5456
Didinga	none	Didinga	30,000	Animism	<1%	4	583
Dinka	New Testament	Dinka	1,940,000	Animism	4%	5	582
Dinka, Agar	none	Dinka, Agar	16,000	Islam	0%	1	5458
Dongjoi	not reported	Dongjoi	9,000	Islam	0%	1	5465
Dongo	not reported	Dongo	100	Islam	0%	1	5490
Eritrean Refugees	+not reported	Galla	150,000	Islam	nr%	4	9007
Feroge	none	Feroge	3,000	Islam	0%	1	5471
Fungor	none	Fungor	5,000	Islam	0%	1	5472
Gbaya-Ndogo	not reported	Gbaya-Ndogo	2,000	Islam	0%	1	5491
Gberi	none	Gberi	600	Islam	0%	1	5473
Ghol	not reported	Ghol	2,000	Islam	0%	1	5460
Ghulfan	none	Ghulfan	3,000	Islam	0%	1	5474
Gumuz	none	Gumuz	40,000	Islam	0%	1	5475
Heiban	New Testament	Heiban	25,000	Islam	<1%	1	5476
Ingassana	none	Tabi	35,000	Animism	0%	5	581
*Jiye	none	Jiye (Karamojong)	7,000	Animism	0%	5	1129
Kadugli	none	Kadugli	19,000	Islam	0%	1	5477
Kanga	none	Kanga	6,000	Islam	0%	1	5479
Karko	none	Karko	2,000	Islam	0%	1	5480

REGISTRY OF THE UNREACHED

NAME	LANGUAGE	SCRIPTURE	GROUP SIZE	PRIMARY RELIGION	% CHR	V	VOL	UP ID
Katcha	Katcha	portions	6,000	Islam	0%	1		5481
Katla	Katla	none	9,000	Islam	0%	1		5482
Keiga	Keiga	none	6,000	Islam	0%	1		5483
Keiga Jirru	Keiga Jirru	none		Islam	0%	1		5484
Kichepo	Kichepo	none	16,000	Animism	0%	3		704
Koalib	Koalib (Nuba)	NT,portions	1,000	Animism	6%	6	79	580
Koma, Central	Koma, Central	none	320,000	Islam	6%	6		5489
Koroma	Koroma	none	3,000	Islam	0%	1		706
Krongo	Krongo	New Testament	30,000	Animism	0%	3		579
Lafofa	Lafofa	not reported	121,000	Animism	1%	4		5494
Laro	Laro	none	2,000	Islam	0%	1		5495
Liguri	Liguri	none	3,000	Islam	0%	1		5496
*Lokoro	Lokoro	none	2,000	Islam-Animist	5%	4		1128
Lori	Lori	none	22,000	Christo-Paganism	0%	1		5447
**Lotuka	Latuka	New Testament	1,000	Islam	6%	5		200
Luac	Luac	not reported	150,000	Other	0%	1		5466
Luo	Luo	portions	700	Islam	<1%	1		5497
Maba	Maba	none	20,000	Islam	0%	1		5498
Maban-Junjun	Maban-Junjun	portions	9,000	Islam	<1%	1		5499
Madi	Madi	portions	20,000	Islam	0%	1		5500
Masakin	Masakin	none	6,000	Islam	0%	1		5501
Masalit	Arabic	none	16,000	Islam	1%	4		5502
Meban	Maban-Junjun	portions	27,000	Animism	0%	1		578
Midob	Midob	none	130,000	Islam	0%	1		5503
Miri	Miri	none	2,000	Islam	0%	1		5504
Modo	Modo	not reported	8,000	Islam	0%	1		5448
Moreb	Moreb	not reported	2,000	Islam	0%	1		5520
Moru	Moru	portions	600	Islam	0%	1		5511
Murle	Murle	not reported	23,000	Animism	1%	4		577
Naka	Naka	none	40,000	Islam	0%	1		5492
Ndogo	Ndogo	not reported	4,000	Unknown	0%	1		5512
Nginyukwur	Nginyukwur	not reported	4,000	Islam	0%	1		5485
Ngirere	Ngirere	not reported	4,000	Islam	0%	1		5486
Ngok	Ngok	not reported	21,000	Islam	0%	1		5467
Ngunduna	Ngunduna	not reported	9,000	Islam	0%	1		5487
Nguwurang	Nguwurang	not reported	8,000	Islam	0%	1		5488

NAME	SCRIPTURE	LANGUAGE	GROUP SIZE	PRIMARY RELIGION	% CHR	VOL V	UP	ID
Njaiguigule	none	Njaiguigule	900	Islam	0%			5513
*Nuer	New Testament	Nuer	844,000	Animism	1%	6	79	576
Nyanusa	not reported	Nyanusa	1,000	Islam	0%			5510
Nyarueng	not reported	Nyarueng	2,000	Islam	0%			5461
Nyzatom	none	Toposa, Donyiro	80,000	Animism	0%	3		705
Otoro	New Testament	Otoro	28,000	Islam	<1%	1		5514
Paloc	not reported	Paloc	14,000	Islam	0%			5468
Rural Refugees from Eritrea	+New Testament	Tigre	300,000	Islam	0%	4	83	9008
Rut	not reported	Rut	500	Islam	0%	1		5469
Sere	none	Sere	4,000	Islam	0%	1		5515
Shatt	none	Shatt	9,000	Islam	0%	1		5516
Shilluk	New Testament	Shilluk	110,000	Islam	<1%	1		5517
Shwai	none	Shwai	3,000	Islam	0%	1		5518
Sopi	none	Sopi	2,000	Islam	0%	1		5449
Sudanese Repatriates	+portions	Tribal Languages	1,000,000	Animism	<1%	4	83	9009
Tabi	portions	Tabi	10,000	Animism	0%	1		5519
Talodi	none	Talodi	1,000	Islam	0%	1		5522
Tegali	none	Tegali	16,000	Islam	0%	1		5523
Temein	none	Temein	2,000	Islam	0%	1		5524
Thoi	not reported	Thoi	400	Islam	0%	1		5470
Thuri	none	Thuri	154,000	Islam	0%	1		5525
Tira	none	Tira	10,000	Islam	0%	1		5526
Tirma	none	Tirma	9,000	Islam	<1%	1		5527
*Topotha	none	Toposa	60,000	Animism	2%	4		575
Tulishi	none	Tulishi	9,000	Islam	0%	1		5528
Tumale	not reported	Tunale	1,000	Islam	0%	1		5521
Tumma	none	Tumma	5,000	Islam	0%	1		5529
Tumtum	none	Tumtum	7,000	Islam	0%	1		5530
Tui	none	Tui	9,000	Islam	0%	1		5462
Uduk	not reported	Uduk	7,000	Islam	9%	4		574
Ugandan Refugees	New Testament	Swahili	100,000	Animism	<1%	4	83	9048
Umm Dorein	not reported	Umm Dorein	500	Islam	0%	1		5507
Umm Gabralla	not reported	Umm Gabralla	9,000	Islam	0%	1		5508
Woro	not reported	Woro	400	Islam	0%	1		5493
Yulu	none	Yulu	2,000	Islam	0%	1		5531

NAME	SCRIPTURE	LANGUAGE	GROUP SIZE	PRIMARY RELIGION	% CHR	VOL V	UP ID
Zaghawa	none	Zaghawa	nr	Islam	<1%	1	5532

Surinam

NAME	SCRIPTURE	LANGUAGE	GROUP SIZE	PRIMARY RELIGION	% CHR	VOL V	UP ID
Djuka	portions	Djuka	20,000	Christo-Paganism	<1%	1	5129
Matawari	none	Matawari	1,000	Animism	0%	1	5130
Saramaccan	portions	Saramaccan	20,000	Christo-Paganism	<1%	1	5131
Trio	portions	Trio	800	Animism	<1%	1	5132
Wayana	portions	Wayana	600	Animism	<1%	1	5133

Switzerland

NAME	SCRIPTURE	LANGUAGE	GROUP SIZE	PRIMARY RELIGION	% CHR	VOL V	UP ID
*Americans in Geneva	Bible	English	45,000	Secularism	<1%	4	4118
Tibetan Refugees	+Bible	Tibetan	1,000	Buddhism	0%	4 83	9015
Turks in Basel	+Bible	Kurdish	3,000	Islam	nr%	6 82	5011

Syria

NAME	SCRIPTURE	LANGUAGE	GROUP SIZE	PRIMARY RELIGION	% CHR	VOL V	UP ID
*Alawites	Bible	Arabic	600,000	Islam	0%	6 79	1104

NAME	SCRIPTURE	LANGUAGE	GROUP SIZE	PRIMARY RELIGION	% CHR	V	VUP	ID
Taiwan								
*Ami	New Testament	Ami	99,000	Buddhist-Animist	2%	5	81	7032
**Chinese Hakka of Taiwan	Bible	Hakka	1,750,000	Traditional Chinese	1%	6	79	746
*Chinese Mainlanders	Bible	Mandarin	2,000,000	Traditional Chinese	8%	4		85
Chinese Muslims	Bible	Mandarin	45,000	Islam	<1%	5	81	7019
*Deviant Youth in Taipei	+Bible	Chinese, Min-Nan	80,000	Folk Religion	nr%	5	82	5044
Fishing Village People	Bible	Amoy	150,000	Traditional Chinese	2%	4		2107
*Industrial Workers	Bible	Taiwanese (Hoklo)	500,000	Secularism	2%	5	81	4121
**Puyuma	none	Puyuma	7,000	Christo-Paganism	nr%	5	81	7033
Saisiat	not reported	Saisiat	3,000	Animism	nr%	5	81	7034
Taiwan-Chinese Un. Stud.	none	Mandarin	310,000	Secularism	nr%	6		7038
*Tsou	none	Tsou	4,000	Animism	<1%	5	81	7035
*Women Laborers	Bible	Amoy	1,200,000	Traditional Chinese	2%	4		2115
Tanzania								
Arusha	New Testament	Arusha	110,000	Animism	8%	5		142
Asu	New Testament	Asu	110,000	Animism	0%	1		5533
Barabaig	none	Tatoga	49,000	Animism	2%	5	79	573
Bena	New Testament	Bena	150,000	Animism	0%	1		5534
Bende	not reported	Bende	9,000	Animism	0%	1		5535
Bondei	portions	Bondei	30,000	Islam	0%	1		5536
Burundian Hutu Refugees	+Bible	Kirundi	120,000	Animism	<1%	4	83	9006
Burungi	none	Burungi	20,000	Animism	7%	4		493
Chagga	New Testament	Chagga	800,000	Animism	0%	1		5537

NAME	SCRIPTURE	LANGUAGE	GROUP SIZE	PRIMARY RELIGION	% CHR	VOL V	UP ID
Dhaiso	Bible	Dhaiso	12,000	Animism	<1%	1	5538
Digo	none	Digo	30,000	Animism	0%	1	5539
Doe	none	Doe	8,000	Animism	0%	1	5540
Dorobo	none	Hadza	3,000	Animism	1%	4	490
Fipa	none	Fipa	78,000	Animism	0%	1	5541
Gogo	Bible	Gogo	280,000	Animism	0%	1	5542
Goroa	none	Goroa	180,000	Animism	0%	1	5543
Ha	portions	Ha	286,000	Animism	0%	1	5544
Hangaza	portions	Hangaza	54,000	Animism	0%	1	5545
Hatsa	none	Hatsa	2,000	Animism	0%	1	5546
Haya	New Testament	Haya	276,000	Animism	0%	1	5547
Hehe	not reported	Hehe	192,000	Animism	0%	1	5548
Holoholo	none	Holoholo	5,000	Animism	0%	1	5549
Ikizu	not reported	Swahili	9,000	Animism	0%	1	5550
Iraqw	portions	Iraqw	218,000	Animism	11%	4	492
Isanzu	none	Isanzu	12,000	Animism	0%	1	5552
Jiji	none	Jiji	3,000	Animism	0%	1	5553
Jinja	portions	Jinja	66,000	Animism	0%	1	5554
Jita	New Testament	Jita	71,000	Animism	0%	1	5555
Kagulu	portions	Kagulu	59,000	Animism	0%	1	5556
Kami	none	Kami	180,000	Animism	0%	1	5557
Kara	not reported	Kara	32,000	Animism	0%	1	5558
Kerewe	New Testament	Kikerewe	35,000	Animism	1%	4	243
Kimbu	not reported	Kimbu	15,000	Animism	0%	1	5559
Kinga	New Testament	Kinga	57,000	Animism	0%	1	5560
Kisankasa	none	Kisankasa	4,000	Animism	0%	1	5561
Kisi	none	Kisi	4,000	Animism	0%	1	5562
Konongo	none	Konongo	20,000	Animism	0%	1	5563
Kuria	portions	Kuria	75,000	Animism	0%	1	5564
Kutu	none	Kutu	17,000	Animism	0%	1	5565
Kwaya	none	Kwaya	35,000	Animism	0%	1	5566
Kwere	none	Kwere	63,000	Animism	10%	5	491
Lambya	none	Lambya	7,000	Animism	0%	1	5567
Langi	none	Langi	95,000	Animism	0%	1	5568
Luo	Bible	Luo	1,522,000	Animism	0%	1	5569
Makonde	not reported	not reported	550,000	Islam	6%	5	144

NAME	SCRIPTURE	LANGUAGE	GROUP SIZE	PRIMARY RELIGION	% CHR	VOL	V	UP ID
Malila	none	Malila	175,000	Animism	0%	1		5570
Mambwe-Lungu	New Testament	Mambwe-Lungu	16,000	Animism	0%	1		5571
Manda	New Testament	Manda	10,000	Animism	0%	1		5572
Matengo	none	Matengo	58,000	Animism	0%	1		5573
Matumbi	not reported	Matumbi	72,000	Islam	8%	4		488
Mbugwe	none	Mbugwe	8,000	Animism	0%	1		5574
Mbunga	none	Mbunga	10,000	Animism	0%	1		5575
Mosi	New Testament	Mosi	240,000	Animism	0%	1		5576
Mpoto	portions	Mpoto	36,000	Animism	0%	1		5577
Muanga	New Testament	Muanga	27,000	Animism	0%	1		5578
Muera	none	Muera	110,000	Animism	0%	1		5579
Nata	none	Nata	10,000	Animism	0%	1		5580
Ndali	none	Ndali	57,000	Animism	0%	1		5581
Ndamba	none	Ndamba	19,000	Animism	0%	1		5582
Ndengereko	none	Ndengereko	53,000	Animism	0%	1		5583
Ndomde	none	Ndomde	12,000	Animism	0%	1		5584
Ngasa	none	Ngasa	1,000	Animism	0%	1		5585
Ngindo	none	Ngindo	85,000	Animism	0%	1		5586
Ngoni	portions	Ngoni	85,000	Animism	0%	1		5587
Ngulu	none	Ngulu	13,000	Animism	0%	1		5588
Ngurimi	none	Ngurimi	12,000	Animism	0%	1		5589
Nguu	none	Nguu	46,000	Animism	0%	1		5590
Nilamba	New Testament	Nilamba	210,000	Animism	0%	1		5591
Nyakyusa	New Testament	Nyakyusa	193,000	Animism	0%	1		5592
Nyambo	none	Nyambo	4,000	Animism	0%	1		5593
Nyamwezi	New Testament	Nyamwezi	590,000	Animism	9%	6	80	487
Nyiha	New Testament	Nyiha	64,000	Animism	0%	1		5594
Pangua	none	Pangua	26,000	Animism	0%	1		5595
Pare	none	Pare	99,000	Animism	0%	1		5596
Pimbwe	none	Pimbwe	13,000	Animism	0%	1		5597
Pogolo	none	Pogolo	65,000	Animism	0%	1		5598
Rulhi	none	Rulhi	71,000	Animism	0%	1		5599
Rungi	none	Rungi	95,000	Animism	0%	1		5600
Rungwa	none	Rungwa	5,000	Animism	0%	1		5601
Rusha	none	Rusha	54,000	Animism	<1%	1		5602
Safwa	New Testament	Safwa	100,000	Animism	3%	4		486

NAME	SCRIPTURE	LANGUAGE	GROUP SIZE	PRIMARY RELIGION	% CHR	VOL	V	UP ID
Sagala	none	Sagala	20,000	Animism	0%	1		5603
Sandawe	none	Sandawe	38,000	Animism	0%	1		5604
Sangu	none	Sangu	30,000	Animism	0%	1		5605
Shambala	New Testament	Shambala	152,000	Animism	0%	1		5606
Sonjo	none	Sonjo	7,000	Animism	5%	5		217
Suba	none	Suba	17,000	Animism	0%	1		5607
Subi	none	Subi	74,000	Animism	0%	1		5608
Sumbwa	none	Sumbwa	64,000	Animism	0%	1		5609
Tatoga	none	Tatoga	22,000	Animism	0%	1		5610
Tongwe	none	Tongwe	8,000	Animism	<1%	1		5611
Turu	portions	Nyaturu	320,000	Animism	0%	4		485
Vidunda	none	Vidunda	11,000	Animism	10%	4		5612
Vinza	none	Vinza	4,000	Animism	0%	1		5613
**Wajita	New Testament	Kijita	65,000	Animism	1%	4		244
Wanda	none	Wanda	8,000	Animism	0%	1		5614
Wanji	none	Wanji	19,000	Animism	0%	1		5615
Wasi	none	Wasi	13,000	Animism	0%	1		5616
*Wazinza	none	Kizinza	2,000	Animism	7%	4		1210
Wungu	none	Wungu	8,000	Animism	0%	1		5617
Zanaki	portions	Zanaki	23,000	Animism	<1%	1		5618
Zarano	portions	Zarano	300,000	Islam-Animist	2%	5		147
Zigwa	portions	Zigwa	112,000	Animism	0%	1		5619

Thailand

NAME	SCRIPTURE	LANGUAGE	GROUP SIZE	PRIMARY RELIGION	% CHR	VOL	V	UP ID
**Akha	New Testament	Akha	10,000	Ancestor Worship	1%	6	79	609
Blind, N.E. Thailand	portions	Northeast Thai	100,000	Buddhist-Animist	<1%	4	84	4810
*Cambodians	portions	Northern Kamer	1,000,000	Buddhist-Animist	1%	5	81	606
*Central Thailand Farmers	Bible	Thai	5,000,000	Buddhist-Animist	1%	5		645
*Chinese in Thailand	Bible	Hakka	3,600,000	Traditional Chinese	2%	4		749
Government officials	Bible	Thai	100,000	Buddhism	0%	3		59
***Hmong Refugee Women, Ban Vinai	+Bible	Miao	12,000	Buddhist-Animist	0%	4	83	9003

NAME	SCRIPTURE	LANGUAGE	GROUP SIZE	PRIMARY RELIGION	% CHR	V	UP	ID
Karen	Bible	Sgaw Karen	80,000	Animism	1%	6	79	613
Karen, Pwo	portions	Pwo Karen	40,000	Animism	1%	5		30
*Khamu	portions	Khamu	6,000	Animism	0%	4		2087
**Khmer Refugees	Bible	Cambodia	30,000	Buddhist-Animist	1%	4		2094
Khmer Refugees, Unaccd. Minors	not reported	Khmer	3,000	Buddhist-Animist	0%	3	83	9050
*Kui	portions	Kui	160,000	Buddhist-Animist	1%	5		607
*Lahu	New Testament	Lahu	23,000	Animism	7%	5	81	2088
*Lao Refugees	Bible	Lao	20,000	Buddhist-Animist	<1%	4		2090
Lawa, Eastern	none	Tibeto-Burman Dialect	3,000	Buddhist-Animist	<1%	5	81	7039
Lawa, Mountain	New Testament	Lawa	10,000	Buddhist-Animist	4%	5		612
*Lepers of Cen. Thailand	Bible	Thai	20,000	Buddhist-Animist	1%	6	81	7003
**Lepers of N.E. Thailand	portions	Northeast Thai	200,000	Buddhism	1%	4		236
*Lisu	not reported	Lisu	13,000	Animism	6%	4		2089
**Meo	New Testament	Meo	30,000	Animism	9%	5		610
Moken of Thailand	none	Local dialects	3,000	Animism	<1%	3		2092
Phu Thai	Bible	Phu Thai	80,000	Buddhist-Animist	<1%	4	84	4809
*Rankanhaeng Un. Students	New Testament	Thai	200,000	Buddhism	<1%	4		4053
Shan	Bible	Shan	300,000	Buddhist-Animist	<1%	4		2086
*Slum Dwellers of Bangkok	Bible	Thai	45,000	Buddhism	<1%	4		4052
*Soh	none	Soh	8,000	Animism	<1%	5	81	2091
T'in	not reported	T'in	25,000	Animism	<1%	5	81	81
Thai Islam (Malay)	portions	Mala, Pattani	1,700,000	Islam-Animist	1%	6	80	39
*Thai Islam (Thai)	none	Thai; Southern	600,000	Islam-Animist	0%	4		2093
*Thai University Students	Bible	Thai	nr	Buddhism	nr%	5	81	7015
**Vietnamese Refugees	not reported	Vietnamese	140,000	Buddhism	4%	4		2083
*Yao	New Testament	Yao (Mien Ua)	20,000	Animism	2%	6	79	611
*Yao Refugees from Laos	none	Yao	7,000	Animism	4%	4		2097

NAME	SCRIPTURE	LANGUAGE	GROUP SIZE	PRIMARY RELIGION	% CHR	V	VOL UP ID
Togo							
Adele	none	Adele	3,000	Islam-Animist	0%	1	5620
Ahlo	none	Ahlo	3,000	Islam-Animist	0%	1	5621
Ana	none	Ana	36,000	Islam-Animist	0%	1	5622
Animere	none	Animere	300	Islam-Animist	0%	1	5623
Anyanga	none	Anyanga	3,000	Islam-Animist	0%	1	5624
Basari	none	Basari	100,000	Animism	10%	5	599
Basila	none	Basila	5,000	Islam-Animist	0%	1	5625
Binoba	portions	Binoba	70,000	Islam-Animist	<1%	1	5626
Bouili	none	Bouili	3,000	Islam-Animist	0%	1	5627
Chakossi in Togo	none	Chakossi	20,000	Animism	3%	4	598
Gangan	none	Gangan	16,000	Islam-Animist	0%	1	5628
Kabre	portions	Kabre	273,000	Animism	9%	5	192
Kasele	none	Kasele	20,000	Islam-Animist	0%	1	5629
Kebu	none	Kebu	20,000	Islam-Animist	0%	1	5630
*Konkomba	not reported	Kom Komba	25,000	Animism	1%	4	253
Kotokoli	none	Kotokoli	150,000	Islam-Animist	0%	1	5631
Kposo	none	Kposo	45,000	Islam-Animist	0%	1	5632
Lamba	portions	Lamba	29,000	Animism	3%	4	425
Moba	portions	Binoba	70,000	Animism	8%	4	597
Naoudem	portions	Naoudem	90,000	Islam-Animist	<1%	1	5633
Natemba	none	Natemba	17,000	Islam-Animist	0%	1	5634
Ntrubo	none	Ntrubo	3,000	Islam-Animist	0%	1	5635
Tafi	none	Tafi	1,000	Islam-Animist	0%	1	5636
Ten	none	Ten	100,000	Islam	5%	4	596
Watchi	Bible	Ge	1,000,000	Animism	5%	4	424
Yanga	none	Yanga	nr	Islam-Animist	<1%	1	5637

NAME	SCRIPTURE	LANGUAGE	GROUP SIZE	PRIMARY RELIGION	% CHR	VOL V	UP ID

Trinidad and Tobago

NAME	SCRIPTURE	LANGUAGE	GROUP SIZE	PRIMARY RELIGION	% CHR	VOL V	UP ID
**Indians, East	Bible	English with Hindi	400,000	Hinduism	5%	6 79	1221

Turkey

NAME	SCRIPTURE	LANGUAGE	GROUP SIZE	PRIMARY RELIGION	% CHR	VOL V	UP ID
Abkhaz	portions	Abkhaz	12,000	Islam	<1%	1	2540
*Anatolian Turks-Istanbul	+Bible	Turkish	2,000,000	Islam	0%	5 82	5041
Circassian	portions	Circassian	113,000	Islam	<1%	1	2541
Kirghiz Afghan Refugees	+portions	Kirghiz	1,300	Islam	<1%	4 83	9060
*Kurds of Turkey	not reported	Kurdish (Kirmancho)	1,900,000	Islam	<1%	6 79	180
Romany	none	Romany	20,000	Folk Religion	<1%	1	2542
Turks, Anatolian	Bible	Turkish, Osmanli	31,20,000	Islam	<1%	6	4022
Yoruk	Bible	Turkish (Danubian)	600,000	Islam	0%	5	4048

USSR

NAME	SCRIPTURE	LANGUAGE	GROUP SIZE	PRIMARY RELIGION	% CHR	VOL V	UP ID
Abazin	none	Abazin	25,000	Islam	0%	1	5821
Abkhaz	portions	Abkhaz	83,000	Unknown	0%	1	5822
Adygei	not reported	Adygei	100,000	Islam	0%	1	5811
Agul	none	Agul	9,000	Islam	0%	1	5823
Akhavakh	none	Akhavakh	5,000	Unknown	0%	1	5824

NAME	SCRIPTURE	LANGUAGE	GROUP SIZE	PRIMARY RELIGION	% CHR	V	VOL UP	ID
Alutor	none	Alutor	2,000	Unknown	0%	1		5825
Andi	none	Andi	9,000	Unknown	0%	1		5826
Archin	none	Archin	900	Unknown	0%	1		5827
Balkars	not reported	Balkar	60,000	Islam	0%	1		5813
Bashkir	portions	Tatar	1,200,000	Islam	0%	5	80	4001
Batsi	none	Batsi	3,000	Unknown	0%	1		5828
Botlikh	none	Botlikh	4,000	Unknown	0%	1		5829
Budug	none	Budug	2,000	Unknown	0%	1		5830
Buriat	portions	Buriat	315,000	Buddhist-Animist	<1%	1		5831
Chamalin	none	Chamalin	6,000	Unknown	0%	1		5832
Cherkess	not reported	Cherkes	40,000	Islam	0%	1		5814
Chukot	none	Chukot	14,000	Unknown	0%	1		5833
Dargin	portions	Dargin	231,000	Islam	0%	1		5834
Didoi	none	Didoi	7,000	Unknown	0%	1		5835
Dolgans	not reported	Dolgan	5,000	Unknown	0%	1		5816
Dungan	none	Dungan	39,000	Islam	0%	1		5836
Evenks	none	Evenk	25,000	Buddhist-Animist	0%	1		5837
Gagauzes	portions	Gagauz	157,000	Christo-Paganism	<1%	1		5838
Gilyak	none	Gilyak	4,000	Unknown	0%	1		5839
Gypsies	not reported	not reported	175,000	Christo-Paganism	0%	1		5810
Ingushes	none	Ingush	158,000	Islam	0%	1		5840
Itelmen	none	Itelmen	1,000	Unknown	0%	1		5841
Izhor	none	Izhor	1,000	Unknown	0%	1		5842
Kalmytz	NT,portions	Kalmytz	137,000	Buddhism	0%	1		5844
Kapuchin	none	Kapuchin	3,000	Unknown	0%	1		5845
Karachay	New Testament	Karachay-Balkan	173,000	Islam-Animist	0%	5	80	4042
Karagas	none	Karagas	600	Unknown	0%	1		5846
Karaim	none	Karaim	1,000	Unknown	0%	1		5847
Karakalpak	not reported	Karakalpak	277,000	Islam	0%	6	80	4011
Karatin	none	Karatin	6,000	Unknown	0%	1		5849
Ket	none	Ket	1,000	Unknown	0%	1		5850
Khakas	none	Khakas	67,000	Unknown	0%	1		5851
Khanti	portions	Khanti	21,000	Unknown	0%	1		5852
Khinalug	none	Khinalug	2,000	Unknown	0%	1		5853
Khvarshin	none	Khvarshin	2,000	Unknown	0%	1		5854
Kirgiz	not reported	Kirgiz	1,700,000	Islam-Animist	0%	6	80	4016

NAME	SCRIPTURE	LANGUAGE	GROUP SIZE	PRIMARY RELIGION	% CHR	V	UP ID
Komi-Permyat	portions	Komi-Permyat	153,000	Christo-Paganism	<1%	1	5855
Komi-Zyrian	NT,portions	Komi-Zyrian	322,000	Christo-Paganism	<1%	1	5856
Koryak	none	Koryak	8,000	Unknown	0%	1	5857
Kryz	none	Kryz	6,000	Unknown	0%	1	5858
Kvanadin	none	Kvanadin	6,000	Unknown	0%	1	5859
Laklans	not reported	Lakian	86,000	Islam	0%	1	5812
Liv	portions	Liv	2,000	Unknown	0%	1	5860
Mansi	portions	Mansi	8,000	Unknown	0%	1	5861
Mari	New Testament	Mari	599,000	Christo-Paganism	<1%	1	5862
Mingat	none	Mingat	4,000	Unknown	0%	1	5863
Nanai	portions	Nanai	12,000	Unknown	0%	1	5864
Nentsy	not reported	Nentsy	29,000	Unknown	0%	1	5815
Nganasan	none	Nganasan	1,000	Unknown	0%	1	5865
Nivkhi	not reported	Nivkhi	4,000	Unknown	0%	1	5817
Oroch	none	Oroch	1,000	Unknown	0%	1	5866
Orok	none	Orok	400	Unknown	0%	1	5867
Rutul	none	Rutul	12,000	Islam	0%	1	5868
Saams	not reported	Saams	2,000	Unknown	0%	1	5819
Selkup	none	Selkup	4,000	Unknown	0%	1	5869
Shor	none	Shor	16,000	Unknown	0%	1	5870
Svan	none	Svan	35,000	Unknown	0%	1	5871
Tabasaran	none	Tabasaran	55,000	Islam	0%	1	5872
Tajik	portions	Persian (Tajiki)	2,500,000	Islam	0%	5	4041
Tat	portions	Tat	17,000	Islam	0%	1	5873
Tatars	Bible	Tatar dialects	6,000,000	Islam	1%	6 80	4008
Tindin	none	Tat	5,000	Unknown	0%	1	5874
Tsakhur	none	Tsakhur	11,000	Islam	0%	1	5875
Tuvinian	none	Tuvin	139,000	Buddhist-Aninist	0%	1	5876
Udegeis	none	Udegeis	2,000	Unknown	0%	1	5877
Udin	none	Udin	4,000	Unknown	0%	1	5878
Udmurt	portions	Udmurt	700,000	Animism	0%	1	5879
Ulchi	portions	Ulchi	2,000	Unknown	0%	1	5818
Veps	not reported	Veps	16,000	Unknown	0%	1	5880
Yagnobi	none	Yagnobi	2,000	Unknown	0%	1	5881
Yazgulyam	not reported	Yazgulyam	2,000	Unknown	0%	1	5882
Yukagirs	not reported	Yukagir	nr	Unknown	0%	1	5820

REGISTRY OF THE UNREACHED

NAME	SCRIPTURE	LANGUAGE	GROUP SIZE	PRIMARY RELIGION	% CHR	VOL V	UP ID
Yurak	none	Yurak	29,000	Unknown	0%	1	5883

Uganda

NAME	SCRIPTURE	LANGUAGE	GROUP SIZE	PRIMARY RELIGION	% CHR	VOL V	UP ID
Acholi	New Testament	Acholi	nr	Animism	1%	1	5638
Adhola	portions	Adhola	200,000	Animism	0%	1	5639
Chiga	portions	Chiga	272,000	Animism	0%	1	5641
Gwere	portions	Gwere	162,000	Animism	0%	1	5642
Jiye	none	Jiye	34	Animism	<1%	4	494
Kunam	portions	Kunam	100,000	Animism	0%	1	5644
Kupsabiny	portions	Kupsabiny	60,000	Animism	0%	1	5645
Lango	portions	Lango	560,000	Animism	<1%	1	5646
Madi	portions	Madi	114,000	Animism	1%	1	5647
Makere	none	Makere	18,000	Animism	0%	1	5648
Masaba	New Testament	Masaba	110,000	Animism	<1%	1	5650
Meje	none	Meje	13,000	Animism	0%	1	5649
Muslims (West Nile Dist.)	Bible	Lugbara	45,000	Islam	1%	4	238
Nyankole	Bible	Nyankole	810,000	Animism	<1%	1	5651
Nyoro	Bible	Nyoro	620,000	Animism	<1%	1	5652
Nyuli	none	Nyuli	140,000	Animism	0%	1	5653
Pokot	New Testament	Pokot	170,000	Animism	<1%	1	5654
Rwamba	none	Rwamba	60,000	Animism	0%	1	5655
Saamia	portions	Saamia	124,000	Animism	0%	1	5656
Soga	portions	Soga	780,000	Animism	0%	1	5657
Tepeth	none	Tepeth	4,000	Animism	0%	1	5658
Teso	Bible	Teso	830,000	Animism	<1%	1	5659

NAME	SCRIPTURE	LANGUAGE	GROUP SIZE	PRIMARY RELIGION	% CHR	V	UP	VOL ID
United Arab Emirates								
Indians in Dubai	+Bible	Malayalam	24,000	Hinduism	6%	5	82	5047
Muslims	Bible	Arabic	752,000	Islam	1%	6	79	365
**Shihu	none	Shihu	10,000	Islam	<1%	1		2543
United Kingdom								
Bengalis in London	+Bible	Bengali	15,000	Islam	0%	5	82	5038
**Chinese Students Glasgow	Bible	Mandarin	1,000	Traditional Chinese	15%	4	84	2078
**Chinese in United Kingdom	Bible	Mandarin	110,000	Traditional Chinese	3%	4	84	1225
**Gujarati	Bible	Gujarati	300,000	Hinduism	1%	6		1239
**Muslim Immigrants in U.K.	not reported	not reported	500,000	Islam	<1%	4		1099
Sylhetti	none	Sylhetti	150,000	Islam	0%	4		6566
Ugandan Refugees	+Bible	English	27,000	Islam	0%	4	63	9021
United States of America								
**Arabs in New Orleans	+Bible	Arabic	1,000	Islam	nr%	5	82	5008
**Bengali, Los Angeles area	Bible	English	4,000	Islam	<1%	4	84	4818
**Casual Laborers-Atlanta	+Bible	English	3,000	Secularism	nr%	5	82	5048
**Chicanos in Denver	+Bible	Spanish	121,000	Nominal Christian	nr%	5	82	5029

NAME	SCRIPTURE	LANGUAGE	GROUP SIZE	PRIMARY RELIGION	% CHR	V	VOL UP	ID
**Chinese in Boston	+Bible	Mandarin	20,000	Secularism	4%	6	82	5019
**Chinese in United States	Bible	Mandarin	550,000	Traditional Chinese	9%	5	82	750
**Ex-Mental Patients in NYC	+Bible	Spanish	20,000	Secularism	nr%	5	82	5007
Gays in San Francisco	+Bible	English	150,000	Secularism	0%	6	82	5010
Haitian Refugees	+Bible	Creole	40,000	Folk Religion	nr%	4	83	9044
*Havasupai	none	English	300	Unknown	3%	4		4083
***Hmong Refugees	+Bible	Miao	35,000	Buddhist-Animist	<1%	4	83	9055
Hmong, Twin Cities	+Bible	Miao	11,000	Nominal Christian	nr%	4		9034
Hopi	New Testament	Hopi	6,000	Animism	4%	5		382
**Japanese Students In USA	Bible	Japanese	nr	Secularism	<1%	4		54
Jemez Pueblo	none	Tewa (Jemez)	2,000	Christo-Paganism	5%	4		401
K'anjobal of Los Angeles	not reported	K'anjobal	5,000	Christo-Paganism	5%	2		8500
***Marielito Refugees in Florida	Bible	Spanish	125,000	Secularism	14%	4	83	6565
Nurses in St. Louis	+Bible	English	3,000	Secularism	<1%	5	82	5031
Paiute, Northern	portions	Paiute, Northern	5,000	Peyote Religion	3%	4		391
**Pro Hockey Players	English	English	600	Secularism	5%	6	82	5020
**Racetrack Residents	Bible	Spanish	50,000	Secularism	10%	5	79	476
Rajneeshees of Oregon	+Bible	English	1,000	New Eastern	0%	4		4806
*Thai Immigrants, Los Angeles	+Bible	Central Thai	60,000	Buddhism	1%	4		4813
Urban Elite Vietnamese	+Bible	Vietnamese	90,000	Ancestor Worship	nr%	4		9035
Urban Street Women/Los Angeles	+Bible	Spanish	100	Secularism	nr%	4	84	4826
Vietnamese Fishermen, Biloxi	+Bible	Vietnamese	1,300	Nominal Christian	nr%	3		4835
**Vietnamese Refugees	Bible	Vietnamese	2,700,000	Buddhism	7%	4		1222
Wandering Homeless	Bible	English	15,000	Secularism	nr%	4	84	4804
Zuni	portions	English	6,000	Animism	1%	4		410

Upper Volta

NAME	SCRIPTURE	LANGUAGE	GROUP SIZE	PRIMARY RELIGION	% CHR	V	VOL UP ID
Birifor	not reported	Birifor	50,000	Islam-Animist	<1%	3	5664
Bolon	none	Bolon	4,000	Islam-Animist	<1%	1	5661
Bousansi	New Testament	Bisa	140,000	Islam-Animist	<1%	1	5660
Buli	portions	Buli	60,000	Islam-Animist	0%	1	5662
Bwa	portions	Buamu (Bobo Wule)	140,000	Animism	9%	6 80	468
Dagari	not reported	Dagari	150,000	Islam-Animist	<1%	1	5663
Doghosie	none	Doghosie	8,000	Islam-Animist	0%	1	5665
Dyan	none	Dyan	8,000	Islam-Animist	0%	1	5666
Fula	portions	Fula	250,000	Islam-Animist	<1%	1	5667
Fulah	not reported	Fulani	300,000	Islam	1%	5	140
Gan	none	Gan	4,000	Islam-Animist	<1%	1	5668
Gouin-Turka	portions	Gouin-Turka	25,000	Islam-Animist	<1%	1	5669
Gourency	not reported	Gourendi	300,000	Animism	5%	4	94
*Karaboro	New Testament	Qurma	250,000	Islam-Animist	1%	4	5670
Kasem	none	Karaboro	40,000	Animism	1%	4	4139
Komono	portions	Kasem	28,000	Islam-Animist	0%	1	5671
Kurumba	none	Komono	6,000	Islam-Animist	0%	1	5672
Marka	none	Kurumba	86,000	Islam-Animist	<1%	1	5673
Mossi	none	Marka	39,000	Islam	0%	1	5675
Natioro	New Testament	Mole	3,300,000	Animism	7%	6 80	4009
*Nouni	none	Natioro	1,000	Islam-Animist	0%	1	5676
Nunuma	portions	Nouni	50,000	Animism	3%	4	4129
Puguli	not reported	Nunuma	43,000	Islam-Animist	<1%	1	5677
Sano, Northern	none	Puguli	5,000	Islam-Animist	0%	1	5678
Sano, Southern	none	Sano, Northern	70,000	Islam-Animist	<1%	1	5679
Sisala	none	Sano, Southern	4,000	Islam-Animist	0%	1	5680
Songhai	New Testament	Sisala	35,000	Islam-Animist	0%	1	5681
		Songhai					5682

703

NAME	SCRIPTURE	LANGUAGE	GROUP SIZE	PRIMARY RELIGION	% CHR V	VOL UP ID
Tiefo	none	Tiefo	7,000	Islam-Animist	0% 1	5683
*Toussian	none	Toussian	20,000	Islam	8% 4	4123
Vige	none	Vige	4,000	Islam-Animist	0% 1	5684
Uara	none	Uara	2,000	Islam-Animist	0% 1	5685
Win	portions	Win	20,000	Islam-Animist	<1% 1	5686

Venezuela

NAME	SCRIPTURE	LANGUAGE	GROUP SIZE	PRIMARY RELIGION	% CHR V	VOL UP ID
Arecuna	none	Arecuna	14,000	Animism	<1% 1	5134
Arutani	none	Spanish	100	Animism	0% 1	5135
**Jivaro (Achuara)	New Testament	Jivaro	20,000	Christo-Paganism	6% 4	385
Mapoyo	none	Mapoyo	200	Animism	0% 1	5136
Maquiritari	New Testament	Maquiritari	5,000	Animism	<1% 1	5137
Motilon	portions	Motilon	3,000	Animism	<1% 1	5138
Mutu	none	Spanish	300	Christo-Paganism	0% 1	5139
Panare	none	Panare	1,000	Animism	<1% 1	5140
Piaroa	portions	Piaroa	12,000	Animism	<1% 1	5141
Saruma	none	Saruma	4,000	Animism	<1% 1	5142
Wapishana	none	Wapishana	20,000	Animism	<1% 1	5143
Warao	New Testament	Warao	15,000	Animism	<1% 1	5144
Yanomamo	portions	Shamatali	nr	Animism	<1% 5	2024
Yaruro	not reported	Yaruro	5,000	Animism	<1% 1	5145
Yuana	none	Yuana	300	Animism	<1% 1	5146
Yukpa	none	Yukpa	3,000	Animism	0% 1	5147

NAME	SCRIPTURE	LANGUAGE	GROUP PRIMARY SIZE RELIGION	% VOL CHR V UP ID

Viet Nam

NAME	SCRIPTURE	LANGUAGE	GROUP SIZE	PRIMARY RELIGION	% CHR	V	UP ID
Cham	portions	Cham	45,000	Hindu-Animist	1X	5	272
**Chrau	portions	Jro	15,000	Animism	14X	4	394
Street Vendors in Saigon	+Bible	Vietnamese	nr	Buddhist-Animist	nr%	5 82	5035

Yemen, Arab Republic

NAME	SCRIPTURE	LANGUAGE	GROUP SIZE	PRIMARY RELIGION	% CHR	V	UP ID
***Akhdam	Bible	Arabic	nr	Islam-Animist	0%	4	4064
Ethiopian Refugees, Yemen	+not reported	Tigre	480	not reported	nr%	3	9040
Sayyids	Bible	Arabic	nr	Islam	<1%	4	4067
Yemenis	New Testament	Arabic (Eastern)	5,600,000	Islam	<1%	5 79	1061

Yemen, Democratic

NAME	SCRIPTURE	LANGUAGE	GROUP SIZE	PRIMARY RELIGION	% CHR	V	UP ID
**Hadrami	Bible	Arabic	151,000	Islam	0%	3	4065
*Mahrah	none	Local dialects	50,000	Islam	0%	3	4066

NAME	SCRIPTURE	LANGUAGE	GROUP SIZE	PRIMARY RELIGION	% CHR	V	V UP	VOL ID
Yugoslavia								
*Albanians in Yugoslavia	portions	Albanian (Gheg)	1,500,000	Islam	<1%	5		4036
*Bosnian	Bible	Serbo-Croatian	1,740,000	Islam	<1%	6	80	4004
Gypsies in Yugoslavia	portions	Romany (Serbian Kaldnash)	800,000	Islam	17%	4		4038
Muslim Gypsies in Skoplje	not reported	Romany Dialects	23,000	Islam	0%	5	82	5026
Zaire								
Baali	none	Baali	38,000	Animism	0%	1		5688
Baka	none	Baka	3,000	Animism	0%	1		5689
Bakongo Angolan Refugees	+Bible	Kikongo	600,000	Animism	nr%	4	83	9026
**Bakuba	Bible	Tshiluba	75,000	Animism	14%	5		1188
Bangba	not reported	Bangba	29,000	Animism	0%	1		5692
Bawoyo	none	Kiwoyo	10,000	Nominal Christian	20%	4		6571
Bembe	portions	Bembe	50,000	Animism	0%	1		5693
Binji	New Testament	Binji	64,000	Animism	0%	1		5694
Bolondo	none	Bolondo	1,000	Animism	0%	1		5696
Boma	none	Boma	15,000	Animism	0%	1		5697
Bugombe	portions	Bugombe	12,000	Animism	0%	1		5699
Buja	none	Buja	200,000	Animism	0%	1		5700
Bulia	none	Bulia	45,000	Animism	0%	1		5701
Bushoong	Bible	Bushoong	100,000	Animism	<1%	1		5702
Bwa	portions	Bwa	35,000	Animism	<1%	1		5703
Bwisi	none	Bwisi	6,000	Animism	0%	1		5704
Dengese	none	Dengese	4,000	Animism	0%	1		5705

NAME	SCRIPTURE	LANGUAGE	GROUP SIZE	PRIMARY RELIGION	% CHR	VOL V	UP ID
**Djandeau	Bible	Tribal dialects	26,000	Animism	3%	4	6559
Dongo	none	Dongo	5,000	Animism	0%	1	5706
Enya	none	Enya	7,000	Animism	0%	1	5707
Fuliro	portions	Fuliro	56,000	Animism	0%	1	5708
Furu	none	Furu	5,000	Animism	0%	1	5709
Havu	New Testament	Havu	262,000	Animism	0%	1	5710
Heso	New Testament	Heso	6,000	Animism	0%	1	5767
Hunde	portions	Hunde	34,000	Animism	0%	1	5711
Karu	none	Karu	4,000	Animism	0%	1	5714
Kaonde	Bible	Kaonde	20,000	Animism	<1%	1	5715
Kari	none	Kari	1,000	Animism	0%	1	5716
Kelah	portions	Kela	100,000	Animism	0%	1	5717
Kumu	portions	Kumu	60,000	Animism	<1%	1	5718
Kusu	none	Kusu	26,000	Animism	0%	1	5719
Kwese	portions	Kwese	60,000	Animism	<1%	1	5720
Lalia	none	Lalia	30,000	Animism	0%	1	5721
Lamba	Bible	Lamba	80,000	Animism	<1%	1	5722
Lega	New Testament	Lega	150,000	Animism	<1%	1	5723
Liko	none	Liko	26,000	Animism	0%	1	5727
Lombi	none	Lombi	8,000	Animism	0%	1	5729
Lombo	none	Lombo	10,000	Animism	0%	1	5730
Luna	Bible	Luna	50,000	Animism	<1%	1	5732
Lwalu	none	Lwalu	21,000	Animism	0%	1	5733
Ma	none	Ma	5,000	Animism	0%	1	5734
Manvu-Efe	portions	Manvu-Efe	40,000	Animism	0%	1	5735
Mangbutu	none	Mangbutu	8,000	Animism	0%	1	5736
Mba	none	Mba	20,000	Animism	<1%	1	5737
Mbala	portions	Mbala	200,000	Animism	0%	1	5738
Mbangwe	none	Mbangwe	2,000	Animism	0%	1	5739
Mbanja	none	Mbanja	81,000	Animism	0%	1	5740
Mbo	none	Mbo	2,000	Animism	0%	1	5741
Mbole	not reported	Mbole	100,000	Animism	0%	1	5742
Mono	none	Mono	30,000	Animism	0%	1	5690
Mundu	NT,portions	Mundu	5,000	Animism	<1%	1	5743
Nandi	none	Nandi	310,000	Animism	0%	1	5744
Ndaaka	none	Ndaaka	5,000	Animism	0%	1	5745

REGISTRY OF THE UNREACHED

NAME	SCRIPTURE	LANGUAGE	GROUP SIZE	PRIMARY RELIGION	% CHR	V	VOL UP ID
Ndo	portions	Ndo	13,000	Animism	<1%		1	5746
Ndoolo	none	Ndoolo	5,000	Animism	0%		1	5747
Ndunga	none	Ndunga	5,000	Animism	0%		1	5748
Ngando	New Testament	Ngando	121,000	Animism	0%		1	5749
Ngbaka	New Testament	Ngbaka	700,000	Animism	<1%		1	5750
Ngbaka Ma'bo	portions	Ngbaka Ma'bo	17,000	Animism	0%		1	5751
Ngbandi	portions	Ngbandi	137,000	Animism	0%		1	5752
Ngbee	none	Ngbee	30,000	Animism	0%		1	5753
Ngiri	none	Ngiri	6,000	Animism	0%		1	5754
**Ngombe	New Testament	Ngombe	5,000	Animism	3%		5	4080
Nkutu	portions	Nkutu	40,000	Animism	<1%		1	5755
Ntomba	portions	Ntomba	50,000	Animism	0%		1	5756
Nyali	none	Nyali	12,000	Animism	0%		1	5757
Nyanga-Li	portions	Nyanga-Li	25,000	Animism	0%		1	5758
***Pakabeti of Equator	none	Pakabeti	3,000	Animism	3%		4	1007
Pende	New Testament	Pende	200,000	Animism	0%		1	5759
Peri	portions	Peri	40,000	Animism	0%		1	5760
Poke	portions	Poke	46,000	Animism	0%		1	5761
*Pygmy (Mbuti)	none	local languages	40,000	Animism	1%	5	79	396
Rwanda	none	Rwanda	48,000	Animism	0%		1	5762
Sakata	portions	Sakata	75,000	Animism	<1%		1	5763
Salampasu	portions	Salampasu	60,000	Animism	0%		1	5764
***Sanga	+Bible	Sanga	35,000	Nominal Christian	nr%	4	84	5765
Sanza	none	Sanza	15,000	Animism	0%		1	5766
Songe	New Testament	Songe	500,000	Animism	0%		1	5768
Songomeno	none	Songomeno	40,000	Animism	0%		1	5769
Songoora	none	Songoora	1,000	Animism	0%		1	5770
Suku	portions	Suku	74,000	Animism	0%		1	5771
Swaga	none	Swaga	121,000	Animism	0%		1	5772
Teke, Eastern	portions	Teke, Eastern	71,000	Animism	0%		1	5773
Tembo	none	Tembo	30,000	Animism	0%		1	5774
Tiene	none	Tiene	25,000	Animism	<1%		1	5775
Togbo	not reported	Togbo	6,000	Animism	0%		1	5691
Wongo	portions	Wongo	8,000	Animism	0%		1	5776
Yaka	none	Yaka	200,000	Animism	<1%		1	5777
Yans	portions	Yans	165,000	Animism	0%		1	5778

NAME	SCRIPTURE	LANGUAGE	GROUP SIZE	PRIMARY RELIGION	% CHR	VOL V	UP ID
Yela	none	Yela	33,000	Animism	0%	1	5779
Zimba	none	Zimba	50,000	Animism	0%	1	5781

Zambia

NAME	SCRIPTURE	LANGUAGE	GROUP SIZE	PRIMARY RELIGION	% CHR	VOL V	UP ID
Ambo	not reported	Ambo	1,000	Animism	0%	1	5786
Bisa	not reported	Bisa	83,000	Animism	0%	1	5789
Cewa	not reported	Cewa	200,000	Animism	0%	1	5803
Chokwe	NT,portions,tracts,other	Chokwe	25,000	Animism	0%	2	5782
Ila	New Testament	Ila	39,000	Animism	0%	1	5783
Iwa	not reported	Iwa	15,000	Animism	0%	1	5800
Kaonde	Bible	Kaonde	116,000	Animism	<1%	1	5784
Kunda	not reported	LaLa-Bisa	21,000	Animism	0%	1	5790
	not reported	Nyanja	8,000	Animism	0%	1	5805
Lala	not reported	Lala	125,000	Animism	0%	1	5785
Lamba	Bible	Lamba	99,000	Animism	0%	1	5791
Lenje	portions	Lenje	79,000	Animism	0%	1	5793
Lima	not reported	Lima	12,000	Animism	0%	1	5792
Lozi	Bible	Lozi	215,000	Animism	0%	1	5794
Luano	not reported	Luano	4,000	Animism	0%	1	5787
Luchazi	Bible	Luchazi	34,000	Animism	<1%	1	5795
Lunda, Ndembu	Bible	Lunda, Ndembu	100,000	not reported	nr%	1	5796
Luvale Refugees from Angola	+Bible	Luvale	11,000	Animism	nr%	4 83	9061
Luyana	portions	Luyana	50,000	Animism	0%	1	5797
Manbwe-Lungu	New Testament	Manbwe-Lungu	121,000	Animism	<1%	1	5798
Mashi	none	Mashi	21,000	Animism	0%	1	5799
Ngoni	not reported	Ngoni	257,000	Animism	0%	1	5804
*Nkoya	New Testament	Shinkoya	nr	Animism	%	4	413
Nsenga	Bible	Nsenga	191,000	Animism	<1%	1	5802
Nyiha	New Testament	Nyiha	59,000	Animism	0%	1	5806
Sala	not reported	Sala	11,000	Animism	0%	1	5807

NAME	SCRIPTURE	LANGUAGE	GROUP SIZE	PRIMARY RELIGION	% CHR	V UP	VOL ID
Sinaa	none	Sinaa	40,000	Animism	0%	1	5808
Soli	portions	Soli	32,000	Animism	0%	1	5809
Swaka	not reported	Swaka	33,000	Animism	0%	1	5788
Tambo	not reported	Tambo	7,000	Animism	0%	1	5801
Tonga, Gwembe Valley	Bible	Chitonga	86,000	Animism	2%	7 79	188
Urban Refugees in Lusaka	not reported	Bantu Dialects	800	Animism	nr%	4 83	9038
Zimbabwean Refugees	+Bible	Tribal Languages	45,000	Christo-Paganism	nr%	4	9029

Zimbabwe

NAME	SCRIPTURE	LANGUAGE	GROUP SIZE	PRIMARY RELIGION	% CHR	V UP	VOL ID
*Bushmen (Hiechware)	none	Kwe-Etshari	2,000	Animism	6%	5	588
*Indians in Rhodesia	Bible	Gujarati	10,000	Hinduism	9%	4	182
Kalanga	portions	Kalanga	87,000	Animism	<1%	1	5410
Kunda	none	Kunda	40,000	Animism	0%	1	5411
Kwe-etshori	none	Kwe-etshori	2,000	Animism	0%	1	5412
Lozi	Bible	Lozi	8,000	Animism	<1%	1	5413
Manyika	New Testament	Manyika	350,000	Animism	<1%	1	5414
**Nambya	portions	Nambya	40,000	Animism	8%	5	1161
Ndau	Bible	Ndau	178,000	Animism	<1%	1	5415
**Ndebele	New Testament	Sindebele	1,000,000	Animism	7%	6 79	1235
Nsenga	Bible	Nsenga	16,000	Animism	0%	1	5416
Nyanja	Bible	Nyanja	252,000	Animism	0%	1	5417
*Tonga	Bible	Chitonga	99,000	Animism	2%	5	1160
Tswa	Bible	Tswa	300,000	Animism	0%	1	5418
Tswana	Bible	Tswana	30,000	Animism	<1%	1	5419
Venda	Bible	Venda	38,000	Animism	0%	1	5420
Zimbabwean Repatriates	+Bible	Tribal Languages	300,000	Christo-Paganism	<1%	4 83	9019

Appendices

he following questions ask if this is a people group and whether it is reached.

Name of this people group?

_____

If there is another name that this group is called, what is it?

_____

What country do these people live in?

_____

What other countries do these people live in?

_____

How many people are there in this group?

_____

What language do they speak?

_____

What religions do the people in the group practice? What approximate percentage of people in the group belong to each of these religions?

Religion	Percentage of People
Christian _____	_____
_____	_____
_____	_____
_____	_____
_____	_____

If a Christian community exists, what is its growth rate?

_____

What are the characteristics that make this people a group?

A shared or common:

language	location	legal status
political loyalty	class or caste	age group
ethnic origin	special interest	problem
religion	economic status	vocation
kinship	discrimination	_____
education level	health situation	_____

Please describe any other characteristics that help define this group.

_____

_____

_____

8. Describe the location of this people group on a blank piece of paper. Use whatever boundaries or landmarks that show where they can be found. Draw a picture of their location. If you can draw boundaries or locate nearby natural features, or even note the longitude and latitude from a map you have, it would be helpful. This information can then be used to help others reach this group.

This section seeks to determine whether there is a good probability that it is feasible to reach this group.

1. What languages do they speak? (Note the name of the language, the proportion of the people group who speak it and also the proportion who read it.)

Name	Percent who speak	Percent who read

2. Are there political or governmental restrictions that prohibit in any way the evangelization of this people? Please describe them.

_____

_____

_____

_____

3. Are there social, economic or other forces at work which will interfere with the proclamation of the gospel? What are they?

_____

_____

_____

_____

4. What organized religious groups or agencies would be opposed to the gospel among this group?

_____

_____

_____

_____

Please list others who have information about this people group.

_____

Name: _____ _____ _____

Address: _____ _____ _____

_____ _____ _____

_____ _____ _____

_____ _____ _____

). Please list books, magazines, pamphlets, etc., that provide information on this group.

Author: _____ _____ _____

Title: _____ _____ _____

Publisher: _____ _____ _____

_____ _____ _____

. May we direct others who desire to know more about this group to you? _____Yes

_____ No

_____ _____
Signature   Date

Please list
your name   _____
and address: _____

_____

_____

_____

Then mail this   Unreached Peoples Desk
questionnaire   MARC-World Vision
to: 919 W. Huntington Dr.
                        Monrovia, CA 91016
                        U.S.A.

It appears there is the following error/omission on page _____ of
Unreached Peoples '84:

_____

_____

_____

_____

_____

_____

I would like to receive more information on the

_____

(name/ID of people group).

Additional Comments:

_____

_____

_____

Name: _____

Date: _____

Address: _____

Please detach, insert in an envelope, and mail to: *Missions Advanced
Research and Communication Center*, 919 West Huntington Drive, Monrovia,
CA 91016 U.S.A.